Colonial
United States of America

IN WHICH IS GIVEN THE HISTORY, GENEALOGY AND
ARMORIAL BEARINGS OF COLONIAL FAMILIES WHO
SETTLED IN THE AMERICAN COLONIES FROM
THE TIME OF THE SETTLEMENT OF
JAMESTOWN, 13TH MAY, 1607,
TO THE BATTLE OF LEXINGTON, 19TH APRIL, 1775

EDITED BY

GEORGE NORBURY MACKENZIE, LL.B.

MEMBER OF THE
AMERICAN HISTORICAL ASSOCIATION, NATIONAL GENEALOGICAL SOCIETY,
OLD NORTH-WEST GENEALOGICAL SOCIETY.
MEMBER OF THE COMMITTEE ON HERALDRY AND GENEALOGY OF
MARYLAND HISTORICAL SOCIETY.

VOLUME VI

CLEARFIELD

Originally published:
Baltimore, Maryland, 1912

Reprinted by Genealogical Publishing Co., Inc.
Baltimore, Maryland, 1966, 1995

Library of Congress Catalog Card Number 66-18423

Reprinted for Clearfield Company by
Genealogical Publishing Company
Baltimore, Maryland, 2012

ISBN, Volume VI: 978-0-8063-1944-5
ISBN, 7-volume set: 978-0-8063-1946-9

Made in the United States of America

Colonial Families of the United States of America

Abbott

CHARLES CONRAD ABBOTT, M.D., of Trenton, New Jersey; *b.* 4th June, 1843; *m.* 13th February, 1867, Julia Boggs OLDEN, *b.* 23d May, 1846, dau. of Job Gardner and Maria Brenton (BOGGS) OLDEN of Princeton, New Jersey.

ISSUE

I. Maria Olden, *b.* 27th December, 1867; *m.* 29th April, 1896, Joseph Paxson CANBY of Hulmeville, Pennsylvania, son of Joseph and Margery (PAXSON) CANBY.

ISSUE

1. Pease CANBY, *b.* 1st July, 1897.
2. Joseph Olden CANBY, *b.* 10th July, 1900.
3. Arthur Brenton CANBY.
4. Edward CANBY.

II. Richard Mauleverer, *b.* 17th January, 1871.
III. Julia Boggs, *b.* 21st August, 1874.
IV. Arthur Brenton, *b.* 1st April, 1883; *d.* 17th February, 1888.

CHARLES CONRAD ABBOTT, Naturalist M.D. University of Pennsylvania, 1865. Made large collection of archaeological specimens, now in Peabody Museum, Cambridge, Massachusetts, where he was Assistant, 1876–1889. Member of the American Philosophical Society, Boston Society of Natural History, Fellow of the Royal Society Antiquaries of the North, Copenhagen (Denmark), Academy of Sciences, Linnean Society, New York. Has written much on archaeological and biological subjects; demonstrated existence of man in Delaware River Valley during glacial and subsequent prehistoric periods. Author: "The Stone Age in New Jersey," 1876; "Primitive Industry," 1881; "A Naturalist's Rambles About Home," 1884; "Upland and Meadow," 1886; "Wasteland Wanderings," 1887; "Days Out of Doors," 1889; "Outings at Odd Times," 1890; "Recent Rambles," 1892; "Travels in a Tree-top," 1894; "The Birds About Us," 1894; "Notes of the Night," 1895; "A Colonial Wooing" (novel), 1895; "Birdland Echoes," 1896; "When the Century

Was New" (novel), 1897; "The Hermit of Nottingham" (novel), 1897; "The Freedom of the Fields," 1898; "Clear Skies and Cloudy," 1899; "In Nature's Realm," 1900; "Archaeological Explorations in the Valley of the Delaware," 1894; "Rambles of an Idler," 1906; "Archaeologica Nova Caesarea," 1907, 1908, 1909; "Ten Years' Diggings in Lenape Land," 1912. He is lineally descended from the following Sureties for the Magna Charter:

William D'Albini	Gilbert De Clare	William De Lan-	Saise De Quincy
Hugh Bigod	Richard De Clare	vallie	Robert De Roos
Roger Bigod	John Fitzrobert	William Malet	Robert De Vere
Henry De Bohun	John De Lacie	William De Mowbray	

Lineage

The founder of this family was John ABBOTT, b. circa 1660, in Farnsfield, Nottinghamshire, England; d. 16th October, 1739; came in the ship called *Bristol Marchant*, William SMITH, commander, arriving in Philadelphia August, 1684; settled in Nottingham Township, New Jersey, in 1684, and was founder of Abbott's Landing on Crosswicks Creek. Was elected Constable of Nottingham, 1691, and Overseer of Highways, 1694, and in 1721 was Surveyor of Highways; *m.* 26th May, 1696, at the Chesterfield Monthly Meeting, Anne MAULEVERER, dau. of Edmund and Anne (PIERSON) MAULEVERER, who was, it is thought, a descendant of Sir Richard MAULEVERER, Knight Templar of the Norman Conquest.

ISSUE

 i. Mary, b. 14th November, 1696; d. 9th February, 1739; m. (firstly) 24th September, 1720, Benjamin ELLIS of Philadelphia; m. (secondly) 12th September, 1730, George WILLIAMS of Shrewsbury, New Jersey.
 ii. Anne, b. 14th September, 1698; d. 10th August, 1767; m. Jonathan BILES.
 iii. Jane, b. 9th March, 1701; d. 3d January, 1780; m. 16th December, 1726, Joseph BURR of Northampton, New Jersey.
 iv. Rachel, b. 1st January, 1704; d. in early infancy.
 v. Rachel, b. 12th June, 1706; d. unmarried 6th October, 1777.
 vi. John, b. 22d September, 1708; d. unmarried 2d November, 1795.
 vii. Elizabeth, b. 5th November, 1711; m. 18th March, 1738, George WILLIAMS, Jr., of Shrewsbury, New Jersey.
 viii. TIMOTHY, b. 9th February, 1717, of whom later.
 ix. Sarah, b. 12th January, 1719; d. 2d May, 1746; m. 22d March, 1740, Hezekiah WILLIAMS, brother of George WILLIAMS, Jr.
 x. Samuel, b. 22d August, 1721; m. 3d April, 1746, Elizabeth HASTINGS, dau. of John HASTINGS, of Philadelphia.

TIMOTHY ABBOTT of Abbott's Landing, Burlington County, New Jersey; b. 9th February, 1717; d. 30th November, 1776; m. 27th September, 1746, Anne SATTER-

COLONIAL FAMILIES OF THE UNITED STATES 5

THWAITE, *d.* 15th September, 1777, dau. of William and Mary (OSBORNE) SATTERTHWAITE of Burlington County, New Jersey.

ISSUE

I. JOHN, *b.* 29th October, 1747, of whom later.
II. Samuel, *d.* in infancy.
III. Samuel, *b.* 3d November, 1749; *d.* 22d February, 1828; *m.* 9th March, 1775, Lucie LAURIE.
IV. Marmaduke, *b.* 2d March, 1753; *d.* 1824.
V. William, *b.* 20th September, 1755; *d.* 6th September, 1793; *m.* 13th March, 1783 (firstly) Helena LAURIE, *d.* 19th September, 1784; *m.* (secondly) 11th January, 1787, Rebecca HOLLOWAY.
VI. Mary, *d.* in infancy.
VII. Rebecca, *d.* in infancy.
VIII. Abel, *b.* 3d October, 1763; *d.* 1823-1824.
IX. Timothy, *b.* 24th August, 1767; *m.* (firstly) 12th May, 1802, Rebecca HOWARD, *d.* 17th ———, 1818; *m.* (secondly) 9th May, 1822, Anne NEWBOLD, *d.s.p.*

ISSUE BY FIRST MARRIAGE

1. Howard, *b.* 10th April, 1803; *d.* 27th November, 1828; *m.* Susan S. STOKES.
2. William, *b.* 30th October, 1804; *d.* 20th June, 1837; *m.* Sarah Ann JONES.
3. Charles, *b.* 10th October, 1806; *d.* 1881; *m.* Rebecca F. PITFIELD.
4. George, *b.* 21st January, 1808; *d.* 3d January, 1860; *m.* Elizabeth W. LONGSTRETH.
5. Rebecca, *b.* 31st August, 1810; *d.* 7th June, 1883; *m.* Joseph PANCOAST, who was one of the world's greatest surgeons.

X. David, *b.* 21st March, 1770; *d.* September, 1846; *m.* 6th January, 1798, Margery SMITH of Philadelphia.

JOHN ABBOTT of Abbott's Landing, Nottingham, New Jersey; *b.* 29th October, 1747; *d.* 26th October, 1809; *m.* 17th September, 1778, Susannah BULLOCK, dau. of Joseph and Elizabeth (WRIGHT) BULLOCK of Burlington County, New Jersey.

ISSUE

I. JOSEPH, *b.* 8th July, 1779, of whom later.
II. Timothy, *b.* 10th December, 1780; *d.* 1803, in South America.
III. Ann, *b.* 25th August, 1782; *d.* 30th July, 1846; *m.* 10th September, 1812, Thomas COLLINS.
IV. Elizabeth, *b.* 18th August, 1785; *d.* October, 1854; *m.* 9th September, 1802, Solomon White CONRAD.

v. Lucy, *b*. 15th March, 1787; *d*. 24th December, 1860.
vi. Susanna, *d*. in infancy.
vii. Edith, *d*. in early childhood.
viii. John, *b*. 23d August, 1792; *d*. 30th July, 1851.
ix. George, *b*. 27th December, 1795; *d*. 1st December, 1851.
x. Hannah, *b*. 23d June, 1799; *d*. 17th September, 1825.

JOSEPH ABBOTT of Nottingham Township, Burlington County, New Jersey, *b*. 8th July, 1779; *d*. 28th October, 1861; *m*. 7th March, 1805, Anne RICKEY, *d*. 20th November, 1846, dau. of John and Amy (OLDEN) RICKEY.

ISSUE

I. Susan, *b*. 20th January, 1806; *d*. 4th November, 1879.
II. John Rickey, *b*. 28th September, 1807; *d*. 15th August, 1876.
III. TIMOTHY, *b*. 3d June, 1809, of whom later.
IV. Ephraim Olden, *b*. 3d June, 1809; *d*. 19th March, 1889; *m*. (firstly) 16th December, 1840, Anne HANCE, *d*. 12th August, 1843; *m*. (secondly) 31st December, 1846, Catherine MOYER, *d*. 3d January, 1887.
V. Joseph Gardner, *b*. 3d April, 1811; *d*. 14th July, 1876; *m*. (firstly) 11th January, 1843, Rebecca HARRISON, *d*. 28th March, 1854; *m*. (secondly) Martha ELLIS, *d*. 13th January, 1883.
VI. Thomas, *b*. 9th March, 1813; *d*. 28th August, 1825.
VII. Amy Ann, *b*. 16th November, 1814; *d*. 12th January, 1892.
VIII. George B., *b*. 10th September, 1816; *d*. 7th January, 1873; *m*. 20th September, 1837, Rebecca COMFORT, *d*. 30th July, 1849.
IX. Elizabeth, *b*. 10th June, 1819; *d*. 10th March, 1882; *m*. 5th September, 1855, Ezekiel COMBS.

TIMOTHY ABBOTT of Trenton, New Jersey; *b*. 3d June, 1809; *d*. 20th November, 1882; Cashier and then President of Mechanics National Bank of Trenton from 1850–1853 and 1870–1882; *m*. 19th November, 1832, Susan CONRAD, *b*. 1st December, 1807, *d*. 19th July, 1864; dau. of Solomon White and Elizabeth (ABBOTT) CONRAD, of Philadelphia, Pennsylvania.

ISSUE

I. Mary G., *b*. 23d December, 1833, unmarried.
II. Joseph, *b*. 15th June, 1837; *d*. 29th August, 1862; *m*. 4th June, 1861 Ann Eliza HUNT of Kingston, Jamaica, British West Indies.

ISSUE

I. Ada Frances, *b*. 7th May, 1862; *m*. 7th May, 1883, Alfred L. BLACK.
III. Frances, *b*. 5th April, 1840; *m*. 10th July, 1865, Julia C. SHEWELL.

COLONIAL FAMILIES OF THE UNITED STATES

ISSUE

1. Joseph de Benneville, *b.* 28th June, 1866; *m.* 18th November, 1899, Helen Shewell KEIM.
2. Francis L., *b.* 7th February, 1870; *m.* Jennie FINE.
3. Charles Shewell, *b.* 9th November, 1871.

IV. CHARLES CONRAD, *b.* 4th June, 1843, the subject of this memoir.

Residence.—Bristol, Pennsylvania, formerly Three Beeches, Trenton, New Jersey, until 13th November, 1914, when residence was destroyed by fire and estate later sold to Pennsylvania Railroad.

Arms (Mauleverer).—Sable three greyhounds courant in pale argent, collared or.

Crest.—A maple branch sprouting from the trunk of a tree all ppr.

Motto.—En Dieu ma foy.

Societies.—Order of Runnemede, American Philosophical (Philadelphia), Natural History (Boston), New York Academy of Sciences, Linnæan of New York, Anthropological of Washington (D. C.), Minnesota Historical of St. Paul, Fellow Royal Societies of Antiquaries of the North, Copenhagen, etc.

Adams

GILMER SPEED ADAMS, of Louisville, Kentucky; *b.* 19th August, 1854, in Mobile, Alabama; *m.* 28th October, 1886, in Louisville, Kentucky, Lettie Reed ROBINSON, *b.* 8th November, 1857, dau. of John McHenry ROBINSON, *b.* 21st September, 1824, *d.* 16th March, 1894, *m.* 22d May, 1856, in Springfield, Kentucky, Maria Louisa BOOKER, *b.* 23d April, 1834.

GILMER SPEED ADAMS, Merchant and Manufacturer, was educated at Louisville, Kentucky; Commissioner of Louisville, Kentucky, Hospital; Director in Citizens National Bank, First National, Fidelity Columbia Trust Company, Kentucky Title Savings Bank and Trust Company, Kentucky Title Company, University of Louisville; Governor of Kentucky Society of Colonial Wars, 1914–1915, Member Chapter (vestry) Christ Church Cathedral (Episcopal).

Lineage

CAPTAIN EBENEZER ADAMS, *d.* 13th June, 1735; emigrated from England to St. Peter's Parish, New Kent County, Virginia, before 1714, and received grants of 3983 acres of land in New Kent and Henrico Counties in that year; subsequently became a vestryman of St. Peter's Parish 11th June, 1718, and remained so and as a warden until his death. In 1731 he became Captain of Colonial Militia; *m.* circa 1718, Tabitha COCKE, dau. of Richard COCKE the younger of Bremo by his first wife Anne BOWLER, dau. of Thomas BOWLER, Esq., of Rappahannock County, a member of the Virginia Council 1670.

ISSUE

I. Richard, *d.* in infancy.
II. Bowler, *b.* 19th April, 1722; *d.* in infancy.
III. William, *b.* 4th July, 1724; *d.* before 25th August, 1763.
IV. RICHARD, *b.* 17th May, 1726, of whom later.
V. Tabitha, *b.* July, 1728; *d.* 1764, *m.* Richard EPPES, Member of House of Burgesses, 1752–1755, 1758–1764; had issue.
VI. Thomas, *b.* in New Kent County, circa 1730; *d.* at his seat "Cow Pasture" August, 1788, in Augusta County; was Clerk of Henrico County, Vestryman and Warden Henrico Parish, Secretary of Indian Treaty at Cataba Town 20th February, 1756; about 1762 went to England and became a merchant in London; returned to Virginia in 1772. May 27th, 1774, one of the Signers of an "Association" entered into by late Members of the House of Burgesses. Chairman of the New

COLONIAL FAMILIES OF THE UNITED STATES 9

Kent County Committee, 1774, Member of the Old Congress, 1778, and signed the Articles of Confederation between the States. Removing to Augusta County, he represented in the Legislature that district comprising Augusta, Rockingham, Rockbridge, and Shenandoah from 1784-1787. He was an earnest patriot; *m.* Elizabeth (FAUNTLEROY) COCKE, Jr.

VII. Anne, *b.* circa 1731; *d.* 1775; *m.* circa 1748 (as second wife), Col. Francis SMITH of South Franham Parish, Essex County, Member of the House of Burgesses 1752-1758; had issue.

VIII. Sarah, *m.* Col. John FRY, *b.* 7th May, 1737, of the Colonial Militia, Member of the House of Burgesses from Albemarle County, Virginia; 1761-1764; was also a Vestryman of St. Anne's Parish, Albemarle County.

ISSUE

1. Joshua FRY, moved to Kentucky; *m.* Peachy WALKER, dau. of Dr. Thomas WALKER, the Kentucky Explorer; had issue.
2. William A. FRY, *m.* and had issue.
3. Tabitha FRY, *m.* Bowler COCKE; no issue.

COLONEL RICHARD ADAMS of Richmond, Virginia; *b.* 17th May, 1726, in New Kent County; *d.* 2d August, 1800, at Richmond. Was a member of the House of Burgesses for New Kent and Henrico Countries from 1752 to 1775; House of Delegates 1776-1778; Convention of 1776; Virginia Senate 1779-1782; was an ardent patriot throughout the Revolution and one of the most enterprising, public spirited, wealthy and influential citizens of Richmond; *m.* 10th April, 1755, Elizabeth GRIFFIN, *b.* 1738, *d.* 23d December, 1800, dau. of Leroy and Mary Anne (BERTRAND) GRIFFIN of Richmond, Virginia, and sister of Judge Cyrus GRIFFIN of Williamsburg. Colonel Richard ADAMS, his wife and many of his descendants are buried in Richmond, Virginia. Leroy GRIFFIN was High Sheriff of Richmond County, Virginia, 1734; his wife Mary Anne BERTRAND was the dau. of John BERTRAND, a Hugenot refugee, who fled from France during the persecution of Louis XIV. Leroy GRIFFIN was son of Thomas GRIFFIN, Burgess from Richmond County, Virginia, 1715, 1718-1723-1726, who was the son of Col. Le Roy GRIFFIN, Justice of Rappahannock County, Virginia, 1680, and Colonel of Militia. His mother was Winifred CORBIN, dau. of Col. Henry CORBIN, Member of the Virginia Council 1663, Burgess 1658-1659.

Griffin Arms.—A lion rampant.
Corbin Arms.—Sable on a chief or three ravens ppr.

ISSUE (OF COLONEL RICHARD AND ELIZABETH (GRIFFIN) ADAMS)

I. Tabitha, *b.* 4th July, 1756; *d.* unmarried 17th February, 1828.
II. Elizabeth Pressin, *b.* 17th December, 1757; *d.* unmarried 1832.

III. Thomas Bowler, b. 18th December, 1759; d. 28th November, 1794, in Richmond; m. Sarah Mowisin, whose mother was a Miss Bland of Prince George County.
IV. Richard, b. 26th November, 1760; d. January, 1817; m. (firstly) Mrs. Elizabeth Southall of Chatsworth; m. (secondly) Mrs. Sarah Travers Daniel Hay; had issue.
V. Anne, b. 27th October, 1762; d. 22d October, 1820; m. 30th September, 1787, Col. Mayo Carrington of "Boston Hill," Cumberland County, Virginia.
VI. William, b. 8th June, 1764; d. unmarried 15th June, 1787.
VII. Sarah, b. 14th January 1766; d. 30th September, 1806; m. 7th February, 1793, William Smith, Governor of Virginia and Member of House of Delegates 1791–1793, who was lost in the Richmond Theatre fire 26th December, 1811; had issue.
VIII. Alice, b. 20th February, 1768; m. 28th June, 1788, William Marshall of Fauquier County, Virginia; had issue.
IX. Ebenezer, d. in infancy.
X. John, b. 14th July, 1773; d. 23d June, 1825; Physician and prominent citizen of Richmond for many years; m. Margaret Winston, dau. of Geddes Winston of Richmond.
XI. Samuel Griffin, b. 5th May, 1776, of whom later.

Samuel Griffin Adams of Richmond, Virginia; b. there 5th May, 1776; d. there 15th July, 1821. Was adjutant 19th Regiment Virginia Militia War of 1812; was projector first water works system of Richmond, 1809; served in Virginia Assembly; m. May, 1797, Katherine Elizabeth Innes, b. 9th May, 1779, d. 5th November, 1836, dau. of Judge Henry Innes, b. in Caroline County, Virginia, 15th January, 1753, d. 20th September, 1816, in Frankfort, Kentucky, m. (firstly) 3d October, 1775, Katherine Elizabeth Callaway, b. 1756, d. 26th December, 1790, niece of Col. James Innes, Lieutenant Colonel in the Revolutionary War, the first Attorney-General of Virginia and was offered the appointment of Attorney-General of the United States by Washington but declined. Judge Innes was a Member of the Virginia Legislature in 1783 and in that year was elected by the Legislature of Virginia as one of the Judges of the Supreme Court for the District of Kentucky. In 1785 was elected by the Virginia Legislature, Attorney-General for the district of Kentucky. In 1789 he was appointed Judge of the United States Court for the District of Kentucky, which office he held until his death in 1816, in the meantime having declined the appointment of Chief Justice of the Court of Appeals, which was offered him when Kentucky became a State in 1792. Was a member of the Kentucky Board of War in 1791; Member of Danville Convention in 1785, 1787 and 1788 looking to the erection of Kentucky into a separate State; and was a Member of the Convention in Frankfort in 1799 which formed the Constitution of Kentucky. His wife, Elizabeth Callaway was the daughter of Col. James Callaway of Bedford County, Virginia, who was a Burgess from that

County in 1766–1768 and who with William Preston Robert ADAMS, Jr. (a descendant of Capt. Ebenezer ADAMS) and Charles LYNCH formed the original LYNCH law, and their acts were condoned and they were granted indemnity by the Virginia General Assembly, October, 1782.

ISSUE OF HARRY INNES AND KATHERINE ELIZABETH CALLAWAY

I. Sarah, *b.* 13th July, 1776; *m.* 1792, Francis THORNTON and had issue.
II. Katherine Elizabeth, *b.* 9th May, 1779; *m.* 7th May, 1797, Samuel G. ADAMS.
III. Elizabeth, *b.* 23d September, 1785; *m.* June, 1805, Thomas ALEXANDER.
IV. Ann, *b.* 6th April, 1787; *m.* October, 1802, John MORRIS.

Innes Arms.—Argent three stars with a bordure, chigney of the first and second.
Crest.—A branch of Palm slipped, ppr.
Motto.—"Ornatus Radix Fronde."

ISSUE OF SAMUEL G. AND KATHERINE ELIZABETH (INNES) ADAMS

I. Elizabeth Innes, *b.* 30th April, 1798; *d.* 20th November, 1803.
II. Richard, *b.* 7th February, 1800; *d.* 11th June, 1851; *m.* (firstly) Mary SELDEN; *m.* (secondly) Lucy W. THORNTON; had issue.
III. Mary Griffin, *b.* 8th February, 1803; *d.* 20th February, 1870; *m.* George POLLARD; had issue.
IV. Innes Callaway, *b.* 6th March, 1807; *d.* 16th August, 1862; *m.* (firstly) Ellen Green WILLIAMS; *m.* (secondly) Hannah W. WOODWARD.
V. Samuel Griffin, *b.* 31st July, 1810; *d.* 24th June, 1839; *m.* Maria GILMER.
VI. John, *b.* 7th July, 1812; *d.* May, 1813.
VII. George William, *b.* 29th March, 1814; *d.* 1853; *m.* Jane Ruffin ROBERTSON; had issue.
VIII. THOMAS, *b.* 15th June, 1816, of whom later.
IX. James Innes, *b.* 18th December, 1818; *d.* 1855; *m.* Henrietta Catherine BICKLEY.

THOMAS ADAMS, of Richmond, Virginia; *b.* 15th June, 1816; *d.* 1st July, 1858; removed from Virginia to Louisville, Kentucky and then to Mobile, Alabama, where he became a prominent merchant and steamboat owner. His health failing he removed to an estate near Louisville, where he died the same year; *m.* 6th October, 1846, at "Farmington" near Louisville, Kentucky, Martha Bell SPEED, *b.* 8th September, 1822, *d.* 31st March, 1903, dau. of Judge John and Lucy Gilmer (FRY) SPEED. Hon. Joshua Fry SPEED who was President LINCOLN's most intimate friend and Hon. James SPEED who was Attorney-General in President LINCOLN's cabinet were brothers of Martha Bell SPEED.

ISSUE

I. Kate, *b.* 29th November, 1848; *d.* 8th February, 1862.
II. Lucy Ness, *b.* 14th February, 1852; *d.* 23d June, 1853.

III. GILMER SPEED, b. 19th August, 1854, the subject of this memoir.
IV. Bessie Innes, b. 7th May, 1857; d. 15th July, 1857.
V. Jessie St. John, b. 10th June, 1858; d. 25th May, 1894; m. 20th November, 1892, Horace SPEED, b. ————; studied law in the office of President Benjamin HARRISON at Indianapolis, Indiana, and when married was the first United States District Attorney for Oklahoma; he was son of Thomas and Margaret (HAWKINS) SPEED.

Arms.—Ermine three cats passant in pale azure.
Crest.—A boar's head argent, couped gules.
Residence.—1355 Third Avenue, Louisville, Kentucky.
Clubs.—Pendennis and Louisville Country.
Societies.—Colonial Wars, Sons American Revolution, Kentucky State Historical Society (Life Member), Virginia Historical Society, Life Member National Geographic Society.

Speed

JOHN SPEED, I, of London, England, the historian, geographer and antiquarian was b. at Farrington, County Cheshire, England, 1552. His great work was the "History of England" with accompanying maps. He was buried in the chancel of the Church of St. Giles, Cripplegate, London, where a monument stands over his grave. The remains of John MILTON rest in the same church. One of his sons,

DR. JOHN SPEED, II, b. 1595, was educated at Oxford and buried in the Chapel of St. John's College, Oxford; one of his sons,

JOHN SPEED, III, M.D., was educated as a physician at St. Johns' College, Oxford, and practiced his profession at Southampton, England, as late as 1694. His son,

JAMES SPEED, b. in England 28th September, 1679, was the emigrant to Virginia about 1695; m. 6th September, 1711, in Surrey County, Virginia, Mary PULLEY, b. 1693, d. June, 1733.

ISSUE

I. James, b. 16th June, 1712.
II. JOHN, b. 5th February, 1714, of whom later.
III. William T., b. 19th February, 1716.
IV. Thomas, b. 28th February, 1719.

JOHN SPEED, b. 5th February, 1714; d. 8th March, 1785; m. 6th October, 1737, Mrs. Mary Minetry TAYLOR who d. 1st July, 1782.

ISSUE

I. John, *b.* 3d August, 1738; a Revolutionary soldier; *m.* Sarah BAIRD, had issue.
II. JAMES, *b.* 4th March, 1739, in Mecklenberg County, Virginia; of whom later.
III. Henry, *b.* 28th March, 1742; Revolutionary soldier; *m.* Elizabeth Julia SPENCER.
IV. Sarah, *b.* 14th February, 1743; *m.* Richard HANSARD.
V. Lewis, *b.* 25th January, 1745; killed as a Revolutionary soldier.
VI. Martha, *b.* 11th August, 1748; *m.* ——— APPERSON.
VII. Joseph, *b.* 27th May, 1750; Member of Virginia Convention, May, 1776; Revolutionary soldier; *m.* Ann BIGNALL; had issue.
VIII. Lucy, *b.* 11th April, 1752; *m.* ——— JETER; had issue.
IX. Mathias, *b.* 18th June, 1754, *m.*, removed to Casey County, Kentucky; had issue.
X. Son, *d.* young.
XI. Mary, *d.* young.

CAPTAIN JAMES SPEED of ———————; *b.* 4th March, 1739, Mecklenberg County, Virginia; *d.* 3d September, 1811. He was a Burgess from Charlotte County, Virginia, 1772-1775. (Stanard's "Colony Virginia Register"). He served in the Revolutionary War, first as Lieutenant and then as Captain and was wounded at the battle of Guilford Court House, North Carolina, 15th March, 1718, while leading his command in battle. One of his family of six brothers who served in the Revolutionary War was killed in this battle. For his military services before and during the Revolutionary War he received large grants of land. He moved to Kentucky with his family in the fall of 1782 from Charlotte Court House, Caroline County, Virginia, over the "Wilderness Road," which led through the mountains of Virginia to Cumberland Gap and thence to Danville, Kentucky, which was then in Lincoln County. He was a member of the early Kentucky Conventions of 1783-1785, 1787. He was a member of the Political Club, a society of the leading men in Kentucky, which met from 1786 to 1790 at Danville, then the capital of Kentucky. He died near Danville 3d September, 1811; *m.* 10th December, 1767, in Charlotte County, Virginia, Mary SPENCER.

ISSUE

I. Thomas, *b.* 25th October, 1768; as a young man was clerk of the Bullett and Nelson Circuit Courts, Secretary of the Political Club of Danville, 1786; was a Major in the War of 1812, Member of Congress 1817-1819; *m.* (firstly) 11th December, 1796, Susan Clayton SLAUGHTER; *m.* (secondly) 9th January, 1810, Mrs. Mary McElroy ALLEN; left issue.

ISSUE

I. A child who died in infancy.

II. Mary, *b.* 8th June, 1770; *m.* 1789, William SMITH; had issue.
III. JOHN, *b.* 17th May, 1772, of whom later.
IV. Elizabeth, *b.* 7th February, 1774; *m.* 1792, Dr. Adams RANKIN; had issue.
V. James, *b.* 7th February, 1774; *d.* 14th September, 1812, unmarried.
VI. Henry, *b.* 15th August, 1777; *m.* Miss SMITH; had issue.

JUDGE JOHN SPEED, *b.* 17th May, 1772; *d.* 30th March, 1840. Served in War against Indians 1791; was early in life a merchant and salt manufacturer at the licks near Shepherdsville, Kentucky; was Judge of Quarter Sessions Court, Jefferson County, Kentucky. Although a slaveholder, was an Emancipationist. He was admired and respected by all who knew him, including Rev. James Freeman CLARK, who eulogizes him in his "Recollections." Judge John SPEED owned a handsome estate of the celebrated "Beargrass" land near Louisville, upon which he built a large house of the old Colonial style of architecture which he called "Farmington" and where was dispensed lavish hospitality; *m.* (firstly) Abby LEMASTER, who *d.* 1st July, 1807; *m.* (secondly) 15th November, 1808, in Mercer County, Kentucky, Lucy Gilmer FRY, *b.* in Albemarle County, Virginia, 23d March, 1788, *d.* 27th January, 1874, dau. of Joshua and Peachy (WALKER) FRY. Joshua FRY, *b.* circa 1760, was a soldier in the War of the Revolution at 14, and was at Cornwallis' surrender. He received the best classical education and had a decided taste for scholarly pursuits. He inherited a large estate and in 1798 left Virginia for Kentucky with his family and settled at Danville and became the owner of very large tracts of fine land. His tastes led him to teaching and he became the most noted educator in Kentucky. Being a man of large means, he would never receive compensation for teaching and gave instruction to hundreds of pupils gratuitously. In the published biographical sketches of many of the most prominent Kentuckians, the fact of being educated by Joshua FRY is especially mentioned. His father was Col. John FRY who commanded the Virginia troops in the early colonial wars, and was a Member of the House of Burgesses 1761 to 1764. His mother was Sarah ADAMS, dau. of Ebenezer ADAMS, of New Kent County, Virginia. The father of Col. John FRY (See Adams line, p. 8) was Col. Joshua FRY. Col. Joshua FRY was educated at Oxford, England, emigrated to Virginia previous to 1710, during which year he was vestryman Essex Parish, Virginia, Magistrate Essex County, Virginia, 1710–1720; here he *m.* Mrs. Mary Micou Hill, of Hugenot descent; Master of Grammar School William and Mary College, 1729; Professor of Natural Philosophy and Mathematics at William and Mary College, 1732 to 1737; Presiding Justice, Surveyor and County Lieutenant for Albemarle County, Virginia, at its formation, February 28th, 1745. Together with his intimate friend Peter JEFFERSON (father of Thomas JEFFERSON) he was Commissioner in 1745–1749 of the Crown in marking boundary lines between Virginia and North Carolina. Joint author of FRY and JEFFERSON's map of Virginia in 1749; Commissioner for Crown at Treaty of Logstown (near Pittsburg) with six Nation Indians in 1752; Member of House of Burgesses, 1745–1754, and Council; commissioned 25th February, 1754, by Governor DINWIDDIE as Colonel and Commander-in-Chief of the Virginia forces in French and Indian War, his compensation being 15 shillings ($3.75) per day and £100 per year for his table. George WASHINGTON was the Lieutenant Colonel, compensation as such per day 12s. 6d. ($3.12½). While in command at Fort Cumberland, Virginia, on the Potomac River, he *d.* 31st May, 1754, and was buried near there. George WASHINGTON, who, by reason of Colonel FRY's death became Commander in Chief, and the Army attended the funeral, and on a large oak tree which served as a tomb and monument to his memory, George WASHINGTON cut the following inscription:

"Under this oak lies the body of
THE GOOD, THE JUST AND THE NOBLE FRY"
("Memoir of Col. Joshua Fry,"—Rev. P. Slaughter.)

PEACHY WALKER, *b.* 6h February, 1767; *m.* Joshua FRY. Was a dau. of Dr. Thomas WALKER, of Castle Hill, by his first wife, Mildred THORNTON, widow of Nicholas MERIWETHER. Dr. Walker's ancestors came from Staffordshire, England. Capt. Thomas WALKER was Burgess from Gloucester County, Virginia, 1662; in 1666 he is called Maj. Thomas WALKER, in the list of Burgesses. Titles were strictly applied because they meant something in those days. His grandson Thomas WALKER, lived in King and Queen, and *m.* there in 1707. He was the father of Dr. Thomas WALKER of Castle Hill, Albemarle County, who was *b.* 25th January, 1714, and *d.* 9th November, 1794; he is believed to be the first white man who explored Kentucky. He was Commissary-General of Virginia troops in Braddock's war; Member of House of Burgesses, of the Virginia Convention of 1775; Commissioner to treat with the Indians after their defeat by Andrew LEWIS, Commissioner to run boundary line between Virginia and North Carolina, known as WALKER's line, and he was the guardian of Thomas JEFFERSON. He *m.* (firstly) 1741, the widow of Nicholas MERIWETHER, whose maiden name was Mildred THORNTON.

ISSUE

I. Mary WALKER, *b.* 24th July, 1742; *m.* Nicholas LEWIS, of Albemarle.
II. Col. John WALKER, of Belvoir; *b.* 13th February, 1744; confidential Aide-de-camp to Washington; Member of Congress and Senator of United States; *m.* Elizabeth MOORE, dau. of Bernard MOORE and granddau. of Governor SPOTSWOOD.
III. Susan WALKER (often called Sukie), *b.* 14th December, 1746; *m.* Henry, often called Harry FRY then Deputy Clerk of Albemarle.
IV. Thomas WALKER, *b.* 17th March, 1748–49; Captain in Revolution, 9th Regiment; *m.* ————, dau. of Thomas HOOPS of Carlisle, Pennsylvania, who educated Benjamin WEST, the painter.
V. LUCY WALKER, *b.* 5th May, 1751; *m.* Dr. George GILMER of Pen Park, Albemarle, the father of Francis Walker GILMER, first Professor of Law, University Virginia, Author and Scholar; and of Mildred, wife of William WIRT, Attorney-General of United States, and grand-

16   COLONIAL FAMILIES OF THE UNITED STATES

      father of Thomas Walker GILMER, Governor of Virginia, and Secretary of the United States Navy.
- VI. Elizabeth WALKER, b. 1st August, 1753; m. Rev. Matthew MAURY, Fredericksville Parish, Virginia.
- VII. Mildred WALKER, b. 5th June, 1755; m. Joseph HORNSBY; no issue.
- VIII. Sarah WALKER, b. 28th March, 1785; m. Col. Reuben LINDSAY.
- IX. Martha WALKER, b. 2d May, 1760; m. George DIVERS of "Framington," Albemarle.
- X. Reuben WALKER, d. in infancy.
- XI. Col. Francis WALKER, Colonel 88th Regiment; residuary legatee of Dr. Thomas WALKER, b. June, 1764; d. 1806; Member of Congress from Albemarle and Orange Counties, Virginia, 1792–1795.
- XII. Peachy WALKER, b. 6th February, 1767; m. Joshua FRY, Danville, Kentucky.

ISSUE OF JOSHUA AND PEACHY (WALKER) FRY

- I. John FRY, m. Judith HARRISON; had issue.
- II. Thomas Walker FRY, m. Elizabeth Speed SMITH; had issue.
- III. Lucy Gilmer FRY, m. Judge John SPEED, of whom later.
- IV. Sally FRY, m. John GREEN; had issue.
- V. Martha FRY, m. David BELL; had issue.
- VI. Ann FRY, m. William C. BULLITT; had issue.
- VII. Susan FRY, d. unmarried.

ISSUE OF JUDGE JOHN AND ABBY (LEMASTER) SPEED

- I. James, d. in infancy.
- II. James, d. in infancy.
- III. Mary, who lived to an advanced age; d. unmarried.
- IV. Eliza, d. unmarried.

ISSUE OF JUDGE JOHN AND LUCY GILMER (FRY) SPEED

- I. Thomas, b. 15th September, 1809; d. 12th July, 1812.
- II. Lucy Fry, b. 26th February, 1811; m. James D. BRECKINRIDGE; no issue.
- III. James, b. 11th March, 1812; d. 25th June, 1887; Attorney-General, LINCOLN's Cabinet; m. ———, 1841, Jane COCHRAN; issue, six boys.
- IV. Peachy Walker, b. 4th May, 1813; d. 18th January, 1891; m. Austin PEAY.
- V. Joshua Fry, b. 14th November, 1814; d. 29th May, 1882; m. 15th February, 1842, Fannie HENNING; no issue.
- VI. William Pope, b. 26th April, 1816; d. in Boonville, Missouri, 28th June, 1863, married.

ISSUE

1. Margaret D. Phillips; no issue.
2. Mary Ellen Shallcross; had issue.
3. Ardell Hutchinson; had issue.

VII. Susan Fry, *b.* 30th September, 1817; *m.* 5th June, 1838, B. O. DAVIS; had issue.
VIII. Philip, a Major in Union Army, Civil War, *b.* 12th April, 1819; *d.* 1st November, 1882; *m.* Emma KEATS, a niece of the poet John KEATS; had issue.
IX. John Smith, *b.* 1st January, 1812; *d.* 26th October, 1886; *m.* (firstly) Elizabeth WILLIAMSON, no issue; *m.* (secondly) Susan PHILLIPS; had issue.
X. Martha Bell, *b.* 8th September, 1822; *d.* 31st March, 1903; *m.* 6th October, 1846, Thomas ADAMS, *b.* 15th June, 1816, *d.* 1st July, 1858 (see Adams Line, page 8, this book); had issue.
XI. Ann Pope, *b.* 5th November, 1831; *d.* 9th October, 1838.

Arms.—Gules on a chief or, two swallows, wing expanded ppr.
Crest.—A swallow, wings expanded ppr.

Alexander

WINTHROP ALEXANDER of Roxbury, Massachusetts; *b.* 15th November, 1861, in Boston; *m.* there (firstly) 23d December, 1889, Elizabeth Blake WOOD, *b.* Brookline, Massachusetts, 15th September, 1866, *d.* Washington, D. C., 13th June, 1895, dau. of Charles Blake WOOD of Boston, *b.* 21st February, 1839, *d.* 24th April, 1876, *m.* 6th October, 1864, Marietta Gridley BOWMAN of Boston, *b.* 13th July, 1839; *m.* (secondly) 25th November, 1897, at Auburn, Maine, Harriet Bethiah BRIGGS, *b.* there, 23d November, 1869, dau. of William Henry BRIGGS of Auburn, Maine, *b* 8th January, 1833, *d.* 19th October, 1906, *m.* 25th September, 1856, Mary Ann DILLINGHAM, *b.* 20th April, 1838, *d.* 1st September, 1909.

ISSUED BY FIRST MARRIAGE

I. Charles Winthrop, *b.* 11th April, 1892 (through maternal line a descendant of Isaac ALLERTON of the *Mayflower*).

II. Marion Louise, *b.* 14th October, 1893; *m.* 14th October, 1915, Arthur Willard SNOW of Boston; (through her maternal line a descendant of Isaac ALLERTON of the *Mayflower*).

ISSUE BY SECOND MARRIAGE

I. Donald Briggs, *b.* 3d November, 1898 (through maternal line descendant of Gov. William BRADFORD and Elder William BREWSTER of the *Mayflower*).

II. Harriet Bradford, *b.* 5th November, 1903 (through maternal line descendant of Gov. William BRADFORD and Elder William BREWSTER, of the *Mayflower*).

WINTHROP ALEXANDER has been engaged in engineering architecture, and building construction. At present Superintendent of the Suffolk County Court House, Boston. Has had thirty-two years military service in Massachusetts, Rhode Island, District of Columbia and Canada, serving from private to colonel.

Lineage

JOHN ALEXANDER, *b.* in Scotland, circa 1615, came to Massachusetts prior to 1644 and later settled at Windsor in the Connecticut Valley.

ISSUE

  I. GEORGE, *b.* in Scotland, of whom later.
 II. John.
III. Thomas.

GEORGE ALEXANDER of Northfield and Northampton, Massachusetts; *b.* in Scotland, circa ——; *d.* 5th May, 1703, in Northfield; *m* 18th March, 1644, Susanna SAGE, *d.* 5th May, 1684.

ISSUE

  I. JOHN, *b.* 25th July, 1645, of whom later.
 II. Abigail, *b.* 1647; *m.* 16th June, 1663, Thomas WEBSTER.
III. Mary, *b.* 20th October, 1648; *m.* 23d September, 1670, Micah MUDGE.
 IV. Daniel, *b.* 12th January, 1651; *d.* circa 1684.
  V. Nathaniel, *b.* 29th December, 1652; *d.* 29th October, 1742; *m.* 20th June, 1679 Hannah ALLEN.
 VI. Sarah, *b.* 8th December, 1654; *m.* 6th July, 1678, Samuel CURTIS.

JOHN ALEXANDER of Windsor, Connecticut, and Northampton, Massachusetts; *b.* 25th July, 1645, in Windsor, Connecticut; *d.* 31st December, 1733, at Northampton; *m.* 18th November, 1671, Sarah GAYLORD, *b.* 18th January, 1652; *d.* 3d November, 1732, dau. of Samuel and Elizabeth (HULL) GAYLORD of Windsor, the son of William of England, whom he accompanied to America.

ISSUE

   I. John, *b.* 24th January, 1673; *d.* 24th January, 1748–1749.
  II. Nathaniel, *b.* 6th April, 1676; *m.* 3d December, 1707, Abigail Searle.
 III. Samuel, *b.* 6th November, 1678; *d.* 1763.
  IV. Joseph, *b.* 16th October, 1681; *d.* 30th September, 1761; *m.* 28th May, 1705, Margaret MATTOON.
   V. EBENEZER, *b.* 17th October, 1684, of whom later.
  VI. Sarah, *b.* 7th February, 1688; *m.* 26th June, 1716; Eleazer HOLTON.
 VII. Thankful, *b.* 29th March, 1691; *m.* 2d June, 1734–1735, Gideon HALE.
VIII. Elizabeth, *b.* 5th October, 1694; *m.* 15th November, 1733, John SUMMERS.

CAPTAIN EBENEZER ALEXANDER, known as the "Fighting Deacon" of Northfield, Massachusetts; *b.* 17th October, 1684; *d.* 22d January, 1768. Lived previously at Wethersfield, and Coventry, Connecticut; he filled many important offices in the town of Northfield, Massachusetts, saw much service in Father RASLE's War, serving as Ensign under Capt. Thomas WELLES and as Lieutenant under the famous Capt. Benjamin WRIGHT; 9th March, 1744–1745, he was commissioned Lieutenant in the expedition against Cape Breton; was at the capture of Louisburg, 17th June, when Sir William PEPPERELL gave him a Captain's Commission, 13th July. In 1746 he served under Governor SHIRLEY in the expedition for the reduction of Canada; in 1748 although then sixty-four years old he was a leader of a company ranging the woods in the search of Indians; was Deacon in Northfield for forty years; *m.* 10th October, 1709, Mehitabel BUCK, of Wethersfield, *b.* 1684; *d.* 6th March, 1767, dau. of Henry and Elizabeth (CHURCHILL) BUCK.

ISSUE

I. Elias or Elisha, *b.* 25th July, 1710; *m.* Ruth, surname unknown.
II. EBENEZER, *b.* 2d September, 1714, of whom later.
III. Anna, *b.* 1720; *m.* 20th September, 1738, Samuel TAYLOR.
IV. Simeon, *b.* 26th May, 1722; *d.* 14th February, 1801; *m.* Sarah HOWE.
V. Thomas, *b.* 30th May, 1727; *d.* 23d March, 1801; *m.* 11th December, 1754, Azubah WRIGHT.

EBENEZER ALEXANDER of Northfield, Massachusetts and Winchester, New Hampshire; *b.* 2d September, 1714; *d.* 29th July, 1788; served in the French and Indian War, 1746-1749; *m.* Abigail ROCKWOOD; *b.* 8th June, 1714, *d.* 27th March, 1788, dau. of Nathaniel and Joanna (ELLIS) ROCKWOOD of Wrentham, Massachusetts.

ISSUE

I. Abigail, *b.* 30th July, 1738; *d.* 23d December, 1739.
II. Reuben, *b.* 14th February, 1739-1740; *m.* Sarah FOSTER.
III. ASA, *b.* 17th October, 1742, of whom later.
IV. Abigail, *b.* 30th August, 1745; *m.* Henry FOSTER.
V. John, *b.* 1748; *d.* 16th December, 1806; *m.* 7th October, 1771, Thankful ASHLEY.
VI. Anna, *b.* 12th July, 1733; *m.* 15th October, 1770, Theodore WATKINS.

ASA ALEXANDER of Winchester, New Hampshire; *b.* there 17th October, 1742; *d.* there 4th November, 1811; served in the expedition against Canada in 1760; *m.* 13th November, 1762, Mary BOND, *b.* 13th November, 1742, *d.* 1st July, 1835, dau. of Henry and Mary (CUTTING) BOND of Watertown, Massachusetts.

ISSUE

I. EBENEZER, *b.* 24th April, 1765, of whom later.
II. Thaddeus, *b.* 15th November, 1766.
III. Mary, *b.* 9th November, 1768; *m.* 1805, Amasa WOOLLEY.
IV. Lucretia, *b.* 11th January, 1771; *m.* 1795, Elisha KNAPP.
V. Asa, *b.* 15th January, 1773; *d.* 25th March, 1849; *m.* 1801, Abigail ALEXANDER.
VI. John, *b.* 6th December, 1774; *d.* 20th May, 1842; *m.* 1800, Polly PRATT.
VII. Amos, *b.* 15th July, 1779; *m.* 5th October, 1809, Betsey L. SWAN.
VIII. Anna, *b.* 4th March, 1781; *m.* Rev. Ezra CONANT.
IX. Solomon, *b.* 8th August, 1783; *m.* 1806, Thankful ALEXANDER.

EBENEZER ALEXANDER of Boston, Massachusetts; *b.* 24th April, 1765, at Winchester, New Hampshire; *d.* 6th December, 1844, in Boston, Massachusetts; lived successively in Winchester, Chesterfield, New Hampshire, and Montague and Boston, Massachusetts; *m.* 3d June, 1788, Rhoda SCOTT, *b.* 10th January, 1770, *d.* 5th July, 1831, dau. of James and Rhoda (ROCKWOOD) SCOTT of Winchester, New Hampshire.

ISSUE

I. Eusebia P., *b.* 28th December, 1788; *d.* 23d March, 1861; *m.* James AIKEN.
II. Emery, *b.* 9th November, 1790; *d.* 28th September, 1848.
III. Oliver Brown, *b.* 24th May, 1795; *d.* 1864; *m.* Susan ADAMS.
IV. Henry Foster, *b.* 23d October, 1797; *d.* 17th December, 1852.
VI. Mary Brown, *b.* 24th January, 1800; *d.* 17th January, 1888; *m.* David GRANGER.
VII. EBENEZER, *b.* 14th September, 1802, of whom later.
VIII. Willard Huntington, *b.* 14th September, 1806; *d.* 10th November, 1891; *m.* Eunice SCOTT.
IX. Octavia, *b.* 2d December, 1808; *d.* October, 1895; *m.* ——— SCOTT.
X. Merab Ann, *b.* 14th July, 1811; *d.* September, 1883; *m.* Willis R. SCOTT.

EBENEZER ALEXANDER of Boston, Massachusetts; *b.* 14th September, 1802; at Montague, Massachusetts; *d.* 7th February, 1835, at Boston, Massachusetts; *m.* 24th December, 1826, Nancy WILSON, *b.* 23d March, 1802, *d.* 16th June, 1860, dau. of Henry Wilson and Jane URANN; she gd. dau. of Capt. Thomas URANN of the "Boston Tea Party."

ISSUE

I. Whittaker Howland, *b.* 12th March, 1828; *d.* 27th August, 1854, unmarried.
II. Willard SCOTT, *b.* 10th March, 1830; *d.* 18th February, 1833.
III. EBENEZER, *b.* 17th February, 1832, of whom later.

EBENEZER ALEXANDER of Boston, Massachusetts; *b.* there 17th February, 1832; *d.* there 30th March, 1906; *m.* 21st October, 1857, Harriet Sherman BURCHSTED, *b.* in Boston, 3d December, 1833, *d.* there 26th January, 1916, dau. of Benjamin and Harriet (SHERMAN) BURCHSTED of Boston.

ISSUE

I. Carrie Adeline, *b.* 2d December, 1858; *m.* 2d December, 1879, Rev. Fred A. DILLINGHAM,, *d.* 10th February, 1903.

ISSUE

I. Mabel, *b.* 30th September, 1880; *m.* 4th August, 1904, Henry CROSBY of Indianapolis, Indiana.

2. Alexander, *b.* 6th August, 1883; *m.* 22d June, 1901, Alveda GREENWOOD of Somerville, Massachusetts.
3. Leslie, *b.* 24th May, 1886; *m.* 15th October, 1913, William H. CONE of Bridgeport, Connecticut.
4. Paul, *b.* 9th May, 1889, *m.* 25th June, 1915, Frances O'Rourke.
5. Sydney, *b.* 15th September, 1892.
6. Edith, *b.* 15th September, 1895.

II. WINTHROP, *b.* 15th November, 1861; the subject of this memoir.
III. Mabel, *b.* 19th December, 1867; *d.* 30th April, 1869.
IV. Hollis Williams, *b.* 26th August, 1871; *m.* 12th August, 1896, Rosemary CONROY of St. Louis, Missouri, *b.* there 21st May, 1871.

1. Eben Roy, *b.* 15th February, 1899.
2. Calvert Page, *b.* 18th September, 1900.
3. John Hollis, *b.* 8th February, 1903.

Arms.—Per pale argent and sable a chevron in base a crescent all counter charged.
Crest.—A bear erect argent.
Motto.—Per mare per terra.
Residence.—No. 3 Wabon Street, Roxbury (Boston), Massachusetts.
Societies.—Colonial Wars, Sons of the American Revolution, Old Guard of Massachusetts, Roxbury City Guard Veteran Association; Ancient and Honorable Artillery Company of Boston (1638), Massachusetts Historic-Genealogical Society, Roxbury Historical; Masonic Algonquin Lodge, Roxbury Council, St. Omer Commandery Knight Templars; Sigma Chi Fraternity.

Atkinson

ROBERT WHITMAN ATKINSON, A.B., of Brookline, Massachusetts; *b.* 14th December, 1868, at Heath Hill, Brookline, Massachusetts; *m.* 5th March, 1904, Elizabeth Bispham PAGE of Philadelphia, *b.* 27th March, dau. of Edward Augustus PAGE and Josephine Augusta BISPHAM.

ISSUE

I. Alice Tucker, *b.* 10th December, 1904.
II. Eliot Heath, *b.* 3rd August, 1907.
III. Samuel Greenleaf, *b.* 17th November, 1911.

ROBERT WHITMAN ATKINSON was educated at Harvard College, A.B., 1891, summis in musicus honoribus; subsequently studied at Munich, Bavaria, under eminent teachers, for several terms. Has served at different times as organist, as theatre music director, as pianist, both in recital and in concert, as choir master, as teacher, translator and essayist on musical subjects. Songs and piano pieces from his pen may be found scattered in various collections and periodicals and also separately. His latest piece, "Cinq Pas" New York, G. Schirmer, 1915, marks a novel departure in musical rhythmics.

Lineage

Among the early settlers of Boston was Theodore ATKINSON, a native of Bury in Lancashire, England; *b.* 1611; *d.* August, 1701; a man of some note in his day. Came to Boston in 1634; was a member of the Artillery Company in 1644. In a deed of gift dated 1674 he says, "On account of the love which I bear to my Nephew, John ATKINSON of Newbury," etc. This John ATKINSON was *b.* about 1640, whether *b.* in England or in America is not known, was according to tradition the son of Henry ATKINSON, Barrister, who came with his brother Theodore and settled in Newbury. Theodore ATKINSON, *m.* Mary (WHEELWRIGHT) LYDE, a dau. of Rev. John WHEELWRIGHT of Salisbury, and widow of ——— LYDE.

ISSUE

1. Theodore II, *b.* April 1644; *d.* May, 1676, in Boston; *m.* ———

ISSUE

1. Theodore, III, *b.* 3d October, 1669; *d.* 1719; was a member of the Council of New Hampshire.

ISSUE

1¹. Theodore, IV, *b.* in Newcastle, New Hampshire, 20th December, 1697; *d.* 22d September, 1779; graduated at Harvard College, 1718; he was a Counsellor, Judge, Secretary of New Hampshire.

ISSUE

1². Theodore, V, who *d.* before his father, 28th October, 1769, without issue. The ATKINSONS in New Hampshire are descended from an adopted son of Theodore ATKINSON, who *d.* 1779.

II. Nathaniel, *b.* 28th October, 1645; *d.* before 1698; graduated at Harvard College, 1667.

JOHN ATKINSON, nephew to the first Theodore ATKINSON, came to Newbury about 1663 and resided on the southwesterly side of the upper green on the spot occupied in 1853 by Capt. Stephen W. LITTLE; *m.* 27th April, 1664, Sara MYRICK.

ISSUE

I. Sara, *b.* 27th November, 1665; *m.* 8th October, 1685, Stephen COFFIN.
II. JOHN, of whom later.
III. Thomas, *b.* 27th December, 1669; *d.* before 1699; graduated at Harvard College, 1691.
IV. Theodore, *b.* 23d January, 1672; was drowned 24th July, 1685.
V. Abigail, *b.* 8th November, 1673; *m.* 1695, Jonathan WOODMAN.
VI. Samuel, *b.* 16th January, 1676.
VII. Nathaniel, *b.* 29th November, 1677; *m.* 22d January, 1707, Deborah KNIGHT.

ISSUE

1. Mary, *b.* 31st October, 1708.
2. Sara, *b.* 10th December, 1710; *m.* 13th May, 1730, Davis STICKNEY.
3. Margaret, *b.* 2d November, 1712; *m.* 19th April, 1737, Elias JACKMAN.
4. Nathaniel, *b.* 19th March, 1717; *m.* (firstly) 1738, Elizabeth GREENLEAF; *m.* (secondly) 1st April, 1756, Sarah MORRIS.

VIII. Elizabeth, *b.* 20th June, 1680; *m.* 1704, Thomas LEAVITT, of Hampton.
IX. Joseph, *b.* 1st May, 1682, was killed by the Indians in Maine in 1706.
X. Rebecca, *m.* (firstly) 14th October, 1714, Israel ADAMS, who *d.* in Waltham, 12th December, 1714; *m.* (secondly) 10th October, 1716, Ensign Joseph HILTON of Exeter.

JOHN ATKINSON, II, *m.* (firstly) 1693, Sara WOODMAN, *m.* (secondly) 3d June, 1700, Hannah CHENEY, widow, *b.* 1643, *d.* 5th January, 1705.

ISSUE BY FIRST MARRIAGE

1. Thomas, *b.* 16th March, 1694; *m.* 5th August, 1719, Mary PIKE, of Salisbury.

ISSUE

1. Humphrey, *b.* 12th June, 1720; *m.* 25th May, 1743, Sarah HALE.
2. Anna, *b.* 5th November, 1722, in Hampton, New Hampshire; *m.* 11th September, 1746.
3. Susanna, *b.* 9th December, 1724; *m.* November, 1742, Robert COLE.
4. Moses, *b.* 29th July, 1727.

II. John, III, *b.* 29th October, 1695; *m.* 13th November, 1721, Judith WORTH. Judith ATKINSON, perhaps the widow of John, *m.* 13th June, 1746–1747, Cutting PETTINGELL.

ISSUE

1. Judith, *b.* 1st November, 1724; *m.* 22d November, 1744, Silas PEARSON.
2. Theodore, *b.* 12th August, 1727; *d.* 7th April, 1753; *m.* 30th January, 1752, Lydia STICKNEY. Lydia (STICKNEY) ATKINSON, *m.* (secondly), 26th May, 1756, Joseph MUSSEY.
3. Lydia, *b.* 12th October, 1729; *m.* 24th October, 1751, Richard STICKNEY.
4. Elizabeth, *b.* 7th December, 1731; *m.* 27th December, 1750, Michael TOPPAN.
5. Sarah, *b.* 1st April, 1734; *m.* 17th June, 1764, Joseph CLEMENT.
6. Mary, *b.* 22d October, 1737; *m.* 14th February, 1764, Moses COFFIN.
7. John, *b.* 30th April, 1740; *m.* 4th October, 1779, Lydia LITTLE.
8. Eunice, *b.* 14th April, 1744; *m.* 5th January, 1775, Dr. Joshua LITTLE.

III. Theodore, *b.* 8th October, 1698.
IV. Sara, *b.* 6th November, 1700.
V. Hannah, *b.* 21st January, 1703; *m.* 4th March, 1731, Joseph CLEMENT.
VI. Abigail, *b.* 31st March, 1705; *m.* 1st April, 1725, Joshua MOODY.
VII. Joseph, *b.* 5th October, 1707; *m.* 23d January, 1744–1745, Hannah HALE.

ISSUE

1. Sarah, *b.* 19th December, 1745.
2. Simeon, *b.* 10th August, 1747.
3. Samuel, *b.* 16th October, 1748.
4. Silas, *b.* 16th October, 1752.
5. Simeon, *b.* 30th March, 1754.
6. Susanna, *b.* 15th June, 1758.
7. Hannah, *b.* 10th June, 1760.

VIII. Mary, *b.* 19th February, 1709; *m.* 1736, Major GOODWIN.
IX. Elizabeth, *b.* 28th June, 1712; *m.* 1736, Samuel PILSBURY.
X. DEACON ICHABOD, *b.* 13th August, 1714; of whom later.

DEACON ICHABOD ATKINSON *b.* 13th August, 1714; *m.* 6th November, 1733, Priscilla BAILEY.

ISSUE

I. Moses, *b.* 22d September, 1734; *m.* (firstly) 19th May, 1757, Mary MERRILL; *m.* (secondly) 1781, Sarah HALE.
II. Matthias, *b.* 6th January, 1735; *m.* 10th April, 1766, Abigail BAILEY.
III. Miriam, *b.* 20th March, 1739; *m.* 20th June, 1757, Ralph CROSS.
IV. Hannah, *b.* 21st September, 1743, *d.* young.
V. Anna, *b.* 16th May, 1746; *m.* before 1797, ―――― NOYES.
VI. Sarah, *b.* 1st November, 1748; *m.* 27th February, 1794, Stephen ATKINSON.
VII. Abigail, *m.* Robert EMERSON.
VIII. Amos, *b.* 20th March, 1754.
IX. Eunice, *b.* 18th September, 1759; *m.* Abner LITTLE.

LIEUTENANT AMOS ATKINSON of Newbury, Massachusetts; *b.* 20th March, 1754; *m.* (firstly) 1778, Anna BAILEY, of Amesbury; *m.* (secondly) 1784, Anna KNOWLTON.

ISSUE BY FIRST MARRIAGE

I. William, *b.* 13th November, 1779, *m.* 10th April, 1804, Nancy LITTLE.

ISSUE

1. Joseph, *b.* 28th August, 1805; *d.* 15th October, 1805.
2. William, *b.* 11th October, 1806; *m.* 1829, Adeline REED.
3. Charles, *b.* 18th May, 1808; *m.* 1830, Eliza Ann BATES.
4. Josua T., *b.* 9th April, 1810; *m.* 1832, Emiline LITTLE.
5. Joseph, *b.* 15th February, 1812; *m.* (firstly) Charlotte SWASEY; *m.* (secondly) 1851, Frances FARRINGTON.
6. Dr. Moses L., *b.* 27th July, 1814; *d.* 18th January, 1852; *m.* 7th May, 1845, Catherine BARTLETT.
7. Judith, *b.* 25th June, 1817; *m.* 1837, Gideon DICKINSON.
8. Rev. George Henry, *b.* 10th May, 1819; *m.* 7th October, 1846, Nancy BATES, and settled in Oregon.
9. Josiah L., *b.* 14th February, 1823.

ISSUE BY SECOND MARRIAGE

I. Charles, *b.* 2d January, 1786; *d.* unmarried.
II. George, *b.* 17th November, 1788; *m.* Eliza RIDER.
III. Amos, *b.* 10th May, 1792, of whom later.
IV. Anna, *b.* 22d July, 1797; *m.* 25th October, 1817, Alfred JOHNSON, of Belfast, Maine. (See "Johnson Genealogy," by Alfred JOHNSON, Boston, Stanhope Press, 1914.)

AMOS ATKINSON, *b.* 10th May, 1792; *d.* 26th June, 1864; *m.* 28th April, 1818, Anna G. SAWYER.

ISSUE

I. William Parsons, *b.* 12th August, 1820; *m.* June, 1843, Sarah Cabot PARKMAN.

ISSUE

1. Charles Follen, *b.* 16th April, 1844; *d.* 6th May, 1915.
2. Emily Cabot, *b.* 5th September, 1847; *d.* 17th November, 1873; *m.* 12th February, 1872, George W. HOLDREGE.

ISSUE

1^1. Henry Atkinson HOLDREGE, *b.* 12th November, 1873; *m.* 26th September, 1899, Annie Mumford HUNT.

ISSUE

1^2. George Chandler HOLDRIGE, *b.* 30th March, 1905.
2^2. Charles Francis HOLDRIGE, *b.* 13th September, 1906.

3. Francis Parkman, *b.* March, 1851; *d.* 29th January, 1874.
4. Susan, *b.* 31st July, 1856.

II. George, *b.* 19th May, 1822; *m.* 19th May, 1852, Elizabeth STAIGG, *d.* 5th June, 1915.

ISSUE

1. Mary, *b.* 27th February, 1853; *d.* 17th March, 1856.
2. George, *b.* 14th March, 1854; *d.* 20th March, 1856.
3. Richard Staigg, *b.* 19th July, 1855.
4. Elizabeth, *b.* 31st December, 1856; *m.* 9th December, 1882, G. O. G. COALE.

ISSUE

1^1. Marian, *b.* 30th October, 1883; *m.* 2d December, 1907, Richard INGLIS, of Detroit, Michigan, *b.* 23d November, 1880.

ISSUE

1^2. Richard INGLIS, *b.* 27th December, 1912.
2^2. Jean INGLIS, *b.* 16th April, 1914.

5. Marian, *b.* 10th September, 1858; *d.* 11th August, 1874.
6. James Sawyer, *b.* 11th December, 1860; *d.* 17th December, 1883.
7. Henry Morrell, *b.* 13th November, 1862, in Brookline; *m.* 5th April, 1888, at Atlanta, Georgia, Mary PETERS, *b.* 14th March, 1868, dau. of Richard PETERS, *b.* in Germantown, Pennsylvania, 10th November, 1810, *d.* in Atlanta, Georgia, February, 1889, by his wife Mary Jane THOMPSON, *b.* 31st December, 1830, *d.* 8th June, 1911.

ISSUE

1^1. Mary Peters, *b.* 16th October, 1889.
2^1. Harry Morell, *b.* 23d February, 1892.

8. George, *b.* 9th May, 1866; *d.* 19th January, 1913.

III. Elizabeth Parsons, *b.* 21st April, 1824; *d.* 1st March, 1903.
IV. EDWARD, *b.* 10th February, 1827, of whom later.
V. Henry, *b.* 1831; *d.* 1832.
VI. Anne, *b.* 16th April, 1837; *m.* 26th June, 1872, Richard Morrell STAIGG, *b.* in Leeds, England, September, 1817; *d.* Newport, Rhode Island, 11th October, 1881.

EDWARD ATKINSON, *b.* 10th February, 1827; *d.* 10th December, 1905; *m.* 4th October, 1855, Mary Caroline HEATH, *b.* 1st June, 1830, *d.* 12th December, 1907, dau. of Charles and Caroline Penniman HEATH.

ISSUE

I. Caroline Heath, *b.* 6th July, 1856; *d.* 12th May, 1857.
II. Anna Greenleaf, *b.* 25th February, 1858; *m.* at Brookline, 8th June, 1882, Ernest WINSOR.

ISSUE

1. Percival WINSOR, *b.* 1st September, 1883; *d.* 10th November, 1891.
2. Anna Greenleaf WINSOR, *b.* 6th February, 1885; *m.* 20th June, 1912, John Baker SWIFT, Jr., *b.* 12th August, 1883.

ISSUE

1[1]. Martha SWIFT, *b.* 28th July, 1914.

3. Edward Atkinson WINSOR, *b.* 19th August, 1889.
4. Helen WINSOR, *b.* 17th July, 1894.

III. Edward William, *b.* 13th October, 1859; *m.* 15th November, 1894, Ellen Forbes RUSSELL, dau. of Henry S. and Mary Forbes RUSSELL.

ISSUE

1. Edward, *b.* 3d October, 1897.
2. Henry Russell, *b.* 12th December, 1899.
3. Mary Forbes, *b.* 19th December, 1900.

IV. Charles Heath, *b.* 2d July, 1862; *d.* 19th July, 1915.
V. Lincoln, *b.* 19th April, 1865; *d.* 12th August, 1865.
VI. William, *b.* 7th July, 1866; *m.* 29th May, 1900, Mittie Harmon JACKSON, (her second marriage), dau. of James Churchill and Caroline March (HARMON) JACKSON, both of Madison, New Hampshire.
VII. ROBERT WHITMAN, *b.* 14th December, 1868, the subject of this memoir.
VIII. Caroline Penniman, *b.* 5th July, 1871.
IX. Mary Heath, *b.* 16th November, 1878; *m.* 25th June, 1901, Richard Goodwin WADSWORTH.

Arms.—Vert, a cross voided, between four lions rampant or.
Crest.—A dove with wings expanded or.
Motto.—Nil facimus non sponte dei.
Residences.—Heath Hill, Brookline, Massachusetts and Mattapoisett, Massachusetts.
Clubs.—Tavern, Boston, Reform (New York).

Avery

SAMUEL PUTNAM AVERY, of Hartford, Connecticut; *b.* 7th October, 1847, in Brooklyn, New York; is Honorary Vice President National Arts Club, New York; Trustee Institute of Arts and Sciences, Brooklyn, New York; Trustee Lincoln Memorial University, Cumberland Gap, Tennessee; Trustee Hartford Atheneum and Morgan Memorial, Hartford, Connecticut; Director Colonial National Bank of Hartford, Connecticut; Director Wheeling and Lake Erie Railroad; Fellow in Perpetuity Metropolitan Museum of Art, New York; Benefactor Numismatic Society.

Lineage

ROBERT AVERY, Yeoman, of Pill (now Pylle), Somerset, England, *d.* previous to 14th October, 1575, this being the date of the proving of his will. His wife evidently predeceased him as she is not mentioned in his will; he names the following children.

ISSUE

I. WILLIAM, of whom later.
II. Richard.
III. Thomas.

WILLIAM AVERY of Congnesbury in Winterstoke Hundred, England, *d.* 1585; wife's name is unknown, he had, however, issue.

ISSUE

I. ROBERT, of whom later.

ROBERT AVERY lived in Wokingham, Berkshire, England; he was by trade a blacksmith; his will found in the Diocese of Doctors Common bears date of 30th March, 1642.

ISSUE

I. WILLIAM, *b.* 1622, of whom later.
II. Robert.
III. Frances.

LIEUTENANT WILLIAM AVERY, M.D., of Dedham and Boston, Mass.; *b.* 1622, in England; *d.* 18th March, 1686, and his tombstone stands in King's Chapel burying ground, Boston; came to Dedham, Massachusetts in 1650, bringing his wife Margaret, who *d.* 28th September, 1678, and three children from Barkham County, Berkshire, England. He is designated as Sergeant in 1669 and was a Deputy to the General Court, 1669, from Springfield; Lieutenant of Dedham County, 1673; Member Ancient and Honorable Artillery Company. He was the earliest educated physician known to have taken up his life in Dedham; he *m.* (secondly), Mrs. Mary (WOODMANSEY) TAPPING, dau. of Mr. Robert (probably) WOODMANSEY.

ISSUE

I. Mary, *bapt.* 19th December, 1645, in England; *d.* 9th September, 1713; *m.* 5th November, 1666, James TISDALE, of Taunton, Massachusetts.
II. William, Deacon, *bapt.* 27th October, 1647; *m.* (firstly) 21st September, 1673, Mary LANE, *d.* 11th October, 1681; *m.* (secondly) 29th August, 1682, Elizabeth WHITE, *d.* 3d October, 1690; *m.* (thirdly) 25th August, 1698, Mehitable (HINCKLEY) WORDEN, dau. of Gov. Thomas HINCKLEY and widow of Samuel WORDEN, *m.* 22d July, 1679, Sybil SPARHAWK, dau. of Secretary Nathaniel and Patience (NEWMAN) SPARHAWK.
III. ROBERT, *bapt.* 7th December, 1649, of whom later.
IV. Jonathan, M.D., *b.* 26th May, 1653.
V. Rachel, *b.* 20th September, 1657.
VI. Hannah, *b.* 27th September, 1660.
VII. Ebenezer, *b.* 24th November, 1663; *d.* before 1683, as he is not mentioned in his father's will.

ENSIGN ROBERT AVERY of Dedham, Massachusetts; *bapt.* 7th December, 1647, in Barkham, Berks, England; *d.* 3d October, 1722; was ensign; *m.* Elizabeth LANE, *b.* circa 1665, *d.* 21st October, 1746, dau. of Job and Sarah LANE of Malden.

ISSUE

I. Elizabeth, *b.* 21st December, 1677; *d.* 28th January, 1746–1747; *m.* 6th August, 1697.
II. Rachel, *b.* 1st September, 1679; *d.* 1775; *m.* 14th May, 1702, Michael DWIGHT.
III. Robert, *b.* 28th November, 1681; killed by the falling of a tree, 21st August, 1723.
IV. JOHN, *b.* 4th February, 1684–1685, of whom later.
V. Jonathan, *b.* 20th January, 1694–1695; *m.* 1st February, 1721–1722, Lydia HEALEY.
VI. Abigail, *b.* 8th May, 1699.

REV. JOHN AVERY of Truro, Massachusetts; *b.* 4th February, 1684–1685; *bapt.* 27th April, 1686; *d.* 23d April, 1754, in the forty-fourth year of his ministry. Was ordained 1st November, 1711, as Pastor of the First Church in Truro; Graduate Harvard College, 1706, and began his ministerial work in Truro soon after; *m.* (firstly) 23d November, 1710, Ruth LITTLE, *b.* 23d November 1686, *d.* 1st October, 1732, dau. of Ephraim and Mary (STURDEVANT) LITTLE of Marshfield and gr. gd. dau. of Mr. Richard WARREN who came in the *Mayflower* in 1620. Ephraim LITTLE was the son of Thomas and Ann (WARREN) LITTLE, she the dau. of Richard WARREN; *m.* (secondly) 3d July, 1733, Ruth KNOWLES, *b.* November, 1694, *d.* 1st November, 1745, dau. of Samuel and Mercy (FREEMAN) KNOWLES of Eastham, gd. dau. of Hon. John FREEMAN and gr. gd. dau. of Governor PRINCE; *m.* (thirdly) 24th June, 1748, Mrs. Mary ROTCH, widow of William ROTCH.

ISSUE BY FIRST MARRIAGE

I. John, *b.* 24th August, 1711; Harvard College, 1731; became "the Boston Merchant;" *m.* 13th June, 1734, Mary DEMING of Boston, who *d.* 2d December, 1763.
II. EPHRAIM, *b.* 22d April, 1713, of whom later.
III. Ruth, *b.* 26th July, 1715; *m.* Rev. Jonathan PARKER.
IV. Elizabeth, *b.* 5th March, 1716–1717; *m.* John DRAPER of Boston.
V. Robert, *b.* 26th May, 1719; removed to Lebanon, Connecticut.
VI. Job, *b.* 14th January, 1722–1723; inherited the homestead.
VII. Mary, *b.* 19th January, 1724–1725; *m.* ——— WEST.
VIII. Abigail, *b.* 1st June, 1727; *m.* Elisha LOTHROP, Norwich, Connecticut,
IX. Ann, *b.* 6th July, 1729; *d.* 25th August, 1747.

REV. EPHRAIM AVERY, of Brooklyn, Connecticut; *b.* 22d April, 1713, in Truro, Massachusetts; *d.* 20th October, 1754; graduated Harvard College, 1731; was the first minister ordained, 24th September, 1735, in Brooklyn, Connecticut; *m.* 21st September, 1738, Deborah LOTHROP, *b.* 9th January, 1716–1717, dau. of Samuel and Deborah (CROW) LOTHROP.

ISSUE

I. John, *b.* 14th July, 1739; *d.* 20th August, 1779; *m.* 26th June, 1769, Ruth SMITH, *b.* 5th May, 1741, *d.* 4th October, 1779, dau. of Jehiel and Kesia (WOOD) SMITH.
II. EPHRAIM (twin), *b.* 13th April, 1741, of whom later.
III. Samuel (twin), *b.* 13th April, 1741, *d.* soon.
IV. Samuel, *b.* 7th November, 1742; *m.* Mrs. Mary (FILLIS) ACKINCLOSS, Nova Scotia.
V. Elisha, *b.* 3d December, 1744; *m.* Emma PUTNAM.
VI. Elizabeth, *b.* 5th December, 1746; *m.* Rev. Aaron PUTNAM.
VII. Septimus, *b.* 21st July, 1749; *d.* 10th October, 1754.
VIII. Deborah, *b.* 5th July, 1751; *m.* Dr. Joseph BAKER.
IX. Ruth, *b.* 13th January, 1754; *m.* Dr. John Brewster HAMPTON.

REV. EPHRAIM AVERY, M.D., of Rye, New York; *b.* 13th April, 1741; *d.* 5th November, 1776; Graduate of Yale, 1761; M.A., King's College, New York, 1767; went to England; was ordained Deacon Priest by Dr. HINCHMAN, Bishop of London; *m.* Hannah PLATT (?).

COLONIAL FAMILIES OF THE UNITED STATES

ISSUE

I. Hannah Platt, *b.* 16th April, 1763; *m.* Stephen BARRITT.
II. Elizabeth Draper, *b.* 29th August, 1765; *m.* (firstly) ——— CHURCH, who *d.* in the West Indies.
III. JOHN WILLIAM, *b.* 24th May, 1767, of whom later.
IV. Elisha Lothrop, *b.* 27th November, 1768.
V. Joseph Platt, *b.* 24th March, 1771.
VI. Deborah Palmer, *b.* 1st June, 1773.

JOHN WILLIAM AVERY of Stratford, Connecticut; *b.* 24th May, 1767; *d.* 1799; the family tradition is that he was a clergyman; *m.* Sarah FAIRCHILD, of Stratford, Connecticut.

ISSUE

I. John William, *b.* 179—; in early life was lost at sea in the *Jeannette*.
II. SAMUEL PUTNAM, *b.* January, 1797, of whom later.
III. Sarah Elizabeth (Betsey), *m.* 1817, Ebenezer R. DUPIGNAC.
IV. Elisha Lothrop, *b.* 1799; *m.* (firstly) 1822, Jane GUNNING, *d.* September, 1837; *m.* (secondly) Sarah COIT, dau. of David COIT, of New London, Connecticut.

SAMUEL PUTNAM AVERY, I, of New York City, *b.* January, 1797; *d.* of cholera, 1832; was proprietor of the hotel called "East River Mansion House;" *m.* 1st January, 1821, Hannah Ann PARK, *b.* 24th April, 1805, *d.* 26th June 1888, dau. of Capt. Benjamin PARK, who *d.* 5th August, 1807, and whose tombstone is still standing in old Trinity Church Yard, New York City.

ISSUE

I. SAMUEL PUTNAM, II, *b.* 17th March, 1822, of whom later.
II. Hannah Stanton, *b.* 12th October, 1824; *m.* 2d May, 1854. Charles Russell CORNELL; *d.* 25th June, 1885.
III. Susan Jane, *b.* 11th December, 1826; *m.* (firstly) 5th December, 1850, Stephen AVERY, *d.* 1st January, 1853; *m.* (secondly) 14th February, 1867, William ROBINSON.
IV. Benjamin Parke, United States Minister to China, *b.* 11th November, 1828; *d.* 8th November, 1875; *m.* Mary A. FULLER.
V. Mary Rebecca Halsey, *b.* 10th August, 1830; *m.* Rev. T. DeWitt TALMAGE.
VI. Charles Russell, *b.* October, 1832; *d.* 5th August, 1833.

SAMUEL PUTNAM AVERY of New York City; *b.* 17th March, 1822; *d.* 11th August, 1904. In 1867 was appointed to go abroad in charge of the American Art Department at the Paris Universal Exhibition; was Secretary of the Art Committee of the Union League Club; one of the Founders and Trustees of the Metropolitan Museum of Art and one of the Committee for the Erection of the Bartholdi "Statue of Liberty" in New York Harbor; was a member of the Century, Union League and Grolier Clubs, and a life member of historical, geographical, free library, archeological and other societies. Author of "Some Notes on the History of the Fine Arts in New York City During Fifty Years." The Avery collection of Oriental porcelain, purchased and presented by his friends to the Metropolitan Museum of Art in New York, is said to have been the most complete ever brought together in this country, consisting of more than 1200 pieces; he *m.* 24th November, 1844, Mary Ann OGDEN, *b.* 1st December, 1825, *d.* 29th April, 1911, dau. of Henry Aaron and Katharene (CONKLIN) OGDEN of New York.

ISSUE

I. Mary Henrietta, *b.* 4th October, 1845; *d.* 7th April, 1900.
II. SAMUEL PUTNAM, *b.* 7th October, 1847, the subject of this memoir.
III. Fannie Falconer, *b.* 3d November, 1849; *m.* 15th February, 1881, Rev. Manfred Philester WELCHER, *b.* 27th October, 1850.

ISSUE

1. Emma Parke Avery WELCHER, *b.* 26th November, 1881.
2. Alice Lee WELCHER, *b.* 17th May, 1884.
3. Lester Groome WELCHER, *b.* 1st of July, 1885.
4. Amy Ogden WELCHER, *b.* 26th March, 1887.

IV. Henry Ogden, *b.* 31st January, 1852; *d.* 30th April, 1890.
V. Emma Parke, *b.* 27th August, 1853; *d.* 31st August, 1857.
VI. Ellen Waters, *b.* 1st January, 1861; *d.* 25th March, 1893.

Arms.—Gules a chevron between three besants, or.
Crest.—Two lions jambs or supporting a besant.
Motto.—Fidelis.
Residences.—61 Woodland Street, Hartford, Connecticut and West Port, New York.
Clubs.—Union League, Grolier and National Arts of New York.
Societies.—Mayflower Descendants of Connecticut, Colonial Wars of New York, Sons of the Revolution of New York, Life Member of New England Society of New York, the New York Historical Society, the Archaeological Institute of America, the New York Geographical Society, the New York Zoological Society, the New York Genealogical and Biographical Society, Member American Science, Historical Preservation Society of New York, New York Academy of Sciences, American Academy of Political and Social Science of Philadelphia and many others.

Avery-Park (maternal)

RICHARD PARK of London, England; *b.* 1602 (?); *d.* 1665, in Newton, Massachusetts. His will was dated 12th July, 1665; was a proprietor in Cambridge, Massachusetts, in 1636, and of Cambridge Farms (Lexington), 1642; his house was near the commons in Cambridge. The very ancient dwelling house which was pulled down about 1800 was supposed to have been built by him. Previous to 1652, he owned a large tract of land in the northwest part of the village of Cambridge. It contained 600 acres which he probably bought of Pastor SHEPARD or his heirs. In 1657 he was one of a committee, with Edward JACKSON, John JACKSON, and Samuel HYDE, to lay out and settle highways in the village. During the contest between the village and Cambridge to be set off, he sent a petition to the Court in 1661 praying to retain his connection with the Cambridge Church; *m.* (firstly) in England and came over in the ship *Defense*, July, 1635, and settled in Cambridge, Massachusetts, where he purchased a large tract of land on the Charles River, a portion of which is now occupied by the Harvard College; *m.* (secondly) Sarah (COLLIER) BREWSTER, dau. of William and Jane COLLIER and widow of Love BREWSTER of Duxbury, his widow Sarah *d.* after 1678 at Duxbury, Massachusetts.

ISSUE BY FIRST MARRIAGE

I. THOMAS, *b.* 1628 or 1629, of whom later.
II. Sarah, *d.* 1699.
III. Isabel, supposed to be 7 years old in 1635; *m.* Francis WHITTEMORE.
IV. Elizabeth, 4 years, in 1635.

THOMAS PARK of Cambridge, Massachusetts; *b.* 1629; *d.* 11th August, 1690; *m.* 1st December, 1650, Abigail DIX, *d.* 3d February, 1691, dau. of Edward and Jane DIX of Watertown, Massachusetts.

ISSUE

I. Thomas, *b.* 2d November, 1654; *d.* 28th August, 1681.
II. JOHN, *b.* 6th September, 1656, of whom later.
III. Abigail, *b.* 3d March, 1658; *m.* 1st December, 1679, John FISKE.
IV. Edward, *b.* 8th April, 1661; *m.* 1679, Martha FISKE, who *d.* 11th August, 1690.
V. Richard, *b.* 21st December, 1663; *d.* 19th June, 1725; *m.* Sarah CUTTER.
VI. Sarah, *b.* 1st January, 1666; *m.* 4th August, 1686; John KNAPP.
VII. Rebecca, *b.* 13th February, 1668; *m.* 1685, John SANGER of Watertown, Massachusetts.

VIII. Jonathan, *b.* 27th August, 1670; *d.* 1719; *m.* 1690, Anne SPRING, of Watertown.
IX. Elizabeth, *b.* 28th July, 1679; *m.* John HOLLAND.

JOHN PARK, *b.* 6th September, 1656; *d.* 21st March, 1718; *m.* 5th April, 1694, Elizabeth MILLER of Watertown, Massachusetts.

ISSUE

I. Elizabeth, *b.* 24th February, 1695; *d.* young.
II. John, *b.* 20th December, 1696; *d.* 21st May, 1747; *m.* Abigail LAURENCE.
III. Solomon, *b.* 16th October, 1699; *d.* 3d January, 1754; *m.* Lydia LAURENCE.
IV. Elizabeth, *b.* 21st February, 1701; *m.* 1724, John MORSE.
V. Abigail, *b.* 20th April, 1702; *m.* Nathaniel WHITTEMORE.
VI. JOSEPH, *b.* 12th March, 1705, of whom later.
VII. Mary, *b.* 17th March, 1708; *m.* 1727, Isaac SANGER.
VIII. Deliverance, no record.

REVEREND JOSEPH PARK, B.A., M.A., of Westerly, Rhode Island; *b.* in Newton, Massachusetts, 12th March, 1704; *d.* 1st March, 1777, in the forty-fifth year of his ministry. Graduated from Harvard College, 1720, with the degree of B.A., subsequently receiving the degree of M.A. in 1724. He studied for the Ministry and was ordained 1730, moved to Westerly, Rhode Island, 1733, where he distinguished himself as a Minister of the Gospel. He was a self sacrificing, patriotic and public spirited man. Ordained 1732. Went to Westerly, Rhode Island, 1733. He organized a Sunday School in connection with his church at Westerly, 1752, nearly thirty years before the experiment of Robert REIKES in England. Having care for a sick woman of smallpox who had been driven away by the town authorities, he was tried for contempt, whereupon he preached a sermon in vindication of his course, which with a narrative of the transaction was published. "April 11th, 1756, Appointed Wednesday 14th as a day of fasting and prayer, to humble ourselves before God, to implore His gracious presence with, and blessings to our young brethren Joseph PARK, Jr., Benjamin PARK, and Thomas PARK and William GARRIT, all who offered their desire in writing to this society, and we believe that God of His Infinite Mercy will hear and answer, and also that God would bless our Army in general, who are going forth against our enemies. The young men here mentioned were in the expedition that went forth for the reduction of Crown Point. It will be noticed that three of them were sons of Rev. Joseph PARK, who was always a man of public spirit." Proceedings of the General Assembly held for the Colony of Rhode Island and Providence Plantations at South Kingstown the 14th day of February, 1758. "Whereas the Rev. Joseph PARK of Charlestown in the County of Kings, presented this Assembly with a memorial setting forth that he hath ever been ready to contribute all of the assistance in his power to stop his Majesty's enemies from their injurious encroachments on his dominion and just rights in America and to defend the Country. That in the year of 1756 he consented to the voluntary service of three of his sons who served in the expedition formed for the reduction of Crown Point; that when they were discharged from the service upon their return homeward, they put their clothing and other furniture to the value of £100 currency, in their chest which was unfortunately lost in the sea. That this summer when the enemy attacked Fort William Henry, they volunteered in the stead of officers who declined, that they did this without any consideration purely to serve their country, that he the memorialist was thereby put to considerable charge, wherefore he prays for such allowance as should be thought proper. On consideration whereof this Assembly do vote and resolve that the sum of £100 be paid said Joseph PARK out of the General Treasury, for the use of his aforesaid, but that nothing be allowed them as officers." After his graduation at Harvard College, Cambridge, he was appointed missionary to the Indians and such English as would attend, in Westerly, Rhode Island. He entered his new field of labor in 1733, occupying a meeting-house on a lot of land given by George NINEGRET, chief sachem of the Indians. The lot comprised twenty acres and was situated near the post-road in the eastern part of the present town. His congregation came from Westerly, Charlestown and Narragansett. His work was slow and difficult until 1740, when the great revival arose in New England. In 1751 he removed and settled at Mattatuck, near Southfield, Long Island, where he labored until 1756, when he returned to Westerly, and was formally settled again, 23d May, 1759. This church established the first Sabbath-school and Mr. PARK was its first and only pastor;" he *m.* 1732, Abigail GREENE, *b.* 1703, *d.* 19th October, 1772.

ISSUE

I. Jonathan Greene, *b.* 30th October, 1733, at Newton, Massachusetts.
II. BENJAMIN, *b.* 1st November, 1735, of whom later.
III. Joseph, Jr., *b.* Westerly, Rhode Island, 1st November, 1735; was at the reduction of Crown Point 1756, and at the defense of Fort William Henry, 1758.
IV. Thomas, *b.* in Westerly, Rhode Island, 1738; was at the reduction of Crown Point, the defense of Fort William Henry, and the siege of Louisburg.
V. Ann, *b.* 1739; *d.* 20th March, 1817; *m.* 7th September, 1758, Peleg PENDLETON of Stonington, Connecticut.
VI. John, Captain, *b.* at Westerly, Rhode Island, 1742; *d.* in 1812 in Searsport, Maine; he commanded a Company of Militia at Charlestown, Rhode Island, 1780; *m.* (firstly) by Rev. Joseph PARK, 4th November, 1772, Abigail CHAPMAN, who *d.* 4th March, 1790, dau. of William CHAPMAN of Westerly, Rhode Island; *m.* (secondly) 29th June, 1794, Sarah HISCOX.
VII. Henry, *b.* in Westerly, Rhode Island, 1744.
VIII. Samuel, *b.* in Westerly, Rhode Island, 1747; *d.* there 29th September, 1747.
IX. Mary (?), no further record.

CAPTAIN BENJAMIN PARK, Jr., of New York City; *b.* 16th September, 1766, at Charlestown, Rhode Island; *d.* 5th August, 1807, in New York City; buried in Trinity Churchyárd, in Broadway, New York City, (about 18 paces north of nearly the west end of the church of which he was vestryman); came to New York City where he engaged in business with his brother Joseph; *m.* Susanna Maria KEENS, *b.* 2d December, 1776, *d.* 17th February, 1807, buried in Trinity Churchyard, dau. of Joseph and Mary KEENS of New York City.

ISSUE

I. Susanna Maria, *b.* in New York City.
II. HANNAH ANNE, *b.* in New York City, 24th April, 1804, of whom later.

HANNAH ANNE PARK, *b.* in New York City, 24th April, 1804; *d.* 26th June, 1888. In the War of the Rebellion of the slave holding States, she was active in sending delicacies to the sick and wounded soldiers, in caring for their widows and orphans, and was the chief instrument in founding a home for the children of the dead soldiers. She subsequently became identified with Mrs. Gen. U. S. GRANT in extending this work, and was at one time Vice-President when Mrs. GRANT was President of the National Organization; *m.* (firstly) at an early age Samuel P. AVERY of New York City, *b.*—January, 1797, *d.* 24th July, 1832; *m.* (secondly) 26th September, 1835, John Nicholas COYNE, *b.* in Ireland, 22d December, 1815, *d.* 31st May, 1854; *m.* (thirdly) 1858, John Owen ROUSE; no issue.

ISSUE BY FIRST MARRIAGE

I. Samual Putnam AVERY, *b.* 17th March, 1822; *d.* 11th August, 1904; *m.* 24th November, 1844, Mary Ann OGDEN, *b.* 1st December, 1825, *d.* 29th April, 1911, dau. of Henry Aaron and Katharene (CONKLIN) OGDEN of New York.

ISSUE

1. Mary Henrietta AVERY, *b.* 4th October, 1845; *d.* 7th April, 1900.
2. SAMUEL PUTNAM AVERY, *b.* 7th October, 1847, the subject of this memoir.
3. Fannie Falconer AVERY, *b.* 3d November, 1849; *m.* 15th February, 1881, Rev. Manfred Philester WELCHER (see Avery record, p. 34).
4. Henry Ogden AVERY, *b.* 31st January, 1852; *d.* 30th April, 1890.
5. Emma Park AVERY, *b.* 27th August, 1853; *d.* 31st August, 1857.
6. Ellen Waters AVERY, *b.* 1st January, 1861; *d.* 28th March, 1893.

II. Hannah Stanton AVERY, *b.* 12th October, 1824; *d.* 25th June, 1825.
III. Susan Jane AVERY, *b.* 11th December, 1826.
IV. Benjamin Parke AVERY, *b.* 11th November, 1828; *d.* 8th November, 1875.
V. Mary Rebecca AVERY, *b.* 10th August, 1830; *d.* 9th June, 1862.
VI. Charles Russell AVERY, *b.* October, 1832; *d.* 5th August, 1833.

ISSUE BY SECOND MARRIAGE

I. A child, *b.* in New York City, in 1837, *d.* in infancy.
II. John Nicholas COYNE, Jr., *b.* in New York City, 14th November, 1839; *d.* March, 1907; *m.* (firstly) in Philadelphia, Pennsylvania, 19th March, 1863, Sallie Johnson MATTHEWS, *b.* 17th May, 1844, in Philadelphia, *d.* 8th November, 1833, youngest dau. of Dr. Caleb B. and Mary (MYERS) MATTHEWS; *m.* (secondly) 6th June, 1894, Pauline Mary HEMINGWAY, *b.* in England, 1st March, 1868, dau. of William and Gertrude HEMINGWAY of Germantown, Pennsylvania.

ISSUE BY FIRST MARRIAGE

1. Saidee Matthews COYNE, *b.* 22d December, 1863, at Philadelphia; *m.* 16th December, 1885, Dr. Samuel Wellman CLARK, who *d.* in Jersey City, 5th December, 1899.
2. Bertha Park COYNE, *b.* 27th September, 1865, in Jersey City; *d.* 5th December, 1866.
3. Anne Augusta COYNE, *b.* 23d January, 1868, in Jersey City; *d.* 3d July, 1868.
4. Maie Park COYNE, *b.* 18th May, 1870, in Jersey City; *m.* there 12th February, 1896, John Murray LINDSAY.

III. William Henry Harrison COYNE, *b.* in New York City, 20th January 1841; *d.* 2d January, 1901; *m.* Jane GOODALE.
IV. Jane Augusta COYNE, *b.* 6th April, 1843; *d.* 14th November, 1851, and was buried in the COYNE family plot, Greenwood.
V. Charles Russell COYNE, *b.* 11th September, 1845; *d.* 4th October, 1899 and was buried in Jersey City Cemetery; *m.* Fanny C. WATERS, of Jersey City, New Jersey.

Arms (Park).—Gules on a pale argent three bucks heads cabossed of the field.
Crest.—A talbot's head gules pierced in the breast with a pheon or.
Motto.—"Virtus"—Courage.

Bacon

CHARLES FRANCIS BACON, deceased, of Waterville, Maine; *b.* 11th July, 1835; *d.* unmarried 6th April, 1913; served four years in the Civil War, in the Union Army. He was badly wounded at Bull Run and was in the hospital for a long period. Upon his recovering from his wounds he returned to the Army and served until the termination of the War.

Lineage

BACON is a Seigniory in Normandy according to the well authenticated genealogy of the great Suffolk family of BACON from which sprung many branches. The founder of the English family is said to have been Grumbaldus, a Norman gentleman related to William DE WARRENE, Earl of Surrey. He came into England at the time of the Conquest and had grants of land at Letheringsete near Holt, County of Norfolk. He had three sons.

   I. Rudueph.
  II. RANUEF, of whom later.
 III. Edmund.

RAN(D)ULF or Reynolds resided at Thorpe, County Norfolk, called Baconsthorpe by distinction, his son Roger had sons ROBERT and William.
ROBERT had JOHN and William.
JOHN I had JOHN II Time of Edward I.
JOHN II had JOHN III.
JOHN III had JOHN IV.
JOHN IV had
JOHN V who had
EDMUND who had
JOHN who had Robert John, THOMAS, Henry and William.

THOMAS BAKON of Helmingham, will proved 27th February ——; *m.* Johan, surname not given, *d.* 1540.

ISSUE

   I. JOHN, will proved 11th March, 1557, of whom later.
  II. Thomas.
 III. Anne, *m.* ——— Dow.
  IV. John.
   V. Henry.
  VI. Mary.
 VII. Agnes.
VIII. Elizabeth.

JOHN BACON, will proved 19th March, 1587; *m.* Margaret, surname not given.

ISSUE

 I. William.
 II. Thomas.
 III. MICHAEL, *bapt.* 31st May, 1566, of whom later.
 IV. Richard.
 V. Barbara.
 VI. Rose.
 VII. William (the younger).

MICHAEL BACON, Yeoman, of Winston, County Suffolk, England, *bapt.* 31st May, 1566, was buried 25th March, 1615, will dated 24th October, 1614; *m.* (firstly) 16th August, 1565, Elizabeth WYLIE, *bapt.* 30th May, 1566; *m.* (secondly) 20th September, 1607, the widow Grace BLOWERSES.

ISSUE BY FIRST MARRIAGE

 I. John, *bapt.* 31st May, 1566.
 II. William.
 III. Thomas.
 IV. MICHAEL, *bapt.* 6th December, 1579, of whom later.
 V. Sarah, *m.* Daniel YORKE.
 VI. Elizabeth, *bapt.* 3d September, 1584.

MICHAEL BACON, Yeoman, of Winston, Suffolk County, England, and Dedham, Massachusetts; *b.* 6th December, 1579, in Winston, Suffolk County, England; *d.* 18th April, 1648; *m.* Alice (surname not given), who *d.* 2d April, 1648.

ISSUE

 I. MICHAEL, *b.* probably 1608, of whom later.
 II. Daniel, *b.* probably 1615; *d.* 7th September, 1691, at Newton; came to New England, 1640; *m.* Mary READ, who *d.* 4th October, 1691, dau. of Thomas READ.

ISSUE

1. Daniel, *b.* probably 1641; *d.* 1720; *m.* 1st August, 1664, Susanna SPENCER, dau. of Michael SPENCER, of Salem.
2. Thomas, *b.* 13th April, 1645, *d.* young.
3. John, *b.* 8th September, 1647; found dead on Boston Marsh 31st August, 1723; *m.* Abigail, surname unknown.
4. Isaac, *b.* 4th April, 1650; *d.* 8th January, 1684; *m.* Abigail, surname unknown.
5. Rachel, *b.* 8th June, 1652; *m.* 24th March, 1680, Thomas PEIRCE, *b.* 21st June, 1645, *d.* 8th December, 1717, son of Thomas and Elizabeth (COLE) PEIRCE.

6. Jacob, *b.* 2d June, 1654; *d.* 5th June, 1709; *m.* Elizabeth KNIGHT, *b.* 3d June, 1656, *d.* 27th January, 1713, dau. of John and Ruhamah (JOHNSON) KNIGHT.
7. Lydia, *b.* 6th March, 1656; *d.* 5th December, 1717; *m.* 9th December, 1680, Samuel PEIRCE, *b.* 7th April, 1656, *d.* 5th July, 1721, brother of Thomas above.

III. John, of Dedham, freeman, 1647; *d.* 17th June, 1683.
IV. Alice, *d.* 29th March, 1648; *m.* 31st March, 1647, Thomas BANCROFT, of Dedham, Massachusetts, *b.* in England, 1622, son of John and Jane BANCROFT.
V. Sarah, *b.* 1652; *m.* 14th April, 1648, Anthony HUBBARD, of Dedham.

MICHAEL BACON, of Woburn, Massachusetts, *b.* in England probably 1608; *d.* 4th July, 1688. Came to New England 1640. Surveyor of Highways, 1644. His sawmill on the Shawsheen River was burned by the Indians at the time of King Philip's War. Selectman, 1659–1665, 1666, 1668 and 1670; *m.* (firstly) Mary, surname not given, who *d.* 26th August, 1655; *m.* (secondly) 26th October, 1655, Mary RICHARDSON, *d.* 19th May, 1670, widow of Thomas RICHARDSON; *m.* (thirdly) 28th November, 1670, Mary (HAINES) NOYES, dau. of Walter and Eliza HAINES and widow of Thomas NOYES.

ISSUE

I. MICHAEL, *b.* in England; *bapt.* 16th February, 1639, at Winston, England, of whom later.
II. Mary, *bapt.* 18th February, 1640, at Winston, England; *m.* March, 1662, Bartholomew GALE, of Salem, as his second wife.
III. Elizabeth, *b.* 4th January, 1642, in Woburn, Massachusetts; *m.* 22d October, 1658, Lieut. John RICHARDSON, *bapt.* 12th November, 1639, *d.* 1st January, 1697, son of Samuel and Joanna RICHARDSON, of Woburn.
IV. Sarah, *b.* 24th August, 1644, in Woburn; *m.* 25th September, 1677, Caleb SIMMONS.

MICHAEL BACON of Woburn and Billerica, Massachusetts; *b.* in England, *bapt.* at Winston, 16th February, 1639. On 19th July, 1682, purchased the farm of five hundred acres in Billerica; *m.* 22d March, 1660, Sarah RICHARDSON, *bapt.* 22d, November, 1640, *d.* 15th August, 1694, dau. of Thomas RICHARDSON, *b.* 1640.

ISSUE (RECORDED IN WOBURN)

I. Mary, *b.* 1st March, 1661; *m.* John LAKIN of Groton.
II. Sarah, *b.* 24th August, 1663.
III. Abigail, *b.* 5th March, 1667; *d.* 6th December, 1743; *m.* 13th December 1686, Josiah WOOD, Jr., of Woburn, who *d.* 9th March, 1740.
IV. Michael, birth unknown, removed to Dorchester, South Carolina, and probably later removed to Georgia.

v. Jonathan, b. 14th July, 1672; d. 12th January, 1754; m. (firstly) 3d June, 1694, Elizabeth GILES, b. 1671, d. 16th December, 1738, dau. of John and Elizabeth GILES; m. (secondly) 22d September, 1739, Elizabeth (HANCOCK) WYMAN, b. 1685, d. 3d March, 1748, dau. of Nathaniel and Mary (PRENTICE) HANCOCK, and widow of Benjamin WYMAN of Coburn.

vi. Nathaniel, b. 18th September, 1675; d. 24th July, 1750, at Lexington; was one of the twelve Billerica soldiers who went to rescue Lancaster when it was attacked by Indians 31st July, 1704. In July, 1706, served two days under Major LANE in an expedition for the relief of Dunstable; m. Judith WYMAN, b. 15th January, 1679, dau. of Francis and Judith (PIERCE) WYMAN of Woburn.

vii. JOSIAH, b. 20th October, 1678, of whom later.

viii. Ruth, b. 24th September, 1681.

ix. Benjamin, birth recorded between 1681 and 1685; d. 27th November, 1727; served in Captain John LANE's Company in Indian War. In Queen Anne's War he served in the relief of Dunstable in 1706; m. 2d December, 1712, Abigail TAYLOR of Concord.

x. Joseph, b. 8th May, 1685; d. 29th November, 1747, in Bedford; m. 9th May, 1716, Rebecca TAYLOR, of Concord, b. 1686, d. 24th August, 1778.

JOSIAH BACON of Billerica, Massachusetts; b. 20th October, 1678; d. 14th October, 1723; was one of the troopers who served under Major LANE for the relief of Dunstable, 4th July, 1706. In August of the same year he served as trumpeter; m. Mary, surname not given.

ISSUE

i. JOSIAH, b. 27th April, 1702, of whom later.
ii. Mary, b. 20th October, 1703; d. 16th November, 1703.
iii. Mary, b. 9th December, 1704; d. 8th January, 1705.
iv. Mary, b. 14th October, 1706.
v. Lydia, b. 6th June, 1710.
vi. Samuel b. 25th March, 1719; d. 19th April, 1719.

JOSIAH BACON of Billerica, Massachusetts; b. there 27th April, 1702; d. previous to August, 1751, as his widow, Sarah DAVIS, m. (secondly) 8th August, 1751, Capt. Enoch KIDDER. Sarah DAVIS was the dau. of Deacon Joseph and Sarah (PATTEN) DAVIS.

ISSUE

i. Josiah, b. 23d April, 1727.
ii. Solomon, b. 27th November, 1728.
iii. David, b. 30th August, 1730.
iv. Joshua, b. 14th September, 1732.

v. William, *b.* 8th August, 1734; *d.* after 1790; was a member of Col. Jacob FOWEL's Regiment October, 1755, Colonial Wars; also in the Revolutionary War Commissioned Captain 22d June, 1775, at Marblehead, Massachusetts; also in Col. John CLOVER's Regiment, 1st August, 1775; commissioned 20th September, 1779, Colonel 5th Essex County Regiment.
vi. EBENEZER, *b.* 15th September, 1736, of whom later.
vii. James, *b.* 30th June, 1738.
viii. Sarah, *b.* 18th August, 1740.
ix. Mary, *b.* 5th February, 1742.
x. Joseph, *b.* 24th March, 1745.
xi. Liday, *b.* 23d August, 1747.

EBENEZER BACON of Sidney and Vassalborough, Maine; *b.* 15th September, 1736, in Billerica, Massachusetts. Will dated 12th February, 1798, probated 2d August, 1798. Appears as enlisted in Capt. Joseph WINSLOW's Regiment, 31st May, 1754 and was in service four months and two days. In 1755 enlisted in Capt. William LITHGOW's Company and was in service at Fort Halifax, Maine, until 19th April, 1755. One of the Constables of Vassalborough 13th July, 1775. In 1777 was Tithing Man and in 1778 Surveyor of Highways; 23d June, 1779, Delegate to County Convention to take measures against the British landing at Penobscot; *m.* 1762, in Boston, Abigail (FARWELL) RICHARDSON, *b.* 11th March, 1734, in Dunstable, dau. of Isaac and Sarah FARWELL and widow of Levi RICHARDSON.

ISSUE

i. Frances, *b.* 21st June, 1763; *m.* 20th August, 1786, Joseph THOMAS.
ii. EBENEZER, *b.* 13th September, 1765, of whom later.
iii. William, *b.* 9th March, 1768; *m.* 1st December, 1794, Abigail LOVEJOY, dau. of Abigail LOVEJOY.
iv. Abigail, *b.* 23d August, 1770; *m.* (firstly) 14th September, 1786, Winthrop ROBINSON; *m.* (secondly) 28th December, 1788, Elnathan SHERWIN.

EBENEZER BACON of Waterville and Fairfield, Maine, *b.* 13th September, 1765, in Vassalborough, Massachusetts; *d.* circa, 1847, in Fairfield, Maine; was Town Treasurer in 1789 and also at a later date; Selectman of Sidney, Maine, 1772 and 1773; Town Clerk in 1796; was Selectman of Waterville, Maine, 1802–1813; Member from Waterville, Maine (territory of Massachusetts at the time) of the Massachusetts Convention in 1819; *m.* 28th November, 1793, Hannah LOVEJOY, *b.* 19th November, 1775, in Pownalboro, Maine, now Wiscasset, Maine.

ISSUE

i. Columbus, *b.* 1794, there is a tradition he went to Australia; probably *m.* 7th May, 1842, in Calais, Maine, Mary Roads STICKNEY, *b.* 2d January, 1806, dau. of Jonathan and Wealthy Chase STICKNEY.
ii. EBENEZER FARWELL, *b.* 22d September, 1796, of whom later.

III. Evelina, *b.* 1800; *d.* 1882; *m.* 1827, Rev. Henry PAINE, a graduate of Colby University in 1823.
IV. Julia A., *b.* 1803; *d.* 1873; *m.* ——— ESTEY.
V. John Hancock, *b.* 1808.
VI. Samuel Adams, *b.* 1808; *m.* 18th January, 1838, at Waterville, Elvira MCLAUGHLIN, who *d.* 19th April, 1869.

EBENEZER FARWELL BACON of Waterville, Maine; *b.* 22d September, 1796, in Sidney, Maine; *d.* in Waterville, Maine, 25th October, 1841; was Sheriff of Kennebec County, 1839, and was holding the office at the time of his death; served on the Fire Board, and Selectman of Waterville, Maine; was elected Ensign of a Company in 1st Regiment of Infantry, 23d February, 1818, and Captain 2d March, 1821; resigned and was discharged 2d April, 1824; made a Master Mason at Waterville, Maine, May 10th, 1827; *m.* 9th November, 1828, Jane FAUNCE, *b.* 11th August, 1807, *d.* 8th January, 1882, dau. of Asa and Miriam FAUNCE.

ISSUE

1. Caroline Frances, *b.* 7th January, 1830 in Waterville, Maine; *d.* 1st October, 1899, in Cambridge, Massachusetts; *m.* 2d December 1853, in Waterville, Maine, James Monroe PALMER, *b.* 5th October, 1822, in Exeter Mills, Maine, *d.* 23d May, 1897, in Kenosha, Wisconsin, son of Jonathan and Martha (PRESCOTT) PALMER.

ISSUE

1. Rev. Charles James PALMER, S.T.B., General Theological Seminary, New York, 1878, of Lanesboro, Massachusetts; *b.* 4th November, 1854, Fairfield, Maine; an Episcopal minister and graduate of Bowdoin College 1874; Deacon, 1878; Priest, 1879 in Protestant Episcopal Church; Pastor St. John's Church, Bangor, Maine, 1879–1880; St. Luke's Church, Lanesboro, Massachusetts, 1880–1899; missionary for Berkshire County, Massachusetts, since 1899; President Berkshire County, Massachusetts Ministers Association; Author of many historical works; *m.* (firstly) 19th January, 1881, Helen M. WATSON of Cambridge, Massachusetts, who *d.* 23d May, 1882; *m.* (secondly) 15th October, 1885, Gertrude S. BARNES of Lanesboro, Massachusetts, who *d.* 7th May, 1915.

ISSUE

1¹. Helen E. PALMER, *b.* 23d January, 1882.
2¹. Edward James Barnes PALMER, *b.* 3d October, 1886; *d.* 3d April, 1913. He was educated in the common schools of Lanesboro, Massachusetts, also attended Prof. A. J. CLOUGH's private school in Pittsfield, Massachusetts, and the Pittsfield High School, where he was graduated in 1907. He also took a brief course in the Berk-

shire Business College. He had been early drawn to physics and chemistry, in which he specialized with marked success. His original intention was to enter the General Electric Works in Pittsfield, but he was advised to secure a more comprehensive education in physics and chemistry. His ambition was that of leadership in his chosen profession. As a special student in the Class of 1911, he entered Bowdoin College, giving special attention to physics and chemistry. He also attended the sessions of the Harvard Summer School. These studies led to an enlarged vision and he determined to enter on a complete college course, and in 1909 was admitted to the Sophomore Class at Harvard, where he remained for three years, giving particular attention to chemistry, but by no means neglecting collateral studies. He was awarded one of the Matthews' Scholarships in 1910 and also in 1911. He received the degree of Bachelor of Science from Harvard on Commencement Day, 1912. In the autumn he was invited to a position as Assistant Professor of Chemistry at Allegheny College, Meadville, Pennsylvania, where he rapidly won friends and was spoken of as a "Master Chemist;" was a member of his College Society Delta Upsilon.

 3^1. Annie G. PALMER, *b.* 9th April, 1893.

2. Edward Francis PALMER, *b.* 15th October, 1857; *d.* 23d March, 1862.
3. Caroline Emma PALMER, *b.* 28th February, 1861; *m.* 17th July, 1894, Rev. Charles Graham GARDNER, at Osaka, Japan; they live in London, England.

ISSUE

 1^1. Charles Graham GARDNER, *b.* 8th May, 1895.
 2^1. Ralph Graham GARDNER, *b.* 15th January, 1900.
 3^1. Emily Beatrice GARDNER, *b.* 6th March, 1903.

4. George Monroe PALMER, *b.* 31st May, 1863; *m.* 27th September, 1893, Anne Wildes BROWN, who *d.* 7th March, 1912.
5. William Lincoln PALMER, *b.* 19th September, 1868; *m.* 14th April, 1892, in Boston, Massachusetts, Jennie C. GIESLER, *b.* 22d July, 1873, dau. of Charles A. and Margaret (DIVES) GIESLER (see memoir, Vol. V, p. 408, "Colonial Families United States of America").

ISSUE

 1^1. Jennie Carolyn PALMER, *b.* 22d November, 1894.
 2^1. Marion Prescott PALMER, *b.* 29th September, 1897.
 3^1. William Lincoln PALMER, Jr., *b.* 7th July, 1909.

6. Frederick Tobey PALMER, *b.* 20th May, 1871; *m.* 31st May, 1900, at Williamstown, Mary E. PRIMMER, who *d.* 8th March, 1904.

ISSUE

1¹. Florence Mary, *b.* 23d March, 1901.

II. Mary Angeline, *b.* 28th March, 1831.
III. Emily Jane, *b.* 14th November, 1832; *d.* 9th October, 1908; *m.* 13th April, 1857, in Berkeley, California, Thomas Barnes BUCK, of Stockton, California.

ISSUE

1. Lizzie BUCK, *b.* 23d January, 1858; *d.* young.
2. Hon. George Faunce BUCK, *b.* 4th March, 1863, in Chinese Camp, California; graduated from Harvard University, 1887; in 1902 he was appointed one of the Judges of the Superior Court of California; *m.* 1895, Blanche E. STAPLES, dau. of Stephen and Emma STAPLES of Stockton, California, who graduated at Wellesley College, 1895.

ISSUE

1¹. George Faunce BUCK, *b.* 15th December, 1898, in Stockton, California.
2¹. Thomas Barnes BUCK, *b.* 20th February, 1900, in Stockton, California.
3¹. Samuel Dutton BUCK, *b.* 9th January, 1902, in Stockton, California.

3. Emily Jane BUCK, *b.* 31st October, 1865; *d.* 5th August, 1876.

IV. Evelina Maria, *b.* 7th January, 1834.
V. CHARLES FRANCIS, *b.* 11th July, 1836, the subject of this memoir.

Bacon

HORACE SARGENT BACON, LL.B., deceased, of Lowell, Massachusetts; *b.* 29th October, 1869, at Lowell, Massachusetts; *d.* there 8th April, 1915, and buried in the Lowell Cemetery; *m.* 7th June, 1911, at North Middletown, Bourbon County, Kentucky, by Rt. Rev. Lewis William BURTON, Bishop of Lexington, Kentucky, Malvina (MENG) HARRISON, *b.* 8th March, 1879, dau. of Charles Henry MENG, *b.* 25th April, 1843, *m.* 21st May, 1873, in Mason County, Kentucky, Sarah Katherine CALVERT, *b.* 29th November, 1852, in Mason County, Kentucky, *d.* 12th June, 1915 (a descendant of Sir George Calvert, 1st Lord Baltimore); both of Bourbon County, Kentucky, and widow of Ellwood Garrett HARRISON of Xenia, Ohio, who *d.s.p.* 5th February 1899.

ISSUE

I. Horace Sargent, Jr., *b.* 25th March, 1912.
II. Stephen Sargent, *b.* 23d October, 1914.

HORACE SARGENT BACON was educated at the public schools of Lowell and Chauncey Hall, Boston, Massachusetts. He was graduated from the Boston University Law School in the Class of 1899 in which he was a class officer. He was president of the Phi Delta Phi Fraternity. After leaving College he returned to his home in Lowell. He never practiced his profession to any extent. Spent much time in study and research and travel in foreign lands. He devoted much time to Free Masonry. He was a member of Kilwinning Lodge, Mt. Horeb R. A. Chapter, Royal and Select Masters; Pilgrim Commandery, Knights Templars and of the 32d degree, Scottish Rite Free Masonry. Besides being Past Master of his Lodge, he was High Priest of his Chapter and also served as District Grand High Priest of the Eleventh District. He was a Past District Deputy Grand Master of the Blue Lodge of the Twelfth Masonic District. He was Past Commander of his Commandery. He was an honorary member of Mother Kilwinning Lodge number nothing, Kilwinning, Scotland. He was a member of Aleppo Temple, N.M.-Shrine, Boston. On the Committee of Curiosities of the Craft in the Grand Lodge of Massachusetts and Rhode Island, and a life member of Massachusetts Consistory. He was one of the Trustees of the Masonic Association of Lowell. A member of the Massachusetts and Rhode Island Association of Knights Templars Commanders; National Masonic Research Society of Anamosa, Iowa; Masonic Relief Association of Lowell and former Vice-President of the Masonic Club of Lowell, and "*Elect of 7.*" He was appointed Commissioner of Deeds, 1892, Register of Deeds, 1909 Middlesex County, North District, Massachusetts. "At the time of his death he

COLONIAL FAMILIES OF THE UNITED STATES 49

was Recorder of his Commandery and also the Most Worshipful Master of Mt. Calvary Chapter of Rose Croix, and was actively engaged in elaborate preparations of the exemplification of the 18th degree and had brought through his individual efforts that degree of rite to a state unequalled in its history in Lowell. His loss to Free Masonry cannot be realized." Honorary Member of the Burbank Society of California, National Geographical Society, Washington, D. C.; Massachusetts Society, Audubon Society (associate), Member Bar Association of County of Middlesex, Automobile Legal Association, Lowell Board of Trade, Boston University Law School Alumni Association, Trustee of Central Savings Bank, Lowell, Massachusetts, and a member of St. Anne's Episcopal Church.

Lineage

ENGLISH ANCESTRY OF MICHAEL BACON OF DEDHAM

"Bacon is a Seignority in Normandy acc. to the well authenticated genealogy of the great Suffolk family of Bacon from wh. sprung many branches."—Kimber's "Baronetage," 1, i.

I. Grimbaldus, a Norman gentleman, related to Wm. DE WARRENE, Earl of Surrey, came into England at the time of the Conquest and had grants of land at Letheringsets near Holt, County Norfolk.—Liber primatus de Binham MSS. nup. in cust. Thos. WITHERINGTON, Kt.

II. Ran(d)ulf or Reynolds resided at Thorpe, County Norfolk, called Baconsthorpe by distinction. Authorities differ as to who first assumed the name Bacon, Ran(d)ulf or his grandson, Robert, son of Roger.

III. George "Gave and released to his sister Agnes, wid. of Sir Roger DE HALIS all the lands belonging to his fam¹. in Normandy"—Reg. Abbot DE LANGLEY, fol. 90.

IV. Roger, son of Geo. "sued by his sister Agnes, wid. of his bro. Thomas for distraining her tenants in Baconsthorpe and Lodue and breaking her park (lusis ap Norwich 5 H, III 3/4). He raised arms with the barons agnst. the Kg. John and had his estates confiscated (Fines 2 John Rot. 13, Clans I, H, III, pt. 2). His lands were returned by favor of Henry III in 1216.

V. JOHN BACON of Herset, Suffolk, m. Alice, surname unknown, by whom he had

VI. JOHN BACON, II, m. Cicily HOO, by whom he had

VII. JOHN BACON, III, m. Helena GEDDING, by whom he had

VIII. JOHN BACON, IV, m. (firstly) Helena TILLOTT; m. (secondly) Julia BARDWELL; he had by first marriage

IX. John Bacon, V, who m. Margarey THORPE, dau. and heir of John THORPE, son of William, son of Sir William THORPE, by the dau. Sir Roger BACON, commissioned in the time of the Wars of Edward II, Edward III. Sir Roger BACON was a son of Sir Henry BACON, son of Sir Henry BACON, a judge itinerant temp. Henry III, lineally descended from Grumbaldus.—(Visitation of Suffolk, Metcalf and Kimber).

x. EDMUND BACON, of Drinkston, County Suffolk, *m.* Elizabeth CROFTS, by whom he had

xi. John Bacon, VI, *m.* Agnes COCKFIELD, dau. of Sir Thomas COCKFIELD. (ibid, and "Visitations of London," 1568—Cooke-Harleson M.S., 1463).

ISSUE

1. Robert.
2. John, will proved June, 1518.
3. THOMAS, of whom later.
4. Henry.
5. William.

THOMAS BACON of Helmingham, County Norfolk, England; will proved 28th February; *d.* 1540; will probated 12th December, 1540; *m.* Joane, surname unknown.

ISSUE

I. JOHN, of whom later.
II. Thomas, *d.* 1557; *m.* Agnes, surname not known.
III. Anne.
IV. John.
V. Henry.
VI. Mary.
VII. Agnes.
VIII. Elizabeth.

JOHN BACON of Helmingham, County Norfolk, England; will proved 19th March, 1557; *m.* Margaret ———.

ISSUE

I. William, of Coddington, *d.* 1618.
II. Thomas.
III. MICHAEL, of whom later.
IV. Richard.
V. William of Winston; *d.* unmarried 13th October, 1574.
VI. Barbaro.
VII. Rose.

MICHAEL BACON of Winston, was buried 25th March, 1615; will dated 20th April, 1615; *m.* (firstly) 16th August, 1565, in Helmingham, Elizabeth WYLIE; *m.* (secondly) 20th September, 1607, the widow Grace BLOWERSES.

ISSUE BY FIRST MARRIAGE

I. John, *bapt.* 31st May, 1566.
II. William.
III. Thomas.

 IV. MICHAEL, of whom later.
 V. Elizabeth, *bapt.* 3d September, 1584; *m.* ――――― BACON.
 VI. Sarah, *m.* Daniel YORKE.
 VII. Rose, *m.* ――――― BALLET.

MICHAEL BACON of Dedham, Massachusetts; *b.* in Winston, Suffolk County, England, where he was *bapt.* 6th December, 1579; *d.* 18th April, 1648. In 1633, his name appears as one of the Signers of the Dedham agreement. In Dedham records he is said to have come from Ireland, where he probably went to take passage to this country. Tradition says he was a Captain of Yeomanry in County Suffolk. In 1644 he granted land to the town of Dedham for a highway who, *m.* Alice, surname unknown, who *d.* 2d April, 1648.

ISSUE

 I. Michael, *b.* in England, circa 1608; *d.* 4th July, 1688; came to New England in 1640; was at Charlestown, 1640; Woburn, 1641; soldier in King Philip's War at "No. 10" Billerica in 1675; *m.* (firstly) Mary, who *d.* 26th August, 1655, surname unknown; *m.* (secondly) 26th October, 1655, Mary RICHARDSON, *d.* 19th May, 1670, widow of Thomas RICHARDSON; *m.* (thirdly) 28th November, 1670, Mary (HAINES) NOYES, dau. of Walter and Eliza HAINES and widow of Thomas NOYES of Sudbury.
 II. Daniel, *b.* in England, probably 1615; *d.* 7th September, 1691; came to New England, 1640, and in that year was one of the original proprietors in the settlement of Woburn. Freeman 26th May, 1647. In 1669 he is mentioned as one of the early settlers of Newton; *m.* Mary REED, *d.* 4th October, 1691, dau. of Thomas READ of Colchester, England.
 III. JOHN, Dedham, freeman, 1647; *d.* 17th June, 1683, of whom later.
 IV. Alice, *d.* 29th March, 1648; *m.* 31st March, 1647, Anthony HUBBARD, of Dedham.

JOHN BACON came to Dedham in 1640, with his father, and was made freeman in 1647. He was sole executor of his father's estate. He was frequently appointed on committees for clearing lands and laying out highways, and is recorded among the Selectmen, 1660–1661; was a surveyor and commissioner ("Dedham Record," Vol. III, p. 141), and one of the signers of the petition of the town of Dedham against the Indians of Natick, sent to the Governor and Assistants and Deputies assembled in General Court at Boston, 7th May, 1662 ("Massachusetts Archives," XXX, 112). He was a member of Capt. Timothy DWIGHT's Company in King Philip's War; stationed at the garrison at Wrentham in 1676 ("Soldiers in King Philip's War," pp. 367–368, by G. M. Bodge). He left no will. There is no record of division of the property, but in the inventory "lands and rights in Wrentham" are mentioned. He remained at Dedham until his death, 17th June, 1683; he *m*. 17th December, 1651, Rebecca HALL of Dedham, who *d*. 27th October, 1694.

ISSUE, BORN AT DEDHAM, MASSACHUSETTS,

I. Mary, *m*. Nathaniel KINGSBURY.
II. John, *b*. 17th July; *bapt*. 3d August, 1656; *d*, 27th October, 1732; *m*. Lydia DEWING.
III. Rebecca, *b*. 10th November, 1658; *m*. 13th February, 1678, John GAY, of Dedham.
IV. Daniel, *b*. 10th March, 1660–1661; *d*. before 21st April, 1700.
V. Sarah, *b*. 31st March, 1663; *m*. John ELLIS.
VI. Samuel, *b*. 8th October, 1665; *m*. Elizabeth ACKERS of Roxbury.
VII. THOMAS, *b*. 23d August, 1667; *d*. at Wrentham, 10th April, 1749, of whom later.
VIII. Susanna, *m*. 7th January, 1692, Jonathan DEWING.
IX. Stephen, *b*. 21st August, 1677; *m*. Mary ———.

THOMAS BACON was *b*. at Dedham, 23d August, 1667; *d*. at Wrentham 10th April, 1749. He removed to Wrentham, and is recorded among the planters there in 1693. He came into possession of some part of the "land and rights in Wrentham" mentioned in his father's inventory. He was one of the Selectmen of Wrentham, Fence Viewer, Surveyor of Highways, Assessor of Rates, and Town Treasurer, and was elected Representative to the Great and General Court, 1719–1720 ("Wrentham Records," Vol. II, p. 97); *m*. (firstly) 22d January, 1691, Hannah FALES, who came from Chester, England, early in the seventeenth century; and was among the first settlers of Dedham; a freeman in 1653, and a soldier in King Philip's War; *m*. (secondly) 16th July, 1746, Mary FISHER, who *d*. 25th March, 1750, in her seventy-sixth year.

ISSUE BY FIRST MARRIAGE

I. Thomas, *b*. 26th November, 1693; *d*. 1784; *m*. Esther THURSTON.
II. Hannah, *b*. 25th April, 1697; *d*. 23d October, 1754; *m*. Nathaniel WRIGHT.
III. James, *b*. 28th October, 1700; *d*. 1785.
IV. Martha, *b*. 8th October, 1703; *d*. 3d April, 1800; *m*. 22d June, 1731, John SHEPARD.
V. Jacob, *b*. 9th September, 1706; *d*. 14th August, 1787, at Rowley; *m*. (firstly) 22d June, 1749, "Mary WOOD of Boxford," *b*. 1717, *d*. 17th February, 1772, tombstone, "Burial Hill;" he *m*. (secondly) Mary WHITNEY, who *d*. at David THURSTON's in Sedgwick, Maine, 6th March, 1815, aged eighty-seven; had issue.
VI. JOHN, *b*. 22d April, 1710, of whom later.
VII. Sarah, *b*. 25th August, 1712 ("Wrentham Records," p. 88).

JOHN BACON of Wrentham, Massachusetts; *b.* there 22d April, 1710; *d.* 1806; *m.* Mary, surname unknown. On 20th March, 1732, he received a deed from his father of several parcels of land, including a dwelling house and barn.

ISSUE

  I. John, *b.* 30th June, 1732; was made a Deacon of the Second Precinct of Brookfield, 3d October, 1766; *m.* (firstly) 25th March, 1763, Mrs. Mary OLDS, who *d.* 30th August, 1779; *m.* (secondly) 25th July, 1781, Mrs. Alice LEACH of Oakham.
 II. Huldah, *b.* 11th April, 1734.
III. DANIEL, *b.* 6th November, 1736, of whom later.
 IV. Asa, *b.* 8th April, 1738; was on the roll of Capt. Obadiah COOLEY'S Company, 20th September to 24th November, 1756; was also in service in 1758 and in the Crown Point Expedition in 1759 in Capt. William PAIGE'S Company.
  V. Rufus, *b.* 6th April, 1740; *d.* 21st February, 1750.
 VI. Elizabeth, *b.* 4th May, 1744; *d.* same day.
VII. Sarah, *b.* 4th November, 1745.
VIII. Thomas, *b.* 26th June, 1747; *m.* 3d February, 1775, Hepisbah BOUTELLE.
 IX. Jarib, *b.* 16th March, 1749; was a Corporal in Capt. John PACKARD'S Company, Col. David BREWER'S Regiment; he enlisted 2d May, 1775, and was in service three months, also enlisted in 1777 for three years and reported discharged 9th April, 1780; in 1779 was in service at Peekskill; *m.* 2d October, 1782, Polly JONES.
  X. Ebenezer, *b.* 16th January, 1752; served as private in Capt. Peter HARWOOD'S Company, Col. Ebenezer LEARNED'S Regiment; enlisted 2d May, 1775, and was in serivice three months and one week; enlisted from the town of Weston, in Capt. COBURN'S Company, Col. James CONVERSE'S Regiment in 1778, and later was in Capt. LANE'S Company, Col. NIXON'S Regiment.

DANIEL BACON of Wrentham, Massachusetts; *b.* 6th November, 1736; *d.* 12th February, 1813; a Muster Roll of a detachment of men from Spencer District which marched to the relief of Fort William Henry in 1759 contains the name of Daniel BACON. He lived in Spencer and afterwards Oxford and then at Charlton. He was Deacon of the Church in Charlton; *m.* February, 1758, Mary BALDWIN, *b.* 2d April, 1739, dau. of David and Abigail (BURR) BALDWIN of Leicester.

ISSUE

  I. Rufus, *b.* 12th September, 1758; *d.* 23d September, 1820; was a fifer in Capt. William CAMPBELL'S Company, Col. Ebenezer LEARNED'S Regiment, enlisted 3d May, 1775, and was in service three months and six days. Was also drum major in Capt. Abijah LAMBIS' Company, Col. Jonathan HOLMAN'S Regiment; enlisted 15th August, 1777, also served as drum major in Capt. Reuben DAVIS' Company, Col. Luke DRURY'S Regiment; enlisted 17th July, 1781; *m.* 17th April, 1782, Eleanor EDWARDS, who *d.* 6th February, 1842, dau. of John EDWARDS.

II. Daniel, *b.* 5th October, 1760; *d.* 9th March, 1834; *m.* (firstly) 16th May. 1782, Anna FAY, *b.* 15th April, 1762, *d.* 6th May, 1807, dau. of Daniel FAY; *m.* (secondly) 21st June, 1808, Mrs. Della (GROW) NICHOLS *b.* 14th September, 1786, *d.* 16th February, 1829; *m.* (thirdly) 6th December, 1831, Mrs. Olivia (CAMPBELL) WITT, *b.* 4th December, 1767, *d.* 5th February, 1848, dau. of Duncan CAMPBELL and widow of Benjamin WITT.

III. Lucy, *b.* 17th February, 1762; *d.* 11th December, 1766.

IV. Jonathan, *b.* 4th December, 1763; *d.* 9th December, 1766.

V. Elihu, *b.* 20th July, 1765; *d.* 13th December, 1766.

VI. John, *b.* 27th May, 1768; *d.* 27th November, 1818; *m.* 14th December, 1786, Abigail KELLY, *b.* 3d July, 1768; *d.* 19th April, 1851, dau. of Joel and Ruth (WHEELOCK) KELLY.

VII. Asa, *b.* 23d December, 1769, *d.* ————; *m.* (firstly) 29th July, 1795, Lois FISK, *b.* 8th February, 1776, *d.* 24th October, 1797, dau. of Deacon Daniel FISK; *m.* (secondly) 24th October, 1799, Elizabeth COMINS, *b.* 30th October, 1778, *d.* 26th May, 1849, dau. of Reuben COMINS.

VIII. ALVAN, *b.* 27th September, 1771, of whom later.

IX. David, *b.* 1st May, 1774; *d.* 18th May, 1848; *m.* (firstly) 13th December, 1802, Ruth WARRINER, *b.* 22d September, 1782, *d.* 26th March, 1808, dau. of William WARRINER; *m.* (secondly) 12th December, 1809, Dorothy BRADBURY, *b.* 1st August, 1782, *d.* 26th November, 1864, dau. of Capt. Joseph and Dorothy (CLARK) BRADBURY.

X. Mary, *b.* 28th April, 1776; *d.* 20th December, 1857; *m.* 3d September, 1797, Barnabus COMINS, *b.* 24th March, 1771; *d.* 10th January, 1829, son of Reuben and Mary (PATKER) COMINS; had issue.

XI. Lucy, *b.* 22d March, 1778; *d.* 12th September, 1817; *m.* February, 1796, Moses BLANCHARD, *d.* 6th August, 1833, son of James BLANCHARD.

ALVAN BACON, M.D., of Scarborough, Maine; *b.* 27th September, 1771, in Charlton; *d.* 15th August, 1858. He had a large practice as a physician. The house in which he lived in Scarborough is still standing at Dunstan's Corner and is a fine specimen of the house of the period. It has twisted bannister balusters in the front hall and a remnant of a large brick oven and fireplace in the kitchen; *m.* October, 1800, Sarah MILLIKEN, *b.* 27th November, 1779, *d.* 27th May, 1853, dau. of Capt. John Mulberry and Sarah (SIMONTON) MILLIKEN of Scarborough.

ISSUE

I. Amanda, *b.* 7th June, 1801; *d.* 29th December, 1802.

II. HORACE, *b.* 29th March, 1804, of whom later.

III. Alvan, *b.* 25th April, 1806; *d.* 24th November, 1880; *m.* (firstly) 26th September, 1836, Mary COMINS, *b.* 3d April, 1811, *d.* 7th May, 1843; *m.* (secondly) 20th November, 1849, Mary A. MAXWELL, dau. of James and Nancy MAXWELL.
IV. Mary Baldwin, *b.* 6th July, 1808; *d.* 16th June, 1869; *m.* 5th October, 1836, Rodney D. HILL, *b.* 22d July, 1805, *d.* 6th January, 1867.
V. Sarah, *b.* 24th May, 1811; *d.* 13th February, 1859; *m.* 26th April, 1841, Seth L. LARABEE, *b.* 12th April, 1813, *d.* 7th December, 1853.

HORACE BACON, M.D., of Biddeford, Maine; *b.* 29th March, 1804, in Scarborough; *d.* 24th April, 1888, in Biddeford. Was a physician and a man of great qualities. At the time of his death he is said to have been the dean of the medical profession of York County; *m.* 22d April, 1828, Mary Emery COFFIN, *b.* 25th July, 1807, *d.* 13th April, 1882, in Dover, New Hampshire, dau. of Edmund COFFIN, who was a descendant of Tristam COFFIN the immigrant.

ISSUE

I. Henry McCobb, *b.* 1st May, 1829; *d.s.p.* 7th December, 1899; graduated at Dartmouth, 1854. At the outbreak of the Civil War entered the army as a contract nurse; was rapidly promoted and at the end of the war was private secretary in the Medical Director's Office in Washington. Later entered the silversmith business; *m.* 24th November, 1892, Annie P. SARGENT, *b.* 5th October, 1839, *d.* 8th May, 1913, dau. of Stephen Pillsburg and Sarah J. (AMES) SARGENT of Lowell.
II. Charles Edward, *b.* 11th March, 1832; *d.* 10th June, 1898; *m.* 15th June, 1856, Susan Nancy CLARK, *b.* 29th September, 1838, *d.* 10th June, 1898.
III. Mary Elizabeth, *b.* 9th November, 1835; *m.* 13th March, 1856, Samuel E. CLARK, of Biddeford.
IV. HORACE BALDWIN, *b.* 11th June, 1841, of whom below.

HORACE BALDWIN BACON of Lowell, Massachusetts; *b.* 11th June, 1841, in Biddeford, Maine; *d.* 24th October, 1885. Learned the jewelry business in Portland, Maine, later went to Dover, New Hampshire, and from there to Laconia and later to Lowell, Massachusetts; *m.* 13th June, 1865, Sarah Elizabeth SARGENT, *b.* 30th December, 1843, *d.* 31st January, 1884, dau. of Deacon Stephen P. SARGENT; she was a descendant of John ALDEN of Plymouth and also of Hannah DUNSTEN.

ISSUE

I. HORACE SARGENT, *b.* 29th October, 1869, the subject of this memoir.
II. Margaret Burnett, *b.* 1st November, 1875; *m.* (firstly) 8th September, 1892, Ralph B. LYMAN of Lowell, Massachusetts, *b.* 1873, in Troy, New York, son of Edward and Carolina LYMAN; *m.* (secondly) 18th October, 1911, Walter E. MURCKLAND, of Lowell, Massachusetts.

ISSUE BY FIRST MARRIAGE

1. Dorothy Bacon LYMAN, *b.* 12th December, 1894.

Arms.—Gules on a chief argent two mullets sable.
Crest.—A boar passant ermine, armed and hoofed or.
Motto.—Mediocria firma.
Residence (family).—Lowell, Massachusetts.
Clubs (formerly member of).—Vesper Country Club, Yorick Club, Middlesex Club, Boston, New England Fat Man's Club, former Secretary of Highland Club and Men's Club of St. Anne's Episcoapl Church.
Societies (formerly member of).—Colonial Wars, Massachusetts Society of Mayflower Descendants, The Alden Family Association, Massachusetts Society Sons of the American Revolution, President Old Middlesex Chapter S. A. C., Lowell, New England Historic Genealogical Society, and Recording Secretary and Clerk, Executive Committee; Sub-Committees; Library, Papers and Publications and Cabinet of Lowell Historical Society.

Baird

MAJOR WILLIAM BAIRD, U. S. A., Retired; *b.* 22d August, 1851, in Philadelphia, Pennsylvania; *m.* 18th June, 1885, at San Francisco, California, Minnie DAWLEY, dau. of Olive Pratt DAWLEY, and gd. dau. of Judge A. C. TWEED of Arizona.

ISSUE

I. Cornelia Wyntje, *b.* 9th April, 1886, at Fort Bayard, New Mexico; *m.* 9th October, 1909, at Annapolis, Maryland, William Whinnery HICKS, Lieutenant in the United States Army.

ISSUE

1. Cornelia Baird HICKS, *b.* 7th June, 1915, at Fort Totten, New York.

II. John Absalom, *b.* 23d June, 1890, at Fort Myer, Virginia; graduated United States Naval Academy, Annapolis, 1911; Ensign United States Navy; was severely injured in an accident on the *U. S. S. Vermont*, September, 1915; resigned from Navy and entered United States Army; second Lieutenant Coast Artillery Corps, 20th December, 1912; served at Fort Monroe, Virginia, and Fort Totten, New York, to 1915, and as an Aide at White House, Washington, D. C., 1916; promoted first Lieutenant, July, 1916.

MAJOR WILLIAM BAIRD, Cadet United States Military Academy, West Point; graduated June 16th, 1875; second Lieutenant 6th United States Cavalry; first Lieutenant, February 15th, 1881; Captain, February 24th, 1891; served in Arizona, New Mexico, Old Mexico, California and Wyoming, participating in the Chiricahua, Chimhuevi, Victoria, and Geronimo campaigns under General CROOK and General MILES. Explorations and surveys for wagon routes in the Tonto Basin, Arizona. In campaigns against White Mountain Apaches, Tontos, Chiricahuas and Navajos. In command of Indian Scouts and of troops detailed to guard the United States mail route to California, 1879. On duty with General WILLCOX in exploration of Grand Canyon of the Colorado. During the Chimhuevi campaign along the Colorado River and in Southern California in 1880, performed the duties of Chief Quartermaster, and received the thanks of the Department Commander; graduate School of Military Signaling, Fort Myer, Virginia, 1881. Adjutant 6th Cavalry, 1884-1886; garrison duty at Fort Myer, Virginia, 1887; frontier duty Fort Washakie, Wyoming, and Inspector of Supplies for Arapahoes and Shoshones, 1891-1894; garrison duty at Fort Leavenworth, Kansas; Infantry and Cavalry School, 1894; retired 1897 (disability in line of duty); Professor Military Science and Tactics, Massachusetts Institute of Technology, 1st September, 1900, to 15th February, 1904; staff duty with Governor of Maryland in connection with organized Militia of the State 18th February, 1904, to 1st July, 1911; Major on Retired List 3d June, 1916.

Lineage

The earliest mention of the name is to be found in an old tradition preserved in the family records. To the effect that King William the Lion whilst hunting in one of the southwest counties became separated from his companions and being alarmed by the sudden approach of a wild boar called for assistance, when a gentleman of the name of BAIRD came up and slew the animal. For this service the king conferred upon him large grants of land and gave him for a Coat of Arms: Gules a Boar passant or. And the Motto: Dominus fecit, with Crest: A Boar's head erased. Which means a red shield with a gilt Boar as if passing upon it. There is a family tradition that the father of Lieut. John BAIRD held a Commission in the British Army and took part in an expedition against Canada, probably returning later to Scotland, where his son was born.

LIEUTENANT JOHN BAIRD probably came Ayr, Scotland, the exact date, however, of his arrival in America is not known; he was *b.* circa 1730, in Scotland; *d.* circa 1760. Entered military service of the Colony of Pennsylvania. Early in 1758 a regiment of three battalions, each of sixteen companies, was raised by the Colony to take part in the expedition of that year under General FORBES against Fort Duquesne; the Hon. William DENNY, Lieutenant-Governor of the Colony was the Colonel in Chief. In the second battalion, in Captain WORK'S Company, John BAIRD was commissioned an Ensign, 13th March, 1758. This battalion joined the Army of General FORBES at Carlisle and a portion of it was present at Grant's defeat in September, 1758. Ensign BAIRD, took part in that engagement. After the successful termination of the expedition his company remained on the frontier and 18th April, 1759, he was promoted to Lieutenancy in the same Company. In 1760 he was reported as having "died in service;" *m.* circa, 1755, Catherine M'CLEAN, *b.* 19th July, 1733, probably in Chester County, Pennsylvania, *d.* 28th November, 1802; she was descended from a Scotch Irish Presbyterian family that had long been located in the North of Ireland, one of her ancestors having taken part in the defense of Londonderry in 1688.

ISSUE

1. ABSALOM, *b.* circa 1756, only child.

DR. ABSALOM BAIRD of Washington, Pennsylvania; *b.* circa 1756, in Kenneth Square, Pennsylvania; *d.* 27th October, 1805, at Washington, Pennsylvania; was a Surgeon in 1776, in the Army of the Revolution; afterwards Colonel and County Lieutenant of Pennsylvania; *m.* 14th July, 1783, at Wilmington, Delaware, Susanna Harlan BROWN, *b.* ———, *d.* in November, 1802, dau. of George and Susanna (HARLAN) BROWN.

ISSUE

I. John, b. 26th July, 1784, at Kenneth Square, Pennsylvania.
II. George, b. 28th October, 1785; d. 2d November, 1860, at Washington, Pennsylvania; was educated at Washington Academy (now Washington College); elected Sheriff of Washington County in 1811 and represented this County in the State Legislature, 1816; later in life filled the office of Magistrate; elected Ruling Elder in the Presbyterian Church, 3d November, 1847, and in 1855 represented the Presbytery of Washington in its General Assembly at Nashville, Tennessee; m. 25th October, 1811, Jane WILSON, b. 18th September, 1793, d. 16th July, 1872.

ISSUE

1. Catherine, b. 8th August, 1812; d. 25th September, 1871; m. 15th March, 1836, George WILSON, who d. 21st June, 1861.
2. Absalom, b. 27th May, 1814; d. 16th June, 1818.
3. John, b. 15th July, 1816; d. 5th March, 1889; m. (firstly) 9th January, 1844, Harriet Newell GILFILLAN; m. (secondly) 14th December, 1858, Harriet Steele CLARK, dau. of Joseph CLARK.
4. Thomas (twin), b. 1st May, 1820; d. 1823.
5. William (twin), b. 1st May, 1820; d. 19th May, 1820.
6. Susan Campbell, b. 7th September, 1818; d. unmarried 19th October, 1895.
7. Martha, b. 2d April, 1822; d. 15th October, 1859; m. 8th August, 1839, Hon. Alfred CALDWELL, son of James and Ann CALDWELL.
8. Ann, b. 8th June, 1824; d. 28th August, 1853; m. 10th September, 1844, Zachariah S. MITCHELL.
9. Sarah, b. 8th April, 1826; d. 27th August, 1862; m. 17th October, 1850, David Shield WILSON.
10. Jane, b. 16th April, 1828, unmarried.
11. George, M.D., b. 30th November, 1829; d. 7th March, 1891, of Wheeling, West Virginia; m. (firstly) January, 1857, Margaretta Montgomery M'CULLOCH.

ISSUE

1^1. Read M'Culloch, M.D., b. 25th October, 1857; m. 6th October, 1885, Laura Rebecca UPDEGRAFF.

ISSUE

1^2. Du Bois, b. 7th July, 1887.

2^1. George Brown, b. 6th December, 1858.
3^1. David Wilson, b. 8th March, 1861; d. 13th May, 1861.
4^1. John M'Culloch, b. 22d July, 1862; d. 13th March, 1864.
5^1. Anna Maria, b. 19th December, 1864; d. 13th March, 1864.

6¹. Jane Wilson, *b.* December, 1866.
7¹. Sarah Wilson, *b.* 4th November, 1868.
8¹. William Jourdan Bates, M.D., *b.* 6th January, 1870; graduated M.D., University of Pennsylvania, 1893; *d.* 30th November, 1893, near Seattle, Washington.
9¹. Louisa Todd, *b.* 18th August, 1874.

12. Andrew Todd, *b.* 25th September, 1831; *d.* 25th March, 1887; *m.* 8th June, 1865, Clara WILSON, dau. of Hugh H. WILSON.
13. Alexander, *b.* 23d September, 1833; *d.* 13th January, 1834.
14. Ellen, *b.* 25th April, 1835; unmarried.

III. Thomas Harlan of "Harlem," Washington County, Pennsylvania; *b.* 15th November, 1878, at Washington, Pennsylvania; *d.* 1866; graduated at Washington Academy; studied law and admitted to the Bar in 1807; was appointed presiding Judge of the Judicial District formed by Washington, Fayette and Green Counties; resigned in 1838 to practice his profession in Pittsburgh, Pennsylvania; *m.* Nancy McCULLOUGH, *b.* in Ireland; had thirteen children.
IV. WILLIAM, *b.* 24th July, 1789, of whom below.
V. Sarah, *b.* 11th March, 1793; *d.* at Mayville, Kentucky, 30th March, 1833; *m.* 30th May, 1826, William HODGE, of Maysville, Kentucky.
VI. Susan, *b.* 14th October, 1796; *d.* at Uniontown, Pennsylvania, 9th July, 1824; *m.* ———— CAMPBELL.

WILLIAM BAIRD "Vir juris peritus, morum suavitate ingernii elegantia studiisque humanitutus ac literarum ornatrisimus;" *b.* 24th July, 1789, in Washington, Pennsylvania; *d.* 11th October, 1834; studied law in the office of his brother, Judge Thomas Harlan BAIRD; admitted to the Bar 18th June, 1812; was a distinguished member of the Pennsylvania Bar; in 1816 succeeded his brother as Deputy Attorney-General for Washington County, holding the office until 1824; *m.* 1st April, 1822, Nancy MITCHELL, *b.* January, 1799, *d.* 16th March, 1881, in Cumberland, Maryland, dau. of John and Maria (JACOB) MITCHELL, of Town Creek, Maryland, and Washington, D. C.

ISSUE

I. Susan, *b.* 10th January, 1823; *d.* August, 1851.
II. ABSALOM, *b.* 20th August, 1824, of whom later.
III. William, *b.* 1st July, 1826; was Captain in the Confederate Army, Acting Adjutant-General of a Brigade, twice captured and exchanged; *m.* Annie NELSON, dau. of Hon. John NELSON of Baltimore.
IV. Jane.
V. Catharine, *b.* 5th November, 1825; *d.* 11th February, 1857.
VI. Maria.
VII. John Mitchell, *b.* 11th October, 1833, *d.* 11th August, 1834.

BRIGADIER-GENERAL ABSALOM BAIRD, U. S. A.; *b.* 20th August, 1824, at Washington, Pennsylvania; *d.* 14th June, 1905, at Relay, Maryland; Cadet Military Academy, West Point; graduated 1st July, 1849; Second Lieutenant, 1st Artillery, 1st April, 1850; First Lieutenant, 24th December, 1853; brevetted Captain, 11th May, 1861; Captain Assistant Adjutant-General, 3d August, 1861; Major Inspector-General, 12th November, 1861; Brigadier-General Volunteers, 28th April, 1862; Lieutenant-Colonel Inspector-General in Regular Army, 13th June, 1867; Colonel Inspector-General, 11th March, 1885; Brigadier-General, 22d September, 1885; brevetted Lieutenant-Colonel for "*gallant and meritorius service in the battle of Chickamauga, Georgia;*" Colonel for "*gallant and meritorius service at the battle of Chattanooga, Tennessee;*" Brigadier-General for "*gallant and meritorius service in the capture of Atlanta, Georgia.*" Major-General, 13th March, 1865, for "*gallant and meritorius* service in the field during the war" and Major-General Volunteers, 1st September, 1864, for *faithful service and distinguished conduct* during the Atlanta *campaign and particularly in the battles of Resaca and Jonesboro* and for general good conduct in the command of his division against Savannah. Awarded "*Medal of Honor*" "*for most distinguished gallantry in action at Jonesboro, Georgia, 1st September, 1864, voluntarily leading a detached brigade in an assault upon the enemy's works while serving as Brigadier-General of Volunteers commanding a division;*" Commander Legion of Honor of the Republic of France, 1888; Retired 20th August, 1888; *m.* 17th October, 1850, Cornelia Wyntje SMITH of New York, *b.* May—, 1828, *d.* 16th May, 1883, dau. of Peter Skenandoh and Anne (PRENTICE) SMITH. Peter S. SMITH was the first white child born in Utica, New York, and was given his middle name after the celebrated Chief of the Oneidas, with whom his father traded in Western New York, where he owned much land. Skenandoh means "a swift running deer." The old Chief in a speech at a Council referred to himself as "like an ancient hemlock, alive in the roots but dead in the branches." And the SMITH Crest contains the deer and hemlock.

ISSUE

1. WILLIAM, *b.* 22d August, 1851, the subject of this memoir (only child).

Arms.—Gules a boar passant or.
Crest.—A boar's head erased or.
Motto.—Dominus fecit.
Residence.—Washington, D. C.
Clubs.—Army and Navy of Washington.
Societies.—Colonial Wars, Sons of the Revolution, Loyal Legion, Order of Indian Wars.

Baker

HON. FRANK BAKER, A.B., LL.B., of Chicago, Illinois; *b.* at Melrose, Seneca County, Ohio, 11th May, 1840; *d.* 9th July, 1916; *m.* 10th November, 1870, in London, Ohio, Eliza WARNER, *b.* 6th May, 1842, dau. of Henry WARNER, of London, Ohio, *b.* 15th July, 1795, *m.* February, 1823, Keturah GOSSLEE, *b.* 10th March, 1806.

ISSUE

I. Ethel, *b.* 31st July, 1871; *m.* 10th October, 1899, Edmund Lathrop ANDREWS of Chicago, Illinois, son of Edmund ANDREWS, M.D., of Chicago.

ISSUE

1. Frank Baker ANDREWS, *b.* 2d March, 1901.
2. Frances Ethel ANDREWS, *b.* 29th November, 1902.
3. Edmund Lathrop ANDREWS, *b.* 30th May, 1904.
4. Edward Wyllys ANDREWS, *b.* 21st April, 1910.

II. Nora, *b.* 22d July, 1873; *m.* 29th October, 1902. Capt. Stephen Morris KOCHERSPERGER, U. S. A., son of William S. KOCHERSPERGER, of Philadelphia, Pennsylvania.

ISSUE

1. Elizabeth KOCHERSPERGER, *b.* 28th November, 1915.

FRANK BAKER received degrees of A.B. Ohio Wesleyan University, 1861; LL.B., Albany Law School, 1863; in practice in Chicago, 1873–1887; Judge of the Circuit Court of Cook County, since 1st June, 1887; assigned to Appellate Court of First District Illinois, June, 1904; re-elected for the sixth time, June, 1915; private, Company D, 84th Ohio Infantry, enlisted May, 1862; Compiler of "The Ancestors of Samuel BAKER of Pleasant Valley, New York," 1914.

Lineage

THOMAS BAKER, *b.* in England, 29th September, 1618; *d.* 30th April, 1700, at Easthampton, Long Island, came from Kent County, England, in 1639. He was the son of Thomas and Frances (DOWNE) BAKER, and was *bapt.* 11th October, 1618, in the parish church at Hothfield; was enrolled as a "Free Planter" at Milford 29th November, 1639; removed to East Hampton, Long Island, 1650, and one of the thirty-four proprietors in 1652. He was an Ensign of East Hampton Militia, Townsman, Magistrate or Assistant of the General Court of Connecticut, 1658–

1663; Justice of the Peace for ten years; Commissioner for Indian Affairs; Commissioner for the Trial of Small Causes; Constable and Foreman of the first Grand Jury empanelled in the Province of New York, 1665; a patentee and corporator in the patent of East Hampton granted by Governor NICOLL in 1666, and in the patent of 1686 granted by Governor Dongan, and a Grantee in the Indian Deeds of Montauk of 1660, 1661, 1670, and 1687; *m.* probably at New Haven, 20th June, 1643, Alice DAYTON, *b.* 22d May, 1620, at Ashford, in Kent, and was *bapt.* at St. Mary's Church, Ashford, 21st May, 1619, *d.* 4th February, 1708-1709, dau. of Ralph and Alice (WILTON) DAYTON of New Haven.

ISSUE

I. Hannah, *b.* 26th 1650; *m.* Ebenezer LEEKE.
II. THOMAS, *b.* 26th July, 1654, of whom later.
III. Nathaniel, *b.* 22d December, 1655; *m.* (firstly) Catherine SCHELLINGER, *b.* 9th April, 1656, *d.* 19th May, 1722; *m.* (secondly) 26th August, 1724, Sarah POST, *b.* circa 1665, *d.* 9th October, 1727.

ISSUE BY FIRST MARRIAGE

1. Jonathan, *b.* 12th February, 1679.
2. Susannah, *b.* 7th July, 1681; *d.* 26th May, 1714.
3. Abigail, *b.* 15th March, 1680.
4. A son, *b.* 16th April, 1686; *d.* about a fortnight after.
5. Katharine, *b.* 4th April, 1687.
6. Mary, *b.* 21st November, 1689.
7. Daniel, *b.* 1st August, 1692.
8. Hannah, *b.* 26th January, 1695.

IV. Abigail, *m.* ———— TUTHILL.

THOMAS BAKER of East Hampton, Long Island, New York; *b.* 26th July, 1654; *d.* 8th September, 1735; *m.* (firstly) 24th April, 1686, Ann TOPPING, of Southampton, dau. of Thomas TOPPING of Southampton, the son of Capt. Thomas TOPPING, the first of the name in that town. Capt. Thomas TOPPING held many offices of trust and importance in New York and Connecticut. In New York he was a Member of the Governor's Council, Captain of the Southampton Train Band, Constable, Deputy to the Hempstead Assembly of 1665, Commissioner in Admiralty and Deputy Commissioner of Indian Affairs of the Province. In Connecticut he was a Representative from Wethersfield to the General Court in 1639; Patentee in the Connecticut Charter, Assistant, Member of the Council of War and Captain of New Haven County Troop. He was an Englishman, and was at Wethersfield in 1636. His name appears with Thomas BAKER's on the roll of the "free planters" of Milford in November, 1639. Later he was at Hempstead, and in 1650 was at Southampton; 18th October of that year he was appointed "Captain of the banded soldiers" of that town. Southampton was then under the jurisdiction of Connecticut, and up to 1662 nominated three men in each year from whom the General Court of Connecticut chose two Magistrates or Assistants who were members of the upper house or the General Court of the Colony. Captain TOPPING was elected Assistant each year from 1651 to 1662. In 1662, Charles II granted to Governor WINTHROP and his associates, under the Great Seal of England, the Charter of Connecticut which remained the fundamental law of the Colony and State until 1817. Edmund ANDROSS, Governor General of New England, in 1686, demanded of the General Court the production and surrender of their charter. It was produced, but during the discussion between the officers of the Colony and the Governor General, the lights were extinguished and the charter seized and hid in a hollow oak. Captain TOPPING was one of the patentees in that charter and was therein named one of the Assistants to the Governor. In 1663, after the charter, he was again chosen an Assistant by the General Court of Connecticut. After the conquest of New Netherlands by the English in 1664, Long Island became a part of the Province of New York. Captain TOPPING was a Deputy from Southampton to the Hempstead Assembly 28th February, 1665, in which Thomas BAKER was a Deputy from Easthampton. In 1665 he was appointed by Governor NICOLL Commissioner of Admiralty of the Province of New York. The next year the Governor appointed him Constable, then, as has been said, an office of much importance; later he was appointed Deputy Commissioner of Indian Affairs of the Province. About 1671 he returned to Milford, and 16th May, 1673, was by the General Court of Connecticut confirmed Captain of the New Haven County Troop. In November of the same year, when war with the Dutch was threatened, he was appointed a member of the Council of War. He went from Milford to Branford about 1671, and was chosen Magistrate or Assistant by the General Court of Connecticut each year from 1678 to 1684. Captain TOPPING's death at Branford in December, 1687, was thus recorded in the town records: "In this town died Thomas TOPPING, one of the Colony to whom King Charles his letters patent of the Colony of Connecticut." THOMAS BAKER *m.* (secondly) 11th July 1711, Elizabeth OSBORN, *b.* circa 1670, *d.* 18th July, 1753, dau. of Joseph OSBORN.

ISSUE BY FIRST MARRIAGE

I. Thomas.
II. Daniel, *b.* 1693; *d.* 16th March, 1740.
III. Nathaniel, *bapt.* 24th December, 1699; *m.* Catherine SCHELLINGER.
IV. Micah, *bapt.* 28th July, 1705.
V. SAMUEL, *bapt.* 5th April, 1702, of whom later.
VI. Jeremiah, *bapt.* 29th April, 1705.
VII. John, *bapt.* 6th July, 1707.
VIII. Mercy, *bapt.* 8th November, 1716.

SAMUEL BAKER of Easthampton, Long Island, and Branford, Connecticut; *bapt.* 5th April, 1702, at Easthampton; *d.* 22d August, 1767, at Branford, to which town he removed with his family in 1728. He was several times chosen selectman of

Branford and in 1765 was a Deputy to the General Court of Connecticut; *m.* (firstly) 18th October, 1721, Mercy SCHELLINGER, *b.* 4th November, 1699, at Easthampton, *d.* 25th August, 1749, at Branford, dau. of Jacob and Hannah SCHELLINGER and gd. dau. of Jacobus and Cornelia (MELYN) SCHELLINGER, who came to New Amsterdam, 1652, and settled at Easthampton before 2d October, 1667. Cornelia MELYN, *b.* 1627, was the dau. of Cornelis MELYN, Patroon of Staten Island, President of the Council of "Eight Men" in Nieuw Netherland, 1643; a native of Antwerp, who came to New Amsterdam in 1639; he returned to Holland and procured from the Amsterdam Chamber of the Dutch West India Company authority to settle a colony on Staten Island. He returned next year to settle his colony and brought with him his family and servants. His family consisted of his wife and three children, the eldest of whom was his daughter Cornelia; 29th June, 1642, Director General KIEFT granted to him a "ground brief" or patent, covering all of Staten Island excepting DE VRIES' reserved "bouwerij" and investing him with all the powers, jurisdictions, privileges and pre-eminence of a patroon. He established a number of settlers on the island and built a house there in which he resided with his family. Trouble with the Indians began as early as 1640. DE VRIES bouwery was attacked and the measures taken by KIEFT only served to further enrage the Indians against KIEFT and the Dutch. These troubles led to the Indian war of 1643, which completely frustrated MELYN'S design to establish a settlement on the island. He held KIEFT responsible for the war, and became the leader of the party opposed to KIEFT's government. He was compelled by the war to abandon his home on Staten Island and retire to Manhattans, or New Amsterdam. He received in 1643 a grant of a double lot in Manhattan, the patent for which was issued 28th April, 1644. In the same year he was made President of the Council of "Eight Men" in Nieuw Netherland. The shore of East River was then about the line of the present Pearl Street, and the present Stone Street east of Broad corresponds nearly with the Hoogh Street of that day. The present Broad Street was not laid out until long afterwards. MELYN'S patent covered the east half of the present Broad Street from the south line of Hoogh Street, extended west, south to the shore of East River. He acquired by purchase in 1644 the property bounded by Hoogh Street (Stone Street) on the north, the lot on which the Great Tavern stood on the east, East River (Pearl Street) on the south, and the double lot granted to him by patent on the west. This property had a frontage on Hoogh Street and on the river of about one hundred and thirty-five feet. On the lot granted him by patent MELYN built a modest two story house, probably of brick. Its location appears to have been in the easterly half of the present Broad Street, midway between Stone and Pearl Streets. In 1657 a canal, the Heere Graft, was dug in the present Broad Street, and the lot granted MELYN by patent was taken for that purpose. In partial compensation the Burgomaster gave to the MELYN family a lot only eighteen feet square at the southeast corner of Stone and Broad Streets. On this lot the second MELYN house was built; 28th May, 1684, after the death of Jannetje, the widow of Cornelis MELYN, this lot was conveyed by her son Jacob. "It is curious fact that this small plat of ground has retained its dim·nsions though the vicissitudes of nearly two centuries and a half, and is today occupied by a small and somewhat dingy brick building with a wealth of rusty iron fire-escapes; it appears to have resisted absorption by the more imposing structure whose blank walls of yellow brick overtower it on two sides." In INNES' "New Amsterdam" is a view of the East River shore in 1652, taken from an old print showing the first house of Cornelis MELYN, and a view of the site of the later MELYN house as it now appears. In 1645, MELYN leased from the Company two acres of ground covering the site of the present Trinity Church, and the northern portion of the church yard and extending to North River, and raised a crop of grain thereon. Samuel BAKER *m.* (secondly) 24th July, 1750, Martha GOODSELL.

ISSUE BY FIRST MARRIAGE

I. Mercy, *b.* at Easthampton, 22d July, 1722.
II. Hannah, *b.* at Easthampton, 24th February, 1724.
III. Esther, *b.* at Easthampton, 17th March, 1727.
IV. Samuel, *b.* at Branford, Connecticut, 24th December, 1729.
V. Jacob, *b.* at Branford, Connecticut, 11th February, 1732.
VI. Elizabeth, *b.* at Branford, Connecticut, 11th March, 1734.
VII. JONATHAN, *b.* at Branford, Connecticut, 10th November, 1736, of whom below.

JONATHAN BAKER of White Creek, Washington County, New York and Canisteo, Steuben County, New York; *b.* 10th November, 1736; *d.* 1820, at Canisteo; *m.* (firstly) 17th September, 1758, Mary BARKER, dau. of Deacon Edward and Hannah (BALDWIN) BARKER of Branford, he, son of Edward BARKER of Branford, the son of Edward BARKER of New Haven and Branford; he *m.* (secondly) Sarah MORRIS.

ISSUE BY FIRST MARRIAGE

I. Caty, *bapt.* at Branford, 20th April, 1762; *m.* ——— FORD.
II. SAMUEL, *bapt.* 24th April, 1763, of whom later.
III. William Pitt, *bapt.* 4th December, 1766.
IV. Peter, *bapt.* 27th August, 1767; *d.* in infancy.

ISSUE BY SECOND MARRIAGE

I. Betsey, *m.* ——— PURDY.

JUDGE SAMUEL BAKER of Pleasant Valley, Steuben County, New York; *b.* 24th April, 1763; *d.* 2d December, 1842; settled first in Tioga County, Pennsylvania, and later removed to Pleasant Valley, New York; was captured August, 1777, by Indians, sold to an officer of General Burgoyne's Army for twelve dollars, where he was retained until Burgoyne surrendered to General Gates at Saratoga, 1781, when he returned to his family. In 1781 he enlisted in Capt. Peter VAN RENSSALAER'S Company, Col. Marinus WILLETT's corps and took part in the battle of Johnstown, 24th October, 1781. Was elected Assessor of the town of Bath, 1797. In 1797,

COLONIAL FAMILIES OF THE UNITED STATES 67

Governor John JAY issued to him a commission of Lieutenant in the regiment whereof Charles WILLIAMSON was Lieutenant-Colonel and Commandant. He was commissioned by Governor Daniel D. TOMPKINS, Loan Commissioner in 1808, and in 1813, by the same Governor, First Judge of the Court of Common Pleas of Steuben County; and by John TAYLOR, Lieutenant-Governor, who became acting Governor on the election of Governor TOMPKINS, Vice-President of the United States, as Surrogate of Steuben in 1817.

ISSUE

I. Mary, b. 6th February, 1787; d. 1861; m. 1810, Joseph BAKER.

ISSUE

1. Seneca.
2. Elizabeth, m. Ethan SMITH.
3. William, b. 1813; m. Elizabeth CHANDLER, d. 1884.
4. Sophia, b. 1815; m. Albert S. FLEET; d. 1895.
5. Eunice, m. Clark LAMPMAN.
6. Irene, m. CHAMBARD.
7. Ruth, m. James McCLUNG.
8. Samuel.
9. Jefferson.
10. Richard, enlisted in United States Volunteers, 1861; d. in the service, 1862.
11. Mary, b. 1833; m. Louis GUILLAUME; d. 1912.

II. Caty, b. 14th June, 1789; d. 1861; m. William FAIRFIELD.

ISSUE

1. Christine FAIRFIELD.
2. Eliza FAIRFIELD, m. Lucius WILLIAMS.
3. Kate FAIRFIELD.
4. Rebecca FAIRFIELD, m. Silas SMITH.
5. Emma FAIRFIELD.
6. Electa FAIRFIELD.
7. Lure FAIRFIELD.
8. Ann FAIRFIELD.
9. John FAIRFIELD.
10. Scott FAIRFIELD.
11. Baker FAIRFIELD.

III. William, b. 24th May, 1791; d. 16th May, 1860; m. Eunice CONGER.

ISSUE

1. Eliza, b. 1816; m. Rev. John G. GULICK.
2. Fanny, b. 1818; m. Alonzo TUNNICLIFF.
3. Azariah C., b. 1819; d. 1863; Lieutenant 164th Ohio Volunteers; m. Harriet KENNEDY.
4. Thomas J., b. 1821; d. 1855; m. Louisa TUNNICLIFF.

68   COLONIAL FAMILIES OF THE UNITED STATES

    5. Benjamin Franklin, *b.* 1823; *m.* Mary BRUNDAGE.
    6. Aaron Y., *b.* 1827; *m.* Maria DORSEY.
    7. Mary Papillon Barker, *b.* 1835; *m.* United States Senator Angus CAMERON, of LaCrosse, Wisconsin.

IV. Trpyhena, *b.* 8th of May, 1793; *m.* Levi GRAY.

ISSUE

1. Samuel Baker, *b.* 1811; *m.* Jane STRYKER.
2. Daniel, *b.* 1813; *m.* Lydia MYRTLE.
3. Franklin, *b.* 1815.
4. Harry, *b.* 1818.
5. Jane, *b.* 1821; *m.* Jonathan B. LaRUE.
6. Lauren, *b.* 1823.
7. Eunice, *b.* 1826; *m.* James NEELY.
8. Elizabeth, *b.* 1828; *m.* Samuel VAN PELT.
9. Lucretia, *b.* 1831; *m.* Abraham BROWN.
10. Richard, *b.* 1838; *m.* Candace BARNEY.

V. Samuel, *b.* 8th October, 1795; *d.* 25th January, 1842; *m.* Catharine HAMMOND.

ISSUE

1. Julianna, *b.* 1819; *m.* Zenas COBB.
2. Elizabeth, *b.* 1821.
3. Sarah, *b.* 1823; *m.* Dr. VAN KEUREN.
4. John H., *b.* 1826; *m.* Roxanna KINGSLEY.
5. Emily Alice, *b.* 1829; *m.* Charles Davenport CHAMPLIN.
6. Kate, *b.* 1835; *m.* Ezra HAWLEY.

VI. Sophia, *b.* 26th ——, 1797; *m* (firstly) George STEARNS; *m.* (secondly) William FLEET, *d.* 5th June, 1839.

ISSUE BY FIRST MARRIAGE

1. John Baker STEARNS.
2. George W. STEARNS, *b.* 1826; *m.* Arvilla KING.
3. Daniel STEARNS, *b.* 1828; *m.* Louisa SIMMONS.
4. Alfred STEARNS, *b.* 1830; *m.* Nancy SLOAT.

ISSUE BY SECOND MARRIAGE

1. Sophia FLEET, *m.* Charles NOLAN.

VII. Franklin, *b.* 13th September, 1799; *d.* 26th December, 1832; *m.* Elizabeth FORD.

ISSUE

1. Edwin, *d*. 1827.
2. Elizabeth, *d*. 1832.

VIII. Thomas Jefferson, *b*. 15th June, 1801; *d*. 16th October, 1863; *m*. Sarah BOYD.

ISSUE

1. Caroline, *b*. 1826; *d*. 1913; *m*. John LAPHAM.
2. Dugald Cameron, *b*. 1828; *d*. 1850.
3. Frances J., *b*. 1831; *m*. Cornelius Y. BRUNDAGE.
4. Franklin, *b*. 1833; *m*. Matilda BLAIR.
5. Samuel, *b*. 1837, Lieutenant 164th Ohio Volunteers; *m*. Lavinia MCCORMICK.
6. Ann, *b*. 1839; *m*. Randolph Fitz EASTMAN, Captain 55th and Lieutenant-Colonel 166th Ohio Volunteers.
7. Elizabeth D., *b*. 1842; *m*. Capt. James H. HALL.
8. Julia Dennison, *b*. 1846; *m*. Albert EWER.

IX. Lucretia, *b*. 1803; *d*. 19th June, 1890; *m*. Silvanus ARNOLD.

ISSUE

1. Ann ARNOLD, *b*. 27th February, 1828; *d*. 21st October, 1903; *m*. Solomon White SHEPARD.
2. John ARNOLD, *b*. 29th July, 1831; *d*. 28th December, 1859.
3. Samuel Baker ARNOLD, *b*. 18th October, 1834; *d*. 4th March, 1847.
4. Nancy Long ARNOLD, *b*. 26th January, 1837; *d*. 18th December, 1881; *m*. Stanfield Pinkhard MCNEILL.
5. Guy Perry ARNOLD, *b*. 6th March, 1843; *m*. Elsie HOWE.

X. John, *b*. 7th January, 1806; *d*. 3d March, 1876; *m*. Mary EATON.

ISSUE

1. Elizabeth, *b*. 20th November, 1832; *d*. 9th June, 1901; *m*. John G. PATTERSON.
2. George E., *b*. 10th June, 1835; *d*. 1910, Sergeant 8th Ohio Volunteers.
3. William F., *b*. 29th July, 1837; *d*. 1913, 164th Ohio Volunteers.
4. Emily, *b*. 8th May, 1840; *m*. James THOMPSON.
5. Thomas Corwin, *b*. 26th March, 1842; Lieutenant 3d Ohio Cavalry.
6. Fanny E., *b*. 27th January, 1856; *d*. 13th December, 1884.
7. Zack, *b*. 16th March, 1852; *d*. 11th August, 1862.

XI. RICHARD, *b*. 1st January, 1809, of whom later.
XII. Ann, *b*. 13th January, 1811; *m*. Zelotes KNAPP.

ISSUE

1. Thomas Jefferson, *b.* 25th March, 1833; *m.* Sylvia MUDGETT.
2. Charles Maurice, *b.* 10th January, 1835, 3d Iowa Cavalry; *m.* Hester Ann WOOLEY.
3. Samuel Baker, *b.* 16th August, 1836; *m.* Frances BURNS.
4. Edward Young, *b.* 30th July, 1838, 3d Iowa Cavalry; *m.* Mary MUDGETT.
5. Lucretia, *b.* 16th June, 1841; *m.* Charles ARMSTRONG.
6. Mary, *b.* 31st October, 1850; *m.* Ladislaus, Count ZICHY, 21st May, 1879.

RICHARD BAKER, of Melmore, Seneca County, Ohio; *b.* January, 1809; *d.* 14th February, 1889; *m.* 20th September, 1836, Fanny WHEELER, dau. of Grattan Henry WHEELER, of Wheeler, Steuben County, New York.

ISSUE

1. Silas Wheeler, *b.* 26th November, 1837; *m.* Delilah BROWN, dau. of Asa BROWN of Crawford County, Ohio.

    1. Robert Anderson.

        ISSUE

        1^1. Jean. 2^1. Helen.

    2. Fanny, *m.* Arthur J. SIMMERS.

        ISSUE

        1^1. Charles J. SIMMERS. 3^1. Anabel SIMMERS.
        2^1. Edith Eliza SIMMERS.

    3. Eliza, *m.* Charles O. LEE.

        ISSUE

        1^1. Roscoe Silas LEE. 4^1. Mary Rocelia LEE.
        2^1. Lyman Charles LEE. 5^1. DeWitt Rodgers LEE.
        3^1. Richard Baker LEE.

    4. Richard, *m.* wife's name unknown.

        ISSUE

        1^1. Paul. 2^1. Dorothy.

II. FRANK, *b.* 11th May, 1840, the subject of this memoir.
III. Job, *b.* March, 1843, 49th and 164th Ohio Volunteers; *m.* Eliza NICHOLS.

ISSUE

1¹. Mary, *m.* Lincoln RHODES.

2. Maud.
3. Monroe; *m.* Delia ASHLOCK.
4. Wheeler, *m.* 2d October, 1902, Gertrude Lucile LaRUE.
5. Nora.
6. Frank.

IV. Grattan Henry, *b.* 15th September, 1848; *m.* Frances FLEET.

ISSUE

1. William Fleet, *m.* (firstly) Catherine PADDOCK; *m.* (secondly) Anne O'CONNOR.
2. Richard Guy, *m.* Jane Elizabeth HEINLY.
3. Eliza Ogden.
4. Florence, *m.* Henry Earl SHELDON.

V. Ralph W., *b.* 7th June, 1851; *d.* 18th May, 1911; *m.* Patience Hatch GRAVES.

ISSUE

1. Richard Selden, *d.* 1913.
2. Gertrude Gretchen, *m.* Brice McDONOUGH.
3. Grattan Henry.
4. Fanny Grace.
5. Margaret Helen.

VI. Richard Ward, *b.* 25th December, 1858.

Arms.—Argent, a tower between three keys erect sable.
Crest.—On a tower sable an arm embowed in armour holding in the hand a flint stone ppr.
Residence.—643 Woodland Park, Chicago, Illinois.
Societies.—Colonial Wars, Sons American Revolution, Grand Army Republic.

Bartlett

EDWIN JULIUS BARTLETT, A.B., A.M., M.D., Chemist, of Hanover, New Hampshire; *b.* 16th February, 1851, in Hudson, Ohio; *m.* 8th July, 1879, in Milwaukee, Wisconsin, Caroline Elizabeth RICE, *b.* 6th June, 1855, in Bangor, Maine, dau. of John Abbott and Elizabeth Emmeline (FOSTER) RICE, of Milwaukee, Wisconsin.

ISSUE

I. Harriette Louise, *b.* 29th July, 1880; *m.* 28th December, 1904, at Hanover, New Hampshire, Moses Bradstreet PERKINS, *b.* 27th May, 1881, in Salem, Massachusetts.

ISSUE

1. Richard Bartlett PERKINS, *b.* 22d September, 1905, in Boston, Massachusetts.
2. Eleanor PERKINS, *b.* 7th April, 1908, in Exeter, New Hampshire.

II. Edwin Rice, *b.* 12th May, 1883; *m.* 2d June, 1915, at Niagara Falls, New York, Margaret Jaffrey PORTER, *b.* 3d March, 1895, dau. of Alexander J. and Maud (LANGMUIR) PORTER.

III. Samuel Colcord, *b.* 26th November, 1886; *m.* 15th February, 1915, at New York City, Dorothy HINMAN, *b.* 22d May, 1889, at Norfolk, Virginia, dau. of Frank H. and Mary M. (COLEMAN) HINMAN.

IV. John Foster, *b.* 17th November, 1889.

EDWIN JULIUS BARTLETT was educated at Dartmouth College, where he graduated A.B., 1872, A.M., 1874, M.D. Rush Medical College, 1879; Instructor of Sciences, Monson Massachusetts Academy, 1872; High School, Glencoe, Illinois, 1874–1875; Lake Forest, Illinois Academy, 1876–1878; Associate Professor and Professor of Chemistry, Dartmouth College, since 1878; Honorary Member New Hampshire Medical Society; President Corporation of Mary Hitchcock Memorial Hospital; Moderator of Town of Hanover, 1906–1912; New Hampshire House of Representatives, 1913; Chairman Committee Public Health. Has published many papers on medical subjects.

Lineage

ADAM BARTTELOT an Esquire came with William the Conqueror and seated himself in Ferring County, Sussex, buried at Stopham, 1100.

WILLIAM BARTTELOT DE STOPHAM buried in Stopham Church.

JOHN BARTTELOT, Esqr., buried in Stopham Church

RICHARD BARTTELOT, Esqr., buried in Stopham Church.
THOMAS BARTTELOT, Esq., buried in Stopham Church; *m.* Assoline, dau. of JOHN DE STOPHAM.
JOHN BARTTELOT, Esqr., captured the Castle of Fontenoy, in France and to him was granted the Castle crest as the Barttelot Arms; *m.* Joan, dau. and co-heir of John DE STOPHAM.
JOHN BARTTELOT, Member of Parliament for Sussex County, 1453; *m.* Joan, dau. and heir of John DE LEWKNOR.
RICHARD BARTTELOT, Esqr., 1459; *m.* Petronilla, heir general of Walton.
JOHN BARTTELOT, Esqr., of Stopham; *d.* 1493; *m.* Olive ARTHUR, dau. of John ARTHUR of London, heiress of Syheston.
RICHARD BARTTELOT, Esqr., of Stopham, *m.* Elizabeth GATES, dau. of John GATES.
EDMUND BARTTELOT of Enly, fourth son; *d.* 1591.

ISSUE

I. Edmund of Ernly, *m.* Elizabeth GORE, dau. of Richard GORE.
II. John.
III. RICHARD, of whom later.
IV. Thomas, *b.* between 1580 and 1590; came to America and settled at Watertown, Massachusetts.

RICHARD BARTLETT, came from Stopham, Sussex, England, settled in Newbury, Massachusetts, in 1635; *d.* 25th May, 1647; wife's name not given. He was descended from Adam DE BARTTELOT, who with William the Conqueror came over from Normandy, and fought at the Battle of Hastings, and who received grants of land at Stopham, Sussex. The original arms of the family in England were sable, three sinister falconers' gloves, argent, arranged triangularly, two above, one below, pendent, bands around the wrists, and tassels, golden. Near the close of the fifteenth century, one of the crests, the castle, was granted to John BARTTELOT who in command of the Sussex troops, captured the castle of Fontenoy, in France. In the sixteenth century, the swan crest was introduced to commemorate the right of the family to keep swans upon the River Arun, a right granted by William the Conqueror. The estates, consisting of several thousands of acres of land, granted more than eight hundred years ago have descended in the male line of the BARTTELOT family to the present day. The present head of the family in England is Sir Walter George BARTTELOT, who owns and occupies the ancestral estate. His father, Sir Walter Balfour BARTTELOT, was killed in the Boer War. His younger and only brother, Commander BARTTELOT of the *Pathfinder*, was killed 9th September, 1914, in the present European war. His ship was torpedoed and sunk by a German submarine in the British Channel.

ISSUE

I. Joanna, *b.* 29th January, 1610; *m.* before 1640, William TITCOMB.
II. John, *b.* 9th November, 1613; *d.* 5th February, 1678.

III. Thomas, *b.* 22d January, 1615.
IV. RICHARD, *b.* 31st October, 1621, of whom later.
V. Christopher, *b.* 25th February; 1623; *d.* 15th March; 1669; *m.* (firstly) 16th, April, 1645, Mary ———, *d.* 24th December, 1661; *m.* (secondly) 1663, Mary HOYT, probably dau. of John and Frances HOYT, of Salisbury.
VI. Anne, *b.* 26th February, 1625.

RICHARD BARTLETT, *b.* 31st October, 1621; *d.* 1698; he lived at first at Oldtown in Newbury, removing to Bartlett's corner near Deer Island, at the Merrimac River. He is said to have been "a facetious and intelligent man," and was four years a Deputy to the General Court; his will dated 19th April, 1695, being proved 18th of July, 1698; *m.* Abigail, surname not given, who *d.* 8th March, 1686.

ISSUE (BORN IN NEWBURY)

I. Samuel, *b.* 20th February, 1645; *d.* 15th May, 1732; was a very active and zealous partisan against Governor ANDROS; *m.* 23d May, 1671, Elizabeth TITCOMB, *d.* 26th August, 1690.
II. RICHARD, *b.* 21st February, 1649, of whom later.
III. Thomas, *b.* 7th September, 1650; *d.* 6th April, 1689; *m.* 21st November, 1685, Tirza TITCOMB.
IV. Abigail, *b.* 14th March, 1653; *d.* in 1723; *m.* 27th May, 1700, John EMERY.
V. John, *b.* 22d June, 1655; *d.* 24th May, 1736; *m.* (firstly) 29th September, 1680, Mary RUST, and she was living in 1693; *m.* (secondly) 13th of November, 1710, Dorcas PHILLIPS, who *d.* 18th January, 1719.
VI. Hannah, *b.* 18th December, 1657; *d.* unmarried between 1698 and 1723.
VII. Rebecca, *b.* 23d May, 1661; *d.* in 1723; *m.* 5th of September, 1700, Isaac BAYLEY.

RICHARD BARTLETT of Newbury, Massachusetts; *b.* there 21st February, 1649; *d.* 17th April, 1724; *m.* 18th November, 1673, Hannah EMERY, *b.* 26th April, 1654, dau. of John EMERY, *b.* in England, 1628, came with parents to Newbury, Massachusetts, 1628, *m.* 2d October, 1648, Mary WEBSTER, dau. of John and Mary (SHATWELL) WEBSTER. John EMERY was made freeman 30th May, 1660, and his will was probated 3d August, 1693.

ISSUE

I. Hannah, *b.* 8th November, 1674; *m.* John ORDWAY.
II. Richard, *b.* 20th October, 1676; *m.* 12th April, 1699, Margaret WOODMAN.
III. John, *b.* 3d September, 1678; *m.* 18th November 1702, Mary ORDWAY.
IV. Samuel, *b.* 8th May, 1680; *d.* 20th November, 1685.
V. Daniel, *b.* 8th August, 1682; *m.* and had issue.

VI. Joseph, *b.* 18th November, 1686; *d.* 1754; served in the French War of 1707; was captured and sent prisoner to Canada, where he remained over four years; *m.* (firstly) a Miss TEWKESBURY, who *d.s.p.*; *m.* (secondly), a Miss HOYT; had issue.
VII. Samuel, *b.* 2d May, 1689; *m.* and had issue.
VIII. STEPHEN, *b.* 21st April, 1691, of whom later.
IX. Thomas, *b.* 14th July, 1695; *m.* a Miss MOODY; had issue.
X. Mary, *b.* 15th September, 1697; *m.* ——— HILL; had issue.

STEPHEN BARTLETT of Newbury, Massachusetts; *b.* 21st April, 1691; *d.* 20th April, 1773; *m.* Hannah WEBSTER of Salisbury, Massachusetts.

ISSUE

I. Stephen, *b.* 1727; *d.* 5th October, 1759; *m.* Miss CURRIER; had issue.
II. JOSEPH, *b.* 18th April, 1720, of whom later.
III. Simeon, *b.* 17th June, 1727; *m.* (firstly) Miss GEORGE; *m.* (secondly) Hannah HERBERT, sister of Lieut. Richard HERBERT of Concord.
IV. Hon. Josiah, M.D., of Kingston, New Hampshire; appointed Colonel of a Regiment by Sir John WENTWORTH. Began his political career in 1765 as a Representative for the town of Kingston; in 1775 chosen as Delegate by the Continental Congress in Philadelphia; one of the Signers of the Declaration of Independence. Returned to Congress in 1776 and again in 1778 at Yorktown, the enemy then occupying Philadelphia. In 1780 appointed Chief Justice of the Court of Common Pleas and in the same year Muster-Master to muster the troops raising for three years. In 1782 appointed a Justice of the Supreme Court and in 1788 Chief Justice. Was an active member of the Convention of 1788 for the adoption of the plan for the government of the Confederation. Was chosen first Senator in 1788; elected President of New Hampshire, 1790–1791, and elected again 1792–1793 as Governor, being the first Governor of New Hampshire. In 1792 was one of the Electors of President and Vice-President; January, 1790, declined to be a candidate for any office; *m.* Mary BARTLETT of Newton, New Hampshire, who *d.* 1789, dau. of Joseph and ——— (HOYT) BARTLETT.

ISSUE

1. Levi, M.D.
2. Josiah, M.D.
3. Ezra, M.D.
4. Mary, *b.* 28th December, 1754; *m.* 12th March, 1780, Jonathan GREELEY; had issue.
5. Lois, *b.* 2d June, 1756; *d.* unmarried.
6. Marian, *b.* 19th June, 1758; *d.* 27th May, 1785; *m.* Joseph CATEF.
7. Rhoda, *b.* 22d May, 1760; *m.* Reuben TRUE.

8. Hannah, *b.* 31st August, 1762; *d.* September, 1762.
9. Sarah, *b.* 29th July, 1773; *m.* 24th April, 1796, Amos GALE, Jr., M.D.

v. Levi, *m.* and had issue.

JOSEPH BARTLETT of Amesbury, Massachusetts; *b.* 18th April, 1720; *d.* 1753; *m.* Jane COLBY, dau. of Ichabod COLBY of Amesbury, Massachusetts.

ISSUE (NO RECORD OF OTHER CHILDREN)

I. JOSEPH, *b.* 14th January, 1751, of whom below.

DR. JOSEPH BARTLETT of Salisbury, New Hampshire; *b.* Amesbury, Massachusetts, 14th January, 1751; *d.* 20th September, 1800. Removed to Salisbury in 1773, where he was the first physician, having studied his profession with his uncle Gov. Josiah BARTLETT. He was enrolled in Capt. Ebenezer WEBSTER's Company in 1775; *m.* 16th December, 1773, Hannah COLCORD of Kingston, New Hampshire, *b.* there 13th March, 1754, *d.* 29th August, 1837, dau. of Samuel B. and Mehitable (LADD) COLCORD.

ISSUE

I. Joseph, M.D., *b.* 8th April, 1778; *d.* 18th March, 1814.
II. Susannah, *b.* 17th April, 1779; *d.* 6th November, 1806; *m.* 12th October, 1800, Moses EASTMAN.
III. SAMUEL COLCORD, *b.* 16th January, 1780, of whom later.
IV. Hannah, *b.* 25th March, 1782; *d.* 12th November, 1802.
V. Levi, *b.* 3d January, 1784; *d.* 21st January, 1864, in Boston; *m.* Clarissa WALKER, *b.* 27th July, 1788, *d.* 28th October, 1845, dau. of Judge Timothy WALKER; had issue.
VI. Hon. Ichabod of Salisbury, *b.* 24th July, 1786; *d.* unmarried 19th October, 1853; graduated at Dartmouth College, 1808; Member of State Legislature; Clerk of the Senate, 1817; Speaker of the House, 1821; Representative in Congress, 1823–1829.
VII. Peter, M.D., *b.* 18th October, 1788; *d.* 8th September, 1868; *m.* August, 1816, Anna PETTENGILL.
VIII. James, *b.* 14th August, 1792; *d.* 17th June, 1837; graduated Dartmouth, 1812; was Member of Legislature and State Senator; *m.* (firstly) Lydia BALLARD; *m.* (secondly) Jane ANDREWS.
IX. Daniel of Boston, *b.* 25th August, 1795.

SAMUEL COLCORD BARTLETT of Salisbury, New Hampshire; *b.* 16th January, 1780; *d.* 31st March, 1867; *m.* 31st July, 1810, Eleanor PETTENGILL, *b.* in Salisbury, 26th December, 1786, *d.* 7th March, 1861, dau. of Amos and Charlotte (TRUE) PETTENGILL, he the son of Capt. Benjamin and Mehitable (KIMBALL) PETTENGILL of Salisbury, and was in Colonel MESERVE's regiment in the expedition against Crown Point in 1757.

COLONIAL FAMILIES OF THE UNITED STATES 77

ISSUE

1. Amos Pettengill, *b.* 14th May, 1812, in Salisbury, New Hampshire; *d.* 11th April, 1895, in Peoria, Illinois; *m.* 4th October, 1836, Sarah Maria ROGERS, *b.* 10th November, 1815, *d.* 16th October, 1905, dau. of Pelatiah and Mary (TALL) ROGERS.

ISSUE

1. Mary Ellen, *b.* 20th August, 1840.
2. Sarah Maria, *b.* 15th September, 1842; *m.* 23d June, 1868, John Sanborn STEVENS, *b.* 16th September, 1839.

ISSUE

1^1. Bartlett STEVENS, *b.* 9th November, 1874; *d.* 13th September, 1875.
2^1. John Sanborn STEVENS, *b.* 10th February, 1879; *d.* 17th February, 1881.

3. Samuel Colcord, *b.* 11th December, 1845; *d.* 19th March, 1893, in Winetka, Illinois; *m.* 22d June, 1876, Laura Amelia BENTON, *b.* 1850.

ISSUE

1^1. Samuel Colcord of Chicago, Illinois; *b.* 1st November, 1882; *m.* 10th July, 1906, Harriet Mary BUCK, *b.* 9th February, 1881, dau. of Ira D. BUCK.

ISSUE

1^2. Harriet Buck, *b.* 11th November, 1913.

2^1. Edmund Benton of Peoria, Illinois, *b.* 27th June, 1888; *m.* 11th October, 1913, Nanette Marie HUSTON, *b.* 11th January, 1888, dau. of James A. HUSTON of Sewickley, Pennsylvania.

4. Anna Frances, *b.* 1st August, 1848; *d.* 5th May, 1849.
5. William Henry, of Vermejo Park, New Mexico; *b.* 27th April, 1850; *m.* 9th September, 1875, in Woodstock, Vermont, Mary Wentworth CAMPBELL, *b.* 20th October, 1852, *d.* 2d December, 1904, in Denver, Colorado, dau. of William M. and Mary Wentworth (WILLIAMS) CAMPBELL.

ISSUE

1^1. Mary Wentworth, *b.* 19th June, 1876; *m.* 6th April, 1899, in Phoenix, Arizona, Charles William Case DEERING, *b.* 18th October, 1876.
2^1. Norman Williams, *b.* 19th July, 1878.
3^1. William Henry, *b.* 22d June, 1880; *m.* 4th November, 1903, Virginia Louise MILLARD, *b.* 2d October, 1881, dau. of Addison MILLARD.

ISSUE

1². Mary Wentworth, *b.* 30th May, 1905.
2². Virginia, *b.* 22d February, 1908.

6. Helen, *b.* 14th December, 1854.

II. Rev. Joseph, *b.* 26th January, 1816; *d.* 12th August, 1882, in Gorham, Maine; *m.* 26th October, 1847, Margaret MOTLEY, *b.* 22d December, 1818, *d.* 1st October, 1894, dau. of Capt. Robert MOTLEY.

ISSUE

1. Ellen Motley, *b.* 7th February, 1849; *d.* 26th August, 1882.
2. Sarah C., *b.* 27th July, 1853; *d.* 31st August, 1853.

III. SAMUEL COLCORD, *b.* 25th November, 1817, of whom later.
IV. Levi James, *b.* 28th August, 1823; *d.* 16th May, 1908, in Griggsville, Illinois; *m.* 4th December, 1860, Harriet Greenleaf CRANE, *b.* 9th June, 1827, *d.* 14th October, 1909, in Franklin, New Hampshire.

ISSUE

1. Albert Joseph, *b.* 20th December, 1862.
2. Grace Greenleaf, *b.* 28th October, 1869.

V. Alfred Henry, *b.* 19th April, 1825; *d.* 19th February, 1826.
VI. William Henry, *b.* 20th August, 1827; *d.* 24th September, 1867, in Concord, New Hampshire, graduated Dartmouth College, 1847; Judge New Hampshire Supreme Court, 1861; *m.* 8th May, 1856, Caroline BAKER, *b.* 1st November, 1824, *d.* 16th January, 1905, dau. of Abell BAKER of Concord.

REV. SAMUEL COLCORD BARTLETT of Hanover, New Hampshire; *b.* 25th November, 1817; *d.* 16th November, 1898, in Hanover, New Hampshire; graduated at Dartmouth College, 1836; was tutor at Dartmouth, 1838–1839; studied divinity at Andover Theological Seminary, graduating in 1842; ordained Pastor of the Congregational Church at Monson, Massachusetts, 2d August, 1843; Professor of Intellectual Philosophy and Rhetoric at Western Reserve College, Ohio, September, 1846, to July, 1852; installed Pastor at Manchester, New Hampshire, 3d November, 1852, where he remained till February, 1858; installed Pastor of the New England Church, Chicago, Illinois, 15th April, 1858, and dismissed 1st March, 1859. He was Professor of Sacred Theology at Chicago Theological Seminary, since May, 1858; President of Dartmouth College, 1877–1892; Dartmouth conferred upon him the degree of D.D., 1861; *m.* (firstly) 16th August, 1843, Laura BRADLEE, *d.* December, 1843, dau. of Nehemiah BRADLEE, of Peacham, Vermont; *m.* (secondly) 12th

COLONIAL FAMILIES OF THE UNITED STATES 79

May, 1846, Mary Bacon LEARNED, dau of Rev. Erastus LEARNED at Fall River, Massachusetts, *b.* in Canterbury, Connecticut, 18th December, 1821, *d.* in Hanover, New Hampshire, 2d April, 1893.

ISSUE

I. Henry Bancroft, *b.* 3d May, 1847; *d.* 23d August, 1847, in Hudson, Ohio.
II. Laura Bradlee, *b.* 21st May, 1848; *d.* 23d June, 1849, in Hudson, Ohio.
III. EDWIN JULIUS, *b.* 16th February, 1851, the subject of this memoir.
IV. Alice Wheaton, *b.* 20th September, 1854, in Hudson, Ohio; *m.* 19th April, 1877, Henry Albert STIMSON, *b.* 28th September, 1842, in New York City.

ISSUE

1. Alice Mary STIMSON, *b.* 6th September, 1879, in Minneapolis, Minnesota.
2. Julia Catherine STIMSON, *b.* 26th May, 1881, in Worcester, Massachusetts.
3. Lucile Hinkle STIMSON, *b.* 19th October, 1882, in Worcester, Massachusetts.
4. Henry Bartlett STIMSON, *b.* 24th November, 1884, in Worcester, Massachusetts.
5. Philip Moen STIMSON, *b.* 1st November, 1888, in St. Louis, Missouri.
6. Dorothy STIMSON, *b.* 10th October, 1890, in St. Louis, Missouri.
7. Barbara Bartlett STIMSON, *b.* 14th February, 1898, in New York City.

V. William Alfred, *b.* 17th February, 1858, in Chicago, Illinois; *m.* (firstly) 4th January, 1888, Susan Lord PITKIN, *b.* 24th January, 1860, *d.s.p.* 19th April, 1889; *m.* (secondly) 23d February, 1892, Esther Adelaide PITKIN, *b.* 28th December, 1864, dau. of John Jay and Susan Jeannette (THOMPSON) PITKIN.

ISSUE BY SECOND MARRIAGE

1. William Pitkin, *b.* 2d January, 1893, in Oak Park, Illinois; *d.* 1st December, 1910, in Hartford, Connecticut.
2. Doris Jeannette, *b.* 24th April, 1894, in Oak Park, Illinois.
3. Richard Learned, *b.* 20th December, 1896, in Lowell, Massachusetts.

VI. Samuel Colcord, *b.* 21st September, 1865; *m.* 11th July, 1894, Fanny GORDON, *b.* 26th August, 1874, in Osaka, Japan, dau. of M. Lafayette and Agnes Helen (DONALD) GORDON.

ISSUE

1. Samuel Colcord, *b.* 13th February, 1896, in Kioto, Japan.
2. Gordon, *b.* 12th March, 1898, in Tottori, Japan.
3. Robert Learned, *b.* 18th December, 1899, in Kioto, Japan.

4. Donald, b. 8th March, 1902, in Tottori, Japan.
5. Agnes Vernon, b. 18th March, 1911, in Kioto, Japan.

Arms.—Sable, three falconers' sinister gloves pendent argent, tasseled or.
Crest.—A swan couched argent, wings expanded.
Residence.—Hanover, New Hampshire.
Clubs.—Dartmouth Graduate and New England Chemical.
Societies.—New Hampshire Historical, Dartmouth Scientific, Fellow of American Association for Advancement of Sciences, American Chemical Society.

Bartlett

RALPH SYLVESTER BARTLETT, A.B., A.M., LL.B., of Boston, Massachusetts; b. 29th April, 1868, in Eliot, Maine; attended town schools of Eliot, 1872-1882; prepared for college at Berwick Academy, South Berwick, Maine, class of 1885; received degree A.B. Dartmouth College, 1889, A.M., 1892, LL.B. Magna cum laude, Law School of Boston University, 1892; admitted to the Suffolk Bar, 1892; admitted to practice in the United States Courts, 1894; associated in practice with former Gov. William E. Russell from 1892 until the latter's death in 1896; since engaged in the practice of his profession in Boston with offices in the Exchange Building; delegate to the National Farmers' Congress at Council Bluffs, Iowa, 1890; Active Member First Corps Cadets, Massachusetts National Guard, 1894-1903; now Honorary and Veteran Member of same; served with this organization in Coast Defence Duty during Spanish-American War, 1898; travelled extensively, in this country and abroad; Republican and unmarried.

Lineage

The lineage of this family in America is traced back to Adam DE BARTTELOT, who came over with William the Conqueror from Normandy, France, to England, and fought at the Battle of Hastings. He received grants of land in Stopham, Sussex, where he settled. The estate of the BARTTELOT family in England, consisting of several thousands of acres of land and granted more than 800 years ago, has descended in the male line of the BARTTELOT family to the present day. The estate is situated in Stopham, Pulborough, Sussex, on the River Arun, and the mansion upon the estate is known as Stopham House. Upon the estate is the old Stopham Church where many members of the early generations of the BARTTELOTS are buried. The subject of this memoir visited the estate in the summer of 1914, just before the outbreak of the war. The present head of the family is Sir Walter BARTTELOT who owns and occupies the estate. He is now serving in the European War with the rank of Major. Lady BARTTELOT, his wife, in a letter to the subject of this memoir under date of September 14, 1915, writes, "My husband, Major Sir Walter, is serving in the Dardanelles on Sir Ian HAMILTON's Staff. He was very badly wounded by a bullet through the lung at the Battle of the Aisne on September 14, 1914. He was then serving with his Regiment, the 2d Coldstream Guards, and went out with them with the Expeditionary Force. He made a most wonderful recovery and returned to active service about three months ago. Sir Walter's brother Lieut. Nigel BARTTELOT, was killed when commanding his Destroyer, *H.M.S. Liberty* at Helgoland." Sir Walter BARTTELOT's father was killed in the

Boer War. In the sixteenth century the swan crest was introduced in the BARTTE-LOT arms to commemorate the right of the family to keep swans upon the River Arun, a right granted by William the Conqueror. Hence, the Barttelot crest—a swan couched argent, wings expanded.

ADAM DE BARTTELOT was buried in Stopham, 1100; his son

WILLIAM BARTTELOT DE STOPHAM, who was buried in Stopham Church; his son

JOHN BARTTELOT, ESQ., who was buried in Stopham Church; his son

RICHARD BARTTELOT, ESQ., who was buried in Stopham Church; his son

THOMAS BARTTELOT, ESQ., who was buried in Stopham Church: *m.* Assoline DE STOPHAM, dau. of John DE STOPHAM; their son

JOHN BARTTELOT, ESQ., who, in command of the Sussex troops, captured the castle of Fontenoy in France. To him near the close of the fifteenth century was granted the castle, one of the crests of the BARTTELOT arms. The original arms of the family in England were sable, three sinister falconers' gloves, argent, arranged triangularly, two above, one below, pendent, bands around the wrist, and tassels, golden. He *m.* Joan DE STOPHAM, dau. and co-heir of John DE STOPHAM; their son

JOHN BARTTELOT, member of Parliament for Sussex County, who died in 1453. He fought at Agincourt; *m.* Joan DE LEWKNOR, dau. and heir of John DE LEWKNOR; their son

RICHARD BARTTELOT, ESQ., who *d.* in 1432; *m.* Petronilla, heir general of Walton; their son

JOHN BARTTELOT, Esq., of Stopham, who died in 1493; *m.* Olive ARTHUR, dau. of John ARTHUR of London and heiress of Syheston; their son

RICHARD BARTTELOT, Esq., of Stopham, *d.* at Tournay, in France in 1514; *m.* Elizabeth GATES, dau. of John GATES, their son

EDMUND BARTTELOT, Esq., of Ernly, who *d.* in 1591; *m.* wife's name not given; their son

RICHARD BARTTELOT, Esq., who was *b.* in England between 1580 and 1590, and emigrated to America in 1635, was the original ancestor of this line of the BARTLETT (formerly spelled B-a-r-t-l-e-t) family in America.

EARLY HISTORY OF THE BARTLETT FAMILY IN AMERICA

RICHARD BARTTELOT, son of Edmund BARTTELOT, who emigrated to America and settled in Newbury, Massachusetts in 1635, spelling his name "Bartlet" instead of "Barttelot." He *d.* in Newbury 25th of May, 1647; his wife's name is not given.

ISSUE

I. Joan, *b.* 29th January, 1610; *m.* before 1640 William TITCOMB.
II. John, *b.* 9th November, 1613; *d.* 5th February, 1678.
III. Thomas, *b.* 22d January, 1615.
IV. RICHARD, *b.* 31st October, 1621, of whom later.
V. Christopher, *b.* 25th February, 1623; *d.* 15th March, 1669.
VI. Anne, *b.* 26th February, 1625.

RICHARD BARTLET, *b.* 31st October, 1621; *d.* in 1698; his will dated 19th April, 1695, being proved 18th July, 1698; he lived first at Oldtown in Newbury, removing to Bartlet's corner near Deer Island, at the Merrimac River. He is said to have been "a facetious and intelligent man," and was for several years a Deputy to the General Court; *m.* Abigail ———, who *d.* 8th March, 1686.

ISSUE (BORN IN NEWBURY)

I. Samuel, *b.* 20th February, 1645; *d.* 15th May, 1732; *m.* 23d May, 1671, Elizabeth TITCOMB.
II. Richard, *b.* 21st February, 1648; *d.* 17th April, 1724; *m.* 18th November, 1673, Hannah EMERY.
III. Thomas, *b.* 7th September, 1650; *d.* 6th April, 1689; *m.* 21st November, 1685, Tirza TITCOMB.
IV. Abigail, *b.* 14th March, 1653; *d.* in 1723; *m.* 27th May, 1700, John EMERY, of Newbury.
V. JOHN, *b.* 22d June 1655, of whom later.
VI. Hannah, *b.* 18th December, 1657; *d.* unmarried between 1698 and 1723.
VII. Rebecca, *b.* 23d May, 1661; *d.* in 1723; *m.* 5th September, 1700, Isaac BAYLEY of Newbury.

JOHN BARTLET was *b.* in Newbury, 22d June, 1655; *d.* 24th May, 1736, at the age of eighty; he was a tanner and innholder and lived in Newbury; *m.* (firstly) 29th September, 1680; Mary RUST, and she was living in 1693; he *m.* (secondly) 13th November, 1710, Dorcas PHILLIPS of Rowley, who *d.* 18th January, 1719.

ISSUE (BORN IN NEWBURY)

I. Mary, *b.* 17th October, 1681; *d.* 29th March, 1682.
II. John, *b.* 24th January, 1682; *d.* in 1752.
III. Mary, *b.* 27th April, 1684; *d.* 19th March, 1707; *m.* July, 1700, John BAILEY.
IV. Nathaniel, *b.* 18th April, 1685; he lived in Exeter, New Hampshire; *m.* Meribah LITTLEFIELD of Kittery.
V. Dorothy, *b.* 13th August, 1686, and was living in 1733; *m.* 6th June, 1707, John ROPES, of Salem, Massachusetts.
VI. Sarah, *b.* 27th November, 1687; *d.* before 1733; *m.* December, 1707, Joseph FOWLER of Ipswich.
VII. Hannah, *b.* 13th March, 1688; *m.* Nathaniel BROWN of Wenham.
VIII. NATHAN, *b.* 23d December, 1691, of whom later.
IX. Abigail, *b.* 12th August, 1693; was living in 1733; *m.* Samuel GOODHUE, of Exeter.
X. Alice, *b.* 18th March, 1694; *d.* before 1733, probably unmarried.
XI. Mary, *m.* 12th January, 1722, Joseph JACOBS of Ipswich; *d.* before 1733.
XII. Gideon, *b.* about 1703; *d.* September, 1793.
XIII. Seth, *d.* in 1759; *m.* Sarah MERRILL.

xiv. Elizabeth, *m.* 13th April, 1725; *m.* Josiah BARTLET.
xv. Rebecca, *m.* 15th July, 1725, Deacon Daniel COFFIN of Newbury and was living in 1753.

CAPT. NATHAN BARTLET, *b.* in Newbury, 23d December, 1691; *d.* 1775; moved to that part of Kittery, now Eliot, in 1713. Captain Bartlet was a ganner and did a prosperous business. He purchased in 1725 60 acres of land at Sturgeon Creek of John WITTUM for £250. The following year he bought 20 acres of land of Peter WITTUM, paying therefor £100. An old deed from John HEARD to his son-in-law, Capt. Nathan BARTLET, in 1725, gives him a tract of land at Third Hill with one-half part of Stoney Brook and one-third part of a saw-mill built by James EMERY and Maj. Charles FROST adding this note "that it is to be understood that the above given and granted premises are not to be reckoned as any part of my daughter, Shuah's, portion." This land and other land which he purchased became the homestead place of his descendants. Captain BARTLET built (about 1718) a brick house near John HEARD's home, the present site of the Bartlett homestead, making the bricks on his land bordering on Sturgeon Creek. This brick house was partially destroyed by an earthquake about 1737, and Captain BARTLET built about 1740 the oak timbered two and a half story Colonial house, now standing, in which five generations of the Bartlett family have been born and reared. He *m.* 10th March, 1714, Shuah HEARD, *b.* 15th January, 1694, dau. of Capt. John and Phebe (LITTLEFIELD) HEARD. Phebe (LITTLEFIELD) HEARD, Maj. Charles FROST and Dennis DOWNING were killed by Indians at Ambush Rock, in that part of Kittery, now Eliot, on Sunday, 4th July, 1697, while returning on horseback from the meeting house in the Parish of Unity, in the Precinct of Berwick, where they had attended divine service. A bronze tablet marks this spot. The body of Phebe LITTLEFIELD HEARD was buried in the old burying ground upon the farm in Eliot, belonging to the heirs of Sylvester BARTLETT. A bronze tablet also marks this spot. These tablets were erected by Ralph Sylvester BARTLETT, the subject of this memoir.

ISSUE

i. Shuah, *b.* 1st January, 1716, *m.* 15th November, 1732, Dr. Edmund COFFIN, *b.* 19th March, 1708; he was a practising physician in Kittery, and his home was near the home of Capt. Nathan BARTLET; they had thirteen children; Dr. Edmund COFFIN was a son of Hon. Nathaniel COFFIN of Newbury, Massachusetts.
ii. Mary, *b.* 1st March, 1718; *m.* (firstly) Thomas DENNETT; *m.* (secondly) ———— LORD.
iii. Nathan, *b.* 30th April, 1720; *d.* 7th May, 1720.
iv. Phebe, *b.* 8th May, 1721; *m.* February, 1739, John DENNETT, of Portsmouth.
v. Abigail, *b.* 6th December, 1723; *d.* 3d June, 1800; *m.* (firstly) in 1741, John SHAPLEIGH, son of Maj. Nicholas SHAPLEIGH; *m.* (secondly) Moses HANSCOM.

vi. John Heard, b. 8th April, 1726; d. 28th July, 1805; he was the first BART-
LET to graduate from Harvard College, graduating therefrom in the
class of 1747. His grandfather, John HEARD, in his will bequeathed
him £50, and then added an additional £50 "in consideration that
his father intends to educate him at the College." After graduation
John Heard BARTLET settled near Third Hill, Kittery (in that part now
Eliot). He was a school teacher, Trial Justice, Clerk of Judicial Court,
and in 1757 was a Lieutenant in Sir William PEPPERRELL's Regiment
called "The Blue Troop of Horse;" he m. (firstly) in 1747, Dorcas
MOULTON of York, who d. 29th January, 1788; m. (secondly) June
15th, 1788, Elizabeth ATKINSON, widow; m. (thirdly) Bertha MIRIAM
in 1799, widow, of Berwick, who d. 11th April, 1817, aged eighty-two
years.

vii. Hannah, b. 29th October, 1728; m. 9th June, 1745, Robert CUTTS, who
was the eldest son of Maj. Richard CUTTS of Cutts Island.

viii. Nathan, b. 3d November, 1730; d. 21st May, 1736.

ix. James, b. 24th May, 1732; d. 17th September, 1738.

x. Sarah, b. 25th December, 1735; d. January, 1736.

xi. NATHAN, b. 31st March, 1737, of whom later.

xii. Sarah, b. 26th May, 1741; m. 17th September, 1762, Capt. John WENT-
WORTH of Kittery.

NATHAN BARTLET b. 31st March, 1737; d. 18th June, 1775; lived in his father's
house; m. 9th June, 1757, Sarah SHAPLEIGH, who d. 17th December, 1805, dau. of
Capt. John and Dorcas (LITTLEFIELD) SHAPLEIGH.

ISSUE

i. Dorcas, b. 9th January, 1758; m. 20th June, 1776, Nathan COFFIN.

ii. JAMES, b. 24th November, 1759, of whom later.

iii. Shuah, b. 11th November, 1761; m. 28th March, 1782, Stephen FERGU-
SON.

iv. Nathan, b. 21st November, 1763; m. Abigail STAPLES.

v. Alice, b. 22d January, 1767; m. ——— GILE of Alfred, Maine; no
children.

vi. Mary, b. 16th March, 1768; m. 19th November, 1799, George LIBBY.

vii. Lucretia, b. 4th November, 1771; m. ——— HODSDON.

viii. Sarah, b. 14th January, 1775; m. 19th February, 1795, George FROST.

JAMES BARTLETT (the spelling of the name "BARTLET" was in this generation
B-A-R-T-L-E-T-T); b. 24th November, 1759; d. 30th October, 1836; was a Revolutionary soldier, a private in Capt. Richard ROGERS' Company of Col. GERRISH's
Regiment; he was nineteen years of age at time of service and was on guard duty
at Winter Hill, Somerville, Massachusetts, from 20th July, to 14th December,
1778; he m. 30th May, 1782, Lois HILL, b. 29th May, 1757, d. 3d October, 1838,

dau. of John and Elizabeth (FERGUSON) HILL. They lived in the old Bartlett homestead in Eliot, Maine, which is now owned by the heirs of James W. BARTLETT.

ISSUE

I. Elizabeth, *bapt.* 6th May, 1784; *m.* 28th December, 1802, Samuel SHAPLEIGH, and moved to Lebanon, Maine; they had seven children.
II. Shuah, *bapt,* 21st June, 1784; *m.* 1st February, 1810, Andrew EMERY and moved to New Portland, Maine; they had four children; Hiram A. EMERY, late of Brooklyn, New York, was one of her sons.
III. James, *b.* 18th June, 1787; *d.* in New Portland 4th March, 1875; *m.* 28th November, 1814, Lucy KNOWLTON; they lived in Portsmouth, New Hampshire, and of this union there were three sons and three daughters.
IV. John Hill, *b.* 9th December, 1789; *d.* 21st January, 1878; *m.* 8th February 1814, Phebe BURBANK; they lived in North New Portland and of this union there were seven sons and five daughters. Mrs. Abbie E. SHAPLEIGH of West Lebanon, Maine, is one of the daughters.
V. NATHAN, *b.* 2d February, 1792, of whom later.
VI. Sarah, *b.* 16th July, 1796; *d.* 24th November, 1883; *m.* 24th December, 1812, Hugh KENNISON; they lived in Temple, Maine; of this union there were seven sons and four daughters, among the living daughters being Miss Myra A. KENNISON.
VII. William, *b.* 4th October, 1797; *d.* 12th March, 1882; *m.* 11th March 1824, Abigail BURBANK; they lived in New Portland, Maine; of this union there were three sons and four daughters.

NATHAN BARTLETT, *b.* 2d February, 1792; *d.* 15th October, 1865; he was a farmer and lived in the Old Bartlett homestead in Eliot, Maine, now owned by the heirs of the late James W. BARTLETT; *m.* 25th December, 1817, Mehitable EMERY, dau. of William and Philomelia (WEBBER) EMERY, who *d.* 1st September, 1857.

ISSUE

I. Lucinda, *b.* 24th May, 1819; *d.* 7th May, 1852.
II. SYLVESTER, *b.* 4th July, 1822; of whom later.
III. Elizabeth S., *b.* 14th June, 1824; *d.* in Eliot, 28th January, 1898; *m.* 11th November, 1873, Edwin P. FARLEY of Lockport, Illinois.
IV. Sarah, *b.* 30th August, 1826; *m.* 1st March, 1860, Hiram W. EMERY, and lived in Lockport, Illinois, where she died 11th January, 1875.
V. James W., *b.* 1st July, 1828; *d.* 2d January, 1915; *m.* (firstly) Caroline A. GOODWIN; *m.* (secondly) Lydia F. WORSTER.
VI. Justin S., *b.* 11th September, 1830; *d.* 3d January, 1866; *m.* 12th January, 1857, Emily D. SHOREY; they had two children who died in childhood.

SYLVESTER BARTLETT was born in the old Bartlett homestead in Eliot, 4th July, 1822; *d.* 24th April, 1901; after his marriage he was actively engaged for several years with his brother, James W. in a large retail meat business; closing that about 1875 he devoted his time to his farm and other business interests. His home was on the site of the John HEARD house and adjoins the old Bartlett homestead. The HEARD family, two early generations of the BARTLETT family and several members of the COFFIN family are buried in an old burying ground in the field opposite the old Bartlett homestead. He was a Republican, and was a Representative from Eliot to the Maine Legislature in 1895–1896; *m.* 30th December, 1855, Clementin RAITT, who *d.* 10th January, 1911, dau. of John and Betsey (FERGUSON) RAITT.

ISSUE

I. Elizabeth Mehitable, *b.* 21st September, 1857; she lives in Eliot, Maine.
II. John Howard, *b.* 29th October, 1860; *d.* 5th February, 1863.
III. Charles Edward, *b.* 19th January, 1863; *m.* 19th January, 1915, Jean McRAE; they live in Eliot, Maine.
IV. RALPH SYLVESTER, *b.* 29th April, 1868, the subject of this memoir.
V. Rolla Willis, *b.* 2d September, 1869; *m.* 25th June, 1912, Mary E. MOULTON; they live in Boston, Massachusetts.
VI. Grace Isabel, *b.* 14th February, 1871; *d.* 28th April, 1874.

Arms.—Sable, three sinister falconers' gloves pendent argent, tasseled, or.
Crest.—A swan couched argent, wings expanded.
Motto.—Mature.
Residence.—139 Beacon Street, Boston, Massachusetts.
Clubs.—University, Dartmouth, Middlesex, Economic.
Societies.—Sons of the American Revolution, Theta Delta Chi, Phi Delta Phi, New England Historic-Genealogical Society, Bostonian Society and Society for the Preservation of New England Antiquities.
Associations.—American Bar Association, Massachusetts Bar Association, Bar Association of the City of Boston, and the Boston Chamber of Commerce.

Betts

SAMUEL ROSSITER BETTS, A.B., LL.B., of New York City; *b.* 5th November, 1854, at New York City; Graduate Yale University, A.B., 1875; Columbia University, LL.B., 1877; member and head of successive law firms located in New York City, and practicing patent law as specialty; now counsel in special matters; United States Commissioner for Southern District of New York since 1877; Master in Equity and Examiner in United States Courts; director of business and charitable institutions; Secretary of New York Institution for Instruction of the Deaf and Dumb.

Clubs.—Union, University, Yale, Century, Players, Bankers of New York, and others out of town.

Societies.—Colonial Wars, Military Order Loyal Legion, Sons of the Revolution, Society War of 1812, Society of Foreign Wars, American Bar Association, New York State Bar Association, Bar Association City of New York, New York County Lawyers Association, American Geographical Society, American Museum of Natural History, New York Botanical Garden, New York Zoological Society, Metropolitan Museum of Art, American Association Advancement of Science.

Arms.—Sable on a bend argent three cinquefoils gules all within a bordure engrailed of the second.

Crest.—Out of a ducal coronet or, a buck's head gules attired or, gorged with a collar argent.

Motto.—Ostendo non ostento.

Residence Address.—University Club, New York City.

Lineage

THOMAS BETTS, *b.* in England, 1618, came to America as early as 1639 and became one of the founders of Guilford, Connecticut; *d.* Norwalk, Connecticut, 1688; *m.* and had issue.

ISSUE

I. Thomas, *b.* in Guilford, 1644; *d.* 1717.
II. Mary, *b.* in Guilford, 1646; *d.* after 1688.
III. John, *b.* in Guilford, 20th June, 1650; *d.* about 1730.
IV. Hannah, *b.* in Guilford, 22d November, 1652; *d.* before 1688.
V. Stephen, *b.* in Guilford, 10th May, 1655; *d.* before 1672.
VI. DANIEL, *b.* in Guilford, 4th October, 1657; *d.* 8th February, 1758, of whom later.
VII. Samuel, *b.* in Milford, 4th April, 1660; *d.* after 1730.
VIII. James, *b.* in Norwalk, early in 1663; *d.* 6th July, 1753.
IX. Sarah, *b.* in Norwalk, about 1664; *d.* after 1706.

DANIEL BETTS of Norwalk, Connecticut; *b.* Guilford, Connecticut, 4th October, 1657; *d.* Wilton, Connecticut, 8th February, 1758; *m.* December, 1692, Deborah TAYLOR, *b.* 1st June, 1671, *d.* circa 1751, dau. of Thomas TAYLOR.

ISSUE

I. Deborah, *b.* 24th October, 1693; *d*, no record.
II. Rebecca, *b.* 4th August, 1696; *d.* after 1731.
III. DANIEL, Jr., *b.* 2d May, 1699, of whom later.

DANIEL BETTS of Wilton, Connecticut; *b.* 2d May, 1699, at Norwalk, Connecticut; *d.* 10th July, 1783, at Wilton; *m.* 1724 or 1725, Sarah COMSTOCK, *b.* 25th March, 1707, *d.* 18th January, 1781, dau. of Capt. Samuel COMSTOCK.

ISSUE

I. Josiah, *b.* 8th March, 1726; *d.* before 1732.
II. Sarah, *b.* 8th March, 1726; *m.* Josiah BURCHARD; no record.
III. Daniel, III, *b.* 28th June, 1728; *d.* 8th October, 1820.
IV. Hannah, *b.* 12th May, 1730; *m.* 20th November, 1750, Ezra GREGORY.
V. SAMUEL COMSTOCK, *b.* 2d March, 1732, at Norwalk; *d.* 16th May, 1823, of whom later.
VI. Elizabeth, no birth record; *d.* March 1818; *m.* 25th January, 1764, Zacharia MEAD, of Balston, New York.
VII. Jesse, *b.* December, 1734; *d.* 6th October, 1742.
VIII. Ruth, *b.* February, 1737; *d.* 2d October, 1742.
IX. Abijah N., *b.* 1740; *bapt.* 13th July, 1740; *d.* 30th December, 1817.
X. Timothy, *bapt.* 8th May, 1743; lived after 13th August, 1817.
XI. Lydia, *b.* 1745; *bapt.* 29th June, 1745; *d.* 1746.
XII. Deborah, *b.* 1748; *bapt.* 5th June, 1748; *d.* 15th April, 1774.
XIII. Reuben, *b.* 27th May, 1753; *d.* after 1792.
XIV. Elijah, no birth record; *d.* after 1799.

SAMUEL COMSTOCK BETTS of Richmond, Massachusetts; *b.* Norwalk, Connecticut, 2d March, 1732; *d.* 16th May, 1823; was a non-commissioned officer in the 2d Company of the 9th Regiment of Connecticut Foot in Revolutionary War; *m.* 5th June, 1754, Mary TAYLOR, *b.* 3d December, 1731, *d.* 11th September, 1807, dau. of Reuben TAYLOR, of Norwalk, Connecticut.

ISSUE

I. Mary, *b.* 1st May, 1755; *d.* 11th December, 1831.
II. Joel, *b.* 4th May, 1756; *d.* 5th April, 1790.
III. Aaron, *b.* 16th September, 1757; *d.* 3d April, 1833.
IV. Preserved, *b.* 12th August, 1759; *d.* 1st February, 1818.
V. URIAH, *b.* 25th February, 1761; *d.* 10th August, 1841, of whom later.
VI. Comstock, *b.* 19th November, 1762; *d.* 18th December, 1845.

VII. Zebulon, *b.* 12th August, 1764; *d.* 27th November, 1828.
VIII. Lydia, *b.* 2d August, 1766; *d.* 22d November, 1861.
IX. Enoch, *b.* 4th May, 1768; *d.* 6th June, 1822.
X. Amos, *b.* 25th September, 1770; *d.* October, 1793.
XI. Daniel, V, *b.* 22d August, 1772; *d.* 8th March, 1792.

URIAH BETTS of Richmond, Massachusetts; *b.* Wilton, Connecticut, 25th February, 1761; *d.* 10th August, 1841, Newburgh, N. Y.; was a soldier in the Revolutionary War, serving in Connecticut and New York; *m.* (firstly) 14th October, 1783, Sarah ROSSETER, *b.* 28th August, 1763, *d.* 11th June, 1796, dau. of Hon. Nathan ROSSETER of Richmond, Massachusetts; *m.* (secondly) 22d September, 1796, Rebekah ROSSETER, *b.* 29th June, 1774, sister of his first wife.

ISSUE BY FIRST MARRIAGE

I. Julia or Juliana, *b.* 5th September, 1784; *d.* April, 1872.
II. SAMUEL ROSSETER, *b.* 8th June, 1786; *d.* 3d November, 1868, of whom later.
III. A son, *b.* and *d.* 7th December, 1790.
IV. Sarah Maria, *b.* 29th March, 1796; *d.* 5th February, 1873.

ISSUE BY SECOND MARRIAGE

I. Amanda E., *b.* 5th February, 1799; *d.* 17th October, 1857.
II. Frederic J., *b.* 2d July, 1803; *d.* 12th October, 1879.
III. Nathan Comstock, *b.* 18th November, 1809; *d.* July, 1882.

SAMUEL ROSSETER BETTS of New York, New York, *b.* 8th June, 1786, at Richmond, Massachusetts; *d.* 3d November, 1868, at New Haven; graduated Williams College, 1806; LL.D., Williams, 1830; was an officer in War of 1812; Member of Congress from 1815–1817; Circuit Judge of the Supreme Court of New York 1823–1827, and Judge of the United States District Court for Southern District of New York for forty years, 1827–1867; *m.* 4th November, 1816, Caroline A. DEWEY, *b.* 8th April, 1798, *d.* 9th June, 1882, dau. of Hon. Daniel DEWEY of Northampton, Massachusetts.

ISSUE

I. Maria Caroline, *b.* 15th August, 1818; *d.* 31st January, 1909; *m.* 12th July, 1842, James W. METCALF.
II. Charles Dewey, *b.* 6th July, 1820; *d.* 16th January, 1845; unmarried.
III. Frances Julia, *b.* 28th November, 1822; *d.* 14th June, 1907; *m.* 18th January, 1854, William HILLHOUSE.
IV. GEORGE FREDERIC, *b.* 14th June, 1827, of whom later.
V. Emily, *b.* 7th October, 1830; *d.* 26th April, 1916; unmarried.

GEORGE FREDERIC BETTS of New York City; *b.* 14th June, 1827, at Newburgh, New York; *d.* 18th January, 1898, at New York City; Graduated Williams College,

1844; was Lieutenant-Colonel of 9th New York Volunteers in the Civil War, serving from 19th April, 1861, to February, 1862; Counsellor at Law, Clerk United States District Court for Southern District New York, 1855–1878; *m.* 19th November, 1851, Ellen PORTER of Boston, Massachusetts, *b.* 4th May, 1829, at Williamstown, Massachusetts, *d.* 15th July, 1899, at New York City, dau. of Prof. William A. PORTER of Williams College and Mary A. NOBLE, his wife, dau. of Hon. Daniel NOBLE of Williamstown, Massachusetts.

ISSUE

I. Mary, *b.* 23d March, 1853; *d.* 7th July, 1855.
II. SAMUEL ROSSITER, *b.* 5th November, 1854, the subject of this memoir.
III. Amy Ellen, *b.* 5th September, 1856; *m.* 23d December, 1883, John Addison PORTER of New Haven, Connecticut, son of Prof. John Addison PORTER, of Yale University, and Josephine Earl SHEFFIELD, his wife, dau. of Hon. Joseph E. SHEFFIELD of New Haven, Connecticut.

ISSUE

1. Constance Elaine PORTER, *b.* 25th August, 1885; *d.* 23d June, 1889.
2. Amy Agnes Sheffield PORTER, *b.* 7th March, 1891.
3. Josephine Earl PORTER, *b.* 17th October, 1892.

IV. Fanny Johnston, *b.* 29th January, 1867; *m.* 8th October, 1895, Wolcott Howe JOHNSON, son of Samuel and Mary (STODDARD) JOHNSON, of Boston, Massachusetts, dau. of Charles and Mary (NOBLE) (PORTER) STODDARD by her second marriage, all of Boston, Massachusetts.

ISSUE

1. Samuel JOHNSON, *b.* 7th December, 1896.
2. George Frederic Betts JOHNSON, *b.* 10th July, 1898.
3. Rosamond Porter JOHNSON, *b.* 16th May, 1900.
4. Beatrice Howe JOHNSON, *b.* 5th July, 1903; *d.* 21st April, 1912.

V. Georgina, *b.* 13th November, 1868; *m.* 8th April, 1894, Thomas Tileston WELLS, son of John and Grace (TILESTON) WELLS, of New York, New York.

ISSUE

1. John WELLS, *b.* 10th May, 1895.
2. Rossiter Betts WELLS, *b.* 18th October, 1900; *d.* 12th June, 1902.
3. Georgina Lawrence WELLS, *b.* 5th October, 1902.

Biddle

NICHOLAS BIDDLE of Noble, Pennsylvania; *b.* 30th July, 1893, in Brookline, Massachusetts; *m.* 11th February, 1915, at 1712 Spruce Street, Philadelphia, Pennsylvania, Sarah LIPPINCOTT, *b.* 14th July, 1894, dau. of Joshua Bertram and Joanna (WHARTON) LIPPINCOTT of Philadelphia and "Melmar," Bethayres, Pennsylvania.

ISSUE

1. Joanna Wharton, *b.* 27th December, 1915.

NICHOLAS BIDDLE was educated at the Newton Grammar School, also Central High School, and is a graduate of the Episcopal Academy of Philadelphia; later entered Princeton College, leaving in the Junior year to enter business life; was connected with the Insurance Company of North America until September, 1915, since which time has been associated with Hutchinson Rivinus and Company, of Philadelphia; is a member of the 1st City Troop of Philadelphia and was ordered into service 6th July, 1916, on the Mexican border.

Lineage

The ancestor of this family was William BIDDLE, *b.* 1630, near London, England; left that city July, 1681, and came to New Jersey; he is said to have been an officer in the Parliamentary Army during the Civil War in England, but soon after its close joined the Society of Friends; his name appears among the list of persons imprisoned by Major BROWN, 1660–1661, for attending "non-conformist" meetings. Esther BIDDLE, his mother, an eminent Friend, suffered persecution for "Truth's Sake" at various periods; he *d.* 1712, at "Mt. Hope," West Jersey; will proved 3d March, 1711–1712. Purchased 23d January, 1676, of William PENN, Garber LAURIE, Nicholas LUCAS and Edward BYLLANGE a one-half share of the lands in Western Jersey and became therefore one of the Proprietors of that Province. His later purchase gave him $1\frac{3}{4}$ shares of the 16 shares into which the Province was divided, entitling him to 43,000 acres. Settled in West Jersey in 1681; Member of the Governor's Council 1682–1685 and 1701. and of the General Assembly of the Province, 1683, 1684–1685 and 1702; was a Justice of Burlington County from 1682 until his death; one of the Trustees selected by the Proprietors to conduct the business of the Proprietorship, 14th February, 1687, and regularly re-elected thereafter, serving as President of the Board of Trustees, 1706–1707.; one of the Board of Commissioners for laying out lands; Member of Council of Proprietary of West Jersey, 1682, re-elected 15th March, 1683; *m.* 7th December, 1665, at Bishopgate Street Friends Meeting in London, England, Sarah KEMP, *b.* 1634, *d.* 27th February, 1709.

ISSUE (ALL BORN IN LONDON)

I. Elizabeth, *b.* 25th June, 1668; *d.* in infancy.
II. WILLIAM, *b.* 4th December, 1669, of whom later.
III. John, *b.* 27th December, 1670; *d.* in childhood.
IV. Joseph, *b.* 6th February, 1672; *d.* in childhood.
V. Sarah, *b.* 2d December, 1678; *d.s.p.* 2d August, 1705, in Philadelphia; *m.* (firstly) 21st October, 1695, William RIGHTON; *m.* (secondly) 14th March, 1703, Clement PLUMSTEAD of Philadelphia.

WILLIAM BIDDLE, II, of "Mt. Hope," New Jersey; *b.* 4th October, 1669, in London, England; *d.* at "Mt. Hope," 1743; was like his father prominent in the affairs of West Jersey; appointed by the Council of Proprietors on 2d November, 1703, to treat with the Indians for lands above the Falls, and at his father's death inherited 12,905 acres of land in the "Lotting Purchase;" *m.* 13th December, 1691, in Shrewsbury, New Jersey, Lydia WARDELL, gd. dau. of Elialim WARDELL, who purchased lands at Newark of the Indians in 1666; was Sheriff of Monmouth, 1688, and Member of the General Assembly, 1692, gr. gd. dau. of Thomas WARDELL, a French Huguenot, who settled in New England about the middle of the seventeenth century.

ISSUE

I. WILLIAM, III, *b.* circa 1698, of whom later.
II. Elizabeth.
III. Sarah.
IV. Penelope, *m.* ——— WHITEHEAD.
V. Joseph, *m.* (firstly) Lydia HOWARD; *m.* (secondly) Sarah ROGERS, remained in New Jersey.
VI. John, *b.* 1707; *m.* 3d March, 1763, Sarah OWEN, dau. of Owen OWEN, a descendant of OWEN, of Dolly Sone, Wales.

WILLIAM BIDDLE, III, of "Mt. Hope," New Jersey, and Philadelphia, *b.* 1698, "Mt. Hope;" *d.* 1756 in Philadelphia, to which city he removed with his family, 1720–1730; *m.* 3d April, 1730, in Philadelphia, Mary SCULL, *b.* 2d August, 1709, *d.* 9th May, 1790, dau. of Nicholas SCULL, *b.* 1687, *d.* 1761, Surveyor-General, participated in the Indian Walk of 1737, elected Sheriff of Philadelphia, 1744, *m.* 1708, Abigail HEAP, who *d.* 21st May, 1753. Nicholas SCULL was the eldest son of Nicholas SCULL who came to Pennsylvania in the ship *Bristol Merchant* arriving at Chester, 10th October, 1685, The progenitor of the family was Sir John SCULL, a Norman, one of the twelve Norman Knights mentioned in Burke's "Landed Gentry," who accompanied Newmarch into North Wales and eventually conquered that country.

ISSUE

I. James, *b.* 18th February, 1731; *d.* 15th June, 1797; *m.* 30th June, 1753, Frances MARKS.

COLONIAL FAMILIES OF THE UNITED STATES

II. Nicholas, *b.* 1733; *d.* in infancy.
III. Lydia, *b.* 1734; *m.* 3d December, 1752, Capt. William McFUNN of the Royal Navy, and later Governor of the Island of Antigua, West Indies.
IV. John, *b.* 1736; *d.* in Nova Scotia; was Deputy Quartermaster in the Provincial Army in General FORBES campaign against Fort Duquense; was a Royalist during the Revolution and sought refuge with the British Army at New York, 1777–1778, and later fled to Nova Scotia.
V. Edward, *b.* 1738; *d.* 5th September, 1779, at the residence of his son-in-law, George LUX in Baltimore; Ensign of Lieut.-Col. WEISER's Company, 3d December, 1757; Lieutenant, 1759; Captain in Col. Hugh MERCER's battalion, 24th February, 1760; was at the capture of Fort Duquense and Fort Morgan; *m.* 1761, Elizabeth Ross, dau. of John Ross, Esq.
VI. CHARLES, *b.* 24th December, 1745, of whom later.
VII. Abigail, *b.* 1747; *d.* 1756.
VIII. Mary, *b.* 1749; *d.* in infancy.
IX. Nicholas, II, *b.* 1750; killed in action at loss of the *Randolph*, February, 1778, in the combat between the American vessel *Randolph* and the vessel *Cornwallis*.
X. Thomas, *b.* 1752; removed to Georgetown, South Carolina; studied medicine with Dr. Thomas BOND of Philadelphia; took degree of M.D. at the University of Pennsylvania and located at Georgetown, South Carolina.

CHARLES BIDDLE, of Philadelphia; *b.* there 24th December, 1745; *d.* there 4th April, 1821; January, 1776, joined Captain COWPERTHWAIT's Company of the Quaker Light Infantry; Vice-President, Supreme Executive Council of Pennsylvania for two years, when Benjamin FRANKLIN was President; *m.* 25th November, 1778, at Beaufort, South Carolina, Hannah SHEPARD.

ISSUE

I. Nicholas, *b.* 1779, Newberne, North Carolina; *d.* in infancy.
II. William Shepard, *b.* 21st February, 1781; *d.* 30th May, 1835; *m.* (firstly) Circe DERONCERAY; *m.* (secondly) Elizabeth B. (HOPKINSON) KEATING.
III. James, *b.* 18th February, 1783; *d.* unmarried, October, 1848.
IV. Edward, *b.* 1784; *d.* on frigate *President*, 14th November, 1800; appointed Midshipman in United States Navy, 14th 1800.
IV. NICHOLAS, *b.* 8th January, 1786, of whom later.
V. Charles, *b.* 1787; *d.* 1836; sent to Isthmus of Panama by President Jackson, 1835, to report a feasible route for railroad and canal crossing the Isthmus; *m.* 1808, Anna H. STOKES.
VI. Thomas, *b.* 1790; Major United States Army; killed in duel with Spencer PITTS, Member of Congress, 29th August, 1831, *m.* Ann MULLANPHY.
VII. John, Major, *b.* 1792; *d.* 21st August, 1859; *m.* Eliza BRADISH.

COLONIAL FAMILIES OF THE UNITED STATES

VIII. Richard, *b.* 1796; *d.* 1847; Member of Congress, 1837–1841; *m.* Ann ANDERSON.
IX. Mary.
X. Ann.

NICHOLAS BIDDLE of Philadelphia, Pennsylvania; *b.* there 8th January, 1786; *d.* 27th February, 1844, at "Andaulusia," Bucks County; Graduated at Princeton with honors in his fifteenth year; went to Europe in 1804 as Secretary to General ARMSTRONG, United States Minister to France, and was present at the coronation of Napoleon at Paris; later Secretary to James MONROE, then Minister at London; returned to Philadelphia in 1807; elected to Pennsylvania Legislature, 1810; elected to State Senate during second war with England; was a writer of ability and took great interest in agriculture and horticulture. Charles J. INGERSOLL, his political opponent, said of him, "Nicholas BIDDLE was as iron nerved as his great antagonist, Andrew JACKSON, loved his country not less—and money as little." Was President of the Bank of the United States, 1823–1836; *m.* October, 1811, Jane Margaret CRAIG, *b.* 1792, in Philadelphia; *d.* 11th August, 1856, dau. of John and Margaret CRAIG of Philadelphia.

ISSUE

I. EDWARD, *b.* 1815, of whom later.
II. Charles John, Colonel 13th Regiment United States Volunteers, 21st June, 1861; served with distinction in the Mexican War, being brevetted Major for gallant and meritorius service at the storming of Chapultepec; *m.* Emma MATHER; *d.* 28th September, 1873.
III. Hon. Craig, A.M., 1841; LL.D., *b.* 10th January, 1823; in 1861 was Major on Staff of Gen. Robert PATTERSON and served in Shenandoah Campaign; later Member of Staff Governor Andrew G. CURTIN; Judge of the Court of Common Pleas of Philadelphia, 1875–1907.
IV. Meta Craig, *m.* her cousin Capt. James BIDDLE, U. S. N., son of Charles BIDDLE, 1787–1836.
V. Adele.
VI. Jane.

EDWARD BIDDLE, II, of Philadelphia, *b.* 1815; *d.* 1872; *m.* 1842, in New York City, Jane Josephine *née* (SARMIENTO) CRAIG, *b.* 1816, *d.* 1884, dau. of James SARMIENTO and widow of John C. CRAIG.

ISSUE

I. Edith, *m.* Philip Schuyler VAN RENSSELAER.
II. Frances.
III. Agnes, *m.* James W. WARD.
IV. EDWARD, III, *b.* 24th November, 1851, of whom later.
V. Mildred.

EDWARD BIDDLE, III, of Philadelphia; *b.* 24th November, 1851; *m.* (firstly) 1872, Emily DREXEL, *d.* 1883, dau. of Anthony J. DREXEL of Philadelphia; *m.* (secondly) 8th June, 1889, Lilian Howard LEE, *b.* 16th May, 1862, in Brookline, Massachusetts, dau. of John R. LEE.

ISSUE BY FIRST MARRIAGE

I. Anthony, *m.* 1895, Cordelia BRADLEY.
II. Livingston.
III. Craig, *m.* Laura WHELEN.

ISSUE BY SECOND MARRIAGE

I. Lilian Lee, *b.* 12th October, 1891.
II. NICHOLAS, *b.* 30th July, 1893, the subject of this memoir.
III. Winthrop Lee, *b.* 11th August, 1896.

Arms.—Argent three double brackets sable.
Crest.—A demi heraldic tiger rampant, ducally gorged.
Motto.—Deus clypeus meus.
Residence.—"Springhead," York Road, Noble, Montgomery County, Pennsylvania.
Clubs.—Rittenhouse, Huntington Valley Country, Merion Cricket, Princeton of Philadelphia and University Cottage Club of Princeton.
Societies.—Colonial Wars, National Security League, National Geographic Society, Upsilon Omega, Cliosophic Society of Princeton.
Military Organization.—1st City Troop of Philadelphia.

Bingham

GENERAL THEODORE ALFRED BINGHAM, M.A., U. S. A.; b. 14th May, 1858, in Andover, Tolland County, Connecticut; m. 15th December, 1881, in St. Louis, Missouri, Lucille RUTHERFURD, b. 21st August, 1859, dau. of Thomas Scott RUTHERFURD of Scotland, b. 1814, d. 1887, m. 18th December, 1840, Lucille Zoe TISON, b. 1819, d. 1885.

ISSUE

I. Rutherfurd, b. 30th August, 1884.

GENERAL THEODORE ALFRED BINGHAM was educated at Yale College, Class 1876; Graduated at West Point Military Academy, 1879; Honorable M.A., Yale, 1896; promoted Second Lieutenant 13th June, 1879; First Lieutenant 17th June, 1881; Captain 2d July, 1889; Major 5th July, 1898, Corps of Engineers. Served in various duties as engineer officer 1879-1890; Military Attaché United States Legation, Berlin, 1890-1892; Rome, 1892-1894; in charge Public Buildings and Grounds at Washington with rank of Colonel 9th March, 1897, to 17th May, 1903; in charge of Engineering District Lake Ontario and Lake Erie; Light House Engineer tenth lighthouse district, 1903-1904; Brigadier-General, United States Army, 11th July, 1904; retired 12th July, 1904; Police Commissioner, New York City, 1st January, 1906, to 1st July, 1909; Chief Engineer Highways New York, 4th May to 4th July, 1911; Consulting Engineer, Department of Bridges, 5th July, 1911, to 1st February, 1915.

Lineage

THOMAS BINGHAM of Sheffield, England, and Norwich and Windham, Connecticut; b. there (Sheffield) 1642; d. 16th January, 1730, at Windham; arrived at Saybrook, Connecticut in 1659; m. 12th December, 1666, Mary RUDD, dau. of Jonathan RUDD.

ISSUE

I. Thomas, b. 11th December, 1667; d. 1st April, 1710; m. 17th February, 1692, Hannah BACKUS, dau. of William BACKUS.
II. Abel, b. 25th June, 1669; m. Elizabeth ODELL.
III. Mary, b. July, 1672; m. John BACKUS.
IV. Jonathan, b. 15th April, 1674; m. Ann HUNTINGTON.
V. Ann, b. August, 1677; m. Hezekiah MASON.
VI. Abigail, b. 4th November, 1679; m. Daniel HUNTINGTON.
VII. Nathaniel, b. 3d October, 1681; m. Sarah LOBDELL.
VIII. Deborah, b. 18th December, 1683; m. Stephen TRACY.
IX. Samuel, b. 28th March, 1685; m. (firstly) Faith RIPLEY; m. (secondly) Elizabeth MANNING.
X. Joseph, b. 15th January, 1688; m. (firstly) Abigail SCOTT; m. (secondly) widow Rachel HUNTINGTON.
XI. STEPHEN, b. 1690, of whom later.

STEPHEN BINGHAM, of Andover, Connecticut; *b.* 1690, in Norwich, Connecticut; *m.* (firstly) Mary KINGSBURY; (secondly) Rebecca BISHOP.

ISSUE

I. ELEAZER, of whom later.

ELEAZER BINGHAM of Andover, Connecticut; *b.* 1719; *d.* 1783; *m.* (firstly) Miriam PHELPS; *m.* (secondly) Hannah DAGGET.

ISSUE

I. STEPHEN, *b.* 1740, of whom later.
II. Rebecca, *b.* 1743; *m.* Israel LOOMIS.
III. Eleazer, *b.* 1745; *m.* Esther LOOMIS.
IV. Miriam, *b.* 1749; *m.* William CLARK.
V. Sarah, *b.* 1751; *m.* Whiting BACKUS.
VI. Esther, *b.* 1752; *m.* Daniel ROCKWELL.
VII. Mary, *b.* 1756; *m.* Joseph PARKER.
VIII. Aaron, *b.* 1758; *m.* —————— MAYNARD.

STEPHEN BINGHAM, of Andover, Connecticut; *b.* 1740; *d.* 1835; *m.* (firstly) Sarah LONG; *m.* (secondly) Jerusha SPRAGUE.

ISSUE

I. Tabitha, *b.* 1763; *m.* Isaac BROOKS.
II. Silas, *b.* 1765; *m.* Betsey RASH.
III. Sarah, *b.* 1767; *m.* Abner BURNAP.
IV. Stephen, *b.* 1770; *m.* Polly WALES.
V. Ezra, *b.* 1772; *m.* name unknown.
VI. Josiah, *b.* 1775; never married.
VII. Hannah, *b.* 1778; *m.* John CONE.
VIII. Flavel, *b.* 1781; *m.* Fanny WHITE.
IX. Harvey, *b.* 1784; *m.* Polly BIDWELL.
X. CYRUS, *b.* 1789, of whom later.

CYRUS BINGHAM, of Andover, Connecticut; *b.* 1789; *d.* 1862; *m.* 15th December, 1814, Abigail FOOTE, *b.* 15th December, 1792, *d.* 1st December, 1889, dau. of Joel FOOTE.

ISSUE

I. William, *b.* 1816; *m.* Elizabeth BEARDSLEY.
II. Caroline, *b.* 1818; *m.* Aaron CLARKE.
III. Edward, *b.* 1821; *m.* Esther SANFORD.
IV. JOEL FOOTE, *b.* 1827, of whom later.

JOEL FOOTE BINGHAM, A.M., D.D., Litt.D., of Hartford, Connecticut; *b.* 11th October, 1827; *d.* October, 1914; Valedictorian, Yale, 1852; A.M., 1855; Student

COLONIAL FAMILIES OF THE UNITED STATES

Theological Seminary, New York; D.D., Western Reserve University, 1869; Litt.D. Trinity College, Connecticut, 1898; Head Master Classical School, Bible House, New York 1852–1858; Pastor, Congregational Church, Cleveland,' 1860–1861; Buffalo, 1861–1867; Augusta, Maine, 1867–1871; ordained Priest, Protestant Episcopal Church, 1871; Rector New Haven, 1871; Portsmouth, New Hampshire, 1872–1875; Waterbury, Connecticut, 1875–1879; on literary work, 1879–1888; Rector, New London, Connecticut, 1888–1890; retired to engage in literary work, 1890; Lecturer on Italian literature, Trinity College, ten years. Author of "Our Fathers House," 1865; "History of Sunday Schools," 1867; "Christian Marriage Ceremony," 1871; "Francesco de Rimini" (translated in verse), six editions, 1897, 1904; "Twin Sisters of Martigny," 1899; "Christian Marriage," 1900; "Gemma della Letteratura Italana" (in Italian), 1903, 1910; "Sacred Hymns and Napoleonic Ode of Alexander Mazzoni," translated in rhyme, 1901; also patriotic discourses, sermons, poems, letters of travel and other contributions to magazines; *m.* 14th July, 1857, Susan GREW of Philadelphia; *b.* 9th November, 1834, dau. of Henry Johnson and Elizabeth Ives (DEMING) GREW. He son of Rev. Henry and Harriet (JOHNSON) GREW. She dau. of Lieut. Jonathan JOHNSON, who served as Sergeant from 28th March until 16th November, 1758, in Capt. Timothy HIERLIHYS Company; served as Lieutenant in same Company from 22d March to 16th December, 1758; 1st Connecticut Regiment, Col. Phineas LYMAN commanding; was commissioned Second Lieutenant by the General Assembly, March, 1759; again commissioned March, 1760 to March, 1761; commissioned First Lieutenant; also served during the Revolutionary War, being at its close Lieutenant-Colonel; was one of the original members of the Society of the Cincinnati of Connecticut.

ISSUE

I. THEODORE ALFRED, *b.* 14th May, 1858, the subject of this memoir.
II. Howard Henry Charles, *b.* 5th December, 1862.

Residences.—59 West 45th Street, New York City; summer, "Edgerston," Chester, Nova Scotia.

Clubs.—Metropolitan, Army and Navy of Washington, D. C.; Century, St. Nicholas, Aero of America, Press Club, and Atlantic Yacht Club, all of New York.

Societies.—Cincinnati, Colonial Wars, Sons of American Revolution, Freemasons.

Brooke

GEORGE BROOKE, II, Ph.B., of Birdsboro, and Philadelphia, Pennsylvania; *b.* 5th July, 1870, in Philadelphia, Pennsylvania; *m.* 16th August, 1914, in London, England, Lucile Stewart POLK. of Baltimore, Maryland, dau. of William Plunket Stewart POLK, *b.* 22d April, 1828, still living, who *m.* Louise Ellen ANDERSON, *b.* 24th May, 1844, still living, dau. of Peter ANDERSON of Virginia.

ISSUE

I. Elizabeth Muhlenberg, *b.* 25th April, 1916.

GEORGE BROOKE, II, received his education at private schools; received degree of Ph.B. from University of Pennsylvania in 1889; appointed 24th February, 1903, Lieutenant-Colonel on Staff of Governor PENNYPACKER of Pennsylvania.

Lineage

JOHN BROOKE, II, and his wife Frances of Hagg in the township of Henley and Parish of Almonbury in Yorkshire, with their two youngest sons, James and Matthew, sailed from Liverpool on the ship *Britannia*, Richard NICHOLAS, commander, in the year 1698; arriving in the early part of 1699 to take up lands he had purchased. In consequence of a contagious disease on board the vessel, the passengers were not permitted to land at Philadelphia, but landed lower down the river on the New Jersey side, about where Gloucester now stands. They at once went to stop at the house of William COOPER, Cooper's Point, New Jersey, a friend of theirs, and in a very short time both died and were buried at Newton Creek Friends Meeting House Cemetery at Haddonfield, New Jersey. JOHN BROOKE is known to have belonged and was an active member of the estimable Society of Friends and it was probably the severe persecution on that point that obliged his leaving. The Vicar of Kirburton Parish, which adjoined Almonbury, the Rev. Joseph BRIGGS, was a stern upholder of the Established Church opinions, and was the most active in the persecution of the Quakers of that section. The estate purchased by John BROOKE before leaving England, from William PENN, consisted of 2,500 acres of land to be taken up anywhere between the Delaware and Susquehanna Rivers, where vacant land should be found; James and Matthew BROOKE, after the death of their parents, took up the land in Limerick Township, County of Philadelphia, now Montgomery County, Pennsylvania, where they settled. The two brothers divided the land between them and Matthew seems to have prospered, as by records he added more land to his estate and built in 1716 the first stone house in all that country. It was situated on the Manatawney Road, and was a large house of Colonial design. It was torn down in 1878.

COLONIAL FAMILIES OF THE UNITED STATES

ISSUE OF JOHN AND FRANCES BROOKE (AMONG OTHERS)

I. James, *b.* in Hagg, England.
II. MATTHEW, I, *b.* in Hagg, England, 1st January, 1680, of whom below.

MATTHEW BROOKE, I, of Limerick Township, County of Philadelphia, Pennsylvania; *b.* 1st January, 1680; *bapt.* at Holmfirth Chapel, 30th January, same year; *d.* 18th June, 1720, at his residence in Limerick Township; was an influential citizen and yet while living on his estate quietly, as an English gentleman, he must have been very prosperous, as at his death, he had so enlarged his land holdings that he left his sons all with large tracts of lands and comfortably off; *m.* 18th May, 1712, at Christ Church, Philadelphia, Ann EVANS.

ISSUE

I. MATTHEW, II, *b.* 1719, of Limerick, of whom later.
II. William.
III. George, died without issue.
IV. John, died without issue.

MATTHEW BROOKE, II, of Birdsboro, Pennsylvania; *b.* 1719, at Limerick; *d.* October, 1806, at Birdsboro; some years before his death, he moved to Birdsboro, as he and his son, Matthew III, had purchased in 1788, part of the iron works of the BIRD family at that place. He represented Philadelphia County in the Provincial Conference of Pennsylvania held at Carpenter Hall in 1776; was one of the committee on removing the public stores from Philadelphia, when the city was threatened by the British troops. He also held and served on many local committees that those stirring times of the Revolution demanded. In the "Pennsylvania Archives," Vol. III, it cites where he sent as a present to the Honorable Council of Safety of Philadelphia, in the year 1776, two cannon, one a twelve and the other an eighteen pounder; the cannon having been made at Hopewell Furnace; *m.* 29th March, 1744, Sarah REESE, dau. of Thomas REESE.

ISSUE

I. Anna, *b.* 1746; *m.* ———— EVANS.
II. Ann, *b.* 1749; unmarried.
III. Thomas, *b.* 1751; *m.* Ann GRANT.
IV. Eleanor, *b.* 1755; *m.* David DAVIS.
V. George, *b.* 1758; *m.* Hanna EVANS.
VI. MATTHEW, III, *b.* 9th February, 1761, of whom later.
VII. Sarah, *b.* 1765; *m.* Daniel BUCKLEY.
VIII. Reese, *d.s.p.*
IX. William, *m.* ———— MOORE.

MATTHEW BROOKE, III, of Birdsboro, Pennsylvania; *b.* 6th February, 1761, in Limerick Township; *d.* 1822, in Birdsboro. In the year 1786 the BIRD family, who owned extensive iron works and great tracts of lands, situated at and about Birdsboro, became financially involved and in 1788 began selling off certain tracts, forges, etc., and a short time after that, Matthew BROOKE, II, and his son Matthew BROOKE, III, purchased one of these tracts and one of the forges and moved from Limerick to Birdsboro, residing in one of the BIRD houses which was situated near where the present rolling mills stand. It was torn down in 1880 to make room for additions to the rolling mills. In the year 1800 he with his brother Thomas and brother-in-law, Daniel BUCKLEY of Philadelphia, purchased from the BIRD family, Hopewell Furnace and an estate of 10,000 acres extending from Hopewell to Birdsboro, a distance of five miles, which had been built about 1760 by Mark BIRD, and ranks among the first furnaces of the country. Cannon and shell were made here for the Revolutionary War. A short time before Matthew BROOKE and his son Matthew made their first purchase, Capt. John Louis BARDE, a retired English army officer, in the year 1788, leased the iron works of the BIRDS together with certain land which embraced the old BIRD Manor House, a very large and handsome house standing in the midst of a great park with sweeping lawn down to the banks of the Schuylkill River. It was in all likelihood one of the finest estates that could be found in Pennsylvania at that date. The old house is still standing, but the grounds have all given way to the march of progress, and it is now in the midst of the thriving borough of Birdsboro. Here Matthew BROOKE met Miss Elizabeth BARDE, and in the year 1805, married her. In the year 1796 Captain BARDE purchased the properties he had under lease, but a few years later sold them to his son-in-law, who had by that time purchased all the other lands of the BIRDS and had thereby, before 1800, become the owner of all the extensive BIRD properties and works. Later, the Hopewell property was divided, Thomas and Daniel BUCKLEY still retaining the furnace and half of the lands, and Matthew BROOKE taking the other half and retiring from the firm. Matthew BROOKE was a man of prominence of his day, giving both time and counsel to his localists and state. When quite young, he joined the Continental Army, but was soon after taken prisoner and placed on board a prison ship where he was held some time; finally being released through an exchange of prisoners but as the war was then drawing to a close, he never saw any active service. His two sons, Edward and George, at his death inherited the properties, but both being very young, the works were leased and so run for a number of years until the coming of age of Edward BROOKE, when he with his brother George took over the management of the business.

ISSUE (OF MATTHEW BROOKE III)

I. Edward, *b.* 1816; *d.* 1878.
II. GEORGE, *b.* 28th June, 1818, of whom later.
III. Ann, never married.
IV. Sarah, never married.
V. Elizabeth Barde, *m.* Hon. Heister CLYMER.

GEORGE BROOKE, I, of Birdsboro, Pennsylvania; *b.* 28th June, 1818; *d.* 10th January, 1912; *m.* 21st April, 1862, Mary Baldwin IRWIN, *b.* 25th June, 1837, *d.* 3d March, 1910, dau. of John Heister and Margaret (BALDWIN) IRWIN.

ISSUE

1. Edward, *b.* 4th June, 1863; *m.* 12th October, 1887, A. Louise CLINGAN, *b.* 12th March, 1864, dau. of Charles M. and Maria Teresa (BROOKE) CLINGAN.

    ISSUE

    1. George, III, *b.* 7th July, 1888.
    2. Edward, *b.* 10th January, 1890.
    3. Charles, *b.* 24th January, 1892.
    4. Mary Baldwin Irwin, *b.* 16th October, 1897.

II. GEORGE, II, *b.* 5th July, 1870, the subject of his memoir.

Arms.—Or, a cross engrailed per pale gules and sable.
Crest.—A sword erect argent, hilted or, entwined by two serpents, respecting each other ppr., scroll around the hilt, bearing the motto.
Motto.—Nec aestu nec astu.
Residences.—Birdsboro, Pennsylvania, and Philadelphia, Pennsylvania.
Clubs.—The Philadelphia, The Racquet, The Rabbit, Philadelphia Country, St. Anthony, and Clam Bake of Newport, Rhode Island.
Societies.—Colonial Wars, Sons of the American Revolution.

Bryan

WILLIAM ALANSON BRYAN, B.Sc., of Honolulu, Territory of Hawaii; b. 23d December, 1875, in New Sharon, Iowa; m. (firstly) 20th June, 1900, Ruth May Goss, b. 23d May, 1875, d. 5th February, 1904, dau. of Howard M. and Julia (———) Goss; m. (secondly) 16th March, 1909, at Buffalo, New York, Elizabeth Jane LETSON, b. 9th April, 1874, at Griffins Mills, Erie County, New York, dau. of Augustus Franklin LETSON, b. 26th May, 1841, d. 26th February, 1900, m. 5th June, 1869, Catherine Ellen WEBB, b. 5th June, 1850.

WILLIAM ALANSON BRYAN was born on a farm near New Sharon, Iowa. Received his early education in the public schools; secured his degree of B.Sc. at Iowa State College, 1896; Assistant, Department of Zoology, in charge of Iowa State College Museum, 1893; on expedition to Big Stone Lake, 1894; special lecturer on museum methods, University of Minnesota, Indiana University, University of Chicago, Purdue University, Iowa College, 1895–1897; Assistant Curator, Department of Ornithology, Field Columbian Museum, Chicago, Illinois, 1898–1899; appointed Representative of United States Department of Agriculture to investigate fauna of the Hawaiian Islands, 1899; travelled extensively in Europe and America studying Museum Administration, 1900; Curator, Bishop Museum of Ethnology and Natural History, 1900–1907; organized and made President Pacific Scientific Institution, 1907; Professor of Zoölogy and Geology at the College of Hawaii since 1909; Candidate for Governor of the Territory of Hawaii, 1912; Candidate for Territorial Senate, 1914; Chairman Territorial Central Committee, 1916; Democrat; Member of Central Union Church, Honolulu, Hawaii. Bibliography exceeds seventy-five titles on Hawaiian and kindred subjects including "Monograph of Marcus Island," "Mission of the Pacific Scientific Institution," "Key to Hawaiian Birds," "Natural History of Hawaii" (600 pages), etc.

Lineage

WILLIAM SMITH BRYAN was a landholder in Ireland, County Clare, at the time of the British invasion under CROMWELL, and for taking the side of Ireland was transported as a "rebellious subject," in 1650, to the American Colonies, with his family, goods and chattels, consisting of a ship load. He settled in Gloucester County, Virginia; he had eleven sons. Morgan BRYAN, who was in Norfolk County in 1693, was probably one of these sons. Francis BRYAN, the oldest son, returned to Ireland, in 1677, and endeavored to recover his hereditary titles and estates, but was so greatly persecuted by the English Government that he sought refuge in Denmark. After a few years he returned to Ireland. His oldest son Morgan was born in Denmark. It is believed that William BRYAN, b. in 1685, was also his son. William BRYAN and his wife, Margaret, lived at Ballyroney, County Down, Ireland. They were Presbyterians. The town of Bryansford near by is said to have been named for some of his family. William and Margaret BRYAN one day sent their little son John into the woods to cut a stick to make a handle for a hook used in weaving, and he was arrested for poaching. After much trouble and expense the father got him clear and immediately sailed for America, where, he said, timber was free and there were no constables. This was in the year 1718. William BRYAN and family settled in New Jersey or Pennsylvania. (From Bryan-Akers Family by Jesse BRYAN.

"The BRYAN family from the ancestral stock has spread into every State in the Union, the District of Columbia, Hawaii and the Philippine Islands. It includes men in every walk of life from President to the humblest citizen; military men of every grade; educators from presidents of Universities to common school teachers, divines, lawyers and doctors; poets, authors and inventors; pioneers, scientists and financiers; railway men, electricians and farmers and the direct descendants from immigrants on the *Mayflower*. BRYANS have fought in all American wars. None has ever been convicted of crime, or in prison (except military prison), or paupers depending on public charity, and none is known as drunkard and but few who drank habitually."

NOTES REGARDING THE BRYAN FAMILY FROM "THE SHEARER-AKERS-BRYAN FAMILY" BY REV. JAMES WILLIAM SHEARER, D.D.

ISSUE OF WILLIAM AND MARGARET BRYAN

I. William Smith, had eleven sons.

ISSUE

I. FRANCIS, of whom below.
II. Morgan.

FRANCIS BRYAN;

ISSUE

I. Morgan, *m.* Martha STRODE.
II. WILLIAM, *b.* 1685, of whom below.

WILLIAM BRYAN, *b.* in Ireland, 1685; *m.* Margaret ―――――.

ISSUE

I. JOHN ANDREW, *b.* 1st May, 1744, of whom later.
II. James.
III. William, *m.* Margaret WATSON.

JOHN ANDREW BRYAN of near Fairfield, Rockbridge County, Virginia; *d.* between 9th October and 9th December, 1779; *m.* Mary MORRISON; was a member of Capt. Peter HOGG's Company of the Virginia troops serving under Washington at the Battle of Great Meadows and at the siege and surrender of Fort Necessity, 4th July, 1754. (Virginia Magazine of History and Biography, volume 1, page 279., Virginia State Records; also Washington Memoirs, II, III, Library of Congress.) He also served in the Revolutionary war in Capt. Thomas MERRIWETHER'S

Company, First Virginia State troops, March, 1777, to serve for three years. (Record United States War Department; his two sons Andrew Morrison BRYAN and John BRYAN were also in the Revolution in Captain LEFTWITCH's Company, Colonel CHRISTIE. The latter John BRYAN, Jr., seeing service in the Battle of Brandywine, was wounded at Guilford Courthouse and was at Jamestown and at the capture of Cornwallis. (U. S. Bureau of Pensions.)

ISSUE

I. William, b. 1st May, 1744; m. Mary ————.
II. ANDREW MORRISON, b. 25th April, 1748, of whom below.
III. Mary, b. 27th May, 1750; died young.
IV. Margaret, b. 14th March, 1752; m. (firstly) Daniel MITCHELL; m. (secondly) Patrick GIBSON.
V. John, b. 19th December, 1756; m. Catherine EVANS.
VI. Jane, b. 16th May, 1761; m. John DAVISON.
VII. Agnes, b. 9th August, 1763; m. (firstly) John AKERS; m. (secondly) Reuben B. BAGBY.
VIII. Catherine, b. 21st October, 1765; m. Samuel COLE.

ANDREW MORRISON BRYAN, of Campbell County, Virginia; b. 25th April, 1748; d. 20th April, 1821; m. Mary AKERS, b. 15th March, 1754, d. 17th February 1823.

ISSUE

I. John, b. 4th March, 1774; m. Rebecca ————.
II. Elizabeth, b. 1st June, 1776; m. John PAGE.
III. William Akers, b. 1st October, 1778.
IV. MORRISON, b. 14th February, 1781; of whom below.
V. James, b. 23d June, 1785; d. 19th April, 1864; m. Mary JOHNSON.
VI. Mary, b. 14th June, 1787; d. 6th September, 1839; m. George EVANS.
VII. Thomas, b. 25th February, 1791; d. 6th October, 1853; m. Mary BRYAN, d. 4th May, 1842.
VIII. David, b. 24th October, 1793; d. 26th February, 1881; m. Mildred JOHNSON, d. 27th February, 1881.

MORRISON BRYAN of Highland County, Ohio; b. 14th February, 1781; d. 7th March, 1822; m. 29th December, 1805, Rhoda JOHNSON, b. 27th May, 1788, d. 25th August, 1863; she m. (secondly) 11th March, 1824, Peyton SHORT.

ISSUE

I. Cynthia, b. 1st November, 1806; d. 15th November, 1852; m. 4th January, 1821; Beedy BURGESS, d. 1853.
II. Alanson, b. 4th February, 1808; of whom later.
III. Clarissa, b. 20th February, 1818; m. 5th March, 1840, Lynch A. JOHNSON.

iv. Talitha, *b.* 12th December, 1809; *d.* 23d November, 1841; *m.* 15th November, 1827, William LOCKHART.
v. Austin, *b.* 19th June, 1812; *d.* 31st July, 1812.
vi. Albert, *b.* 29th July, 1815; *m.* Ann PARKER.
vii. Neri, *b.* 11th March, 1820; *m.* (firstly) 21st May, 1840, Sarah MENDENHALL; *m.* (secondly) Margaret KIRK.

ALANSON BRYAN, *b.* 4th February, 1808; *d.* 16th August, 1897; *m.* 14th November, 1827, Easter MENDENHALL, *b.* 14th January, 1809, *d.* 25th November, 1874.

ISSUE

i. Morrison Gabriel, *b.* 11th June, 1828; *d.* 10th January, 1849.
ii. John Mendenhall, *b.* 10th August, 1829; *m.* Tacy Jane SMITH.
iii. Dennis, *b.* 23d June, 1832; *m.* (firstly) Sitnah Ann PEARSON, *b.* 12th April, 1832, *d.* 18th October, 1868; *m.* (secondly) Sedellia MARTIN, *b.* 17th October, 1835.
iv. Rachel, *b.* 19th December, 1830; *d.* 25th March, 1896; *m.* Joseph BONE.
v. Beedy, *b.* 28th February, 1834; *d.* 16th November, 1914; *m.* Margaret A. VICTOR, *b.* 13th October, 1834.
vi. WILLIAM ALBERT, *b.* 18th October, 1835, of whom later.
vii. Rhoda, *b.* 1st April, 1838; *d.* 27th March, 1839.
viii. Neri, *b.* 27th February, 1840; Union solider; *m.* Mary Elizabeth JOB.
ix. Talitha, *b.* 22d November, 1841; *m.* (firstly) Samuel S. ROBERTS, lost in Red River raid, Arkansas; *m.* (secondly) Andrew HARNER.
x. Andrew Alanson, *b.* 30th April, 1843; Union soldier: *m.* Harriet HARNER, dau. of Andrew HARNER.
xi. James Johnson, *b.* 6th May, 1845; *d.* 14th August, 1846.

WILLIAM ALBERT BRYAN, *b.* 18th October, 1835; *d.* 22d January, 1914; *m.* 25th December, 1856, Catherine M. PEARSON, *b.* 7th December, 1838.

ISSUE

i. Lillian Augustine, *b.* 29th September, 1857; *m.* 18th January, 1878, Alice A. KIRK.
ii. Charles Fremont, *b.* 10th September, 1859; *d.* 16th June, 1882; *m.* 2d February, 1881, Hannah M. ADAMSON.
iii. Elma Alfaretta, *b.* 25th February, 1862; *d.* 26th December, 1876.
iv. Arthur Channing, *b.* 29th August, 1864; *d.* 2d September, 1865.
v. Frederick Homer, *b.* 21st July, 1866; *d.* July, 1906; *m.* (firstly) 27th January, 1887, Elizabeth M. COBB; *m.* (secondly) 19th February, 1908, Lillian ———.
vi. Ernest Edwin, *b.* 10th August, 1869; *m.* 1st March, 1889, Sarah MOORMAN.
vii. WILLIAM ALANSON, *b.* 23d December, 1875, the subject of this memoir.

VIII. Walter Emmett, *b.* 3d September, 1878; *m.* 25th October, 1899, Gertrude Leo PARKHURST.
IX. Clarence W., *b.* 15th January, 1881; *d.* 9th August, 1881.

Residence.—1013 Punahou Street, Honolulu, Hawaii.

Clubs.—Cosmos Club, Washington, D. C., Aero Club of Hawaii (Charter Member).

Societies.—President, Hawaiian Society of Sons of the American Revolution; Member New York State Society Colonial Wars; Vice President, Hawaiian Historical Society; Fellow, American Association for the Advancement of Science; Member National Geographical Society; American Ornithological Union; American Fisheries Society; Hawaiian Entomological Society; American Museums Association; National Audubon Society.

Bye

ARTHUR EDWIN BYE, B.A., M.A., Ph.D., of Princeton, New Jersey; *b.* 18th December, 1885, at Philadelphia; *m.* 4th July, 1911, at Amsterdam, Holland, Maria Catherine HELDRING, *b.* 9th June, 1886, dau. Rt. Rev. Dr. Jan. Lodewijk HELDRING, *b.* 26th March, 1852, *m.* 1884, Geertruide Margarethe Jacoba VAN EEGHEN, *b.* 7th November, 1854, *d.* 17th November, 1911, both of Amsterdam, Holland.

ISSUE

I. Ottho Gerhard Heldring-Bye, *b.* 13th June, 1912.
II. Margaret, *b.* 21st December, 1913.
III. Ranulph de Bayeux, *b.* 17th June, 1916.

ARTHUR EDWIN BYE, Landscape Painter and Writer on Art History, was educated at George School; Graduated 1904; studied drawing and painting at the School of Industrial Art of Philadelphia and at the Pennsylvania Academy, 1904–1907; studied under COURTEOIS and COLLIN at Paris, 1907; then at Oxford, England, 1910–1911; and at the University of Pennsylvania and graduated B.A., 1911; Assistant Professor at Lafayette College, 1911–1913; studied at Princeton and received degrees M.A., 1914, and Ph.D., 1916.

Lineage

This family was an ancient one among the gentry of England. A direct pedigree is recorded in the College of Heraldry of the Byes of Basingstoke, dating from a remote period up to 1622. Among the ancestors of the American emigrant were:

THOMAS BYE, Member of Parliament for Reading, 1403.
THOMAS BYE, Mayor of Reading, 1516.
JOHN BYE, Bailiff of Basingstoke, 1516, 1535, 1540 and 1542.
JOHN BYE, Steward of the Royal Manor of Basingstoke and "Deputy of the Most Noble William," Marquess of Winchester, 1585 and 1603.
JOHN BYE. Quaker preacher, imprisoned 1675 in Reading jail for preaching.
THOMAS BYE, *b.* circa 1650, probably at "Copyngedbridge House," Basingstoke, Hampshire, England; *d.* 25th June, 1726; emigrated to America from Horselydown, Southwark, England in 1699, with son John; his wife, Margaret, *b.* in England, *d.* 6th October, 1724, she and daughters followed to America in 1701; he settled on an estate of 1,000 acres in Buckingham, Bucks County. The history of the life of Thomas BYE is practically the story of the rise of Quakerism in England.

ISSUE

I. JOHN, *b.* in England, circa 1675, of whom later.
II. Nathaniel, *b.* in England, circa 1677; *m.* Martha surname not known; ancestor of the BYES of Buckingham, the younger branch of the family.
III. Elizabeth, *b.* 20th May, 1678, at Horselydown, Southwark, England; *d.* 2d June, 1678.
IV. Elizabeth (twin), *b.* March, 1680, at same place; *d.* 14th September, 1681.
V. Mary (twin), *b.* March, 1680, at same place; *d.* 30th September, 1680.
VI. Sarah, *b.* 11th August, 1683, at same place.
VII. Elizabeth, *b.* 1685, at same place; *m.* Nehemiah BLACKSHAW of the Falls, Bucks County, Pennsylvania, son of Randall BLACKSHAW, of Holingee Manor, Cheshire, and The Falls, Bucks County, Pennsylvania.
VIII. Ann, *b.* 1706.

JOHN BYE of Solebury, Bucks County, Pennsylvania; *b.* in England, circa 1675; *d.* 1732; *m.* 4th March, 1704, Sarah PEARSON, dau. and co-heiress of Thomas PEARSON of Marsden, Lancashire, and Grace VIPONT, dau. of John VIPONT of Briarcliffe, Westmoreland, England, descended from the ancient family of DE VIPONT, Barons of Westmoreland.

ISSUE

I. Elizabeth, *b.* 1st January, 1705; *m.* George MITCHELL.
II. Sarah, *b.* 27th January, 1707.
III. Deborah, *b.* 30th January, 1709; *m.* Jonathan INGHAM of Ingham Spring.
IV. John, *b.* 6th December, 1710; *d. s.p.*
V. Samuel, *b.* 5th January, 1713; *d.s.p.*
VI. Mary, *b.* 19th July, 1715.
VII. HEZEKIAH, *b.* 17th November, 1717, of whom later.
VIII. Martha, *b.* 7th March, 1720.
IX. Enoch, *b.* 1722.

HEZEKIAH BYE of Solebury, Pennsylvania, *b.* 17th November, 1717; *d.* September, 1790; *m.* 11th March, 1743, Mary INGHAM, *d.* 1790, dau. of Jonas INGHAM of Ingham Spring.

ISSUE

I. Rachel, *b.* 31st August, 1743; *m.* 1764, Zachariah BETTS, son of Thomas and Sarah Stevenson BETTS.

ISSUE

I. Jesse BETTS, *m.* Hannah PAXSON; had issue.

ISSUE

1^1. John BETTS, *b.* 23d July, 1745; *m.*, no known issue.
II. Jonas, *b.* 22d March, 1748; removed West, no record.

III. Jemima, *b.* 16th June, 1751.
IV. Hezekiah, *b.* 27th March, 1754; *m.* 1778, Sarah PETTIT, dau. of William PETTIT; their dau., Charity, was the mother of Gov. William F. PACKER of Pennsylvania.
V. ENOCH, *b.* 27th September, 1757, of whom later.
VI. Jonathan, *b.* 22d January, 1761; *m.* Sarah KINSEY, dau. of Benjamin KINSEY of Buckingham.

ENOCH BYE of Solebury, Bucks County, Pennsylvania; *b.* 27th September, 1757; *d.* 12th January, 1837; he removed to East Nottingham, Chester County, Pennsylvania; *m.* 1781, Abigail KINSEY, *d.* 1824, dau. of Samuel and Elizabeth (CREW) KINSEY of Buckingham.

ISSUE

I. Amos, *b.* 1781, of whom later.
II. Albert, *b.* circa 1783; *m.*, name unknown, had issue.
III. Samuel Kinsey, *b.* circa 1785; *d.s.p.*
IV. Jemina, *m.* ———— PEARSON.
V. Anne, *d.s.p., m.* ———— SCOTT.

AMOS BYE of East Nottingham, Pennsylvania; *b.* 1781; *d.* 4th December, 1861 at "Hickory Hill," Chester County, Pennsylvania; *m.* 23d August, 1806, Deborah PAXSON, *b.* 3d September, 1780, *d.* 28th March, 1859, dau. of Benjamin PAXSON of Solebury and Deborah TAYLOR of Taylorsville.

ISSUE

I. Charles Paxson, *b.* 1st April, 1807; *m.* Mary Anne WOOLENS, dau. of Jesse WOOLENS of "Hickory Hill."
II. Mary Anne, *b.* 14th June, 1809; *m.* Amos PUGH of East Nottingham.
III. JOHN HOWARD, *b.* 28th April, 1812; *m.* Sarah Moore WOOLENS, dau. of Jesse WOOLENS.
IV. Deborah, *b.* 23d April, 1815; *m.* William TAYLOR, of Philadelphia.
V. ENOCH MORTIMER, *b.* 3d January, 1818, of whom later.
VI. Benjamin Tilghman; *m.* Mary Elizabeth COLEMAN, dau. of John COLEMAN of Wilmington, Delaware.
VII. William Thompson, *m.* Susan GATCHELL, dau. of Henry GATCHELL of Fairhill, Maryland.

ENOCH MORTIMER BYE of East Nottingham, Pennsylvania, and of Wilmington, Delaware; *b.* at "Hickory Hill," 3d January, 1818; *d.* 6th November, 1894, at Wilmington, Delaware; *m.* 24th March, 1843, at "The Brick Meeting House," Phoebe Pusey PASSMORE; dau. of Andrew and Judith (MOORE) PASSMORE. She was descended from the ancient Welsh family of LEWIS of royal descent.

ISSUE

1. Ruth Anna, *b.* 23d February, 1844; *m.* 15th October, 1868, Charles Follen THOMAS of Wilmington, Delaware.
2. Pusey Passmore, *b.* 30th July, 1846, *m.* 11th December, 1872, Caroline SPEAKMAN, dau. of Thomas and Anna (JENKINS) SPEAKMAN.
3. ANDREW MOORE, *b.* 24th September, 1850, of whom later.
4. Rosalie Paxson, *b.* 7th October, 1853, unmarried.
5. Colin Taggart, *b.* 8th October, 1856; *m.* 19th April, 1882, Isabel PYLE dau. of Cyrus and Mary Bassett (MUMFORD) PYLE; have issue.

ANDREW MOORE BYE of Wilmington, Delaware; *b.* 24th September, 1850, in the PASSMORE homestead, East Nottingham; *d.* 11th May, 1914; *m.* 22d April, 1880, Alva May TAYLOR, *b.* 15th December, 1860, dau. of Benjamin Field, and Elizabeth (DICKINSON) TAYLOR, of Langhorne Manor, Bucks County, Pennsylvania.

ISSUE

1. ARTHUR EDWIN, *b.* 18th December, 1885, the subject of this memoir.
2. Margaret Taylor, *b.* 3d April, 1890.
3. Raymond Taylor, *b.* 29th January, 1892.

Arms.—Quarterly of six: 1st quarter, Azure a chevron between three bees volant or (for Bye of Basingstoke); 2d quarter, or and azure, on a bend of the second three fleur de lys of the first (for Bay of Lincoln and Oxford); 3d quarter, Or, a bend vair cottised sable, (Bowyer, Basingtoke) three spades; 4th quarter, three spades; blades or handles ppr. (for Knypersley of Knypersley); 5th quarter, ermine, on two bars gules, three plates, two and one—for Pearson of Marsden; 6th quarter, Azure, a chevron between three bees, bees volant or (for Bye).

Crest.—A dragon's head or pierced by an arrow shaft or, pheoned gules and argent.

Residence.—"Boxstead," Princeton, New Jersey.

Societies.—Bucks County Historical, Genealogists of London, Pennsylvania Historical and Princeton Architectural Association.

Cabell

JAMES BRANCH CABELL, of "Dumbarton Grange," Dumbarton, Virginia; *b.* Richmond, Virginia, 14th April, 1879; *m.* 8th November, 1913, Priscilla BRADLEY, *b.* 6th September, 1877, dau. of William Joseph and Mary Susan (WADDILL) BRADLEY of "Auburn," Charles City County, Virginia, and widow of Emmett Albin SHEPHERD.

ISSUE

I. Ballard Hartwell, *b.* 25th August, 1916.

JAMES BRANCH CABELL graduated from the College of William and Mary, 1898; on staff Richmond (Virginia) *Times*, 1898; New York *Herald*, 1899–1901; Richmond (Virginia) *News*, 1901; writer for magazines since 1902, having contributed over one hundred short stories, considerable verse, translations, and numerous papers upon historical and biographical subjects; has personally conducted much genealogical work and original research in America, France and England; has published four novels, four series of romances, three genealogical works, and one book of poems. Author (fiction): "The Eagle's Shadow," "The Cords of Vanity," "The Soul of Melicent," "The Rivet in the Grandfather's Neck;" "The Line of Love," "Gallantry," "Chivalry," and "The Certain Hour;" (genealogy) "Branchiana," "Branch of Abingdon," and "The Majors and Their Marriages;" (verse) "From the Hidden Way."

Lineage

RICHARD CABELL of Cayford and Frome, in the County of Somerset, England, born circa 1480; has various deeds from 1510 to 1528; and died in 1530, leaving issue.

RICHARD CABELL of Cayford and Frome, eldest son and heir; deeds from 1545 to 1557; buried 2d May, 1561; *m.* Thomasin, surname unknown, and had issue.

RICHARD CABELL of Cayford and Frome, eldest son and heir; in 1562 elected member of Parliament for the Borough of Heytesbury in Wiltshire, which he represented from 11th January, 1563–1564 to 2d January, 1567–1568, and again 2d April to 29th May, 1571; removed, circa 1575, to the manor of Brooke, in the parish of Buckfastleigh, in the County of Devon, and *d.* 17th February, 1612–1613; Inq. p. m. 11 Jas., pt. I, No. 37; will dated 28th August, 1610; probated 5th May, 1613; P. P. C., Capell 39; *m.* circa 1580, Susannah PETER, dau. of John PETER of Buckfastleigh, she *d.* 7th August, 1597.

ISSUE

I. RICHARD, *b.* 1582, of whom later.
II. Samuel, *d.s.p.*, will dated 30th March, 1638; probated 6th June, 1638, P. P. C., Barrington 54.

III. Bridget, *m.* Thomas MARTIN of Totnes.
IV. Susan, *m.* Thomas TURGIS of Buckfastleigh.
V. Anne, *m.* John HELE of Brooke.

RICHARD CABELL of Brooke in the Parish of Buckfastleigh in the County of Devon; *b.* 1582; *d.* 24th August, 1655; matriculated at Exeter College, Oxford, 12th December, 1600, aged 18; a student of the Middle Temple, 1604; held the Manor of Maynebow in Warnecombe, Somerset, in 1618; in 1620 gave in the pedigree of his family at the Heralds' Visitation of Devonshire; in 1649 compounded for his estates in the sum of £1430; *m.* Mary PRESTWOOD, dau. of George PRESTWOOD of Whetcombe Parish of North Huish, Devon, marriage license 4th December, 1618, Exeter.

ISSUE

I. Richard, *b.* 1620; *d.* 1677; *m.* Elizabeth FOWELL; will dated 6th May, 1671; probated 9th March, 1677–1678, P. P. C., Eure 71.
II. Samuel, *bapt.* 4th May, 1623; *d.s.p.* April, 1699; will dated 16th March, 1698–1699; probated 22d April, 1699, P. P. C., Pett 55.
III. George, *bapt.* 15th September, 1628; buried 8th March, 1631–1632.
IV. WILLIAM, *bapt.* 4th January, 1630–1631, of whom later.
V. John, *bapt.* 27th December, 1636, living in 1671.

WILLIAM CABELL of "Bugley," *b.* 1630; *d.* September, 1704; removed circa 1660 from Buckfastleigh to Bugley, near Warminster in the County of Wilts, and was buried at Warminster 4th September, 1704; *m.* circa 1650 Mary surname unknown, who survived him, and was buried at Warminster 5th December, 1704; her will, dated 29th September, 1704, recorded in the court of the Archdeacon of Sarum.

ISSUE

I. William, *d.* unmarried, December, 1734.
II. Anthony, twice married but had no issue.
III. Christopher, *bapt.* at Warminster 21st February, 1664–1665.
IV. NICHOLAS, *bapt.* 29th May, 1667, of whom later.
V. Elizabeth, *m.* ——— YEATMAN, and *d.* February, 1739–1740.

NICHOLAS CABELL of Warminster, *b.* May, 1667; *d.* 30th July, 1730; will dated 9th July, 1730; probated in the Court of the Archdeacon of Sarum 26th October, 1730; *m.* at Frome-Selwood, 15th November, 1697, Rachel HOOPER, dau. of George HOOPER, who survived him, and was buried 27th October, 1737.

ISSUE

I. William, *b.* 24th August, 1698; *d.* 8th December, 1698.
II. WILLIAM, *b.* 9th March, 1699–1700 of whom later.
III. Joanna, *b.* 6th February, 1702–1703; *d.* 2d July, 1728.

IV. Mary, *b.* 21st December, 1704; *m.* Christopher CARTER.
V. Joseph, *b.* 14th March, 1706–1707; *d.* 10th July, 1762.
VI. Elizabeth, *b.* 5th July, 1709; *d.* 12th October, 1709.
VII. Sarah, *b.* 26th December, 1710; buried 9th August, 1715.
VIII. Elizabeth, *b.* 30th January, 1712–1713; *d.* 1741; *m.* ——— DAVIS.
IX. Sarah, *b.* 6th August, 1715.

WILLIAM CABELL of "Warminster" in Virginia; *b.* 9th March, 1699–1700; *d.* 12th April, 1774; was graduated from the London Royal College of Surgery and Medicine, and served as a Surgeon in the English Navy; immigrated to Virginia in 1726, and settled in that portion of Henrico County which was sub-divided into Goochland in 1728; into Albemarle in 1745, and into Amherst in 1761 (and is now Nelson County); Under-Sheriff of Henrico, 1726; County Coroner for Goochland, 1729; Justice of the Peace for Goochland 1728–1745; served in the Indian Wars against the Tuscaroras or Monican Indians in 1730, and was Captain in the Goochland Militia in and before 1745; settled and christened the present "Warminster," Virginia, in 1742; Justice of the Peace for Albemarle, 1745–1761; Burgess for Albemarle for the sessions beginning 25th March, 1756; 20th September, 1756; 30th April, 1757, and 30th March, 1758; a resident of Amherst after 1761, and Burgess for Amherst for the sessions beginning 3d November, 1761; 14th January, 1762; 30th March, 1762; 2d November, 1762; 19th May, 1763; 12th January, 1764; 1st May, 1765, and October 1765; *m.* (firstly) in 1726, Elizabeth BURKS, *b.* in 1705, *d.* 21st September, 1756, dau. of Samuel and Mary (DAVIS) BURKS of Hanover County, Virginia; *m.* (secondly) 30th September, 1762, Margaret MEREDITH; by whom he had no issue.

ISSUE BY FIRST MARRIAGE

I. Mary, *b.* 13th February, 1727–1728; *m.* William HORSLEY.
II. William, *b.* 13th March, 1730–1731; *d.* 23d March, 1798; *m.* Margaret JORDAN.
III. Joseph, *b.* 19th September, 1732, *d.* 1st March, 1798, *m.* Mary HOPKINS.
IV. John, *b.* circa 1740; *d.* May, 1815; *m.* Paulina JORDAN.
V. George, *d.* in infancy.
VI. NICHOLAS, *b.* 29th October, 1750, of whom later.

NICHOLAS CABELL of "Liberty Hall," *b.* 29th October, 1750; *d.* 18th August, 1803; a graduate of the College of William and Mary, 1771; Captain of the Amherst Minute-Men, 1775; ordered out in May, 1776, and served till October, 1776, around Westham and Jamestown; Lieutenant-Colonel of Amherst Volunteers, 25th June, 1778; Colonel, September, 1780; served under La Fayette in Virginia April to November, 1781; taking part in siege at Yorktown; Member of the Cincinnati; State Senator, 1785–1803; *m.* 16th April, 1772, Hannah CARRINGTON, *b.* 28th March, 1751, *d.* 7th August, 1817, dau. of George and Anne (MAYO) CARRINGTON.

ISSUE

I. WILLIAM H., *b.* 16th December, 1772, of whom later.
II. George, *b.* 5th October, 1774; *d.* February, 1827; *m.* Susanna WYATT.
III. Elizabeth, *b.* 5th May, 1776; *d.* 28th November, 1802; *m.* William B. HARE.
IV. Joseph Carrington, *b.* 26th December 1778; *d.* 5th February, 1856; *m.* Mary CARTER.
V. Nicholas, *b.* 24th December, 1780; *d.* 25th June, 1809; *m.* Margaret VENABLE.
VI. Mary Anne, *b.* 2d January, 1783; *d.* 6th February, 1850; *m.* Benjamin CARRINGTON.

HON. WILLIAM H. CABELL of "Montevideo;" *b.* 16th December, 1772; *d.* 12th January, 1853; a graduate of the College of William and Mary, 1793; Member of the Assembly, 1796–1798 and 1802–1805; Governor of Virginia from 1st December, 1805, to 1st December, 1808; Judge of the General Court, 1808–1811; Judge of Supreme Court of Appeals, 1811–1851, and the President of Supreme Court of Appeals, 1842–1851; *m.* (firstly) 9th April, 1795, Elizabeth CABELL, dau. of William and Margaret (JORDAN) CABELL, she *d.* 5th November, 1801; *m.* (secondly) 11th March, 1805, Agnes Sarah Bell GAMBLE, *b.* 22d August, 1783, *d.* 15th February, 1863, dau. of Robert and Catharine (GRATTAN) GAMBLE of Augusta County, Virginia, and, after 1790, of Richmond, Virginia.

ISSUE BY FIRST MARRIAGE

I. Nicholas Carrington, *b.* 9th February, 1796; *d.* unmarried, 13th October, 1821.
II. Louisa Elizabeth, *b.* 19th February, 1798; *d.* 8th January, 1865; *m.* Henry CARRINGTON.
III. Abraham Joseph, *b.* 24th April, 1800; *d.* unmarried, October, 1831.

ISSUE BY SECOND MARRIAGE

I. Catherine Anne, *b.* 12th August, 1806, *d.* 1807.
II. Emma Catherine, *b.* 10th March, 1808; *m.* Paul S. CARRINGTON.
III. ROBERT GAMBLE, *b.* 9th December, 1809, of whom later.
IV. Elizabeth Hannah, *b.* 9th September, 1811; *d.* 7th November, 1892; *m.* William DANIELS.
V. William Wirt, *b.* 1st November, 1813; *d.* unmarried.
VI. Edward Carrington, *b.* 5th February, 1816; *m.* Anna Maria WILCOX.
VII. John Grattan, *b.* 17th June, 1817; *m.* Agnes C. COLES.
VIII. Henry Coalter, *b.* 14th February, 1820; *d.* 31st January, 1889; *m.* Jane ALSTON.

ROBERT GAMBLE CABELL of Richmond, Virginia; *b.* 9th December, 1809; *d.* 16th November, 1889; a graduate of the College of William and Mary, 1829; in

Medicine of the University of Virginia, 1833, and of the College of Philadelphia; for years a practicing physician and Member of the Board of Aldermen and Common Council of Richmond, Virginia; *m.* 19th January, 1843, Margaret Sophia CASKIE, *b.* 22d September, 1823, *d.* 3d July, 1867, dau. of James and Elizabeth (PINCHAM) CASKIE of Stewarton, Scotland.

ISSUE

I. James Caskie, *b.* 9th February, 1844; *m.* Nannie ENDERS; no issue.
II. William H., *b.* 13th November, 1845; killed at battle of Newmarket, 15th May, 1864.
III. ROBERT GAMBLE, *b.* 16th July, 1847, of whom later.
IV. Edward Carrington, *b.* 4th January, 1850; *d.* 13th June, 1883; *m.* Isa CARRINGTON; no issue.
V. Elizabeth Caskie, *b.* 1st May, 1851; *m.* Albert RITCHIE.

ISSUE

1. Albert Cabell RITCHIE, *b.* 29th August, 1876.

VI. Arthur Grattan, *b.* 12th May, 1853; *d.* unm. 19th June, 1906.
VII. Agnes Bell, *b.* 18th November, 1856; *m.* John D. LOTTIER; no issue.
VIII. Henry Landon, *b.* 3d November, 1858; *m.* 27th April, 1897, Adah WYMOND.

ISSUE

1. William Wymond, *b.* 2d April, 1898.
2. Henry Landon, *b.* 23d July, 1903.
3. Robert Gamble, *b.* 21st April, 1905.

IX. Margaret Constance, *b.* 2d December, 1862; *m.* Boykin WRIGHT.

ISSUE

1. Marguerite Cabell WRIGHT, *b.* 7th November, 1889; *m.* 25th November, 1914, James Frayer HILLMAN.
2. Boykin Cabell WRIGHT, *b.* 20th September, 1891.
3. Constance Cabell WRIGHT, *b.* 9th October, 1902.

ROBERT GAMBLE CABELL of Richmond, Virginia; *b.* 16th July, 1847; a graduate of the Virginia Military Institute, 1865; took part in the cadet's charge at the battle of Newmarket, 15th May, 1864; graduate in Medicine of the Medical College of Virginia; formerly Superintendent of the Virginia State Central Lunatic Asylum and now Superintendent of the City Home of Richmond, Virginia; *m.* 14th November, 1877, Anne Harris BRANCH, *b.* 31st December, 1859, *d.* 14th February, 1915, dau. of James Read and Martha Louise (PATTESON) BRANCH of Richmond, Virginia.

ISSUE

I. JAMES BRANCH, *b.* 14th April, 1879, the subject of this memoir.
II. Robert Gamble, *b.* 27th April, 1881; *m.* 24th February, 1910, Maude Crenshaw MORGAN; no issue.
III. John Lottier, *b.* 27th February, 1883; *m.* 23d April, 1913, Anna Elizabeth BELL; has issue.

1. John Bell, *b.* 13th February, 1916.

Arms.—Sable, a horse upright argent, bitted and bridled or.
Crest.—A horse upright argent, bitted and bridled or.
Motto.—Impavide.
Residences.—"Dumbarton Grange," Dumbarton, Henrico County, Virginia; (summer) "Numerocinq," Rockbridge Alum Springs, Virginia.
Societies.—Colonial Wars, Sons of the American Revolution, Kappa Alpha (Southern).

Calhoun

JOHN CALDWELL CALHOUN of New York City; *b.* 9th July, 1843, near Demopolis, Marengo County, Alabama; *m.* 8th December, 1870, Linnie ADAMS, dau. of David ADAMS, of Lexington, Kentucky, who *m.* Elizabeth JOHNSON, dau. of Joel JOHNSON, a brother, Richard M. JOHNSON, was Vice-President of the United States.

ISSUE

I. James Edward, *b.* 1st May, 1878; Captain United States Army.
II. David Adams, *b.* 14th January, 1881; *m.* Olga DININY.

ISSUE

1. John Caldwell, II. *b.* 16 June, 1908.

III. John Caldwell, II, *b.* 22d April, 1887.
IV. Julia Johnson, *b.* 14th January, 1884; *m.* 8th December, 1914, Baron E. de NAGELL of Shaffelaar, Holland, in the Diplomatic Service, is now Secretary of Legation for the Netherlands, and is located in London, England.

JOHN CALDWELL CALHOUN in the fall of 1860, at the age of seventeen years, entered the South Carolina College at Columbia as a Sophomore. In the subsequent spring of 1861 the Civil War broke out and he immediately volunteered for the Confederate Army in a company of cadets which hastened to Charlestown, where they arrived at the time of the bombardment of Fort Sumter. After the cadets were disbanded, he proceeded to Columbia and joined Capt. Thom TAYLOR's Company, which formed a part of the Hampton Legion Cavalry, of which he was appointed Color Sergeant; he was, however, discharged on account of his extreme youth. Hastily returning to his home, he organized a fine cavalry troop of 160 men and was on his way to the front within one month of his discharge. His company was assigned to Adams Battalion commanded by Maj. James P. ADAMS, and afterwards merged into the 4th Regiment, South Carolina Cavalry, under command of Col. B. H. RUTLEDGE, which was one of the Regiments composing Gen. M. C. BUTLER's Brigade (since United States Senator from South Carolina), and it was under this commander Captain CALHOUN led the charge at Trevillion Station and continued to serve until the end of the war. When LEE surrendered, he returned to Fort Hill, only to find his ancestral home devastated, and the entire fortune of the family swept away. In addition, was the recent death of his father, which imposed upon him the immediate care and support of his widowed mother, together with provision for and the education of his young brothers, Andrew, James and Patrick, and sisters, Margaret and Lucrecia. Captain CALHOUN courageously assumed the life of a planter after the war, with restricted means and under absolutely changed conditions of labor, and by his energy, industry and integrity produced the resources to efficiently discharge the obligations of nature and affection. In 1866 he went to Alabama and entered into a co-partnership with James R. POWELL at Montgomery, for the purpose of colonizing negroes in the Yazoo Valley, Mississippi, to work plantation lands on the coöperative plan. This undertaking proved so successful that he sold out his interest to his partner in less than one year for $10,000. He then went to Arkansas and repeated the enterprise on a much larger scale, retaining immediate supervision of and managing vast plantations, while inaugurating and effecting an imigration movement of negroes, which resulted in the removal of over 5,000 of them from the Carolinas, Georgia and Alabama to the Mississippi Valley. During the fourteen years of his connections with these undertakings, all his agricultural operations were carried on under the system of coöperative tenantry, which proved profitable to both land owner and laborer, while it was the first practical solution of the way to efficiently assist the freed men upward in citizenship and to land proprietorship, and has since been generally adopted in that section. Previous to withdrawing from this occupation he organized his agricultural interests into the Calhoun Land Company and the Florence Planting Company, while occupying the position of President of each corporation for some time. So important was Mr. CALHOUN'S experience regarded by Senator BLAIR'S Senate Committee on Education and Labor, while sitting in 1885, in New York City, that he was called as a leading witness before the Committee and his testimony was given great weight and prominence in their reports to Congress, and is now quoted as standard authority on the subject. In 1884 Captain CALHOUN disposed of his plantation interests at a surplus net profit of over $100,000 and removed to New York City to enter the greater arena of finance. Among his first operations was the organization of a syndicate to settle and refund the state debt of Arkansas, which was successfully accomplished. His marked abilities soon brought him into prominence in Wall Street, where his efforts were largely directed toward financial interests of his beloved South, in bringing Southern securities into favor with capitalists and investors. He soon developed extraordinary capacity in his clear grasp of transportation problems and railroad management, especially in the South, and this promptly led to his classification among the giants of the street. His first notable operation was in inaugurating a combination to acquire control of the Richmond Terminal Railroad properties. These were afterwards utilized to absorb the Richmond & Danville and Eastern Tennessee Railway System. Simultaneously he led the movement to obtain control of the Central Railroad and Banking Company of Georgia and its tributaries, and under this régime he became a leading Director, its Vice-President and Chairman of its Finance Committee. He was also elected a Director of the Richmond and Danville Railroad and the West Point Terminal Company, which brought him into contact with the most prominent railroad magnates of America; so that, in 1891, he had a dominating influence in the management of 9,000 miles of railway. From this time on

Captain CALHOUN rapidly became recognized as a leading citizen of New York. He was elected a member of the Manhattan, Reform, Lawyers, New and other Clubs in the Metropolis, of the Metropolitan Museum of Art, and of the New York Genealogical and Biographical Society. He was one of the chief originators of the Southern Society, which was established for the purpose of promoting fraternal friendships among Southerners resident in the city and the enlargement of amicable relations with citizens generally. He was President of the Society for some time and a leading spirit in its membership, and the interest and enthusiasm he inspired among them was always characteristic of his ancestry. At the fourth annual banquet of the Society on 22d February, 1890, when he was both the President of the Society itself and presiding over an assembly of 600 distinguished guests, with President CLEVELAND on his right and Bishop Henry C. POTTER on his left, his loyal and affectionate eulogy upon Jefferson DAVIS and Henry W. GRADY, who had died during the previous year, without offending courtesy or arousing partisan feeling, was regarded as a marvel of delicacy and oratorical skill. In 1873 Captain CALHOUN was appointed by Governor BERRY a Delegate from Arkansas to the Louisville, Kentucky, Cotton Exposition, and the succeeding year fulfilled a similar mission at the New Orleans Exposition. He was Vice-President of the Convention at Washington, which petitioned Congress in 1884 for the improvement of the Mississippi River and its tributaries, and was for several years, during his residence in Arkansas, President of the Levee Board of Improvements for the State and in all his business career has devoted untiring energy to the advancement and prosperous development of his beloved South. In 1890 he was selected as a member of the World's Fair Committee of One Hundred, by the citizens of New York, under the leadership of Hon. Chauncey M. DEPEW, and from them, was chosen as one of the Executive Committee of twelve. Captain CALHOUN was also one of the originators of the Sons of the American Revolution Societies, and has always taken a keen interest in whatever incites Americans to loyal pride in their forefathers. In 1897 he was appointed Special Ambassador to France by the Sons of the American Revolution, to confer with the President and Cabinet of the French Republic and also with the representatives of descendants of Lafayette, Rochambeau and De Grasse and of the Society of Arts, Science and Literature, asking their coöperation in commemorating the 119th Anniversary of the signing of the treaty between France and the Colonies.

Lineage

The origin of the family has been distinctly traced back to the reign of Gregory the Great and connects with the Earl of Lexon in Dumbartonshire, Scotland, and one of the younger sons of King Conock of Ireland, who came to the same region at that period. The name of CONOCK soon became corrupted into COLQUOHOUN, COLQUHOUN, COLCHOUN and finally CALHOUN. The first ancestor who obtained the barony of COLQUHOUN in Dumbartonshire, was Umphredies, who lived in the time of Alexander II and his posterity have enjoyed successive possession ever since. His son Robert, who lived in the reign of King David, was ordered by that king to storm and take the castle of Dumbarton, which was strongly fortified. His written reply to the King, was "Si je puis."—"If I can." He effected the capture of the castle by strategy. Collecting his trusted friends and followers, he arranged for a great hunt in the immediate neighborhood, which drew out temporarily from the castle most of the defending warriors and retainers, and when the chase was at its height, he suddenly sounded the recall of his clan and hounds and took unresisting possession of Dumbarton Castle of which he was subsequently created Earl. For this deed of personal valor and warlike strategy, the crest was bestowed upon him. This consists of a Stag's Head, indicative of the chase, supported by two ratch hounds, with the motto, "Si je puis," and below this the words, "Snock Locken" the war cry of the COLQUHOUN Clan. Succeeding Sir Robert was Sir Humphrey and after him Sir John, a man of parts and Governor of Dumbarton Castle in the reign of James II. Then came Sir John of Luss, who was made a Knight of Nova Scotia by Charles in 1602. He became such a zealous loyalist during the Civil War that he was fined £2,000, by Oliver CROMWELL. Following these was Sir James, and after him Humphrey, fourth Baronet of Luss. From him came Patrick, who was given an estate near Glasgow, and then his son Patrick, IV, and succeeding him was Sir James again, who became Principal Clerk of Sessions and married Mary FALCONER of Edinburgh. His son Patrick, a lawyer, was the father of James CALHOUN, who came to this country from Donegal, Ireland, in 1733, bringing with him his wife, Catherine MONTGOMERY, with four sons and one daughter, James, William, Ezekiel, Patrick and Catherine. The cognomens of James and Patrick have had the preference for eldest sons in the family. Their first settlement was in Pennsylvania and from thence they removed to the waters of Kenhawa, Wythe County, Virginia. They were driven from there by the Indians after Braddock's Defeat, and established Calhoun Settlement, in Abbeville County, South Carolina, February, 1756. Their settlement here was again devastated and broken up in 1760 after a desperate encounter, with the Indians, in which James, the eldest son, and his mother were slain. Subsequent to this, Patrick, the youngest son, father of the celebrated statesman and great-grandfather of our subject, was appointed to the command of a body of rangers by the Provincial Government for the defense of the frontiers at the time of the Revolution, and rendered conspicuous and sanguinary service in fighting both Indians and Tories in defense of his country. On his mother's side, Captain CALHOUN's lineage goes back distinctly to the reign of King William III, at which time a census of the officers of the Court and Government, both civil and clerical, shows the name of William Green (in 1693-1694) among the select body guard of one hundred under command of Charles, Earl of Manchester, in daily waiting upon the King. They were required to be men of the best quality and not less than six feet high. Their attire consisted of scarlet coats to the knee, scarlet breeches, richly mounted with black velvet, broad crown caps with velvet bands, and distinguished by ribbons of the King's color. Robert, the son of the above William, was born in 1695, and emigrated to Virginia with his uncle, Sir William DUFF, a Quaker, about the year 1717. Sir William settled in what is now King

George County, Virginia, and acquired large landed possessions. Duff GREEN, son of the above Robert, was next in line of maternal ancestry. He married for his second wife, Ann, dau. of Col. Henry WILLIS, founder of Fredericksburg, Virginia, whose wife, Mildred WASHINGTON was aunt and god mother of Gen. George WASHINGTON, which thus brought his children into blood relations with the Father of his Country; these ties also exist with the LEES, LEWISES and HENRYS of Virginia. John GREEN, the eldest son of this Duff GREEN, by his first marriage was father of the distinguished jurist and scholar, William GREEN, LL.D., of Richmond, Virginia (*b.* in 1809 and *d.* 1880) who left a conspicuous history in jurisprudence. The above John GREEN was appointed a Captain of the Culpepper Minute Men, in the War of the Revolution and had reached the rank of Colonel of the First Virginia Regiment, when leading the advance of the storming party at Great Bridge. He was also seriously wounded in the engagement at Mamorouk. The previously mentioned William GREEN, who is next in direct maternal line of Captain CALHOUN's ancestry, was the youngest son of the above Duff. He became a Revolutionary soldier at the age of fifteen and was with Washington at Valley Forge in the winter of 1777–1778, and afterwards with General MORGAN at Cowpens. He *m.* Ann MARSHALL, who was a cousin of Chief Justice John MARSHALL and also of the celebrated Humphrey MARSHALL of Kentucky. Next in line was Gen. Duff GREEN, the noted diplomat, soldier and editor of Gen. JACKSON's time, who served with General HARRISON's command in the War of 1812. Gen. Duff GREEN's maternal grand father was Markham MARSHALL, whose wife was Ann BAILEY, and these resided for some time in the Shenandoah Valley, Virginia, from whence they removed to Wayne County, Kentucky. It is said that the descendants of Ann BAILEY and Mildred WASHINGTON include more distinguished names than any other families in America. Gen. Duff GREEN of Kentucky was the father of Margaret Maria GREEN, who was his second child and Colonel CALHOUN's mother. Her mother was Lucretia EDWARDS, a sister of Ninian EDWARDS, a distinguished jurist and first Governor of Illinois.

ISSUE OF JAMES AND CATHERINE (MONTGOMERY) CALHOUN

I. James, of Pennsylvania, killed in 1755, while holding a command at Braddock's Defeat.
II. William, of South Carolina, Justice of the Peace; *m.* 19th October, 1749, Agnes LONG.

ISSUE

1. Joseph, *b.* 22d October, 1750; *d.* 14th April, 1817; was several times a Member of the Legislature of South Carolina, serving in both House and Senate; was Colonel of Militia and elected to Congress in 1807 in place of Gen. Levi CASEY, who *d.* 1st February, 1807, served until 4th March, 1811, when he was succeeded by his cousin, John C. CALHOUN; *m.* (firstly) Catherine CALHOUN; *m.* (secondly) 26th May, 1802, Patsey MOSELEY, dau. of William MOSELEY of Virginia.

ISSUE BY FIRST MARRIAGE

1^1. Ann, *m.* William PERRIN.
2^1. Joseph, *b.* 22d July, 1787; was educated by Dr. Moses WADDEL; was commissioned in the United States Army and attained the rank of Captain; was in the Richmond Theatre the night of the fire and escaped by jumping out of a window; was severely wounded at the battle of Lundy's Lane; received a bullet in his arm in a duel; his winter home was "Calhoun's Mills," his summer home "Ben Lomond;" *m.* 29th January, 1819, Frances DARRICOURT, *b.* 1st May, 1800, at Vienna, Abbeville District, *d.* 21st March, 1885, at Mt. Carmel, Abbeville District.

ISSUE

1^2. Rebecca, *d.* at the age of sixteen years.
2^2. Thomas Smith, *d.* at the age of four years; named for an army friend.
3^2. Joseph Selden, *d.* at the age of seven years; named for an army friend.
4^2. Louise, *d.* early.
5^2. Eliza, from whom these records were obtained.
6^2. Elizabeth Mary, *d.* unmarried at the age of twenty-one years.
7^2. Frances Josette, *m.* Dr. J. W. MARSHALL.
8^2. Ann, *d.* young.
9^2. John Joseph.

3^1. Catherine, *d.* unmarried.
4^1. Mary, *d.* unmarried.

ISSUE BY SECOND MARRIAGE

1^1. Eliza, *m.* James HOLT.
2^1. John Ewing, *m.* Mary SPEED.

ISSUE

1^2. Elizabeth, *m.* James LeRoy.
2^2. Martha, *m.* George BROWN.
3^2. Margaret.
4^2. John Ewing.

3^1. Martha, *m.* John SPEED.
4^1. Samuel, *d.* unmarried.
5^1. William, Captain in the Seminole War; *d.* unmarried.
6^1. Jane, *m.* James McKELVEY.

2. Catherine, b. 4th February, 1753; is said to have been killed in the Indian Massacre on Long Cane Creek, 1st February, 1760.
3. Anne, b. 18th May, 1755; d. 19th December, 1830; was taken captive by the Indians in the Long Cane Massacre and was held captive for fourteen years; m. 12th October, 1784, Isaac MATTHEWS, who d. 1801; had issue.
4. Mary, b. 1st November, 1757; captured at the Long Cane Massacre and probably died in captivity.
5. Patrick, b. 18th February, 1760; killed by the Indians, 26th June, 1776, while serving as an Ensign in Capt. James McCALLS' Expedition in the Cherokee Country.
6. Rachel, b. 19th September, 1762; m. Patrick NORRIS; had issue.
7. Esther, b. 30th September, 1756; m. William LOVE; had issue.
8. William, b. 5th April, 1768; m. Rebecca TONNYHILL.

ISSUE

1^1. Ezekiel.
2^1. Catherine.
3^1. Rachel, m. Handy HARRIS.
4^1. William P.
5^1. James Montgomery.
6^1. Joseph.
7^1. Rebecca.
8^1. Sarah.
9^1. Mary Elizabeth, m. Nathan MASSEY.

9. Ezekiel, b. 27th November, 1770; d. 25th January, 1817; m. Frances HAMILTON, dau. of Maj. Andrew HAMILTON.

ISSUE

1^1. William, d. unmarried.
2^1. Joseph, d. unmarried.
3^1. Harriet, m. Thomas DAVIS, of Washington, D. C.
4^1. Jane Hamilton, b. 2d September, 1798; d. 11th January, 1846; m. Dr. Joseph Webb SIMONDS, b. in Boston, Massachusetts, 8th April, 1781, d. 7th March, 1840.
5^1. Ephraim.
6^1. Catherine, m. Dr. John W. PARKER, of Columbia, South Carolina.
7^1. Andrew.

10. Agnes, b. 29th August, 1773; m. General HUTTON; had issue.
11. Alexander, b. 21st December, 1776; m. Kitty JOHNSON.

ISSUE

1^1. Kitty, m. Edward TILLMAN.

III. John, *m.* and had two children.
IV. Catherine, *m.* in Ireland, John NOBLE, and had three children; the oldest Alexander NOBLE was born on the passage over.
V. Ezekiel, of South Carolina, *b.* 1720; will proved 25th May, 1762; *m.* prior to his arrival in South Carolina, Jean EWING of New Jersey.

ISSUE

1. John Ewing, *b.* 1750; *d.* 26th October, 1802; first Senator from the up-country of South Carolina; he adopted COLHONE as his style of spelling the name, United States Senator, etc., 16th August, 1775; was a member of Capt. Charles DRAYTON'S Company of Militia at the organization in Charlestown, 16th August, 1775, where he came to study law but was not admitted to the Bar until 1783, the Revolution interfering with his studies; was elected a Member of the Privy Council in February, 1775, and also served as a Commissioner of Fortified Estates; sent to the House of Representatives in the Fall of 1781 from Ninety Six District; February, 1785, elected a Member of the Privy Council by the State Legislature, several times in the Legislature between 1785 and 1800 and in December, 1796, was supported for Governor; 8th December, 1800, elected United States Senator by the Legislature for the full term beginning 1st March, 1801; *m.* 8th October, 1786, Floride BONNEAU, dau. of Samuel BONNEAU, Esq., of St. John's Parish.

ISSUE

1^1. Benjamin, *d.* young.
2^1. Caroline, *d.* young.
3^1. Floride Bonneau, *b.* 15th February, 1792; *m.* her father's first cousin, John Caldwell CALHOUN.
4^1. John Ewing, Colonel; *b.* 1791, in Charleston, South Carolina; *m.* 21st February, 1822, Martha Maria DAVIS, who *d.* 13th November, 1853, dau. of Capt. William Ransom DAVIS.

ISSUE

1^2. John Ewing, *d.* young.
2^2. Martha Maria, *d.* unmarried.
3^2. William Ransom, *b.* 22d July, 1827; educated at West Point, was an Aid to Gov. J. L. MANNING; was sometime Secretary of Legation and Acting Minister to France; was first a Captain and then a Colonel of the 1st Regiment South Carolina Regular Artillery; was killed in a duel with Lieut.-Col. Alfred RHETT, 5th September, 1862.
4^2. Susan.
5^2. John Ewing.

6^2. Florence, *d.* young.
7^2. Warren Davis.
8^2. Henry Davis.
9^2. Edward Boiseau, served as Lieutenant in Major of T. B. FERGUSON'S battalion of light artillery during the Civil War and attained the rank of Captain; *m.* Sarah C. NORWOOD.

ISSUE

1^3. Martha Maria (twin).
2^3. Sarah Louise (twin), *m.* Allen McLee SHOEN, of Richmond, Virginia; had issue.
3^3. Floride Bonneau (twin).
4^3. Willie Norwood (twin).

5^1. James Edward, *b.* 4th July, 1798; some time an officer in the United States Navy; *d.* 31st October, 1889, at Millwood, South Carolina; *m.* Maria SIMKINS.

ISSUE

1^2. A child, *d.* young.
6^1. William Sheridan, *d.* young.

2. Patrick, probably Ensign in Capt. James MCCALL'S Company; sent into the Cherokee Country in 1776 to capture Alexander CAMERON, the British Indian Agent, and who was captured, tortured and finally killed by the Indians.
3. Ezekiel.
4. Mary, *m.* ——— CARR; had issue.
5. Rebecca, *m.* 19th March, 1765, Andrew Pickens; who subsequently obtained during the Revolution the rank of Brigadier-General of the Militia of South Carolina; had issue.
6. Catherine, *m.* 7th January, 1768, Alexander NOBLE, son of John and Mary (CALHOUN) NOBLE, her first cousin; had issue.
7. Jean, *m.* John STEADMAN.

VI. PATRICK, *b.* 27th June, 1727, of whom later.

PATRICK CALHOUN, of South Carolina, *b.* June, 1727; *d.* 15th February, 1796; appointed by the Provincial Government as Commander of a body of Rangers, 5th June, 1764, for defense of the frontier; Justice of the Peace; Member of the Assembly, 1769–1772; Deputy to First Provincial Congress, 11th January, 1775 to 1st November, 1775; re-elected to Second Provincial Congress, 1st November, 1775, to 21st October, 1776; Member of First General Assembly of South Carolina, 26th March, 1776 to 21st October, 1776; subsequently served in every House of the General Assembly until his death. In 1791 was one of the Judges from Asheville; *m.* (firstly) Miss CRAIGHEAD, *d.* 10th September, 1766, of miscarriage of twins, dau. of Rev. Alexander CRAIGHEAD; *m.* (secondly) Martha CALDWELL of Newberry, South Carolina. Her oldest brother John was murdered by Tories; the second brother was killed in the battle of Cowpens, where his body bore the marks of thirty sabre wounds; the third was imprisoned by the English for nine months in the dungeons of St. Augustine.

ISSUE BY SECOND MARRIAGE

1. James, *m.* 4th May, 1802, Sarah Caldwell MARTIN, who *d.* 11th March, 1845, dau. of Dr. James MARTIN, Surgeon of the 3d Regiment, South Carolina Continentals.

ISSUE

1. Patrick, *b.* 25th January, 1803; *d.* same day.
2. James Martin, lawyer, *b.* 25th January, 1805, at Vienna, South Carolina; *d.* 20th November, 1877; *m.* Susan PICKENS, who *d.* 7th September, 1877.

ISSUE

1^1. Susan Wilkinson, *m.* Alexander NOBLE.
2^1. Andrew, *m.* Frances E. LEE.
3^1. Sarah L., *m.* William T. WADE.
4^1. James F.
5^1. John C.

3. John Alfred, *b.* 8th January, 1807.
4. Caroline, *b.* 1st April, 1811; *d.* 13th July, 1823.
5. William Henry, M.D., *b.* 15th November, 1813; *d.* 24th September, 1869; *m.* 18th June, 1837, Jane ORR.

ISSUE

1^1. Florence C., *m.* John T. TANKERSLEY, of Mississippi.
2^1. James Lawrence.
3^1. Martha J.
4^1. J. Christopher.
5^1. Sarah Caroline, *m.* L. T. TAYLOR, of Mississippi.
6^1. John Caldwell, *d.* unmarried.
7^1. William Henry.

6. Benjamin, *b.* 13th July, 1815; killed accidentally when a boy.
7. Sarah, *b.* 9th May, 1818.
8. George McDuffie, *b.* 25th July, 1820; *d.* 25th July, 1824.

II. Catherine, *m.* Rev. Moses WADDEL; subsequently a noted Teacher and Doctor of Divinity; they had one child who died young.
III. William, *m.* Catherine Jenne DE GROFFENREID.

ISSUE

1. Tescharner, *d.* unmarried.
2. Patrick, *d.* unmarried.
3. Mary, *d.* unmarried.
4. Jane, *d.* unmarried.
5. Lucretia Ann, *m.* (firstly) Dr. Henry TOWNES, of Greenville; *m.* (secondly) Dr. Tescharner DE GROFFENREID, of Alabama.
6. Thomas.
7. Mary Catherine; *m.* 12th March, 1827, Armistead BURT.
8. James Lawrence.
9. Sarah, *m.* Ezekiel Pickens NOBLE; had issue.
10. Eugenia, *m.* Dr. Edwin PARKER; had issue.
11. George McDuffie.

IV. JOHN CALDWELL, *b.* 18th March, 1872, of whom later.
V. Patrick, *m.* Nancy DE GROFFENREID, sister of his brother William's wife.

ISSUE

1. Martha, *m.* Dr. BONNER.
2. Catherine, *m.* Dr. William TENNENT; had issue.
3. Edward.
4. Ludlow.
5. Francis Augustus.
6. Benjamin Alfred, *m.* Miss YARBOROUGH; had issue.

JOHN CALDWELL CALHOUN, of Fort Hill, Pendleton, South Carolina; *b.* 18th March, 1782, in Abbeville District, South Carolina; *d.* 30th March, 1850, in Washington, D. C.; was prepared for College by his brother-in-law, Rev. Moses WADDEL; entered the junior class at Yale College in 1802 and was graduated as A.B., 12th September, 1804; studied law at Litchfield Law School, Litchfield, Connecticut, 22d July, 1805, to 28th July, 1806; then in Charleston and Asheville; was admitted to the bar in 1807; elected to the South Carolina House of Representatives, 13th October, 1809; appointed aid on the Staff of Governor DRAYTON with the rank of Lieutenant-Colonel, 15th December, 1808; elected to the House of Representatives of the United States in 1810, taking his seat 4th March, 1811; re-elected in 1812, 1814, and 1816, serving to 8th October, 1817, when he became Secretary of War in President MONROE'S Cabinet, serving 4th March, 1825, when he was inaugurated as Vice-President of the United States; was re-elected Vice-President in 1828 and served to 28th December, 1832; resigned as Vice-President 16th July, 1832; elected United States Senator from South Carolina, 12th December, 1832, to succeed Robert Y. HANE, who had been elected Governor and took his seat in the Senate, 4th January, 1833; was re-elected in 1834 and 1840, but resigned in 1842, serving until 4th March, 1843; was a candidate for the Presidency in 1844 but withdrew, 20th January, 1844; was Secretary of State under President TYLER from 6th March, 1844 to 6th March, 1845; was elected to the United States Senate, 26th November, 1845, to succeed Judge Daniel Elliott HUGER, who resigned in order that Mr. CALHOUN might be returned to the Senate; *m.* 11th January, 1811, Floride Bonneau CALHOUN, *b.* 15th February, 1792, *d.* 25th July, 1866, dau. of John Ewing and Floride (BONNEAU) CALHOUN, M.D.

ISSUE

I. ANDREW PICKENS, *b.* 15th October, 1812, of whom later.
II. Anna Maria, *b.* 13th February, 1817; *d.* 22d September, 1875; *m.* Thomas G. CLEMSON; had issue.
III. Patrick, Major in United States Army; *b.* 9th February, 1821; *d.* unmarried 1st June, 1858.
IV. John Caldwell, M.D., *b.* 17th May, 1823; *d.* 31st July, 1855; *m.* (firstly) Anzie ADAMS, who *d.s.p.*; *m.* (secondly) January, 1853, in Trinity Church, St. Augustine, Florida, Kate Kirby PUTNAM, only dau. of B. A. PUTNAM, Esq. of St. Augustine.

ISSUE BY SECOND MARRIAGE

1. John C., married.
2. Benjamin P., *m.* Julia PETERMAN; had issue.

V. Martha Cornelia, *b.* 22d April, 1824; *d.* 2d May, 1857, in Abbeville.
VI. James, *d.* unmarried, in California.
VII. William Lowndes, of Abbeville District, *b.* 13th August, 1829; *d.* 19th September, 1858; *m.* (firstly) Margaret CLOUD of HINSBOROUGH, S. C., *m.* (secondly) Kate Kirby (Putnam) CALHOUN, widow of his brother, John Caldwell CALHOUN, M.D.

ISSUE BY SECOND MARRIAGE

1. William Lowndes.

ANDREW PICKENS CALHOUN of Fort Hill, Pendleton District, Pickens County, South Carolina; *b.* 15th October, 1812; *d.* 16th March, 1865; Cotton Planter and Commissioner from South Carolina to Alabama, 1860, at the beginning of the Civil War; educated at Yale and South Carolina College; *m.* (firstly) Miss CHAPPELL, who *d.s.p.*; *m.* (secondly) 5th May, 1836, Margaret Maria GREEN, *b.* 18th February, 1816, *d.* 27th July, 1891, dau. of Duff GREEN of Kentucky and Washington, D. C., who *m.* Lucretia EDWARDS of Kentucky, sister of Ninian EDWARDS, first Governor of Illinois.

ISSUE

1. Duff Green, *b.* 21st April, 1839; *d.* 25th August, 1873; *m.* 1871, Elizabeth Marshall BEASELEY of Texas.

ISSUE

1. Andrew Pickens II, *b.* 10th April, 1872; *m.* 14th August, 1895, Floride LEE, dau. of Gideon and Floride (CLEMSON) LEE, gd. dau. of Mrs. Anna Calhoun CLEMSON.

ISSUE

1^1. Margaret Maria, *b.* 6th July, 1896.
2^1. Patrick, *b.* 19th August, 1899.
3^1. Creighton Lee, *b.* 31st October, 1901.

II. JOHN CALDWELL, financier, *b.* 9th July, 1843, the subject of this memoir.
III. Margaret Maria.
IV. Andrew Pickens, *b.* 22d August, 1852, at Fort Hill, South Carolina; *d.* 4th April, 1872, at Dalton, Georgia; *d.* unmarried.
V. Patrick, of Charleston, South Carolina, Euclid Heights, Cleveland, Ohio and 88th Street, New York City; *b.* 21st March, 1856, at Fort Hill, the plantation of his grandfather near Pendleton District, South Carolina; removed to Dalton, Georgia, in 1871; admitted to Georgia Bar, 1875; Missouri bar, 1876; went to Atlanta, Georgia, practiced there, 1878–1894, and became one of the leading corporation lawyers in the South and prominent in politics, prominent in consolidation of railway and traction interests, notably the Central Railroad of Georgia, Richmond & Danville, and Richmond & West Point Terminal Railway & Warehouse Company for all of which was counsel, 1889–1892; since then has devoted attention chiefly to consolidation and development of street railways, taking part in the consolidation of street railway systems in Pittsburg, St. Louis, Baltimore and San Francisco; Director, Philadelphia Company, United Railways of Pittsburg; President, United Railroads of San Francisco; Director, United Railways Investment Company of San Francisco, Houston Oil Company of Texas; Calhoun Falls Investment Company, and Calhoun Mills; owner of Euclid Heights, Cleveland, Ohio; Director, Euclid Heights Realty Company, and largely interested in South Carolina, Georgia and Texas; *m.* 4th November, 1885, Sarah Porter WILLIAMS, dau. of George W. WILLIAMS of Charleston.
VI. James Edward, *b.* 18th March, 1857, at Fort Hill, South Carolina; *d.* 3d June, 1877, at Dalton, Georgia.

ISSUE

1. Martha.
2. Margaret Green.
3. Patrick.
4. George Williams.

VII. Mary Lucretia, b. 21st February, 1862; d. 17th July, 1865.

Arms.—Argent, a saltire engrailed sable.
Crest.—A hart's head couped gules, attired argent, supporters two grey hounds argent, collared sable.
Motto.—Si je puis, Snock elachan.
Residence.—200 West 58th Street, New York City.
Clubs.—Manhattan, Lawyers, Tilden of New York and Gate City of Atlanta.
Societies.—Military Order Foreign Wars, Sons of the American Revolution, New York Southern Society, Genealogical and Biographical Society (life); South Carolina Historical Society, The Virginia, The Carolina, The Pilgrims, The France America, Honorable Life Member of The United Military Order of America

Capp

SETH BUNKER CAPP of Devon and Philadelphia; b. in Philadelphia, 23d May, 1875; educated at De Lancey School, Philadelphia, Class of 1893; has resided abroad for a number of years, making Paris, his home, he retains however a residence also in Philadelphia; is an expert in antiques and has a valuable personal collection; takes a deep interest in the advancement of the Arts and Sciences; is a member of over sixty associations and societies in America and Europe.

Lineage

SETH BUNKER CAPP is descended from JOHN HOWLAND of the *Mayflower*.

GEORGE BUNKER, 1632, son of William BON COEUR, a French Huguenot, for whom Bunker Hill was named.

CAPTAIN LAWRENCE WILKINSON, one of the founders of The Providence and Rhode Island Plantation, who claimed descent from Henry DE BOHUN, Earl of Hereford, a Magna Charta Baron, through Ida Estelle STITT, dau. of Seth Bunker and Sarah Wilkinson (WALL) STITT. Ida Estelle STITT *m.* 4th March, 1868, William Musser CAPP, M.D. of Philadelphia (see "Mayflower Descendants," "Huguenot Society of America" and "Baronial Order of Runnemede.") Seth Bunker CAPP is also descended from Capt. George MUSSER and John SINGER, soldiers of the American Revolution, through Sarah SINGER, who *m.* 1829, John Charles CAPP. The CAPP family were Scotch and trace their origin and Arms to the days of Bruce. Owing to religious differences they went to the Palatinate and became Germanized. The first of the name of Capp in America was Andreas KAPP, who with his wife Regina Sophia, left the Palatinate and moved with many others to America in 1710, settling first on the Hudson River, New York; becoming dissatisfied with property conditions, they purchased land in Pennsylvania and under the leadership of Andreas KAPP in 1728 they marched through the unbroken wilderness, assisted by friendly Indians, and settled in the Lebanon Valley about twenty miles from the present city of Reading, calling their settlement Heidelberg. Andreas *d.* 1746, without issue, leaving a considerable landed estate. His two younger brothers John Michael and George Frederick had previously come to America by the ship *Pennsylvania*, arriving in 1732, at Philadelphia, and purchased 425 acres of land adjoining Andreas' holdings. Their surname in autograph signature on passenger list, to oath of allegiance and on title to lands was spelled CAPP and this spelling has ever since been retained by the descendants of John Michael. George Frederick CAPP *m.* Eva Marie and by his will left his estate to his widow and their children, John Frederick, John George and George Michael. John Michael was educated at the University of Heidelberg; nineteen years after his settlement in America he visited Europe and his native town of Heidelberg in 1751; he d. in 1764. he bequeathed a considerable estate to his widow and children; *m.* 1737, Margaret, surname unknown, *d.* 1785.

ISSUE

I. CHRISTOPHER, *b.* 5th October, 1738, of whom later.
II. Barbara, *m.* ——— DINGIRT.
III. George.
IV. Valentine.
V. John Andreas.
VI. John Michael.
VII. Anthony .
IX. Peter, *m.* Christina BEFF.
X. Susanna, *m.* John GUNDRUM.
XI. Catherine, *m.* Martin FRY.
XII. Christina, *m.* Michael NEFF.

CHRISTOPHER CAPP of Harrisburg; *b.* Heidelberg, 5th October, 1738; *d.* 13th May, 1806, at Harrisburg; was an active man in Council and of considerable wealth and largely increased his landed holdings; he built a commodious stone Colonial Mansion which is still (1916) in excellent preservation; *m.* 1764, Anna FABER, *d.* 1792, dau. of Elizabeth FABER, widow, *d.* 1775.

ISSUE

1. Jacob, *b.* 1765, of Jonestown, Pennsylvania; *d.* 16th March, 1826; established a store at Jonestown, and also had large landed holdings; *m.* Elizabeth ZIMMERMAN, *b.* 1767, *d.* 1841.

ISSUE

1. Michael, *b.* 1790; *d.* 1844; *m.* Catherine BROWN.

ISSUE

1^1. Mary, *b.* 1819, *d.* 1844.
2^1. Sabina.
3^1. Susan.
4^1. Jacob, *b.* 1825; *m.* Caroline BOWMAN, of Lebanon.

ISSUE

1^2. Henry M., *b.* 1852; *m.* Emma DEAN, a descendant of Gen. Israel PUTNAM.

ISSUE

1^3. Henry M.
2^3. Emma.
3^3. Ninian.
4^3. Dean.

2. Sabina, *m.* John STEIN.
3. Catherine, *m.* John CONRAD.
4. Joseph, no issue.
5. John, *b.* 1801; *d.* 1864; *m.* Sallie SELTZER, *b.* 1804; *d.* 1863.

ISSUE

1¹. George Thomas, *b.* 1825; was a man of prominence in his community; *m.* Sarah BICKNEL.

  1². George S.
  2². John A., M.D., of Lancaster, Pennsylvania.
  3². Hon. Thomas H., Lawyer, of Lebanon, Pennsylvania; Member of the State Legislature for several years, and was the presiding officer of that body, and a Judge.

II. JOHN, *b.* 1768, of whom later.
III. Christopher, Jr., *b.* circa 1770; *d.s.p.*

JOHN CAPP, *b.* 1768; *d.* 14th February, 1826; was educated at Dickinson College, m which institution he was offered a professorship; he served as a Burgess and was appointed a Commissioner for the Eastern States to settle all claims of officers and soldiers who served under Col. George WASHINGTON in the French and Indian Wars from 1754 to 1764; he established a bank in Harrisburg; was the first President of the Turnpike Roads Company of Pennsylvania; *m.* 1793, Sarah CHAMBERLAIN, *d.* 1821, dau. of Charles CHAMBERLAIN, who was regarded as a Tory and whose house in Philadelphia was occupied by General HOWE, during the British occupancy of that town.

ISSUE

I. Sarah Elizabeth, *b.* 1876; unmarried.
II. Samuel, *b.* 1796; *d.* 1854; unmarried.
III. Mary Ann, *b.* 1807; *d.* 1870; *m.* Dr. William GALLAHER, a descendant of General MONTGOMERY who fought at Quebec.

ISSUE

1. Sarah Elizabeth GALLAHER, unmarried.
2. Stephen GALLAGHER, unmarried.
3. Samuel Capp GALLAHER, who makes his residence in London, England.

IV. JOHN CHARLES, *b.* 26th June, 1800, of whom later.

JOHN CHARLES CAPP, of Philadelphia, *b.* Harrisburg, 26th June, 1800; *d.* 3d March, 1876; engaged in the banking business; at the time of his death was the dean of the Philadelphia Stock Exchange; *m.* 28th July, 1829, Sarah SINGER, *b.* 16th November, 1798; *d.* 8th April, 1876, dau. of John and Anna Maria Musser SINGER.

ISSUE

I. Charles Singer, of San Francisco, California; *b.* 19th December, 1831; *d.* 1912; went to California in 1849; was a Lawyer and for many years connected with newspaper work; *m.* 6th August, 1889, Lillian E. STILLWELL, *b.* 1864, *d*au. of Rev. ——— STILLWELL.

ISSUE

1. Lillian, *b.* 20th May, 1890.
2. Charles, *b.* 7th December, 1893.
3. Miriam, *b.* 4th December, 1891; *m.* 1915, Rev. Clifton Alden DOUGLAS, a missionary to Colombia, South America.

II. John Singer, Banker of Philadelphia; *b.* 29th April, 1833; *d.* 10th January 1882; served in the Civil War as Lieutenant; *m.* 22d November, 1860 Mary MICHENER.

ISSUE

1. Sarah Emma, *b.* 21st December, 1882; *m.* Traff HAVERSTICK, son of, Rev. Alexander HAVERSTICK.

III. Allen, Electrical Engineer, *b.* 14th January, 1870; Graduate University of Pennsylvania.
IV. Alfred, *b.* 13th February, 1840; *d.* 2d April, 1852.
V. Samuel, *d.* in infancy.
VI. Samuel M., of San Francisco, *b.* 2d March, 1836; *d.* 1908.
VII. Rev. Edward Payson, *b.* 12th September, 1837; *d.* 26th October, 1873, and is buried at Yokohoma, Japan; Graduate University of Pennsylvania, and Princeton Theological Seminary; with his brother-in-law Rev. S. MATEER established a school in Tung Chow, which has since become a University with fifty-five professors and several hundred students; also built a Presbyterian Church at Tung Chow which is in a flourishing condition; *m.* at Tung Chow, China, Margaret BROWN, *d.* 17th February, 1882, a missionary.
VIII. WILLIAM MUSSER, M.D., *b.* 20th November, 1842, of whom later.

DR. WILLIAM MUSSER CAPP, of Philadelphia; *b.* 20th November, 1842; a graduate of Jefferson College of Medicine in Philadelphia; *m.* 4th March, 1868, Ida Estelle STITT, *b.* 29th November, 1845, dau. of Seth Bunker STITT of Philadelphia and Sarah Wilkinson WALL.

ISSUE

1. Estelle, *m.* 3d November, 1902, Frederick JOST, of New York, *b.* 1870; *d.* 1908, a graduate of the University of Berlin, Prussia, son of Frederick W. JOST, and a descendant of Anika JANS and Peter STUYVESANT, who *m.* ——— KIP.

ISSUE

1. Gordon JOST, *b.* 1st October, 1903.

II. William Edgar, *b.* 19th August, 1872; *d.* 30th September, 1891, while a Junior at the University of Pennsylvania.

III. Louise Thayer, *b.* 10th September, 1879; *d.* 18th September, 1879.
IV. SETH BUNKER, *b.* 23d May, 1875, the subject of this memoir.

Arms.—Noir, three spurs or.
Crest.—A winged spur or.
Motto.—Nunquam non paratus.
Residence.—Devon, Pennsylvania.
Clubs.—Merion Cricket Club (Proprietary Member), Bay Head Yacht Club, The American Kennel Club.
Societies.—Mayflower Descendants, Colonial Society of Pennsylvania, Sons of the American Revolution, Baronial Order of Runnemede, 32d degree Mason.

Chisolm

WILLIAM GARNETT CHISOLM, LL.B., of Baltimore, Maryland; *b.* there 19th November, 1890; LL.B. Baltimore Law School, 1912; Member of 1st Company Coast Artillery, Maryland National Guard; is Editor of "Chisolm Genealogy," Knickerbocker Press, 1914; is associated with the Baltimore Trust Company.

Lineage

The CHISHOLMS are of Anglo-Norman origin and came soon after the Conquest, A. D. 1066, from Tyndale, England, and settled in Roxburgheshire, Scotland, and later in Inverness-shire, where they founded a small but independent Highland Clan; their principal seat being Erchless Castle, and the chief being known as "The Chisolm." The first on record is

JOHN DE CHISHOLME, A. D. 1254, Berwick; *m.* Emma DE VIPOUNT, dau. of William DE VIPOUNT, Lord of Bolton, the descendant of a valiant and powerful Norman house, who accompanied the Conqueror to England; his son

RICHARD DE CHISHOLME, swore fealty to Edward III, 1296, signing the Ragman's Roll; his son

SIR JOHN DE CHISHOLME, Knt., fought with Bruce at Bannockburn, 1314; his son

ALEXANDER DE CHISHOLME had a son

SIR ROBERT DE CHISHOLME, Knt., described as one of the "Magnates of Scotland;" taken prisoner with King David II at Neville's Cross, Durham, 1346; *m.* Anne DE LAUDER, dau. of Sir Robert DE LAUDER, Constable of Urquhart Castle, Loch Ness; his son

SIR ROBERT DE CHISHOLME, Knt., Constable of Urquhart Castle, Sheriff of Inverness and Justiciary of Moray, 1358–1376; *m.* Margaret HALIBURTON, dau. of Sir Walter HALIBURTON, Member of King's Council and Ambassador to England.

ISSUE

I. John, *m.* Catherine BISSET, with issue an only dau. Muriel, who *m.* Alexander SUTHERLAND, Baron Duffus, gr. gd. son of Nicholas, Earl of SUTHERLAND.
II. ALEXANDER, of whom later.
III. Robert, *m.* Marion Douglas, dau. of Sir William DOUGLAS, ancestor of the Dukes of Queensbury, and became the ancestor of the Border Chisholmes of Stirches, Chisholme and Cromlix, now represented in the female line by the Viscounts Strathallan, the Earls of Kinnoul and the Earls of Perth.

ALEXANDER DE CHISHOLME, Constable of Urquhart Castle, *m.* Lady Margaret DE L'AIRD, gd. dau. of Malise, Earl of Stratherne, Orkney and Caithness, a direct descendant of the ancient Kings of Norway and Denmark; his son

THOMAS DE CHISHOLME, Constable of Urquhart Castle, 1391; *m.* Margaret MACKINTOSH, dau. of Lauchlan MACKINTOSH, VIII, of Mackintosh.

ISSUE

I. Alexander, Lord of Kinrossy, Strathglass and the Aird, *m.* with issue an only daughter, Catherine, who *m.* Walter HALIBURTON, son of Lord Dirleton, one of the hostages for the ransom of King James I, High Treasurer of Scotland, 1439, by his wife, Lady Margaret, widow of David, Duke of Rothesay and dau. of Archibald, third Earl of Douglas.
II. WILAND, of whom below.

WILAND DE CHISHOLME, who *m.* with issue; his son
WILAND DE CHISHOLME, the first to be designated "The Chisholm," 1509; his son
JOHN CHISHOLM, who under date of 13th March, 1538, had a charter under the Great Seal of James V erecting his lands into a barony; his son
ALEXANDER CHISHOLM succeeded to estates, 31st May, 1555; *m.* Janet (MACKENZIE) MACDONALD, widow of Aeneas MACDONALD, and dau. of Sir Kenneth MACKENZIE, X Baron of Kintail by his wife, Lady Elizabeth STEWART, dau. of John, Earl of Athol.

ISSUE

JOHN CHISHOLM, served as heir 19th December, 1590; *m.* (secondly) the eldest dau. of Alexander MACKENZIE of Coul and Applecross.

ISSUE

ALEXANDER CHISHOLM, *m.* 1639, the dau. of Alexander MACKENZIE, V, of Gairloch.

ISSUE

I. Colonel Angus, Commander of the forces in Inverness-shire.
II. Alexander, who succeeded as Chief of Clan, inheriting Erchless Castle and the main family estates.
III. COLIN, of Knockfin, of whom below.

COLIN CHISHOLM, progenitor of the house of Knockfin, redeemed for the Chief the estates of Strathglass, etc., after they had been confiscated, owing to the part the clan took in the Rising of 1715 under the Earl of Mar; *m.* Mary GRANT, dau. of Patrick GRANT, IV, of Glenmoriston.

ISSUE

ARCHIBALD CHISHOLM of Fasnakyle House, *m.* dau. of Kenneth MACRAE.

ISSUE

ALEXANDER CHISHOLM m. Janet FRASER, dau. of FRASER of Ballindorn, and about 1717 emigrated to the Province of Carolina and settled near Charles Town on the Wando or Cooper River.

ISSUE

ALEXANDER CHISOLME of Charles Town, d. September, 1772; m. 15th February, 1742, Judith RADCLIFFE.

ISSUE

I. Ann, b. 31st December, 1743; d. 27th November, 1806; m. 8th April, 1759, Dr. Robert WILSON, with issue.
II. CHRISTINA, b. 21st November, 1745, of whom below.
III. Alexander, b. 30th May, 1747.
IV. Judith, b. 14th June, 1748.

CHRISTINA CHISOLM, b. 21st November, 1745; d. 1778–1786; m. 5th October, 1766, a cousin, Alexander CHISOLM, Jr., of Charleston, b. in Inverness, Scotland, 1738, and said to have been a son of John Ban and Catherine (MACRAE) CHISHOLM, and a gr. gd. son of Colin I of Knockfin. He came to Carolina about 1746 accompanied by his mother, d. 10th December, 1810, and is buried in Scotch Presbyterian Churchyard, Charleston.

ISSUE

I. Alexander Robert, b. 1767; d. 1814; m. 1789, Sarah G. MAXWELL, with issue.
II. Dr. William, b. 8th December, 1770; d. 3d September, 1821; m. Marianne PORCHER; had issue.
III. GEORGE, b. 19th February, 1772, of whom later.
IV. Dr. Robert Trail, d. 1821; m. Margaret Elizabeth EDINGS.

ISSUE

1. Susan Matilda Harriet, m. 1828, Oliver Hering MIDDLETON, son of Hon. Henry MIDDLETON, Member of Congress, Minister Plenipotentiary to Russia and Governor of South Carolina (see Middleton, Vol. II); had issue.

V. Captain Thomas, d. 1816.
VI. Ann, m. Mungo MACKIE, with issue.

GEORGE CHISOLM, b. in Charleston, 19th February, 1772; d. 31st October, 1835; lived in Charleston on East Bay and at his plantation, "The Retreat" on Cooper River, which had been the headquarters of Sir Richard LEE, during the Revolution; m. 21st January, 1796, Providence Hext PRIOLEAU, b. 28th July, 1776, d. 6th December, 1860, dau. of Lieut. Hext PRIOLEAU, of Charleston Light Infantry, 1776; gd. son of Col. Samuel PRIOLEAU, 1690–1752, Colonel of His Majesty's Royal Horse Guards and Member of His Majesty's Council; he son of Rev. Elias PRIOLEAU,

COLONIAL FAMILIES OF THE UNITED STATES

founder of Huguenot Church in Charleston, who emigrated from Pons, France in 1685; he being a descendant of the noble Venetian house of Priuli, who furnished three Doges, many generals, ambassadors and prelates to the Republic, and whose history can be traced back to a period prior to A. D. 1000.

ISSUE

I. GEORGE, b. 22d October, 1796 of whom later.
II. Robert Trail, b. 16th July, 1798; m. (firstly) 10th October, 1827, Harriet Emily SCHUTT, dau. of Caspar C. SCHUTT; m. (secondly) 2d January 1851, Lynch Helen BACHMAN, b. 19th September, 1828, d. 20th August, 1901, dau. of Rev. John BACHMAN, D.D., LL.D., Ph.D. 1790–1874, Pastor of St. John's Church Charleston, a naturalist and ornthologist of note, close friend of Agassi and Audubon, writing many of the descriptions in the latter's "Book of Birds." Two of Mrs. CHISOLM's sisters, Maria and Eliza BACHMAN, m. John W. and Victor G. AUDUBON, the sons of the naturalist.

ISSUE BY FIRST MARRIAGE

1. Henry Lewis, b. 16th October, 1828; d. 25th April, 1891; m. 1852, Caroline E. MOODIE, with issue.
2. John Julian, b. 16th April, 1830, for whom see later.
3. Robert George, b. 30th November, 1831; m. Mary GREGG, with issue.
4. Caspar A., b. 16th October, 1833; d. 18th March, 1910; m. 26th September, 1866, Mary Bellinger GREGG, with issue an only son.

ISSUE

1^1. William Gregg, b. 10th January, 1868; d. 4th November, 1901; m. 6th December, 1892, Nannie MILES, dau. of Rev. Wm. Porcher MILES, D.D.
5. Emily Providence, b. 12th November, 1835; m. 1867, Stephen L. HOWARD.
6. Evelyn Z., b. 17th August, 1839; unmarried.

ISSUE BY SECOND MARRIAGE

1. John Bachman, b. 24th October, 1851; m. 5th October, 1882, Octavia DE SAUSSURE, gr. gd. dau. of Hon. Henry Wm. DE SAUSSURE, 1763–1839, Member of South Carolina Convention, 1789, Director of United States Mint, 1795, Mayor of Charleston, 1797–1798, one of founders of South Carolina College, Chancellor and Chief Justice of South Carolina, 1808–1838; with issue.
2. Alfred de Jouve, b. 26th May, 1853; d. 2d May, 1882; unmarried.
3. William Bachman, b. May, 1858; m. (firstly) 1877, Felicia O. HALL; m. (secondly) 1911, Katherine A. REED, with issue.
4. Katherine Prioleau, b. 11th August, 1867; m. 8th September, 1900, Benjamin Deford WEBB.

III. Samuel Prioleau, *m.* (firstly) Martha CHAPLIN, with issue; *m.* (secondly) Mrs. Sarah Porteous (CUTHBERT) DANA; no issue.
IV. Alexander, *d.* young.
V. Elizabeth Prioleau, *m.* Samuel E. CROCKER of Boston; *d.s.p.*
VI. Christina, *d.* unmarried.
VII. Alexander Hext, *d.* 12th March, 1885; had an adopted daughter, Alexina Pauline, who *m.* Count John B. LEONETTI of Florence, Italy.
VIII. William S., *b.* 1821; *d.* 8th April, 1901.
IX. Thomas Hanscome, *d.* young.
X. Providence Hext, *d.* young.
XI. Octavius, *m.* in Ireland, Miss LODGE.
XII. Mary Maria, *m.* Charles EDMONDSTON, Esq., with issue.

GEORGE CHISOLM, *b.* in Charleston, 22d October, 1796; *d.* 31st August, 1837; graduated from South Carolina College, 1814; *m.* 14th January, 1823, Sarah Maynard EDINGS, *b.* 8th May, 1802, *d.* 19th January, 1835, dau. of William and Sarah (EVANS) EDINGS, and a descendant of William EDINGS, Captain of Militia on Edisto Island, and one of the founders of Edisto Presbyterian Church, 1732, and son of William EDINGS, a Scotchman, who came to Carolina in the latter part of the seventeenth century, receiving a large grant of land in the vicinity of Beaufort.

ISSUE

1. William Edings, *b.* 30th December, 1823; *d.* 13th November, 1895; *m.* 23d February, 1848, Mary Ann ROGERS, *b.* 14th September, 1827, *d.* 21st May, 1913, dau. of John ROGERS and his wife Mary Ann C. MUHLENBERG, sister of Rev. William Augustus MUHLENBERG, D.D., LL.D., S. T. D., founder of St. Luke's Hospital, New York, also of St. Johnland, and St. Paul's College, and gd. dau. of Hon. Frederick Augustus MUHLENBERG, 1750–1801, first speaker of United States House of Representatives, 1789.

ISSUE

1. Mary Fredericka, *b.* 10th February, 1851; *m.* 27th April, 1871, Charles Miller SCHIEFFELIN, New York; with issue.
2. Jessie Edings, *b.* 1854; *d.* 1855.
3. John Rogers, *b.* 1856; *d.* 1866.
4. George Edings, *b.* 13th June, 1858; *m.* 18th November, 1890, Edith LAWRENCE, dau. of Henry Effingham and Lydia (UNDERHILL) LAWRENCE, New York; with issue.
5. William Augustus Muhlenberg, *b.* 1862; *d.* 1866.
6. Margaret Willing, *b.* 17th October, 1863; *d.* 5th January, 1904; *m.* 30th April, 1888, James Hooker HAMERSLEY, Esq., *b.* 26th January, 1844, *d.* September, 1901, son of John William and Catherine Livingston (HOOKER) HAMERSLEY, New York; with issue.

7. Benjamin Ogden, *b.* 1st June, 1865; *m.* 12th November, 1888, Elizabeth RHOADES dau. of John Harsen and Anne G. (WHEELWRIGHT) RHOADES, New York, with issue.

II. JAMES JULIUS, *b.* 7th June, 1827; of whom later.
III. George Edings, *b.* 4th June, 1831; *m.* Catherine BRYAN, dau. of Col. John and Eliza (LEGARÉ) BRYAN; with issue.
IV. Mary Edings, *b.* 21st February, 1833; *d.* 29th March, 1888; *m.* 3d February, 1852, her cousin, John Julian CHISOLM, M.D., LL.D. of Baltimore, *b.* 16th April, 1830, son of Robert Trail and Harriet S. CHISOLM, Surgeon, Confederate States of America; Dean of Medical Faculty University of Maryland, 1869–1874; founder of Baltimore Presbyterian Eye, Ear and Throat Hospital; President of Ophthalmology Section, Pan American Medical Congress, 1893; Chairman of Ophthalmology Section, International Medical Congress, 1887; Dr. J. J. Chisolm *m.* (secondly) 14th June, 1894, M. Elizabeth STEELE, of Petersburg, Virginia.

ISSUE

1. Julia, *b.* 18th January, 1854; *d.* 3d July, 1903; *m.* 16th June, 1875, Glover Holmes TRENHOLM, *b.* 5th October, 1849, son of Edward L. and Eliza Bonsall (HOLMES) TRENHOLM of Charleston, South Carolina, and nephew of Hon. George A. TRENHOLM, Secretary of the Treasury, Confederate States of America; with issue.
2. Francis Miles, M.D., *b.* September, 1867; *m.* 29th November, 1890, Lillian Bevan BAUGHER; with issue.
3. Katherine Imogen, *b.* 14th January, 1898.

JAMES JULIUS CHISOLM, *b.* in Charleston, 7th June, 1827; *d.* 23d February, 1862, educated under Rev. William Augustus MUHLENBERG at St. Paul's College, Long Island; lived at "Indian Field," near Beaufort, a part of the original EDINGS' grant, which he inherited from his mother; Captain of Stony Scouts, 1861, a company of volunteers raised on John's Island; *m.* 17th June, 1847, Margaret Swinton BRYAN, *b.* 20th May, 1829, *d.* 24th August, 1860, dau. of Col. John BRYAN, 1791–1848 of "Campvere," Member of South Carolina Legislature, Collector of Port of Charleston and his wife, Eliza Catherine LEGARÉ, sister of Hon. Hugh Swinton LEGARÉ, 1797–1843, Editor of *Southern Review*, Member of Congress, Minister to Belgium, Attorney-General of United States and Secretary of State ad interim under TYLER, and dau. of Solomon LEGARÉ and Mary SWINTON, the gd. dau. of William SWINTON, Surveyor-General of Carolina 1721–1732, and holder of a barony of land in the Colony.

I. Catherine Bryan, *b.* 12th July, 1850.
II. Mary Edings, *b.* 29th December, 1851; *d.* 25th June, 1880; unmarried.

III. Rev. James Julius, D.D., b. 8th December, 1852; A.B., Princeton, 1874; d. 10th August, 1915; m. 4th June, 1885, Mary Virginia TWEED, dau. of Robert TWEED, a Scotchman, and his wife, Virginia SHOEMAKER, of Philadelphia.

ISSUE

1. James Julian, b. 24th December, 1889; A.B., Princeton University, 1911; Phi Beta Kappa; M.D., Johns Hopkins University, 1915.

IV. WILLIAM EDINGS, b. 31st May, 1855, of whom later.
V. Paul Hamilton, b. 4th May, 1858; d. September, 1892; unmarried.

WILLIAM EDINGS CHISOLM, b. in Charleston, 31st May, 1855; d. 12th October, 1903; m. 28th December, 1886, Helen GARNETT, b. 16th May, 1860, dau. of Edgar Malcolm and Emily Dennis (HAYWARD) GARNETT, he son of Muscoe GARNETT, 1786–1869, of "Prospect Hill," Essex County, Virginia, and his wife, Maria BATTAILE, the gd. dau. of Lieut.-Col. Lewis WILLIS, of the 10th Virginia Continental Line, 1776, son of Col. Henry WILLIS and his wife Mildred WASHINGTON, aunt and sponsor of Gen. George WASHINGTON. Muscoe GARNETT was a brother of Hon. James Mercer GARNETT, Member of Virginia Constitutional Convention, 1829, Member of Congress, 1805–1809, and of Hon. Robert Selden GARNETT, Member of Congress, 1817–1827, and the son of Muscoe GARNETT, 1736–1803, of "Mount Pleasant," Member of Essex County Committee of Safety, 1774–1775, and his wife, Grace Fenton MERCER, sister of Hon. John Francis MERCER, Member of Continental Congress, Member Constitutional Convention, 1787, Governor of Maryland, 1801–1803, and of Hon. James MERCER, President of General Court and Judge of Virginia Court of Appeals, gr. gr. gd. dau. of James GARNETT, 1692–1765, Justice of Essex, Member of House of Burgesses and son of John GARNETT, the immigrant, who came to Gloucester County, Virginia, from England in the latter part of the seventeenth century. Through her mother, Emily Dennis HAYWARD, she was descended from many of the early colonists, among them Sir George YEARDLEY, Governor of Virginia, 1618; Col. Nathaniel LITTLETON of His Majesty's Council; Col. Obedience ROBINS, 1600–1662, Chief Magistrate of Northampton County; Capt. Adam THOROUGHGOOD of the Virginia Council, 1639–1640; Capt. Edward WATERS, 1610, and Ensign Thomas SAVAGE, who was the first white settler on the Eastern Shore of Virginia and who came to the Colony with Capt. Christopher NEWPORT in January, 1608.

ISSUE

1. WILLIAM GARNETT, b. 19th November, 1890, the subject of this memoir.

Arms.—Gules a boar's head erased argent.
Crest.—A dexter hand holding a dagger erect ppr. on the point a boar's head couped gules.

Mottoes.—"Vi aut virtute;" over crest "Feros ferio."
Residence.—925 Cathedral Street, Baltimore, Maryland.
Clubs.—Bachelor's Cotillon.
Societies.—Colonial Wars, Sons of the Revolution, American Historical Association, American Red Cross, General Alumni Association, University of Maryland.

Churchill

HERMAN CHURCHILL, of Kingston, Rhode Island; *b.* 9th October, 1869, in the town of Scott, Cortland County, New York; *m.* 15th June, 1898, at Menomonie, Wisconsin, Cora Mae BOYCE, *b.* 26th August, 1876, at Sandy Hill, New York, dau. of Joseph C. and Lydia Ida (LANGDON) BOYCE of Sandy Hill, New York. Joseph C. BOYCE, *b.* January, 1852, Poultney, Vermont; *d.* 3d April, 1910, Bolton, New York. Lydia Ida LANGDON, *b.* at Kingsbury, New York, 23d October, 1853; *m.* 22d December, 1872, at Sandy Hill, New York.

ISSUE

I. Irving Lester, *b.* 9th April, 1901, at Madison, Wisconsin.
II. Florence Hermia, *b.* 16th April, 1905, at Cortland, New York.
III. Arthur Chester, *b.* 29th December, 1911, at University Place, Nebraska.

HERMAN CHURCHILL, A.B., Syracuse University, 1894; A.M., University of Wisconsin, 1902; Instructor English Department, Northwestern University, 1903–1907; Head of Department of English, Southwestern College, 1907–1909; and of Nebraska Wesleyan University, 1909–1912; Department of Rhetoric and Composition, Rhode Island State College, since 1912.

Lineage

JOSIAH CHURCHILL, *b.* in England, circa 1615; his will was executed 17th November, 1683; *d.* before January, 1687. We hear of him first in Wethersfield, Connecticut, prior to 1640; he was a gentleman of more than medium estate for the time in which he lived, and of reputation in the Colony; was a juror of the Particular Court, 1643, 1649 and 1651; at the Quarter Court 1664–1665, and at the County Court 1666–1670 and 1675; served in the Wethersfield Company of Troops in the Pequot War; was Constable in 1657 and 1670, and was elected one of the two Town Surveyors in 1666 and 1673; *m.* circa 1638, Elizabeth FOOTE, *b.* circa 1616, and *d.* 8th September, 1700, at Wethersfield, dau. of Nathaniel FOOTE of Wethersfield, who came from Shalford, in Colchester, England: and settled in Watertown, Massachusetts, and became one of the first settlers of Wethersfield; he was deputy to the General Court of Connecticut, 1641–1644.

ISSUE

I. Mary, *b.* 24th March, 1639; *d.* 1690; *m.* Samuel Church who. *d.* 13th April, 1684.
II. Elizabeth, *b.* 15th May, 1642; *m.* Henry BUCK, of Wethersfield.
III. Hannah, *b.* 1st November, 1644; *d.s.p.*; *m.* January, 1667, Samuel ROYCE.

IV. Ann, b. 1647; m. ——— RICE.
V. JOSEPH, b. 7th December, 1649, of whom later.
VI. Benjamin, Lieutenant; b. 16th May, 1652; m. Mary, surname unknown.
VII. A son, d. in infancy.
VIII. Sarah, b. 11th November, 1657; m. ———WICKHAM.

JOSEPH CHURCHILL, husbandman, of Wethersfield, Connecticut; b. there 7th December, 1649; d. 1st April, 1699; Town Surveyor, Constable, Assessor, Selectman; was designated on the town records as Sergt. Joseph CHURCHILL; m. 13th May, 1674, Mary, surname not given.

ISSUE

I. Mary, b. 6th April, 1675; m. April, 1699, Josiah EDWARDS.
II. Nathaniel, b. 9th July, 1677; m. Mary HURLBUT.
III. Elizabeth, b. 1679; m. Richard BUTLER.
IV. Dinah, b. 1680; m. 23d November, 1709, Jacob DEMING.
V. SAMUEL, b. 1688, of whom later.
VI. Joseph, b. 1690; m. 12th January, 1714, Lydia DICKERMAN.
VII. David, b. 1692; m. Dorothy, surname unknown.
VIII. Jonathan, b. 1692; m. Mrs. Sarah DEMING.
IX. Hannah, b. 1696; d. unmarried.

ENSIGN SAMUEL CHURCHILL of Newington Parish, Connecticut, b. 1688, Wethersfield; d. 21st July, 1769; appointed Ensign, 1746, of the local military company by the General Assembly; m. 26th June, 1717, Martha BOARDMAN, b. 19th December, 1695, d. 14th December, 1780, dau. of Daniel and Hannah (WRIGHT) BOARDMAN and gd. dau. of Samuel Boardman of Clydon, England, one of the first settlers of Wethersfield.

ISSUE

I. Giles, b. 11th June, 1718; m. and settled in Stamford, New York.
II. SAMUEL, b. 27th April, 1721, of whom later.
III. Captain Charles, b. 31st December, 1723; m. 19th November, 1747, Lydia BELDEN.
IV. Jesse, b. 31st August, 1726; m. (firstly) 8th November, 1750, Jerusha GAYLORD; m. (secondly) 29th November, 1769, Sarah (BOARDMAN) CADY, widow; m. (thirdly) 15th June, 1778, Elizabeth BELDEN, widow.
V. Benjamin, b. 10th April, 1729; m. (firstly) 19th April, 1753, Abigail BARNES; m. (secondly) Hulda BEECHER.
VI. William, b. 6th November, 1732; m. (firstly) 25th September, 1760, Ruth TRYON; m. (secondly) Abiah WILDMAN.

SAMUEL CHURCHILL of Hubbardton, Vermont; b. 27th April, 1721, in Wethersfield; d. at Hubbardton, Vermont, about 1800; m. 1747, in Sheffield, Massachusetts, Thankful (HEWIT) SEAGER, widow of Joseph Seager of Newington. In the French and Indian War was a volunteer in 1757 and went to the relief of Fort Edward, New York (for authority see H. R. Stiles, "History of Ancient Wethersfield," Vol. II, part 1, page 233, appendix); was taken prisoner in battle of Hubbardton in Revolutionary War and was taken to Fort Ticonderoga, from which he later made his escape.

ISSUE

I. Martha, *b.* 14th January, 1748; *m.* Abigail WEBSTER.
II. Joseph, *b.* 14th February, 1750; *d.* 20th March, 1821; served in Revolutionary War; *m.* 7th December, 1773, Amy STYLES, *b.* 23d March, 1755.
III. Lydia, *b.* 1st June, 1751; *m.* Abner ASHLEY.
IV. Lois, *b.* 30th May, 1753; *m.* David BALDWIN, New Marlborough, Massachusetts.
V. Thankful, *b.* 7th March, 1755; *d.* unmarried, at a great age.
VI. Samuel, *b.* 20th May, 1756; *d.* 1797; *m.* Anna CAMP.
VII. JOHN, *b.* 12th March, 1758, of whom later.
VIII. Silas, *b.* 18th June, 1760; *m.* Elizabeth CULVER.
IX. William, *b.* 10th February, 1763; was in the battle of Hubbardton; *m.* 26th March, 1787, Eunice CULVER, *b.* 31st December, 1762.
X. Ezekiel, *b.* 24th June, 1764; *d.* 12th February, 1813; *m.* 1786, Elizabeth DYER, *b.* 30th August, 1766, *d.* 25th October, 1843.

JOHN CHURCHILL, of Tully, New York, *b.* 12th March, 1758, in Sheffield, Massachusetts; *d.* 27th September, 1817, in town of Scott, New York; was in the battle of Hubbardton, 7th July, 1775; taken prisoner and carried to Ticonderoga, where he was kept until the following October; served later in the war in Col. Heman SWIFT's Regiment of Connecticut; *m.* 29th May, 1786, Martha BALDWIN, who was the daů. of Jehiel, *b.* 21st June, 1716, at Milford, Connecticut, and Bridget (GOODWIN) BALDWIN and was born in Meriden Parish, Massachusetts, 16th August, 1766, *d.* town of Scott, New York, 13th February, 1839.

ISSUE

I. John, *b.* 13th April, 1787; *d.* 27th September, 1817; *m.* 1813, Mary HOUSE; lived in Portland, Chautauqua County, New York.
II. Sylvester, *b.* 7th October, 1788; *d.* 3d November, 1829; *m.* January, 1816, Theodosia HOUSE, dau. of Deacon John HOUSE, lived at Portland, Chautauqua County, New York.
III. Anice, *b.* 14th October, 1790; *m.* Chester SHARP; family moved to Michigan.
IV. Electa, *b.* 19th December, 1792; *m.* Clark TOWN; family moved to Ohio.
V. Alvin, *b.* 7th November, 1794; *d.* 26th March, 1878; *m.* Sally SEELEY of the Town of Spafford, New York.
VI. Sylvina, *b.* 25th August, 1796; *d.* 14th October, 1797.
VII. Joab, *b.* 10th November, 1798; *d.* 24th November, 1816.

VIII. Sarah, *b.* 4th January, 1801; *d.* 26th May, 1890; *m.* 15th November, 1825, John BACON of Spafford, New York, *b.* August, 1800, *d.* 22d April, 1844, son of Amos and Abigail (CADY) BACON.
IX. Irena, *b.* 8th October, 1802; *d.* 8th May, 1881; *m.* Lucius VAIL, of Spafford, New York.
X. Jotham, *b.* 29th December, 1804; *m.* ———— RANDALL; family moved to Iowa.
XI. CHAUNCEY, *b.* 3d October, 1808, of whom below.

CHAUNCEY CHURCHILL, of East Scott Cortland County, New York; *b.* 3d October, 1808, at Tully, New York; *d.* 18th February, 1896; *m.* 17th March, 1834, Catharine MERRY, *b.* 9th May, 1812, *d.* 23d May, 1865, dau. of John and Clarinda (DAVIS) MERRY of Minaville, Montgomery County, New York. John MERRY was born 5th November, 1785; *d.* 22d November, 1844, son of Benjamin and Mary MERRY. Clarinda (DAVIS) MERRY was born 24th April, 1790; *d.* 23d November 1847; *m.* 24th October, 1808.

ISSUE

I. Sylvester, *b.* 20th December, 1834; still living, 1916, town of Scott, New York; *m.* 28th March, 1866, Helen DOWD, dau. of Richard DOWD.
II. John Wesley, *b.* 13th August, 1836; *d.* 3d September, 1910; *m.* (firstly) 13th April, 1871, Alice P. MARTINIE, *d.* 1st August, 1886, dau. of David and Mary (TRIPLET) MARTINIE; *m.* (secondly) March, 1890, Catherine WATSON, lived in Champaign County, Illinois.
III. Olive C., *b.* 16th February, 1838; *d.* 11th May, 1838.
IV. SYLVANUS AMOS, *b.* 26th November, 1839, of whom later.
V. Oliver Clinton, *b.* 22d March, 1841; *d.* 28th February, 1905, Homer, New York; *m.* 26th October, 1865, Delphine ROE, dau. of John ROE.
VI. Martha Asenath, *b.* 24th November, 1842; *d.* 12th December, 1893, Champaign County, Illinois; *m.* 8th November 1871, James SHAWHAN.
VII. Olive Clarinda, *b.* 6th August, 1844; *d.* 1875; *m.* 10th November, 1864, William S. KELLOGG, of Homer, New York.
VIII. La Fayette Marion, *b.* 17th March, 1846; *m.* 9th March, 1870, Eliza PRATT, dau. of Orrin and Ruth E. (CAPRON) PRATT, lives in Michigan.
IX. Chloe Irene, *b.* 4th October, 1847; lives in New York City; *m.* 18th November, 1869, William A. KELLOGG, son of Cyrus and Amanda (SALISBURY) KELLOGG.
X. Catharine Helen, *b.* 10th April, 1849; *m.* 28th March, 1871, George BURROUGHS, son of John BURROUGHS, lived in Cortland County, New York.
XI. Caleb Washington, *b.* 27th November, 1850; *m.* (firstly) 28th March, 1881, Achsah EADIE, *b.* 16th February, 1844, *d.* 11th August, 1882, dau. of John and Abigail (DOTY) EADIE; *m.* (secondly) 6th November, 1884, Minnie BROWN, lives in Cortland County, New York.

XII. Benjamin Franklin, *b*. 30th July, 1852; *d*. 4th October, 1910; *m*. 21st November, 1878, Carrie CHURCHILL, *b*. 25th July, 1856, dau. of James CHURCHILL and Chloe (CARR) CHURCHILL, who were *m*. 7th February, 1854.

XIII. Jason Merry, *b*. 2d April, 1855; *d*. August, 1911; *m*. 25th September, 1878, Jennie E. FRENCH, dau. of Jason C. and Emily (RICE) FRENCH.

SYLVANUS AMOS CHURCHILL, farmer, of East Scott, New York; *b*. 26th November, 1839, at Scott, New York; educated in common schools and the academy at Homer, New York; taught many terms in the public schools of central New York; *m*. (firstly), 22d November, 1867, Caroline EADIE, *b*. 16th December, 1844, *d*. 2d September, 1888, dau. of John *b*. February, 1816, *d*. 20th October, 1873, and Abigail (DOTY) EADIE; *m*. (secondly) 7th September, 1892, Sarah Erminie WOODWORTH, *b*. 12th August, 1865, dau. of Joel Cyrenus, *b*. 1st August, 1838, *d*. 27th June, 1902, and Charlotte (NORTON) WOODWORTH.

ISSUE BY FIRST MARRIAGE

I. HERMAN, *b*. 9th October, 1869, the subject of this memoir.
II. Edith (twin), *b*. 20th August, 1875, Onondaga Valley, New York.
III. Eadie (twin), *b*. 20th August, 1875; *m*. 4th December, 1902, May Sarah CROSLEY, of Homer, New York, dau. of Fred. CROSLEY and Emeline (COTRELL) CROSLEY.

ISSUE

1. Doris May, *b*. 5th October, 1903; *d*. 12th March, 1916.
2. Muriel Jean, *b*. 1st October, 1905.

ISSUE BY SECOND MARRIAGE

I. Sylvanus Woodworth, *b*. 14th July, 1894.
II. Leo, *b*. 29th April, 1896.
III. Gladys Erminie, *b*. 8th May, 1902.

Arms (Foote).—Argent a chevron sable on the dexter chief a trefoil slipped.
Crest.—An oak tree ppr.
Motto.—Loyalty and Truth.
Residence.—Kingston, Rhode Island.
Societies.—Colonial Wars, Mayflower Descendants, Sons of American Revolution, Phi Beta Kappa and Beta Theta Pi, Syracuse Chapter; Charter Member Phi Kappa Phi, Rhode Island Chapter.

Claiborne

JOHN HERBERT CLAIBORNE, M.D., of New York City; *b.* at Louisbourg, North Carolina, 29th June, 1861; *m.* 16th April, 1901, Marie Louise CLAIBORNE, dau. of Maj. William Charles Cole CLAIBORNE of New Orleans and his wife, Jeanne ROBLOT:

ISSUE

I. John Herbert, *b.* 1st July, 1902.

JOHN HERBERT CLAIBORNE graduated at the University of Virginia, M.D., 1883; volunteered for Spanish American War and passed through grades of the Line, Second Lieutenant, First Lieutenant, Regimental Adjutant and Captain of a Company; securing honorable discharge 15th October, 1898. Author of numerous papers on the subject of eye diseases; editor of several medical journals; author of "The Theory and Practice of the Ophthalmoscope," "The Functional Examination of the Eyes," "Cataract Extraction," "Three Months' Experience at Camp Thomas, Georgia," etc.

Lineage

EDMUND CLIBURNE, *b.* 1544; *d.* 1590, at Cliburne Hall, County, Westmoreland and Killerby, County York; Administration granted at York, 22d September, 1590, son of Richard CLIBURNE, of Killerby and descended from Bardolph, Lord of Ravensworth and other manors in Richmondshire. Bardolph is of the family of the Earls of Richmond (Gale's "Honorisde Richmond" and Whittaker's "Richmondshire"). This Bardolph was seventh son of Eudo, who was second son of Geoffrey, Duke of Brittany, whose wife was Aricia, sister of Richard, Duke of Normandy (see O'Hart's "Irish Peerages," p. 100, Dabbin, 1888). The first son of Geoffrey was Alan and Bardolph had among others two brothers, named Alan, viz., Alan Niger and Alan Rufus, hence the name Alan dictus Claiborne. The first Claiborne who resided at Cliburn, Westmoreland was Alan dictus Cleburne, he was third son of Hervey Fitz Akaris (1165– o.b. 1182) who was son of Akaris (1140), who was the son of said Bardolph (Le Nave, MSS. III, 114). Edmund CLIBORNE, through Elizabeth CURWEN, who *m.* John, son of Rowland CLIBORNE, dau. of Sir Thomas CURWEN of Workington Hill, was descended from Cospatrick "The Great," Maldred and Elgiva, dau. of Ethelred the "Unready" (Jacksons, Curwens of Workington, Symeon of Durham II, 307; Freeman's "Norman Conquest," IV, 98). Edmund CLIBORNE matriculated at Queen's College, Oxford, 1572, and *m.* September, 1576, Grace BELLINGHAM, dau. of Sir Alan BELLINGHAM of Helsington and Levins, Treasurer of Berwick and Deputy Warden of the Marches.

ISSUE

I. Thomas, *m.* Agnes LOWTHER, dau. of Sir Richard LOWTHER, of Lowther, had issue.
II. WILLIAM, *b.* 1587, of whom later.
III. Robert.

COLONEL WILLIAM CLAIBORNE of Romancoke, Virginia; *b.* 1587; *d.* 1676; engaged by the Virginia Company as Surveyor, 1621; arrived in Virginia with Governor WYATT in 1621; appointed by Governor YEARDLEY, Secretary of State for the Colony, and Member of the Council, 1625-1637; Treasurer of Virginia, 6th April, 1642; *m.* (in London, 1638, it is said, Jane BULLER, but 11th June, 1644, a grant of land in Elizabeth City County was made to Elizabeth CLAIBORNE, the wife of Capt. William CLAIBORNE, Esq., his Majestie's Treasurer of this Colony of Virginia).

ISSUE

I. William, Lieutenant-Colonel, of King William County, New Kent, 1663, 1666; in 1676, appointed with Maj. George LYDELL to command the fort at Indiantown, New Kent; *m.* probably Elizabeth, surname unknown.

ISSUE

1. William
2. Ursula, *m.* William GOOCH.
3. Mary.

II. THOMAS, *b.* 17th August, 1647, of whom later.
III. Leonard, settled in Jamaica, West Indies; *d.* 1694; *m.* Martha, surname unknown.

ISSUE

1. Katherine, *m.* Hon. John CAMPBELL, of Inverary, Scotland.
2. Elizabeth.

IV. Jane, *d.* before 20th May, 1671; *m.* Col. Thomas BRERETON, of Northumberland County.

LIEUTENANT-COLONEL THOMAS CLAIBORNE, *b.* 17th August, 1647, of King William County; killed by the Indians, 7th October, 1683, and buried at tomb near Smokers King, King William County, Virginia, aged 36 years; *m.* Sarah DANDRIDGE; who *m.* (secondly) Thomas BRAY of New Kent.

ISSUE

I. THOMAS, *b.* 16th December, 1680, of whom below.

CAPTAIN THOMAS CLAIBORNE of Sweet Hall, King William County, Virginia; *b.* 16th December, 1680; *d.* 16th August, 1732; said to have been married three times and to have had twenty-seven children, but this is doubtful; on his monument he is described as "Captain;" *m.* as his last wife, Ann Fox, *b.* 20th May, 1684, *d.* 4th May, 1733, dau. of Henry Fox, and Anne West, she the dau. of Col. John West.

ISSUE BY THIRD MARRIAGE

I. Thomas, *b.* 9th January, 1704; *d.* 1st December, 1735; Clerk of Stafford County.
II. William, of Romancocke, whose will was proved 16th June, 1745; *m.* Mary, probably a dau. of Col. Philip Whitehead.
III. Nathaniel, Colonel, of Sweet Hall; *b.* 1755; *m.* Jane Cole, dau. of William Cole; had issue.
IV. Leonard, Sheriff of King William County, 1732; Member of the House of Burgesses, 1736; is said to have moved to Georgia; *m.* Martha Burnell, *d.* 3d April, 1720, aged 19 years, 3 months and 2 days, dau. of Maj. Francis Burnell.
V. Bernard, *m.* Martha (Ravenscroft) Poythress, widow of Maj. William Poythress.
VI. Augustine, *b.* 1721, of whom below.

Colonel Augustine Claiborne, of "Windsor," *b.* at Sweet Hall, 1721; *d.* 3d May, 1787; removed to Surrey County; Member of the House of Burgesses, 1748–1754; Clerk of Sussex County, 1754; Member of State Senate, 1780; *m.* Mary Herbert, dau. of Buller Herbert of Puddlecock, Dinwiddie County.

ISSUE

I. Mary, *b.* 1745; *m.* 1763, Gen. Charles Harrison; had issue.
II. Herbert, of "Chestnut Grove," New Kent; *b.* 7th April, 1746; *m.* (firstly) Mary Ruffin, dau. of Robert Ruffin, of "Sweet Hall;" *m.* (secondly) Mary Browne, dau. of William Burnett Browne, of "Elsing Green," King William County, *b.* 7th October, 1738, at Salem, Massachusetts, *d.* 6th May, 1784, at his seat in Virginia, his wife was a dau. of Governor Burnett of New York.
III. Augustine, *b.* 2d February, 1748; *d.* 1796; *m.* Martha Jones, dau. of Frederick Jones of Dinwiddie; had issue.
IV. Colonel Thomas, *b.* 1749; Sheriff of Brunswick, 1789; Member of Congress, 1793–1805; *m.* ———— Scott, dau. of ———— Scott, a native of Nova Scotia.
V. Anne, *b.* 30th December, 1749; *m.* 19th November, 1768, Col. Richard Cocke; had issue.
VI. Susanna, *b.* 29th November, 1751; *m.* Frederick Jones of Dinwiddie County; had issue.
VII. William, *b.* 2d November, 1753; *m.* dau. of Robert Ruffin; had issue.
VIII. Buller, *b.* 27th October, 1755; Major in the Revolutionary War and Aide de Camp to General Lincoln; Commanded a Squadron of Cavalry at

the defeat of TARLETON at Cowpens; Justice of the Peace for Dinwiddie County, 1789; Sheriff, 1802–1804; *m.* Patsy RUFFIN, dau. of Edward RUFFIN of Sussex County; had issue.

IX. Richard, *b.* 1757; *d.* 1818; Major Continental Army; Member of the House of Delegates from Brunswick, 1775–1778; *m.* Miss HAYWARD, of South Carolina; had issue.

X. Lucy Herbert, *b.* 22d August, 1760; *m.* Col. John COCKE; had issue.

XI. Elizabeth, *b.* 1761; *m.* Thomas PETERSON; had issue.

XII. JOHN HERBERT, *b.* 3d May, 1763, of whom later.

XIII. Sarah, *b.* 1765. *m.* Charles ANDERSON of Virginia, and had issue.

JOHN HERBERT CLAIBORNE *b.* 3d May, 1763; *m.* Mary GREGORY, dau. of Roger GREGORY of Chesterfield, Virginia.

ISSUE

I. JOHN GREGORY, *b.* 1798, of whom later.
II. Maria, *m.* John D. WILKINS.
III. Martha Jane, *m.* Nicholas LEWIS.

JOHN GREGORY CLAIBORNE of Roslin, Virginia; *b.* 1798; *m.* Mary E. WELDON.

ISSUE

I. JOHN HERBERT, *b.* 16th March, 1828, of whom later.
II. Weldon, *d.s.p.*
III. Anna Augusta; *m.* Gabriel THOMAS.

JOHN HERBERT CLAIBORNE, *b.* 16th March, 1828; *d.* 24th February, 1905; graduated at the University of Virginia, 1849; Jefferson Medical College, 1850; settled in Petersburg, Virginia, 1851; Member of Virginia Senate, 1857; Surgeon and Major in the Confederate States Army during the Civil War; *m.* (firstly) Sarah Joseph ALSTON, *d.* 2d February, 1869, dau. of Joseph John ALSTON, of Halifax, North Carolina and Louisa Dandridge THOMAS, of Louisburg, North Carolina; *m.* (secondly) Annie Leslie WATSON, 1887.

ISSUE BY FIRST MARRIAGE

I. Mary Louisa, *b.* 16th August, 1855, at Petersburg, Virginia; *d.* 29th June, 1902; *m.* 8th June, 1876, Herbert H. PAGE, of Edenton, North Carolina, and "Pagebrook," Clarke County, Virginia.

ISSUE

1. Herbert Claiborne PAGE, Lieutenant, in Constabulary Philippine Islands.
2. Byrd Alston PAGE, Lieutenant, United States Army, resigned.
3. Weldon Bathurst PAGE, United States Army.

COLONIAL FAMILIES OF THE UNITED STATES 155

4. Matthew PAGE, United States Army.
5. Randolph Rosewell PAGE.

II. Anne Augusta, *b.* 21st February, 1858, in Petersburg, Virginia; *m.* December, 1877, Dr. Philip Howell LIGHTFOOT, *d.* 1881, son of John Bernard LIGHTFOOT of Port Royal, Caroline County, Virginia, and his wife, Harriet FIELD; *m.* (secondly) 1895, Charles Albert ENGLISH; no issue by second marriage.

ISSUE BY FIRST MARRIAGE

1. Herbert Claiborne LIGHTFOOT, *m.* 8th June, 1904, Mary Waller MERCER of Williamsburg, Virginia; no issue.
2. Philip Howell LIGHTFOOT, *m.* 1909, Helen Bertha QUILLIAN, of English parentage.

ISSUE

1^1, Anne Claiborne LIGHTFOOT.
2^1. Philip Howell LIGHTFOOT.
3^1. Helen Bernard LIGHTFOOT.

IV. JOHN HERBERT, *b.* 29th June, 1861, the subject of this memoir.
V. Elizabeth Weldon, *b.* 14th January, 1867, in Petersburg, Virginia; *m.* there 24th of February, 1886, Bernard MANN, son of John and Catharine Frances (BERNARD) MANN.

ISSUE

1. Elizabeth Weldon Claiborne MANN, *b.* 28th October, 1887; *m.* 27th June, 1911, Lewis Parke CHAMBERLAYNE.

ISSUE

1^1. Mary Gibson CHAMBERLAYNE.
2^1. Elizabeth Claiborne Mann CHAMBERLAYNE.

2. Catharine Frances Bernard MANN, *b.* 21st March, 1891.
3. David Meade Bernard MANN, *b.* 28th October, 1893.
4. John Herbert Claiborne MANN, *b.* 22d August, 1900.

III. Sarah Joseph Alston, *b.* 25th October, 1859; *m.* 28th December, 1882, William Baird McILWAINE of Petersburg; *b.* 4th October, 1854, son of Robert Dunn and Lucy Atkinson (PRYOR) McILWAINE of Petersburg, Virginia; Member of Virginia Society Colonial Dames, Daughters of American Revolution, United Daughters of the Confederacy, Ladies Memorial Association of Petersburg, Virginia.

ISSUE

1. Joseph Alston Claiborne McILWAINE, *b.* 26th September, 1880; *m.* 7th February, 1912, Miss Edgar Simeon BOWLING.

ISSUE

1¹. Josephine Claiborne McIlwaine BOWLING, *b.* 13th November, 1912.

2. William Baird McILWAINE, Jr., *b.* 6th February, 1885; *m.* 5th October, 1910, Isabella Louisa MARTIN.

ISSUE

1¹. William Baird, *b.* 15th August, 1911.
2¹. Isabella Martin, *b.* 12th December, 1912.

3. Lucy Atkinson McILWAINE, *b.* 13th September, 1886.
4. Anne Claiborne McILWAINE, *b.* 11th September, 1889; *m.* 15th June, 1910, William Taliaferro THOMPSON.

ISSUE

1¹. Julia Elizabeth Adams THOMPSON, *b.* 25th July, 1911.
2¹. William Taliaferro THOMPSON, III (twin), *b.* 26th May, 1913.
3¹. William McIlwaine THOMPSON (twin), *b.* 26th May, 1913.

5. Hibernia McILWAINE, *b.* 2d April, 1891; *d.* in infancy.
6. Elizabeth Herbert McILWAINE, *b.* 3d March, 1897; *d.* in infancy.

ISSUE BY SECOND MARRIAGE

I. Robert Watson, *b.* December, 1888; unmarried; residence, Union Street, Petersburg, Virginia.
II. Donald Fraser, (dau.) *b.* November, 1890; *m.* 10th June, 1915, Stephen West HOLDEN of Petersburg, Virginia.

Arms.—Quarterly, first and fourth argent, three chevronels interlaced in base sable, a chief of the last, second and third argent a cross engrailed vert.

Crest.—A demi-wolf rampant reguardant proper.

Motto.—Lofe Clibbor na Sceame.

Residence.—17 West 11th Street, New York City.

Clubs.—Union, University, Calumet, Rockaway Hunting Club.

Societies.—Cincinnati, Colonial Wars, Foreign Wars, Naval and Military Order of Spanish American Wars, Uniformed Detachment of the War of 1812 (veteran corps of artillery), Sons of Confederate Veterans, United Military Order of America. Member of American Medical Association, American Ophthalmological Society, American Academy of Ophthalmology, New York County and State Medical Society, New York Academy of Medicine, Medical Society of Virginia, Fellow American College of Surgeons, Associate ex-Member of Squadron A, National Guard of New York.

Clark

ORLANDO ELMER CLARK, B.S., A.M., of Appleton, Wisconsin; *b.* 9th November, 1850, in Darien, Genessee County, New York; *m.* 5th December, 1883, in Appleton, Wisconsin, Leda Amanda BALLARD, *b.* 6th October, 1854, dau. of Anson BALLARD, of Appleton, Wisconsin, *b* 20th December, 1821, *d.* 4th April, 1893, *m.* 1st May, 1851, Harriet STORY.

ISSUE

I. Tilden Ballard, *b.* 31st December, 1885; *m.* 29th August, 1912, Alice CUMMINGS, dau. of James CUMMINGS.

ISSUE

1. Alice M., *b.* 30th June, 1914.
2. John Cummings, *b.* 23d March, 1916.

ORLANDO ELMER CLARK graduated B.S. at Rochester University, 1876; Law Student, Batavia, New York, 1876–1877; admitted to the Bar at Green Bay, Wisconsin, 1st February, 1878; to United States Circuit Court, Milwaukee, 15th September, 1898; United States Court of Appeals, Chicago, 3d March, 1899; United States Supreme Court, Washington, 23d October, 1914; Regent of University of Wisconsin since 3d February, 1892; on Board of Commissioners for Erection of Wisconsin State Historical Library Building, 1897–1901; A.M., Rochester University, 1907.

Lineage

JOHN CLARK from the Parish of Great Munden, Hertfordshire, England; *b.* 1608, Chelmsford (?), England; *d.* Milford, Connecticut, 1672–1673; was of Newtown, now Cambridge, Massachusetts, 1629; in 1635 one of Rev. Thomas HOOKER'S Company of 100 that founded the town, now City of Hartford, Connecticut; was of Saybrook, Connecticut, 1647–1669; was one of the petitioners to Charles II for Charter and one of the nineteen patentees named therein when granted 23d April, 1662; was one of the forty-two men to whom land was granted for service in the Pequot War from Hartford, in Soldiers' Field. This was the first bounty paid to American soldiers for service in war (see "Hartford in History," p. 33). He took the Freeman's Oath at General Court at Newtown, Massachusetts, 6th November, 1632; he was First Secretary of Connecticut under the Charter of 1662, and was re-elected 11th May, 1665 (see Dwight's "History of Connecticut," pp. 153–163). His will, one of the notable ones of the Colony of Connecticut, is printed in full in the "Pratt Genealogy," p. 340; from the Probate Records of New Haven, Vol. I, pt. 2, p. 50; *m.* (firstly) Mary COLEY; *m.* (secondly) Mary (WARD) FLETCHER, dau. of Joyce WARD and widow of John FLETCHER of Milford.

ISSUE

I. JOHN, of whom later.
II. John, d. 1663, lost at sea.
III. Elizabeth, m. (firstly) William PRATT of Hartford, 1637, d. 17th October, 1678; m. (secondly) William PARKER.
IV. Sarah, m. Simon HUNTINGTON, October, 1653; d. 1721.

JOHN CLARK of Saybrook, Connecticut; b. 2d February, 1644; killed by upsetting of a cart, 21st September, 1677; m. 16th October, 1650, Rebecca PARKER, d. 9th January, 1683; she m. (secondly) Thomas SPENCER.

ISSUE

I. Rebecca, b. 26th January, 1653; d. 1704; m. 1674, Abram WATROUS.
II. JOHN, b. 17th November, 1655, of whom later.
III. James, b. 29th September, 1657; d. August, 1659.
IV. Samuel, b. 25th April, 1675; d. 1750; m. 14th December, 1699, Mary KIRTLAND.

MAJOR JOHN CLARK, of Saybrook, Connecticut; b. 17th November, 1655; d. 1736; was Lieutenant of Saybrook Fort; nominated and appointed by the General Court of Connecticut and commissioned by Robert TREAT, Governor of Connecticut, 9th February, 1693–1694; accepted to be Lieutenant of Train Band of Saybrook by General Assembly of Connecticut and commissioned by Governor John WINTHROP of Connecticut, 1699; accepted to be Captain of Saybrook Fort by the Connecticut Assembly and commissioned by Governor John WINTHROP 1702; afterward commissioned Major of Train Band of Saybrook and as such commanded the troops to protect the Library of Yale College in its removal from Saybrook to New Haven in 1718 by order of Governor Guerdon SALTONSTALL, dated 4th December, 1718; the original commissions of Lieutenant and Captain and the order for the removal of the Library are now in the possession of Mr. Orlando Elmer CLARK; m. 16th December, 1684, Rebecca BEAUMONT, dau. of William BEAUMONT.

ISSUE

I. Abigail, b. 23d September, 1685; d. 6th February, 1688.
II. Rebecca, b. 26th May, 1687; d. 10th January, 1716; m. 4th April, 1710. Samuel LYNDE.
III. John, b. 21st June, 1689; d. 16th December, 1777; m. (firstly) Sarah JONES; m. (secondly) Phoebe NOTT.
IV. Joseph, b. 23d January, 1692; d. 21st August, 1772; m. 25th September, 1772, Lydia GRENELL.
V. NATHANIEL, b. 19th July, 1694, of whom later.
VI. Temperance, b. 1698.
VII. Samuel, b. 26th June, 1702; m. Mary MINOR.

NATHANIEL CLARK of Saybrook and Essex, Connecticut; *b.* 19th July, 1694; *d.* 21st August, 1772; *m.* Mary VRENNE, *b.* 1690 (?), *d.* 30th December, 1754, dau. of ———— VRENNE, a Huguenot of Norwich, Connecticut. Nathaniel CLARK was one of the first fifty-five graduates of Yale, while it was located at Saybrook; he was ten times deputy to General Assembly, 1733-1743.

ISSUE

I. JOHN, *b.* 30th January, 1719, of whom later.
II. Nathaniel, *b.* 23d December, 1716.
III. William, Lieut., *b.* 1725; *d.* 16th September, 1803; *m.* (firstly) Jane TURNER; *m.* (secondly) Naomi CARTER.
IV. Peter, *b.* 14th November, 1723; *d.* 8th May, 1814; *m.* Thankful PRATT, *d.* 11th March, 1813.
V. Andrew, *b.* 17th July, 1721; *d.* 9th May, 1799.
VI. Christopher, *b.* 1736; *d.* 22d February, 1820; *m.* Penniah NOTT, *b.* 5th June, 1743, *d.* 27th May, 1834, dau. of John NOTT.
VII. George, *b.* 1729; *d.* 7th July, 1789; *m.* Bethsheba PRATT.
VIII. Beaumont, *b.* 1739; *d.* 10th September, 1827; *m.* Hannah BULL.
IX. Annah, *d.* 20th June, 1781; *m.* (firstly) Daniel CLARK; *m.* (secondly) Stephen ATWATER of Cheshire, Connecticut.

LIEUTENANT JOHN CLARK, of Saybrook, Connecticut; *b.* 30th January, 1719; *m.* (firstly) Elizabeth WILLIAMS; *m.* (secondly) Mary PRATT.

ISSUE

I. PAUL, *b.* 29th August, 1750, of whom later.
II. Nathaniel, *d.* April, 1827; *m.* Sarah JONES.
III. Elizabeth, *m.* Joseph SPENCER.
IV. Hester, *d.* 20th May, 1820; *m.* Benajah PRATT.
V. Phoebe, *m.* Thomas RATHBONE.
VI. John, *d.* unmarried.
VII. Mary, *m.* ———— JONES.

PAUL CLARK of Essex, Connecticut; *b.* 29th August, 1750; *d.* 1st March, 1804 *m.* Sarah WHEELER, *b.* 28th March, 1774, *d.* 14th August, 1827.

ISSUE

I. Jesse, *b.* 5th May, 1777; *d.* 17th December, 1853; *m.* Lydia MALLORY, *d.* 11th December, 1849.
II. EZRA, *b.* 8th March, 1783, of whom later.
III. Sarah, *b.* 29th August, 1775; *d.* 3d March, 1842; *m.* Ephraim STANNARD,
IV. Asa, *b.* 12th January, 1779.
V. Betsy, *b.* 4th April, 1783; *d.* October, 1835, unmarried.
VI. Irene, *b.* 17th March, 1785; *d.* 30th November, 1835; *m.* Joseph DENNISON.

vii. Elizabeth, *b.* 5th June, 1787; *d.* 5th May, 1852; *m.* Ezra SPENCER.
viii. John, *b.* 5th June, 1787; *d.* at sea; unmarried.
ix. Benjamin, *b.* 5th October, 1789; *d.* 16th April, 1828; Polly DEWOLF.
x. Ada, *b.* 5th February, 1793; *d.* 7th July, 1856; *m.* Job STANNARD.

EZRA CLARK, of Saybrook, Connecticut, and Darien, New York; *b.* 8th March, 1783; *d.* 17th October, 1832; *m.* 12th March, 1812, Cinderilla CARTER, *b.* 13th March, 1796, *d.* 1st January, 1879, dau. of Barzillai CARTER, and Mary CRARY.

ISSUE

i. Sarah, *b.* 10th July, 1814; *d.* 1899; *m.* (firstly) Alfred BEBE; *m.* (secondly) Isaac DUMONT.
ii. Fanny, *b.* 7th March, 1816; *d.* 12th January, 1843; *m.* Peter D. OYER.
iii. Diana, *b.* 7th May, 1818; *d.* 8th September, 1846; *m.* Elisha DELAND.
iv. RUFUS, *b.* 5th March, 1820, of whom later.
v. Ezra, *b.* 20th June, 1823; *d.* 30th July, 1886; *m.* Diadama COLEMAN.
vi. Henry, *b.* 11th December, 1827; *d.* 24th July, 1835.
vii. Mary, *b.* 10th May, 1825; *d.* 27th July, 1816; *m.* Albert CASE.
viii. Norman, *b.* 11th May, 1831; *d.* 14th July, 1906; *m.* Delia M. TAYLOR.

RUFUS CLARK, of Darien, Genesee County, New York; *b.* 5th March, 1820; *d.* 15th April, 1893; *m.* 4th April, 1844, Eunice Amelia WHEELER, *b.* 5th August, 1821, *d.* 26th December, 1904, dau. of Jacob and Hannah (DRURY) WHEELER, she dau. of Ebenezer and Marian (GOODALE) DRURY, he son of Capt. Zedekiah and Hannah (WOOLEY) DRURY, gr. gd. son of Lieut. John DRURY, who served in King Philip's War, 1675.

ISSUE

i. ORLANDO ELMER, *b.* 9th November, 1850, the subject of this memoir.

Arms.—Argent on a fesse between three crosses pattee sable, three plates.
Crest.—A cross pattee or between two wings azure.
Motto.—Absit ut glorier nisi in cruce.
Residence.—Appleton, Ontagamie County, Wisconsin.
Clubs.—University Club of Madison, Wisconsin.
Societies.—Colonial Wars, Sons of American Revolution, Founders and Patriots of America, Theta Delta Chi, American Bar Association, American Historical Association, Wisconsin Bar Association, State Historical Association of Wisconsin.

Cone

JAMES BREWSTER CONE, M.A., B.A., *b.* 6th January, 1836, at Hartford, Connecticut; *m.* 27th January, 1863, in New York City, Harriet Elizabeth UHLHORN, *b.* 24th June, 1838, dau. of Casper Frederick and Maria (GOODRICH) UHLHORN of New York.

JAMES BREWSTER CONE received his education at Dudley's School, Northampton, Massachusetts, M.A. and B.A., Yale; Trustee Wadsworth Athenæum, Watkins Library and Insane Retreat of Hartford; Vice-president of the School for the Deaf, and Director of Hartford-Aetna National Bank of Hartford.

Lineage

This family is of Scotch ancestry and is descended from Daniel MACKHOE, who later was known as Daniel CONE, *b.* in Edinboro, 1626, *d.* 24th October, 1706, settled in East Haddam, Connecticut; he was an officer in the Scottish Army and was at the battle of Dunbar; *m.* Mehitable SPENCER, dau. of Jared SPENCER of Lynn, Massachusetts.

ISSUE AMONG OTHERS

I. NATHANIEL, *bapt.* 6th June, 1675.

NATHANIEL CONE, of East Haddam, Connecticut; *bapt.* 6th June, 1675; *d.* 1730-1733; *m.* Sarah HUNGERFORD, *d.* 25th September, 1753, dau. of Thomas HUNGERFORD of Lyme, Connecticut.

ISSUE AMONG OTHERS

I. JAMES, *b.* 14th August, 1693.

LIEUTENANT JAMES CONE of East Haddam, Connecticut; *b.* 14th August, 1693; *d.* 4th April, 1775; it is said served under Sir William Pepperell 25th July, 1724, as Lieutenant at the siege of Louisburg; *m.* before 1729, Elizabeth WARNER, dau. of John WARNER.

ISSUE AMONG OTHERS

I. SYLVANUS, *b.* 21st January, 1731.

SYLVANUS CONE, of East Haddam, Connecticut; *b.* 21st January, 1731; *d.* 4th May, 1812; he enlisted for the Fort Edward Expedition in Capt. Ichabod PHELPS Company, 4th Regiment, 4th September, 1755, and was discharged 11th November, 1755; on 30th May, 1756, enlisted for the Crown Point Expedition in Capt. Edward WELLS Company, 4th Regiment; was mustered at Fort William Henry, 13th October, 1756, and was discharged 26th November, 1756; was at the Battle of Bunker Hill; *m.* 13th November, 1755, Hannah ACKLEY, *b.* 18th March, 1742 (?), *d.* 24th June, 1790, at Millington, Connecticut, dau. of Gideon ACKLEY.

ISSUE AMONG OTHERS

I. JOSEPH WARREN, *b.* 3d July, 1755.

JOSEPH WARREN CONE, of East Haddam, Connecticut; *b.* 3d July, 1775; *d.* 4th August, 1848, at West Hartford; *m.* 17th November, 1796, Mehitable SWAN, *b.* 3d May, 1778; *d.* 11th September, 1849, dau. of Jabez SWAN.

ISSUE AMONG OTHERS

I. WILLIAM RUSSELL, *b.* 22d June, 1810.

WILLIAM RUSSELL CONE, of Hartford, Connecticut; *b.* 22d June, 1810, at East Haddam; *d.* 10th January, 1890; *m.* 7th October, 1883, Rebecca Daggett BREWSTER, *b.* 22d April, 1814, *d.* 15th May, 1890, dau. of James BREWSTER, of New Haven.

ISSUE

I. JAMES BREWSTER, *b.* 6th January, 1836, the subject of this memoir.

Arms.—Gules a fesse engrailed between a cinquefoil in chief and crescent in base argent.
Crest.—A pine cone.
Motto.—Truth with trust.
Residence.—640 Farmington Avenue, Hartford, Connecticut.
Clubs.—Union League of New York, Hartford Club, Farmington Country Club, Hartford Golf Club.
Society.—Colonial Wars.

Corwin

REV. CHARLES EDWARD CORWIN, A.B., A.M., B.D.; *b.* 7th September, 1868, in Millstone, New Jersey; *m.* 15th June, 1898, at Gloverville, New York, Ellen Gibb KINGSLEY, *b.* 5th January, 1868, dau. of Henry KINGSLEY, *b.* 3d November, 1809, *d.* 27th March, 1894, *m.* 12th February, 1866, Mary Hull GIBB.

ISSUE

I. A son, *b.* and *d.* 22d January, 1910.

REV. CHARLES EDWARD CORWIN, Minister of the Reformed Church in America, received degree of A.B. in 1892 from Rutgers College; B.D., 1895; and A.M., 1907, Pastor of Cuddeback New York, 1895–1897, and of Greenport, Columbia County, New York, 1897–1905; Stated Supply, Second Presbyterian Church, New Brunswick, New Jersey, 1905–1907; Pastor North Branch, New Jersey, 1907–1915; engaged 1st July, 1915, by Collegiate Reformed Church to edit their documents from 1628 to present time; Associate Editor of *Somerset Church News*.

Lineage

MATTHIAS CORWIN, *b.* in England, 1590–1600; *d.* at Southold, Long Island, New York, 12th September, 1658; came to America, it is said, from Warwick, England, and was at Ipswich, Massachusetts, 1634; *m.* Margaret (MORTON)?

ISSUE

I. JOHN, *b.* circa 1630, of whom later.
II. Martha, *b.* 1630–1640; *m.* November, 1658 (firstly) Henry CASE; *m.* (secondly) 11th January, 1665–1666, Thomas HUTCHINSON.
III. Theophilus, *b.* before 1634; *d.* before 1692; *m.* Mary, surname unknown.

JOHN CORWIN, of Southold, Connecticut; *b.* circa 1630; *d.* 25th September, 1702; *m.* 4th February, 1658, Mary GLOVER, *d.* probably before 1690, dau. of Charles GLOVER.

ISSUE

I. Mary, *b.* 15th December, 1659; *d.* probably before 1690; *m.* Jacob or Jabez MAPES.
II. Sarah, *b.* circa 1660; *m.* before 1690, Jacob OSMAN.
III. JOHN, *b.* 1663, of whom later.
IV. Rebecca, *b.* 1660–1670; *m.* before 1690, Abraham OSMAN.
V. Hannah, *b.* 1660–1670.

VI. Abigail, *b.* 1660–1670.
VII. Samuel, *b.* 12th August, 1674.
VIII. Matthias, *b.* 1676; *d.* 9th March, 1769; *m.* circa 1708, Mary, surname not given.

CAPTAIN JOHN CORWIN of Southold, Long Island, *b.* 1663; *d.* 13th December, 1729; *m.* before 1698, Sarah, surname not given.

ISSUE

I. Hester, *b.* circa 1685.
II. Benjamin, *b.* 1685–1700; *d.* 1721.
III. Elizabeth, *b.* circa 1700.
IV. JOHN, *b.* 10th July, 1705, of whom later.
V. David, *b.* circa 1705–1710; *d.* before 1782; *m.* 1732, Deborah WELLS, *b.* 1717, *d.* 24th November, 1798.
VI. Sarah (?), *b.* 29th October, 1838; *m.* Peter SIMMONS.

JOHN CORWIN, of Southold, Long Island, New York; *b.* 10th July, 1705; *d.* 22d December, 1755; *m.* (firstly) probably Hester CLARK; *m.* (secondly) 1732, Elizabeth GOLDSMITH.

ISSUE

I. Elizabeth, *b.* circa 1730.
II. John, *b.* 1735; *d.* 22d December, 1718; *m.* (firstly) 20th March, 1755, Sarah HUBBARD, *b.* 1731, *d.* 28th December, 1760; *m.* (secondly) 9th September, 1767, Deborah BROWN, *b.* 1733, *d.* 22d February, 1823.
III. Sarah, *b.* circa 1739; *m.* 26th October, 1786, John PENNY.
IV. JAMES, *b.* 22d August, 1741, of whom later.
V. William, of Chester, New Jersey; *b.* 21st February, 1744; *d.* 1st December, 1818; was a soldier in the French and Indian Wars; Lieutenant in the Revolution and a Representative in the New Jersey Legislature; *m.* 14th January, 1768, Hannah REEVES of Middletown, *b.* 23d May, 1747, *d.* circa 1840.

JAMES CORWIN, of Middletown, Orange County, New York; *b.* 22d August, 1741; *d.* 9th November, 1791; *m.* 1763, Mehetable HORTON, *b.* 29th September, 1743; *d.* 27th October, 1795, dau. of William and ——— (WELLS) HORTON.

ISSUE

I. William, *b.* 19th March, 1764; *d.* 17th May, 1800; *m.* Leah JOHNSON.
II. George, *b.* 27th June, 1766; *d.* 2d December, 1834; *m.* 10th October, 1805, Betty BRUSH, *b.* 25th February, 1772, *d.* 15th May, 1852.
III. Martin Luther, *b.* 22d December, 1768; *d.* 14th August, 1845; *m.* Rebecca Jane NEWMAN.
IV. JAMES, *b.* 14th July, 1771, of whom later.
V. Mehetable, *b.* 1773; *d.* 1794; *m.* James BOAAK.

COLONIAL FAMILIES OF THE UNITED STATES 165

- VI. Benjamin, *b.* 1780; *d.* 24th June, 1804.
- VII. Elizabeth, *b.* 1781; *d.* 1820; *m.* Eliphalet WARNER.
- VIII. John, *b.* 11th September, 1782; *d.* 11th October, 1850; *m.* Elizabeth WICKHAM, *b.* 28th August, 1788.
- IX. Moses, *b.* 16th January, 1785; *d.* 29th March, 1866; *m.* 28th September, 1809, Martha STUART, *b.* 22d January, 1791.

JAMES CORWIN, of New York City; *b.* 14th July, 1771; *d.* at Long Island, 8th July, 1848; was a deacon in New York City at the Spring Street Presbyterian Church; *m.* (firstly) 17th December, 1793, Mary SIMVALL, *b.* 10th September, 1769, in New York City, *d.* 22d July, 1825, dau. of William SIMVALL, *b.* 5th May, 1743, *d.* 2d July, 1814, *m.* Bethia OWEN, *b.* 9th January, 1749; *m.* (secondly) 10th December, 1833, Mary GARLAND, *b.* circa 1784, *d.* 1869.

ISSUE

- I. Henry Wisner, *b.* 25th October, 1794; *d.* July, 1842; *m.* Eliza Ann KELLY.
- II. Gabriel, *b.* 10th October, 1795; *d.* 2d November, 1820; *m.* Olivia GLADEN.
- III. A dau., *b.* 9th April, 1797; *d.* 24th April, 1797.
- IV. Laura, *b.* 2d September, 1798; *d.* 12th August, 1799.
- V. William Owen, *b.* 10th August, 1800; *d.* 20th May, 1835; *m.* Amanda CHAPPEL.
- VI. A child, *b.* and *d.* 19th April, 1802.
- VII. Eliza, *b.* 7th May, 1804; *d.* 30th November, 1842; *m.* 13th July, 1834, Henry Corwin WETHERBY, *b.* 12th February, 1812, *d.* 21st August, 1869.
- VIII. Maria, *b.* 7th May, 1804; *d.* 27th June, 1805.
- IX. James H., *b.* 12th August, 1812; *d.* 13th September, 1870, in Memphis, Tennessee; *m.* (firstly) 8th September, 1842, Sarah L. SINNERD, of Hamilton, Ohio, *d.* 14th July, 1843; *m.* (secondly) 13th September, 1853, name not given.
- X. EDWARD CALWELL, *b.* 30th December, 1807, of whom later.
- XI. Lewis B.

EDWARD CALWELL CORWIN, of New York City; *b.* 30th December, 1807, near Middletown, Orange County, New York; *d.* 22d August, 1856, in Jersey City; *m.* 16th June, 1829, Mary Ann SHUART, dau. of Christian SHUART, who lived near Patterson, New Jersey, a descendant of Olferts SUERT, living on Broadway, below Trinity Church in New York City in the year 1687.

ISSUE

- I. James Horton, *b.* 17th March, 1830; *d.* 21st February, 1861; *m.* 31st January, 1854, Annie M. GARRETSON, *b.* 9th May, 1833, dau. of John and Catherine Ann (RIKER) GARRETSON.

II. Leah Margaret, *b.* 24th March, 1832; *m.* George S. Corwin, who *d.* November, 1900.
III. Edward Tanjore, *b.* 12th July, 1834, of whom later.
IV. George Brainard, *b.* 12th June, 1836; *d.* 22d March, 1839.

Rev. Edward Tanjore Corwin, of New York City, *b.* 12th July, 1834, in New York City; *d.* there 22d June, 1914; graduated from the College of New York, 1853, in the first class that institution sent forth; graduated from the Theological Seminary of the Reformed (Dutch) Church at New Brunswick, New Jersey, 1856; was installed 22d September, 1857, Pastor of the Reformed Church of Paramus, New Jersey; published in 1869, "The Manual of the Reformed Church in America," with about one hundred sketches or characterizations of deceased ministers, with an introductory chapter on the history of the denomination, and appendices, containing the history of Rutgers College, of the New Brunswick Theological Seminary, and of the several Benevolent Boards of the Church; *m.* 25th July, 1861, at Geneva, New York, Mary Esther Kipp, *b.* 21st August, 1840, at Geneva, New York, dau. of Nicholas and Mary (Freshour) Kipp. He descended from Roeloff de Kype, of Bretagne, France.

ISSUE

I. Euphemia Kipp, *b.* 26th June, 1863.
II. A son, *b.* 25th June, 1866; *d.* 26th June, 1866.
III. Charles Edward, *b.* 7th September, 1868, the subject of this memoir.
IV. Francis Huntington, *b.* 19th January, 1879; *d.* 22d July, 1879.

Arms.—Argent, a fretty gules, a chief azure.
Crest.—A unicorn's head erased argent, armed or.
Motto.—Si je n'estoy.
Residence.—New Brunswick, New Jersey.
Societies.—Phi Beta Kappa, American Society of Church History.

Crosby

JUDGE GEORGE STEPHEN CROSBY, of Thompson, Windham County, Connecticut; *b.* in Thompson, 17th February, 1844; *m.* in East Thompson, Connecticut, 29th October, 1879, Mary Bailey JACOBS, *b.* 3d November, 1844, dau. of Capt. Joseph Dresser JACOBS of East Thompson, *b.* 29th March, 1806, *d.* 21st October, 1890, *m.* 27th October, 1828, Sarah Crosby CARROLL, *b.* 6th November, 1809, *d.* 25th April, 1887, dau. of Wyman and Sarah (CROSBY) CARROLL.

ISSUE

I. Sarah Carroll, *b.* in East Thompson, Connecticut, 16th February, 1882; Graduate of Roxbury High School, Boston, Massachusetts, and the Department of Hygiene and Physical Education, Wellesley College, Wellesley, Massachusetts; Supervisor of Physical Education in the Northampton Public Schools, Northampton, Massachusetts.
II. Mary Larned, *b.* in East Thompson, Connecticut, 8th November, 1884; *d.* 7th April, 1885.

JUDGE GEORGE STEPHEN CROSBY received his education in the public and private schools of Thompson, Connecticut, in which place he has always resided. On finishing his education he entered into the hotel business with his father, Stephen CROSBY, who had bought the Vernon Styles' Tavern at Thompson Center. He continued in this business until his father's death in 1884, when he sold the hotel business and became interested in farming. He bought the ancestral estate of his maternal grandfather, George LARNED, and later owned by his paternal grandfather, Stephen CROSBY. He joined the Thompson Congregational Church early in life and was elected Deacon of the same in 1892. He was Director of the Thompson National Bank; an Incorporator of the Thompson Dime Savings Bank; in 1902 was elected Judge of the Probate Court of the District of Thompson, which position he held until he reached the age limit of seventy. He is a descendant of Roger WILLIAMS, who founded the city of Providence in 1636; of Rev. Chad BROWN, who was one of the thirteen original settlers of Providence and the first settled pastor of the First Baptist Church in America, he was ordained in 1640 and buried in 1650 in the home lot, which is the site of the present Court House; of William WICKENDON who was one of the thirteen original settlers of Providence, he signed an agreement for the form of government and was ordained pastor of the First Baptist Church in 1647; of Cabel CARR who was treasurer and Governor of the Providence Plantation.

Lineage

THOMAS CROSBY, the emigrant, came from England and settled first in Cambridge, and later in Rowley, Massachusetts. CROSBY, or CROSBIE, is a well known name throughout York County, England, and for several generations we find them at Holme-on-Spalding Moor. Here Thomas CROSBY was born about 1575. He was the son of Anthony and Alison CROSBY. He *m.* 19th October, 1600, Jane SOTHERON *bapt.* 4th March, 1581, in England, and was buried in Rowley, Massachusetts, ,2d May, 1662, dau. of William and Constance (LAMBERT) SOTHERON. Tradition says that Thomas CROSBY came over in company with the Rev. Ezekiel ROGERS in 1638. That he was a man of wealth for those days is shown by his advancing a considerable sum of money for the first printing press brought and set up in America. He spent his last years in the home of his grandson Dr. Anthony CROSBY, of Rowley, and *d.* there 6th May, 1661.

ISSUE

I. Anthony, *b.* about 1602, in Holme; *d.* 23d June, 1632, in Holme.
II. Thomas, *b.* about 1604, in Holme; *d.* 28th December, 1658, in Holme; *m.* about 1633, Prudence ———.
III. WILLIAM, *b.* about 1606, of whom later.
IV. Simon, *b.* about 1608, in Holme; *d.* September, 1639, in Cambridge, Massachusetts; *m.* 21st April, 1634, Anne BRIGHAM.

WILLIAM CROSBY was born in Holme-on-Spalding Moor, County York, England about 1606; *d.* about 1640; *m.* in Seaton, County York, 2d April, 1633, Anne WRIGHT, who was buried in Holme, 22d June, 1636..

ISSUE

I. Thomas, *bapt.* in Seaton, 18th December, 1633; *d.* 20th December, 1633.
II. ANTHONY, *bapt.* in Holme, 5th October, 1635, of whom later.

DR. ANTHONY CROSBY, *bapt.* 5th October, 1635, in Holme-on-Spalding Moor, County York, England. He was left an orphan early in life and was adopted by his grandfather, Thomas Crosby, who brought him to New England. He was a prominent physician of Boston, Rowley and vicinity. He inherited his grandfather's entire estate and died in Rowley, 16th January, 1672–1673; *m.* in Rowley, Massachusetts, Prudence WADE, 28th December, 1659, *b.* in 1638 in Ipswich, Massachusetts, dau. of Jonathan and Susanna WADE, *d.* in Watertown, Massachusetts, 1st September, 1711. After the death of Dr. Anthony CROSBY, she *m.* (secondly) the Rev. Seaborn COTTON, oldest son of the Rev. John COTTON, the most eminent of all the Puritan divines, as his second wife. He died in 1686, and she *m.* (thirdly) Lieutenant John HAMMOND.

ISSUE

I. Thomas, *b.* 4th March, 1660–1661.
II. Jonathan, *b.* 26th January, 1663–1664; *d.* 27th May, 1664.

III. Jonathan, b. 28th October, 1665–1666.
IV. Nathaniel, b. 5th February, 1666–1667; d. April, 1667.
V. NATHANIEL, b. 27th September, 1668, of whom below.

NATHANIEL CROSBY was b. in Rowley, Massachusetts, 27th September, 1668; d. in Rowley, 7th March 1699–1700; m. 13th December, 1693, Elizabeth BENNETT, b. 10th November, 1672, dau. of Dr. David and Mary BENNETT. After Nathaniel CROSBY'S death she m. (secondly) John SCOTT, 24th September, 1701.

ISSUE

I. Jonathan, b. 11th September, 1694.
II. Elizabeth, b. 7th August, 1697.
III. NATHANIEL, b. 21st August, 1699, of whom later.

NATHANIEL CROSBY, II, was b. in Rowley, Massachusetts, 31st August, 1699; d. in Thompson, Connecticut, 24th August, 1770; he moved to Connecticut soon after his marriage and purchased in 1722 land on the French River near the present site of Grosvenor Dale; he assisted in building the church at Thompson Centre and united with the same in 1731; m. in February, 1721, Hephsibah PEARSON, dau. of Stephen and Mary (FRENCH) PEARSON, b. in Rowley, Massachusetts, 20th January, 1699, d. in Thompson, Connecticut, 30th October, 1771.

ISSUE

I. Jane, b. 26th December, 1723; d. 12th November, 1788.
II. Nathaniel, b. 14th June, 1729; d. 22d October, 1774.
III. Richard, b. 9th March, 1731; d. 10th December, 1736.
IV. STEPHEN, b. 5th January, 1734; d. 15th September, 1776, of whom later.
V. Jonathan, b. 1st May, 1737; d. 13th September, 1742.
VI. Richard, b. 22d July, 1740; d. 7th September, 1742.

CAPTAIN STEPHEN CROSBY was b. in Thompson, Connecticut, 5th January, 1734; d. on the retreat from New York, 15th September, 1776; Capt. Stephen CROSBY was one of the most prominent men of his day in Thompson and represented his town in the Legislature of 1776 as Representative; at the first call of the Lexington Alarm he went out as Sergeant of Captain ELLIOTT'S Company, and in June, 1776, was commissioned Captain in WADSWORTH'S Brigade, 3d Regiment, Col. Comfort SAGE. On the retreat through Harlem, General PUTNAM'S Division suffered sorely, and Captain CROSBY was one of those who died. His body was never sent home, but a monument is erected to his memory in the cemetery at West Thompson, Connecticut; m. 16th February, 1755, Hannah CARROLL dau. of John and Rebecca CARROLL, b. 24th August, 1736, d. in Thompson, Connecticut 27th December, 1813, she m. (secondly) 8th May, 1783, Jacob MASCRAFT.

ISSUE

I. Elijah, *b.* 19th May, 1756; *d.* 16th August, 1831; *m.* Celia BATES.
II. Sarah, *b.* 4th December, 1758; *d.* 24th December, 1758.
III. Sybil, *b.* 8th March, 1760; *d.* 5th April, 1829; *m.* Capt. William RUSSELL.
IV. Pearson, *b.* 14th February, 1763; *d.* 19th September, 1829; *m.* Hannah BATES.
V. Betty, *b.* 16th October, 1765; *d.* 28th April, 1785; *m.* David WHITE.
VI. Hannah, *b.* 16th August, 1768; *d.* 8th July, 1843; *m.* Jothan JOHNSON.
VII. STEPHEN, *b.* 9th October, 1772; *d.* 15th September, 1849, of whom later.
VIII. Sarah, *b.* 20th November, 1776; *d.* 22d December, 1854; *m.* Capt. Wyman CARROLL.

STEPHEN CROSBY, II, *b.* in Thompson, Connecticut, 9th October, 1772; *d.* 15th September, 1849; he was a man well known in the community and was held in the highest esteem; he carried on a grist mill, saw mill, and fulling mill business; was frominently identified with the Brandy Hill Baptist Church and was chosen Deacon in 1815, which office he held until his death; in 1836 he assisted in the erection of the Central Baptist Church of Thompson Center; *m.* 29th November, 1792, Susanna JOHNSON, dau. of Diah and Susanna (CONVERSE) JOHNSON.

ISSUE

I. Talcott, *b.* 23d June, 1794; *d.* 16th November, 1795.
II. Talcott, *b.* 24th August, 1796; *d.* 8th December, 1870; *m.* 29th November, 1818, Attaresta DIKE.
III. STEPHEN, *b.* 27th April, 1802; *d.* 29th November, 1884, of whom below.

STEPHEN CROSBY, III, *b.* in Masonville, Connecticut, but moved early in life to Thompson; he was a highly repected gentleman, and at various times he was Assessor, Selectman and Justice of the Peace; was Director of the Thompson National Bank; of the Thompson Savings Bank and was President of the same at the time of his death; was Treasurer of the Thompson Ecclesiastical Society for many years and settled estates to the satisfaction of all concerned; *d.* in Thompson, 29th November, 1884; *m.* (firstly) 15th March, 1829, Susan Mason LARNED, *b.* 10th March, 1810, *d.* 18th April, 1849, dau. of George and Anna Dorinda (BROWN) LARNED, she was a half-sister of Ellen D. LARNED, the author of the "History of Windham County;" *m.* (secondly) in 1859, Polly GREEN, *d.* in 1888, leaving no children, widow of Joseph GREEN of Thompson.

ISSUE

I. Annie Dorinda Brown, *b.* 1st April, 1830; *d.* 15th March, 1889; *m.* 12th May, 1852, Jonathan NICHOLS.

ISSUE

1. Frank Herbert, *b.* July, 1853; *d.* in infancy.
2. Edgar Crosby, *b.* 3d February, 1858; *d.* 23d August, 1898.
3. Susan Georgianna, *b.* 20th July, 1869.

II. John, *b.* 29th April, 1838; *d.* October, 1842.
III. GEORGE STEPHEN, 17th February, 1844, the subject of this memoir.

Arms.—Sable, a chevron ermine, between three rams trippant argent, armed and hoofed or.
Crest.—A ram trippant as of the arms.
Residence.—Thompson, Connecticut.

Davenport

CHARLES BENEDICT DAVENPORT, B.S., A.B., A.M., Ph.D., of Cold Spring Harbor, Long Island, New York; *b.* 1st June, 1866, at Stamford, Connecticut; *m.* 23d June, 1894, at Burlington, Kansas, Gertrude CROTTY, *b.* 28th February, 1855, dau. of William CROTTY, *b.* 29th March, 1836, *m.* 7th November, 1861, Millia ARMSTRONG, *b.* 29th November, 1842.

ISSUE

I. Millia Crotty, *b.* 30th March, 1895.
II. Jane Joralemon, *b.* 10th September, 1897.
III. Charles Benedict, *b.* 8th January, 1911; *d.* 5th September, 1916.

CHARLES BENEDICT DAVENPORT, Biologist; B.S., Polytechnic Institute, Brooklyn, 1886; A.B., Harvard 1889; A.M., Ph.D., 1892; Engineer, Survey of Duluth South Shore and Atlantic Railway, 1886–1887; Assistant in Zoology, 1888–1890; Instructor, 1891–1899, Harvard; Assistant Professor Zoology and Embryology, 1899–1901; Associate Professor and Curator of Zoological Museum, 1901–1904; University of Chicago; Director Station for Experimental Evolution (of Carnegie Institution) Cold Spring Harbor, New York, since 1904; Director Biological Laboratory, Brooklyn Institute of Arts and Sciences, since 1898; Organizer and Resident Scientific Director of Eugenics Record Office; Associate Editor *Journal Experimental Zoology* since 1898; *American Breeders' Magazine*, 1910; New York Zoological Society; Author of "Graduate Courses—A Handbook for Graduate Courses," 1893; "Experimental Morphology," part 1, 1897; part 2, 1899; "Statistical Methods in Biological Variation," second edition, 1904; "Introduction to Zoology" (with G. C. Davenport), 1900; "Elements of Zoology," 1911; "Inheritance in Poultry," 1906; "Inheritance of Characteristics of Fowl," 1909; "Eugenics," 1910; "Heredity in Relation to Eugenics," 1911; "Heredity of Skin Color in Negro White Crosses," 1913; contributor to biological journals.

Lineage

REV. JOHN DAVENPORT, *b.* in Coventry, England, 1597; *d.* 15th March, 1670; Vicar of St. Stephen's Coleman Street, London, 1624–1633; was bred at Oxford, entered Brazen Nose College, 1613; at Merton College, thence after two years removed to Magdalen Hall, where he procured D.B., fled to Holland and resided in Amsterdam, 1633–1637; he came to Boston with Governor EATON, 26th June 1637, in the ship *Hector* and settled at New Haven, 14th April, 1638; *m.* Elizabeth WOLLEY, *b.* 1673, *d.* 15th September, 1676, buried in King's Chapel burying ground, Boston, Massachusetts.

ISSUE

I. JOHN, *b.* in England, of whom later.
II. Joseph, *d.* 15th March, 1670.

JOHN DAVENPORT, Merchant, of Boston, Massachusetts; *b* 1635 (?), in London; *d.* 1676 at New Haven; arrived in New Haven from London, in 1639; Freeman, 1669; was Register of Probate for Boston from 31st January, 1670, to August, 1676; *m.* 27th November, 1663, Abigail PIERSON, dau. of Rev. Abraham PIERSON of Brandford, *d.* 9th August, 1678, bred at Trinity College, Cambridge, A.B., 1632.

ISSUE

I. John, *b.* 7th and *bapt.* 11th June, 1665; *d.* in a few days.
II. Elizabeth, *b.* 7th October; *bapt.* 18th November, 1666; *m.* December, 1700, Warham MATHER.
III. REV. JOHN, *b.* 22d February, 1668, of whom later.
IV. Abraham, *b.* 5th March, 1671.
V. Abigail, *b.* 15th September, 1672; *m.* 27th October, 1691, Rev. James PIERPONT, of New Haven and *d.* within four months.
VI. Mary, *b.* 17th September, 1676; *m.* 22d May, 1694, Nathaniel WOOD.

REV. JOHN DAVENPORT, of Stamford, Connecticut; *b.* 22d February, 1668; *d.* 5th February, 1731; ordained, 1694; was Minister at Stamford, Harvard College, 1687; *m.* (firstly) 18th April, 1695, Martha (GOULD) SELLICK, *d.* 1st December, 1712, dau. of Maj. Nathan GOULD and widow of John SELLICK; *m.* (secondly) Mrs. Elizabeth (MORRIS) MALTBY, dau. of John MORRIS.

ISSUE BY FIRST MARRIAGE

I. Abigail, *b.* 14th July, 1696, *d.* 26th August, 1766, *m.* 3d July, 1718, Rev. Stephen WILLIAMS, who had been carried away by the Indians in the raid on Deerfield, Massachusetts, May, 1693, and was redeemed after two years.
II. JOHN, *b.* 21st January, 1696, of whom later.
III. Martha, *b.* 10th February, 1700; *d.* 1796; *m.* 6th October; 1731, Rev. Thomas GOODSELL.
IV. Sarah, *b.* July, 1702; *m.* (firstly) Capt. William MALTBY; *m.* (secondly) in 1735, Rev. Eleazer WHITLOCK.
V. Theodora, *b.* 2d November, 1703; *d.* 15th February, 1712.
VI. Deodate, *b.* 23d October, 1706; *d.* 3d December, 1761; *m.* 1730, Lydia WOODWARD.
VII. Elizabeth, *b.* 28th August, 1708; *d.* 6th July, 1747; *m.* Rev. William GAYLORD.

ISSUE BY SECOND MARRIAGE

I. Abraham, *b.* 1715; *d.* 20th November, 1789; Yale College, 1732; represented Stamford in the Legislature for twenty-five sessions; State

Senator, 1766–1784; in 1777 on Committee of Safety for Connecticut; *m.* 1750, Elizabeth HUNTINGTON, whose mother was a sister of Jonathan EDWARDS.

 II. James, *b.* 1716; Evangelist; Yale College, 1732.

JOHN DAVENPORT, of Stamford, Connecticut; *b.* 21st January, 1696; *d.* 17th November, 1742; retired to lands at "Davenport Ridge," bequeathed to him by his father; one of the original four members who organized a Congregational Church in New Canaan; *m.* 6th September, 1722, Sarah BISHOP.

ISSUE

 I. John, *b.* 15th January, 1724, of whom later.
 II. Joseph, *b.* 9th August, 1725; *m.* 5th July, 1753, Hannah AMBLER.
 III. Nathan, *b.* 15th January, 1727.
 IV. Gould, *b.* 6th September, 1728.
 V. Deodate, *b.* 5th January, 1730; *m.* (firstly) 16th June, 1757, Lydia RAYMOND, *d.* 10th March, 1808; *m.* (secondly) 28th September, 1774, Mrs. Elizabeth JONES.
 VI. Martha, *b.* 20th February, 1731; *m.* 7th April, 1757, John CRISSEY.
 VII. Eleazar, *b.* 15th March, 1732.
 VIII. Thaddeus, *b.* 3d February, 1734.
 IX. Elizabeth, *b.* 1st April, 1735.
 X. Silas, *b.* 13th May, 1736; *m.* 7th March, 1765, Mary WEBB.
 XI. Hezekiah, *b.* 14th January, 1738; *m.* 7th December, 1763, Ruth KETCHAMS *d.* in battle of Danbury, 1777.
 XII. Josiah, *b.* 6th August, 1739.
 XIII. Stephen, *b.* 9th April, 1741.
 XIV. Sarah.

JOHN DAVENPORT, Farmer and Landowner, of Stamford, Connecticut; *b.* 15th January, 1724; *d.* 23d June, 1756; *m.* 7th March, 1742, Deborah AMBLER.

ISSUE

 I. John, *b.* 15th January, 1749, of whom later.
 II. Sarah, *b.* 7th January, 1751; *d.* 1819; *m.* Monmouth LOUNSBURY.
 III. Stephen, *b.* 9th March, 1752; *d.* unmarried, 1777.
 IV. Rhoda, *b.* 4th January, 1754; *m.* 19th November, 1775, Thaddeus HUESTED.

JOHN DAVENPORT, Carpenter, Farmer, Deacon, of Stamford, Connecticut; *b.* 24th May, 1749; *d.* 6th February, 1820; *m.* Prudence BELL of Stamford, Connecticut.

ISSUE

 I. John, *b.* 27th October, 1773; *d.* 1784, by falling from a horse.
 II. Ralph, *b.* 1775; *d.* 1779.

III. Theodora, *b.* 27th September, 1779; *d.* 29th October, 1809; *m.* William DAVENPORT, son of Lieut. Hezekiah DAVENPORT.
IV. WILLIAM, *b.* 25th March, 1781, of whom later.
V. Sarah, *b.* 5th March, 1783; *d.* 17th February, 1839; *m.* Jonathan BATES of Darien.
VI. James, *b.* 20th February, 1787; *d.* 27th October, 1845; *m.* Martha WARREN of Norwalk.
VII. Julia Ann, *b.* 30th November, 1794; *d.* 2d July, 1868; *m.* 4th January, 1817, Jonathan HOYT.
VIII. John Gaylord, *b.* 6th March, 1799; *d.* 1st April, 1799.
IX. Elizabeth, *b.* 4th March, 1802; *d.* 12th April, 1818.

WILLIAM DAVENPORT of Stamford, Connecticut; *b.* 25th March, 1781; *d.* 16th January, 1860; *m.* Abigail BENEDICT, dau. of Deacon Isaac BENEDICT of New Canaan, Connecticut.

ISSUE

I. Isaac Gould, *b.* 17th January, 1804; *d.* 28th April, 1839; *m.* 12th October, 1831, Hannah WILSON.
II. John William, *b.* 22d July, 1807; *d.* 26th May, 1826.
III. Theodore, *b.* 15th January, 1810; *d.* 20th August, 1830.
IV. Lewis Benedict, *b.* 24th June, 1812; *d.* 17th December, 1836.
V. Mary Jane, *b.* 7th March, 1814; *d.* 25th April, 1836.
VI. AMZI BENEDICT, *b.* 30th October, 1817, of whom later.
VII. Julius, *b.* 26th May, 1821; *m.* 4th June, 1846, Mary Ann BATES.
VIII. Harriet, *m.* 3d October, 1842; Elisha COMSTOCK of Norwalk.

AMZI BENEDICT DAVENPORT, Teacher, Genealogist, one of the organizers of Plymouth Church, Brooklyn; Deacon, and Abolitionist of New Canaan, Connecticut; *b.* 30th October, 1817; *d.* 20th August, 1894; *m.* 30th October, 1850, Jane Joralemon DIMON, *b.* 1st March, 1828, dau. of John DIMON, who *m.* Margaret JORALEMON, dau. of Judge Tuenis JORALEMON.

ISSUE

I. Henry Benedict, President of Real Estate Title Insurance Company, Bank Director and Lawyer; *b.* 1st June, 1854; *m.* 6th June, 1877, Flora Dwight LUEFKIN, dau. of A. D. LUEFKIN, of Cleveland, Ohio.

ISSUE

1. Maurice, *b.* 1878.
2. Henry Joralemon, *b.* 1880.

II. James Pierpont, *b.* 27th July, 1856; Yale College, 1877; Judge, Lawyer and Editor; *m.* 1886, Lemoine FARWELL.

ISSUE

1. Dorothy. 3. Pierrepont.
2. Margery. 4. Farwell.

III. William Edwards, social worker; *b.* North Stamford, Connecticut, 31st August, 1862; unmarried; educated academic department, Brooklyn Polytechnic Institute, 1875–1881; three years special student, Union Theological Seminary, 1897–1899; Clerk in New York Post Office, 1881–1896; licensed by North New Jersey Congregational Association, 1889; in 1901 founded the Brooklyn Italian Settlement, consolidated, 1910, with other organizations as the United Neighborhood Guild, maintains the Italian settlement of the Guild, of which he is in charge; Foreign correspondent, 1902, 1904, 1909 for New York *Evening Post* and Brooklyn *Daily Eagle;* lecturer on subjects relating to Italian immigration in New Jersey, Connecticut, and New York, since 1901; Independent Republican; President of Republican District Association. Author: "The New Dispensation," 1884; "Visions of the City," 1884; "The Perpetual Fire," 1886; "The Praise of Plymouth," 1892; "The Poet and His Friends," 1893; "Beecher—An Ode," 1891; "Poetical Sermons," 1896, 1897; "The Beggar Man of Brooklyn Heights," 1904; "More Outcries from Brooklyn Hollow," 1905; Moral Effects of the Messina Earthquake." Contributor to magazines. Address, 90 Adams Street, Brooklyn, New York.

IV. Mary Vere, *b.* 2d May, 1864; *m.* 1893, Charles CRANDALL.

ISSUE

1. Roland CRANDALL.
2. Clarence CRANDALL.

V. CHARLES BENEDICT, *b.* 1st June, 1866, the subject of this memoir.

VI. Frances Gardiner, historian; *b.* Stamford, Connecticut, 30th April, 1870; Barnard College, New York, 1890–1891; A.B., Radcliffe College, Cambridge, Massachusetts, 1894; A.M., 1896; London (England) School of Economics, 1897; Association of Collegiate Alumnae, European fellowship, 1902–1903; studied at Cambridge, England; Fellow of University of Chicago, 1903–1904; Ph.D., 1904; Instructor in History, Erasmus Hall High School, Brooklyn, 1898–1901; Vassar College, 1904–1905; Assistant in Department of History Research, Carnegie Institute, 1905—. Member of American Historical Association, 'Lyceum Club' London. Author: "The Economic Development of a Norfolk Manor," 1906; compiler of List of Printed Original Materials for English Manorial and Agrarian History," 1894; (joint) Guide to the Manuscript Materials for the History of the United States to 1873, in the British Museum, etc.," 1908; Editor of a collection of European treaties bearing on the early history of the United States; articles on English agrarian history, etc.

Arms.—Argent, a chevron sable, between three cross-crooslets fitchee of the second.
Crest.—A felon's head couped at the neck ppr. haltered or.
Motto.—Audaces fortuna juvat.
Residence.—Cold Spring Harbor P. O., Town of Oyster Bay, Long Island, New York.
Clubs.—Huntington Country and Harvard of New York
Societies.—National Academy of Sciences, American Philosophical Society, American Academy of Arts and Sciences, New York Academy of Medicine, American Zoological Society, National Institute of Social Sciences, Nassau County Association.

Deming

JUDSON KEITH DEMING, Litt.D., of Dubuque, Iowa; *b*. 18th September, 1858, in Sheldon, Vermont; *m*. 10th January, 1884, at Winona, Minnesota, Mary Colebrook WORTHINGTON, *b*. 11th February, 1853, dau. of Edward WORTHINGTON, *b*. 17th March, 1812, *d*. 20th September, 1884, *m*. 24th November, 1841, Jane Maria SHEPARD, *b*. 1st September, 1821, *d*. 15th January, 1871.

ISSUE

I. Elsa Louise, *b*. 6th December, 1885.
II. Keith Worthington, *b*. 29th June, 1887; *d*. 13th November, 1909, at Amherst, Massachusetts (Class of 1912 Amherst).

JUDSON KEITH DEMING was educated at public schools and by private tutors; President Second National Bank, Dubuque Savings Bank; Vice-President Dubuque Casket Company; President Board of Trustees, Dubuque German College and Seminary; President Board of Education in 1906; Treasurer Dubuque Benevolent and Humane Society; Dubuque Boys Welfare Association; Trustee Linwood Cemetery Association; Trustee and Treasurer Iowa Episcopate Fund; Trustee American Red Cross in Iowa; Member Standing Committee Diocese of Iowa; Deputy to General Convention Episcopal Church, 1910–1913 and 1916; Vice-President American Bankers Association for Iowa, 1892; President Iowa Bankers Association, 1896–1897; President Society of Sons of Revolution, 1903–1904; Governor Society of Colonial Wars, 1894; Degree Litt.D. conferred by Dubuque German College, 1915; Compiler of "Deming Genealogy." Author (under nom de plume of "Jay Cady") "Moving of the Waters," 1909; "The Stake," 1912, and short stories.

Lineage

JOHN DEMING of Wethersfield, Connecticut; *b*. circa 1610; *d*. circa 1705; one of the early settlers; recorded his homestead there in 1641; was one of the patentees named in the Royal Charter of Connecticut, 1662; 2d March, 1642, one of the jury of the "Particular Court;" 1st December, 1645 one of the deputies to the General Court; will proved 21st November, 1705; was a representative at fifty sessions of the General Court; his name appears upon many of the records with the prefix of "Mr." a courtesy only paid to men of some prominence; no accurate date of birth or death or where he emigrated from; Trumbull speaks of him as one of the Fathers of Connecticut, and Hinman says that in 1654 he held the office of Constable, showing he had the full confidence of the Governor; *m*. 1637, Honor TREAT, dau. of Richard and ———— TREAT.

ISSUE

I. John, *b.* 9th September, 1638; *d.* 23d January, 1712; *m.* 12th December, 1657, Mary MYGATT, dau. of Joseph and Ann MYGATT.
II. Jonathan, *b.* circa 1639; *d.* 8th January, 1700; *m.* (firstly) 21st November, 1660, Sarah GRAVES, dau. of George GRAVES; *m.* (secondly) 25th December, 1673, Elizabeth GILBERT, *b.* 28th March, 1654, *d.* 8th September, 1714, dau. of Josiah and Elizabeth GILBERT.
III. A dau., *b.* circa 1643; *m.* ——— BECKLEY of Wethersfield.
IV. Rachel, *b.* circa 1644; *m.* 16th November, 1655, John MORGAN of Wethersfield.
V. Samuel, *b.* circa 1646; *d.* 6th April, 1709; *m.* 29th March, 1694, Sarah BUCK, dau. of Enoch and Mary (KIRBY) BUCK, *b.* 1st April, 1669, she *m.* (secondly) Capt. Jonathan CHURCHILL.
VI. Mary, *b.* circa 1648; *m.* circa 1670, John HURLBURT of Wethersfield.
VII. Mercy, *b.* circa 1651; *d.s.p.* 17th December, 1714; *m.* Thomas (or Joseph) WRIGHT of Wethersfield.
VIII. David, *b.* circa 1652; *d.* 4th May, 1725; removed to Boston, before 1707; *m.* 14th August, 1678, in Wethersfield, Mary ———, *b.* circa 1652, *d.* 14th October, 1724.

ISSUE

1. David, *b.* 20th July, 1681.
2. Samuel, *b.* 9th August, 1683.
3. Honour, *b.* 9th May, 1685; *d.* 13th May, 1713.
4. Martha, *m.* 15th December, 1709, Henry HOWELL of Boston (see Howell family, "Colonial Families," Vol. III, pp. 244-255).

IX. Sarah, *b.* circa 1654; *d.* 29th September, 1717, in Hadley, Massachusetts; *m.* Samuel MOODY of Hartford.
X. EBENEZER, *b.* circa 1659, of whom later.

EBENEZER DEMING of Wethersfield, Connecticut; *b.* there, circa, 1659; *d.* there, 2d May, 1705; Constable of Wethersfield, 1692; *m.* there, 16th July, 1677, Sarah, surname not discovered.

ISSUE

I. Ebenezer, *b.* 5th May, 1678; *d.* 16th April, 1765; *m.* 27th December, 1704, Rebecca TREAT, *b.* 1686, *d.* 26th December, 1753, dau. of Lieut. James and Rebecca (LATIMER) TREAT.
II. John, Deacon, *b.* 26th July, 1679; *d.* 1st May, 1761; *m.* (firstly) 5th June, 1712, Mary CURTIS, *b.* 2d September, 1677, *d.* 21st December, 1723; *m.* (secondly) 12th August, 1731, Catherine (BECKLEY) DEWEY, *b.* 1685, *d.* 24th December, 1768, dau. of John BECKLEY and widow of Daniel DEWEY.
III. Sarah, *b.* 6th July, 1681; *d.* 19th March, 1755; *m.* 1st April, 1701, Joseph TALCOTT.

IV. Prudence, *b.* circa 1683; *d.* 24th October, 1706; *m.* 4th October, 1705, Thomas WRIGHT.
V. EPHRAIM, *b.* circa 1685, of whom later.
VI. Josiah, *b.* circa 1688; *d.* 12th August, 1761; *m.* (firstly) 8th December, 1714, Prudence STEELE, *b.* 17th January, 1693, *d.* 10th July, 1752, dau. of Capt. James and Ann (WELLES) STEELE.

LIEUTENANT EPHRAIM DEMING, of Wethersfield, Connecticut; *b.* there, 1685; *d.* there, 14th November, 1742; Lieutenant of Newington Train Band, commissioned 13th October, 1726, by the Connecticut General Assembly; *m.* there, 19th January, 1716, Hannah BELDING, *b.* 12th September, 1692, *d.* 6th November, 1771, dau. of John and Dorothy (WILLARD) BELDING.

ISSUE

I. Dorothy, *b.* 21st October, 1716; *d.* 8th September, 1788; *m.* Daniel WILLARD.
II. Janna, Sergeant West Indies Expedition, 1741; *b.* 2d November, 1718; *d.* 24th July, 1796; *m.* 14th June, 1750, Anna KILBOURN, *b.* 20th June, 1728, *d.* 12th April, 1813, dau. of Ebenezer and Eunice (HALE) KILBOURN.
III. Honour, *b.* 18th May, 1721; *m.* 4th May, 1749, Samuel STEELE.
IV. Stephen, *b.* 25th August, 1723; *d.* 24th April, 1790; served in Captain STODDARD's Company, Colonel MOSELEY's Regiment, during the Revolution; *m.* 29th January, 1747, Hannah GOODRICH, *b.* 15th May, 1725, *d.* 16th December, 1799, dau. of Ephraim and Hannah (STEELE) GOODRICH.
V. WAITSTILL, *b.* 18th May, 1726, of whom later.
VI. Hannah, *b.* 4th August, 1728; *d.* 26th June, 1776; *m.* 16th November, 1757, Capt. Peter BURNHAM.
VII. Lydia, *b.* 26th March, 1732; *m.* 4th April, 1757, Elisha WELLES.

WAITSTILL DEMING, farmer, of Newington, Connecticut; *b.* 18th May, 1726, in Wethersfield; *d.* 10th March, 1776, in Newington, Connecticut; *m.* 1st September, 1758, Hannah LUSK, *b.* circa 1739, *d.* 10th December, 1826, dau. of Thomas and Isabel LUSK.

ISSUE

I. Elizabeth, *b.* 17th May, 1759; *m.* 14th June, 1779, Silas WALTON of Norwich, Connecticut.
II. Ephraim, *b.* 26th February, 1761; *m.* (firstly) Elizabeth, surname unknown; *m.* (secondly) 28th October, 1801, Asenath SCOVILLE.
III. Ezekiel, *b.* 4th April, 1763; *d.* unmarried, 21st June, 1814.
IV. Frederick, *b.* 7th May, 1765; *d.* 21st September, 1823; *m.* a Miss WARE.
V. Lucretia, *b.* 19th March, 1767; *m.* 23d September, 1784, Silas SANFORD.
VI. SELAH, *b.* 7th March, 1769, of whom later.

VII. Roger, *b.* 19th July, 1771; *d.* 19th December, 1837; *m.* firstly, Esther, surname unknown, *d.* 19th January, 1797; *m.* (secondly), Mabel, surname unknown, *d.* 26th January, 1811, aged 44 years.
VIII. Lyman, *b.* 2d June, 1773; *d.* young.

SELAH DEMING, Farmer, of Sheldon, Vermont; *b.* 7th March, 1769, in Newington, Connecticut; *d.* 29th July, 1854, in Sheldon, Vermont; moved from Newington, to Northern Vermont where he bought 200 acres of land in 1795 in the town of Sheldon and there settled; *m.* (firstly), 24th February, 1793, Sarah JEROME, *b.* 18th March, 1777, *d.* 26th December, 1804, dau. of Asahel and Sarah (BRONSON) JEROME; *m.* (secondly), Thankful TRACY, *b.* 28th June, 1772, dau. of Hezekiah and Annie (ROOD) TRACY, *d.* 28th August 1836; *m.* (thirdly), Philinda BENNETT.

ISSUE BY FIRST MARRIAGE

I. Sarah, *b.* 26th October, 1794; *m.* Ezekiel TRACY.
II. Jedediah, *b.* 6th March, 1796; *d.* 1877; *m.* (firstly), Electa COLTON, *b.* 10th June, 1802, *d.* 9th June, 1843; *m.* (secondly), the widow of ——— DIGGINS.
III. Edna, *b.* 12th March, 1798; *m.* Barnabas GRAVES.
IV. ERI JEROME, *b.* 21st December, 1799, of whom later.
V. Anne, *b.* 17th February, 1802; *d.* 22d August, 1837, in Brighton, New York; *m.* her cousin, Alonzo Decalvis DEMING, *b.* 21st July, 1804, *d.* 22d September 1856, son of Frederick and ——— (WARE) DEMING.
VI. Selah, *b.* 27th May, 1804; *d.* young.

ERI JEROME DEMING, Farmer, of East Sheldon, Vermont; *b.* 21st December, 1799, in East Sheldon, Vermont; *d.* there, 16th January 1853; *m.* 6th December 1822, Eliza GOODSELL, *b.* 30th November 1804, *d.* 19th December 1889, dau. of Elihu and Anna (ATHERTON) GOODSELL.

ISSUE

I. Sarah Ann, *b.* 28th September, 1824; *d.* 8th June, 1865; *m.* 8th June, 1853, Rev. Charles KIMBALL.
II. Edna, *b.* 24th November, 1825; *d.* 12th March, 1891; unmarried.
III. ANSON HARRINGTON, *b.* 9th January, 1828, of whom later.
IV. Elihu Goodsell, of St. Albans, Vermont; *b.* 26th July, 1829; *d.* 6th September, 1893; *m.* 15th January, 1855, Laura Sophia HERRICK, *b.* 29th December, 1830, *d.* 22d September, 1892, dau. of Samuel Bellows and Alma (HULL) HERRICK.
V. Lucy Willard, *b.* 24th July, 1831; *d.* 26th October, 1861; *m.* 24th May, 1859, Israel NORTHROP.
VI. William Morrison, of Paso Robles, California; *b.* 28th March, 1833; *d.* 12th May, 1911; *m.* 28th May, 1861, Charlotte Louise NORTHROP, dau. of Harmon and Sarah (WOOSTER) NORTHROP.

VII. Zama Eliza, *b.* 28th October, 1834; *d.* 24th June, 1849; unmarried.
VIII. Mary Goodsell, *b.* 6th March, 1837; *d.* 22d February, 1897; *m.* 6th June, 1861, Joseph NORTHROP.
IX. Nelson Jerome, *b.* 23d October, 1838; *d.* 15th December, 1854; unmarried.
X. Caroline Matilda, *b.* 24th June, 1842; *d.* 26th November, 1861; unmarried.

ANSON HARRINGTON DEMING, Merchant, of Sheldon, Vermont; *b.* there, 9th January, 1828; *d.* there, 29th May, 1860; *m.* there, 18th September, 1854, Hannah Keith JUDSON, *b.* there, 15th September, 1833, dau. of Dr. Frederick William and Lois (KEITH) JUDSON. Mrs. Deming *m.* (secondly) 5th March, 1867, Alonzo John VAN DUZEE, of Dubuque, Iowa.

ISSUE (ONLY CHILD)

I. JUDSON KEITH, *b.* 18th September, 1858, the subject of this memoir.

Arms.—Sable, three stags heads erased argent, a crescent of the second.
Crest.—A lion's head erased.
Motto.—Of the name of Deming.
Residence.—125 Grove Terrace, Dubuque, Iowa.
Clubs.—Dubuque Commercial, Dubuque Country, Shawondasee.
Societies.—Colonial Wars, Cincinnati, Sons of the Revolution.

Dixon

WILLIS MILNOR DIXON, of Los Angeles, California; *b.* 5th September, 1846, in New Lisbon, Ohio; *m.* 23d December, 1877, Los Angeles, California, Regina MAST, *b.* 19th April, 1851, in East Liverpool, Ohio, *d.* 7th July, 1911, in Los Angeles, dau. of Lieut. John MAST, *b.* 17th June, 1804, in Hochdorf, Württemburg, Germany, *d.* 26th June, 1889, *m.* 26th March, 1835, in Pittsburg, Pennsylvania, Regina KOENIG, *b.* 18th December, 1806, Württemburg, Germany, *d.* 1899, in East Liverpool, Ohio.

ISSUE

I. Lucile Mast, *b.* 9th March, 1880; *m.* 14th October, 1909, in Los Angeles, California, Ralph William STEWART, *b.* 24th March, 1878, in Washington County, Wisconsin.

ISSUE

1. Dixon STEWART, *b.* 10th November, 1910.
2. Ralph William STEWART, II, *b.* 20th March, 1912.
3. John Keith STEWART, *b.* 1st November, 1914.

WILLIS MILNOR DIXON, retired capitalist, was engaged extensively in real estate and mining enterprises in California.

Lineage Maternal

ISAAC CUMMINGS, the emigrant ancestor, supposedly of Scotch ancestry is first mentioned in Essex County records by the Town Clerk of Watertown, where he received a grant of land in 1636; in July 1638 he received another grant of land and in 1639 he owned a house and lot in the village of Ipswich. His wife's name is not known.

ISSUE

I. JOHN, *b.* 1630, of whom later.
II. Isaac, *b.* 1633.
III. Elizabeth, *m.* 2d April, 1661, to John JEWETT.
IV. Ann, *d.* 29th June, 1689; *m.* 8th October, 1669, John PEASE, Jr.

JOHN CUMMINGS, of Boxford, Massachusetts; *b.* 1630; *d.* 1st December, 1700; *m.* Sarah HOWLETT, *d.* 7th December, 1700, dau. of Ensign Thomas and Alice (FRENCH) HOWLETT.

ISSUE

I. JOHN, *b.* 1657, of whom later.
II. Thomas, *b.* 6th October, 1658, at Boxford; *d.* 23d October, 1722; *m.* 19th December, 1688, Priscilla WARNER.

III. Nathaniel, b. 10th September, 1659, m. 14th April, 1697, Abigail PARKHURST.
IV. Sarah, b. 27th January, 1661; m. 28th December, 1682, Lieuteant Samuel FRENCH, b. 1645.
V. Abraham, d. circa 1706–1707; m. 28th February, 1687, Sarah WRIGHT.
VI. Isaac, killed by Indians, 2d November, 1688.
VII. Ebenezer, killed by Indians, 2d November, 1688.
VIII. William (twin), b. 1671, d. 3d March, 1672.
IX. Eleazer (twin) b. 1671.
X. Benjamin, b. 1673.
XI. Samuel, b. 1677.

JOHN CUMMINGS, of Chelmsford, Massachusetts; b. in Boxford, Massachusetts, 1657; m. 13th September, 1680, Elizabeth KINSLEY, b. 22d November, 1657. d. 3d July, 1706, dau. of Samuel and Hannah (BROCKETT) KINSLEY.

ISSUE

I. John, b. 7th July, 1682.
II. SAMUEL, b. 6th October, 1684, of whom later.
III. Elizabeth, b. 5th January, 1687; m. 10th November, 1687, Joseph FRENCH.
IV. Hannah, b. 20th May, 1690.
V. Ebenezer, b. 17th September, 1695, at Woburn; d. 5th September, 1724.
VI. Ann, b. 14th September, 1698.
VII. Lydia, b. 24th March, 1701; d. April, 1701.
VIII. William, b. 24th April, 1702.

SAMUEL CUMMINGS, of Groton, Massachusetts; b. 6th October, 1684, in Chelmsford, Massachusetts, d. 1718; m. 14th January, 1708, Elizabeth SHEDD, dau. of Samuel and Elizabeth SHEDD of Billerica and Chelmsford.

ISSUE

I. Samuel, b. 6th March, 1709.
II. Jerahameal, b. 10th October, 1711.
III. James, b. 14th July, 1713.
IV. LEONARD, b. 1714, of whom below.

LEONARD CUMMINGS, of Londonderry, New Hampshire; b. 1714, in Dunstable (?); d. 1758; m. circa 1738, Jane, surname unknown.

ISSUE

I. Mary, b. 3d September, 1739; m. 1760, Eleazer FAREWELL.
II. Leonard, b. 10th May, 1742; d. young.
III. Betty, b. 6th October, 1744; d. 4th October, 1837; m. 19th October, 1762, Joel PARKHURST.

IV. James, *b.* 4th April, 1747; *d.* young.
V. JERAHAMEAL, *b.* 20th September, 1750, of whom later.
VI. Rachel, *b.* 1st January, 1752; *d.* 28th February, 1838; *m.* January, 1771, Eleazer REED.
VII. Silas, *b.* 6th February, 1754; *m.* circa 1775, Hannah KENDALL.

LIEUTENANT JERAHAMEAL CUMMINGS, of Amherst, New Hampshire, and Windsor, Vermont; *b.* 20th September, 1750, in Londonderry (?); *d.* Windsor, Vermont; he was First Lieutenant in 1781 of a company of Vermont Militia under Capt. Samuel Stow SAVAGE, 3d Regiment, Col. Ebenezer Hood (see "Vermont Records," pp. 351 and 359); *m.* 13th May, 1771, Deborah KENDALL, *b.* 13th May, 1751, dau. of John and Hannah (WHITTEMORE) KENDALL.

ISSUE

I. Deborah, *b.* 28th March, 1772, in Amherst.
II. Leonard, *b.* 4th June, 1773, in Amherst; *d.* 25th January, 1854; *m.* circa 1794, Lydia SPENCER.
III. Jane, *b.* 28th February, 1777.
IV. Jerahameal, *b.* 24th January, 1779; *m.* Susan WHITE.
V. JOSEPH, *b.* 15th January, 1781, of whom later.
VI. John, *b.* 20th October, 1782.
VII. Asa, *b.* 9th August, 1784.
VIII. Bera, *b.* 9th April, 1786.
IX. Hannah, *b.* 15th November, 1787; *m.* 14th May, 1807, Joel HINCKLEY.
X. Polly, *b.* 17th August, 1789.
XI. Fanny.

JOSEPH CUMMINGS, of Randolph, Vermont; *b.* 15th January, 1781, in Windsor; *m.* 2d October, 1808, Hannah CONVERSE, *b.* 8th April, 1785, *d.* 31st August, 1856, dau. of Col. Israel CONVERSE, 6th in descent from Deacon Edward CONVERSE, *b.* 30th January, 1590, at Wakerly County, Northampton, England, *d.* 10th August, 1663, at Woburn, Massachusetts.

ISSUE

I. Solon, *b.* 3d December, 1810; *d.* 20th June, 1873; *m.* (firstly) Hannah MARSH; *m.* (secondly) ——— MOORE.
II. Laura, *b.* 4th April, 1813; *d.* 23d March, 1885; *m.* Horner H. PAINE.
III. Edwin, *b.* 28th August, 1815; *d.* 13th November, 1893.
IV. Marion Orinda, *b.* 8th September, 1818; *d.* 9th December, 1888; *m.* 11th February, 1847, Dr. Marvin CHAPIN.
V. Lucinda, *b.* 14th July, 1820; *d.* 3d October 1785; *m.* Cornelius WILBUR.
VI. CHARLOTTE CONVERSE, *b.* 30th December, 1822-1823, of whom later.
VII. Theron, *b.* 12th July, 1825; *d.* 3d August, 1898; *m.* (firstly) Josephine HARRIS; *m.* (secondly) Louisa GILL.

CHARLOTTE CONVERSE CUMMINGS, *b.* 30th December, 1822-1823, in Royalton, Vermont; *d.* 23d November, 1900, in Los Angeles, California; *m.* 24th October, 1845, in Parkman, Ohio, Lot DIXON, *b.* 11th February, 1914, in Columbiana, Ohio, *d.* 14th August, 1853, in Bucyrus, Ohio, son of John and Hannah (BEAL) DIXON.

ISSUE

I. WILLIS MILNOR DIXON, *b.* 5th September, 1846, the subject of this memoir.
II. J. Theron DIXON, *b.* 25th October 1848; *d.* 24th October, 1853.

Residence.—1200 Arapahoe Street, Los Angeles, California.
Clubs.—Sierre Madre, Los Angles, California.
Societies.—Colonial Wars, Sons of the Revolution, Order of Washington National Genealogical Society, New Jersey Society, Order of Founders and Patriots, California Genealogical Society, Shedd Family Association, National Geographical Society. All branches of the Masonic Fraternity.

Douglas

GEORGE WILLIAM DOUGLAS, B.A., M.A., D.D., S.T.D., of New York City; *b.* New York City, 8th July, 1850; *m.* 3d September, 1884, in Trinity Church, Newport, Rhode Island, Cornelia De Koven DICKEY, dau. of Judge Hugh T. DICKEY, *b.* 30th May, 1811, *d.* 2d June, June, 1892, *m.* 18th April, 1850, Frances Russell DE KOVEN, *b.* 21st June, 1829, *d.* 12th October, 1900.

GEORGE WILLIAM DOUGLAS graduated from St. Paul's School, Concord, New Hampshire, in 1868, and from Trinity College, Hartford, Connecticut, B.A. (valedictorian) 1871; M.A., 1874; D.D., 1895. He received the degree of S.T.D. from Hobart College in 1885 and D.D. from the University of the South in 1899; he graduated from the General Theological Seminary, New York City, in 1874. From then until 1876, he studied at Oxford, England, and the University of Bonn, Germany. He was ordained Deacon by Bishop Horatio POTTER in 1874; ordained Priest in 1878, becoming assistant minister to the Rev. Edward A. WASHBURN, D.D., at Calvary Church, New York City. In 1879 he was Assistant of Trinity Parish as Vicar of Trinity Church, New York, 1879–1886. He resigned in 1886 on account of ill health and spent two years in Europe. From 1889 to 1892 he was Rector of St. John's Church, Washington, D. C., and Trustee of Washington Cathedral; and of Trinity Church, New Haven, Connecticut, from 1895 to 1898. He was Select Preacher at Grace Church, New York City, and Instructor in the Training School for Deaconesses from 1898 to 1904. In 1904 he became Senior Canon Residentrary of the Cathedral of St. John the Divine, New York City. He declined the Presidency of Hobart College, Geneva, New York, 1885. Lecturer Union Theological Seminary, New York; Philadelphia Divinity School; Episcopal Theological School, Cambridge, Massachusetts. He is the author of "Sermons Preached in St. John's Church, Washington," 1893; "Prayers for Children," 1884; "Hints to Sunday School Teachers," 1883; "Essays in Appreciation" 1912, and also various sermons, addresses, magazine articles. He was Chaplain of the District of Columbia Society, Sons of the American Revolution, 1890–1891.

Lineage

DEACON WILLIAM DOUGLAS, the immigrant ancestor, was *b.* 9th August, 1610, doubtless in Scotland; *m.* probably about 1636, Ann MATTLE, dau. of Thomas MATTLE of Ringstead, England. In 1640, with his wife Ann and two children, Ann and Robert, William DOUGLAS went to New England. Tradition says that they landed at Cape Ann. They settled first in Gloucester, but removed within the year to Boston, where he is first mentioned in the Boston records on 31st June, 1640, when he was made a Freeman. He removed shortly to Ipswich where he was entitled to a share of the public land, 28th February, 1641. There he remained for about four years, returning to Boston in 1645. He was a cooper by trade and on 1st May, 1646, there is record of his purchasing from Walter MERRY and Thomas ANCHOR, a dwelling house, shop and land. Later he went to New London, Connecticut, and obtained considerable property through purchase and grants from the town. One of his farms was inherited by his son William and has remained in the hands of descendants for over two centuries. In 1662-1663 he was appointed one of the Appraisers of Property for the town of New London. The land for a new church was purchased from him and the graveyard still remains on that place. He and Mr. WILLERBY were appointed to deliver provisions to Commissary TRACY at Norwich during King Philip's War. His education for the times was liberal. He held many important offices in the town at different times. He was Deputy to the General Court in 1672 and once or twice later. In May, 1670, his wife, then sixty years old made a journey to Boston to establish her claim as heir to her father's property. She *d.* in New London in 1685 and William DOUGLAS himself *d.* there on 26th July, 1682.

ISSUE

I. Ann, *b.* in Scotland, 1637; *m.* 14th October, 1658, Nathaniel GEARY, of Roxbury.
II. Robert, *b.* in Scotland, 1639; *m.* in 1665, Mary HEMPSTEAD, dau. of Robert HEMPSTEAD.
III. Elizabeth, *b.* in Ipswich, Massachusetts, 26th August, 1641; *m.* 16th February, 1659, John CHANDLER.
IV. Sarah, *b.* in Ipswich, 8th April, 1643; *m.* 1661, John KEENY, of New London.
V. WILLIAM, *b.* 1st April, 1645, of whom below.

WILLIAM DOUGLAS, of New London, Connecticut, *b.* in Boston, 1st April, 1645; *d.* there 9th March, 1725. William DOUGLAS, Jr. received lands at Voluntown, 29th March, 1706, which he afterwards sold to his son William 3d; *m.* (firstly) at New London, Connecticut, 18th December, 1667, Abiah HOUGH, dau. of William and Sarah (CAULKINS) HOUGH of New London, and gd. dau. of Edward HOUGH of Westchester, Cheshire, England. She was *b.* 15th September, 1648, *d.* 21st February, 1715. William DOUGLAS *m.* (secondly) July, 1715, the widow Mary BUSHNELL, who survived him. His children were all born in New London.

ISSUE BY FIRST MARRIAGE ONLY

I. Elizabeth, *b.* 25th February, 1668-1869; *m.* 4th August, 1686, Daniel DART of New London.
II. Sarah, *b.* 2d April, 1671; *m.* August, 1702, Jared SPENCER of Saybrook.
III. WILLIAM, *b.* 19th February, 1673, of whom later.

IV. Abiah, *b.* 18th August, 1675; *d.* 12th August, 1689.
V. Rebecca, *b.* 14th June, 1678; *d.s.p.* after 15th March 1725.
VI. Ann, *b.* 24th May, 1680; *m.* 3d September, 1702, Thomas SPENCER of Saybrook.
VII. Richard, *b.* 19th July, 1682; *m.* 7th December, 1704, Margaret ABELL.
VIII. Samuel, *b.* circa 1684; *m.* 18th July, 1714, Sarah OLCOTT.

WILLIAM DOUGLAS, of Plainfield, Connecticut; *b.* in New London, Connecticut, 19th February, 1673; *d.* 10th August, 1719, at Plainfield; he removed in 1699 to Quinnebaug, afterwards Plainfield, Connecticut, where he had land on the east side of the river; he also owned the lands of his father at Voluntown; *m.* Sarah PROCTOR, who *d.* after 1729.

ISSUE

I. Hannah, *b.* 7th September, 1696; *m.* 9th February, 1713–1714, Thomas WILLIAMS of Plainfield.
II. William, *b.* 19th February, 1697–1698; *m.* 26th March, 1716, Mary HANOVER.
III. Samuel, *b.* 13th April, 1699; *d.s.p.* June, 1703.
IV. Abiah, *b.* 26th February, 1701–1702; *m.* 3d May, 1720, Henry HOLLAND of Plainfield.
V. John, *b.* 28th July, 1703; *m.* 13th January, 1724–1725, Olive SPAULDING.
VI. Sarah, *b.* 7th December, 1704.
VII. Jerusha, *b.* 26th April, 1706.
VIII. Samuel, *b.* 3d December, 1707; *m.* Mary, surname unknown.
IX. Benajah, *b.* 17th September, 1710; *m.* name unknown.
X. James, *b.* 20th May, 1711; *m.* 4th December, 1732, Rachel MARSH.
XI. Thomas, *b.* 26th November, 1712; *m.* 4th January, 1737, Martha GALLUP.
XII. ASA, *b.* 11th December, 1715, of whom later.

ASA DOUGLAS, of Stephentown, New York; *b.* at Plainfield, Connecticut, 11th December, 1715; *d.* 12th November, 1792; he removed from Plainfield to Old Canaan about 1746; about twenty years later he removed to what was then Jericho Hollow, Massachusetts, now Stephentown, New York; during the Revolution the cellar of his house was used as the jail; he led a company of thirty Silver Grays in the Battle of Bennington, 16th August, 1777, when the British and Indians sent to seize the stores collected there and were defeated by the Americans under Col. John STARK; *m.* in 1737, Rebecca WHEELER, *b.* 26th August, 1718, at Concord, Massachusetts, *d.* 12th June, 1809, at Stephentown, New York, dau. of Jonathan and Sarah (———) WHEELER.

ISSUE

I. Sarah, *b.* at Plainfield, 26th February, 1738; *m.* George (?) STEWART.
II. Major Asa, *b.* at Plainfield, 24th December, 1739; he was a Major in the Continental Army; he made himself so troublesome to the British

that a large reward was offered for his apprehension; when BURGOYNE went from Canada to meet Clinton at Albany, Major Asa had to take to the woods for several weeks, staying no two nights in the same place to avoid capture; *m.* Sarah ROBBINS.

III. Rebecca, *b.* at Plainfield, 3d January, 1741–1742; *d.s.p.* 28th April, 1826.
IV. William, *b.* at Plainfield, 22d August, 1743; *m.* Hannah COLE.
V. Hannah, *b.* at Plainfield, 17th January, 1744–1745; *m.* Hon. J(ames?) BROWN.
VI. Lucy, *b.* at Canaan, 12th January, 1746–1747; *d.* 1749.
VII. Olive, *b.* at Canaan, 7th September, 1748; *m.* Gen. Samuel SLOANE.
VIII. WHEELER, *b.* 10th April, 1750, of whom later.
IX. Jonathan, *b.* at Canaan, 14th February, 1752; *m.* Rhoda HANCOCK.
X. Nathaniel, *b.* at Canaan, 11th August, 1754; *m.* (firstly) Prudence BROWN; *m.* (secondly) ——— TRAVAISSA.
XI. John, *b.* at Canaan, 2d August, 1758; *m.* Hannah BROWN.
XII. Benajah, *b.* at Canaan, 15th December, 1760; *m.* Martha ARNOLD.
XIII. Lucy, *b.* at Canaan, 10th May, 1762; *m.* Maj. Jonathan BROWN.

WHEELER DOUGLAS, *b.* at Canaan, 10th April, 1750; he removed from Stephentown to Albany, New York, in 1780, where he opened the firm of Douglas and Wheeler with one of his cousins; in 1798 his property was destroyed by fire; he then went to Brant's Ford, Canada, where he remained about a year with the famous Chief of the Six Nations, Capt. Joseph BRANT; in 1799 he removed his family to Canada and settled on the Grand River, where Brantford is now situated; he made his home among the Indians for a few years, but later leased some five hundred acres, lying about eight miles west of their settlement from Brant; he and his wife both *d.* at the home of their dau. Harriet; he *m.* 7th August, 1773, at Stonington, Martha RATHBONE, *b.* 7th August, 1753, at Stonington, Connecticut, *d.* 1st December, 1837, at Smithville, Canada, dau. of Rev. John and Content (BROWN) RATHBONE.

ISSUE

I. Content, *b.* at Stephentown, 4th September, 1772; *m.* Gen. Samuel STEWART.
II. Martha, *b.* at Stephentown, 26th September, 1774; *m.* Jesse TRACY.
III. John Hancock, *b.* at Stephentown, 26th April, 1776; he was a physician in New York City and *d.* about 1865; *m.* Elizabeth WILLIAMS.
IV. ALANSON, *b.* 11th February, 1779, of whom later.
V. Mary, *b.* at Albany; *m.* Roger SELDEN.
VI. George, *b.* at Albany; *d.s.p.*
VII. Charlotte, *b.* at Albany, 15th July, 1785; *m.* Joseph SMITH.
VIII. Minerva, *b.* at Albany, 17th October, 1787; *m.* ——— MATHEWS.
IX. Stephen van Rensselaer, *b.* at Albany, 24th March, 1790; *m.* Caroline H. Whitehead.
X. Harriet, *b.* at Albany, 15th June, 1793; *m.* Smith GRIFFIN.

ALANSON DOUGLAS, *b.* at Stephentown, New York, 11th February, 1779; *d.* at Troy, New York, 7th April, 1856; he studied law; settled first in the village of Lansinburgh, in 1806 he was Surrogate of Rensselaer County, New York, in 1811; he was elected Cashier of the newly incorporated Bank of Troy; in 1827 he was invited to become the Cashier of the Chemical Bank of New York City, but not caring for New York, gladly accepted the call of the Merchants' and Mechanics' Bank of Troy in 1829, just after it received its charter; here he stayed until 1836 when he resigned and was succeeded by his son Charles Selden DOUGLAS. Alanson DOUGLAS declined the offer of President VAN BUREN of Secretaryship of the Treasury in the latter's Cabinet; *m.* at Stanford, New York, 12th June, 1803, Ann SUTHERLAND, *b.* at Stanford, 7th April, 1784, *d.* at Irvington, New York, 28th February, 1869, dau. of the Hon. Solomon and Tamma (THOMPSON) SUTHERLAND.

ISSUE

I. Sutherland, *b.* at Lansingburgh, 25th October, 1804; *m.* Harriet L. STAPLES.
II. Mary Ann, *b.* at Lansingburgh, 7th February, 1807; *m.* Hon. Samuel MILLER.
III. George Henry, *b.* at Lansingburgh, 12th September, 1809; *d.s.p.* 1st September, 1837.
IV. Charles Selden, *b.* at Lansingburgh, 17th August, 1812; *m.* (firstly) Sarah A. HOLLISTER; *m.* (secondly) Mary WARNER, widow of ———— WELLS.
V. WILLIAM BRADLEY, *b.* 26th December, 1818, of whom later.
VI. Julia, *b.* at Troy, 17th September, 1823, *m.* George MERRITT.

WILLIAM BRADLEY DOUGLAS, of New York City and Rochester, New York; *b.* at Troy, New York, 26th December, 1818; he early entered his father's bank; in 1842 he was elected Cashier of the Bank of Ithaca; at the expiration of its charter he removed to New York City, and in January, 1850, with others, set about organizing the Mercantile Bank, of which he became first President; in 1856 he retired because of ill health; he went to live in Geneva for some years, but in 1869 removed to Rochester; *m.* 3d June, 1841, Charlotte Cornelia Dickinson FERRIS, dau. of Orange and Sophia (RATHBONE) FERRIS, of St. Albans, Vermont.

ISSUE

I. GEORGE WILLIAM, *b.* 8th July, 1850, the subject of this memoir.
II. Mary Hawley, *b.* 29th April, 1852, *m.* 31st December 1872, Frank A. WARD.

ISSUE

1. William Douglas WARD, *b.* 25th August, 1874.
2. Frank Hawley WARD, *b.* 13th December, 1876.
3. Charlotte Ferris WARD, *b.* 22d March, 1879.
4. Emma Wilder WARD, *b.* 28th October, 1881.

5. Edward Smith WARD, b. 27th April, 1884; d. 19th July, 1913.
6. George Merritt WARD, b. 18th December, 1885.
7. Mary Antoinette WARD, b. 15th September, 1887.
8. Sutherland Douglas WARD, b. 27th March, 1890; d. December, 1890.
9. Cornelia de Koven WARD, b. 5th February, 1893.
10. Dudley Livingston WARD, b. 11th August, 1894.

III. Anna Sutherland, b. 22d May, 1856; d. 5th December, 1856.

Arms.—Argent, a man's heart gules ensigned with an imperial crown proper; on a chief azure three stars of the first.

Crest.—A heart encrowned or.

Motto.—Jamais arriere.

Residence.—5 East 88th Street, New York City, Tuxedo Park, New York.

Clubs.—Century, Grolier, Tuxedo, University, Union League (New York City); Chicago (Chicago); Automobile of America, Metropolitan (Washington). Clerical Club, Churchman's Association, Vice President of Clergy Clubs of New York and Neighborhood.

Societies.—Colonial Wars, Sons of the American Revolution; Psi Upsilon (Beta Beta Chapter), Phi Beta Kappa, Philothean.

Douglas

HARRY DOUGLAS, of Doric House, Great Barrington, Massachusetts; *b.* 28th February, 1857; *m.* 11th December, 1884, in New York, Anne Grace PAGE, dau. of Kingman Fogg and Grace (MARSHALL) PAGE.

ISSUE

I. Grace Josephine, *b.* 30th September, 1887; *m.* 15th April, 1914. James Sheldon POTTER of New York, son of Asa P. POTTER.

II. Marion, *b.* 22d June, 1889; *m.* 19th September, 1908, William Floyd KENDALL, son of William Beals KENDALL.

ISSUE

1. Douglas KENDALL, *b.* 30th June, 1910.

III. Anne, *b.* 1st June, 1892.

HARRY DOUGLAS was educated at Edwards Place School, Stockbridge, Massachusetts, and public school No. 35, New York City; entered College of the City of New York and later Columbia University, but compelled to give up college owing to ill health; studied law under David Dudley FIELD, for four years, then took up journalism as a profession; established the *Berkshire News* at Great Barrington, Massachusetts, in 1889, sold the paper five years later; was a delegate to the Indianapolis Convention in 1896 of the National Democratic Party; declined a Democratic Congressional nomination in 1894. Author of "Some Old Masters of Greek Architecture," and other works.

Lineage

The emigrant ancestor of this family was Deacon William DOUGLAS, I, *b.* in Scotland, 1610; *d.* 1682. His father's name is supposed to have been Robert DOUGLAS, *b.* in Scotland in 1588. The exact date of Deacon William DOUGLAS' arrival in America and the name of the ship are uncertain. The tradition is that the company landed at Cape Ann. William settled at Gloucester, but removed to Boston the same year. As the date of his residence in Boston is given as 1640 it is to be assumed that he reached this country in that year. The next year he removed to Ipswich, Massachusetts, where he was entitled to a share of the public lands. In December, 1659, he purchased of William HOUGH of New London, Connecticut, the house that was Robert ISBELL's in New Street. Soon after in 1660 he removed to New London; Townsman of New London, 1663, 1666, 1669; Deputy to General Court 1672; m. Ann MATTLE of Ringstead, Northamptonshire, England, dau. of Thomas MATTLE, Esq.

ISSUE

I. Ann, b. in Scotland, 1637; m. 14th October, 1658, Nathaniel GEARY.
II. Robert, b. in Scotland, 1639; m. Mary HEMPSTEAD.
III. Elizabeth, b. Ipswich, Massachusetts, 26th August, 1641; m. 16th February, 1659, Deacon John CHANDLER of Roxbury.
IV. Sarah, b. Ipswich, 8th April, 1643; m. 1661, John KEENY of New London.
V. WILLIAM, II, b. Boston, 1st April, 1645, of whom later.

WILLIAM DOUGLAS, II, of New London, Connecticut; b. 1st April, 1645, in Boston; d. 28th February, 1734; m. (firstly), 1667, Abiah HOUGH; m. (secondly) Mary BUSHNELL of New London.

ISSUE BY FIRST MARRIAGE

I. Elizabeth, b. 25th February, 1668.
II. Sarah, b. 2d. April, 1671.
III. William, b. 19th February, 1672.
IV. Abiah, b. 18th August, 1765.
V. Rebecca, b. 14th June, 1678.
VI. Ann, b. 24th May, 1680.
VII. RICHARD, b. 19th July, 1682, of whom later.
VIII. Samuel, v. 1684.

RICHARD DOUGLAS, of New London, Connecticut; b. 19th July, 1682; d. 26th February, 1734; Sea Captain and Surveyor of Highways; m. Margaret ABELL of New London.

ISSUE

I. Jonathan, b. 30th October, 1705.
II. WILLIAM, III, b. 1st January, 1708, of whom later.
III. Abiah, b. 1710.
IV. Caleb, b. 1714.
V. Margaret, b. 1717.
VI. Richard, b. 1720.
VII. Samuel, b. 1722.
VIII. Elizabeth, b. 1725.

WILLIAM DOUGLAS, III, New London, Connecticut; b. 1st January, 1708; d. 27th November, 1787; was Constable and Deacon of Old Presbyterian Church and a man of importance in the town; m. 4th March, 1730, Sarah DENISON, dau. of George DENISON, d. 12th May, 1796.

ISSUE

I. William, *b.* 7th February, 1731.
II. Elizabeth, *b.* 26th November, 1733.
III. Margaret, *b.* 4th October, 1735.
IV. Jonathan, *b.* 4th July, 1737.
V. George, *b.* 16th July, 1739.
VI. Abiah, *b.* 5th January, 1741.
VII. Lucy, *b.* 27th November, 1743.
VIII. Sarah, *b.* 7th February, 1745.
IX. Eunice, *b.* 1748.
X. RICHARD, *b.* 1750, of whom later.
XI. Lydia, *b.* 1752.

CAPTAIN RICHARD DOUGLAS, of New London, Connecticut; *b.* 1750, *d.* 1st March 1816; derived his title from service in the Revolutionary War (see Year Book of New York Society, Sons of the Revolution); *m.* (firstly) Abigail STARR, *d.s.p.* 1799; *m.* (secondly) 2d September, 1804, Lucy (WAY) PALMER, *b.* 6th March, 1774, dau. of John WAY and widow of Samuel PALMER. John WAY was annually elected one of the New London City Council from its incorporation until his death at the age of forty-eight years.

ISSUE

I. EARL, *b.* 27th May, 1805, of whom later.
II. Alfred, *b.* 15th January, 1807.
III. Erskine, *b.* 26th August, 1812.

EARL DOUGLAS, of New London, Connecticut; *b.* 27th May, 1805; *d.* 5th November, 1865, at Grammercy Park Hotel, New York City; *m.* 20th August, 1827, Julia HEMPSTEAD, *b.* in Hartford, 28th April, 1809, *d.* 22d January, 1869, dau. of Josiah and Mary HEMPSTEAD of Hartford, Connecticut, descended from Sir Robert HEMPSTEAD, founder of the towns of Hempstead, Long Island, moved to New London in June, 1645, with John WINTHROP, later Governor of Colony of Connecticut, Sir Richard SALTONSTALL and others.

ISSUE

I. ALFRED, *b.* 10th February, 1829, of whom later.
II. Richard, *b.* 28th April, 1831.

ALFRED DOUGLAS, of New York; *b.* 10th February, 1829; *d.* 3d October; 1876; *m.* 1852, Josephine CHEESEMAN, dau. of a New York merchant.

ISSUE

I. Malcolm, *b.* 1855.
II. HARRY, *b.* 28th February, 1857, the subject of this memoir.
III. Josephine, *b.* 1861.

Arms.—Argent, a man's heart gules ensigned with an imperial crown ppr. on a chief azure three stars of the first.
Crest.—A heart encrowned or.
Motto.—Jamais arriere.
Residence.—Doric House, Great Barrington, Massachusetts.

Duke

WILLIAM BERNARD DUKE of "Wilbermar Fields," Riderwood, Baltimore County, Maryland; *b.* 4th July, 1873, at Leonardtown, St. Mary's County, Maryland; *m.* (firstly) at Church of the Immaculate, Towson, Maryland, Jennie (WEBB) ABELL, *d.s.p.*, dau. of George WEBB and widow of George ABELL, both of Baltimore; *m.* (secondly) at the Cathedral, Baltimore, Maryland, 11th February, 1913, Katherine Marie TURNER, dau. of Joseph Joshua TURNER of Baltimore Maryland, and Virginia Agnes MUMFORD, of Snow Hill, Worcester County, Maryland, *m.* 12th November, 1867, she dau. of William and Eleanor (HOLLAND) MUMFORD. Joseph Joshua TURNER was son of Joshua Joseph and Catherine (HERTER) TURNER, she dau. of Ignatius HERTER, he son of J. J. TURNER of Baltimore, who was the son of William, the son of Matthew TURNER.

ISSUE

I. William Bernard, *b.* 31st May, 1914.

WILLIAM BERNARD DUKE was educated at the schools in St. Mary's County, Maryland; came to Baltimore and engaged in the bicycle business under the firm name of EHRMAN and DUKE; later founded the firm of DUKE, MONTAGUE and GILLETT, manufacturers of straw goods, and also the DUKE-PETERSON Hardware Company in 1904; was for three years a Director and Vice-President of the National Bank of Baltimore; Director in the Third National Bank; Vice-President Mercantile Security Company; President German Savings Bank; in 1914 he organized the Seaboard Bank of Baltimore of which he has been President since its organization. He has large farming and stock raising interests in St. Mary's County.

Lineage

The DUKES of Maryland are supposed to have originated in Devonshire, England, and DUKE of Lake is presumed to be the head of the American branch. Richard DUKE came to Maryland with Father WHITE's party in the *Ark*, 1634, and settled at St. Mary's; it is the family tradition he was Father WHITE's private secretary; he was also a close friend and advisor of Governor Leonard CALVERT, who called him "my trusted friend;" he was on Kent Island in 1641; he was a Member of the Assembly 1637 to 1653 and a leading spirit thereat and was otherwise a prominent man in the affairs of the colony; his wife's name is unknown; in 1653 he returned to England with his wife and his sons Thomas and Richard, who *d.* young, it is believed, in London, and never returned to Maryland.

ISSUE

I. Richard, returned to England, no further record.
II. Thomas, returned to England, no further record.
III. Andrew, no record.
IV. JAMES, I, *d.* after 1672, of whom later.
V. William, returned to England, no further record.

JAMES DUKE, I, of Calvert County, Maryland, in 1652; will proved there in 1672; *m.* Margaret, surname unknown.

ISSUE

I. JAMES, II, *d.* 1693, of whom later.
II. John, no record.
III. Joseph, no record.
IV. William, no record.

JAMES DUKE, II, of "Brooke Place Manor," Calvert County; *d.* after 1693; *m.* Mary DAWKINS, dau. of Joseph and Mary (HALL) DAWKINS, of Calvert County, Maryland; James was sometimes called Captain, and was a very active man of affairs; was one of Michael TANEY'S advisers in the controversy between the Sheriff and COADE, for which he suffered arrest and imprisonment; he acquired large landed estates, his plantation was called "Brooke Place Manor."

ISSUE

I. Andrew, *d.* probably before his father, no record.
II. Basil, *d.* probably before his father, no record.
III. John, *d.* probably before his father; no record.
IV. Joseph, *d.* probably before his father; no record.
V. JAMES, III, *d.* prior to 1731, of whom below.

JAMES DUKE, III, of "Brooke Place Manor," Calvert County, Maryland; *d.* prior to 1730; inherited the major part of the estate of his father and added largely to his landed possessions; *m.* Martha MACKALL, dau. of Benjamin and Barbara (SMITH) MACKALL; he *d.* prior to 1731.

ISSUE

I. JAMES, IV, *d.* circa 1754, of whom later.
II. Martha, *m.* William GRAY, of Calvert County.
III. Catherine, *m.* ———— BEALE, of Calvert County.
IV. Elizabeth, *m.* ———— ROWLAND, of Calvert County.

JAMES DUKE, III, of "Brooke Place Manor," Calvert County, Maryland; *d.* 1754; was a prominent man of affairs and was styled Captain; one of the Justices of Calvert County, 1731-1754; of the Quorum from 1736 to 1752; is said to have been the first Protestant member of the family; was a Vestryman of Christ Church; he *m.* (firstly) Martha, surname unknown; *m.* (secondly) Esther PARRAN, widow of John PARRAN, she *d.s.p.*

ISSUE BY FIRST MARRIAGE

I. James, V, *b.* circa 1728; *d.* circa 1769; *m.* Mary (BROWNE) WILSON, widow of Nathaniel BROWNE.
II. BENJAMIN, *b.* circa 1730; of whom later.
III. Leonard, *b.* circa 1732; *d.* unmarried, 1763, leaving his estate to his brother Basil.
IV. JOHN, *b.* circa 1734, of whom later.
V. Basil, *m.*, wife's name unknown.

ISSUE

1. Richard.
2. Moses Parran.

VI. Andrew, moved to Harpers Ferry, Virginia.
VII. Martha, *m.* John MACKALL, son of James and Ann (BROOKE) MACKALL.
VIII. Mary, *m.* ─── HELLEN.

JOHN DUKE, of Calvert and St. Mary's Counties, Maryland; *b.* circa 1734–1735; *d.* after 1780; owing to the complete destruction by fire of all the official County, State and Church records of Calvert and St. Mary's Counties, there is no evidence other than family history of John Duke; it is known he had three sons, two of whom James and Basil remained in Calvert County, while he removed to St. Mary's County, where he married.

ISSUE

I. JOHN, *b.* 1778, of whom later.
II. James, who remained in Calvert County.
III. Basil who probably later moved to Kentucky.

JOHN DUKE of Whitemarsh, St. Mary's County; *b.* in Calvert County, circa 1778; *d.* in St. Mary's County, 1837; *m.* 1799, Mary Priscilla EGERTON of St. Mary's County.

ISSUE

I. Mary, *m.* Col. John WALTON of Annapolis, Maryland.

ISSUE

1. Roland WALTON.
2. Randolph WALTON.
3. Edward WALTON.

II. A son, name not given.
III. JOHN of Whitemarsh, *b.* circa 1800, of whom later.

JOHN DUKE of Whitemarsh, St. Mary's County, Maryland; *b.* circa 1800, *d.* circa 1838; *m.* circa 1823, Mary Ann DENT, dau. of George and Elizabeth Temperance (MILLS) DENT of Trent Fort," St. Mary's County, Maryland.

ISSUE

I. Susanna, *m.* John L. ABELL.
II. George Dent, *m.* Nannie HEBB.
III. James Thomas, *m.* Martha DENT.
IV. Mary Priscilla, *m.* Robert H. WATHEN.
V. Betie Ann, *d.* young.
VI. JOHN FRANCIS, *b.* 25th July, 1835, of whom later.

JOHN FRANCIS DUKE, Planter, of Prospect Point, St. Mary's County, Maryland; *b.* 25th July, 1835; *d.* 18th December, 1915; during the Civil War, when the "Maryland Line" was organized, he became a member of Company B, 2d Maryland Infantry, Confederate States of America; served throughout the war until his capture and imprisonment at Point Lookout; was a Teacher for nearly half of a century; served as School Commissioner for fourteen years; *m.* 30th December, 1865, Margaret Ann NUTHALL, *b.* 4th January, 1844, *d.* 5th March, 1898, dau. of William and Matilda (ABELL) NUTHALL of St. Mary's County, Maryland, she dau. of Thomas ABELL of St. Mary's County.

ISSUE

I.. James Roland of Leonardtown; *b.* 12th December, 1867; *m.* 20th October, 1892, Catherine Carroll COUNCELL, dau. of George Montgomery COUNCELL, and Henrietta (PRICE) COUNCELL of Talbot County.
II. Mary Mabel, *b.* 17th December, 1869; *m.* 21st April, 1900, Joseph Cottman HOBBS of St. George's Island, St. Mary's County, Maryland, son of Joseph COTTMAN and Sarah Jane HOBBS.
III. John Thomas of Leonardtown, *b.* 11th January, 1872; *m.* 29th August, 1894, Elizabeth Stuart HAYDEN of Greenville, South Carolina, *b.* 14th May, 1876.
IV. WILLIAM BERNARD, *b.* 4th July, 1873, the subject of this memoir.
V. Ann Eleanora of Baltimore, *b.* 22d February, 1875; unmarried.
VI. Margaret Martine, *b.* 16th October, 1876; *d.* 11th May, 1906; *m.* 28th June, 1905, Lynwood J. STERLING, son of J. Edward N. STERLING of Cape Charles, Virginia.
VII. Benjamin Hooper of Valley Lee, St. Mary's County; *b.* 12th August, 1878; served with Company I, 1st Maryland National Guard, in Spanish American War, 1898; *m.* 6th January, 1902, Grace Arline DENT, dau. of Thomas and Amy Frances (ALLSTON) DENT.
VIII. Elisabeth Matilda (Sister Michaella), *b.* 30th January, 1880, of St. Catherine's Academy, Lexington, Kentucky.

IX. Agnes Bernadette, *b.* 17th July, 1881; *d.* 12th October, 1881.
X. Maud Francis (Sister Margaret Francis); *b.* 18th November, 1882, of St. Mary's School, Paris, Kentucky.
XI. John Jenkins of Leonardtown, Maryland; *b.* 28th February, 1884; *m.* 10th September, 1910, Lilian Paret TURNER, dau. of Rev. Barker and Fannie (THOMAS) TURNER.
XII. Charles Clarence, *b.* 10th February, 1886; *m.* 16th June, 1913, Anna Bissell BALDWIN, dau. of Dr. Joseph and Anna (BISSELL) BALDWIN.

Arms.—Per fesse argent and azure three chaplets countercharged.
Crest.—A demi-griffin or, holding a chaplet azure.
Motto.—Always faithful.
Residence.—"Wilbermar Fields," Riderwood, Baltimore County, Maryland.
Societies.—Sons of the American Revolution.

Dent

JOHN DENT, "Gentleman," of St. Mary's County, Maryland; *b.* 1651; *d.* 1712; probably was the John DENT who came to Maryland in 1661 to inherit lands from his uncle Thomas DENT, who was *b.* circa 1630, in Gisborough. Yorkshire. John DENT was Commissioner and Justice of the Peace, 1679; served against the Indians at Susquehanna Fort, 1681; Captain to regulate Military Affairs in Chaptico Hundred, St. Mary's County, Maryland, 1694; was a witness against FENDALL, in 1687; Member of the King's Council for Maryland, appointed by King William, 1691; Vestryman of King and Queen's Parish; Member of Committee for St. Mary's County, 1689, etc.; he was quite a large land holder, leaving lands to all his children; *m.* Mary SHERCLIFFE, *b.* 1647, dau. of John and Anne (SPINKE) SHERCLIFFE, he mentions her in his will as "my loving wife."

ISSUE

I. John, to whom he leaves some 1500 acres.
II. Peter, who was living outside of Maryland at the time his father's will was made.
III. Mary, he leaves "Ashmans Freehold."
IV. Lydia, he leaves "St. Anns," 100 acres.
V. Anna, he leaves "St. Stephens," "Colmans," and "Evans Resource," 300 acres.
VI. Abigail, he leaves "Love's Adventure," 136 acres.
VII. Christianna, "Cold Wells," 556 acres.
VIII. GEORGE, "Haphazard," and "Freestone Point," 374 acres, of whom below.

GEORGE DENT, Planter of "Freestone Point" and "Haphazard," St. Mary's County, Maryland; will dated 5th April, 1746; proved 7th June, 1750; was a large land owner as shown by his will; *m.* Mary surname unknown.

ISSUE

I. John.
II. George.
III. Peter.
IV. THOMAS, *b.* circa 1730, of whom later.
V. William.
VI. Mary, *m.* ———— ARMSTRONG.
VII. Lydia.
VIII. Charity.

THOMAS DENT of St. Mary's County, Maryland; *b.* circa 1730; living in 1774; *d.* prior to 1790; *m.* Elizabeth EDWARDS, who *d.* 1823–1824; they had a son.

GEORGE DENT of "Trent Fort," St. Mary's County, Maryland; *b.* 21st December, 1756; *d.* 15th October, 1842; served as a private in the American Revolution from 25th May 1778 to 3d April, 1779, in Capt. John DAVIDSON's Company, 2d Maryland Regiment, commanded by Colonel WOOLFORD; served subsequently for two weeks under Lieut. Benjamin EDWARDS and again for two months under Captain MILLS; *m.* Elizabeth Temperance MILLS.

ISSUE (SURVIVING AT HIS DEATH)

I. William.
II. Hezekiah.
III. Mary Ann, *m.* John DUKE (see DUKE family for descendants), page 200.
IV. Eliza T., *m.* John Amory BURROUGHS.

Dunton

WILLIAM RUSH DUNTON, II, M.D., of Govans, Maryland; *b.* 24th July, 1868, in Philadelphia, Pennsylvania; *m.* 1st July, 1897, Emma Drusilla HOGAN, *b.* 12th September, 1862, dau. of Jonathan Elmer HOGAN, *b.* 19th December, 1840, *d.* 2d February, 1916, *m.* 9th May, 1860, Helen Rowena McCLEAN, *b.* 9th May, 1836, *d.* 28th December, 1892.

ISSUE

I. Helen McClean, *b.* 2d May, 1899.
II. William Rush, III, *b.* 26th May, 1903.
III. Stephen Morgan, *b.* 6th November, 1904; *d.* 6th April, 1905.
IV. Henry Hurd, *b.* 30th December, 1905.

WILLIAM RUSH DUNTON, M.D., was educated at private schools; Haverford College, B.S., 1889; M.A., 1890; University of Pennsylvania, M.D., 1893; Interne at several hospitals; Assistant Physician Sheppard and Enoch Pratt Hospital since 1895; Organizer and first Secretary of Haverford Society of Maryland and President of same; Organizer and Secretary of Maryland Psychiatric Society; Associate Editor *Maryland Psychiatric Quarterly;* Instructor in Psychiatry, Johns Hopkins University.

Lineage

WILLIAM DUNTON of Philadelphia; *b.* 20th June, 1748; *d.* 8th July, 1807; it is supposed that he came from Boston but this has not yet (1916) been proved; the Philadelphia Directory for 1793, where his name first appears, gives William DUNTON, Lieutenant of the *General Green*, Revenue Cutter, 19 Queen Street, Southwark; in that of 1796 as Sea Captain, same address; in that of 1797 as William DUNCAN, Shipmaster; in that of 1801 William DUNCAN, Shipmaster Brown's Street, leading north from Front Street, next to 404; in that of 1802 and 1803 William DUNTON, Sea Captain, 54 Brown Street; in that of 1805 the address is given as Brown Street; in that of 1805 the address is given as 60 Brown Street; it is known that he was taken prisoner by the British. He and his wife were members of the First Moravian (United Brethren) Church of Philadelphia, and from the records much of the following information is derived.

ISSUE

I. JACOB, *b.* 14th August, 1773, of whom later.
II. Thomas, *b.* 14th December, 1774: *bapt.* 18th December, 1774, by Rev. Jacob FRIES, *d. s. p.*
III. William, *b.* 18th May, 1776; *bapt.* 26th May, 1778, by Jacob FRIES, *d. s. p.*
IV. Sarah, *b.* 14th May, 1778; *bapt.* 24th May, 1778; *m.* 15th September, 1796, to Francis HUNT by J. MEDER.

COLONIAL FAMILIES OF THE UNITED STATES

- v. George, b. 23d August, 1780; bapt. 3d September, 1780, by D. LYDICK; d. 28th April, 1854; m. to Anna Mary FRIBERG.
- vi. Elizabeth, b. 31st March, 1783; bapt. 27th April, 1783, by D. LYDICK.
- vii. Margaretha, b. 25th February, 1785; bapt. 13th March, 1785, by J. FRIES.
- viii. Amelia, b. 22d October, 1787; bapt. 4th November, 1787, by John MEDER.
- ix. Maria, b. 4th April; bapt. 25th April, 1790, by John MEDER; m. Isaiah DOANE, b. 1785; d. 1839.
- x. William, b. 13th December, 1792; bapt. 20th January, 1793, by John MEDER; d. 14th March, 1855.
- xi. Anna, b. 28th November, 1794; bapt. 21st December, 1794, by John MEDER.

JACOB DUNTON, b. 14th August, 1773; bapt. 15th August, 1773, by Rev. Jacob FRIES; d. 1st January, 1852; buried in lot G. 207, Laurel Hill; m. (firstly) Bridget FLANAGAN, b. 30th September (?), 1775, d. 20th November, 1805; m. (secondly) 2d October, 1806, Anna Maria MCCARTY, b. 1786, d. 1873.

ISSUE BY FIRST MARRIAGE

- i. William, b. 28th February, 1796; bapt. 6th March, 1796, by John MEDER; d. 3d December, 1796, d.s.p.
- ii. John, b. 24th June, 1797; bapt. 2d July, 1797 by John MEDER; d.s.p. 24th November, 1798.
- iii. Jacob, b. 27th April, 1800; bapt. 1st June, 1800, by J. F. FRUEAUF; d. 31st January, 1854, in New York; m. 10th October, 1821, Caroline DE LA MATER, b. 21st March, 1802, d. 19th February, 1892, in New York; she was the second dau. of John DE LA MATER of Philadelphia, formerly of New York.
- iv. ISAAC, b. 26th May, 1802, of whom later.

ISSUE BY SECOND MARRIAGE

- i. Anna Maria, d.s.p., b. 8th June, 1807; bapt. 2d July, 1807, by Jos. ZESLINE; b. 6th October, 1879; m. (firstly) James Ritchie GEMMILL, b. 27th December, 1805, d. 11th May, 1855; m. (secondly) William Henry ALLEN (widower), b. 27th March, 1808, d. 29th August, 1882. He was President of Girard College for many years before and until his death.
- ii. Abraham, b. 29th July, 1808; bapt. 29th August, 1808; d. 11th April, 1827, bapt. by J. ZESLINE.

ISAAC DUNTON, b. 26th May, 1802, of Philadelphia; bapt. 18th July, 1802, by J. F. FRUEAUF; d. 14th November, 1846; m. Mary Simpson RUSH, dau. of William RUSH the eminent carver. She was b. 3d March, 1803, d. 15th January, 1887.

ISSUE

I. Martha, *b.* 8th May, 1826; *m.* 20th October, 1859, Edward H. LEWIS, of Radnor, Pennsylvania, *b.* 30th November, 1820, *d.* 29th May, 1893.
II. Mary, *b.* 23d September, 1827; *d.* 13th August, 1896; *m.* 23d December, 1856, John H. WESTCOTT, *b.* 11th October, 1825, *d.* 18th January, 1867.
III. Elizabeth, *b.* 8th August, 1829; *d.* 9th August, 1884; *m.* 23d December, 1856, Rev. Lorenzo WESTCOTT, *b.* 1829, brother of John H. WESTCOTT, *d.* 5th June, 1879.
IV. William Rush, *b.* 10th March, 1830.
V. JACOB, *b.* 3d August, 1833, of whom below.

JACOB DUNTON, *b.* 3d August, 1833; *d.* 18th January, 1897; *m.* 23d September, 1858, Anna Maria Gordon GEMMILL, *b.* 28th November, 1833, *d.* 10th December 1893.

ISSUE

I. James Gemmill, *b.* December, 1860.
II. Elizabeth Worrell, *b.* 10th October, 1884.
III. WILLIAM RUSH, Jr., *b.* 24th July, 1868, the subject of this memoir.

Arms (RUSH of England).—Gules on a fesse or, between three horses courant argent as many annulets azure.
Crest.—A wolf's head erased ermine.
Residence.—714 East Evesham Avenue, Govans, Maryland.
Clubs.—Florestan.
Societies.—Colonial Wars, Sons of the American Revolution, American Medical Association, Baltimore County Medical Association, Medical and Chirurgical Faculty of Maryland, American Philatelic Society, Baltimore Philatelic Society, Inter-State Psychiatric Society, Maryland Historical Society.

Rush

JOHN RUSH commanded a troop of horse in CROMWELL'S Army. At the close of the war he married Susanna LUCAS at Horton in Oxfordshire 8th January, 1648. He embraced the principles of the Quakers in 1660 and came to Pennsylvania in 1683 with seven children and several grand children and settled at Byberry, thirteen miles from Philadelphia. In 1691 he and his whole family became Keithians and in 1697 most of them became Baptists. He *d.* at Byberry in 1699. His sword was in possession of Jacob RUSH and his watch in possession of Gen. William DARK of Virginia, but both were later in Independence Hall, Philadelphia.

ISSUE

I. Elizabeth, *b.* 16th June, 1649; *m.* 27th May, 1680, Richard COLLET.
II. WILLIAM, *b.* 21st July, 1652, of whom later.
III. Thomas, *b.* 7th November, 1654; *d.* in London 18th April, 1676.

IV. Susanna, *b.* 28th December, 1656; *m.* John HART in England.
V. John, *b.* 1st March, 1660.
VI. Francis, *b.* 8th February, 1662.
VII. James, *b.* 21st July, 1664; *d.* and was buried at Banbury, 24th January, 1671.
VIII. Joseph, *b.* 26th October, 1666.
IX. Edward, *b.* 27th September, 1670.
X. Jane, *b.* 27th December, 1673–1674; *m.* John DARKE.

WILLIAM RUSH, *b.* 21st July, 1652; *m.* in England; *d.* at Byberry, Pennsylvania, 1688, five years after his arrival in America.

ISSUE BY FIRST MARRIAGE

I. Susanna, *m.* (firstly) John WEBSTER; *m.* (secondly) ———— GILBERT.
II. James, *d.* 1727; *m.* Rachel PEART.
III. Elizabeth, *m.* Timothy STEVENSON, who afterwards *m.* Rachel RUSH, widow of his brother-in-law James RUSH.

ISSUE BY SECOND MARRIAGE

I. Sarah, called Aurelia until her marriage and baptism; *m.* David MEREDITH.
II. WILLIAM, of whom below.

WILLIAM RUSH, *d.* 31st January, 1733, at Boston, Massachusetts; *m.* 1st March, 1711–1712, Elizabeth HODGES, who *d.* 15th April, 1735, in Philadelphia. The wedding took place at a Quaker meeting held at the house of his brother, James RUSH, at Byberry, as appears by a certificate in the possession of James IRVINE.

ISSUE

I. Mary, *b.* 9th February, 1712–1713; *d.* 5th January, 1766; *m.* 24th May, 1733, George IRVINE, who *d.* 2d October, 1740.
II. William, *b.* 24th February, 1717–1718; *d.* 30th November, 1791; *m.* (firstly) Esther CARLISLE; *m.* (secondly) Frances DECORNE.
III. JOSEPH, *b.* 3d January, 1719–1720; of whom later.
IV. Elizabeth, *b.* and *d.* 6th January, 1721–1722.
V. Elizabeth, *b.* 12th February, 1722–1723; *d.* 8th December, 1754.
VI. Francis, *b.* 3d November, 1725; *d.* 27th August, 1726.

JOSEPH RUSH, *b.* 3d January, 1719–1720; *m.* (firstly) 19th September, 1750, Rebecca LINCOLN, probably a dau. of Abraham LINCOLN of Springfield Township, now Delaware County, Pennsylvania; *m.* (secondly) Elizabeth HILTON.

ISSUE BY FIRST MARRIAGE

I. Elizabeth, *m.* William ALLEN.
II. WILLIAM, *b.* 1759, of whom later.

III. Mary, *m.* Joseph TATUM.
IV. Abraham, *d.* young.
V. Catherine, *m.* John COCHRAN.

ISSUE BY SECOND MARRIAGE

I. Joseph, *d.* unmarried.
II. Susanna, *d.* unmarried.
III. George, *d.* young.
IV. Esther, *d.* young.
V. Rebecca, *d.* young.
VI. Benjamin, *m.* Rebecca JONES.
VII. Esther, *m.* John LOUGHERY.
VIII. Sarah, *d.* unmarried.
IX. James Irvine, *m.* Ann EVANS.

WILLIAM RUSH of Pennsylvania, *b.* 1759; *d.* 17th January, 1833; *m.* Martha WALLACE.

ISSUE

I. John, *b.* 1782; *d.* 2d January, 1853; *m.* Mary, surname unknown.
II. Rebecca, drowned.
III. William, *m.* and had issue, six children.
IV. Martha.
V. Joseph.
VI. Benjamin.
VII. Samuel W., *m.* Elizabeth REES.
VIII. Elizabeth, *b.* 10th March, 1801; *d.* 31st October, 1878.
IX. MARY SIMPSON, *b.* 3d March, 1803, of whom below.

MARY SIMPSON RUSH, *b.* 3d March, 1803; *d.* 15th January, 1887; *m.* Isaac DUNTON, *b.* 26th May, 1802, son of Jacob DUNTON, *b.* 14th August, 1773, *m.* (firstly) Bridget FLANAGAN, *m.* (secondly) Anna Maria MCCARTY.

ISSUE

I. Martha DUNTON, *b.* 8th May, 1826; *d.* 13th November, 1917; *m.* 20th October, 1859, Edward H. LEWIS, of Radnor, Pennsylvania, *b.* 30th November, 1820, *d.* 29th May, 1893.
II. Mary DUNTON, *b.* 23d September, 1827; *d.* 13th August, 1896; *m.* 23d December, 1856, John H. WESTCOTT, *b.* 11th October, 1825, *d.* 18th January, 1867.
III. Elizabeth DUNTON, *b.* 8th August, 1829; *d.* 9th August, 1884; *m.* 23d December, 1856, Rev. Lorenzo WESTCOTT, *b.* 1829, *d.* 5th June, 1879, brother of John H. WESTCOTT.
IV. William Rush DUNTON, *b.* 10th March, 1830; *d.* 14th May, 1911, at Montrose, Pennsylvania.

v. JACOB DUNTON, *b.* 3d August, 1833, of whom later.
vi. Anna Maria Gemmill DUNTON, *b.* 25th October, 1885; *m.* 16th April, 1857, James McCullough FARR, of Philadelphia, afterwards living in New York.
vii. Isaac DUNTON, *b.* January, 1839; *d.* 21st February, 1864; *m.* 30th December, 1863, Belle FARR, *b.* 9th December, 1836.
viii. Susan Ritchie DUNTON, *b.* 1842; *d.* 1845.
ix. Emma DUNTON, *b.* 1845; *m.* 19th January, 1881, Wallace Williams LOVEJOY.

JACOB DUNTON of Philadelphia, Pennsylvania; *b.* 3d August, 1833; *d.* 18th January, 1897; *m.* 23d September, 1858, Anna Maria Gordon GEMMILL, *b.* 28th November, 1833, *d.* 10th December, 1893.

ISSUE

i. James Gemmill DUNTON, *b.* December, 1860; *m.* (firstly) name unknown, no issue; *m.* (secondly) Mary LILLIE.

ISSUE

1. Thomas.   2. Elizabeth.

ii. Elizabeth Worrell DUNTON, *b.* 10th October, 1864.
iii. WILLIAM RUSH DUNTON, JR., *b.* 24th July, 1868; *m.* 1st July, 1897, Edna Drusilla HOGAN, *b.* 12th September, 1862, dau. of Jonathan Elmer and Helen Ruhamah (MCCLEAN) HOGAN.

ISSUE

1. Helen McClean DUNTON, *b.* 2d May, 1897.
2. William Rush DUNTON, III, *b.* 26th May, 1903.
3. Stephen Morgan DUNTON, *b.* 6th November, 1904; *d.* 6th April, 1905.
4. Henry Hurd DUNTON, *b.* 30th December, 1905.

Earle

HENRY MONTAGUE EARLE, L.B., of York City; *b.* 28th March, 1870, in Greenville, South Carolina; Lawyer; educated Georgetown University, District of Columbia, where he graduated L.B., 1893; *m.* 19th April, 1897, Mary Louise COE, dau. of Elmore Frank COE.

Lineage

The ancestor of this branch of the American family was John EARLE, a Royalist of the ancient house of ERLE or DE ERLEIGH, who came from Somersetshire, England, to Northumberland County, Virginia, in 1649; *d.* in Westmoreland County, Virginia, September or October, 1660; granted four patents of 1600 acres of land on Yocomoco Neck, 16th November, 1652, for the transportation of thirty-two persons; was a planter and kinsman of Sir Walter EARLE, a member of the Board of Managers of the Virginia Colony; *m.* Mary, surname unknown in England.

ISSUE

I. SAMUEL, *b.* in England, 1638, of whom later.
II. John, *b.* in England.
III. Mary, *b.* in England.

SAMUEL EARLE of Westmoreland County, Virginia, Planter and Merchant; *b.* in England, 1638; *d.* in Westmoreland County, 1697; *m.* Bridget, surname unknown.

ISSUE AMONG OTHERS

I. SAMUEL, *b.* circa 1670.

SAMUEL EARLE, of Westmoreland County, Virginia; *b.* there circa 1670; *d.* there 1746; was a Planter, Surveyor of Highways, Grand Juror many times; was a large land owner; *m.* Phillis, surname unknown.

ISSUE AMONG OTHERS

I. SAMUEL, *b.* circa 1692.

MAJOR SAMUEL EARLE, of Frederick County, Virginia; *b.* in Westmoreland County, circa 1692; *d.* Frederick County, Virginia, circa 1771; Attorney-at-Law, Justice on the same bench in Frederick County with Thomas and Lord FAIRFAX, Baron of Cameron; one of the earliest members of the House of Burgesses from Frederick County; Major of Militia, Sheriff, Church Warden, Collector of Tobacco for the Crown; *m.* Anne SORRELL, dau. of Thomas and Elizabeth SORRELL. Thomas SORRELL was clerk of the County Court for many years beginning with 1718.

ISSUE AMONG OTHERS

I. BAYLIS, *b.* August, 1734.

COLONEL BAYLIS EARLE, of Spartansburgh County, South Carolina; *b.* 8th August, 1734, New Winchester, Virginia; *d.* 6th January, 1825, in Spartansburgh County; was lieutenant in the Virginia Militia before the Revolutionary War and Colonel in the South Carolina Militia after the War; the battle of Earle's Ford was fought upon his place; was one of the early Judges of Spartansburgh County; Graduate of William and Mary College; *m.* 16th April, 1757, Mary PRINCE, dau. of John PRINCE of Frederick County, Virginia, and sister of Capt. Frank PRINCE, 5th Regiment South Carolina Continental Troops, and of Lieut. Thomas PRINCE of the same Regiment who was killed in the battle of Stono, during the American Revolution.

ISSUE

I. Samuel, *b.* 28th November, 1760; *d.* 24th November, 1838; Commissioned 11th June, 1777, Ensign in Capt. John BOWIE's Company, 5th South Carolina Continental Regiment; *m.* 12th March, 1793, Harriet HARRISON, dau. of James and Elizabeth (HAMPTON) HARRISON.

ISSUE

I. Samuel M., *b.* 5th March, 1815.
II. ASPHASIO, of whom later.

ASPHASIO EARLE, wife's name unknown.

ISSUE AMONG OTHERS

I. HENRY M., *b.* 1802.

HENRY M. EARLE, *b.* 1802; *d.* 1890; *m.* wife's name not given.

ISSUE AMONG OTHERS

I. WILLIAM EDWARD, *b.* 1841.

WILLIAM EDWARD EARLE, of Greenville, South Carolina; *b.* 1841; *d.* 1894; was Captain and Major of Artillery in the army of the Confederate States, 1861–1865; Assistant United States District Attorney of South Carolina; *m.* Elizabeth PRICE; *d.* 1878.

ISSUE AMONG OTHERS

I. HENRY MONTAGUE, *b.* 28th March, 1870, the subject of this memoir.

Arms.—Gules, three escallops within a bordure engrailed argent.
Crest.—A lion's head erased or, transpierced by a broken spear.
Motto.—Vulneritus non victus.
Residence.—239 Madison Avenue, New York City.
Clubs.—City, Country of New York, Metropolitan of Washington.

Fullam

REAR ADMIRAL WILLIAM FREELAND FULLAM, United States Navy; *b.* 20th October, 1855, in Monroe County, New York; *m.* 15th April, 1885, Mariana Winder ROBINSON, dau. of the late Judge John Mitchell ROBINSON, Maryland Court of Appeals and Mariana Stoughton EMORY his wife, both of the Eastern Shore of Maryland. John Mitchell ROBINSON was the son of Peter ROBINSON, Caroline County, Maryland, who *m.* Sarah MITCHELL, the dau. of Dr. John MITCHELL of Dorchester County, Maryland. Peter ROBINSON was the son of Ralph ROBINSON of Sussex County, Delaware, who *m.* Caroline POTTER of Caroline County, Maryland. Mariana EMORY was the dau. of Thomas and Mariana Stoughton (WINDER) EMORY, the son of Thomas EMORY of Poplar Grove, Queen Anne County, Maryland.

ISSUE

I. Mariana Emory, *b.* Brooklyn, New York; *m.* Austin Ledyard SANDS, Esq., of Newport, Rhode Island.
II. Rhoda, of Annapolis, Maryland.

WILLIAM FREELAND FULLAM entered the Naval Academy in 1873; graduated 1877, at the head of his Class. 1877 to 1879, cruise in the Mediterranean, *U.S.S. Marion* and *Trenton;* returned to Annapolis for final graduation in 1879; cruise to China, *U. S. S. Swatara,* 1879 to 1882. 1883 to 1887 at Naval Academy, Department of Mathematics, and in charge of Battalion of Midshipmen. 1887 to 1891, cruise in *U. S. S. Boston, Yorktown, Vesuvius* and *Trenton.* 1891 to 1894, Naval Academy, Department of Mathematics and in charge of Battalion of Midshipmen. 1894 to 1897, served on board *U. S. S. Raleigh* and *Miantonomoh;* then to Naval Academy, Department of Ordnance. 1898, served on board *U. S. S. New Orleans,* Spanish War, Santiago Campaign, blockade and bombardment of Santiago and San Juan; then to Naval Academy, Department of Ordnance. 1899 to 1901, Executive Officer, *U. S. S. Lancaster.* 1902 to 1905, Naval Academy, Head of Department of Ordnance; commanded practice ships, *Chesapeake* and *Terror.* 1906, prepared dry dock *Dewey* for the trip to Philippines; commanded *U. S. S. Marrietta* in West Indies and Central America, receiving special letters of commendation for work protecting American interests in those waters, in Cuba and Honduras. 1907 to 1909, commanded Naval Training Station, Newport, Rhode Island. 1909 to 1911, commanded *U. S. S. Mississippi*; received three letters of commendation for efficiency on that ship. 1911 to 1912, Commanded Naval Training Station, Great Lakes, Illinois. 1913, Aid to Secretary, Navy Department. 1914, ordered Superintendent, United States Naval Academy. June to

September, 1914, commanded practice squadron, battleships *Missouri*, *Idaho* and *Illinois*, with Midshipmen to Europe. July to September, 1915, commanded practice squadron, battleships, *Missouri*, *Wisconsin* and *Ohio*, with Midshipmen to San Francisco and return. These were the first battleships to pass through the Panama Canal. October, 1915, ordered to duty Commander-in-Chief United States Pacific Reserve Fleet, and assumed command at San Francisco, 15th October, while fleet was on duty in connection with the Panama-Pacific International Exposition. April, 1917, ordered command Patrol Force, United States Pacific Fleet.

Lineage

HON. FRANCIS FULLAM or FULHAM, of Weston, Massachusetts; *b.* in Fulham, England, 1670; *d.* in Weston, 15th January, 1758; was Judge of the Court of Common Pleas of Weston, Massachusetts; *m.* Sarah LIVERMORE, *b.* 18th February, 1671, *d.* 10th March, 1724.

ISSUE AMONG OTHERS

1. JACOB, *b.* 19th November, 1692, of whom later.

JACOB FULLAM, of Weston, Massachusetts; *b.* there 19th November, 1692; *d.* 8th May, 1725; was enrolled in Captain LOVEWELL'S Company in a campaign against the Indians in 1725; this company left the vicinity of Boston and on 8th May, 1725, met the Indians at Fryesburg, Massachusetts, where a battle was fought which is known in song and story as "Lovewell's Fight;" young Fullam was killed in this fight in a hand-to-hand encounter with an Indian Chief; in 1726 an account of the fight was published in the *"Worcester Magazine"* which is to be found in the Boston Public Library; *m.* 28th February, 1715, in Weston, Tabitha WHITNEY, *b.* 22d August, 1696.

ISSUE AMONG OTHERS

1. ELISHA, *b.* 26th June, 1725, of whom later.

ELISHA FULLAM, of Harvard, Massachusetts; *b.* there 26th June, 1725; *d.* there 22d September, 1801; *m.* 21st January, 1744, Sarah HAGAR, *bapt.* 13th October, 1723.

ISSUE AMONG OTHERS

1. ELISHA, *b.* 14th February, 1752, of whom later.

ELISHA FULLAM, of Harvard, Massachusetts; *b.* 14th February, 1752, Penfield, New York; *d.* 20th May, 1824, in Penfield; *m.* Abigail NICHOLS.

ISSUE

1. NELSON, *b.* 2d November, 1805, of whom later.

NELSON FULLAM, of Rochester, New York; b. in Penfield, 2d November, 1805; d. 15th May, 1878, in Rochester; m. 2d March, 1828, Alexina SEYMOUR, b. 1812, d. 1886.

ISSUE AMONG OTHERS

1. NATHAN SEYMOUR, b. 1831, of whom later.

NATHAN SEYMOUR FULLAM, of Rochester, New York; b. in Penfield, New York, 1831; m. 1854, Rhoda Ann STOWITZ, b. 1831, d. 1881.

ISSUE AMONG OTHERS

1. WILLIAM FREELAND, b. 20th October, 1855, the subject of this memoir.

Arms.—Argent a cross sable between four trefoils slipped vert, a bordure engrailed azure.
Residence.—Annapolis, Maryland.
Clubs.—New York Yacht, Army and Navy (Washington); Naval Academy (Annapolis).
Societies.—Colonial Wars.

Fulton

WILLIAM EDWARDS FULTON, of Waterbury, Connecticut; *b.* 8th August, 1852, in Brooklyn, New York; *m.* 23d October, 1877, Ida Eleana Lewis, *b.* 25th November, 1852, dau. of Edward Cuffin and Harriet Maria (PHIPPENEY) LEWIS.

ISSUE

I. Lewis Edwards, *b.* 22d January, 1879; graduated from Yale, 1901.
II. William Shirley, *b.* 23d November, 1880; graduated from Yale, 1903; *m. m.* 10th January, 1906, Rose Hinckley HAYDEN.

ISSUE

1. William Hayden, *b.* 12th March, 1907.
2. Elizabeth Hayden, *b.* 14th January, 1910.

III. Irving Kent, *b.* 17th December, 1882; graduated from Yale, 1906; *m.* 11th October, 1910, Elizabeth Harrison WARNER, *b.* 27th November, 1886, in Salisbury, Connecticut.

ISSUE

1. Wells, *b.* 4th December, 1911.

WILLIAM EDWARDS FULTON was educated at The College of the City of New York; President of the Waterbury Farrel Foundry and Machine Company since 1902; Vice-President Manufacturers National Bank of Waterbury, Connecticut; Member St. John's Protestant Episcopal Church; is descended from the following Colonial Founders:

Matthew BECKWITH	John ROBERTS	Henry HERRICK
John BENT	Richard SEYMOUR	William HOLT
Thomas BLISS	John SMITH	Robert JENNISON
William CHITTENDEN	John STEVENS	Joseph KERLEY
Robert CROSS	Francis WAINWRIGHT	Oliver MAINWARING
William EAGER	John WARNER	Isaac MIXER
Thomas FORD	Thomas WOODFORD	Thomas NEWELL
William GOODRICH	Samuel WRIGHT	Richard RAYMOND
Adam HAWKES	John ALLEN	William ROCKWELL
Abraham HILL	John BEEBE	Robert STARKWEATHER
William HUNTER	Thomas BIRD	John STRONG
William KEENEY	Edward BRAGG	William WARD
Robert LONG	Nicholas CLAPP	William WHITREDD
John MEIGS	John DANIELS	Matthew WOODRUFF
John MOORE	Alexander EDWARDS	Thomas WRIGHT
Thomas NORTON	Robert FULTON	Thomas BEEBE
William PHELPS	Walter HALLIDAY	John BISSELL

George CHAPPELL
Edward COGSWELL
Anthony DORCHESTER
Sylvester EVELETH
Edward GARFIELD
Walter HARRIS
George HEYWOOD

Abraham HOWE
Solomon JOHNSON
Hugh LASKIN
Matthew MARVIN
Richard MONTAGUE
John NORTH
Joseph PARSONS
Edward RICE

William THOMPSON
Isaac SHELDEN
Rowland STEBBINS
Mark SYMONDS
Andrew WARNER
William WOODBURY
John WOODS

Lineage

The Scottish line of FULTON originated in Ayrshire and Lanarkshire and migrated in various directions. The Protestant Colonies in the North of Ireland, received from this source several families of FULTON, and from these sprang the Scotch-Irish FULTONS who were destined to bear their share in the flood of immigration which was reaching the shores of America during the seventeenth and eighteenth centuries. Several branches of the FULTON lines reached Pennsylvania between 1730 and 1760, who show by their close similarity of names, immediate relationship with the families of FULTON who settled in Massachusetts some twenty or thirty years previously. The Georgia and South Carolina FULTONS very evidently migrated from the Pennsylvania branch. From the families located in Eastern Pennsylvania, came the Robert FULTON, who was soon to make his name famous for all time in connection with the first vessel operated by steam. His father *d*. in Lancaster, Pennsylvania, in 1767, and the family removed to the western part of the State. The relationship between this branch and that of the Massachusetts branch of John and Robert FULTON, is close, and it is in this branch of Massachusetts FULTONS that we are interested. In this connection a chart prepared by Sir Theodore HOPE, K.C., S.J.C., J.E., of London, England, shows the line of descent to the Robert FULTON branch of the Massachusetts line, from which the subject of this memoir descends. It is as follows:

WILLIAM FULTON, of Kilkenny, Ireland, from the Scottish family of the name, lived at Diviaghy, and *d*. in 1638; *m*. Elizabeth (surname not given) who was buried 31st July, 1674.

ISSUE

I. JOHN, of Lisburn; *b*. 1623, of whom later.
II. Richard, of Lisburn, *b*. 1624; buried 25th September, 1711; *m*. (firstly) Dorotie, who was buried 30th May, 1662; *m*. (secondly) Mary, who was buried 21st August, 1712.

ISSUE

1. Matthew.
2. Richard.
3. William.
4. Isabel.
5. Dorothy.
6. Thomas.
7. George.

III. James.
IV. Thomas, *b.* before 1638; had son William of Cork.
V. William, *b.* before 1638; had son William of Kilkenny.

JOHN FULTON, of Lisburn, Ireland; *b.* 1623; *m.* (firstly) name not given; *m.* (secondly) Margaret HOMER; *m.* (thirdly) 13th December, 1676, Sarah COSLET.

ISSUE

I. Paul.
II. Janet.
III. John, *b.* 1653; *m.* (firstly) 18th December, 1687, Margaret ENGLISH; *m.* (secondly) 1690, Margaret CARNAC.

ISSUE

1. Elizabeth.
2. Mary Ann.
3. James Carnac.
4. John.
5. Mary.
6. Margaret.
7. John.

IV. Robert.

ISSUE

1. James.
2. Thomas.

V. HUGH, *b.* 1659, of whom later.
VI. Ann.
VII. Thomas, of Blaris; *b.* 1663; *m.* 15th December, 1687, Ann MEREDITH of Blaris.

HUGH FULTON, *b.* 1659; *m.* 20th February, 1681, Elinor JOHNSON of Denaghy.

ISSUE

I. William, *bapt.* 1683; son John *bapt.* 1709, at Diviaghy.
II. ROBERT, *bapt.* 1685, of whom later.
III. Jane, *bapt.* 1686.
IV. James, *bapt.* 1690.
V. John, *bapt.* 1692.
VI. Thomas, *bapt.* 1694.

ROBERT FULTON, *bapt.* 1685; was in Boston, Massachusetts, as late as 1754, when he sold land on Orange Street, where he lived, which he had purchased in 1751. No record can be found of his death or of any probate. His sons (?) were in Boston as early as 1730, and in 1732 John was *m.* by Rev. John MOORHEAD, pastor of the First Presbyterian Church, which was organized in 1728 on Brattle Street, and which later became the Arlington Street Unitarian Church. Robert FULTON, *m.* Elizabeth (surname not given).

COLONIAL FAMILIES OF THE UNITED STATES

ISSUE

I. John, b. about 1710; d. about 1760; m. 3d August, 1732, at Boston, Massachusetts, Ann WYER; had issue.

1. John, who d. in 1760.
    1¹. Sarah.
    2¹. John A.
2. Robert, d. Boston, 1808; m. (firstly) 3d August, 1769, Elizabeth INGRAHAM; m. (secondly) 27th December, 1783, Polly ORALL. He was a distiller (?).

II. ROBERT, b. 1713, of whom later.
III. Samuel, m. Elizabeth (surname not given).

ISSUE

1. John, b. 1736; d. 9th February, 1790; was a soldier in the War of the Revolution from Medford; m. 25th July, 1762, Boston, Massachusetts, Sarah BRADLEY, b. 1740, d. November, 1835, at Medford, Massachusetts, dau. of Samuel BRADLEY. The present Daughters of the American Revolution Chapter of Medford is named from her, The Sarah Bradley Fulton Chapter; she left one son and four daughters who were m. at Medford, and another dau. Nancy (Ann W.), b. 1767, d. 13th November, 1845.
2. Samuel, m. at Boston (int.), 3d July, 1760, Mary CORBET; d. probably in 1764.

ROBERT FULTON, b. 1713, in North of Ireland; descended from the Scotch FULTONS of Ayrshire and Lanarkshire; d. 1st December, 1776, at Colrain, Massachusetts; he came to America about 1730, with his father and brothers, and settled at Boston, Massachusetts, and about 1742, he removed to Colrain, Massachusetts, where he held various offices, such as Assessor, Selectman and Constable. He served in the French and Indian War, and was stationed at the South Fort at Colrain, Massachusetts, during the years 1747, 1748 and 1749. Among his companions in the Fort was John MILLS, who was killed 22d June, 1747, and his widow became the second wife of Robert FULTON in 1748. He m. (firstly) about 1742, Hannah (surname not given), b. 1713-1714, d. 10th May, 1748; m. (secondly) Margaret (―――――) MILLS, widow of John MILLS.

ISSUE OF FIRST MARRIAGE

I. Sarah, b. 21st September, 1743; m. 2d January, 1766, at Greenfield, Massachusetts, John COCHRAN.
II. JOHN, b. 19th August, 1746, of whom later.
III. Robert, b. May, 1748; m. Sarah EMERSON; was a soldier in the War of the Revolution from Colrain and in 1802 he lived in Camillus, New York.

ISSUE

1. A daughter.
2. Eleazer Emerson, *b.* 28th February, 1789, and there were other children later.

ISSUE BY SECOND MARRIAGE

1. James, *b.* 24th May, 1749; *d.* 20th March, 1834, at Colrain; *m.* Hannah ELLIS, dau. of Richard ELLIS.

ISSUE

1. Robert, *b.* 23d May, 1773.

ISSUE

1^1. Henry of Thetford, Vermont.
2^1. Stephen of Thetford, Vermont.
3^1. Jesse of Boston.
4^1. Elijah of Maine.

2. James, *b.* 7th May, 1775, of Champion, New York; was in War of 1812; *m.* Sally CHOATE.

ISSUE

1^1. Samuel, *b.* 1801; *d.* 1881.
2^1. George, *b.* 1803; *d.* 1879.
3^1. Richard, *b.* 1807; *d.* 1871.
4^1. Jesse, *b.* 1812.

3. Caleb of Wilna, New York; *b.* 11th May, 1777; *d.* 1863; was in War of 1812; *m.* Polly BARNES.

ISSUE

1^1. Simeon.
2^1. James, *d.* June, 1865, of Jefferson County, New York; *m.* Caroline NICHOLAS.
3^1. Elisha of Wilna, New York.

4. David, *b.* 25th December, 1779; *m.* Jennie TAGGART, of Jefferson County, New York.

ISSUE

1^1. John.
2^1. David, *b.* 1817; *d.* 8th October, 1886; *m.* Sarah ELLIS, of Belleville, New York.
3^1. Luke.

5. Daniel, *b.* 21st March, 1784; *d.* 1875, in Ohio; *m.* Polly WOOD.

ISSUE

1¹. Hiram, *d.* 1876; *m.* Polly JONES, of Champion, New York.
2¹. Elijah, *b.* 1811; *m.* Betsey HEALD, of Antwerp, New York.
3¹. Robert, *m.* Lois VAUGHAN, of Pittsfield, Ohio.
4¹. Ruel, *m.* Mary HUMPHREY; in Civil War.
5¹. Gaylord, *d.* about 1885, of Ohio.

6. Elijah, *b.* 2d February, 1788; *d.* about 1829; *m.* Phebe BENNETT of Jefferson County.

ISSUE

1¹. Sylvia. 3¹. Harriet D.
2¹. Bennett D. 4¹. John.

7. Nathan, *b.* 25th April, 1790; *d.* about 1844; *m.* Philena HASTINGS, of Keokuk, Iowa.

ISSUE

1¹. Harry of Keokuk.

8. Jesse, *b.* 25th July, 1792; *d.* 12th March, 1834; *m.* Sophronia FRANKLIN, of Colrain, Massachusetts.

ISSUE

1¹. Aaron. 4¹. Sophronia.
2¹. Robert. 5¹. Jesse Leroy.
3¹. Eunice.

II. Moses, *b.* 175– (?); was in the War of the Revolution; *m.* (firstly) 18th November, 1777, at Pelham, Massachusetts, Lydia CLARK, *b.* 1753, *d.* 1782, at Colrain, Massachusetts; *m.* (secondly) Martha (surname unknown).

ISSUE BY FIRST MARRIAGE

1. Sarah, *b.* 19th August, 1778, at Colrain, Massachusetts.
2. Margaret, *b.* 11th August, 1780, Colrain, Massachusetts.
3. Lydia, *b.* 15th May, 1782; *d.* 1783, Colrain, Massachusetts.

ISSUE BY SECOND MARRIAGE

1. Daniel, *b.* 5th March, 1784, at Colrain, Massachusetts.
2. William, *b.* 1786–1787; *d.* 20th March, 1787.

III. William, *b.* 175– (?); was in War of the Revolution from Colrain, Massachusetts, and in 1790, lived at Salem, New York; *m.* 177 (?), Elizabeth ———.

ISSUE

1. Andrew, *b.* 5th April, 1782.
2. William, *b.* 3d September, 1783; also several daughters.

JOHN FULTON, *b.* 19th August, 1746, at Colrain, Massachusetts; *d.* 27th August, 1805, at Pittsfield, Massachusetts; was in the War of the Revolution throughout the War from Colrain, Massachusetts, and then settled in the village of White Creek, in the town of Cambridge, Albany County (now Washington County, New York), whence he removed in 1791 to Pittsfield, Massachusetts, where he *d.* in 1805; *m.* (firstly) 15th December, 1768, at Greenfield, Massachusetts, Susanne STEWART, *b.* 18th May 17 (?), *d.* about 1770, leaving no issue; *m.* (secondly) 1781–1782, Anne (GOODRICH) AUSTIN, widow of Benjamin AUSTIN, by which first *m.* she had had issue, Benjamin, *b.* 1772, Anna, *b.* 1774, Moses, *b.* 1776, and Goodrich, *b.* 1778, *d.* 4th January, 1795.

ISSUE OF JOHN AND JANE (GOODRICH) AUSTIN FULTON

I. Sarah, *b.* February, 1783; *d.* about 19th August, 1805.
II. Eunice, *b.* 21st April, 1785; *m.* 29th January, 1809, Joseph WINSLOW.
III. Elizabeth, *b.* 20th March, 1789; *m.* 23d June, 1813, John Whitney ROSE.

ISSUE

1. A son, *b.* 22d May, 1814 (?); *d.* 22d May, 1814 (?).
2. Ann Maria ROSE, *b.* 24th May, 1815.
3. William Fulton ROSE, *b.* 3d June, 1817.
4. Lucy Whitney ROSE, *b.* 12th June, 1819.
5. Royal Nelson ROSE, *b.* 4th November, 1821.
6. Martha Elizabeth ROSE, *v.* 6th July, 1825.

IV. William, *b.* 13th January, 1791, at Pittsfield, Massachusetts; *d.* February, 1817, at Pittsfield, Massachusetts.
V. JOHN, *b.* 15th November, 1793, of whom later.
VI. Nancy, *b.* 17th November, 1795, at Pittsfield, Massachusetts; *d.* 1876, at Marshall, Michigan; *m.* 21st February, 1816, at Pittsfield, Massachusetts, Daniel SACKETT, *b.* 1792, *d.* 1879, of Pittsfield, Massachusetts, and Marshall, Michigan.

ISSUE

1. Daniel SACKETT of Melrose, Wisconsin.

   1^1. John Fulton SACKETT.

   ISSUE

2. Robert SACKETT of Pittsford, New York, and Eckford, Michigan.

ISSUE

1[1]. Levi Wallace SACKETT, *d.* March, 1908.

3. Ann SACKETT.
4. Roxana SACKETT, *m.* 1846, Albert HEATH, of Lima, Livingston County, New York.

ISSUE

1[1]. William D. HEATH, *b.* 1848.
2[1]. James M. HEATH, *b.* 1853.
3[1]. Edward N. HEATH, *b.* 1859.

5. William Fulton SACKETT.
6. Lucy SACKETT, *m.* ——— HUGGETT.

ISSUE

1[1]. Mary HUGGETT, *m.* ——— SWEET.

JOHN FULTON, *b.* 15th November, 1793, at Pittsfield, Massachusetts; *d.* January, 1823; *m.* 25th November, 1818, at Hartford, Connecticut, Clarissa DANIELS, *b.* 1800, Windsor, Connecticut, *d.* 4th August, 1882, Brooklyn, Connecticut.

ISSUE

1. WILLIAM GOODRICH, *b.* 31st August, 1819, of whom later.

WILLIAM GOODRICH FULTON, *b.* 31st August, 1819, at Hartford, Connecticut; *d.* 31st January, 1914, at Brooklyn, New York; *m.* 1st October, 1851, Chesterfield, Massachusetts, Eliza EDWARDS, *b.* 11th November, 1829, Chesterfield, Massachusetts, *d.* 30th December, 1900.

ISSUE

1. WILLIAM EDWARDS, *b.* 8th August, 1852, Brooklyn, New York, the subject of this memoir.

Residence.—150 Hillside Avenue, Waterbury, Connecticut.
Societies.—Colonial Wars, Alpha Delta Phi (college fraternity), Founders and Patriots of America, Sons of the American Revolution.

Gardiner

GEORGE SCHUYLER GARDINER, of Laurel, Jones County, Mississippi; *b.* 12th April, 1854, at Penn Yan, New York; *m.* 24th April, 1877, Catherine Larison MARSHALL at Clinton, Iowa, *b.* 30th September, 1858, dau. of Charles Boss and Theresa Lucretia (BAILEY) MARSHALL of Port Byron, Illinois, later of Dallas, Texas.

ISSUE

I. Juliet, *b.* 14th June, 1878; *m.* 10th May, 1899, Hanford Newell ROGERS, son of James Newell and Florence (WALLINGFORD) ROGERS of Indianapolis, Indiana.

ISSUE
1. Catherine Fletcher ROGERS, *b.* 7th May, 1900.
2. Jane Gardiner ROGERS, *b.* 12th October, 1906.

II. Rachel, *b.* 22d May, 1884; *m.* 9th December, 1908, Charles GREEN, of Laurel, Mississippi, son of Gilbert and Annie (HUNTON) GREEN of New Orleans.

ISSUE
1. George Gardiner GREEN, *b.* 29th October, 1910.
2. Annie Hunton GREEN, *b.* 18th November, 1912.

GEORGE SCHUYLER GARDINER was educated at Penn Yan, New York, and Clinton, Iowa.

Lineage

LIEUTENANT LION GARDINER, I, First Lord of the Manor of Gardiner's Island, New York, and the founder of the American branch of the family, was *b.* in England circa 1599; *d.* 1663 at East Hampton, Long Island. He was an officer in the English Army in Flanders under Lord DE VERE, and an Engineer and Master of Fortifications of the Prince of Orange in the Low Countries. Assisted as Engineer in the construction of fortifications on Fort Hill, Boston, Massachusetts, in 1636. He erected in 1636 Fort Saybrook at mouth of Connecticut River and commanded the said Fort throughout the Pequot Indian War. Lieut. Lion GARDINER'S command of Fort Saybrook continued for four years, his wife sharing the dangers and privations of frontier life with him. Two of their children, David and Mary, were born during that time, David being the first child of English parents to be born in Connecticut. GARDINER then bought of the Indians, the Isle of Wight afterwards, and now, called Gardiner's Island, which purchase was later confirmed by Royal grant, thus becoming its first English proprietor. Here he lived fourteen years and then joined the colony of settlers at East Hampton, Long Island, where he often performed valuable services in quieting Indian uprisings; *m.* Mary WILEMSEN, of Woerden, Holland, dau. of Derike WILEMSEN DUERCANT, and his wife Hachim BASTIANS.

ISSUE

I. DAVID, *b.* 29th April, 1636, of whom later.
II. Mary, *b.* 30th August, 1638; *d.* 15th June, 1727; *m.* circa 1658, Jeremiah CONKLING, son of Ananias CONKLING.
III. Elizabeth, *b.* 14th September, 1641; *d.* February, 1657-1658; *m.* circa 1657, Arthur HOWELL, son of Edward HOWELL of Southampton, Long Island.

DAVID GARDINER, of Hartford, Connecticut; *b.* 29th April, 1636; *d.* 10th July, 1689; was Second Lord of the Manor of Gardiner's Island; *m.* 4th June, 1657, in Westminster, England, Mary LERINGMAN, a widow, of the Parish of St. Margaret of Westminster, England.

ISSUE

I. John, *b.* 19th April, 1661; *d.* 29th June, 1737, or 25th June, 1738; third Proprietor of Gardiner's Island; *m.* (firstly) Mary KING, of Southold, New York; *m.* (secondly) Sarah (CHANDLER) COIT, widow; *m.* (thirdly) Elizabeth (ALLYN) ALLEN; *m.* (fourthly) Elizabeth (HEDGES) OSBORNE.
II. David, *d.* 1st May, 1733; *m.* Martha YOUNG, dau. of Capt. Thomas YOUNG.
III. LION, II, *d.* 23d September, 1723, of whom later.
IV. Elizabeth, *m.* James PARSHALL of Southold, Long Island.

LION GARDINER, II, of East Hampton, Long Island; *d.* 23d September, 1723, from an accidental shot while hunting deer; *m.* wife's name unknown, who was *b.* circa 1668, *d.* 20th September, 1733, at East Hampton, aged about 65 years.

ISSUE

I. LION, III, *b.* 1688, of whom later.
II. Giles, *d.* unmarried.
III. Mary, *b.* 1693-1694; *d.* 14th May, 1714, aged 20 years.
IV. A child, *b.* 1700-1701; *d.* within two days.

LION GARDINER, III, of East Hampton, Long Island; *b.* 1688; *d.* 1781; *m.* 11th January, 1720-1721, Hannah MERRY, *bapt.* 28th April, 1700, when probably five or six years old; *d.* 11th January, 1774, dau. of John and Puah MERRY of East Hampton, Long Island. John MERRY was the son of Cornelius MERRY, *b* in Ireland, was in the Falls Fight, 18th May, 1676, served in King Philip's War, 1675-1676, he *m.* Rachel BALLARD.

ISSUE

I. John, *bapt.* 10th February, 1722; *d.* 24th November, 1780; aged 59 years; *m.* 30th January, 1745–1746, Elizabeth DAYTON.
II. Lion, IV, *bapt.* 11th May, 1728–1729, *d.* young.
III. JEREMIAH, *b.* 5th February, 1727–1728, of whom later.
IV. Mary, *bapt.* 19th September, 1725; *m.* John STRATTON, Jr., or "Master STRATTON."

JEREMIAH GARDINER, of East Hampton, Long Island; *b.* 5th February, 1727–1728; *d.* 29th January, 1815; *m.* (firstly) 16th November, 1750, Mary PARSONS, *bapt.* 10th November, 1729; *d.* 21st January, 1771, dau. of Samuel and Hannah (BAKER) PARSONS of East Hampton, she dau. of Nathaniel and Catalyntje (SCHELLINGER) BAKER, of East Hampton, Long Island, he son of Thomas BAKER of East Hampton, and she dau. of Jacobus and Cornelia (MELYN) SCHELLINGER, who was dau. of Cornelis MELYN, Patroon of Staten Island; *m.* (secondly) Jemima (HOWELL) STRATTON, dau. of Edward and Abigail HOWELL and widow of David STRATTON of Easthampton.

ISSUE BY FIRST MARRIAGE

I. Samuel, *b.* 29th January, 1752; *d.* 1st August, 1753.
II. Samuel, *b.* 10th April, 1754; *d.* unmarried, aged 80 years.
III. Mary, *b.* 10th September, 1756; *m.* Thomas EDWARDS of Easthampton.
IV. Hannah, *b.* 17th April, 1759; *m.* Daniel STRATTON.
V. Jeremiah, *b.* 30th September, 1761; *d.* 22d July, 1848, at Bowman's Creek, New York; date of marriage and wife's name not known.
VI. LION V., *b.* 19th July, 1764, of whom later.
VII. Henry, *b.* 10th January, 1771; *d.* 8th June, 1817; *m.* 4th September, 1796, Elizabeth ENSIGN.
VIII. An unnamed dau., *bapt.* 3d October, 1773.

ISSUE BY SECOND MARRIAGE

I. Howell, *b.* 28th September, 1773; *d.* young.
II. Howell, *b.* 6th January, 1776; *d.* 26th February, 1866; *m.* (firstly) Elinor GROSBECK, *d.* 25th June, 1816; *m.* (secondly) 6th November, 1817, Phebe WEED, widow.

LION GARDINER, of East Hampton, Long Island, New York; *b.* Strieben, New York, 19th July, 1764; *d.* 24th May, 1858; *m.* (firstly) Mary SANFORD, *b.* 3d December, 1764; *d.* 29th January, 1815; *m.* (secondly) Sarah (HODGE) SCHUYLER, *b.* 3d May, 1789; *d.* 19th April, 1869, widow of ———— SCHUYLER, of Canajoharie, New York, and dau. of Reuben and Amy (HAVEN) HODGE of Canajoharie, New York.

ISSUE BY FIRST MARRIAGE

I. David, *b.* 3d September, 1785; *d.* 15th August, 1810.
II. Mary, *b.* 30th October, 1787; *m.* Stephen GRIFFITH.

III. John, *b.* 4th December, 1789; *d.* 6th November, 1810.
VI. Abraham, *b.* 7th May, 1791; *d.* 5th March, 1815.
V. Jeremiah, *b.* 11th January, 1793; *d.* 8th November, 1880; *m.* (firstly) Keziah WILLIAMS; *m.* (secondly) Paulina COLLINS.
VI. Samuel, *b.* 21st June, 1796; *d.* 8th February, 1815.
VII. Sanford, *b.* 17th July, 1798; *b.* 12th February, 1815.
VIII. Alanson, *b.* 31st July, 1801; *d.* 5th September, 1876; *m.* Marilla Etta TRUESDELL.
IX. Clarissa, *b.* 12th July, 1804; *d.* 8th February, 1815.
X. Harriet (twin) *b.* 22d June, 1806; *d.* 28th February, 1815.
XI. Alfred (twin), 22d June, 1806; *d.* 12th October, 1835; *m.* Eleanor TEMPLE.

Mary (Sanford) Gardiner and five children, Abraham, Samuel, Sanford, and Clarissa and Harriet, d. of camp fever between 29th January and 5th March, 1815.

ISSUE BY SECOND MARRIAGE

I. Abraham Sanford, *b.* 17th February, 1817; *d.* 23d April, 1891, at Weston, New York; *m.* Ann ACKERSON; *m.* (secondly) Susan GRIFFITH, widow of Henry GRIFFITH.
II. STIMSON BROCKWAY, *b.* 28th August, 1819, of whom later.
III. Sarah, *b.* 12th November, 1821; *d.* 1883; *m.* W. FULLER, at Wayne, New York.
IV. Alvina, *b.* 16th January, 1825; *m.* Cornelius MARGISON of Cameron, New York.
V. Franklin, *b.* 10th September, 1826; *d.* 19th November, 1846.
VI. James Lyon, *b.* 9th March, 1829; *m.* Marinda COLE.
VII. Stephen Griffith, *b.* 1831; *d.* 7th August, 1896; *m.* Celesta RICHARDSON.
VIII. Howell, *b.* 19th September, 1834; *d.* 19th March, 1892; *m.* Esther FULLER at Wayne, New York.

STIMSON BROCKWAY GARDINER, of Clinton, Iowa; *b.* 28th August, 1819, at Wayne, New York; *d.* 12th November, 1903; *m.* 2d May, 1844, Nancy BONNEY, *b.* 10th October, 1824, at Jerusalem, New York, *d.* 5th May, 1899, at Clinton, dau. of Jethro and Abigail (GENUNG) BONNEY of Penn Yan, New York.

ISSUE

I. Silas Wright, of Clinton, Iowa; *b.* 20th August, 1846; *d.* 12th June, 1907; *m.* 9th November, 1870, Louisa Catherine HENKEL, *b.* 5th May, 1850, dau. of Philip M. and Charlotte (EMERICK) HENKEL.

ISSUE

I. Philip Stimson, *b.* 23d. February, 1872; *m.* 9th July, 1895, Margaret HENCH, dau. of George and Rebecca (ALLISON) HENCH of Carl'sle, Pennsylvania.

ISSUE

1^2. Lyon, *b.* 21st May, 1896.
2^2. Eleanor, *b.* 22d October, 1898.

2. Elizabeth, *b.* 22d December, 1873; *m.* 14th November, 1895, Arthur John Cox, of Iowa City, Iowa, *b.* there 14th January, 1870, son of Thomas Jefferson and Sarah Eliza (HERSHIER) COX.

ISSUE

1^1. Frederick Gardiner Cox, *b.* 28th October, 1896.
2^1. Sarah Elizabeth Cox, *b.* 27th May, 1903.
3^1. Thomas Gardiner Cox, *b.* 12th December, 1905.
4^1. Louisa Catherine Cox, *b.* 3d January, 1910.

3. Mary Jeanette, *b.* 21st August, 1875, Clinton, Iowa; *m.* 28th September, 1897, at Lyons, Iowa, Frank George WISNER, of Laurel, Mississippi, *b.* 5th March, 1873, in Clinton, Iowa, son of George E. D. and Mary Elizabeth (HEUPLE) WISNER, the son of Anthony D. and Katherine (SCHAETZEL) WISNER of Waukesha County, Wisconsin. Katherine SCHEATZEL was *b.* in Guntersblum, Germany, 1819.

ISSUE

1^1. George Brockway WISNER, *b.* 22d February, 1899; *d.* 30th May, 1900.
2^1. Elizabeth Gardiner WISNER, *b.* 23d May, 1903.
3^1. Louise Gardiner WISNER, *b.* 1st June, 1907; *d.* 19th March, 1908.
4^1. Frank Gardiner WISNER, *b.* 23d June, 1909.

4. Charlotte Margaret, *b.* 8th September, 1888; *m.* 22d December, 1909, Revd. George Duryee HULST, *b.* 17th February, 1885, son of George DURYEE and Magdalen Hulst (STOOLHOFF) HULST.

ISSUE

1^1. Jeanette Gardiner HULST, *b.* 26th February, 1912.
2^1. George Duryee HULST, *b.* 7th June, 1915.

II. Sarah Elizabeth, *b.* 9th March, 1848; *m.* 17th October, 1866, Lauren Chase EASTMAN of Penn Yan, New York, son of Moses W. and Matilda A. EASTMAN.

ISSUE

1. Nina Louise EASTMAN, *b.* 15th May, 1871; *m.* 22d November, 1893, Wallace Brown ROGERS, *b.* 16th May, 1870, son of Thomas Brown and Mary (BYRD) ROGERS.

ISSUE

1¹. Lauren Eastman ROGERS, *b.* 13th August, 1895.

2. Ida Gardiner EASTMAN, *b.* 20th April, 1873; *d.* 5th February, 1902.

III. GEORGE SCHUYLER, *b.* 12th April, 1854, the subject of this memoir.

Arms.—Argent, a chevron between three bugle horns stringed gules.
Crest.—An arm in armour grasping in the hand a broken shaft of a lance.
Motto.—Nil Desperandum (or sometimes, By the Name of Gardiner).
Residence.—Laurel, Mississippi.
Clubs.—Boston Club, New Orleans; Lotus Club, New York; New York Club, New York; Banker's Club, New York; Automobile Club, New York.

Gibbes

ROBERT WALLER GIBBES, M.D., of Columbia, South Carolina; *b.* 20th August, 1872.

Lineage

JENKIN GIBBES, of Combe, in the parish of Folkestone, County Kent, descended from the ancient family of GIBBES of Exeter, *m.* Anne UDEN.

ISSUE

 I. THOMAS, of whom later.
 II. John, *m.* and had issue.
       ISSUE
  I. William, of Sturry, County Kent.

THOMAS GIBBES, of Combe, County Kent; *m.* Alice TREWNWALL, dau. and heiress of ———— TREWNWALL.

ISSUE

 I. JOHN, of whom below.

JOHN GIBBES, of Patrixbourne, County Kent; *d.* 1526, and was buried at Capelle Ferne, County Kent; *m.* Margaret CHAMPNEY, dau. and heiress of Richard CHAMPNEY, Gloucester King of Arms.

ISSUE

 I. WILLIAM, of whom later.
 II. Thomas, from whom descended the GIBBS of Ash, County Kent.

WILLIAM GIBBES, acquired the Manor of Elmeston, *m.* ———— Jane GASON, dau. and heiress of Simon GASON, of Ash; his will was proved in 1599.

ISSUE

 I. John, *d.* at Saltwood Castle; buried at Capel-le Ferne; *m.* Mary ELHAM, dau. of Richard ELHAM, of Dover.
 II. Edmund, *d.* 1623; *m.* Judith PORTER, and had issue.
 III. Henry, *m.* and had issue.
 IV. STEPHEN, *v.* 1562, of whom later.
 V. Ellen.
 VI. Bennet.

STEPHEN GIBBES, of Bekesbourne, County Kent; *b.* 1562; *m.* ———— (M.L. 10th February, 1585), Jane TURNEY, dau. of Thomas TURNEY of Brockhill, in the parish of Saltwood.

COLONIAL FAMILIES OF THE UNITED STATES

ISSUE

I. Thomas, Councillor of Barbados, 1561.
II. ROBERT, b. 27th November, 1594, of whom later.
III. John.
IV. Alice, m. Thomas BEDDINGFIELD.
V. Anne.
VI. Elizabeth.

ROBERT GIBBES, of Barham, County Kent, and afterwards of Barbados; b. 27th November, 1594; m. 26th February, 1639, Mary COVENTRY, dau. of Thomas COVENTRY of Ash.

ISSUE

I. Basil, Lieutenant, b. 9th January, 1640; d. unmarried 16th January, 1687.
II. Thomas, b. 24th April, 1642.
III. Alice, b. 28th December, 1643; d. 30th October, 1661; m. John DANIEL.
IV. ROBERT, b. 9th January, 1645, of whom later.
V. Stephen, M. D., b. 19th February, 1646.
VI. John, Captain, b. 25th October, 1647; d. unmarried 25th May, 1693.
VII. William, b. 20th November, 1648; d. young.
VIII. Mary, b. 1st April, 1653.
IX. Jane, b. 1st July, 1654; d. in infancy.
X. Nicholas, b. 21st November, 1655; d. 28th June, 1717; m. 19th February, 1679, Elizabeth SEAY, d. 19th March, 1691, left issue.

ROBERT GIBBES, b. 9th January, 1645; d. 24th January, 1715; settled in South Carolina, where he obtained grants of land, 5th October, 1681, and 1st March, 1682; Chief Justice of South Carolina, 1708; Governor, 1709–1712; m. (firstly) name not given; m. (secondly) Mary, surname not given.

ISSUE BY FIRST MARRIAGE

I. Robert, d. young.
II. Mary, m. Thomas ELLIOTT, and had issue.

ISSUE BY SECOND MARRIAGE

I. WILLIAM, b. 2d February, 1689, of whom later.
II. Elizabeth, b. 4th February, 1691; m. Col. John FENWICK.
III. John, b. 21st June, 1696; d. 18th December, 1764; m. (firstly) 25th July, 1719, Mary WOODWARD, and had issue; m. (secondly) 25th August, 1748, Elizabeth BEDON, d. 6th October, 1757; m. (thirdly) 29th August, 1760, Ann WIGG, widow of ——— WIGG.

WILLIAM GIBBES, of South Carolina; b. 2d February, 1689; d. 31st August 1733; m. 8th August, 1716, Anne CULCHETH.

ISSUE

I. Robert, *b.* 21st August, 1718; *d.* November, 1751; *m.* 2d April, 1741, Elizabeth HADDRELL.
II. Mary, *b.* 24th December, 1719; *d.* 11th June, 1743, *m.* William TILLY.
III. WILLIAM, *b.* 8th January, 1725, of whom later.
IV. Culcheth, *b.* 17th October, 1724; *d.* 5th June, 1777; *m.* (firstly) Jane (JACKSON) BUTLER, widow of ———— BUTLER, and had issue; *m.* (secondly) Martha, surname not given.
V. John, *b.* 12th November, 1729; *d.s.p.* December, 1770; *m.* (firstly) Martha FREER; *m.* (secondly) 6th July, 1760, Elizabeth WHITE.

WILLIAM GIBBES, of Charleston, South Carolina; *b.* 8th January, 1723; *d.* 20th February, 1780; was one of the Secret Committee of Five of the Council of Safety in Charleston at the Commencement of the Revolution; *m.* (firstly) 3d March, 1744, Mary BENISON, *d.s.p.*; *m.* (secondly) 12th February, 1748, Elizabeth HASELL, *d.* 3d June, 1762; *m.* (thirdly) 30th October, 1762, Mary COOK, *d.* October, 1799.

ISSUE BY SECOND MARRIAGE

I. Constantia, *b.* 24th July, 1749; *d.* young.
II. Ann, *b.* 6th January, 1752; *d.* 15th February, 1781; *m.* 27th September, 1767, Edward THOMAS; left issue.
III. WILLIAM HASELL, *b.* 16th March, 1754, of whom later.
IV. Elizabeth, *b.* 22d July, 1756; *m.* (firstly) September, 1775, Capt. Charles SHEPHERD, who was killed at Savannah, 1779; *m.* (secondly) Samuel HUNT.
V. Mary, *b.* 19th January, 1758; *m.* 17th July, 1784, William C. WARHAM, and had issue.

ISSUE BY THIRD MARRIAGE

I. Robert, *b.* 18th November, 1763; *d.* 23d September, 1780.
II. Henry, *b.* 25th December, 1764; *m.* 30th August, 1791, Mary DUNBAR, widow.
III. Catherine Elizabeth, *b.* 5th June, 1768; *d.* 14th October, 1786.

WILLIAM HASELL GIBBES, of Charleston, South Carolina; *b.* 16th March, 1754; *d.* 14th February, 1834; student of the Inner Temple, London, 1774; was one of the thirty Americans resident in London who petitioned the King against the Acts of Parliament which were the immediate cause of the Revolution; was Captain-Lieutenant of the Ancient Battalion of Artillery at Charleston; fought at Beaufort and Savannah; admitted to the Bar prior to 1783; Master in Chancery of South Carolina, 1783-1825; *m.* (firstly) 29th August, 1782, Elizabeth ALLSTON, *d.* 1806; *m.* (secondly) 21st January, 1808, Mary Philip WILSON, *d.* 21st April, 1844.

ISSUE BY FIRST MARRIAGE

I. Anne, *b.* 17th September, 1783; *d.* in infancy.
II. William Allston, *b.* 4th May, 1785; *d.* in infancy.
III. Eliza, *b.* 15th December, 1787; *d.* 14th May, 1853; *m.* 22d January, 1811, John WILSON; left issue.
IV. Harriet, *b.* 16th March, 1789.
V. William, *b.* 3d August, 1790; *d.* young.
VI. Allston, *b.* 16th February, 1793; *m.* 31st December, 1819, Sarah CHISOLM, *d.s.p.* 21st July, 1822.
VII. Washington, *b.* 31st January, 1795.
VIII. Henry, *b.* 19th March, 1797; *d.s.p.* 1833; *m.* 15th May, 1820, Ann Isabella MAYRANT.
IX. Edwin, *b.* 7th October, 1799; *d.* 1st June, 1831, leaving issue; *m.* 30th November, 1821, Caroline S. THAYER.
X. Benjamin, *b.* 17th September, 1801; *d.* in infancy.
XI. Sarah Postell, *b.* 15th November, 1804; *d.* 1862; *m.* 1852, William F. HEINS.

ISSUE BY SECOND MARRIAGE

I. ROBERT WILSON, *b.* 8th July, 1809, of whom later.
II. Ann Isabell, *b.* 12th March, 1811; *m.* (firstly) 25th June, 1829, Thomas How, *d.* September, 1834; *m.* (secondly) 7th March, 1837, James M. WILSON, *d.* 20th October, 1887.

ISSUE

1. Robert, WILSON, D.D., *b.* 28th October, 1838, Rector of St. Luke's Church, Charleston, South Carolina; *m.* (firstly) 22d November, 1859, Mary Susan GIBBES, dau. of James Wilson GIBBES; *m.* (secondly) 22d April, 1862, Anne Jane SHAND, dau. of Rev. Peter Johnson SHAND, D.D.

ISSUE BY FIRST MARRIAGE

1¹. Sue Guignard WILSON, *b.* 17th October, 1860.

ISSUE BY SECOND MARRIAGE

1¹. Mary How WILSON, *b.* 26th January, 1863; *m.* 2d April, 1891, Elias BALL.
2¹. Peter Johnson Shand WILSON, *b.* 7th February, 1865; *d.* 1885.
3¹. James Mazyck WILSON, *b.* 1st May, 1866; *d.s.p.* 1897; *m.* (firstly) 18th December, 1890, Susan Wilson GIBBES, dau. of Dr. Robert W. GIBBES; *m.* (secondly) 12th November, 1895, Julia WHITE, dau. of Isaac WHITE.
4¹. Robert WILSON, *b.* 23d August, 1867; *m.* 27th November, 1895, Harriet Chisolm CAIN, dau. of John Calhoun CAIN.
5¹. Henry Ravenel WILSON, *b.* 17th September, 1869; *d.* in infancy.

6¹. Nanna Shand WILSON, *b.* 22d March, 1871; *d.* in infancy.
7¹. Rebecca Wright WILSON, *b.* 15th March, 1874; *d.* in infancy.
2. Samuel WILSON, *b.* 16th February, 1840; *d.* young.
3. Susan Ravenel WILSON, *b.* 27th April, 1843.
4. Emily Thurston WILSON, *b.* 4th February, 1845; *d.* in infancy.

ROBERT WILSON GIBBES, of Columbia, South Carolina; *b.* at Charleston, South Carolina, 8th July, 1809; *d.* 15th October, 1866; graduated at South Carolina College, 1827, and at the Medical College of South Carolina, 1830; twice Mayor of Columbia, South Carolina; Surgeon General of the State, 1861, till the end of the war; *m.* 20th December, 1827, Caroline Elizabeth GUIGNARD, *d.* 1st February, 1865.

ISSUE

I. JAMES GUIGNARD, *b.* 6th January, 1829, of whom later.
II. Robert Wilson, *b.* in Columbia, South Carolina, 10th June, 1831; *d.* 24th October, 1875; graduated at South Carolina College, 1849, and at the Medical College of South Carolina, 1852; Professor of Surgery at the University of South Carolina, 1872–1873; *m.* (firstly) 6th February, 1855, his cousin Mary How, *d.* 1st November, 1862, dau. of Thomas How; *m.* (secondly) 23d December, 1863, Caroline S. SCOTT.

ISSUE BY FIRST MARRIAGE

1. Ann Isabel, *b.* 2d February, 1856; *d.* young.
2. Robert Wilson, *b.* 12th March, 1857; *d.* in infancy.
3. Mary How, *b.* 26th April, 1858; *d.* young.
4. Elizabeth, *b.* 5th June, 1859; *d.* young.
5. Susan Wilson, *b.* 27th June, 1861; *d.* 11th August, 1891; *m.* 18th December, 1890, James Mazyck WILSON.

ISSUE BY SECOND MARRIAGE

1. Calhoun Scott, *b.* 31st October, 1864.
2. Robert Wilson, *d.* in infancy.
3. James Wilson, *b.* 15th April, 1866; *m.* 2d January, 1889, Hannah J. LAMAR.
4. Sarah Eliza, *b.* 17th April, 1868; *m.* 26th May, 1897, Dr. John LAWSON.
5. Caroline Scott, *b.* 10th March, 1870; *m.* 26th April, 1893, James E. HUNTER, *d.* 3d January, 1897.
6. Jennie Guignard, *b.* 15th September, 1871.
7. Marion Farrar, *b.* 29th October, 1873.
8. Robert Wilson, *b.* 24th October, 1875.

III. Samuel Wilson, *b.* 6th February, 1833; *d.* in infancy.
IV. Mary Caroline, *b.* 7th April, 1835; *d.* 7th September, 1890; *m.* 20th November, 1855, Col. John P. THOMAS.

ISSUE

1. Mary Gibbes THOMAS, *b.* 22d August, 1856; *d.* unmarried 21st November, 1894.
2. John Peyre Thomas THOMAS, *b.* 9th December, 1857; *m.* 29th January, 1879. Mary S. WATIES.
3. Robert Gibbes THOMAS, *b.* 22d July, 1859.
4. Hasell THOMAS, *b.* 22d February, 1861; *m.* 22d May, 1889, Emma I. WOLFE.
5. Juliet Elliott THOMAS, *b.* 9th January, 1863; *d.* in infancy.
6. Benjamin Gibbes THOMAS, *b.* 17th December, 1864.
7. Caroline Elizabeth THOMAS, *b.* 3d November, 1866.
8. Walter Couturier THOMAS, *b.* 8th May, 1868.
9. Harriet Couturier THOMAS, *b.* 19th March, 1870; *m.* 1st October, 1889, Rev. A. R. MITCHELL.
10. Dwight THOMAS, *b.* 15th August, 1875; *d.* in infancy.
11. Harold THOMAS, *b.* 14th September, 1876.
12. Eleanor Walter THOMAS, *b.* 11th September, 1880.

v. Wade Hampton, *b.* 3d April, 1837; *m.* 14th November, 1860, Jane A. MASON, *d.* 26th December, 1887.

ISSUE

1. Wade Hampton, *b.* 14th October, 1861; *m.* (firstly) 30th November, 1887, Susan K. HAYWARD, *d.* 21st February, 1896; *m.* (secondly) 3d January, 1898, Heloise WESTON.

ISSUE BY FIRST MARRIAGE

1¹. James Hayward, *b.* 7th October, 1888.
2¹. Virginia Mason, *b.* 29th January, 1890.
3¹. Wade Hampton, *b.* 19th September, 1892.
4¹. Nathaniel, *b.* 21st February, 1896; *d.* in infancy.

ISSUE BY SECOND MARRIAGE

1¹. Heloise Weston, *b.* 19th October, 1898.

2. Jane Mason, *b.* 11th February, 1863.
3. Lucy Elizabeth, *b.* 30th December, 1868; *d.* in infancy.
4. Francis Guignard, *b.* 12th October, 1870.
5. Alexander Mason, *b.* 11th December, 1878.
6. Frank Huger, *b.* 27th March, 1882.

vi. William Moultrie, *b.* 25th March, 1839; *m.* 26th April, 1864, Mary H. CLARK.

ISSUE

1. William Moultrie, *b.* 14th December, 1869.

VII. Washington Allston, *b.* 7th December, 1841; *m.* 21st April, 1869, Elizabeth P. HUNT.
VIII. De Veaux, *b.* 2d May, 1844; *d.* young.
IX. Benjamin Taylor, *b.* 8th June, 1846; *d.* unmarried, 14th March, 1864.
X. Harriet Hampton, *b.* 29th June, 1848; *m.* 21st July, 1868, John R. DOZIER.
XI. Thomas Hasell, *b.* 17th November, 1850; *m.* 2d December, 1873, Eugenia TALLEY.
XII. Alice Eliza, *b.* 11th June, 1853; *m.* 2d September, 1872, William G. CHILDS.

JAMES GUIGNARD GIBBES, of Columbia, South Carolina; *b.* 6th January, 1829; *m.* (firstly) 17th April, 1856, Mary E. MCCULLOUGH, *d.* 19th December, 1866; *m.* (secondly) August, 1870, Elizabeth (WALLER) KILCREANA, dau. of ——— WALLER, and widow of R. KILCREANA.

ISSUE BY FIRST MARRIAGE

I. James Guignard, *b.* 31st January, 1857; *d.* unmarried, December, 1895.
II. Mary Eugenia, *b.* 8th December, 1858; *m.* 1885, David A. CHILDS.
III. Robert Wilson, *b.* 21st August, 1863; *d.* in infancy.

ISSUE BY SECOND MARRIAGE

I. Elizabeth, *b.* 22d July, 1871; *m.* 9th July, 1892, W. S. MONTGOMERY.
II. ROBERT WALLER, M.D., *b.* 20th August, 1872, the subject of this memoir.
III. Daisy (twin), *b.* 16th October, 1874.
IV. Sallie (twin), *b.* 16th October, 1874; *d.* in infancy.
V. Hunter Allston, *b.* 25th January, 1876.
VI. Ethel, *b.* 1st January, 1878.

Arms.—Argent, three battle axes erect two and one, sable.
Crest.—A dexter arm embowed in armour sable, garnished or, holding in the hand a battle axe of the last, headed argent.
Residence.—Columbia, South Carolina.

Gist

JAMES BLACK GIST, of Los Angeles, California; *b.* 8th August, 1868, in Tompkinsville, Kentucky; *m.* 17th April, 1890, at Tulare, California, Luella A. HATCH, *b.* 8th April, 1869, dau. of Charles Melzer HATCH and Clara P. DUGANS, at San Andreas, California.

ISSUE

I. Melville, *b.* 2d February, 1891; *d.* 2d February, 1891.
II. Charles Wooster, *b.* 27th March, 1892; living.
III. Laura Velma, *b.* 6th July, 1897; living.

JAMES BLACK GIST removed from Kentucky in November, 1875, to Woodland, in Yolo County, California, and in September, 1881, to Tulare, California, where he attended Grammar and High School. Naturally fitted for a business career, he obtained employment as a clerk in the Motive Power Accounting Department of the Southern Pacific Company in 1887, from which he was promoted as Chief Clerk in 1890. He then resided at Tulare, California, but retaining the same position, he moved to Bakersfield in 1891, and to Los Angeles, California, in 1894 His success in this capacity drew attention to him and an opportunity arose to enter the banking business. He was appointed, 1st January, 1902, Assistant Cashier of the Central Bank of Los Angeles, and upon 1st August, 1907, Cashier of the Central National Bank of Los Angeles. He was elected October, 1906, as Secretary and Manager of the Los Angeles Clearing House Association, and both of these positions were retained by him until 1st February, 1915. On the latter date he became Manager for Frank W. EMERY, of Los Angeles, a capitalist, and engaged in extensive business enterprises. He has occupied a prominent position in the civic and business world of Los Angles and has been particularly active in his Masonic relationships. He is Treasurer of the Sons of the American Revolution in the State Society of California.

Lineage

CHRISTOPHER GIST, the immigrant ancestor of all the name in America, emigrated to America some time before 1682 and settled in Baltimore County. From land conveyances as early as 1682 he lived on the south side of Patapsco River and in the same is called "planter." He was a member of the Grand Jury for Baltimore County 6th March, 1682; was commissioned one of the justices of the County. 4th September, 1689. *d*; in Baltimore County in 1691, having *m.* Edith CROMWELL, *d.* in Baltimore County in 1694, credited with being a dau. of Richard CROMWELL, of the family of Oliver CROMWELL, Lord Protector of England. She had brothers

William, John and Richard Cromwell, who settled in Maryland, and was thrice married, *m.* (secondly) to Joseph WILLIAMS, *d.* in 1692, and *m.* (thirdly) to John BEECHER, *d.* in 1694. By Christopher GIST she only had one child.

ISSUE

I. RICHARD, CAPTAIN, *b.* 1684; *d.* 28th August, 1741, of whom later.

CAPTAIN RICHARD GIST, of Baltimore County, Maryland, was *b.* in 1684, and *d.* 28th August, 1741; he was a surveyor of the Western Shore of Maryland; one of the seven commissioners in 1729 for laying out Baltimore Town and was commissioned in 1727 one of the justices of Baltimore County, which position he occupied continuously until his death, being Presiding Magistrate in 1736; he represented his county in the Provincial Assembly, 1740–1741; in 1737 and also in 1741 he was styled "Captain" and held a commission as Captain in the County Militia; he owned extensive tracts of land in Baltimore County, of which he made conveyance at different times to his sons; *m.* 7th December, 1704, Zipporah MURRAY, dau. of James MURRAY, of Baltimore County and Jemina MORGAN, his wife, dau. of Capt. Thomas MORGAN. She survived her husband and was living 25th April, 1760.

ISSUE

I. CHRISTOPHER, Colonel, *b.* circa, 1706, of whom later.

II. Nathaniel, *m.* Mary HOWARD, dau. of Joshua HOWARD and sister to the wives of his brothers, Christopher and William.

ISSUE (AS RECORDED IN ST. PAUL'S REGISTER)

1. Zipporah, *b.* 24th December, 1732.
2. Christopher, *b.* 21st September, 1734.

III. William, *b.* 1711; *d.* 19th November, 1794; according to a deposition made in 1767, wherein he gives his age as 56 years (Chancery, D.D. No 2, 179); *d.* 19th November, 1794, and the date is recorded in the register of St. Thomas' Parish, Baltimore County, where his marriage and the births of his children are also recorded; *m.* 22d October, 1737, Violetta HOWARD, dau. of Joshua HOWARD, named in his will as "my daughter Violetta GIST." She was an aunt of Col. John Eager HOWARD of Revolutionary fame.

ISSUE

1. Joseph, Major, *b.* 30th September, 1738, (St. Thomas'); he was commissioned 25th May, 1776, Quartermaster of Soldiers' Delight Battalion, Militia of Baltimore County (Maryland Archives, xi, 443); First Lieutenant, 6th June, 1776 (ibid., 467); and Major, 10th September, 1779 (ibid. xvi, 368); *m.* 30th August, 1759, Elizabeth, dau. of John (*d.* 1762) and Jemima ELDER, and his issue as recorded in St. Thomas's register.

COLONIAL FAMILIES OF THE UNITED STATES

ISSUE

1^1. John Elder, b. 1st January, 1761; m. 13th November, 1783, Frances TRIPPE; St. Paul's Register records his marriage, and the births of his two children, both of whom d. young.

ISSUE

1^2. Elizabeth, b. 17th October, 1784; d. 25th October, 1784.
2^2. John, b. 14th December, 1785; d. 14th August, 1786.

2^1. Cecil, b. 12th November, 1762.
3^1. Joseph, b. 12th August, 1764; d. 15th December, 1786 (St. Paul's).
4^1. Jemima, b. 4th May, 1765.
5^1. Joshua Howard, b. 3d February, 1768.
6^1. Cornelius Howard, b. 25th January, 1770; was Sheriff of Baltimore in 1797, and subsequently removed to Brooke County, Virginia, where he d. in 1830; m. Clara REINECKER; in his will, proved 26th October, 1830, and recorded in Baltimore (Lib. 13, fol. 474), he names the following children (order of birth uncertain).

ISSUE

1^2. Cornelius Howard.
2^2. William.
3^2. George Reinecker.
4^2. Joshua.
5^2. Joseph.
6^2. Louisiana.
7^2. Pamela, m. Conrad FITE.
8^2. Emeline, m. Rev. Joseph BOYLE, D.D.

7^1. William, b. 6th June, 1772; d. 13th October, 1773.
8^1. Violetta, b. 6th June, 1772.
9^1. Elizabeth, b. 21st March, 1774.
10^1. Owen, b. 9th January, 1778.

2. William b. 23d September, 1742.
3. Anne, b. 25th November, 1747; m. 18th November, 1766, James CALHOUN, First Mayor of Baltimore.
4. Thomas, b. 19th May, 1750; d. 1808; intestate, his estate was administered by his widow Ruth and his son Thomas; the inventory was filed 5th October, 1808; m. Ruth BOND, dau. of John BOND.

ISSUE

1^1. Thomas.
2^1. Ruth, a minor in 1811.
3^1. William, a minor in 1811.

5. Elizabeth, b. 19th May, 1750; d. 16th February, 1794; m. 26th November, 1775, Ramsey McGee.
6. John, b. 26th July, 1752; d. unmarried 1782.
7. Violetta, b. 13th March, 1755.
8. Ellen, b. 26th September, 1757.
Sarah Gist, whose m. to Andrew McClure, 28th May, 1772, is recorded in St. Thomas' register, was probably also a dau. of William GIST.

IV. Thomas, b. in 1713, according to a deposition made in 1767, wherein he gives his age as 54 years (Chancery, D.D. No. 2, 179); his will, dated 19th February, 1787, was proved 9th April, 1788 (Baltimore, IV 297); was a Member of the Baltimore County Committee in 1776 (Maryland Archives, XI, 363); m. 2d July, 1735 (St. Paul's) Susan COCKEY, dau. of John COCKEY of Baltimore County, b. 2d Novem- ber, 1714, d. 1803, her will, dated 7th March, 1799, was proved 12th February, 1803 (Baltimore, VII, 152).

ISSUE

1. Elizabeth, b. 14th February, 1736–1737; d. 6th March, 1826.
2. John, b. 22d November, 1738; d. 16th July, 1890.
3. Thomas, Colonel, b. 30th March, 1741; d. 22d November, 1813; commissioned 4th February, 1777, Colonel in Baltimore County Militia (Maryland Archives, XVI, 114).
4. Mordecai, General, b. 22d February, 1742–1743; had a most worthy military career; in 1774 was a Member of the Baltimore Independent Cadets; also Member at the same time of the Non-Importation Committee of Baltimore; 1st January, 1776, he was made Major of General SMALLWOOD's 1st Maryland Battalion; in the Battle of Long Island, August, 1776, he commanded the immortal Maryland Regiment of 450 men, the enemy were completely routed; in WASHINGTON's Retreat through New Jersey; at the battle near Camden Hill, South Carolina, 7th August, 1780, Baron DE KALB led a bayonet charge with Colonel GIST and the 2d Maryland Brigade. In 1777 he had been promoted to Colonel and was made Brigadier-General, 9th July, 1779. He was present at the surrender of Cornwallis at Yorktown, and after the war settled near Charleston, South Carolina. He was Vice President of the Maryland Society of the Cincinnati upon its formation in 1783. He m. (firstly) Cecil CARMAN, b. 1742, d. 21st July, 1770, of Baltimore County, dau. of Charles and Prudence CARMAN of London, England; m. (secondly) 23d January, 1778, Mary STERRETT, dau. of James and Mary STERRETT of Baltimore; m. (thirdly) 1783, Mary (McCALL) CATTELL, b. 2d June, 1749, widow of Capt. Benjamin CATTELL, dau. of George and Ann (YATES) McCALL.

COLONIAL FAMILIES OF THE UNITED STATES

ISSUE BY FIRST MARRIAGE

1¹. Cecil Carman, *b.* 1770; *d.* aged 7 months.

ISSUE BY SECOND MARRIAGE

1¹. Independence, *b.* 8th January, 1779; *d.* 16th September, 1821.

ISSUE BY THIRD MARRIAGE

1¹. Susannah, *b.* 12th November, 1784; *d.* 23d July, 1785.
2¹. States, *b.* 1787; *d.* 1st February, 1882.

5. Joshua, Major, commissioned 4th February, 1777; First Major of Baltimore County Militia.
6. David, commissioned 30th of August, 1777, Second Lieutenant of Baltimore County Militia.
7. Rachel.

v. Edith, *m.* Abraham VAUGHN.
vi. Jemima, *m.* William SEABROOKE.
vii. Ruth, *m.* William LEWIS.
viii. Sarah, *m.* John KENNEDY.
ix. A daughter, *m.* as alleged, James CALHOUN, the first Mayor of Baltimore.

COLONEL CHRISTOPHER GIST of Mt. Braddock, Fayette County, Pennsylvania; *b.* in Maryland about 1706, and *d.* in 1759, of smallpox in South Carolina or Georgia. He was first a merchant in Baltimore Town, but failed in business and made an assignment to his relatives, CROMWELL and STANSBURY, in 1745. In 1750 he styled himself as "late of Baltimore County but then in the Colony of Virginia" and conveyed to Tobias STANSBURY the "Gist Limepits" in Baltimore County. He later settled on the Yadkin, in Virginia, and was undoubtedly the most famous scout and first renowned explorer of the Ohio River and Valley through the present states, West Virginia, Kentucky and Ohio, as agent of the Ohio Company. This was in 1750; and he was associated with Gen. George WASHINGTON as Indian scout and forest ranger, being his guide and companion on the journey to Lake Erie in 1753. He was made Captain of the Rangers, organized in Virginia for the defense of frontier, and served through 1756 and until the company was discharged in 1757. He received various titles of "Scout," "Captain" and "Colonel." With his sons, Nathaniel and Thomas, he took part as guide and scout in BRADDOCK's expedition. He served with George WASHINGTON in his victory at Great Meadows and in his disaster the next day, 4th July, 1754, at Fort Necessity, when WASHINGTON surrendered to the French, in superior numbers, but with the honors of war. At the battle of BRADDOCK's Defeat, 9th July, 1755, he was present with his sons, and afterwards raised a Company of Scouts in Maryland and Virginia and rendered efficient service. 1st October, 1755, he was commissioned Lieutenant of the Virginia forces and in 1756 was made Captain of a Company of Scouts. The same year he went to the Carolinas to enlist the Cherokee Indians for the English service, and as late as 1758 was Deputy Agent for Indian Affairs at Fort Frederick, Maryland; he acquired lands in Fayette County, Pennsylvania, which were inherited by his son Thomas; *m.* Sarah HOWARD, dau. of Joshua and Joanna (O'CARROLL) HOWARD of Baltimore County, Maryland, whose will of 1738 names his daughters, Sarah, Mary and Violetta, who had *m.* Col. Christopher GIST and his two brothers, Nathaniel and William respectively.

ISSUE

I. Richard, *b.* 2d September, 1729; killed at Battle of Kings Mountain, whose descendants lived in South Carolina.
II. Violetta, *b.* 4th July, 1731; *m.* William CROMWELL.
III. Nathaniel, General, *b.* 15th October, 1733, of Canewood, Bowling County, Kentucky; was Colonel in the Virginia line during the Revolution and was present, with his father and brother Thomas, at BRADDOCK'S defeat on the Monongahela, in 1755; he later served with distinction in the Revolution; he was commissioned, 11th January, 1777, Colonel of the Additional Continental Regiment; was taken prisoner at Charleston, 12th May, 1780; and was retired 1st January, 1781 (Heitman's Register); he settled in Kentucky where he built his homestead "Canewood;" *d.* early in the nineteenth century, at an advanced age. Colonel GIST *m.* Judith Cary BELL, dau. of David and Judith (CARY) BELL, and grandniece of Archibald CARY, mover of the Bill of Rights in the Virginia House of Burgesses. They had issue.

ISSUE

1. Henry Cary.
2. Thomas Cecil.
3. Sarah Howard, *m.* Hon. Jesse BLEDSOE, United States Senator from Kentucky.
4. Judith Cary, *m.* Dr. Joseph BOSWELL, of Lexington, Kentucky.
5. Anne Cary, *m.* Nathaniel HART; a brother of Mrs. Henry CLAY.
6. Eliza Violet, *m.* Francis P. BLAIR; their sons were Hon. Montgomery BLAIR, Postmaster General, and Gen. Francis P. BLAIR, Jr.
7. Maria Cecil, first wife of Benjamin GRATZ, of Lexington, Kentucky.

IV. THOMAS. *b.* circa 1735, of whom later.
V. Nancy (also called Anne), *d.* unmarried in Kentucky.

LIEUTENANT THOMAS GIST of Fayette County, Pennsylvania; *b.* in Maryland, 1735; lived temporarily in Kentucky; *d.* in Fayette County, 1786-1787. As a boy he was taken prisoner by the Indians and lived with them until fifteen or sixteen years of age, in the wilds, and possibly was taken into Canada. He served from Virginia in the Colonial Wars, as Lieutenant about 1762, and in the Revolutionary War for three years as a Private in Captain REED's Company, 10th Regiment, Virginia Continental Line, for which he received a bounty warrant for land within the present state of Kentucky. He was, like his father, a frontiersman and scout, and was with his father and brother, Gen. Nathaniel GIST at the Battle of BRADDOCK's Defeat, 9th July, 1755. He gave a most interesting affidavit to be found in the Court Records of Yohogannia County, Virginia, under date of April, 1780, in which he proved to the satisfaction of the court that he served as a Cadet in the year 1757, as an Ensign in 1758 and as a Lieutenant in 1760 in a regiment raised in Virginia service and employed in the last war; that he continued therein until regularly discharged. In 1762 he again served as Lieutenant in another regiment raised and employed in similar service and continued therein until regularly discharged: that he never received any satisfaction or advantage under the King's proclamation of 1763, except a warrant from Lord DUNMORE for two thousand acres of land; and that he has ever continued an inhabitant of this State (i.e., Virginia); he later removed to Pennsylvania); in Fayette County, Pennsylvania, he acquired land originally granted to his father; *m.* Elizabeth (surname not given).

ISSUE (AMONG OTHERS)

I. Thomas.
II. Benjamin, of whom later.
III. Jacob.
IV. Solomon.
V. David.
VI. Joseph.
VII. Elizabeth Johnson, *m.* Andrew McKEWN.

BENJAMIN GIST, *b.* in Fayette County, Pennsylvania, was a taxpayer in Fayette County, 1784–1785; later removed to Kentucky and Tennessee, where other members of the family had settled; was in Washington County, Tennessee, in 1784–1785, with John CHISOLM, whose son married his daughter. The name of Benjamin GIST's wife is unknown.

ISSUE

I. RHODA, of whom later.

RHODA GIST of Washington County, Tennessee, *m.* John A. CHISOLM, son of John CHISOLM, she *m.* (secondly) ——— THOMPSON, and moved to California.

ISSUE

I. JABEZ CHISOLM, *b.* 27th February, 1826, of whom below.

JABEZ CHISOLM, *b.* 27th February, 1826; *d.* 28th May, 1903; who after being adopted by his grandfather, Benjamin GIST, took his mother's family name and was thenceforth known as Jabez Chisolm GIST; *m.* Kitty Malinda MARRS, *b.* 8th February, 1827, *d.* 6th April, 1899.

ISSUE

1. JAMES BLACK, *b.* 8th August, 1868, the subject of this memoir.

Arms.—Per pale gules and sable on a chevron engrailed erminois between three swan's heads and necks erased ermine as many fleur-de-lis azure.

Crest.—A swan's head and neck erased ermine, collared gules between two palm branches vert.

Residence.—400 South Serrano Avenue, Los Angeles, California.

Clubs.—Union League of Los Angeles, Los Angeles Chamber of Commerce.

Societies.—Colonial Wars; Sons of the American Revolution in the State of California, Knight Commander of the Court of Honor (Masonic) 32d Degree, Scottish Rite Mason and Member of the Shrine.

Henry

WILLIAM WIRT HENRY of "Saints Hill Farm," Broad Run, Virginia, B.A., and B.L.; *b.* 11th January, 1860; *m.* (firstly) 10th July, 1894, Anner Lee DULANY, *d.* 17th October, 1894, dau. of Bladen Tasker and Jane Moss (LOVE) DULANY, of Fauquier County, Virginia; *m.* (secondly) 17th June, 1903, Mary Bladen DULANY, sister of first wife; educated at Hampden Sidney College, 1875–1877; taking degree of B.A., University of Virginia, 1877; Law School Richmond College, 1878–1880, taking degree of L.B.; practiced Law in Roanoke and Richmond, Virginia, for three years, gave up profession on account of ill health and is now engaged in farming.

Lineage

JOHN HENRY of "The Retreat," near Richmond, Virginia, son of Alexander and Jean (ROBERTSON) HENRY, of Aberdeen, Scotland; Jean ROBERTSON was a sister of Rev. William ROBERTSON of the Old Gray Friars' Church, Edinburgh, emigrated to Virginia before 1730; Colonel of Militia; for many years Presiding Magistrate of Hanover County; *m.* Sarah (WINSTON) SYME, dau. of Isaac and Mary (DABNEY) WINSTON and widow of Col. John SYME, who *d.* 1730. Isaac WINSTON came to Virginia early in the eighteenth century from Yorkshire, England.

ISSUE

I. William, *d.s.p.*
II. PATRICK, *b.* 29th May, 1736, of whom later.
III. Jane, *m.* Col. Samuel MEREDITH, and had issue.
IV. Sarah, *m.* Thomas THOMAS of Bristol.
V. Susanna, *m.* Gen. Thomas MADISON, and had issue.
VI. Mary, *m.* Luke BOWYER.
VII. Anne, *m.* Col. George William CHRISTAIN, who was killed by the Indians, near Louisville, Kentucky, in 1784.
VIII. Elizabeth, *m.* (firstly) Gen. William CAMPBELL; *m.* (secondly) Gen. William RUSSELL, and had issue.
IX. Lucy, *m.* Col. Valentine WOOD, of Goochland County, Virginia, and had issue.

PATRICK HENRY, Statesman, *b.* 29th May, 1736; *d.* in Red Hill, Charlotte County, Virginia, 6th June, 1799; being unsuccessful in farming he took up the study of law and within six weeks after taking up "Coke Upon Littleton" and "Digest of the Virginia Acts," he appeared at Williamsburg to be examined for admission to the bar and the license was signed by George WYTHE and John RANDOLPH; he however continued his studies for some months before beginning to practice; elected a Member of the Virginia House of Burgesses, 1765, nine days after taking his seat he offered resolutions, which were carried during the night, to enforce the Stamp Act in Virginia. On 3d November, 1763, was retained by the Colony in the celebrated "Parsons Case," which he won for the plaintiff. It was in this speech he struck the keynote of the American Revolution. Delegate to the First Continental Congress, 1774–1776; appointed by the State Convention Colonel of the 1st Virginia Regiment and Commander of all the Virginia forces; elected to the Virginia Convention, May, 1776; appointed first Governor of the State, 1776, to which office he was re-elected 1777, 1778, 1784 and 1785 and in 1786 declined re-election. He was one of the greatest orators of his day. In 1777 he planned and sent out the George Rogers CLARKE expedition, which conquered the northwest and would not ratify the treaty with Great Britain until the northwest ports were surrendered as agreed by treaty in 1794; declined the appointment of United States Senator made Gov. Henry LEE and withdrew to private life. In 1795 declined the position of Secretary of State in President WASHINGTON's Cabinet; in 1796 the position of Justice of United States Supreme Court and the nomination for Governor of Virginia and in 1797 the mission to France offered by President ADAMS. In 1799 allowed himself to be elected to the State Legislature in order to oppose the Virginia resolutions of 1798 which he deemed dangerous, but *d.* before taking his seat; *m.* (firstly) 1754, Sarah SHELTON, who *d.* 1775, dau. of John SHELTON; *m.* (secondly) 9th October, 1777, Dorothea Spotswood DANDRIDGE, *b.* 25th September, 1757, *d.* 1831, dau. of Col. Nathaniel West and Dorothea (SPOTSWOOD) DANDRIDGE and dau. of Governor Alexander and Anne Butler (BRAYNE) and gr. gd. dau. of Col. William and Unity (WEST) DANDRIDGE, SPOTSWOOD, she *m.* (secondly) Judge Edmund WINSTON, of the Court of Appeals (see DANDRIDGE, "Colonial Families, Volume I, page 117).

ISSUE BY FIRST MARRIAGE

I. Martha, *m.* John FONTAINE, son of Rev. Peter FONTAINE.
II. John, *m.*, wife's name not given.
III. William, *m.* and left issue.
IV. Anne, *m.* Spencer ROANE, Judge of Court of Appeals of Virginia, who *d.* 4th September, 1822, and had issue.
V. Elizabeth, *b.* 23d April, 1769; *d.* 24th October, 1842; *m.* 12th October, 1786, Philip AYLETT, of King William Company, and had issue.
VI. Edward, *d.* unmarried.

ISSUE BY SECOND MARRIAGE

I. Dorothea Spotswood, *b.* 2d August, 1778; *m.* 1799, George Dabney WINSTON, and had issue.
II. Sarah Butler, *b.* 4th January, 1780, *d.s.p.*; *m.* (firstly) Robert CAMPBELL, brother of Thomas CAMPBELL, the poet; *m.* (secondly) Alexander SCOTT of Fauquier County, Virginia, and had issue.

III. Martha Catherine, *b.* 3d November, 1781; *m.* Edward HENRY, son of Judge James and Sarah (SCARBOROUGH) HENRY of Northumberland County, and had issue.
IV. Patrick, *b.* 15th August, 1783; *m.* Elvira CABELL, dau. of Col. William CABELL, of Union Hill, Nelson County, and had issue.
V. Fayette, *b.* 29th October, 1785; *m.* ———— ELEAN; *d.s.p.*
VI. Alexander Spotswood, *b.* 2d June, 1788; *m.* Paulina CABELL, dau. of Dr. George CABELL, of Lynchburg, Virginia, and had issue.
VII. Nathaniel, *b.* 7th April, 1790; *d.* 1850; *m.* Virginia WOODSON, and had issue.
VIII. Richard, *b.* 27th March, 1792; *d.* in infancy.
IX. Edward Winston, *b.* 21st January, 1794; *m.* Jane YOUILLE, and had issue.
X. JOHN, *b.* 16th February, 1796, of whom later.
XI. Jane Robertson, *b.* 15th January, 1798; *d.* in infancy.

JOHN HENRY of Red Hill, Charlotte County, Virginia; *b.* 16th February, 1796; *d.* 7th January, 1868; *m.* 19th October, 1826, Elvira Brice MCCLELLAND, *d.* 1871, dau. of Hon. Thomas S. MCCLELLAND and gd. dau. of Thomas Stanhope and Margaret (CABELL) MCCLELLAND, she dau. of Col. William CABELL.

ISSUE

I. Margaret Ann, *b.* 4th October, 1827; *m.* 29th November, 1849, William A. MILLER, of Lynchburg, Virginia, and had issue.
II. Elvira Bruce, *b.* 2d July, 1829; *m.* (firstly) 9th May, 1848, Jesse A. HIGGINBOTHAM, of Amherst County, Virginia, who *d.s.p; m.* (secondly) 19th November, 1851, Alexander F. TAYLOR, and had issue.
III. WILLIAM WIRT, *b.* 14th February, 1831, of whom later.
IV. Thomas Stanhope, *b.* 22d July, 1833; *m.* January, 1858, Mary E. GAINES, dau. of R. F. GAINES, of Charlotte County, Virginia.

ISSUE

1. Mary Gaines, *b.* 29th May, 1859.
2. Thomas Stanhope, *b.* 4th May, 1863.
3. Robert Gaines, *b.* 4th December, 1866.

V. Laura Helen, *b.* 15th March, 1836; *d.s.p.* 4th July, 1856; *m.* March, 1855, Dr. James W. CARTER, and had issue.
VI. Emma Cabell, *b.* 14th February, 1838; *m.* 22d December, 1858, Maj. James B. FERGUSON, of Richmond, who was agent for the Confederate Government in Europe, and had issue.

WILLIAM WIRT HENRY, A.M., LL.D. of Richmond, Virginia; Lawyer and Historian; *b.* at Red Hill, Charlotte County, Virginia, 14th February, 1831; *d.* 5th December, 1900; educated at the University of Virginia, which he entered in 1847 and where he graduated A.M., 1850; admitted to the bar, 1853; he opposed secession in 1861 but joined his State's movement and enlisted in an artillery company commanded by Capt. Charles BRUCE, serving in North Carolina and Georgia; State Attorney for Charlotte County, removed to Richmond, 1873, and represented that city in the House of Delegates, 1877–1878, and the State Senate 1879–1880; was President of the Virginia Historical Society and the American Historical Association; Trustee of the Peabody Educational Fund; received the Honorary Degree of LL.D., from Washington and Lee University. Author of "Reply to Attack of Thomas JEFFERSON on Patrick HENRY's Rescue of Captain SMITH by Pocahontas;" Patrick Henry the Earliest Advocate of Independence," "The First Legislative Body in America;" "The Trial of Aaron BURR for Treason;" "The Westminster Assembly of Divines;" "The Life, Correspondence and Speeches of Patrick Henry," and of numerous magazine articles; *m.* 8th November, 1854, Lucy Gray MARSHALL, dau. of Col. James Pulliam and Elizabeth Edmunds (WATKINS) MARSHALL of Charlotte County, Virginia. Colonel MARSHALL was a soldier in the War of 1812.

ISSUE

I. Elizabeth Watkins, *b.* 22d October, 1855; Hon. Vice-President of Colonial Dames of Virginia; Honorable Vice-President of Association for Preservation of Virginia Antiquities; Member of Richmond Art Club, of Woman's Club, of Daughters of the American Revolution, of Authors League of America, etc.; *m.* 9th October, 1879, Hon. James LYONS, *d.* 28th October, 1913, Member of the House of Delegates of Virginia, son of Judge William Henry and Mary Morrison (MABEN) LYONS. Residence, 508 Seminary Avenue, Ginter Park, Richmond, Virginia.

ISSUE

1. William Wirt Henry LYONS, *b.* 17th June, 1883; *d.* 31st March, 1901.
2. Henningham LYONS, *b.* 3d September, 1885; *d.* 23d October, 1900.

II. Lucy Gray, *b.* 17th October, 1857; *m.* 26th October, 1886, Matthew Bland HARRISON, *d.* 29th February, 1892, of Petersburg, Virginia, son of Robert Wiley HARRISON of Brunswick County, Virginia, and Louise Christine BLAND of Nottoway County, Virginia.

ISSUE

1. Louise HARRISON, *b.* 1st December, 1888.

III. WILLIAM WIRT, *b.* 11th January, 1860, the subject of this memoir.
IV. James Marshall, *b.* 10th April, 1867 (twin), *d.* 9th July, 1909; *m.* 1904, Annie HOLMES, she *m.* (secondly) Robert E. GILLIAM, of Brookneal, Virginia.

ISSUE

1. James Marshall, *b.* 5th August, 1905.

2. William Wirt, III, *b.* 8th April, 1908.

v. John, *b.* 10th April, 1867 (twin), *d.* 20th August, 1868.

Residence.—"Saints Hill Farm," Broad Run, Virginia.
Societies.—Sigma Chi.
Arms.—Per pale indented argent and gules, on the dexter side a rose of the second, a chief azure charged with a lion passant of the first.
Crest.—Out of a crown ppr a demi lion rampant argent, holding between the paws a ducal coronet or.
Motto.—Vincit veritas.
(These arms were furnished the late William Wirt HENRY, Esq., by his cousin Sir Mitchell HENRY of Kylemore Castle, Letterfrack County, Galway, Ireland.)

Holmes

EDWIN BRADFORD HOLMES of Boston, Massachusetts; *b.* 3d January, 1853, at North Abington, Massachusetts; *m.* 12th January, 1880, Sarah Frances PRATT, *b.* 17th March, 1854, dau. of Isaac Reed and Sarah Williams (FORD) PRATT.

ISSUE

I. Mary Frances, *b.* 25th October, 1882.
II. Edwin Pratt, *b.* 9th February, 1886.
III. Francis B., *b.* 27th December, 1887.

EDWIN BRADFORD HOLMES was educated at public schools in Abington, Massachusetts, and Eaton's Commercial College, Boston, Massachusetts; was Grand Master of Masons in Massachusetts, 1895–1896; first President of the Shoe Wholesalers' Association of New England; first President of the National Wholesale Boot and Shoe Dealers of the United States; Vice-President and Director of the John Hancock Mutual Life Insurance Company of Boston, Massachusetts; Director of the Boylston National Bank and of the Grand Lodge of Masons of Massachusetts; Treasurer of the Masonic Education and Charity Trust; Senior member of the firm of Parker, Holmes and Company, Wholesale Boots and Shoes, Boston, Massachusetts.

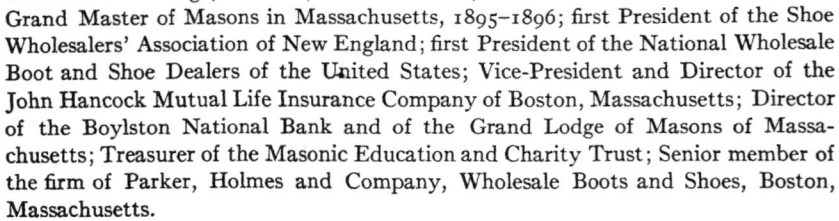

Lineage

THOMAS HOLMES of Colchester, Essex County, England; *d.* 1637; *m.* wife's name not given.

ISSUE

I. JOHN, of whom later.
II. Susan.
III. Frances.

JOHN HOLMES, Gent., of Plymouth, Massachusetts; *d.* 13th October, 1667; was in Plymouth, 1632; first Messenger of the General Court in 1638; *m.* Sarah, Surname unknown.

ISSUE

I. NATHANIEL, *b.* in Plymouth, 1643, of whom later.
II. Thomas, *b.* in England.
III. John, *b.* in Plymouth.

NATHANIEL HOLMES of Plymouth, Massachusetts; *b.* 1643; *d.* 25th July, 1727; *m.* 29th December, 1667, Mercy FAUNCE, dau. of John and Patience (MORTON) FAUNCE and gd. dau. of George MORTON, both of whom came to Plymouth in ship *Ann* in 1623 and fourth in descent from Alexander CARPENTER of Wrentham.

ISSUE

I. ELEAZER, b. 16th October, 1688, of whom later.
II. Elisha, b. 19th April, 1670.
III. Mercy, b. 10th September, 1673.
IV. Nathaniel, b. 10th November, 1676.
V. Sarah, b. 20th October, 1680.
VI. John, b. 17th April, 1682.
VII. Elizabeth, b. 25th April, 1686.

ELEAZER HOLMES of Plymouth, Massachusetts; b. 16th October, 1688; d. 21st August, 1754; m. 6th December, 1711, Hannah SYLVESTER, dau. of Joseph and Hannah (BARTLETT) SYLVESTER, who came to Plymouth in 1664, and fifth in descent from Richard WARREN of the *Mayflower*.

ISSUE

I. JOB, b. in Plymouth, 27th May, 1728, of whom later.
II. Hannah, b. 1712.
III. Eleazer, b. 1714.
IV. Lydia, b. 1715.
V. Lemuel, b. 1719.
VI. Elizabeth, b. 1723.
VII. Ichabod, b. 1726.
VIII. Jonathan, b. 1731.
IX. Joshua, b. 1735.

JOB HOLMES of Plymouth, Massachusetts; b. 27th May, 1728; d. circa 1800; at Hebron; was an original settler of Hebron then called Shepardsfield; purchased land from the proprietor Alexander SHEPARD in 1786; m. (firstly) 1752, Mehitable STUART, dau. of James STUART of Sandwich, Massachusetts; m. (secondly) Judith TUCKER, of New Gloucester, Massachusetts.

ISSUE BY FIRST MARRIAGE

I. Lydia, b. 1753.
II. JONATHAN, b. 3d January, 1755, of whom later.
III. Job, b. 1757.
IV. James, b. 6th August, 1759; d. 8th August, 1827, at Hebron; served in Revolutionary Army; some time afterwards walked from Plymouth to Hebron, 175 miles, with all his possessions on his back; m. 1792 Jerusha RAWSON; whose wife was a gd. aunt of Chief Justice Salmon P. CHASE.
V. Eleazer, b. 1762.
VI. Caleb, b. 1764.
VII. Sarah, b. 1766.
VIII. Molly, b. 1768.

IX. Bradford, *b.* 1771.
X. Bartlett, *b.* 1773.
(The records of the Town of Plympton give the names and dates of birth of all except Lydia and Job, and contain a note saying that Lydia and Job were born elsewhere. Without doubt they were born in Plymouth. It is impossible from the records to determine the issue by first wife or by second wife.)

JONATHAN HOLMES of Plympton, also given Kingston; *b.* 3d January, 1755; *d.* 16th October, 1836; served in the Continental Army; service as recorded in Department at Washington:—Capt. Peleg WADSWORTH's Company, Col. Theophilus COTTON's 16th Regiment; enlisted 7th June, 1775, service 1 month, 26 days; also company returns dated 7th October, 1775; also order for bounty coat or its equivalent in money dated Roxbury, 6th November, 1775; also return of the men raised to serve in the Continental Army from Capt. James HARLOW's Company (3d Plympton Company), Colonel COTTON's (1st Plymouth Company) Regiment; residence, Plympton; engaged April, 1777; joined Colonel PUTNAM's Regiment, term three years; also list of men mustered between 5th March and 22d March, 1777, by James HATCH, Muster Master for Plymouth Company, Colonel PUTNAM's Regiment, enlisted by Capt. N. BROWN; also as private, Captain GARDNER's Company, Col. Rufus PUTNAM's Regiment; listed in the Continental Army pay accounts for service from 8th January, 1777 to 31st December, 1779; commissioned as Corporal by Col. Rufus PUTNAM, 20th July, 1778; also recorded as being in Capt. Benjamin GATES' Company, Colonel PUTNAM's 4th Regiment; also as Corporal in Captain GARDNER's Company, Colonel PUTNAM's Regiment; in Continental Army pay accounts for service from 1st January, 1780, to 31st December, 1780; also mentioned in descriptive list dated West Point, 10th January, 1781, Captain TROTTER's Company, Colonel PUTNAM's Fifth Regiment with rank of corporal; enlisted again 8th January, 1777, by Lieutenant HOWARD, enlistment during war; also list dated Boston, 18th February, 1804, returned by John AVERY, Secretary, and J. Jackson, Treasurer, of men who furnished satisfactory evidence of their service as soldiers and were entitled to gratuities under resolves of 4th March, 1801, and 19th June, 1801, 5th Massachusetts Regiment, addressed Kingston.

ISSUE

I. Caleb, *b.* 1786.
II. Eleazer, *b.* 1788.
III. Mercy, *b.* 1790.
IV. Sally, *b.* 1793.
V. JONATHAN, *b.* 26th September, 1794, of whom later.
VI. Gamaliel, *b.* 1796.
VII. Esther, *b.* 1802.
VIII. Lydia, *b.* 1804.
IX. Zenas, *b.* 1807.
X. William, *b.* 1810.
XI. Harriet, *b.* 1814.

JONATHAN HOLMES, Oxford, Maine; *b.* 26th September, 1794; *d.* 2d March, 1887; served in War of 1812 and enlisted in State Militia, 14th September, 1812, Colonel HOLLAND's Regiment under Lieut. Charles TOWNSEND and Capt. Cyrus THOMPSON, and was stationed at Portland; *m.* Mahala REED, *b.* 11th May, 1798, dau. of Sampson and Jane (ELLIS) REED. Jane ELLIS was a descendant of Gov. William BRADFORD and Mahala REED was therefore descended in the seventh generation from Gov. William BRADFORD of Massachusetts.

ISSUE

I. Sullivan R., *b.* 1818.
II. Mercy, *b.* 1820.
III. Lewis Atwood, *b.* 1823.
IV. BRADFORD REED, *b.* 1st August, 1825, of whom later.
V. Sarah Ellis, *b.* 1828.
VI. Mahala R., *b.* 1830.
VII. Freeland S., *b.* 1833.
VIII. Jonathan, Jr., *b.* 1836.

BRADFORD REED HOLMES of Hartford, Maine; *b.* 1st August, 1825; *d.* 5th June, 1913; *m.* Mary Elizabeth FORD, dau. of Noah Perry and Phoebe (GURNEY) FORD.

ISSUE

I. EDWIN BRADFORD, *b.* 3d January, 1853, the subject of this memoir.

Arms.—Barry of eight or and azure; on a canton argent a chaplet gules.
Crest.—A lion's head erased gules, langued azure, ensigned with a cap of maintenance.
Residence.—33 Winthrop Road, Brookline, Massachusetts.
Clubs.—Algonquin, Exchange, Brae-Burn, Boston Yacht, United States Power Squadron, Beacon Society.
Societies.—Masonic.

Hoover

THEODORE JESSE HOOVER of Casa del Oso, Swanton, California, and London, England; *b.* 28th January, 1871, at West Branch, Iowa; *m.* 6th June, 1899, at San Francisco, California, Mildred Crew BROOKE, dau. of Thomas Snowden BROOKE, who was *b.* 10th April, 1829, at Sandy Springs, Maryland.

ISSUE

I. Mildred Brooke, *b.* 13th May, 1901, Palo Alto, California.
II. Hulda Brooke, *b.* 10th August, 1906, Palo Alto, California.
III. Louise Brooke, *b.* 29th March, 1908, London, England.

THEODORE JESSE HOOVER was educated at The Pacific Academy, Oregon; at Penn College, Iowa; and at The Leland Stanford, Jr., University, California, where he received the degree of A.B. Geology in 1901. Among his various activities may be mentioned: Manager, Standard Consolidated Gold Mines, Bodie, California; Consulting Engineer, Cosmopolitan Proprietary, Ltd., of Mexico; Minerals Separation, Ltd., of London: Chairman, Central American Mines, Ltd., of Nicaragua; Babilonia Gold Mines, Ltd., of Nicaragua; Carnon Valley, Ltd. of Cornwall; Sulphur Syndicate, Ltd., of London; British Sulphur Co. Ltd. of London; Dunderland Iron Ore Co. Ltd.; Managing Director, Zinc Corporation Ltd. of London; Lake View and Oroya Exploration, Ltd. of London. Director, Broken Hill South Blocks, Ltd. of New South Wales; Intercontinental Trust, Ltd. of London; Maikop Apsheron Oil Company, Ltd.; Maikop Mutual Oil Transport Company, Ltd.; Maikop Shirvansky Oil Company, Ltd.; Mountain Queen, Ltd.; Oroya Links, Ltd.; Trinidad Cedros Oil Company, Ltd.; Trinidad Forest Reserve Oil Company, Ltd.; Oroville Dredging Company, Ltd.; Star Explorations, Ltd.; Pato Mines, Columbia, Ltd.; Lake View and Star, Ltd.; Nechi Mines, Columbia, Ltd.; Yuanm Gold Mines, Ltd.; Burma Mines, Ltd.; Burma Trust, Ltd.; Inter-California Trust, Ltd.; Inter Yukon Syndicate Ltd.; Lagunitas Oil Company, Ltd.; Magneta Guarantee Syndicate, Ltd.; Mawchi Tin and Wolfrom Mines, Ltd.; Burma Corporation, Ltd.; Brixworth Ironstone Company, Ltd. Author: "Concentrating Ores by Flotation" (three editions) and various papers in technical and scientific journals.

Lineage

There is a tradition that the family originated in France under the name of HUBER leaving there with the first exodus of the Huguenots and going to Switzerland, from Switzerland to Germany, and from Germany emigrating to Maryland.

ANDREW HOOVER, *b.* in Baden, Germany, came to Maryland circa 1740; *m.* Margaret FOUTZ.

ISSUE

1. Jonas, *d.* in North Carolina; *m.* Rachel BRILES.

COLONIAL FAMILIES OF THE UNITED STATES

ISSUE

1. John, *m.* (firstly) Millicent WINSLOW, *d.* 2d February, 1842; *m.* (secondly) Rachel BRILES-WHISENHURST, *d.* 16th February, 1851.
2. Andrew, *m.* Kate, surname unknown.
3. David, *m.* Pollie, surname unknown.
4. Rachel, *m.* Miller DAVIS.
5. Rebecca, *m.* Samuel HARDESTY.
6. Elizabeth, *m.* Frederick WAYMIRE.

II. Andrew, of Richmond, Virginia, *b.* circa, 1751; *d.* 1834, at Whitewater, Indiana; *m.* Elizabeth WAYMIRE.

ISSUE

1. Mary, *b.* 3d March, 1777; *d.* circa, 1803; *m.* Thomas NEWMAN.
2. Elizabeth, *b.* 25th December, 1778; *d.* circa, 1857; *m.* William BULLA.
3. David, of Whitewater, Indiana, *b.* 14th April, 1781, Randolph County, North Carolina; *d.* 12th September, 1866; *m.* Catherine YOUNT.
4. Frederick, a farmer, *b.* 24th September, 1783, in Randolph County, North Carolina; *d.* 30th April, 1868; *m.* (firstly) Catherine YOUNT; *m.* (secondly) wife's name unknown.
5. Susanna, *v.* 1785; *d.* 1870; *m.* Elijah WRIGHT.
6. Henry, of Richmond, Indiana, Member of the Legislature, *b.* 22d September, 1788; *d.* 23d July, 1888; *m.* (firstly) Susanna Clark; *m.* (secondly) Mrs. Lydia VAUGHAN.
7. Rebecca.
8. Andrew, *b.* 6th June, 1793; *d.* 1866; *m.* Gulielma RATLIFF.
9. Catherine, of Illinois, *b.* 4th January, 1796; *d.* 1865; *m.* John McLANE.
10. Sarah, *b.* 15th July, 1798; *m.* Jacob SANDERS.

III. Jacob, *d.* in North Carolina; *m.* wife's name unknown.

ISSUE

1. Jacob, *b.* 1777, in Stillwater; *d.* 1852; in Iowa; *m.*, wife's name unknown.
2. Joseph, *d.* in North Carolina.
3. Samuel, Clerk of Court of Lafayette, Indiana.
4. John owned a mill on Wea Creek.

IV. Daniel, *d.* in Stillwater, Ohio; *m.*, wife's name unknown.

ISSUE

1. Andrew, *m.* (firstly) ——— YOUNT; *m.* (secondly) Mrs. William SHEETS.

V. David, *d.* in Stillwater, Ohio; *m.*, wife's name unknown.

ISSUE

1. David, *d.* at South Bend, Indiana.
2. Alfred (probably).

VI. JOHN, *b.* in North Carolina, of whom later.
VII. Peter, *d.* in Green's Fork; *m.* and had issue.

ISSUE

1. Absalom.   3. Susan.
2. Ensley.   4. Mrs. Shubael JULIAN.

VIII. Henry, *d.* in Green's Fork.

JOHN HOOVER, *b.* in North Carolina; *d.* in West Milton, Ohio; *m.* in North Carolina, Sarah (BURKET?).

ISSUE

I. John.
II. Noah, *b.* 23d June, 1796, in North Carolina; *d.* 8th August, 1866, at West Milton, Miami County, Ohio; *m.* 1815, Michal YOUNT, at West Milton.

ISSUE

1. Mahala.
2. Celia.
3. Absalom.
4. Mary.
5. Frederick, *b.* 30th March, 1826, at Miami, Ohio; *d.* 20th June, 1904, at New London, Indiana; *m.* 1851, Deborah TUCKER of Howard County, Indiana.
6. Enos.
7. Deborah.
8. William Jason.
9. Andrew.

III. Abram.
IV. JESSE, *b.* 1799, of whom later.
V. Joseph.
VI. Henry.
VII. Elizabeth, *m.* ———— CURTIS.
VIII. Catherine, *m.* Henry YOUNT.

JESSE HOOVER, *b.* 1799, in Hugh Wara River, North Carolina; *d.* November, 1856, in West Branch, Iowa; *m.* 1819, Rebecca YOUNT, at West Milton, Miami County, Ohio; removed to Iowa in 1854.

ISSUE

I. ELI, *b.* 6th October, 1820, of whom later.
II. Delilah, *d.* unmarried.
III. Solomon Y., *m.*, wife's name unknown.

ISSUE

1. Susie.
2. William.
3. Elva.
4. Clark.

IV. Elizabeth, *b.* 1827, in Ohio; *d.* 1903, at West Branch, Iowa; *m.* 1850, William MILES, of West Milton, Ohio.

ISSUE

1. Anzinetta M. MILES, *b.* 23d November, 1851; *m.* 21st November, 1877, in Humboldt, Kansas, Morris Edkin FOULKE.
2. Sarah Jane MILES, *b.* 9th September, 1854, West Branch, Iowa; *m.* 28th September, 1879, in Chanute, Kansas, Marshall McWITHY.
3. Ella N. MILES *b.* 29th December, 1857, West Branch, Iowa; *m.* 1912, T. CORCORAN.
4. Rebecca E. MILES, *b.* 5th October, 1861, West Branch, Iowa; *m.* there, 27th May, 1882, Frank E. WILSON.
5. Mary Della MILES, *b.* 14th February, 1865, at Oskaloosa, Iowa; *m.* (firstly) 13th December, 1883, William H. HARGRAVE; *m.* (secondly) 28th November, 1901, John HARGRAVE.
6. Sabina Iowa MILES, *b.* 18th April, 1872, West Branch, Iowa; *d.* 1911; *m.* 19th September, 1894, at Cedar Rapids, William C. SMITH.

V. Mary H., *m.* Enoch P. MILES.

ISSUE

1. Jesse E. MILES, *m.* 5th October, 1876, Eliza A. E. REEVE.
2. S. Emma MILES, *b.* 18th February, 1858; *d.* 26th July, 1896.
3. Anna Mary MILES, *b.* 21st August, 1863, Miami County, Ohio; *m.* 22d July, 1888, at Fairmount, Indiana, Robert KNIGHT.

VI. Sarah, *m.* Samuel JAY.

ISSUE

1. ELLEN.
2. Delilah JAY; *m.* ———— PEMBERTON.
3. Mary JAY; *m.* ———— WILSON.
4. Alonzo.
5. Olive.

VII. John Y., a minister in the Society of Friends; *b.* 7th June, 1834, in West Milton, Ohio; *m.* 19th July, 1855, at West Branch, Iowa, Mary JAY.

ISSUE

1. Anna Maria, *b.* 12th April, 1856; *d.* 4th January, 1876; *m.* 24th September, 1874, Franklin M. HEALD.
2. Elizabeth A., *b.* 4th December, 1860; *m.* 31st December, 1882, at West Branch, Jesse Walter VORE.
3. Charles E., *b.* 28th December, 1862, at West Branch; *m.* there, 25th March, 1882, Ida BERKHEIMER.
4. Olive Mary, *b.* 12th August, 1865; *d.* 15th September, 1902; *m.* Joe HINCHMAN.
5. Aldus Joel, *b.* 16th November, 1867; *m.* 8th February, 1894, Lillian SAUNDERS.
6. Bertha Laura, *b.* 17th July, 1870; *d.* 1st December, 1896; *m.* 1st January, 1890, Joe HINCHMAN; had issue.
7. John Farnum, *b.* 27th March, 1875; *d.* 16th December, 1904.

VIII. Benajah, *b.* 1836, West Milton, Ohio; *d.* 27th May, 1896, West Branch, Iowa; *m.* 23d October, 1866, in Iowa City, Margaret Ella ALBIN.

ISSUE

1. George, Attorney at Law and Mayor of New Branch, Iowa, *b.* 16th August, 1867; *m.* 12th September, 1894, at West Branch, Ruth E. DARONE.
2. Vernon, *b.* 1878; *d.* January, 1899.

IX. Frederick.

ELI HOOVER of Hubbard, Iowa; *b.* 6th October, 1820, in Miami County, Ohio; *d.* 24th July, 1892, at Hubbard, Iowa; *m.* (firstly) Mary DAVIS, who *d.* 3d March, 1852, in Ohio; *m.* (secondly) 17th August, 1854, in Iowa, Hannah LEONARD, *b.* 14th February, 1832, in Ireland.

ISSUE BY FIRST MARRIAGE

I. Eunice.
II. Allen, *b.* 4th February, 1844, in Miami County, Ohio; *m.* 9th January, 1868, Amelia GIFFORD.

ISSUE

1. Alice M., *b.* 30th November, 1870, in Dysart, Iowa; *m.* 9th January, 1890, at West Branch, Elmer Elsworth Robert SLOAT, *b.* 14th September, 1864, in New York.
2. Walter, *b.* 1st September, 1874, in Benton County, Iowa; *m.* 5th September, 1894, at Quincy, Iowa, Bertha A. WEST.
3. Cora.
4. Ella, *m.* ———— DEVALL.
5. Clyde.

COLONIAL FAMILIES OF THE UNITED STATES 257

III. JESSE CLARK, *b.* 2d September, 1847, of whom later.
IV. Rebecca, *m.* Evan PRICE.
V. Henry Davis, *b.* 2d February, 1852, at West Milton, Ohio; *m.* 5th September, 1873, at Marshaltown, Iowa, H. Maria PLUMMER.

ISSUE

1. Mary Lillian, *b.* 15th January, 1879; *m.* 6th December, 1899, at Legrand, Iowa, Arthur W. HAMMOND.

VI. William L., *b.* 16th May, 1855, at West Branch; *d.* 31st August, 1892, at Spirit Lake, Iowa; *m.* 10th February, 1875, at West Branch, Esther E. BRANTINGHAM.

ISSUE

1. Arthur Eli, *b.* 25th January, 1876; *m.* 19th June, 1898, in Arkansas, Dora Ellen FARMER.
2. Lillian B., *m.* ——— JONES.
3. Jennie M., *b.* 10th March, 1885, Norway, Iowa.
4. William E., *b.* 2d December, 1889, Dickinson County, Iowa.

VII. Joseph; *m.*, wife's name unknown.
1. Clyde.   2. Roy.   3. Ila.
VIII. Infant son.
IX. Mary Jane, *b.* 8th April, 1862, West Branch; *m.* 10th September, 1883, at Hubbard, Iowa, Jerry E. HARVEY.

ISSUE

1. Guy William HARVEY, *b.* 1884; *m.* 1st March, 1906, at Legrand, Iowa, Mary Ogier ARMSTRONG.
2. Hester Maria HARVEY, *b.* 11th November, 1888; *m.* 26th February, 1907, Walter E. WRITZELL.
3. Alvaretta HARVEY, *b.* 9th February, 1887.
4. Charles Davis HARVEY, *b.* 5th November, 1893.

X. Hannah Martha, *b.* 10th September, 1866; *m.* 28th September, 1886, at Hartland, Iowa, Albert H. PEMBERTON.

ISSUE

1. Roland Leigh PEMBERTON, *b.* 10th January, 1891.
2. Hannah Mabel PEMBERTON, *b.* 29th January, 1893.

JESSE CLARK HOOVER, *b.* 2d September, 1847, in Miami County; Ohio; *d.* 13th December, 1880, at West Branch, Iowa; *m.* 12th March, 1870, Hulda Randall MINTHORN, a Minister in the Society of Friends, *b.* 4th May, 1848, *d.* 22d February, 1883.

ISSUE

I. THEODORE JESSE, *b.* 28th January, 1871, the subject of this memoir.
II. Herbert Clark, *b.* 10th August, 1874, at West Branch, Iowa; A.B. Geologist, Stanford University; extensive exploration in interior of China; took part in defense of Tiensin during Boxer disturbances; General Manager Chinese Engineering and Mining Company, Managing Director Zinc Corporation, Ltd.; Trustee Stanford University, Chairman American Commission for Relief in Belgium. Residence, "Red House," Hornton Street, London; *m.* 10th February, 1899, at Monterey, California, Lou HENRY, dau. of Charles D. HENRY.

ISSUE

1. Herbert Charles.
2. Allan Henry.

III. Mary, *b.* West Branch, Iowa; *m.* 8th March, 1899, at Newberg, Oregon, Van Ness LEAVITT.

ISSUE

1. Van Ness Hoover LEAVITT.

Residences.—65 Addison Road, W. London, W. England, and "Casa del Oso," Swanton Post Office, California.

Clubs.—Engineers (New York), University (San Francisco); Royal Automobile (London).

Societies.—American Institute of Mining Engineers, Institution of Mining and Metallurgy, Societé des Ingenieurs Civils de France, Societé Belge des Ingenieurs et des Industrials, National Geographic Society, Cooper Ornithological Club, Fellow Royal Geographic Society, Fellow Royal Zoölogical Society.

Houghton

WILLIAM ADDISON HOUGHTON, A.M., of St. Petersburg, Florida; *b.* 10th March, 1852, in Holliston, Massachusetts; *m.* 11th July, 1876, in New Haven, Connecticut, Charlotte Johnson MORRIS, *b.* 22d July, 1856, dau. of DeWitt Clinton MORRIS, *b.* 1821, in Philadelphia, Pennsylvania, *d.* 28th July, 1868, *m.* 27th August, 1846, in New Haven, Connecticut, Charlotte Augusta JOHNSON, *b.* 5th July, 1823, *d.* 18th March, 1857.

ISSUE

1. William Morris, *b.* 4th October, 1882, Lucerne, Switzerland; graduate Phillips Academy, Andover, 1899; A.B., at Bowdoin, 1902, and A.M., Harvard 1905; *m.* 1st September, 1909, Mary Motte PRINGLE, dau. of Edward Jenkins PRINGLE, San Francisco, California.

ISSUE

1. Hess Pringle, *b.* 27th June, 1910, New York City.
2. William Pringle, *b.* 4th May, 1916, Plainfield, New Jersey.

II. Charles Andrew Johnson, *b.* 8th January, 1884, Holliston, Massachusetts, graduate Bowdoin 1906; *m.* 25th November, 1913, Grace Mabel CARR, dau. of Robert W. CARR, Bowdoinham, Maine.

III. Harriet Cecil, *b.* 7th June, 1886, Montclair, New Jersey.

WILLIAM ADDISON HOUGHTON, graduate Holliston High School, 1868; Phillips Academy, Andover, Massachusetts, 1869 (valedictorian); A.B., Yale College, 1873 (class orator); A.M., on examination 1889; Principal of Preparatory Department, Olivet College, Michigan, 1873-1875; Tutor in Latin, Yale, 1876; Professor of English Literature, Imperial University, Tokio, Japan, 1877-1882; studied Latin at University of Berlin, Prussia, 1882-1883; Associate Professor of English Literature and afterwards of Latin, New York University, 1884-1892; Winkley Professor of Latin Language and Literature, Bowdoin, 1892-1907; Member of Managing Committee American Classical School at Rome, since 1894. Author of miscellaneous poems and articles and published lectures on literary, historical and educational subjects.

Lineage

Tradition says the American founder of this family is descended from Sir Richard HOGHTON, Bart., of Houghton Tower, Lancashire, England. His family fought for the King although Ralph HOUGHTON of Lancashire is said to have fought against the King. The HOGHTONS of Hoghton Tower are descendants of Roger DE BUSLI, one of the followers of William the Conqueror, A.D. 1066. The earliest ancestors of John the emigrant, known in the genealogy and his descent through three generations is: John HOUGHTON, I, buried at Eaton Bray, 23d April, 1618, no further record. John HOUGHTON, II, christened May, 1593, m. Damaris BUCKMASTER and had ten children. He was a passenger on the *Abigail*, 1635, where his age was entered by mistake as four years, an error probably through carelessness. He was in 1629 and 1630 Warden of St. Mary's Church, Eaton Bray. During his wardenship the tower of this ancient church was repaired. This church was built in the beginning of the twelfth century. In the year 1635 the ship *Abigail* 300 tons, Capt. Sir David KIRK'S flagship, sailed from London with many families and servants because of the religious troubles disturbing old England. Many of those who came out were Puritans and others had Puritanical leanings, and among those who sailed from London in the *Abigail* was John HOUGHTON, II, the progenitor of Capt. Timothy HOUGHTON. This John was christened 19th May, 1593, in St. Mary's Church at Eaton Bray, Bedfordshire, where his father, John HOUGHTON, I, was buried 28th April, 1618. The following is a transcription of the passenger list 28th June, 1635, passengers from London to New England in the ship *Abigail*, HACKWELL, Master, John HOUGHTON, III, four years old, certificate of his conformity from Justice of the Peace and Minister of Eaton Bray, in county of Bedford, England. This gentleman did not remain in New England but returned to England, where he had left his family, after the trouble had subsided. 24th December, 1624, John HOUGHTON, III, son of John II, who sailed in the *Abigail* was born. He came to New England about the year 1647 with his wife, Beatrix and his cousin Ralph HOUGHTON, with his wife Jane STOWE. The inscription on his tombstone in the old Granary Burying Ground, shows that John, III, died on the old Common 29th April, 1684, aged sixty years. An incidental proof of John HOUGHTON's connection with the Houghtons of Lancashire, England, is found in the fact that one of his descendants in this country has now a sword said to have been brought from England by John, as the eldest son and heir. It has the rose and thistle on it, previously mentioned as belonging to the family coat of arms granted by King James I in 1612, by writ under the privy seal, to Sir Roger as an augmentation to his coat of arms. This sword is now in the possession of one of his descendants in Washington, D. C. He m. Beatrix, surname unknown, circa 1648–1649; after her husband's death she m. Benjamin BOSWORTH and d. 8th January, 1711–1712.

ISSUE

I. John, b. circa 1650, in England; d. 3d February, 1736–1737; m. 22d January, 1671, Mary FARRAR, b. 1648, d. 1724, dau. of Jacob FARRAR, of Lancaster, b. in England circa 1634, he son of Jacob Farrar, who was killed by the Indians, 22d August, 1675; was known widely as Justice HOUGHTON; represented Lancaster, 1690, and many years after New Charter.

II. ROBERT, b. 28th March, 1658, of whom later.

III. Jonas, b. 1660.
IV. Mary, b. 22d March, 1661-1662.
V. Beatrix, b. 3d December, 1665.
VI. Benjamin, Sen., b. 25th May, 1665.
VII. Sarah, b. 30th July, 1672.

ROBERT HOUGHTON of Lancaster; b. 28th March, 1658, at Dedham; d. 7th November, 1723; was an architect and builder and served in King Philip's War, 1675-1676; m. 1680, Esther LEFFINGWELL of Woburn, b. 1657, d. 13th January, 1741, dau. of Michael LEFFINGWELL.

ISSUE TWELVE CHILDREN OF WHOM

III. Was EBENEZER, b. 2d February, 1693, of whom later.

EBENEZER HOUGHTON of Lancaster, Massachusetts; b. there circa 1700, d. there 13th October, 1723; m. 23d March, 1720, Mary PRIEST, dau. of John PRIEST of Woburn.

ISSUE

I. CYRUS, bapt. 8th September, 1723, of whom below.

CYRUS HOUGHTON of Berlin, Massachusetts; b. in Lancaster, September, 1723, d. 1786-1787, in Berlin; served in the Crown Point Expedition, 1759; m. circa 1744; Miriam BUTLER, b. March, 1724-1725, in Lancaster, dau. of James BUTLER of Bolton, Massachusetts, was living 1774.

ISSUE

I. CYRUS, b. 1745, of whom below.
II. Lavina, b. 22d February, 1747.
III. Oliver, m. Lucy WILDER.
IV. Abigail.
V. Mary.
VI. Ebenezer.
VII. Aaron.

CYRUS HOUGHTON of Berlin, Massachusetts; b. there, 1745; d. there, 10th June, 1834, was called Deacon Cyrus; m. (firstly) Experience PIKE, b. 9th November, 1743, Framingham, d. before 1790, dau. of William and Sybilla (FROST) PIKE; m. (secondly 1790, Mary TAYLOR, b. 1752 of Boylston, Massachusetts; d. 25th May, 1838.

ISSUE BY FIRST MARRIAGE

I. William.
II. Achsa.
III. Eunice.
IV. CALEB, b. 1780, of whom later.

ISSUE BY SECOND MARRIAGE

I. Jonah.

CALEB HOUGHTON of Berlin, Massachusetts; *b.* 1780, in Framingham; *d.* Berlin, August, 1823; *m.* (firstly) 3d October, 1803, Susanna SAWYER, *b.* 19th November, 1781, *d.* 23d August, 1818, dau. of Josiah SAWYER, Jr., who served in Revolution, she was sixth in descent from Ralph HOUGHTON, first Representative of Lancaster in the General Court and Clerk of Writs, etc.; *m.* (secondly) 19th January, 1819, Abigail MERRIAM.

ISSUE BY FIRST MARRIAGE

I. CYRUS, *b.* 12th July, 1804, of whom later.
II. Persis, *b.* 4th January, 1808.
III. George B., *b.* 18th January, 1810.
IV. Rev. William Addison, *b.* 2d June, 1812; graduated Yale 1840; *d.* 21st March, 1891, Berlin.
V. Amory B., *b.* 1816, *d.* 1819.

ISSUE BY SECOND MARRIAGE

I. Lewis M., *b.* 23d October, 1820.
II. A daughter, *d.* young.
III. A daughter, *d.* young.

CYRUS HOUGHTON of Holliston, Massachusetts; *b.* 12th July, 1804, Berlin; *d.* 6th December, 1868, at Holliston; representative to General Court at Boston; 1862; *m.* 20th January, 1829, Eliza Adeline SAWIN of Gardner, Massachusetts, *b.* 25th February, 1807, *d.* 15th August, 1893, at Holliston, dau. of Lieut. Samuel SAWIN.

ISSUE

I. Edward, *b.* 8th November, 1829, in Lancaster; Graduate of Phillips Andover Academy, 1848; of Yale College, 1852, and Yale Law School; *d.* at Lancaster, 2d February, 1910; *m.* 1859, Martha S. OSGOOD, Lancaster, Massachusetts.
II. Eliza, *b.* 14th September, 1831, Lancaster, *d.* 2d August, 1853, at Holliston.
III. Frederick, *d.* in infancy.
IV. George Frederick, *b.* 18th December, 1834, in Lancaster; *d.* 1st November, 1882, at Clinton.
V. Mary W., *b.* 11th April, 1837, in Holliston; *d.* 2d February, 1882, at Holliston.
VI. William Joslin, *d.* in infancy.
VII. Lucius Heywood, *b.* November, 1842; *d.* 27th May, 1908, at Boston.
VIII. Emily F., *b.* 1845; *d.* July, 1870, at Lancaster.
IX. WILLIAM ADDISON, *b.* 10th March, 1852, the subject of this memoir.

Arms.—Sable, three bars argent.
Crest.—A bull passant argent.
Motto.—Malgré le tort.
Residence.—St. Petersburg, Pinnellas County, Florida.
Societies.—Colonial Wars, American Philological Association, Maine.

Hubbard

CHARLES DUNLAP HUBBARD of Wyncote, Pennsylvania; *b.* in New York City, 3d May, 1868; Special Agent Phoenix Assurance Company, Ltd. of London; *m.* 6th January, 1891, at Brooklyn, New York, Gertrude Robbins PITCHER, dau. of William Robinson PITCHER, descendant of Elder William BREWSTER of the *Mayflower*, 1620, and also of Rev. John ROBINSON, first Pastor of the Pilgrims in Holland.

ISSUE

I. Charles Pitcher, *b.* 22d January, 1893, at Brooklyn, New York.

Lineage

From Sir James HOBART of Hales Hall, Norfolk, Attorney General and of the Privy Council to Henry VII have sprung the several branches of the Hobarts. A branch, settled in Massachusetts in 1633, still survives in America. ("Burke's Peerage," 1905, page 236.)

HON. EDMUND HOBART, *b.* in Hingham, England, 1570; *d.* 8th March, 1646; came from Hingham, Norfolk County, England, to Charlestown, Massachusetts, 1633; Freeman at Charlestown, 4th March, 1634; Constable the same year and one of the first settlers of Hingham, 1635; Deputy to the General Court of Commonwealth of Massachusetts, 1639–1642; *m.* 7th September, 1600 (some records say 1597) Margaret DEWEY.

ISSUE

I. Rebecca.
II. Nazareth, *b.* in England; *m.* (firstly) Robert TURNER, 1626, he died 1627; *m.* (secondly) John BEALE, 1630; had eight children.
III. Sarah.
IV. A daughter.
V. Edmund, *b.* 13th October, 1604; *m.* Elizabeth, surname unknown.
VI. Rev. Peter, *b.* 13th October, 1604; Cambridge University, England, A.B. 1626; A.M., 1629; Pastor, Hingham, Massachusetts, 1635–1679; *m.* (firstly) name unknown; *m.* (secondly) 3d July, 1646, Rebecca IBROOK. (Mr. C. D. HUBBARD descended also from Rev. Peter, through son Lieutenant David, whose son Rev. Nehemiah HOBART had dau. Lydia, *m.* Nehemiah RIPLEY, who had a son John RIPLEY, whose dau. Amelia Jane RIPLEY *m.* Hon. Charles HUBBARD of Boston).

VIII. THOMAS, *bapt.* 26th February, 1605–1606, of whom later.
IX. Mary, *b.* 1608.
X. Mehitabel, *b.* 1610.
XI. Elizabeth, *b.* 1612.
XII. Joshua, Captain, *b.* 1614.

THOMAS HOBART of Hingham, Massachusetts; *b.* 26th February, 1605–1606 in Hingham, England; *d.* 3d July, 1689, came to Hingham, Massachusetts, 1633; was a private in the Hingham Company, Indian Wars, 1645; *m.* (firstly) 2d June, 1629, Ann PLOMER; *m.* (secondly), Jane, surname unknown.

ISSUE BY FIRST MARRIAGE

I. CALEB, *b.* 1630, of whom later.
II. Hannah.
III. John, *b.* 1635.
IV. Rebecca, *b.* 1637.
V. Joshua, *b.* 4th February, 1638–1693.

ISSUE BY SECOND MARRIAGE

I. Thomas, *b.* 28th October, 1649.
II. Mehitable, *b.* 4th July, 1651; *m.* 18th June, 1674, John LANE.
III. Isaac, *b.* 25th April, 1653.
IV. Hannah, *b.* 17th January, 1654; *m.* 16th July, 1677, John RECORD of Weymouth.
V. Moses, *b.* 2d December, 1656.
VI. Elias, *b.* 9th December, 1658.
VII. Aaron, *b.* 30th June, 1661.
VIII. Nathaniel, *b.* 25th May, 1665; *m.* 31st May, 1695, or 1696, Mary (BEAL) STOWELL, widow of John STOWELL.

HON. CALEB HOBART, *b.* 1630, in Wymondham, England; *d.* 24th December, 1711; came to Hingham, Massachusetts, in 1633 with his father; Deputy to General Court of Massachusetts 1694. removed to Braintree, Massachusetts; where he died; *m.* (firstly) 20th January, 1657, Elizabeth CHURCH, *d.* in childbirth; *m.* (secondly) 19th April, 1662, Mary ELIOT, dau. of Francis ELIOT; *m.* (thirdly) 15th January, 1676, Elizabeth, widow of Richard FAXON.

ISSUE BY FIRST MARRIAGE

I. Jonathan, *b.* February, 1658–1659; *d.* same year.

ISSUE BY SECOND MARRIAGE

I. Mary, *b.* 12th February, 1663.
II. Caleb, *b.* 23d March, 1665.
III. Elizabeth, *b.* 4th February, 1666.
IV. Hannah, *b.* 10th December, 1668.
V. Josiah, *b.* 11th December, 1670.

COLONIAL FAMILIES OF THE UNITED STATES

ISSUE BY THIRD MARRIAGE

I. BENJAMIN, *b.* 13th February, 1677, of whom later.
II. Peter, *m.* 15th May, 1700, Deborah HAYWARD.

BENJAMIN HOBART, *b.* 13th February, 1677, at Braintree, Massachusetts; *d.* 19th September, 1718; *m.* 5th April, 1699, Susannah NEWCOMB, *b.* 22d June, 1673, dau. of Peter NEWCOMB, of Braintree, who was son of Francis NEWCOMB of England.

ISSUE

I. Ann, *b.* 4th July, 1699.
II. Benjamin, *b.* 6th September, 1701.
III. Caleb, *b.* 9th February, 1704.
IV. Susanna, *b.* 3d December, 1706.
V. PETER, *b.* 3d April, 1709, of whom later.
VI. Israel, *b.* 15th April, 1713.
VII. Joshua, *b.* 15th May, 1716.

PETER HOBART (or HUBBARD), *b.* 3d April, 1709, in Braintree; *d.* 5th September, 1756; served from May, 1756, in the French and Indian Wars, until his death at Fort William Henry, New York; *m.* Desire COPELAND, dau. of Samuel COPELAND, the son of John, who was the son of Lawrence COPELAND of England and Boston, Massachusetts.

ISSUE

I. Mercy, *b.* 15th November, 1733.
II. Benjamin, *b.* 14th February, 1734–1735.
III. Daniel, *b.* 7th February, 1736–1737.
IV. WILLIAM, *bapt.* 15th June, 1740, of whom later.
V. Peter, *bapt.* 21st November, 1742.
VI. Isaac, *bapt.* 10th February, 1744–1745; *d.* same year.
VII. Rebecca, *bapt.* 10th February, 1744–1745; *d.* same year.
VIII. Joshua, *bapt.* 10th August, 1746.
IX. Susanna, *bapt.* 3d June, 1750.
X. Elisha, *b.* 28th April, 1752.

LIEUTENANT WILLIAM HOBART (or HOBARD), *bapt.* 15th June, 1740, in Braintree, Massachusetts; *d.* there, 19th May, 1812; served as private and Sergeant in French and Indian Wars, 1756–1762; also a "Minuteman," Sergeant and Lieutenant in Revolutionary War, 1775–1777; *m.* (firstly) 11th October, 1762, Abigail CURTIS of Boston, Massachusetts, dau. of John CURTIS, son of Theophilus, son of Henry CURTIS, of Boston, Massachusetts; *m.* (secondly) 17th June, 1776, Mercy BURRILL.

ISSUE BY FIRST MARRIAGE

I. Samuel, *b.* 12th November, 1762.
II. WILLIAM, *b.* 17th October, 1764, of whom later.

III. Peter, b. 29th April, 1767.
IV. Benjamin, b. 9th July, 1769.
V. Abigail, b. 13th December, 1771.
VI. Sally, b. 8th May, 1774.

ISSUE BY SECOND MARRIAGE

I. Elisha, b. April, 1777.
II. Daniel, b. 1st September, 1778.
III. Thomas, b. 14th June, 1780.
IV. Charley, b. 26th February, 1782; d. same year.
V. Polly, b. 1st September, 1784.
VI. Charley, b. 20th March, 1877; d. 21st January, 1801.
VII. Hannah, b. 26th May, 1790.

WILLIAM HOBARD (or HUBBARD) of Braintree, Massachusetts; b. there, 17th October, 1764; d. 1809, at Brighton, Massachusetts; served as gunner in Col. Paul REVERE'S Artillery Regiment, 1779-1783, Revolutionary War; m. 2d September, 1792, Elizabeth CAPEN, dau. of John CAPEN, a descendant of John and Priscilla ALDEN of the *Mayflower*, 1620.

ISSUE

I. William, b. 9th April, 1796; m. wife's name unknown, had son Sheldon, who was Captain of the Liverpool packet ship *American Union* of the Grinnell and Minturn Line.
II. Elizabeth Williams, b. 1798; m. (firstly) Rev. James COLMAN; m. (secondly) Rev. Amos SUTTON.
III. Emeline, b. March, 1799; m. Caleb STOWELL.
IV. Mary Capen, b. March, 1799; m. Charles BADGER.
V. CHARLES, b. 18th March, 1801, of whom later.
VI. John Capen, b. 15th January, 1803; m. wife's name unknown; had a son Capen who was Captain of the merchant clipper ships *Sparkling Wave* and *Thorndyke;* Capt. Capen HUBBARD later entered service of Japanese government, having command of one of the government vessels.
VII. Daniel, b. 10th October, 1804.

HON. CHARLES HUBBARD of Boston, Massachusetts; b. 18th March, 1801, at Brighton, Massachusetts; d. 27th December, 1875, Chelsea, Massachusetts; Artist, Captain 2d Massachusetts Regiment, 1829-1831; Massachusetts State Senator, 1851-1852; m. 19th January, 1826, Amelia Jane RIPLEY, dau. of John and Jane (MOLINEUX) RIPLEY of Boston, Massachusetts.

ISSUE

I. Jane Ripley, b. 23d January, 1827; m. 20th December, 1848, Moses Augustus HERRICK, of Winchester, Massachusetts.
II. Ellen Maria, b. 18th August, 1828; m. 4th August, 1847, Hon Rufus Smith FROST, of Chelsea and Boston, Massachusetts.

III. Abigail James, *b.* 27th November, 1831; *m.* 21st May, 1855, Simeon Dickenson HASKELL, of Boston and Chicago.
IV. CHARLES, *b.* 3d January, 1835, of whom later.
V. Elizabeth Capen, *b.* 17th December, 1838; *m.* 17th December, 1859, Col. George Carlos WINSLOW, of the United States Army.
VI. Florence Amelia, *b.* 3d August, 1841; *m.* 10th September, 1868, Courtland Ewart HASTINGS, of New York and Montclair, New Jersey.

CHARLES HUBBARD of New York City, *b.* 3d January, 1835, in Boston, Massachusetts; removed to New York City in 1856; *d.* 22d October, 1915, Larchmont Manor, New York; *m.* at New York City, 7th November, 1866, Martha Jane PACK, dau. of Joseph Sayre PACK, and gr. gr. gd. dau. of Judge Adrian BANCKER, a Deputy to the second New York Provincial Congress, 1775-1776.

ISSUE

I. CHARLES DUNLAP, *b.* New York City, 3d May, 1868, the subject of this memoir.
II. Florence Hastings, *b.* New York, 27th July, 1871; *m.* 2d April, 1891, Capt. George Sibell TOWLE, 7th Regiment National Guard of the State of New York, of Larchmont Manor, New York, *b.* 9th January, 1869, son of Francis Ellingwood TOWLE, *b.* 5th August, 1839.

ISSUE

1. Ellingwood Hubbard TOWLE, *b.* 6th January, 1893.
2. Francis Bartram TOWLE, *b.* 24th May, 1896.
3. Priscilla Alden TOWLE, *b.* 7th March, 1904.
4. John Alden TOWLE, *b.* 21st August, 1905.
5. Charles Sibell TOWLE, *b.* 18th February, 1907.
6. Elizabeth de Peyster TOWLE, *b.* 9th October, 1911.

Arms.—Sable, an estoile of eight points, or, between two flaunches ermine.
Crest.—A bull passant per pale sable and gules, bezantee, ringed or.
Motto.—Auctor pretiosa facit.
Residence.—Wyncote, Pennsylvania.
Clubs.—Underwriters, of Philadelphia.
Societies.—Mayflower Descendants, New England, of Pennsylvania, Underwriters Association of the Middle Department, Fire Insurance Society of Philadelphia.

Hundley

JOHN BARRET HUNDLEY of Louisville, Kentucky; *b.* in Greensburg, Kentucky, 26th May, 1855; *m.* in Louisville, Kentucky, 30th April, 1908, Lucile Pearce ROBINSON, *b.* 8th June, 1883, dau. of Worthington ROBINSON of Louisville, Kentucky, *b.* 7th December, 1849, *d.* 27th August, 1909, *m.* at Covington, Kentucky, 5th December, 1872, Eliza PEARCE, *b.* 3d November, 1850.

ISSUE

I. John Barret, Jr., *b.* 28th April, 1909.

JOHN BARRET HUNDLEY, Banker, educated in the public schools of Greensburg, Kentucky; Deputy Clerk in the Green Circuit Court from 1873 to 1877; read law during that time and was admitted to the bar in 1875; entered Bank of Kentucky, of Louisville, Kentucky, 5th November, 1877, where he has been continuously connected for the past thirty-nine years. A Director in the Robinson-Pettet (wholesale) Drug Company, was elected Director in 1900 of Louisville Gas Company; Member of the Board of Trustees of the Fourth Avenue Presbyterian Church, Louisville, Kentucky, and served as President of said board for fourteen years; Member of Finance Committee Louisville Commercial Club; Treasurer of the Sons American Revolution for a number of years, also elected President of said Society, June, 1913; October, 1913 and 1914.

Lineage

JOSIAH HUNDLEY, I, Planter, of Amelia County, Virginia; *b.* 1756; *d.* in Mecklinburg County, Virginia, 11th August, 1827; served in the American Revolution; enlisting at nineteen years of age from Amelia County, Virginia, September, 1775, in Regiment of Virginia Militia commanded by Col. Patrick HENRY and served until 7th September, 1776; *m.* (firstly) Elizabeth MOTLEY, who *d.* after 30th August, 1888; *m.* (secondly) 28th July, 1791, Ann HOLMES, *b.* 13th May, 1768, *d.* 19th January, 1852.

ISSUE BY FIRST MARRIAGE

I. JOSIAH, *b.* 3d November, 1779, of whom later.
II. Ann, *b.* 22d December, 1780; *d.* 19th October, 1824.
III. Louisa, *b.* 6th April, 1782.
IV. Elizabeth, *b.* 22d October, 1783.
V. Sylvia W., *b.* 30th July, 1785.
VI. Catherine, *b.* 19th February, 1787.
VII. Asa, *b.* 30th August, 1788.

ISSUE BY SECOND MARRIAGE

I. Samuel Holmes, *b.* 24th July, 1792.
II. Jincy Holmes, *b.* 2d January, 1794.

COLONIAL FAMILIES OF THE UNITED STATES

   III. Susanna Holmes, *b.* 15th August, 1796.
   IV. John Holmes, *b.* 9th April, 1800.
   V. Nancy Holmes, *b.* 10th December, 1801.
   VI. William Holmes, *b.* 25th May, 1803.
   VII. Mary Holmes, *b.* 28th July, 1806.

JOSIAH HUNDLEY, II, of Amelia County, Virginia; *b.* 3d November, 1779; *d.* 9th November, 1850; was a planter; participated in the War of 1912; *m.* 3d February, 1803, Elizabeth Archer OGILBY, *b.* 1789, *d.* 25th July, 1837.

                  ISSUE

   I. John Ogilby, M.D., *b.* 19th January, 1804; *d.* on a journey returning from Greensburg, Kentucky, to Richmond, Virginia, 1845; unmarried.
   II. Judith Farrer, *b.* 3d February, 1805; *d.* 18th November, 1880; *m.* Henry W. WATKINS.
   III. Elizabeth Motley, *b.* 7th February, 1807; *d.* 22d April, 1885; *m.* Justus WATKINS.
   IV. Josiah, III, *b.* 6th November, 1808; *d.* 19th August, 1849; *m.* in Amelia County, Virginia, Cornelia JEFFERSON, *b.* 26th March, 1810, *d.* August, 1842, dau. of John Garland JEFFERSON, of Amelia County, Virginia, a Lawyer by profession and a second cousin of President Thomas JEFFERSON under whom he read law at Monticello; he *m.* Nancy BOOKER of Amelia County, Virginia, and a gd. dau. of Elizabeth GILES, the only sister of Governor William B. GILES of Amelia County, Virginia.

                  ISSUE

   1. Calhoun, *b.* May, 1834; *d.* unmarried, January, 1910.
   2. Francis A., *b.* 13th May, 1836; *d.* 6th January, 1912.
   3. Hon. George Jefferson, Lawyer, of Farmville, Virginia, *b.* and reared in Amelia County, Virginia, 22d March, 1838; Judge of the 3d and later of the Fifth Judicial District of Virginia; served in the Confederate Army; received his academic education at Hampden Sidney and his professional preparation at Judge BROCKENBROUGH's law school in Lexington, Virginia. General HUNDLEY left this law school just in time to enter the Confederate Army in April, 1861, where he served until the surrender at Appomatox. Was badly wounded at Brandy Station. After the war, began the practice of his profession. In 1870 was elected to the Virginia Senate to represent the counties of Buckingham, Appomatox and Fluvanna. After the expiration of his term as Senator he moved to Richmond, Virginia, and entered into partnership with ex-Governor Walker. In 1895 he was elected to the Legislature to represent the counties of Nottoway and Amelia. In May, 1898, was appointed by the Governor, Judge of the Third Judicial Circuit and was elected by

the Virginia Legislature, December, 1899. General HUNDLEY acquired his rank by appointment by the Governor in 1873, for his faithful service in the Virginia Volunteers; *m.* 5th October, 1881, Lucy Waller BOYD.

ISSUE

1¹. Waller Massie, *b.* 5th September, 1882.
2¹. Juliet Jefferson, *b.* 10th November, 1884.
3¹. Robert Garland, *b.* 21st July, 1893; now practicing law at Harlan, Kentucky.

4. Elizabeth, *b.* 1840; *d.* 1844.

v. A son, *b.* 10th January, 1810; *d.* same day.
vi. RICHARD OGILBY, *b.* 17th February, 1811, of whom later.
vii. Martha Louisa, *b.* 16th February, 1813; *d.* 6th August, 1836; *m.* John CHAFFIN.
viii. A daughter, *b.* 30th January, 1815; *d.* same day.
ix. Jefferson, *b.* 25th March, 1816; *d.* 28th March, 1816.
x. Mary Chastain, *b.* 20th March, 1817; *d.* 16th March, 1851; *m.* Josiah BRUMMAL.
xi. Frances Archer, *b.* 31st January, 1820; *d.* 2d April, 1872; *m.* Edwin W. POINDEXTER.
xii. Hon. Patrick OGILBY of Oroville, Butte County, California, *b.* 13th April, 1822; *d.* 14th March, 1899, at Oroville, Lawyer; received his education in the State of Virginia until sixteen years of age; in 1838 removing to Greensburg, Kentucky, and while in that State his early schooling was supplemented by a thorough legal course in the University of Louisville, from which he graduated in 1848. The year previous to graduation he was admitted to practice law and as soon as he was graduated entered at once upon a professional career in Green County, Kentucky, but the following spring a spirit of adventure and ambition led him to join with others in a trip to the El Dorado of the West. After an eventful overland journey Sacramento was reached in October, 1849, and a little more than a month later at Dry Creek the first search for gold was commenced. After mining in Nevada, Plumas and Butte Counties with varied success it was finally concluded that this life was not the most suitable for him, and consequently, in July, 1854, he was found in Plumas County settled down to the practice of the law, where he remained (a resident of Quincy, the county seat) for nine years, or until 1863. After that, until, July, 1869 he was occupied in following the legal profession at Virginia City, Nevada, at which time he removed to Oroville and on the 12th of the month opened his law office here. In 1861 while in

COLONIAL FAMILIES OF THE UNITED STATES 271

Plumas County he was elected District Attorney, and held the office until his removal to Nevada. In 1872 he was chosen to a like position in Butte County, where he served for two years. In 1878 upon the death of Judge SEXTON, he was appointed District Judge with jurisdiction in Tehama and Butte Counties, and when the new constitution was adopted he was elected to the position of Judge of the Superior Court of the County, where he discharged his official duties for five years, declining a re-nomination. In fall of 1888 at the general election held to elect a successor to Judge Leon D. FREER, deceased, he was the choice of the Democratic party to fill the unexpired term, and was elected to the position. In 1859 he was elected as a Democrat to the Legislature, where his services were marked by an honest opposition to the Bulkhead bill; *m.* (firstly) 2d September, 1855, Kate Taintor RUSSELL, *b.* 21st February, 1836, *d.* 14th March, 1889, dau. of Gen. Henry Pierrepont RUSSELL and Catherine Elkins MUSIER, dau. of John and Sarah (GUEST) MUSIER; *m.* (secondly) 12th December, 1889, Lucy R. BOBO, *d.* 21st April, 1917.

1. Mary Silvia, *b.* 15th January, 1857; *d.* 3d January, 1901; *m.* 22d December, 1880, at Oroville, California, Dr. J. A. DAWSON.

ISSUE

1^1. Helen DAWSON, *b.* 15th February, 1883; *m.* 20th January, 1907, at Oakland, California, Walter Frank WHIPPLE.

ISSUE

1^2. Helen Dorothy WHIPPLE, *b.* 26th June, 1908.
2^2. Nathan Frank WHIPPLE, *b.* 28th February, 1912.

2. Harriett Elizabeth, *b.* 18th November, 1858; *d.* 2d April, 1860.
3. Eugene Russell, *b.* 26th October, 1860; *d.* 19th March, 1917; *m.* 14th October, 1891, at Leadville, Colorado, Lillie Elizabeth POWERS.

ISSUE

1^1. Dorothy, *b.* 3d October, 1892, at Oakland, California.
2^1. Katherine Taintor (twin), *b.* at Oakland, California, 9th December, 1894.
3^1. Harriett Elizabeth (twin), *b.* at Oakland, California, 9th December, 1894.

4. Josiah Brummal, *b.* 20th March, 1862; *d.* 17th December, 1874.
5. Virginia, *b.* 17th March, 1864; *d.* 27th December, 1898; *m.* 30th April, 1884, at Oakland, California, Alexander Thorn BUSWELL.

ISSUE

1¹. Walter Hundley BUSWELL, b. 21st February, 1885.
2¹. Claiborne Watkins BUSWELL, b. 1887; d. 1911.
3¹. Alice Thorne BUSWELL, b. 17th November, 1889.

6. William Patrick, b. 30th April, 1867; m. 25th December, 1895, at Petaluma, California, Mary Emily HOLAND; no issue.
7. Kate Thompson, b. 21st April, 1870; m. 22d November, 1906, at Farmington, Utah, Leonard Gamble RYLAND; no issue.
8. John Ogilby, b. 27th July, 1872; d. June, 1899.
9. Edgar Archer (twin), b. 25th September, 1875; d. 9th October, 1910.
10. Elner Musier (twin), b. 25th September, 1875; m. 7th September, 1907, at Oakland, California, Carolina Magretha GULDAGER.

ISSUE

1¹. Elner Eugene, b. 4th July, 1910.
2¹. Albert Roy, b. 3d January, 1912.

11. Harry Lee, b. 27th May, 1875; d. 1st March, 1881.

XIII. Rebecca Porterfield, b. 12th February, 1826; d. 22d September, 1913; m. 19th September, 1847, Capt. William Edward SPEARS, Planter and Captain in Confederate Army, b. 16th September, 1819, d. 24th May, 1904.

ISSUE

1. Bettie Thomas SPEARS, b. 27th December, 1850; m. 19th February, 1890, Edwin Josiah ELLETT; has one son William Hundley ELLETT.
2. Fannie Poindexter SPEARS, b. 1st February, 1867; m. 17th June, 1885, James Madison COFER.
3. Mary Willie SPEARS, b. 6th November, 1859, m. 5th June, 1883, Walter Abbott WATKINS.
4. Julian Austin SPEARS, b. 4th July, 1861; m. 12th October, 1890, Virginia Meredith TURNER.

RICHARD OGILBY HUNDLEY of Greensburg, Kentucky; b. Amelia Court House, Amelia County, Virginia, 17th February, 1811; d. 24th January, 1881, in Greensburg, Kentucky; was a merchant-director in the Bank of Kentucky, Greensburg Branch, until 1861; appointed and qualified as Clerk of the Green Circuit Court 2d September, 1867; was an officer in the Methodist Church, also a Master Mason; m. 20th August, 1846, in Greensburg, Kentucky, Martha America (PATTIE) BARRET, b. 26th May, 1826; d. 27th July, 1899, dau. of John and Mary Walker (WOOD) BARRET (see BARRET).

ISSUE

I. Mary E., *b.* 26th July, 1847; *m.* 6th September, 1870, in Greensburg, Kentucky, Robert E. YOUNG, of Lebanon, Kentucky, *b.* 10th June, 1846, Planter, President Citizens National Bank, Elder in Presbyterian Church.

ISSUE

1^1. Annie, *b.* 21st October, 1872; *m.* 29th October, 1896, in Lebanon, Kentucky, William G. CLELAND, *b.* 14th February, 1867, Fayette, Mississippi, Elder in Presbyterian Church.

ISSUE

1^2. Robert Ray CLELAND, *b.* 19th August, 1900.

II. An infant son, *b.* 23d March, 1850; *d.* same day.
III. Virginia, *b.* 17th May, 1852; *m.* in Greensburg, Kentucky, 9th October, 1877, Abraham Hite BARRET, Civil Engineer, *b.* 11th December, 1853, Chief Engineer Louisville Gas and Electric Light Company, and Director in the Bank of Kentucky for a number of years.

ISSUE

1. Thomas L. BARRET, Jr., Civil Engineer, *b.* 20th September, 1878.

IV. JOHN BARRET, *b.* 26th May, 1855, the subject of this memoir.
V. Infant daughter, *b.* 5th April, 1865; *d.* same day.

Residence.—967 South Fourth Street, Louisville, Kentucky.
Clubs.—Pendennis, Country, Cherokee Golf and Louisville Commercial Clubs of Louisville, Kentucky.
Societies.—Sons of the American Revolution, Society of Colonial Wars.

Barret

The earliest information which we have, as yet been able to obtain of this particular family is that Robert BARRET "a dauntless sailor in the English Navy" is mentioned as being a Master of one of the ships of the fleet which Admiral Sir John HAWKINS commanded, and which sailed from Plymouth on the 2d October, 1567. This particular fleet consisted of six ships, namely, *The Jesus*, Admiral HAWKIN's flagship, Robert BARRET, Master; *The Mignon*, Capt. Thomas HAMPTON, John GARNETT, Master; *The William and John*, Capt. Thomas BOLTON, James POUNCE; Master; *The Judith*, Capt. (afterwards Sir) Francis DRAKE; *The Angel* and *The Swallow;* he was evidently in the "West India Trade" and must have amassed more or less a fortune; *m.* Penelope GILBERT.

ISSUE

1. WILLIAM, *b.* in Wales, 22d June, 1566; *d.* 1642.

WILLIAM BARRET, *b.* in Wales, 22d June, 1566; *d.* 1642. The greatest part of his life was spent in London, but it appears that he spent a portion of it at least in America and was practically the first of the BARRETS in this county. Was a member of the London Company, one of the companies organized for the purpose of colonizing the "New World," under the auspices of which that part of America now known as Virginia was settled. This is the same company that sent out expeditions under the leadership of Lord DELAWARE, Capt. John SMITH, of Pocohontas fame. William BARRET appears to have had an eloquent and graphic pen, and that he, in the "True Declaration" painted the Bermuda Isle, with the wrecks there, the glories of the new Atlantas, the smooth glossy bosom of the magnificent Chesapeake, the verdure of the broad and beautiful James, woods full of song, gives a glowing picture of the future and promise of aggrandizement, and the dire shame of the abandonment of the enterprise, gives the causes of the previous failures and his active genius and auspicious patronage did ably aid, in money, the planting of the first vital germ of the civilization and permanent settlement in the New World. He *m.* Dorothea PAYNE.

ISSUE

1. WILLIAM, *b.* 1590, of whom below.

WILLIAM BARRET, *b.* 1590; *d.* 1640; *m.* Ann FERREL, known to have been an American wife.

ISSUE

1. WILLIAM, *b.* at Barret's Ford, near Appomattox, Virginia, in 1623, of whom below.

WILLIAM BARRET was *b.* at Barret's Ford, near Appomattox, Virginia, in 1623; *d.* there, in 1705; Land Office Richmond, Virginia, 700 acre head rights, Warrency Old Town, 1646; he was Burgess, 1644-1646; Councillor, April, 1652. (Reference HENNING. William and Mary College *Quarterly*, Vol. 7, No. 3, page 202); *m.* Ann LUDWELL.

ISSUE

1. ROBERT, *b.* 1682; *d.* 1757, of whom below.

REV. ROBERT BARRET, *b.* 1682, at Barret's Ford; *d.* 1757; was a Clergyman of the Established Church; held large landed possessions in Louisa, Hanover and Goochland Counties; he is said to have been very eloquent and that his sermons were greatly relished and eagerly borrowed by his fellow clergymen, when borrowing was the fashion; he preached at Fort Chute, Hanover and Hollowing Creek Church, Louisa County; *m.* Nancy DANGERFIELD of the "Northern Neck."

COLONIAL FAMILIES OF THE UNITED STATES

ISSUE

1. ROBERT, *b.* 1710, of whom below.

REV. ROBERT BARRET, *b.* 1710; *d.* 1797, in Hanover County, Virginia; he was Rector of Saint Martin's (Louisa County) and Trinity Parishes; co-laborer with Rev. James MAURY, usher of William and Mary College, 1729, Master of same; *m.* (firstly) Elizabeth LEWIS, dau. of Robert and Catherine (FAUNTLEROY) LEWIS and cousin of Capt. Merewether LEWIS of Lewis and Clark fame, Governor of Louisiana and Secretary to Thomas JEFFERSON; *m.* (secondly) Anne LEE, *d.* 1795, sister of Light Horse Harry LEE, dau. of Henry LEE, cousin of Richard Henry and Arthur LEE and Mary BLAND of Jordans, Prince George County, Maryland.

ISSUE BY SECOND MARRIAGE

1. FRANCIS, *b.* 22d February, 1762; *d.* 6th July, 1833, in Greensburg, Kentucky, of whom below.

FRANCIS BARRET, *b.* 22d February, 1762; *d.* 6th July, 1833, in Greensburg, Kentucky; was a soldier in the Revolutionary War at the age of sixteen years, serving in Capt. Robert BARRET's Company, "Virginia Convention Guards," 13th January to 10th September, 1779, and in Gen. Thomas NELSON's Life Guard; *m.* Elizabeth LOWRY. He and his wife died within a few hours of each other during the epidemic of cholera and were buried in same grave in the family grave yard in Greensburg, Kentucky.

ISSUE

1. JOHN, *b.* in Albemarle County, Virginia, 27th November, 1785, of whom later.

JOHN BARRET, *b.* in Albemarle County, Virginia, 27th November, 1785; *d.* Greensburg, Kentucky, 6th April, 1860; was Clerk of the Green County and Circuit Courts for thirty-nine years; also President of Bank of Kentucky, Greensburg Branch; *m.* 1818, Mary Walker WOOD, *b.* 6th October, 1798, in Albemarle County, Virginia, *d.* 8th March, 1883, in Greensburg, Kentucky, dau. of William J. WOOD and Elizabeth TWYMAN, she dau. of George and Mary (WALKER) TWYMAN and gd. dau. of John and Ellena (ISRAEL) WOOD.

ISSUE

1. William Francis, *b.* 5th April, 1820, in Greensburg, Kentucky; *d.* 28th September, 1882, in Louisville, Kentucky; Lawyer, several times elected Member of the Kentucky Legislature; *m.* (firstly) 8th July, 1846, Maria Elizabeth GOODLOE, of Richmond, Kentucky, *b.* 12th December, 1827, *d.* 28th March, 1865; *m.* (secondly) 18th May, 1871, Margarette BROWN, of Frankfort, Kentucky.

ISSUE BY FIRST MARRIAGE

1. William Goodloe, *d.* in infancy.
2. Henry Owsley, *b.* 1st June, 1849; *d.* 10th August, 1863.
3. Mary Walker, *b.* 6th September, 1861; *d.* 8th December, 1911; *m.* J. Speed SMITH.
4. John, Lawyer and Member of Kentucky Legislature; Postmaster of the City of Louisville, Kentucky, four years; *b.* 11th December, 1854; *d.* 22d November, 1906; unmarried.
5. William Goodloe, *b.* 20th April, 1857; *m.* Brooks BURKE.
6. Maria Elizabeth, *b.* 1st November, 1864; *m.* 1st January, 1900, F. S. MUNIER.

ISSUE BY SECOND MARRIAGE

1. Mason Brown, Lawyer, *b.* 8th April, 1872; *m.* 3d December, 1907, Rosa Johnson ROBINSON, of Louisville, Kentucky.

ISSUE

1[1]. Rosa Robinson, *b.* 25th October, 1908.

2. William Francis, *b.* 8th November, 1874; *d.* 23d November, 1902; *m.* 19th December, 1900, Ella JOHNSON, of Frankfort, Kentucky; no issue.

II. Elizabeth, *b.* 10th June, 1823, in Greensburg; *d.* 13th September, 1898, at Walkerville, Canada; *m.* at Greensburg, Kentucky, 1st January, 1843, Judge Henry Crutcher WOOD, *b.* 27th November, 1821, at Munfordsville, Kentucky, *d.* at Munfordsville, Kentucky, February, 1861.

ISSUE

1. Henry Crittenden WOOD, *b.* 7th November, 1844; *d.* unmarried, September, 1866.
2. Thomas John WOOD, unmarried, *b.* 17th September, 1848.
3. George Twyman WOOD, *b.* 26th December, 1854; *m.* 21st January, 1890.
4. Lizzie Boyle WOOD, unmarried, *b.* 3d November, 1856.

III. Martha America (Pattie), *b.* 26th May, 1826, in Greensburg, Kentucky; *d.* 27th July, 1899, in Lebanon, Kentucky; *m.* 20th August, 1846, Richard Ogilby HUNDLEY, *b.* 17th February, 1811 (see Hundley).

IV. John Garnett, Lawyer, *b.* 27th August, 1829, in Greensburg, Kentucky; *d.* 14th May, 1890, in Louisville, Kentucky; founder and President of the Citizens National Bank of Louisville; Elder in Presbyterian Church; *m.* 5th May, 1855, Anne E. RODES, *b.* 13th March, 1830, in Danville, Kentucky, *d.* 30th December, 1915, at her residence, Cherokee Park, Louisville, Kentucky.

COLONIAL FAMILIES OF THE UNITED STATES

ISSUE

1. Amanda, *b.* 18th February, 1856; unmarried.
2. Clifton Rodes, *b.* 4th November, 1859; unmarried.
3. Henrie, *b.* 5th April, 1861; *d.* 19th September, 1900, in Dublin, Ireland and buried in Louisville, Kentucky; *m.* 25th October, 1887, Richard MONTFORT, Chief Engineer for a number of years and at present time Consulting Engineer of the Louisville and Nashville Railroad Company, *b.* 4th March, 1855, near Dublin, Ireland.

ISSUE

1^1. John Barret MONTFORT, Civil Engineer, *b.* 6th March, 1890; unmarried; studying Law at University of Virginia.

v. Virginia, *b.* 5th February, 1832, in Greensburg; *d.* same day.
vi. George Twyman, Lawyer and Planter, *b.* 5th May, 1835, in Greensburg, *d.* 6th July, 1903, near Grove City, Illinois; *m.* 26th December, 1886, Lura A. BARRET; no issue.
vii. Mary Washington, *b.* 4th July, 1837, in Greensburg, *d.* unmarried, 1st January, 1891, in Lebanon, Kentucky.
viii. Daniel Thompkins, Captain in Union Army, Sheriff of Jefferson County, Kentucky, Farmer in Christian County, Illinois; *b.* 21st September, 1839; *d.* 26th July, 1892, near Grove City, Illinois; *m.* 29th November, 1866, Maria MCKENZIE, who *d.* 5th December, 1885.

ISSUE

1. John McKenzie, *b.* 30th September, 1868.
2. Zachariah Wood, *b.* 23d October, 1871.
3. George Arthur, *b.* 25th February, 1875.
4. Edgar Lee, *b.* 17th February, 1877.
5. Mary Edith (twin), *b.* 20th June, 1880.
6. Leah Ethel (twin), *b.* 20th June, 1880.

Isaac

WILLIAM MOORE ISAAC, deceased, of Towson, Baltimore County, Maryland; b. 12th March, 1834, near Ellicott City, Maryland; d. 4th January, 1911, at Baltimore; m. 29th September, 1859, Eleanor Penny PHILLIPS, b. 11th October, 1837, dau. of Thomas PHILLIPS and Amy (PENNY) PHILLIPS, son of James PHILLIPS, Lanceston, England, and Catherine ———. James PHILLIPS d. 1825. Thomas PHILLIPS, b. 25th November, 1790, Cornwall, England, d. 13th August, 1847, in Baltimore County, Maryland, m. (firstly) Jane, dau. of Peter and Jane NICHOLLS (secondly) Amy PENNY, b. 10th September, 1798, in Baltimore County, d. there 28th May, 1873, dau. of Alexander and Susan Ford PENNY. He son of Henry PENNY, and Elizabeth, surname unknown, Vestryman of Old St. Paul's Church, Baltimore. She dau. of Samuel Fortt and Susannah, surname unknown, who afterwards m. George Bramwell, the son of Chief Justice Bramwell of London.

ISSUE

I. Amy Phillips, b. 20th July, 1860.
II. William Thomas, b. 12th October, 1862; d. 12th June, 1863.
III. Mary Ware, b. 7th January, 1865.
IV. Randolph Moore, b. 12th July, 1867; d. 10th February, 1906.
V. Zedekiah Howard, b. 28th July, 1870; d. 7th November, 1914.
VI. Eleanor Phillips, b. 25th December, 1871; m. 25th October, 1900, Edward Boteler PASSANO, b. 11th August, 1872.

ISSUE

1. William Moore PASSANO, b. 12th June, 1902.
2. Edward Magruder PASSANO, b. 22d December, 1904.
3. Howard Isaac PASSANO, b. 27th June, 1906; d. 21st August, 1907.

WILLIAM MOORE ISAAC, Attorney-at-Law, was Deputy Register of Wills of Howard County, Maryland; Deputy Register of Wills, Baltimore County; Deputy Clerk and Clerk Circuit Court of Baltimore County; Clerk United States Treasury Department; Secretary and Treasurer Maryland Title Insurance and Trust Company; Grand Secretary of Grand Lodge of Ancient Free and Accepted Masons; Past Grand Master of Independent Order of Odd Fellows; Vestryman of Trinity Church, Towson; President of Baltimore County School Commissioners.

COLONIAL FAMILIES OF THE UNITED STATES

Lineage

The original progenitor in Maryland, of this line of the ISAAC family, is believed to have been Joseph ISACKE, who came to Maryland during the latter part of the seventeenth century. There is a tradition in this branch of the family that the first settlers of the name, to come to this State, were two brothers, who came from England as officers of the English Government, in charge of certain political prisoners, among whom was the founder of the BOWIE family in Maryland. The tradition, so far as it relates to the BOWIE family, is also alluded to by the author of "The Bowie Family and Their Kindred."

JOSEPH ISACKE is believed to have been the brother of Edward ISACKE, whose will, dated 3d December, 1693 (Wills, Record No. 2, folio 322, Land office, Annapolis), mentioned his wife, Jane, and his son, Sutton. The brother referred to in Edward ISACKE's will is not named, but there is no doubt that he was the Joseph ISACKE who *d.* in 1689 in Calvert County. Joseph ISACKE lived and *d.* in that part of Calvert County which, about 1705, became Queen Anne's Parish, in Prince George's County. Joseph ISACKE's name first appears upon the Maryland Records in his will bearing date 29th December, 1688, and probated 23d February, 1689 (Land Office, Wills, 6, folio, 53, and Test. Prob. 14, folio, 131). In his will, Joseph ISACKE mentioned his wife, Margaret, his sons, Richard and Joseph, his daughters, Elizabeth and Rebecca, and his sons-in-law (that is to say, his stepsons), Joseph BROWN and James CLIFFORD, all children minors. It is evident from this will that Margaret, the wife of Joseph ISACKE, had been married before she became the wife of Joseph, first to one BROWN, and secondly to a certain CLIFFORD. Her maiden name is unknown.

ISSUE

I. Elizabeth, *b.* circa 1677-1678, otherwise unknown.
II. RICHARD, *b.* 1679; *d.* June, 1759.
III. Rebecca, *b.* 1680; *m.* Charles WALKER, Jr., of Bacon Hall, Prince George's County, Maryland, *b.* 1668, according to his deposition in Prince George's County (Chancery Record, P. L., folio 27), and *d.* 1730.
IV. Joseph, *b.* 1681; *d.* 1703, probably unmarried, as on 30th September, of that year, Richard ISAAC, his brother, filed in Prince George's County his administrator's bond on Joseph ISAAC's estate.

RICHARD ISAAC, Gentleman Planter; *b.* 1679, in Queen Anne's Parish, Prince George's County, Maryland; *d.* there, June, 1759; was a Vestryman of that Parish, and in 1753 was a Justice of the Peace, as appears from Deed Book N.N., p. 306; in all the old records he is styled "Gentleman;" *m.* circa 1710, Sarah POTTENGER, *b.* 20th July, 1688, *d.* after 1743 (but before her husband), eldest dau. of John POTTENGER, *b.* 1642; *d.* in Prince George's Co., Md., 1732 (see POTTENGER, Vol. II, "Colonial Families of the U. S. A.") and Mary BEALL, his wife, a dau. of Col. Ninian BEALL.

COLONIAL FAMILIES OF THE UNITED STATES

ISSUE

I. Mary, b. 1st May, 1712; m. 17th February, 1725-1726, Joseph PEACH.
II. Sarah, b. 1714; m. Westal RIDGLEY, son of William RIDGLEY, II, and Jane WESTAL, his wife, dau. of George WESTAL, of South River, Anne Arundel County. William RIDGLEY, II, was the son of William RIDGLEY, a brother of Col. Henry RIDGLEY. Westal RIDGLEY of Frederick County, Maryland, and Sarah ISAAC, his wife, were the parents of Jane RIDGLEY, the wife of William WOODWARD, and were ancestors of James T. WOODWARD, of New York, and Rignal D. WOODWARD, and others, of Anne Arundel County, Maryland.
III. Rachel, b. 2d July, 1716; m. ——— JONES.
IV. Kezia, b. 5th February, 1719; m. 24th September, 1734, Benonii FOWLER.
V. Richard, b. 21st January, 1720; was a Justice of the Peace of Prince George's County, Maryland, in 1770, and a large landowner; m. Sarah JACOB, dau. of Benjamin JACOB and Alice WESTAL (who was the dau. of George WESTAL of South River), and gd. dau. of Capt. John and Ann (CHANY) JACOB, of "All Hallows Parish," Anne Arundel County, Maryland.
VI. Drusilla, b. 5th April, 1723; m. 10th February, 1738, Jeremiah FOWLER.
VII. JOSEPH, b. 1725; d. 1771-1774.
VIII. Jemima, b. 21st May, 1727; m. 7th December, 1745, Mordecai JACOB.

JOSEPH ISAAC, Gentleman Planter, of Queen Anne's Parish, Prince George's County, Maryland; b. circa 1725; d. probably 24th October, 1774, on his dwelling plantation "Stony Plains;" he owned many tracts of land and much personality; was Justice of the Peace; m. prior to 1763, Hannah BRYANT, dau. of Richard BRYANT. After his death she m. Richard BRICE, who d. in 1788. She survived both her husbands, and in her will, dated 19th December, 1798, probated 30th April following, and recorded in Prince George's County Wills, 1770, p. 418, she mentioned all of her children by both marriages, except Sarah, who was then probably deceased.

ISSUE

I. Richard, b. 1760-1763; d. 1836.
II. Joseph.
III. Sutton, m. 6th February, 1795, Elizabeth CLARKE.
IV. Sarah.
V. Mary.
VI. JOHN H., b. 22d September, 1774, of whom later.

JOHN H. ISAAC, Howard County, Maryland; b. 22d September, 1774; d. 31st May, 1855; m. 30th March, 1801, Elizabeth MOORE, b. 12th August, 1779, d. 28th October, 1863, dau. of Thomas MOORE, b. 2d June, 1745, m. 28th January, 1773, Hester, surname unknown, was a sailor on ship *Defense* 1776, Member of House of

Delegates, 1777, was a brother of Zedekiah MOORE, Lieutenant 2d Maryland Regiment, son of George Moore. The tradition of the family is that the father and both sons served in the Revolutionary War.

ISSUE

I. Eliza, *b.* 28th June, 1802, *m.* (firstly) 18th December, 1821, John CARROLL *m.* (secondly) Benjamin MARLOW; *d.* 18th September, 1838.
II. Thomas Jefferson, *b.* 18th March, 1804; *d.* 27th July, 1887; *m.* (firstly) 16th February, 1830, Maria (PEDDAICK) ROCKEY, widow, of New Jersey, who *d.* 14th February, 1864; *m.* (secondly) 22d February 1866, Martha B. WARE, she *d.* 6th April, 1887.
III. George Washington, *b.* 4th July, 1806; *d.* 4th March, 1891; *m.* (firstly) Ann HILL, *b.* 13th March, 1807, *d.* 10th July, 1862; *m.* (secondly) 18th November, 1862, Elizabeth VOLZ.
IV. ZEDEKIAH MOORE, *b.* 12th July, 1808, of whom later.
V. Sarah, *b.* probably 1810; *d.* in infancy.
VI. Mary, *b.* 19th October, 1812; *m.* her brother-in-law, Benjamin MARLOW.
VII. Sarah, *b.* 19th October, 1815; *m.* 4th June, 1835, William CAMPBELL.
VIII. WILLIAM ANDREW JACKSON, *b.* 8th January, 1817: *m.* Susan OLIVER.
IX. Harriet *b.* 1819, *d. unm.* 24th December, 1901.
X. Ann Elizabeth, *b.* 20th August, 1826, *m.* John S. FARREE, 16th October, 1851, *d.* 21st December, 1855.

ZEDEKIAH MOORE ISAAC of Howard County, Maryland; *b.* 12th July, 1808; *d* 2d July, 1892; *m.* 28th March, 1833, Mary Roach WARE, *b.* 12th May, 1811, *d.* 5th August, 1889.

ISSUE

I. WILLIAM MOORE, *b.* 12th March, 1834, the subject of this memoir.
II. Caroline, *b.* 7th October, 1835; *d.* September, 1836.
III. Uriah Randolph, *b.* 7th October, 1838; *d.* 17th June, 1853.
IV. Martha Ann, *b.* 14th May, 1840.
V. Mary Gertrude, *b.* 2d December, 1846; *m.* 19th June, 1873, Benjamin Cosmo SUNDERLAND.

Arms (Isaak of England).—Sable, a bend or, on a canton argent a leopard's face gules.
Crest.—A leopard's head erased or, pellettée and ducally collared gules.
Motto.—Florescat.

Izard

RALPH IZARD of Goodes, Bedford County, Virginia; *b.* at Goodes, Virginia, 19th March, 1860; *m.* there, 1891, N. J. LYONS.

ISSUE

I. Sarah Lyons, *b.* 14th May, 1892.
II. Annie, *b.* 14th August, 1894.
III. Laura, *b.* 3d of February, 1903.

Lineage

RALPH IZARD, *d.* 1699; "Citizen and Grocer of London;" his will was proved 8th November, 1699; *m.* Elizabeth, surname not given.

ISSUE

I. John, "Citizen and Salter of London;" *m.* Mary, surname not given, and had issue; will proved 13th April, 1706.
II. RALPH, *d.* 1711, of whom later.
III. Benjamin, of Wassamsaw, Berkley County; settled in Carolina, where he was a tax-payer, 1704; *d.* 1724; *m.* Elizabeth, surname not given, who *d.* 1726.
IV. Dorothy, *m.* Calverley BEWICKE, of Close House, County Northumberland, and Urpeth Lodge, County Durham, who *d.* 1729, leaving issue.

RALPH IZARD, *d.* 1711, of Berkley County, South Carolina; *b.* in England; emigrated to Carolina, 1682; arrived at Charleston 3d October, of that year; settled in St. James' Parish, where he acquired large plantations; Justice of the Peace; Member of the House of Representatives, and President of the Indian Commission; his will was proved 24th January, 1711; *m.* (firstly) Mary MIDDLETON, widow of Arthur MIDDLETON, her will was proved 26th of July, 1700; *m.* (secondly) Dorothy SMITH, who *d.s.p.*, widow of Christopher SMITH.

ISSUE BY FIRST MARRIAGE

I. RALPH, *b.* 1688, of whom later.
II. Walter (see Izard, Ralph).

RALPH IZARD, *b.* 1688; *d.* 1743; was *b.* in Carolina about 1688; his will was proved 9th December, 1743; succeeded to his father's large estates; appointed Deputy, 1712; Member of Council for several years; Attorney General, 1737; *m.* Magdalene Elizabeth CHASTAIGNER, dau. of Alexandre Thesee CHASTAIGNER. Her will was proved 12th December, 1746.

COLONIAL FAMILIES OF THE UNITED STATES 283

ISSUE

I. HENRY, b. circa 1717, of whom later.
II. Charles, b. 11th January, 1719; m. 7th October, 1742, Mary IZARD, who m. (secondly) 4th March, 1746, Thomas BROUGHTON, she was dau. of Walter IZARD, and d.s.p.; her will proved 16th July, 1744.
III. Charlotte, b. 30th September, 1720; d. unmarried.
IV. Anne, b. 10th April, 1722; buried 9th October, 1722.
V. Martha, m. Hon. Edward FENWICKE, and had issue.
VI. Catherine, bapt. 27th January, 1729; d. in infancy.
VII. John, bapt. 7th August, 1730; d. in infancy.

HENRY IZARD, b. in Carolina about 1717; d. 1749; Commissioner of Taxes, 1738; Member of the House of Representatives, 1742–1748; m. (firstly) 26th September, 1739, Margaret JOHNSON, d. 12th June, 1743; dau. of Col. Robert JOHNSON, Governor of South Carolina; m. (secondly) Charlotte BROUGHTON, of Mulberry, who d. 10th August, 1801.

ISSUE BY FIRST MARRIAGE

I. RALPH, b. 23d January, 1742, of whom later.
II. Margaret, d.s.p. 6th March, 1760; m. 1758, Hon. Daniel BLAKE, who d. 1780.

ISSUE BY SECOND MARRIAGE

I. Nathaniel, b. 29th June, 1746; d. in infancy.
II. Charlotte, b. 15th August, 1747; d. in infancy.

RALPH IZARD, b. near Charleston; 23d January, 1742; d. 30th May, 1804; was educated in England and graduated at Cambridge University; returned to America, but came again to England, 1771, where he remained until 1774; appointed United States Commissioner at the Court of the Grand Duke of Tuscany, 1776; returned to the United States, 1780; Delegate to the Continental Congress 1782–1783; United States Senator from South Carolina, 1789–1795; m. 1st May, 1767, Alice DE LANCEY, d. 1st April, 1832, dau. of Peter DE LANCEY, of Westchester, New York.

ISSUE

I. Margaret, b. 12th February, 1768; d. 3d May, 1824, leaving issue; m. 1st May, 1785, Gabriel MANIGAULT of Charleston.
II. Elizabeth, b. 22d February, 1769; d. in infancy.
III. Charlotte, b. 16th February, 1770; d. 8th January, 1792, leaving issue; m. 1st May 1786, Hon. William Loughton SMITH, United States Minister to Spain.
IV. HENRY, b. 15th May, 1771, of whom later.
V. Ralph, b. in London, 5th August, 1772; d. in infancy.
VI. Charles, b. in London, 15th September, 1773; d. 19th July, 1784.

VII. George, b. in England, 21st October, 1776; d. 22d November, 1828; Colonel of the 2d Artillery in the War of 1812; became Brigadier-General, 1813; Major-General, 1814; Governor of Arkansas Territory, 1825–1828; m. 6th June, 1803, Elizabeth Carter (FARLEY) SHIPPEN, who d. 24th June, 1826, dau. of Maj. James Parke FARLEY, and widow of Thomas Lee SHIPPEN; left issue.
VIII. Elizabeth, b. 11th October, 1777; d. 1st November, 1784.
IX. Anne, b. 1st February, 1779; d. 1863; leaving issue; m. Hon. William Allen DEAS, d. 1863.
X. Ralph, b. at Charleston, South Carolina, 26th February, 1785; d. 6th August, 1824; Lieutenant in United States Navy; m. (firstly) 1808, Elizabeth LIDDLETON, d. 21st January, 1822, dau. of Gen. Charles Cotesworth PINCKNEY, United States Minister to France.
XI. Caroline, b. 24th September, 1786; d. in infancy.
XII. Henrietta, b. 15th May, 1788; d. in infancy.
XIII. Charlotte Georgina, b. 16th September, 1792; d. 15th September, 1832; leaving issue; m. 1st May, 1809, Joseph Allen SMITH.

HENRY IZARD of Charleston, b. 15th May, 1771; d. 30th December, 1826; Member of the House of Representatives, 1800–1802 and 1821–1826; Member of Senate 1807; m. (firstly) 1st June, 1795, Emma Philadelphia MIDDLETON, d. 1st May, 1813, dau. of Hon. Arthur MIDDLETON, of Middleton Place, South Carolina; m. (secondly) Claudia SMITH, who d.s.p., dau. of Thomas Loughton SMITH.

ISSUE BY FIRST MARRIAGE

I. Henry, b. 12th May, 1796; d. in infancy.
II. Henry, b. 6th August, 1797; d. in infancy.
III. Mary, b. 7th November, 1798, d.s.p., 29th September, 1822; m. Thomas MIDDLETON of Charleston.
IV. Walter, b. 6th May, 1800; d. young.
V. Alice, b. 2d March, 1802; d.s.p., 1863; m. 6th January, 1824, Joseph HEYWARD.
VI. WALTER, b. 7th August, 1804, of whom later.
VII. Eliza Caroline, b. 18th January, 1808; d. unmarried, 1823.
VIII. Margaret Emma, b. 3d August, 1811; d. 18th July, 1836; left issue; m. 18th January, 1832, Hon. Nathaniel Russell MIDDLETON, LL.D.
IX. Martha, b. 18th April, 1813; d. in infancy.

WALTER IZARD, b. 7th August, 1804; d. 1835, of Charleston, South Carolina; m. 10th October, 1827, Mary Cadwallader GREEN, dau. of Allen Jones GREEN, of Rose Hill, South Carolina.

ISSUE

I. Walter, b. at Rose Hill, near Landsford, South Carolina, 28th September, 1828; m. 22d October, 1853, Sallie GOODE, dau. of John GOODE.

ISSUE
1. Walter, b. 12th October, 1854; d. 11th February, 1890; m. Annie SALE.

ISSUE
1¹. Lucy, b. 21st November, 1881.
2¹. Walter, b. 7th November, 1882.
3¹. John, b. October, 1884.

2. John, b. 17th August, 1856; d. 22d November, 1899; m. Roberta JOHNSTON.

ISSUE
1¹. John, b. 27th April, 1887.
2¹. Alice deLancey, b. 11th July, 1888.
3¹. Mary Fowler, b. 11th May, 1892.
4¹. James Johnston, b. 29th July, 1894.

3. Lucy, b. 31st July, 1858; d. unmarried, 30th April, 1874.
4. RALPH, b. 19th March, 1860, the subject of this memoir.

II. Henry, b. 29th May, 1830; d. in infancy.
III. Henry, of Meridan, Mississippi; b. 25th September 1831; d. 28th April, 1899, leaving issue; m. Laura LIPSCOMB.

ISSUE
1. George. 2. Henry. 3. Irene.

IV. Lucy Green, b. 26th February, 1833; m. 7th November, 1850, Edward Barnwell HEYWARD, and had issue.
V. Allen Cadwallader, b. 13th July, 1834; d. 28th February, 1901; left issue; Captain of Company I, 9th South Carolina Regiment; promoted Major after the Battle of Pocotaligo, and Lieutenant-Colonel, 1863; m. 1857, Julia Davie BEDON, dau. of Col. Richard Stobo BEDON.

ISSUE
1. Allen Cadwallader, m. Florence BEHRE.
2. de Lancey.
3. Julia Davie, m. William T. WILLIAMS, of Savannah, Georgia, and has issue.
4. Mary Green.
5. Alice Heyward, m. John SOLOMONS.
6. Josephine Bedon, m. A. B. JOSEY, of Columbia, South Carolina.
7. Mattie Perry.
8. Ruth, m. J. A. KLEIN, of Greenwood, South Carolina.

Arms.—Argent, six leopards faces vert, three, two and one.
Crest.—A dolphin embowed ppr.
Residences.—Goodes, Bedford County, Virginia, New York, 1898–1903; Central America, 1903–1907; Chicago, Ill., U. S. Depart. of Justice.

Jackson

RIGHT REVEREND HENRY MELVILLE JACKSON, D.D., Bishop Coadjutor of the Diocese of Alabama; *b.* at Leesburg, Virginia, 28th July, 1849; *d.* at "Roseland," Eufaula, Alabama, 4th May, 1900; *m.* (firstly) 24th July, 1873, Rebecca LLOYD, dau. of John and Eliza Armistead (SELDEN) LLOYD, and gd. dau. of Wilson Cary and Mary Bowles (ARMISTEAD) SELDEN. (See ARMISTEAD and SELDEN, "Colonial Families," Volume II). *m.* (secondly) 21st April, 1880, Violet Lee PACE, dau. of James Baker and Elizabeth (NEAL) PACE; *m.* (thirdly) 17th April, 1895, Caroline Toney COCHRANE, dau. of Judge John and Caroline (TONEY) COCHRANE.

CALVERT ARMS

ISSUE BY FIRST MARRIAGE

I. Henry Melville, II, *b.* 23d October, 1874; *d.* 3d June, 1875.

ISSUE BY SECOND MARRIAGE

I. Violet Pace, *b.* 9th September, 1883; *d.* 4th October, 1884.
II. James Pace, *b.* 21st September, 1885; *d.* 11th August, 1887.
III. Elizabeth Melville, *b.* 28th July, 1887.
IV. William Congreve, *b.* 21st May, 1890; *m.* 10th December, 1912, Marguerite WOODS.

ISSUE BY THIRD MARRIAGE

I. Henry Melville, III, *b.* 22d January, 1896.
II. Caroline Cochrane, *b.* 15th August, 1897.

BISHOP HENRY MELVILLE JACKSON was educated at the Virginia Military Institute, Lexington, and the Theological Seminary, Alexandria; ordained Deacon in 1873 and Priest in 1874; had charge of Montgomery Parish, Virginia, and Christ Church, Greenville, South Carolina; returned to Virginia and became Rector of Grace Church in Richmond from 1876 to 1891; elected Assistant Bishop of Alabama in 1890 and was consecrated, in 1891, Bishop Coadjutor, which office he resigned a month before his death; received degree of D.D., from Randolph-Macon College and was an Editor of the "Southern Pulpit" and later on the Staff of the "Southern Churchman." Bishop Jackson was a brilliant preacher and much beloved by his people in Virginia and Alabama.

Calvert Lineage

The first known ancestor of this famous family is John CALVERT of Danby Wiske, Yorkshire, England, temp. Henry VIII; he *m.*, wife's name not given.

ISSUE

I. LEONARD, *b.* circa 1550, of whom below.

LEONARD CALVERT, I, *b.* circa 1550; he was also of Danby Wiske; *m.* circa 1575, Grace CROSSLAND, who was descended from Roger DE CROSSLAND, temp. Henry III, being the dau. of Thomas and Joanna CROSSLAND of "Crossland Hill," Yorkshire, which Thomas was buried 2d September, 1587, his wife, Joanna having been buried 11th July, 1575; by which alliance he became possessed of the Estate of Kipling in the Valley of the Swale, Yorkshire, where he lived and died.

ISSUE

I. GEORGE, *b.* 1579, of whom later.
II. Mary (?), *b.* 1586; *m.* 1606, Capt. Isaac CHAPLINE, Royal Navy (see CHAPLINE, "Colonial Families," Volume II).

ISSUE

1. John CHAPLINE, *b.* 1607; migrated to Virginia.
2. Isaac CHAPLINE, *b.* 1609.
3. Mary CHAPLINE, *b.* 1623; *m.* ANTHONY WYATT.
4. William CHAPLINE, *b.* 1625; *d.* 1669; migrated to Maryland; *m.* 1650, Mary HOPPER.

GEORGE CALVERT, I, *b.* 1579; *d.* 15th April, 1632; graduated from Oxford and became private secretary to Sir Robert Cecil, through whose influence he was introduced to court life; in 1613 he was Clerk of the Crown and Assize in the County of Clare, Ireland, and Clerk of the Privy Council in 1617; in the latter year he was knighted at Hampton Court by King James I, and was a Member of the Commission for winding up the affairs of the Virginia Company; he was Member of Parliament for Yorkshire in 1621 and later was Principal Secretary of State to James I, which office he resigned in 1625; the same year he was created Baron Baltimore of Baltimore. From his friend, the King, he obtained a grant of land in Newfoundland, which he called Avalon; his settlement there having proved a failure, the grant of Maryland was given to him, but he died before it had passed the Great Seal and was buried in the Chancil of St. Dunstan's in the West, London. Lord Baltimore was twice married, *m.* (firstly) 22d November, 1604, Anne MYNNE

(Lady Calvert was *b.* 20th November, 1579 and *d.* 8th August, 1622), dau. of George and Elizabeth (WROTH) MYNNE and gd. dau. of Sir Thomas WROTH of Durance in Enfield, Essex, whose wife was the Lady Mary RICH, dau. of Lord Chancellor RICH. Lord Baltimore *m.* (secondly) circa 1625, a lady whose name is variously stated as Joan, Arabella, etc.; this Lady Baltimore is supposed to have been drowned returning from Virginia in 1630.

ISSUE BY FIRST MARRIAGE

I. Cecilius, *b.* 8th August, 1605; *d.* 30th November, 1675; he succeeded his father as the second Lord Baltimore and *m.* in 1629, Lady Anne ARUNDEL, *b.* 1615, *d.* 1649, dau. of Thomas, Lord ARUNDEL of Wardour Castle and a Count of the Holy Roman Empire; from them descended the succeeding Lords (Barons of) Baltimore extinct in 1771.

ISSUE

1. John, third, Lord Baltimore, *b.* 1630; *d.s.p.*, 1694.
2. Charles, fourth, Lord Baltimore; *b.* 1631; *d.* 1715; *m.* (firstly) 1656, Mary DARNALL; *m.* (secondly) 1666, Jane (LOWE) SEWALL; *m.* (thirdly) 1701, Mary BANKS; *m.* (fourthly) 1712, Margaret CHARLETON, who survived him and *d.* 1721.
3. Mary, *b.* 1632; *d.* 1663; *m.* circa 1650, Sir William BLAKISTON, of Gibside, in Durham, *d.s.p.*, 1692.

II. LEONARD, II, *b.* 1606, of whom later.
III. George, II, *b.* 1608; *d.* unmarried 1634, in Maryland.
IV. Elizabeth, *m.* Samuel MATTHEWS.
V. Francis, *d.s.p.*
VI. Helen, *m.* (?) Thomas GREEN, second Governor of Maryland.
VII. Henry, *d.* unmarried, before 1635.
VIII. Anne, *m.* William PEASLEY.
IX. Dorothy, *m.* James TALBOT.
X. Grace, *b.* 1614, *m.* before 1632, Sir Robert TALBOT, a brother of the Duke of Tyrconnel, and became ancestress of the Lords Talbot DE MALAHIDE.

ISSUE

1. Frances TALBOT, *b.* circa, 1634; *d.* 1718; *m.* circa 1650, her cousin, Richard TALBOT, *d.* 1703.

ISSUE

1^1. Richard TALBOT, *d.s.p.*
2^1. Robert TALBOT, *d.s.p.*
3^1. John TALBOT, *m.* Frances WOGAN, a quo the Lords Talbot DE MALAHIDE.
4^1. Valentine TALBOT, *d.* 1749; *m.* Mary TOBIN.

5[1]. Frances TALBOT, *d.* 1749; *m.* James BUTLER.
6[1]. Mary TALBOT, *m.* 1706, Robert DILLON.
7[1]. Susan TALBOT, *m.* Nicholas MORRIS.
8[1]. Anne TALBOT.
9[1]. Elizabeth TALBOT.

XI. John, II, *b.* 1622; migrated to Maryland with Philip CALVERT.

ISSUE BY SECOND MARRIAGE

1. Philip, *b.* 1626; *d.* 1682; *m.* (firstly) Anne WOLSELEY; *m.* (secondly) Jane SEWELL, step-dau. of his uncle, Charles, Lord Baltimore.

ISSUE BY SECOND MARRIAGE

1[1]. William, a Burgess of Maryland.

LEONARD CALVERT, II, *b.* 1606; *d.* 1647; he was Prothonotary and Keeper of the Writs in Connaught and Thomond, Ireland, in 1621, and was Governor of Maryland from 1633 to 1647, having been appointed by his brother, Cecilius, Lord Baltimore; he came with the *Ark* and the *Dove* in 1633 and in 1641 returned to England, so it must have been about this time that he was *m.* to Anne BRENT (who predeceased him), a dau. of Richard and Elizabeth (REED) BRENT of Larke Stoke and Admington, Gloucestershire, and a sister of "Mistress Margaret Brent," Mary, Giles and Fulke BRENT, who migrated to the Province.

ISSUE

I. WILLIAM, *b.* 1642, of whom later.
II. Anne, *b.* 1644; *d.* circa 1714; *m.* (firstly) 1664, Baker BROOKE, *b.* 1628, *d.* 1679; *m.* (secondly) circa 1680, her cousin, Henry BRENT, *d.* 1693; *m.* (thirdly) circa 1694, Richard MARSHAM, *d.* 1713; *m.* (fourthly) Judge TASKER.

ISSUE BY FIRST MARRIAGE

1. Charles BROOKE, *d.* unmarried, 1698.
2. Leonard BROOKE, *d.* 1718; *m.* Anne BOARMAN.
3. Baker BROOKE, Jr., *d.* 1698; *m.* Katherine MARSHAM.
4. Mary BROOKE, *d.* 1693; *m.* Raphael NEALE, *d.* 1743.

WILLIAM CALVERT of "Calvert's Rest;" *b.* 1642; was a Member of the House of Burgesses; Deputy-Governor of the Province; Councillor, and Principal Secretary from 1669 to 1682, when he was drowned in the Wicomico River; in or about 1664, he *m.* Elizabeth STONE, who survived him, a dau. of Governor William STONE, *b.* 1603, *d.* 1695, and his wife Verlinda Sprigg COTTON.

ISSUE

I. Elizabeth, *m.* 1681, Capt. James NEALE, whose second wife was Elizabeth LORD.
II. Charles, *b.* 1666; *d.* 1733; living in Stafford County, Virginia, in 1705; *m.* (firstly) Mary HOWSON; *m.* (secondly) Barbara DOANE, who *m.* (secondly) Andrew FOY.

ISSUE BY FIRST MARRIAGE

1. Sarah.   2. Anne.

III. Cecilius, untraced.
IV. GEORGE, III, *b.* 1672, of whom later.
V. Richard, *d.s.p.* before 1718.

GEORGE CALVERT, III, *b.* 1672; *m.* circa 1695, Anne NOTTLEY, a member of a prominent family, one of whom was Thomas NOTTLEY, Governor of the Province of Maryland in 1679.

ISSUE

I. JOHN, *b.* circa, 1700, of whom later.
II. George IV.
III. Thomas.

JOHN CALVERT, III, *b.* circa 1700; *d.* 1739, *m.* circa 1720, Elizabeth HARRISON, evidently a dau. of Benjamin HARRISON, III, *b.* 1673, *d.* 1710, and his wife, Elizabeth BURWELL of Virginia, whither he had moved and where he *d.*, in Prince William County.

ISSUE

I. GEORGE, V., *b.* circa 1722, of whom later.
II. Cecilius.
III. William.
IV. Thomas (?).

GEORGE CALVERT, V, *b.* circa 1722; *d.* 1782; he lived at "Deep Hole Farm," Prince William County, Virginia, and in 1752, in Hamilton Parish, where he was a Member of the House of Burgesses; and late in life moved to Culpeper County, where he *d.* and was buried at Calvert's Mills; in 1781 he was appointed a Captain in the Culpeper Revolutionary Militia by Thomas JEFFERSON, then Governor of Virginia; he *m.* (firstly) circa 1740, Anne CRUPPER; *m.* (secondly) circa 1779, Mrs. Mary (STROTHER) DEATHERAGE, widow of Robert DEATHERAGE, *d.* 1777, and dau. of Francis and Susannah (DABNEY) STROTHER of St. Mark's Parish (see STROTHER, "Colonial Families," Volume V). Mrs. Mary (STROTHER) DEATHERAGE-CALVERT was a great aunt of President Zachary TAYLOR, and a great-great-aunt of the first wife of President Jefferson DAVIS, Confederate States of America (see DAVIS, "Colonial Families," Volume III).

COLONIAL FAMILIES OF THE UNITED STATES

ISSUE BY FIRST MARRIAGE

1. John, IV, *b.* 1742; *d.* 1790; *m.* (firstly) 1765, Sarah BAILEY; *m.* (secondly) 1772, Hellen BAILEY, her sister, the dau. of John and Mary (NEWSOME) BAILEY of "Hunting Ridge," Baltimore, and gd. daus. of George BAYLEY, *d.* 1754, of Baltimore County, whose will shows a seal bearing the crest of the BAYLEYS of Northallerton, Yorkshire, viz: "A griffin sejant ermine, wings and forelegs or." John CALVERT, IV, was a Captain in the War of the Revolution and lived part of his life in Virginia, dying in Culpeper County.

ISSUE BY FIRST MARRIAGE

1. Cecilius, *b.* 31st December, 1767; *d.* 14th February, 1852; *m.* 1797, in Culpeper County, Virginia, his cousin, Nancy Beck CALVERT, *b.* 1773, *d.* 1835, the dau. of George and Lydia Beck (RALLS) CALVERT.

ISSUE

1¹. John, V, *b.* 29th April, 1799; *d.* unmarried, 15th March, 1846.
2¹. Ziba, *b.* 31st August, 1804; *d.* 11th October, 1886; *m.* 25th December, 1834, Mary Elizabeth FERGUSON, *b.* 1811, *d.* 1875.
3¹. George, VII, *b.* 25th April, 1809; *d.* 29th April, 1865; *m.* 1835, Willie Anne WOODS.

ISSUE

1². John Strother, *b.* 1836; *d.* 1886.
2². George Washington, *b.* 1838; *d.* 1913.
3². Benjamin Franklin, *b.* 1840, of Willows, California.
4². Sarah Anne, *b.* 1842; *m.* her cousin, Samuel Ralls CALVERT.

4¹. Sarah Anne, *b.* 24th July, 1810; *m.* James WOOD.
5¹. Elizabeth, *b.* 6th June, 1812; *d.* 1850; *m.* Elijah PEPPER.
6¹. Gabriel, *b.* 27th January, 1814; *d.* 3d November, 1898.

2. Henrietta, *b.* 1769; *m.* ——— BIRCH, *d.s.p.*

ISSUE BY SECOND MARRIAGE

1. Sarah, *b.* 1774; *m.* 1803, John HEATON, *d.s.p.*
2. Anne, *b.* 1776; *d.* 1848; *m.* 1799, Capt. David J. COXE, *d.s.p.*
3. Elizabeth, *b.* 1777; *d.* 1833; *m.* 1802, Capt. Joseph NICKLIN, *b.* 1776, *d.* 1853 (see NICKLIN, "Colonial Families," Volume IV).

ISSUE

1¹. John Bailey NICKLIN, *b.* 1803; *d.* 1891; *m.* 1830, Catharine Thornton PENDLETON (see PENDLETON, "Colonial Families," Volume IV).
2¹. Joseph Marshall NICKLIN, *b.* 1805; *d.* 1846; *m.* 1830, Mary Newton LANE.

COLONIAL FAMILIES OF THE UNITED STATES

3^1. Levi Orme Connor NICKLIN, *b*. 1807; *d*. 1876; *m*. 1832, Margaretta SHRIVER.
4^1. Martha Anne NICKLIN, *b*. 1809; *d*. 1843; *m*. 1837, James Leake POWERS.
5^1. Jacob Richards NICKLIN, *b*. 1811; *d*. 1887; *m*. (firstly) 1843, Susan EASTHAM; *m*. (secondly) 1855, Susan Maria HUNTER.
6^1. William Henry Harrison NICKLIN, *b*. 1813; *d*. 1881; *m*. 1838, Mary Jane NELSON.

4. Hannah, *b*. 1778; *d*. 1861; *m*. 1793, John JETT.

ISSUE

1^1. James JETT, *b*. 1795; *m*. 1821, Julia Anne LANE.

ISSUE

1^2. Eliza Lane JETT, *d*. unmarried.
2^2. John JETT, *m*. Isabel ROBERTS, "A Real Daughter of the Revolution."
3^2. Mary Frances JETT, *m*. her cousin, Judge James William GREEN.
4^2. Lavinia JETT, *m*. Thomas Scott WITHEROW.

ISSUE

1^3. Cecil Calvert WITHEROW.

5^2. Hannah Calvert JETT, *m*. Atcheson POLLOCK.
6^2. William Armistead Lane JETT, *m*. Alice HOPPER.
7^2. Ellen JETT, *m*. Edward McCORMICK.
8^2. Elvira JETT, *m*. Bushrod TAYLOR.
9^2. James JETT, *d*. unmarried.

2^1. Lavinia JETT, *b*. 1798; *m*. 1812, John Strother GREEN.
3^1. John JETT, *b*. 1799; *d*. 1881.

5. Delia, *b*. 1780; *d*. unmarried, 1873.
6. Gettie, *b*. 1785; *d*. 1816; *m*. 1801, Gabriel SMITHER.

ISSUE

1^1. Evelina SMITHER, *b*. 1802.
2^1. Anne SMITHER, *b*. 1804; *m*. Nathaniel Beck RALLS.
3^1. John SMITHER, *b*. 1806.
4^1. Gabriella SMITHER, *b*. 1808; *m*. (firstly) Irving POAGUE; *m*. (secondly) Joseph ABERNATHY.
5^1. Richard SMITHER, *b*. 1810.
6^1. Lucy SMITHER, *b*. 1812; *m*. Robert RUDICILL.

COLONIAL FAMILIES OF THE UNITED STATES 293

II. GEORGE, VI, b. 1744, of whom later.
III. Jane, b. 1746; m. (firstly) circa 1768, Capt. John MADDOX, of the Royal Navy; m. (secondly) ——— SETTLE; m. (thirdly) ——— GRYMES.

ISSUE BY FIRST MARRIAGE

1. Jane MADDOX, b. 1770.
2. Mary MADDOX, b. 1772; d. 1816; m. 1789, William DEATHERAGE.
3. Sarah MADDOX, b. 1774.

ISSUE BY SECOND MARRIAGE

1. John Calvert SETTLE, b. circa, 1780; m. 1806, Sarah TURNER.

ISSUE

1¹. Jane SETTLE, m. her cousin, George THORNE.

IV. Lydia, b. 1748; m. Archibald BIGBEE.
V. Sarah, b. 1749; m. ——— ROOKARD.
VI. Anne, b. 1751; d. 1822; m. 1766, William LINDSAY, d. 1792, of "Colchester," Prince William County, and "Laurel Hill," Culpeper County, Virginia.

ISSUE

1. George Waller LINDSAY, b. 1771; d. 1810; m. 1801, Judith GRAYSON.
2. William Henry LINDSAY, b. 1773; d. 1823; m. 1804, Catherine Washington SANFORD.
3. Sarah Calvert LINDSAY, b. 1785; d. 1840; m. 1805, Maj. George TRIPLETT of Fairfax County.
4. Maria LINDSAY, b. 1787; d. 1849; m. 1806, William LINDSAY of Fairfax County.
5. Catherine LINDSAY, b. 1791; d. 1867; m. 1807, Reynold GRYMES of Barbadoes.

ISSUE BY SECOND MARRIAGE OF GEORGE CALVERT V

1. Mary, b. 1780; d. 1809; m. 1805, Nicholas THORNE.

ISSUE

1. George THORNE, b. 1806; m. his cousin, Jane SETTLE.
2. Mary THORNE, b. 1808.

GEORGE CALVERT, VI, b. 6th February, 1744; d. 1821; m. 1766, Lyd'a Beck RALLS; he was a Captain in the Revolutionary Army from Virginia and lived and died in Culpeper County.

ISSUE

I. RALLS, b. 1767, of whom 'ater.
II. Margaret, b. 1770; m. 1794, John ADAMS.

ISSUE

1. Mariah ADAMS, *m.* 1816, her cousin Nimrod HAMBRICK, Jr.
2. Elizabeth ADAMS, *m.* 1822, Lewis Davis MASSIE.

ISSUE

1¹. Margaret Elizabeth MASSIE, *m.* 1843, her cousin, Oliver Hazard Perry SMITH, *b.* 1815, *d.* 1887.

ISSUE

1². Mary Elizabeth Frances SMITH, *b.* 30th April, 1845; *d.* 18th March, 1913; *m.* 1869, David STEELE.
2². John Perry SMITH, *b.* 29th April, 1847; *m.* 1881, Frances M. BELL.
3². Anna Melvina SMITH, *b.* 25th May, 1849; *m.* 16th January, 1875, John Hanger RUSH, gr. gd. son of Dr. Benjamin RUSH, Signer of the Declaration of Independence.
4². Lewis Edward SMITH, *b.* 1851; *d.* 1914; *m.* 1878, Clara WEIR.
5². Robert Issacher SMITH; *b.* 1853; *d.* 1863.
6². Virginia Emma SMITH, *b.* 5th June, 1855; *d.* 8th September, 1909; *m.* 8th December, 1886, Samuel McCLURE.
7². William Bernard SMITH, *b.* 1858; *d.* 1859.

2¹. Mary Virginia MASSIE, *d.s.p.*
3¹. John W. MASSIE, *m.* Mary CLOUD.
4¹. Thomas Bernard MASSIE, *m.* Margaret BRAGG.

III. George, VIII, *b.* 1771; *m.* 1809, Anne (JENNINGS) NORMAN.
IV. Anne Beck, *b.* 1773; *d.* 1835; *m.* 1797, her first cousin, Cecilius CALVERT, *q.v.*
V. John, *b.* 1775, *m.* 1804, Anne ASKINS.
VI. Lydia, *b.* 1777; *m.* 1794, George WHEELER.
VII. Elizabeth, *b.* 1779; *m.* 1800, Charles WILLIAMS.
VIII. Catherine, *b.* 1781; *m.* (firstly) 1801, Henry GREEN, *d.* 1806; *m.* (secondly) 1809, Jacob MATHEWS.

ISSUE BY FIRST MARRIAGE

1. Caroline GREEN, *b.* 1802.
2. Edward Pendleton GREEN, *b.* 1804.
3. Mary Elizabeth GREEN, *b.* 1806.

ISSUE BY SECOND MARRIAGE

1. Elvira MATHEWS, *b.* 1812.
2. Rufus MATHEWS, *b.* 1813.
3. Hiram MATHEWS, *b.* 1814.
4. Henry MATHEWS, *b.* 1816.
5. George Washington MATHEWS, *b.* 1822.

COLONIAL FAMILIES OF THE UNITED STATES 295

IX. Hannah, b. 1783; m. 1805, Peter LINK.
X. Jane, b. 1785; m. 1804, George CRAVER.
XI. Sarah, b. 1786; d. 1856; m. 1803, John KAYLOR, b. 1784, d. 1866.

ISSUE

1. Margaret Anne KAYLOR, b. 1805; d. 1835.
2. Robert KAYLOR, b. 1807; d. 1881.
3. Josephus KAYLOR, b. 1808; d. 1808.
4. George KAYLOR, b. 1809; d. 1874; m. 1823, Mary Elizabeth CORBIN.
5. William KAYLOR, b. 1812.
6. German KAYLOR, b. 1814.
7. Lydia Beck KAYLOR, b. 1816; m. 1834, John M. COOPER.
8. James Calvert KAYLOR, b. 1819.
9. Jane Calvert KAYLOR, b. 1822; m. 1843, David WOOD.
10. Hannah KAYLOR, b. 1824.
11. Gideon KAYLOR, b. 1829.
12. Mary Louise KAYLOR, b. 1831.

XII. Cecilius, b. 1789; United States Army, 1814, 16th Virginia Regiment of Militia.
XIII. Mariah, b. 1791; m. (firstly) 1808, Jacob MYERS; m. (secondly) Nimrod HAMBRICK.

RALLS CALVERT, b. 9th October, 1767; d. 29th June, 1815; m. 15th November, 1790, Mary Wade STROTHER, dau. of Capt. John and Anne (STROTHER) STROTHER of Culpeper County, gd. dau. of John and Mary Willis (WADE) STROTHER and gr. gd. dau. of Francis and Susannah (DABNEY) STROTHER of St. Mark's Parish, Culpeper County, Virginia (see STROTHER "Co'onial Families," Volume V); Ralls CALVERT was Postmaster at Washington, Virginia, where he died.

ISSUE

I. Jeremiah Strother, b. 1791; m. 1816, Priscilla SMITHER.

ISSUE

1. Priscilla, m. Col. Jack HAYES, "The Texas Ranger."
2. Elizabeth, m. John TWOHIG, of San Antonio, Texas.
3. James Lockhart, killed during the Civil War.
4. Katherine, m. Col. Thomas JOHNSON.
5. Jeremiah.
6. Mary, m. James WATKINS.
7. Matilda.
8. William Launcelot, killed in Civil War.

II. Anne Strother, b. 1793; d. 1861; m. (firstly) 1811, Issacher SMITH; m. (secondly) 1823, Henry SPILLER.

ISSUE BY FIRST MARRIAGE

1. John Ralls SMITH, *b.* 1812; *m.* 1837, Lucy Anna ALLEN.
2. Mary Catherine SMITH, *b.* 1813; *m.* 1836, John RUDICILL.
3. Oliver Hazard Perry SMITH, *b.* 1815; *d.* 1887; *m.* 1843, his cousin, Margaret Elizabeth MASSIE
4. Elizabeth SMITH, *b.* 1819; *m.* 1844, Enoch BROWN.

ISSUE BY SECOND MARRIAGE

1. Nehemiah SPILLER, *b.* 1825.
2. Anne Sophia SPILLER, *b.* 1827; *d.* 1882.
3. Martha Elvira SPILLER, *b.* 1829.

III. GEORGE, IX, of whom later.
IV. Lydia Beck.
V. Martha.
VI. Patsy, *b.* 1803; *d.* 1870.
VII. John Strother, Major 10th Virginia Regiment, Confederate States of America; *m.* 1833, Catherine SALVAGE.
VIII. Edward, *m.* Mary Frances JENKINS.
IX. Ralls.
X. Mary.
XI. Katherine Kennerley, *m.* ———— HOLLINGSWORTH.
XII. Lucy, *d.* 1848; *m.* 1844, James Leake POWERS, *b.* 1799; *d.* 1889, whose first wife was her cousin, Martha Anne NICKLIN (*q.v.*), dau. of Joseph and Elizabeth (CALVERT) NICKLIN.

GEORGE CALVERT, IX, *b.* 20th October, 1795; *d.* 23d September, 1871; *m.* 11th May, 1819, Elizabeth Lovell CARR, dau. of Joseph and Delia (STROTHER) CARR and gd. dau. of Enoch and Mary (KEY) STROTHER.

ISSUE

I. Olivia Jane, *b.* 16th March, 1820; *d.* 28th April, 1881; *m.* William CHAMBLIN.
II. ANNA MARIA, of whom later.
III. Amanda Carr, *b.* 18th November, 1823; *d.* 24th January, 1904, unmarried.
IV. Joseph Carr, *b.* 8th June, 1825, *d.s.p.* 18 August, 1892.
V. Robert Singleton, *b.* 13th September, 1829; *d.* 23d May, 1830.
VI. Caldwell Carr, *b.* 23d January, 1831; *d.* 14th September, 1909; *m.* 25th June, 1879, Mary Landon Armistead ROSSER, dau. of Joseph Travis and Mary Walker (ARMISTEAD) ROSSER, gd. dau. of Walter Keith and Elizabeth (STANLEY) ARMISTEAD (see ARMISTEAD, "Colonial Families," Volume I, page 14, line 9).

ISSUE

1. Mary Rosser.
2. Landon Ralls.
3. Elizabeth Lovell, *d.* in infancy.

ANNA MARIA CALVERT, *b.* 2d December, 1821; *d.* 7th February, 1900; *m.* 7th April, 1840, Dr. Samuel Keerl JACKSON of Norfolk, Virginia, son of the Rev. Dr. Edward JACKSON.

ISSUE

I. Edward Calvert JACKSON, *b.* 1841, of Upperville, Virginia.
II. William Congreve JACKSON, I, *b.* 1843; *d.* 1861.
III. Anne Sophia JACKSON, *b.* 1845; *d.* 1897; *m.* Robert J. TUCKER, of Bermuda and Virginia.
IV. HENRY MELVILLE JACKSON, I, the subject of this memoir.
V. Churchill Calvert JACKSON, *b.* 1850; *d.* 1897; *m.* Elizabeth WILSON.

ISSUE

1. Anna Calvert JACKSON, *m.* James B. WARWICK.
2. William Congreve JACKSON, III.

VI. Olive Caldwell JACKSON, *b.* 1857; *m.* Francis Taliaferro STRIBLING, *d.s.p.*
VII. Marshall Parks JACKSON, *b.* 1860; *d.* 1907; *m.* Josephine Ross.
VIII. George Calvert JACKSON, *d.* in infancy.

Arms.—Quarterly, first and fourth, Paly of six, or and sable, a bend counterchanged for Calvert; second and third, Argent and gules, a cross flory counterchanged for Crossland.
Crest.—Out of a ducal coronet or, two pennons, the dexter of the first, the other sable, staves gules.
Motto.—Fatti maschi, parole femine.

DESCENT OF ANNE (BRENT) CALVERT FROM EDWARD III OF ENGLAND

I. Edward III, King of England, *m.* Phillipa of Hainault.
II. John Plantagenet, Duke of Lancaster, *m.* Katherine (ROET) SWYNFORD.
III. Joane Plantagenet DE BEAUFORT, *m.* Ralph DE NEVILLE, Earl of Westmoreland.
IV. George DE NEVILLE, Lord Latimer, *m.* Elizabeth DE BEAUCHAMP of Warwick.
V. Henry DE NEVILLE, Lord Latimer, *m.* Joane BOURCHIERS of Berners.
VI. Richard DE NEVILLE, Lord Latimer, *m.* Anne STAFFORD of Grafton.
VII. Margaret DE NEVILLE, *m.* Edward WILLOUGHBY DE BROKE.
VIII. Elizabeth WILLOUGHBY, *m.* Sir Fulke GREVILLE of Milcote.
IX. Katherine GREVILLE, *m.* Giles REED, Lord of Tusburie and Witten.
X. Elizabeth REED, *m.* Richard BRENT, of Larke Stoke and Admington.
XI. Anne BRENT, *m.* Leonard CALVERT (*q.v.*), first Governor of Maryland.

Jacobs

LUTHER MORSE JACOBS, deceased, of New York City; *b.* 12th June, 1831, in Thompson, Connecticut; *d.* 20th December, 1907, in New York City; *m.* in New York, 20th January, 1857, Sarah Elizabeth RAND, *b.* 12th July, 1836, in Sacketts Harbor, New York, *d.* 8th February, 1917, dau. of Hanson and Elizabeth Adeline (KIRTLAND) RAND.

ISSUE

I. Luther William, *b.* 29th October, 1859.
II. Harrie Kirtland, *b.* 31st May, 1863; *d.* 5th August, 1890.
III. Lillian Julia, *b.* 30th November, 1865.
IV. Daisy Monell, *b.* 6th January, 1868; *d.* 23d August, 1868.
V. Hervey Wyman, *b.* 30th September, 1871; *d.* 18th September, 1872.
VI. Elmer Rand, *b.* 5th September, 1878.

LUTHER MORSE JACOBS spent his boyhood and youth on the farms of his forefathers; after a brief residence in Norwich, Connecticut, he came to New York in 1852, when stage coaches were the only means of transportation in the city, and street cars were unknown.

Lineage

The immigrant ancestor was Nicholas JACOB, who was *b.* in England; *d.* 5th June, 1657, in Hingham, Massachusetts; came from Hingham, County Norfolk, England, where the parish register shows that "John the sonne of Nycolas JACOB, was baptized the 26th February 1629." He settled first in Watertown, in 1633, but soon removed to Bare Cove, subsequently called Hingham; he was a Freeman 1635; Selectman in 1637; Deputy to the General Court in 1648 and 1649; Commissioner in 1655; *m.* in England, Mary (GILMAN?) who *d.* 15th June, 1681, in Hingham, Massachusetts.

ISSUE

I. John, *b.* or *bapt.* 26th February, 1629; *d.* 18th September, 1693; *m.* (firstly) 1653, Margery EAMES; *m.* (secondly) 1661, Mary RUSSELL.
II. Elizabeth, *b.* or *bapt.* 1632; *d.* 24th November, 1725; *m.* (firstly) 1648, John THAXTER; *m.* (secondly) 1691, Daniel CUSHING.
III. Mary, *b.* or *bapt.* 1636; *d.* after 1683; *m.* 1653, John OTIS.
IV. Sarah, *b.* or *bapt.* 1638; *d.* 8th August, 1701; *m.* 1653, Matthew CUSHING.
V. Hannah, *b.* or *bapt.* 23d February, 1640; *d.* 20th October, 1720; *m.* 1657, Thomas LORING.
VI. Josiah, *bapt.* 6th November, 1642; *d.* 24th November, 1642.

VII. Deborah, b. or bapt. 26th November, 1643; d. 17th June, 1696; m. 1664, Nathaniel THOMAS.
VIII. JOSEPH, b. or bapt. 1st May, 1646, of whom later.

JOSEPH JACOB of Bristol, Rhode Island; b. 1st May, 1646, in Hingham, Massachusetts; d. 9th February, 1708, in Bristol, Rhode Island; of which place he was one of the first settlers and founders, September, 1681; he removed from Hingham about the same time as his father-in-law, Nathaniel BOSWORTH, who built the first house in Bristol in 1680, which is still standing (1916) in good condition and occupied by some of his descendants; was a Freeman in 1680 and a Constable in 1685; m. circa 1670, in Hull, Massachusetts, Hannah BOSWORTH, b. 30th April, 1650, in Hull, Massachusetts, d. after 1722, dau. of Nathaniel and Bridget BOSWORTH.

ISSUE

I. Joseph, b. or bapt. 20th February, 1672; d. young.
II. Joseph, b. or bapt. 10th April, 1675; d. 1st November, 1703.
III. Benjamin, b. or bapt. 27th June, 1677; d. young.
IV. Benjamin, b. or bapt. 10th April, 1680; d. 17th August, 1703.
V. NATHANIEL, b. or bapt. 29th June, 1683, of whom later.
VI. Mary, b. or bapt. 16th September, 1686; d. 22d March, 1696.

NATHANIEL JACOB of Thompson, Connecticut, b. 29th June, 1683, in Hingham, Massachusetts; d. 22d February, 1772, in Thompson; was one of the first settlers and founders of Thompson, Connecticut; was in Bristol in 1722 and Woodstock before 1737; in 1741 he purchased a part of the Saltonstall tract for £900, and when he and his five sons took possession of this wild tract, wild animals were not infrequent; it afterward became known as the Jacob's District; Nathaniel m. 22d October, 1713, in Hull, Massachusetts, Mercy WHITMAN, b. 1689, d. 21st February, 1774, at Thompson, Connecticut, dau. of Rev. Zachariah and Sarah (ALCOCK) WHITMAN.

ISSUE

I. Mary, b. or bapt. 28th August, 1715; m. 1735, James ORCUT.
II. Joseph, b. or bapt. 12th July, 1717; d. 10th October, 1739.
III. Benjamin, b. or bapt. 26th April, 1719; m. (firstly) Hulda BOSWORTH; m. (secondly) 1750, Dorothy ARNOLD.
IV. Nathaniel, b. or bapt. 26th April, 1721.
V. Hannah, b. or bapt. 20th February, 1723.
VI. JOHN, b. 29th May, 1725, of whom later.
VII. Whitman, b. or bapt. 3d May, 1727; d. 28th March, 1801; m. (firstly) 1749, Rebecca, surname unknown; m. (secondly) 1773, Rebecca GROW; he was the organizer and pastor of the first Baptist church in the State of Connecticut.
VIII. Mercy, b. or bapt. 20th April, 1729; d. 29th May, 1810; m. 1751, Joseph DRESSER.
IX. Elnathan, b. or bapt. 5th January, 1731; d. 1st August, 1745.

300   COLONIAL FAMILIES OF THE UNITED STATES

JOHN JACOBS, Farmer, of Thompson, Connecticut; *b.* 29th May, 1725; *d.* in Thompson, Connecticut, 3d March, 1820; was active in town affairs and held several of the local offices; in the Revolutionary Wars, he was on the Continental Frigate *Confederacy* and his sons John, Jesse and Asa took an active part in the war with the Army; *m.* 24th January, 1751, Sarah PLANK, *b.* 1726, *d.* 3d June, 1789, dau. of Robert and Hannah (COOPER) PLANK, of Killingly, Connecticut.

ISSUE

I. Jesse, *b.* or *bapt.* 23d November, 1752; *d.* March, 1842; *m.* Louise MARTIN.
II. John, *b.* or *bapt.* 12th September, 1754.
III. Jerusha, *b.* or *bapt.* 17th September, 1756.
IV. ASA, *b.* or *bapt.* 18th April, 1758, of whom later.
V. Mercy, *b.* or *bapt.* 26th April, 1760; *m.* Israel TOURTELLOT.
VI. Abel, *b.* or *bapt.* 11th April, 1762, *d.* 19th October, 1832.
VII. Sarah, *b.* or *bapt.* 10th February, 1764; *m.* (firstly) Alex MASON; *m.* (secondly) Joseph CHAPLIN.
VIII. Amasa, *b.* 1766; *d.* 12th June, 1837; *m.* 1792, Eunice JOSLIN.

ASA JACOBS, Farmer, of Thompson, Connecticut; *b.* there 18th April, 1758; *d.* there 27th November, 1844; was active all through the Revolutionary War and served through five enlistments; *m.* 11th September, 1791, Sarah EMERSON, *b.* 7th August, 1767, *d.* 5th January, 1835, dau. of Simeon and Persis (DAVENPORT) EMERSON; *m.* (secondly) 1836, Phebe GREENWOOD.

ISSUE

I. Asa, *b.* 10th October, 1790; *d.* 10th May, 1792.
II. Sarah, *b.* 10th October, 1791; *d.* 19th May, 1793.
III. Mary, *b.* 5th January, 1793; *d.* 20th September, 1820; *m.* Thomas ELLIOTT.
IV. Sarah, *b.* 1st April, 1796; *d.* 26th December, 1834, unmarried.
V. John R., *b.* 19th October, 1798; *d.* 8th November, 1847; *m.* Hannah MCLEAN.
VI. Asa, *b.* 1st February, 1800; *d.* 10th September, 1875; *m.* (firstly) Sarah MORSE; *m.* (secondly) ——— ALLEN; *m.* (thirdly) Lucy COOPER.
VII. Hiram, *b.* 12th March, 1801; *d.* 1st April, 1874; *m.* Emma SABINE.
VIII. Betsy, *b.* 13th October, 1804; *d.* 1st November, 1820; unmarried.
IX. JOSEPH D., *b.* 29th March, 1806, of whom later.
X. William, *b.* 9th January, 1808; *d.* 22d August, 1895; *m.* (firstly) 1836, Harriet P. PENHALLOW; *m.* (secondly) 1849, Adeline H. CROCKER.
XI. Nelson, *b.* 1st August, 1809; *d.* 22d June, 1814.

CAPT. JOSEPH D. JACOBS, Farmer, Thompson, Connecticut; *b.* there 29th March, 1806; *d.* 21st October, 1890; was for many years a Captain in Connecticut State Militia; he was active in church and town affairs, and was a Member of the Connecticut Legislature, representing Windham County in 1872; *m.* 27th October,

1828, in Thompson, Connecticut, Sarah C. CARROLL, b. 6th November, 1809, in Thompson, Connecticut, d. 25th April, 1887, in Thompson, Connecticut, dau. of Wyman and Sarah (CROSBY) CARROLL.

ISSUE

I. Frank W., b. 10th September, 1829; d. 1st October, 1904; m. 1855, Nancy GOULD.
II. LUTHER MORSE, b. 12th June, 1831, the subject of this memoir.
III. Everett P., b. 19th January, 1833; d. 30th March, 1875; m. 1861, Phebe A. DEAN.
IV. Ann M., b. 7th March, 1834; d. 9th August, 1910; m. 1860, John N. ALTON.
V. Bela H., b..3d May, 1836; d. 22d December, 1901; m. 1879, Ida PILLSBURY.
VI. Hervey F., b. 3d August, 1838; d. 5th July, 1863, never married; while a student at Brown University, Class of 1863, joined the 26th Connecticut Regiment; he was made Lieutenant of Company F, and while acting Captain of Company A, was wounded 14th June, 1863, at the assault on Port Hudson; d. of his wounds in the hospital at Baton Rouge, Louisiana, 5th July, 1863.
VII. Sarah C., b. 18th February, 1840; d. 1st January, 1917; m. 1870, Luther R. CASE.
VIII. Wyman D., b. 23d December, 1841; d. 7th July, 1863; never married; was a member of Company F, 50th Massachusetts Regiment, and died of the measles in the same hospital as his brother Hervey, at Baton Rouge, 7th July, 1863.
IX. Emma A., b. 11th August, 1843; d. 24th July, 1877; never married.
X. Mary B., b. 3d November, 1844; m. 1879, George S. CROSBY.
XI. Silas B., b. 23d November, 1846; m. 1870, Ella L. GALE.
XII. Lucy E., b. 20th July, 1848; d. 2d August, 1848.
XIII. Helen L., b. 7th February, 1852; d. 22d November, 1852.

Arms.—Argent a chevron gules, between three heraldic tigers heads erased ppr., maned and tusked or.
Crest.—Or, an heraldic tiger, passant proper maned and tusked or.
Motto.—Parta tueri.

Jay

PIERRE JAY, of New York City, b. 4th May, 1870; graduated at Yale University, 1892; *m.* 23d November, 1897, Louisa Shaw BARLOW, dau. of the late Maj.-Gen. Francis Channing BARLOW.

ISSUE

I. Ellen, *b.* 23d August, 1898.
II. Anna Maricka, *b.* 19th June, 1900.
III. Frances, *b.* 27th December, 1904.
IV. Louisa, *b.* 3d May, 1908.

Lineage

AUGUSTUS JAY, of La Rochelle, France; *b.* 23d March, 1665; *d.* 10th March, 1751; second son of Pierre and Judith (FRANCOIS) JAY; emigrated to America upon the revocation of the Edict of Nantes, 1685; ultimately settling in New York as a merchant in 1686; *m.* 1697, Anna Maria BAYARD, dau. of Balthazer BAYARD, Alderman of Amsterdam, 1691.

ISSUE

I. Judith, *b.* 29th August, 1698; *d.* August, 1757; *m.* 6th April, 1735, Cornelius J. VAN HORNE.
II. Mary, *b.* 31st August, 1700; *d.* 5th June, 1762; *m.* 27th June, 1723, Peter VALETTE.
III. Frances, *b.* 26th February, 1702; *m.* 19th January, 1724, Frederick VAN CORTLANDT.
IV. PETER, *b.* 3d November, 1704, of whom later.
V. Ann, *d.* young.

PETER JAY of New York; *b.* 3d November, 1704; *d.* 17th April, 1782; Alderman of New York, 1738–1739; purchased a farm at Rye, Westchester County, New York, where he established his country seat in 1745; *m.* 20th January, 1728, Mary VAN CORTLANDT, dau. of Jacobus VAN CORTLANDT.

ISSUE

I. Eve, *b.* 9th November, 1728; *d.* 7th April, 1810; *m.* 31st March, 1766, Rev. Harry MUNRO.
II. Augustus, *b.* 12th April, 1730; *d.* unmarried 23d December, 1801.
III. James, *d.* young.
IV. James, *b.* 16th October, 1732; *d.* 20th October, 1815.
V. Peter, *b.* 19th December, 1734; *d.s.p.* 8th July, 1813; *m.* 1789, Mary DUYCKINCK.

COLONIAL FAMILIES OF THE UNITED STATES

VI. Frederick, *d.* young.
VII. Anna Maricka, *b.* 20th October, 1737; *d.* 4th September, 1791.
VIII. JOHN, *b.* 12th December, 1745, of whom later.
IX. Frederick, *b.* 19th April, 1747; *d.s.p.* 14th December, 1799; *m.* (firstly) 17th November, 1773, Ann Margaret BARCLAY, dau. of Andrew BARCLAY; *m.* (secondly) Euphemia DUNSCOMB.
X. Mary, *b.* 10th November, 1748; *d.* 18th May, 1752.

HON. JOHN JAY, Patriot, of New York City; *b.* 12th December, 1745; *d.* 17th May, 1829; graduated at King's College, 1764; admitted to the Bar, 1768; Delegate to the First Continental Congress, 1774; Chief Justice of the State of New York, 1777; President of Congress, 1778; Minister to Spain, 1779-1782; with John ADAMS and Benjamin FRANKLIN negotiated the Treaty of Peace between the United States and Great Britain, 1783; Secretary of Foreign Affairs, 1784-1789; First Chief Justice of the Supreme Court of the United States, 1789-1795; Minister Plenipotentiary to Great Britain, 1794-1795; Governor of New York State, 1795-1801; *m.* 28th April, 1774, Sarah Van Brugh LIVINGSTON, dau. of William LIVINGSTON, afterwards Governor of New Jersey.

ISSUE

I. Peter Augustus, *b.* 24th January, 1776, of whom later.
II. William, *b.* 16th June, 1779; *d.* 14th October, 1858; *m.* Augusta McVICKAR, dau. of John McVICKAR.

ISSUE

1. John, United States Minister to Austria, 1870; *m.* Eleanor Kingland FIELD, dau. of Hickson W. FIELD, *d.* 1892.

ISSUE

1⁶. William, *m.* Lucie OELRICHS, and has issue.
2⁶. Eleanor, *m.* 1905, Arthur ISELIN.

2. Anna, *m.* Rev. Lewis P. W. BALCH, D.D.
3. Maria, *m.* John F. BUTTERWORTH.
4. Sarah Louisa, *m.* Alexander M. BRUEN, M.D.
5. Eliza, *m.* 5th October, 1858; *d.* 22d December, 1869; *m.* Henry Edward PELLEW, M.A. Cambridge, son of the Very Reverend the Honorable George PELLEW, Dean of Norwich and gd. son of the first Viscount Exmouth.
6. Augusta, *m.* 14th May, 1873, Henry Edward PELLEW.

III. Susan, *d.* young.
IV. Maria, *b.* 20th February, 1782; *m.* 22d April, 1801, Goldsborough BANYER.
V. Ann, *b.* 13th August, 1783; *d.* 13th November, 1856.
VI. Sarah Louisa, *b.* 20th February, 1792; *d.* 22d April, 1818.

PETER AUGUSTUS JAY of New York City; *b.* 24th January, 1776; *d.* 20th February, 1843; Private Secretary to John JAY on his mission to England, 1795; Member of Assembly, State of New York 1816; Recorder of New York, 1819, Delegate to New York Constitutional Convention, 1821; *m.* 29th July, 1807, Mary Rutherfurd CLARKSON, dau. of Gen. Matthew CLARKSON.

ISSUE

I. JOHN CLARKSON, *b.* 11th September, 1808, of whom later.
II. Mary Rutherfurd, *b.* 16th April, 1810; *d.* 9th September, 1835; *m.* 10th April, 1829, Frederick PRIME.
III. Sarah, *b.* 19th December, 1811; *d.* 9th January, 1846; *m.* 11th February, 1836, William DAWSON; had issue.
IV. Catherine Helena, *b.* 11th June, 1815; *d.* September, 1889; *m.* 17th December, 1835, Henry Augustus DU BOIS, M.D.
V. Anna Maria, *b.* 12th September 1819; *d.* 1902; *m.* 1st December, 1841, Henry Evelyn PIERREPONT; had issue.
VI. Peter Augustus, *b.* 23d October, 1821; *d.* 31st October, 1855; *m.* 13th January, 1848, Josephine PEARSON of Washington, D. C.

ISSUE

1. Augustus, *b.* 17th October, 1850; Secretary American Legation, Paris, 1886–1892; *m.* 3d October, 1876, Emily Astor KANE, dau. of Oliver de Lancey KANE.

ISSUE

1¹. Peter Augustus, Diplomat; *b.* 23d August, 1877; student Eton College, England; A.B., Harvard, 1900; Third Secretary American Embassy at Paris, October, 1902–June, 1903; Second Secretary Legation, June–September, 1903; Secretary, September, 1903–June, 1906; Secretary Embassy, June, 1906–June, 1907, at Constantinople; Secretary Embassy at Tokyo, 1907–1909; Diplomatic Agent and Consul-General at Cairo, Egypt, December, 1909–December, 1913; Secretary American Embassy at Rome, Italy, December, 1913—; authorized by full powers July 7, 1908, while Charge d'Affaires ad interim at Tokyo to effect the exchange of ratifications of the conventions with Japan for the protection of inventions, designs, trade marks, and copyrights in China and Korea; Episcopalian; Member of the Metropolitan Club (Washington) Knickerbocker, Racquet, and Tennis, Harvard (New York); *m.* 16th March, 1909, Susan Alexander McCOOK, of New York.
2¹. De Lancey Kane, *b.* 1881, Private Secretary to the American Ambassador to Great Britain: *m.* and has issue.

VII. Elizabeth Clarkson, *b.* 2d July, 1823; *d.* unmarried 20th October, 1891.
VIII. Susan Matilda, *b.* 29th November, 1827; *m.* 14th April, 1852, Matthew CLARKSON; have issue.

JOHN CLARKSON JAY of New York City; M.D., b. 11th September, 1808; d. 1891, Trustee Columbia College, 1859-1880; m. 8th November, 1831, Laura PRIME, dau. of Nathaniel PRIME.

ISSUE

I. Laura, b. 10th August, 1832; m. 8th February, 1854, Charles Pemberton WURTS.
II. John, d. young.
III. Augustus, d. young.
IV. Mary, b. 3d June, 1837; m. 5th June, 1861, Jonathan EDWARDS, d. 1897.
V. Cornelia, b. 3d April, 1839.
VI. Anna Maria, d. young.
VII. REV. PETER AUGUSTUS, b. 16th June, 1841, of whom later.
VIII. John Clarkson, M.D., b. 20th October, 1844; m. 12th December, 1872, Harriette Arnold VINTON, dau. of Maj.-Gen. David H. VINTON, United States Army.

ISSUE

1. Maria Arnold, b. 18th September, 1873; d. 2d January, 1878.
2. Edith Van Cortlandt, b. 2d June, 1875.
3. John Clarkson, b. 20th January, 1880; m. 1903, Marguerite SOLEIAC.

ISSUE

1¹. Sarah Livingston, b. 1904, and others.

IX. Alice, b. 12th July, 1846.
X. Sarah, b. 12th January, 1848; d. 1883.
XI. Matilda Coster, d. young.

PETER AUGUSTUS JAY of New York City, b. 16th June, 1841; d. 11th October, 1875, Rector of Christ Church, Warwick, New York, 1869-1872; Rector of Grace Church, Fair Haven, Connecticut, 1872-1875; m. 30th March, 1869, Julia POST, 3d dau. of Alfred C. Post, M.D.

ISSUE

I. PIERRE, b. 4th May, 1870, the subject of this memoir.
II. Mary Rutherfurd, b. 16th August, 1872.
III. Laura Prime, b. 30th August, 1874; m. 1899, Frederic DeWitt WELLS.
IV. John, b. 19th November, 1875.

Arms.—Azure, a chevron or, in chief a demi-sun in its splendor, between two mullets of the last; in base on a rock, two buds, all ppr.
Crest.—A cross sable, on a cavalry of three steps ppr.
Motto.—Deo duce perseverandum.
Residences.—New York City, and Mt. Kisco, Westchester County, New York.
Clubs.—University and Century of New York.

Johnson

ALBA BOARDMAN JOHNSON, B.A., LL.D., of "Castana," Rosemont, Pennsylvania; *b.* in Pittsburg, Pennsylvania, 8th February, 1858; *m.* (firstly) 30th April, 1883, Elizabeth Thomas REEVES, *b.* 20th July, 1862, *d.* 1908, dau. of Biddle and Ruthanna (THOMAS) REEVES; *m.* (secondly) 23d June, 1910, Leah GOFF, dau. of Richard W. Petherbridge and Eliza Cathcart (ELLIOTT) GOFF.

ISSUE BY FIRST MARRIAGE

I. Reeves Kemp, *b.* 26th February, 1884; *m.* 6th January, 1915, Eleanor B. PETERSON.
II. Alba Boardman, Jr., *b.* 21st June, 1887; *m.* 19th October, 1912, Helen PAXSON.
III. Ruth Anna, *b.* 6th January, 1896.

ALBA BOARDMAN JOHNSON, A.B., Central High School, Philadelphia, 1876; LL.D. Ursinus College, Collegeville, Pennsylvania, 1909; Elder of Bryn Mawr Presbyterian Church, 28th November, 1909; entered Baldwin Locomotive Works (then owned by firm of Burnham, Parry, Williams and Company) as junior clerk, 14th May, 1877; wlth Edgemoor Iron Works, Wilmington, Delaware, 1878-1879, when he returned to Baldwin Locomotive Works; admitted to partnership as successor firm Burnham, Williams and Company, 1896, and upon incorporation 1st July, 1909, became Vice-President and Treasurer and President, 1st July, 1911; Director, Standard Steel Works; Republican; President, Presbyterian Social Union, 1906-1907; Trustee Jefferson Medical College and Hospital; President, 1907-1909, Geographical Society of Philadelphia; President, 1912-13, New England Society of Pennsylvania; Director, Federal Reserve Bank of Philadelphia; Trustee, Philadelphia Saving Fund; Director, Southwork Foundry Manufacturing Company; New York Life Insurance Company; Vice-President, Philadelphia Chamber of Commerce.

Lineage

The American ancestor of this family was Timothy JOHNSON, *b.* in Hern Hill, County Kent, England; *d.* 15th March, 1688, in Andover, Massachusetts; *m.* there 15th December, 1674, Rebecca ASLETT, *b.* there 6th May, 1652, *d.* there after 25th March, 1705, dau. of John ASLETT, who *m.* 8th October, 1648, Rebecca AYER, dau. of John and Hannah AYER of Ipswich.

ISSUE AMONG OTHERS

1. TIMOTHY, *b.* 25th May, 1679, of whom later.

TIMOTHY JOHNSON of Andover, Massachusetts; *b.* there 25th May, 1679; *d.* there prior to 2d April, 1771, on which date his will was proved; he was a representative to the General Court or Assembly of Massachusetts 1737-1738, 1740 and 1745; Lieutenant of the Andover Troop of Horse and served in that command in His Majesty's service "Eastward" under Capt. Richard KIMBALL in 1725; Muster Roll of Company dated 23d June to 23d July, 1725, being presented to the General Court it was "Resolved that the sum of £213, 6s. 3d. be paid out of the Treasury to Lieutenant Timothy JOHNSON to be by him paid to the respective officers and soldiers born on the Roll." He was advanced to a Captaincy before 1737, and is styled "Captain Timothy JOHNSON" in the official list of Representatives to the General Court in 1737. In the expedition to Cape Bolton in which Louisberg was taken, he served as Lieutenant in the Seventh Company, 4th Massachusetts Regiment of Militia under Col. Samuel WILLARD, 1745; *m.* 3d May, 1705, Catherine SPRAGUE, *d.* 22d February, 1758.

ISSUE AMONG OTHERS

1. ASA, *b.* 27th March, 1716, of whom below.

ASA JOHNSON of Andover, Massachusetts; *b.* there 27th March, 1716; *d.* there 2d March, 1749; *m.* 6th December, 1736, in Charlestown, Massachusetts, Anna KETTLE, *bapt.* 11th January, 1719, in Charlestown, *d.* 10th April, 1792, in Topsfield, Massachusetts.

ISSUE AMONG OTHERS

1. BENJAMIN, *b.* 24th May, 1744, of whom below.

BENJAMIN JOHNSON of Limerick, Maine; *b.* 24th May, 1744; *d.* at Andover, 21st October, 1832; at Limerick, *m.* (record of intention of marriage) 27th July, 1766, Elizabeth BOARDMAN, *b.* Topsfield, *d.* there 7th March, 1820.

ISSUE AMONG OTHERS

1. BOARDMAN, *b.* 23d September, 1769, of whom below.

BOARDMAN JOHNSON of Canterbury, New Hampshire; *b.* there 23d September, 1769, *m.* Kezia FOSTER.

ISSUE AMONG OTHERS

1. BOARDMAN, *b.* 29th December, 1799, of whom below.

BOARDMAN JOHNSON of Jackson, Maine; *b.* 29th December, 1799, in Alfred, Maine; *d.* 4th May, 1853, in Jackson; *m.* 10th January, 1823, Hepzibah PAGE, *b.* 25th March, 1802, *d.* 22d February, 1886, in Windham, Vermont.

ISSUE

1. SAMUEL ADAMS, *b.* 16th February, 1825, of whom later.

SAMUEL ADAMS JOHNSON, *b.* 16th February, 1825, in Atkinson, Maine; *d.* 29th December, 1908, in St. Petersburg, Florida; *m.* 22d July, 1855, in West Townsend,

Vermont, Alma Sarah KEMP, *b.* 25th July, 1822, in Sullivan County, New York, *d.* 5th July, 1882, in Philadelphia, Pennsylvania.

ISSUE

1. ALBA BOARDMAN, *b.* 8th February, 1858, the subject of this memoir.

Residence.—"Castana," Rosemont, Pennsylvania.

Clubs.—Union League, University, Manufacturers, Merion Cricket (Haverford, Pennsylvania), St. David's Golf, Railroad of New York; India House, City, Penn of Philadelphia, cotemporary Fairmount Park Association.

Societies.—Colonial Wars, Sons of the American Revolution, American-Asiatic (Vice-President), Five O'Clock, International Law Association, New Society of Pennsylvania, Pennsylvania Society of New York, American Academy Political and Social Science, American Master Mechanic Association, Geographic of Philadelphia, American Philosophical, etc.

Johnson

CHARLES WILLIAMSON JOHNSON, Civil Engineer, of St. Paul, Minnesota; b. 20th January, 1845, at Johnstown, New York; m. 14th June, 1875, at Menasha, Wisconsin, Maria Cornelia BRONSON, b. 18th February, 1856, dau. of Nelson C. and Maria (MATTISON) BRONSON of Menasha, Wisconsin.

ISSUE

I. Harriet Livermore, b. 18th December, 1876; m. 24th May, 1899, Frederick E. MAHLER of St. Paul, Minnesota.

ISSUE

1. Margaret Livermore MAHLER, b. 26th June, 1900.
2. Charles Frederick MAHLER, b. 13th November, 1902.

II. William Lobdell, b. 26th July, 1878; m. 14th June, 1905, Cora HUBBELL, dau. of Albert C. and Mary (LYON) HUBBELL of Duluth, Minnesota.

ISSUE

1. Louise Cotton, b. 23d May, 1906.

III. Maria Louise, b. 26th October, 1882; m. 9th January, 1901, Arthur E. GILBERT of Duluth, Minnesota.
IV. Elizabeth Ker, b. 6th June, 1891; m. 30th September, 1911, Lieut. Walter Reed WEAVER of the United States Army.

CHARLES WILLIAMSON JOHNSON was educated at Johnstown Academy, Johnstown, New York; resided in France, 1860–1861; graduated from Union College, Schenectady, New York, in 1866 with degree of C.E.; in Engineering Department of the Lake Shore and Michigan Southern Railway from January, 1867, for more than three years and from that time continuously engaged in practice of his profession with Rock Island Railway; Wisconsin Central Railway, and from 1st March, 1879, to 1st November, 1913, Chief Engineer of the Chicago, St. Paul, Minneapolis, and Omaha Railway; since 1st November, 1913, Consulting Engineer of same road.

Lineage

ELIHU JOHNSON of Windsor, Ellington and Tolland, Connecticut; served in the French and Indian War, 1757, and as a private from 1777 to 1780 in the 2d Connecticut Regiment, Continental Line, during the American Revolution; m. 23d June,

1762, at Windsor, Connecticut, Mrs. Sarah (WEBB) CONVERSE, b. 2d April, 1741, at Stafford, Connecticut, dau. of Zebulon and Judith (HOWARD) WEBB of Stafford, Connecticut.

ISSUE

I. Joshua Converse, b. 26th January, 1764; m. (firstly) 29th July, 1787, Polly CARPENTER; m. (secondly) 28th October, 1792, Polly PRENTICE.
II. Noah.
III. Anna, m. ——— CHAPMAN.
IV. Sally, m. (firstly) ——— DAVIS; m. (secondly) ——— NEWELL.
V. Elihu, b. 30th September, 1772; m. (firstly) 12th April, 1795, Eleanor ATCHESON; m. (secondly) Alice BUMP.
VI. Guy, b. 14th May, 1775.
VII. Dolly, b. 19th October, 1777.
VIII. David, b. 21st March, 1781; m. 18th December, 1816, Anna EATON.
IX. ORAN, b. 29th March, 1783, of whom below.

ORAN JOHNSON, M.D., of Johnstown, New York; b. at Tolland, Connecticut, 29th March, 1783; d. at Johnstown, 12th May, 1835; m. 22d September, 1811, Sarah LOBDELL of Johnstown, b. there 21st September, 1793, d. thêre 21st September, 1793, d. there 7th May, 1867.

ISSUE

I. WILLIAM HENRY, b. 6th March, 1814, of whom later.
II. Charles Webb, b. 16th August, 1815; d. 19th July, 1854, unmarried.
III. Mary Chapman, b. 16th June, 1817; d. 12th March, 1865; unmarried.
IV. Elizabeth Little, b. 8th October, 1824; d. 31st October, 1832.
V. Sarah, b. 8th October, 1824; d. 11th July, 1866; m. 12th February, 1846, John J. YOUNG.
VI. James Oran, b. 24th September, 1829; d. 18th April, 1908; m. 29th March, 1853, Evaline GARDINER.
VII. Ann Frances, b. 26th January, 1832; d. 10th December, 1902; m. 10th May, 1855, Lucien BERTRAND.

WILLIAM HENRY JOHNSON, M.D., of Johnstown, New York; b. there 6th March, 1814; d. there 6th May, 1868, up to which time he had practiced his profession there; Graduate M.D. Jefferson Medical College, Philadelphia, Pennsylvania; m. 15th January, 1843, Harriet Livermore McCARTHY, b. 16th May, 1817, and is still (September, 1916) living there, dau. of John and Elizabeth (KER) MCCARTHY of Johnstown, New York.

ISSUE

I. William Lobdell, M.D., b. 17th November, 1843; d. 26th June, 1910; m. Mary A. CLARK of Johnstown, New York.
II. CHARLES WILLIAMSON, b. 20th January, 1845, the subject of this memoir.

III. Margaret Souder, *b.* 31st March, 1847; *d.* 12th April, 1888; *m.* 11th August, 1872, John H. DORN, M.D.
IV. Henry Converse, *b.* 21st June, 1850; *d.* 4th April, 1854.
V. Louis Sterling, *b.* 23d July, 1852; *d.* 10th April, 1904, unmarried.
VI. Harriet, *b.* 12th February, 1855; *d.* 10th November, 1910; *m.* Thomas BILLINGTON.
VII. Samuel Maxwell, M.D., *b.* 9th July, 1856; *m.* Elizabeth GASTLIN.

Residence.—118 Virginia Avenue, St. Paul, Minnesota.
Clubs.—Minnesota of St. Paul, Chicago Engineers Club.
Societies.—Colonial Wars, Sons of the American Revolution, Delta Phi.
Arms.—(Johnson of New England).—Gules three spear heads a chief Ermine.
Crest.—A pair of raven's wings sable.
Motto.—Servabo fidem.

Adams

HENRY ADAMS came from England to this country in 1634 and settled at Braintree, Massachusetts; *d.* 6th October, 1646; *m.* wife's name unknown.

ISSUE, ALL BORN IN ENGLAND

I. Henry, *b.* 1604; *d.* 21st February, 1676; *m.* 17th November, 1643, Elizabeth PAINE.
II. Thomas, *b.* 1612; *d.* 20th July, 1688; *m.* Mary BLACKMORE.
III. SAMUEL, *b.* 1617, of whom later.
IV. Jonathan, *b.* 1619; *d.* 1691; *m.* (firstly) Elizabeth ———; *m.* (secondly) Mary ———.
V. Peter, *b.* 1622; *d.* 1690.
VI. John, *b.* 1624.
VII. Joseph, *b.* 1626.
VIII. Edward, *b.* 1630.
IX. Ursula.

CAPTAIN SAMUEL ADAMS, *b.* in England, 1617; came with his parent to America in 1634 and settled in Braintree, Massachusetts; *d.* at Chelmsford, Massachusetts, 24th January, 1689, where he had lived since 1634; *m.* (firstly) Rebecca GRAVES of Charlestown, Massachusetts, who *d.* in 1664; *m.* (secondly) Esther SPARHAWK of Cambridge, Massachusetts, 7th May, 1668.

ISSUE

I. Thomas, *d.* 19th March, 1686, aged thirty-two years.
II. Rebecca.
III. Susanna.
IV. MARY, *b.* 9th October, 1663, of whom later.

MARY ADAMS was born in Chelmsford, Massachusetts, 9th October, 1663; d. 21st December, 1744; m. 16th December, 1686, Samuel WEBB of Braintree, Massachusetts, son of Christopher WEBB and Hannah (SCOTT) WEBB.

ISSUE

I. Rebecca WEBB, b. 25th September, 1687; d. March, 1688.
II. SAMUEL WEBB, b. 14th May, 1690.
III. Mary WEBB, b. 25th November, 1694.
IV. Nathaniel WEBB, b. 20th February, 1696.
V. Zebulon WEBB, b. 1698; d. 10th May, 1760.

Bridge

JOHN BRIDGE, b. in England; lived in Cambridge, Massachusetts, in 1632; d. in Cambridge, 1685; Representative, 1637, and Deacon of Cambridge Church; m. Elizabeth, surname unknown, she was living in 1683.

ISSUE

I. MATHEW, d. 1700, of whom later.
II. Sarah, b. 16th February, 1648.
III. Thomas, d. 1656.

MATHEW BRIDGE, d. 28th April, 1700; Member of Artillery Company, 1643; m. circa 1643, Anna DANFORTH, who was b. in 1620 and d. 2d December, 1704.

ISSUE

I. John, b. 16th March, 1644-1645.
II. ANNA, b. 1646, of whom later.
III. Martha, b. 19th January, 1648.
IV. Matthew, b. 5th May, 1650, d. 2d May, 1738.
V. Samuel, b. 17th February, 1653; d. 25th February, 1671.
VI. Thomas, b. 1st June, 1656; d. 28th March, 1673.
VII. Elizabeth, b. 17th August, 1659; m. 1677.

ANNA BRIDGE, b. 1646; d. 1727; m. 4th June, 1668, Samuel LIVERMORE, b. 11th May, 1640. (See LIVERMORE, page 318.)

Browne-Brown

ABRAM BROWNE, b. at Swan Hull near Bury St. Edmunds, England; he was one of the first settlers of Watertown, Massachusetts, and was admitted Freeman, 6th March, 1631-1632; d. in Watertown, 1650; m. Lydia surname unknown, who d. there 27th September, 1686.

ISSUE

I. Sarah, b. in England; m. 16th December, 1643, George PARKHURST, Jr.
II. Mary, b. in England; m. 10th April, 1650, John LEWIS of Charlestown, Massachusetts.
III. Lydia, b. in Watertown, Massachusetts, 22d March, 1632–1633, m. Lieut. Wm. LEKIN, Jr.
IV. JONATHAN, b. 15th October, 1635, of whom later.
V. Hannah, b. 1638–1639; d. March, 1638-1639.
VI. Abram, b. 6th March, 1639-40; d. 1667.

JONATHAN BROWNE, of Watertown, Massachusetts; b. 15th October, 1635; m. 11th February, 1661–1662, Mary SHATTUCK, b. 25th August, 1645, d. 23d October, 1732. His sons dropped the final "e" of the name.

ISSUE

I. Mary, b. 5th October, 1662; m. (firstly) John WARREN; m. (secondly) Samuel HARRINGTON.
II. Elizabeth, b. 19th September, 1664; m. Daniel BENJAMIN.
III. Jonathan, b. 25th October, 1666; d. young.
IV. Patience, b. 6th March, 1669.
V. Abraham, b. 26th August, 1671; d. 27th November, 1729.
VI. Samuel, b. 21st October, 1674.
VII. Lydia, b. 31st March, 1677; m. Benjamin WELLINGTON.
VIII. Ebenezer, b. 10th September, 1679.
IX. Benjamin, b. 27th February, 1681; d. 11th March, 1753.
X. WILLIAM, b. 1684, of whom below.

WILLIAM BROWN, b. in Watertown, Massachusetts, 3d September, 1684; d. 28th October, 1756; m. (firstly) 10th January, 1704, Hannah PEASE of Cambridge, she d. 10th March, 1717–1718, he m. (secondly) 11th December, 1718, Sarah BOND, dau. of Col. Jonas and Grace (COOLIDGE) BOND.

ISSUE

I. Ebenezer, b. 23d October, 1705; d. 17th December, 1785; m. 20th May, 1727, Abigail ADAMS of Lexington.
II. HANNAH, b. 1706, of whom later.
III. Sarah, b. 6th July, 1708.
IV. William, b. 27th September, 1710; m. Mary FESSENDEN.
V. Isaac, b. 5th December, 1711; d. 6th October, 1759; m. April, 1736, Mary BALCH.
VI. Susanna, b. 16th May, 1714; d. 1774; m. 12th January, 1737, Henry PRENTICE of Cambridge.
VII. Samuel, b. 1716; d. 1786.
VIII. Grace, b. 1719; d. 1769; m. 13th May, 1742, George LAWRENCE.

IX. Jonas, *b.* 9th December, 1721.
X. Josiah, *b.* 2d August, 1724; *d.* 16th March, 1776.
XI. Sarah, *b.* 14th March, 1727; *d.* 1802, *m.* Col. Benjamin HAMMONDS.
XII. Thankful, *b.* 23d April, 1730; *m.* 3d September, 1751, Abijah PIERCE of Waltham.

HANNAH BROWN, *b.* 22d January, 1706; *d.* 2d November, 1762; *m.* 10th November, 1726, Samuel LIVERMORE. (See LIVERMORE.)

Burwell

JOHN BURWELL came from Hertfordshire, England; lived in Milford, Connecticut, in 1639; *d.* circa 1679; *m.* Alice surname unknown.

ISSUE

I. John, *b.* in England.
II. Zarachiah, *b.* in England.
III. SAMUEL, *b.* 1640, of whom later.
IV. Ephraim, *b.* 19th May, 1644.
V. Nathan, *b.* 1646.
VI. Elizabeth, *b.* 1647.
VII. Mary, *b.* 5th December, 1653.

LIEUTENANT SAMUEL BURWELL, *b.* in Milford, Connecticut, 1640; *d.* there 5th May, 1715; *m.* Sarah FENN.

ISSUE

I. Sarah, *b.* 6th April, 1663.
II. Samuel, *b.* 12th January, 1666.
III. MARY, *b.* 20th October, 1667, of whom later.
IV. Joseph, *b.* 20th September, 1676.
V. John, *b.* 1678.

MARY BURWELL, *b.* 20th October, 1667; *m.* Joshua LOBDELL. (See LOBDELL.)

Danforth

NICHOLAS DANFORTH of Farmingham, Suffolk County, England, came to America in 1634 and settled in Cambridge, Massachusetts; *d.* in Cambridge, Massachusetts, April, 1637; Representative, 1636 and 1637; *m.* Elizabeth surname unknown, who. *d.* in England, 1629.

ISSUE (ALL BORN IN ENGLAND)

I. Elizabeth, *b.* 1618; *d.* 26th June, 1680.
II. ANNA, *b.* 1620, of whom later.
III. Thomas, *b.* 1622; *d.* 5th November, 1699; *m.* Mary WITHINGTON. He was President of Maine and Lieutenant-Governor of Massachusetts.

COLONIAL FAMILIES OF THE UNITED STATES

IV. Samuel, *b.* 1626; *d.* 1674, Graduate of Harvard, 1643.
V. Jonathan, *b.* 29th February, 1628; *d.* 7th September, 1712; *m.* Elizabeth POULTER.

ANNA DANFORTH, *b.* in England circa 1620; *d.* December, 1704; *m.* circa 1643, Mathew BRIDGE. (See BRIDGE.)

Ker

WALTER KER, *b.* in Scotland, 1656; banished from there as a Noncomforist, 3d September, 1685; came with his wife Margaret name unknown and children to America, December, 1685, and settled at Freehold, New Jersey, where he *d.* 10th June, 1748; his wife was *b.* in Scotland in 1661, *d.* in Freehold in 1734. He was from the Parish of Dalsert, Lanarkshire.

ISSUE
I. WILLIAM, of whom later.
II. Samuel, *m.* Catherine MATTISON.
III. Joseph, *m.* Margaret CRAIG.
IV. John.

WILLIAM KER lived at Freehold, New Jersey; *m.* (firstly) name unknown; *m.* (secondly) Catherine LOOFBOUROW.

ISSUE BY FIRST MARRIAGE
I. Margaret, *bapt.* 18th April, 1731.
II. Mary, *bapt.* 4th November, 1733.

ISSUE BY SECOND MARRIAGE
I. NATHAN, *b.* 1736, of whom later.
II. Elizabeth, *bapt.* 19th April, 1738.
III. Hannah, *bapt.* 31st August, 1740.
IV. Lydia, *bapt.* February, 1742.
V. Nathaniel, *bapt.* 15th September, 1745.
VI. Walter, *bapt.* 18th December, 1748.

REV. NATHAN KER, *b.* in Freehold, New Jersey, 7th September, 1736, o.s.; *d.* in Goshen, New York, 14th December, 1804; he was a Graduate of Princeton, 1761, and was Pastor of a Presbyterian Church at Goshen, New York, from 1766 to 1804; *m.* 1765, Anna LIVERMORE of Waltham, Massachusetts, *b.* 16th January, 1743, *d.* 23d February, 1812.

ISSUE
I. Oliver Livermore, *b.* 5th March, 1766; *d.* 21st October, 1796, unmarried; Graduate of Princeton, 1785.
II. Catherine, *b.* 9th August, 1767; *d.* 20th May, 1795; *m.* Rev. Simon HOSACK.

III. Hannah, b. 20th January, 1769; d. 24th January, 1858; m. (firstly) Theodorus VAN WYCK of New York; m. (secondly) James E. CALDWELL.
IV. Margaret Clark, b. 7th March, 1770; d. 27th April, 1830; m. Rev. Jonathan FREEMAN.
V. Mary, b. 30th May, 1772; d. 26th February, 1793.
VI. Elizabeth, b. 14th March, 1774; d. 23d February, 1864.

ELIZABETH KER, b. at Goshen, Orange County, New York, 14th March, 1774; d. at Johnstown, New York, 23d February, 1864; m. John McCARTHY, b. in Ireland, 1763, d. at Johnstown, New York, 7th January, 1832.

ISSUE

I. Charles McCARTHY, b. 6th June, 1798, d. 1st October, 1821.
II. William McCarthy, b. 31st July, 1799; d. 25th September, 1821.
III. Ann Catherine McCARTHY, b. 2d February, 1801; d. 21st May, 1801.
IV. Maria Eleanor McCARTHY, b. 6th March, 1802; d. 17th December, 1822.
V. Catherine Hosack McCARTHY, b. 7th December, 1803; d. 5th September, 1821.
VI. Anna McCARTHY, b. 25th October, 1805; d. 12th May, 1875; m. James CAMPBELL, Jr.
VII. John McCARTHY, b. 15th September, 1807; d. 25th December, 1877.
VIII. Elizabeth Van Wyck McCARTHY, b. 25th September, 1809; d. 26th July, 1821.
IX. Hannah Caldwell McCARTHY, b. 21st May, 1815; d. 1st January, 1864.
X. Margaret Ker McCARTHY, b. 5th May, 1812; d. 11th November, 1821.
XI. HARRIET LIVERMORE McCARTHY, b. 1817, of whom below.

HARRIET LIVERMORE McCARTHY, b. in Johnstown, New York, 16th May, 1817; and is now (October 1916) living there; m. 15th January, 1843, Dr. William Henry JOHNSON of Johnstown.

Little

THOMAS LITTLE of Springfield, Massachusetts; m. Ann BAILEY.

ISSUE

I. WILLIAM, of whom below.

WILLIAM LITTLE, b. in Springfield, Massachusetts; m. (firstly) Molly BRATTAN and removed to Curry Bush, Albany (now Schenectady) County, New York; m. (secondly) Nelly NELSON.

ISSUE BY FIRST MARRIAGE

I. JOHN, b. 1745, of whom later.
II. Thomas, m. Lucretia CRAWFORD.
III. Ann.

ISSUE BY SECOND MARRIAGE

I. Sarah, *m.* William GLASSFORD of Cornwall, Canada.

MAJOR JOHN LITTLE, *b.* in 1745; *d.* at Johnstown, New York, 29th September, 1822; was Captain of the 3d Battalion, Tryon County, New York, 1781; previously First Lieutenant, 2d Regiment Schenectady District; was in the Army all through the Revolutionary War and Commandant of the fort at Johnstown, New York; also served in Captain DUNCAN's Company, Schenectady, New York, in 1767; commissioned Major in New York Militia by Governor CLINTON; *m.* (firstly) Leah CRAWFORD, dau. of Joseph and Catherine (NELSON) CRAWFORD; *m.* (secondly) Catherine McINTYRE.

ISSUE BY FIRST MARRIAGE

I. Ann, *m.* Chauncey HUTCHINSON.
II. MARY, *b* 14th June, 1771, of whom later.
III. Catherine, *m.* (firstly) Joseph LOUP; *m.* (secondly) Benjamin EATON.

ISSUE BY SECOND MARRIAGE

I. Leah, *m.* Benjamin CHAMBERLIN.
II. Elizabeth, *m.* Clark SUTLIFF.

MARY LITTLE, *b.* 14th June, 1771; *d.* at Johnstown, New York, 21st July, 1849; *m.* Abijah LOBDELL of Johnstown, New York (See LOBDELL.)

Livermore

JOHN LIVERMORE, *b.* in England, 1606; *d.* at Watertown, Massachusetts, 14th April, 1684; embarked at Ipswich, England, for New England in April, 1634, in the *Francis;* settled in Watertown, Massachusetts; *m.* in England, Grace SHERMAN a daughter of Edward SHERMAN and wife Grace (MAKIN) SHERMAN, who had both lived in Dedham and Colchester, County Essex, England and came to America in 1634. John LIVERMORE's wife Grace was *b.* in England in 1615 and *d.* at Chelmsford, Massachusetts, 14th January, 1690. John Livermore lived a while in New Haven, Connecticut.

ISSUE

I. Hannah, *b.* 1633.
II. Elizabeth.
III. John, *b.* 1638.
IV. Nathaniel, *d.* 12th February, 1736.
V. Sarah, *b.* 1645, in New Haven.
VI. SAMUEL, *b.* 1640, of whom later.
VII. Edmund, *b.* 8th March, 1659.
VIII. Daniel, *b.* 7th October, 1643.
IX. Mary, *b.* 12th September, 1647.
X. Martha, *d.* 26th October, 1740.

SAMUEL LIVERMORE, *b.* 11th May, 1640, in New Haven, Connecticut; *d.* 5th December, 1690, in Watertown, Massachusetts; *m.* 4th June, 1668, Anna BRIDGE, of Cambridge, Massachusetts, who was *b.* circa 1646 and *d.* 28th August, 1727.

ISSUE (ALL BORN IN WATERTOWN)

I. Anna, *b.* 29th March, 1669.
II. Grace, *b.* 28th September, 1671.
III. Samuel, *b.* 27th April, 1673.
IV. Daniel, *b.* 3d February, 1675.
V. Thomas, *b.* 5th January, 1676.
VI. JONATHAN, *b.* 1678, of whom later.
VII. Mathew, *b.* 12th January, 1680.
VIII. John, *b.* 24th February, 1681; *d.* 18th April, 1717.
IX. Abigail, *b.* 9th October, 1683.
X. Nathaniel, *b.* 29th December, 1685; *d.* 26th February, 1712.
XI. Lydia, *b.* 26th July, 1687.
XII. Anna, *b.* 1690.

JONATHAN LIVERMORE, *b.* 19th April, 1678, in Watertown, Massachusetts; *d.* there 8th November, 1705; *m.* in Watertown, 23d November, 1680, Rebecca BARNES, *b.* 1680, *d.* 9th December, 1765.

ISSUE

I. Jonathan, *b.* 16th August, 1700.
II. SAMUEL, *b.* 14th March, 1702, of whom later.
III. Rebecca, *b.* 8th December, 1703.
IV. Grace, *b.* 15th March, 1706.

SAMUEL LIVERMORE, *b.* at Watertown, Massachusetts, 14th March, 1702; *d.* 7th August, 1773, in Waltham, Massachusetts; *m.* (firstly) in Watertown, 10th November, 1726, Hannah BROWN, *b.* 22d January, 1707, *d.* 2d November, 1762.

ISSUE BY FIRST MARRIAGE

I. Hannah, *b.* 27th April, 1728; *d.* 24th February, 1799; *m.* (firstly) Rev. Nathaniel PATTER; *m.* (secondly) Robert PIERPONT.
II. Samuel, *b.* 6th September, 1729; *d.* 1731.
III. Elijah, *b.* 4th March, 1731; *d.* 5th August, 1808.
IV. Samuel, *b.* 15th May, 1732; *d.* 1803.
V. Isaac, *b.* 28th January, 1735; *d.* 1763.
VI. William, *b.* 9th October, 1737; *d.* 10th August, 1761.
VII. Sarah, *b.* 30th March, 1741; *d.* 9th October, 1761.
VIII. ANNA, *b.* 16th January, 1743; *d.* 23d February, 1812.
IX. Jonathan, *b.* 21st January, 1746; *d.* 22d June, 1751.

Anna Livermore, *b.* in Waltham, Massachusetts, 16th January, 1743; *d.* 23d February, 1812, at Bridgeton, New Jersey; *m.* in 1765 Rev. Nathan Ker of Goshen, New York (See Ker, page 12).

Lobdell

Simon Lobdell, from Hereford, England, in 1645; secured a lot in Milford, Connecticut, in 1646; *d.* there in 1717; *m.* Persis Pierce, dau. of Thomas and Elizabeth Pierce of Charlestown, Massachusetts.

ISSUE

I. Mary, *b.* 1667; *d.* 1711.
II. Elizabeth, *b.* 7th October, 1669.
III. Joshua, *b.* 1671, of whom later.
IV. Anna, *b.* 23d December, 1674.
V. Rebecca, *bapt.* 29th April, 1677; *d.* 2d February, 1740.
VI. Samuel, *bapt.* 7th September, 1679.
VII. Caleb, *bapt.* 26th November, 1682.
VII. Ann, *bapt.* 29th November, 1685.

Joshua Lobdell, *b.* 23d December, 1671; *m.* 11th August, 1695, Mary Burwell, *b.* 20th October, 1667, dau. of Lieut. Samuel Burwell of Milford, Connecticut.

ISSUE

I. Samuel, *b.* 2d February, 1699.
II. Sarah, *b.* 1st February, 1702.
III. Joshua, *b.* 16th March, 1703, of whom later.
IV. Mary, *b.* 30th October, 1704.
V. Ebenezer, *b.* 24th February, 1707.
VI. Susannah, *b.* 27th February, 1709.

Captain Joshua Lobdell, *b.* in Milford, Connecticut, 16th March, 1703; he was Captain of the 7th Company of Militia in the Upper Battalion Westchester County, New York, and served in the French and Indian wars, 1755–1760; *m.* Mary Reynolds, dau. of Joseph Reynolds of Ridgefield, Connecticut; moved from Milford to Ridgefield, Connecticut, and from there about 1730 to Cortland Manor, Westchester County, New York.

ISSUE

I. Mary, *b.* 6th December, 1726.
II. Joshua, *b.* 23d April, 1727, of whom later.
III. Ebenezer, *b.* 1st December, 1730; *m.* Deborah Palmer.
IV. Jacob, *b.* 1732; *m.* Ruth Boughton.
V. Simon, *d.* young.
VI. Sarah, *d.* young.
VII. Hannah, *d.* young.

VIII. Daniel, *m.* Elizabeth LOCKWOOD, 12th January, 1764.
IX. John, *b.* 10th March, 1743; *m.* Elizabeth SHERWOOD.
X. Rachel, *m.* Jacob RUNDELL.

JOSHUA LOBDELL, *b.* in Ridgefield, Connecticut, 23d April, 1727; he was a Corporal in his father's company in the Westchester County Militia, 1755–1760; also Private in Westchester County Militia, 1783 (Captain WILTZ's Company), and was in active service during the Revolutionary War; *m.* circa 1750, Sarah SCOTT; dau. of David SCOTT, of Ridgefield, Connecticut; she was *b.* 1719, and *d.* 3d February, 1823, 103½ years old.

ISSUE

I. Sarah, *b.* 2d July, 1751.
II. Joshua, *b.* 1752; *d.* 13th May, 1813.
III. Isaac, *b.* 8th March, 1755.
IV. James, *bapt.* 13th July, 1757; *m.* ——— VENABLE, moved to Mississippi.
V. Hannah, *bapt.* 24th June, 1759.
VI. Simon, *b.* 25th February, 1762.
VII. Huldah, *bapt.* 1763.
VIII. Abraham, *bapt.* 25th August, 1765.
IX. Abijah, *b.* 1767; *d.* 184—.
X. Rachael.
XI. Rebecca, *d.* 4th November, 1770.
XII. Mary, *bapt.* 4th November, 1770.

ABIJAH LOBDELL, *b.* at Cortlandt Manor, Westchester County, New York, 30th April, 1767; *m.* Mary LITTLE of Johnstown, New York, *b.* 14th June, 1771, *d.* there 21st July, 1849; he *d.* a short time before. She was the daughter of Maj. John LITTLE and wife Leah CRAWFORD of Johnstown.

ISSUE

I. Abijah, *b.* 10th June, 1789; 9th April, 1836.
II. John Little, *b.* 7th May, 1791; *d.* 5th September, 1867.
III. SARAH, *b.* 1793, of whom later.
IV. James Alexander, *b.* 18th September, 1798; *d.* young.
V. Dr. William S., *b.* 3d March, 1801; *d.* 1878.
VI. Henry Milton, *b.* 26th September, 1803; *d.* young.
VII. Charles Sidney, *b.* 1806; *d.* 15th May, 1898.

SARAH LOBDELL, *b.* 21st September, 1793, at Johnstown, New York; *d.* there 7th May, 1867; *m.* 22d September, 1811, Dr. Oran JOHNSON. (See JOHNSON.)

Webb

CHRISTOPHER WEBB came from England previous to 1645 and settled in Braintree, Massachusetts; *d.* June 1671; Freeman, 1645; *m.* Humility surname unknown, *b.* 1588, *d.* November, 1687.

COLONIAL FAMILIES OF THE UNITED STATES

ISSUE

I. CHRISTOPHER, of whom later.
II. Sarah, *m.* Zachariah BUCKWATER.
III. Thomas.
IV. Mary.

CHRISTOPHER WEBB, *b.* in England, 1630; came to America with his parents; he lived in Braintree, Massachusetts; was Representative from Braintree, 1689 and 1690; *d.* 30th May, 1694; *m.* 18th November, 1654, Hannah SCOTT, *d.* in 1718.

ISSUE

I. John, *b.* 23d October, 1655; *m.* May, 1680, Bethia ADAMS.
II. Peter, *b.* 1st December, 1657.
III. SAMUEL, *b.* 1660, of whom later.
IV. Christopher, *b.* 25th March, 1663.
V. Hannah, *b.* 5th September, 1665; *m.* Capt. John ADAMS.
VI. Benjamin, *b.* 2d February, 1667.
VII. Mary, *b.* 6th September, 1669; *m.* 12th February, 1694, Capt. Peter ADAMS.
VIII. Joseph, *b.* 15th March, 1672.
IX. Abigail, *b.* 13th August, 1675.

SAMUEL WEBB, *b.* in Braintree, Massachusetts, 6th August, 1660; *d.* in Windham, Connecticut, in 1739; *m.* 16th December, 1686, Mary ADAMS, who was *b.* at Chelmsford, Massachusetts, 9th October, 1663, and *d.* 21st December, 1744, dau. of Capt. Samuel ADAMS.

ISSUE

I. Rebecca, *b.* 25th September, 1687; *d.* March, 1688.
II. Samuel, *b.* 14th May, 1690.
III. Mary, *b.* 25th November, 1694.
IV. Nathaniel, *b.* 10th February, 1696.
V. ZEBULON, *b.* 1698, of whom below.

ZEBULON WEBB, *b.* in Braintree, Massachusetts, 1698; *d.* 10th May, 1760; he went with his parents to Wyndham, Connecticut; *m.* in Wyndham, 19th December, 1722, Judith HOWARD of that place.

ISSUE

I. Mary, *b.* 14th January, 1723.
II. Zebulon, *b.* 30th July, 1725.
III. Judith, *b.* 28th December, 1727.
IV. Napthali, *b.* 30th July, 1729.
V. Nathan, *b.* 9th October, 1731.
VI. Abner, *b.* 21st September, 1733.

VII. Bethia, *b.* 13th May, 1736.
VIII. Abigail, *b.* 12th June, 1738.
IX. SARAH, *b.* 2d April, 1741, of whom later.
X. Eliphalet, *b.* 20th February, 1742.
XI. Jemima, *b.* 20th April, 1745.
XII. Stephen, *b.* 17th March, 1747.

SARAH WEBB, *b.* 2d April, 1741; *m.* (firstly) 7th May, 1759, Joshua CONVERSE, *d.* 10th December, 1760; *m.* (secondly) 23d June, 1762, at Windsor, Connecticut, Elihu JOHNSON. They lived at Tolland, Connecticut; he served as a volunteer for the relief of Fort William Henry in the French and Indian War in August, 1757, in Captain STOUGHTON's Regiment; he served three years, during the Revolutionary War, in the 2d Connecticut Regiment, Captain HINCKLY's Company, as a private and gave other military service.

ISSUE

I. Joshua Converse JOHNSON, *b.* 26th January, 1764.
II. Noah JOHNSON.
III. Anna JOHNSON.
IV. Sally JOHNSON.
V. Elihu JOHNSON, *b.* 30th September, 1772.
VI. Guy JOHNSON, *b.* 14th May, 1775.
VII. Dolly JOHNSON, *b.* 19th October, 1777.
VIII. David JOHNSON, *b.* 21st March, 1781.
IX. ORAN JOHNSON, *b.* 29th March, 1783; *d.* 1835. (See JOHNSON.)

Kelton

LT.-COL. ROBERT HALL CAMPBELL KELTON, U. S. A.; *b.* 28th January, 1872, in San Francisco, California; *m.* 15th December, 1910, at Newburyport, Massachusetts, Edith Russell WILLS, *b.* 12th June, 1872, dau. of George Edward WILLS, *b.* 9th February, 1849, *d.* September, 1877, *m.* 19th September, 1871, Mary Ella RUSSELL, *b.* 18th January, 1853, both of Newburyport. Mrs. Edith Russell WILLS KELTON is a lineal descendant from Elder William BREWSTER, Governor Thomas PRENCE and Governor Thomas HINCKLEY of the Plymouth Colony and of Anne HUTCHINSON, of Boston. Is a member of Massachusetts Society of Mayflower Descendants and Founder and First Regent of Old Newbury Chapter, Daughters of the American Revolution.

ISSUE

I. John Cunningham Russell, *b.* 14th December, 1911.

LT.-COL. ROBERT HALL CAMPBELL KELTON was educated at Public Schools of San Francisco, California; Washington, D. C., and Washington University of the District of Columbia; commissioned Second Lieutenant, United States Artillery, 9th July, 1898; First Lieutenant, Coast Artillery Corps, December, 1902; Special Duty Pan-American Exposition, 1900-1901; awarded diploma for service; commissioned Captain, Coast Artillery Corps, United States Army, 20th December, 1902; graduated Coast Artillery School, 1903; graduated Field and Staff College, 1905. Served in Philippines, October, 1907, to December, 1909; special duty in Japan and China, 1910; commissioned Major of Coast Artillery Corps 1st July, 1916; Graduate Army War College, 1917.

Lineage

JAMES KELTON was *b.* in Scotland in 1695; *d.* 1781; went to the North of Ireland and from thence to America in 1735; he settled in Londongrove, Chester County, Pennsylvania; *m.* (firstly) in Scotland, Margaretta, surname not given, *b.* therein 1699; *m.* (secondly) Mary HACKETT, of New Garden, near Avondale, Pennsylvania.

ISSUE BY SECOND MARRIAGE

I. JAMES, *b.* 1776, of whom later.
II. Margaret, *m.* John MENOUGH.

JAMES KELTON of Londongrove, Pennsylvania; *b.* 1776; *d.* 1844; served ten years in the House of Assembly and four years in the Senate of Pennsylvania; *m.* 7th

February, 1793, Agnes MACKEY, d. 1823, dau. of Major David MACKEY of Londongrove.

ISSUE

 I. David, b. 9th November, 1793; m. Margaret TURNER.
 II. John M., b. 1st February, 1795.
 III. James, b. 1st August, 1796; m. Mary FULTON.
 IV. Mary, b. 1st May, 1798; m. David JACKSON.
 V. ROBERT, b. 4th March, 1800, of whom later.
 VI. Joseph, b. March, 1802; m. Phoebe ESSINGER.
 VII. Agnes, b. September, 1805; m. Thomas LAMBSON.
 VIII. Julia, d. young.
 IX. George, b. 24th June, 1810; m. Christian JOHNSON.
 X. Margaretta, b. 12th July, 1812; d. young.
 XI. Rachel, b. 1st December, 1814; m. Elyah MCCLENACHAN.

ROBERT KELTON of Londongrove, Pennsylvania; b. 4th March, 1800; d. 1861; m. 8th April, 1824, Margaretta Ross CUNINGHAM, b. 29th October, 1801; d. 3d April, 1885, dau. of Gen. John Welsh CUNINGHAM, b. 11th June, 1779, in New London, Pennsylvania, d. there 26th April, 1840, m. Elizabeth Ross, dau. of John and Margaret (YOUNG) ROSS.

ISSUE

 I. JOHN CUNINGHAM, b. 24th June, 1828, of whom later.
 II. James, b. 14th October, 1833; d. 24th May, 1856.
 III. Annie Elizabeth, b. 19th May, 1831; d. September, 1908.
 IV. Allen Cuningham, b. 19th March, 1836; d. 6th November, 1836.
 V. Henry Clay, b. 29th September, 1837; d. 14th September, 1838.
 VI. Robert, b. 7th July, 1841; d. 15th May, 1849.
 VII. Francis, b. 2d October, 1843; d. 17th August, 1896.
 VIII. Allen Cuningham, b. 28th June, 1846; Colonel in United States Marine Corps; m. Lottie DILLINGHAM.

ADJUTANT-GENERAL JOHN CUNINGHAM KELTON, U. S. A.; b. 24th June, 1828; d. 15th July, 1893, in Washington, D. C.; graduated United States Military Academy, 1851; June, 1851, Second Lieutenant, 6th United States Infantry; 1855, First Lieutenant; Captain, 1860; Brevet Brigadier-General, 1865; after service through entire Civil War, 1866, Lieutenant-Colonel in Adjutant-General's Department; June, 1880, Colonel in Adjutant-General's Department; 1889, Adjutant-General of the United States Army; Retired in 1892 and was appointed Governor of United States National Soldiers Home, Washington, D. C.; m. 20th April, 1870, in Dresden, Saxony, Josephine Parmly CAMBPELL, b. 4th August, 1852, in Rotterdam, Holland, dau. of Hon. William Shaw and Josephine (RABINEAU) CAMPBELL, both b. in New York. Hon. William Shaw CAMPBELL was for twenty years Consul in Rotterdam, Holland, and from 1862 to 1871 he was Consul at Dresden, being in the consular service of the United States thirty-four years; he *d.* 22d March, 1904, in Washington, D. C.

ISSUE

I. ROBERT HALL CAMPBELL, *b.* 28th January, 1872, the subject of this memoir.
II. Josephine Campbell, *b.* 26th February, 1871.
III. Margaretta Nataline, *b.* 3d January, 1873; *m.* 28th June, 1899, Thales L. AMES, Major in United States Army, son of James Furman and Mary Jane (KIRK) AMES.

ISSUE

1. Adelaide AMES, *b.* 3d June, 1900.

IV. Mary Adelaide, *b.* 20th September, 1875.
V. Anna Campbell, *b.* 8th March, 1876; *m.* 27th February, 1911, Harvey W. WILEY, M.D.
VI. John Victor, *b.* 22d March, 1882; *d.* 4th June, 1883.
VII. William Sutherland, *b.* 17th February, 1885, member Earlington Golf Club and Beta Theta Pi Fraternity; *m.* 21st December, 1910, Phoebe Owen JONES, *b.* 5th October, 1886, in Newtown, North Wales, dau. of Rev. Owen and Jane (OWEN) JONES, *m.* in London, 2d July, 1875, and came to the United States in 1887.
VIII. Atlee Sanford, *b.* 9th August, 1887; *d.* 30th November, 1909.

Arms.—Ermine, three cinque foils in fesse sable, pierced argent.
Crest.—A lion passant per pale ermine and ermines.
Residence (legal).—Washington, D. C.
Clubs.—Chevy Chase and Army and Navy, Washington, D. C., and St. Botolph of Boston. Member of the Kappa Alpha Fraternity.

Kendall

WILLIAM BEALS KENDALL of New York City; *b.* 5th January, 1857, at Charlestown, Massachusetts; *m.* 6th February, 1883, at the Church of the Transfiguration, New York City, Kate Varnum WHITNEY, dau. of Rufus Hayden WHITNEY of Westborough and Boston, Massachusetts, *b.* 25th January, 1826, *d.* 20th November, 1911, *m.* October, 1845, Emily Burton STEVENS, *b.* 21st May, 1823, *d.* 11th March, 1911. Mrs. KENDALL is a descendant of John WHITNEY of Watertown, Massachusetts, 1636, of Richard WARREN, a *Mayflower* descendant and of four Revolutionary and many Colonial soldiers. She is descended from George VARNUM who came from England in 1635 and settled near Ipswich, Massachusetts, also a gr. gd. niece of Generals James M. and Joseph B. VARNUM, both Revolutionary soldiers and the latter also Speaker of the House and President pro tem of the Senate at Washington.

ISSUE

I. William Floyd, *b.* 8th November, 1883; *m.* 19th September, 1908, Marion DOUGLAS, dau. of Harry and Anne (PAGE) DOUGLAS, dau. of the late Col. Kingman PAGE of New York City.

ISSUE

1. Douglas, *b.* 20th June, 1909.

II. Katherine Varnum, *m.* 28th September, 1907, Archibald Marshall DENNY of Pittsburgh, Pennsylvania.

ISSUE

1. Archibald Marshall DENNY, *b.* 22d August, 1908.
2. Katherine Varnum DENNY, *b.* 27th January, 1910.
3. Kendall Whitney DENNY, *b.* 8th December, 1912.

III. Marjory Stevens, *m.* 3d November, 1909, Maitland Lathrop BISHOP, of New York and Pasadena, California.

ISSUE

1. Audrey BISHOP, *b.* 7th May, 1912.
2. Maitland Lathrop BISHOP, *b.* 24th December, 1915.

IV. Elinor Whitney.

WILLIAM BEALS KENDALL was educated at Noble's School in Boston and at Lancy, Switzerland; he went to New York in December, 1880, and organized the firm of HATCH and KENDALL, bankers and brokers, with which he remained for eleven years; on 19th May, 1890, he was admitted to membership in the New York Stock Exchange and, the year following, organized the firm of KENDALL and WHITLOCK, of which he was the senior partner for twenty-two years; he has travelled much in Europe and as a boy, was in Paris during the entire siege of 1870; for several years he has been a member of the Third Panel, Sheriff's Jury.

Lineage

The KENDALL family, which is very old in England, derives its name from the town of Kendall on the Kent River in Westmoreland County; among the best known of its early representatives was John KENDALL, Sheriff of Nottingham, who was killed at the Battle of Bosworth 1485, while fighting in the army of Richard III. Branches of the family are found in many parts of England and America.

JOHN KENDALL, ancestor of the New England family, was living in Cambridgeshire, England, in 1646, and *d.* there in 1660.

ISSUE

I. FRANCIS, *b.* circa 1620, of whom later.
II. Thomas, emigrated to Reading, Massachusetts, where he was one of the most influential of the early settlers; a Deacon of the church and for many years a Selectman; his only son *d.* an infant, but, through his eight daughters, he has a large posterity.

FRANCIS KENDALL, *b.* in England, circa 1620; came to America and was living at Charlestown, Massachusetts, in 1640; he emigrated under the name of MILES in order, it is said, to conceal his intentions from his family. At Charlestown he signed the town orders for the new town of Woburn and was one of its first and most prominent inhabitants, serving for eighteen years on the Board of Selectmen and on various town Committees. He owned and operated a mill on one of the streams at Woburn and is described by Sewell, as "a gentleman of great respectability and influence in the place of his residence." In a strict Puritan community, he had the courage to differ slightly in faith from the majority for which he was duly fined. He *m.* 24th December, 1644; Mary, dau. of Sergt. John TIDD, the first man in Woburn to bear a military title. Francis KENDALL *d.* in 1708, at the age of 88. His wife *d.* in 1705.

ISSUE

I. John, *b.* 2d July, 1646; *d.* circa 1732; a soldier in King Philip's War; *m.* (firstly) 1668, Hannah BARTLETT, dau. of Ensign Thomas BARTLETT; *m.* (secondly) 1681, Elizabeth COMEY; *m.* (thirdly) Eunice (BROOKS) CARTER, widow of Samuel CARTER, eldest son of Rev.

Thomas CARTER, Woburn's first pastor. She dau. of John BROOKS who, at the age of 67, was a soldier under Phipps in the expedition to Quebec.

II. Thomas, b. 10th January, 1648–1649; d. 1730; m. (firstly) 1673, Ruth BLODGETT, dau. of Samuel and Ruth (EGGLEDEN) BLODGETT; m. (secondly) 1696, Abigail (RAYNOR) BROUGHTON, widow of Capt. John BROUGHTON and dau. of Rev. John RAYNOR. He was gd. father of Rev. Samuel KENDALL, Harvard College, 1731, of New Salem and gr. gd. father of Rev. Samuel KENDALL, Harvard College, 1782, of Weston. Another gd. son, Ephraim KENDALL, was a soldier and d. in the French and Indian War in 1758.

III. Mary, b. 20th January, 1650–1651; m. Israel REED, son of William and Mabel (KENDALL) REED, son of Sir Thomas REED, Bart., of Brocket Hall, Herts, England.

IV. Elizabeth, b. 15th January, 1652–1653; d. 1715; m. (firstly) 1675, Ensign Ephraim WINSHIP, son of Lieut. Edward WINSHIP of Cambridge; m. (secondly) Joseph PIERCE of Watertown.

V. Hannah, b. 26th January, 1654–1655; m. William GREEN, Jr., of Woburn.

VI. Rebekah, b. 2d March, 1657; d. 1690; m. 1678, Joshua EATON, Selectman and Representative to the General Court from Woburn, son of Jonas and Grace EATON.

VII. Samuel, b. 8th March, 1659–1660; d. 1749; m. (firstly) 1683, Rebecca MIXER of Watertown, dau. of Isaac and Rebecca (GARFIELD) MIXER, her uncle, Benjamin GARFIELD was a direct ancestor of President GARFIELD; m. (secondly) 1692, Mary LOCKE, dau. of Deacon William and Mary (CLARK) LOCKE of Woburn, she was aunt of Samuel LOCKE, Eleventh President of Harvard College.

VIII. JACOB, b. 25th January, 1660–1661, of whom later.

IX. Abigail, b. 6th April, 1666; m. 1686, Capt. William REED, Selectman, Justice of the Peace and Representative to the General Court; son of George REED of Woburn.

JACOB KENDALL, b. 25th January, 1660–1661, at Woburn; lived at Woburn and Dunstable, Massachusetts; m. (firstly) 2d January, 1683–1684, Persis HAYWOOD. who d. 19th October, 1694; m. (secondly) 10th January, 1694–1695, Alice TEMPLE, widow of Christopher TEMPLE of Dunstable, who was killed by the Indians in 1691, and dau. of Richard HASSELL, an early resident of Cambridge and afterwards of Dunstable.

ISSUE BY FIRST MARRIAGE

I. Persis, b. 24th August, 1685; m. Timothy REED of Woburn, and d. 16th September, 1748.

II. Jacob (twin), b. and d. 1686–1687.

III. Jacob (twin), b. 12th January, 1686–1687; lived at Billerica, Massachusetts, and Litchfield, New Hampshire, where he was Selectman; d. 1742; m. Alice HASSELL, dau. of Christopher and Alice HASSELL.

COLONIAL FAMILIES OF THE UNITED STATES 329

IV. JOSEPH, b. 17th December, 1688, of whom later.
V. Jonathan, b. and d. 1690.
VI. Daniel, b. 23d October, 1691, lived in Dunstable.

ISSUE BY SECOND MARRIAGE

I. Ebenezer, b. 9th November, 1695.
II. John, b. 9th January, 1696–1697; d. 1759; settled at Dunstable, where he was Selectman; m. 1718, Deborah RICHARDSON, dau. of John and Deborah RICHARDSON and gr. gd. dau. of Ezekiel RICHARDSON, one of the seven commissioners who founded Woburn. A son, Temple KENDALL, was a Lieutenant in the Revolution and took part in the battle of Bunker Hill. Another son, Lieut. John KENDALL was gd. father of the Hon. Amos KENDALL of Kentucky, Lawyer, Journalist, Philanthropist and Statesman, Postmaster-General under President Jackson.
III. Sarah, b. 18th July, 1698; m. 1723, Benjamin WHITTEMORE, son of John and Ruth (BASSET) WHITTEMORE of Malden, Massachusetts, and gr. gd. son of Thomas WHITTEMORE of Hitchin, Hertfordshire, England.
IV. Esther, b. 20th November, 1699.
V. Hezekiah, b. 26th May, 1701.
VI. Nathan, b. 12th December, 1702; one of the early settlers of Litchfield, New Hampshire, where he had a family.
VII. Susanna, b. 27th October, 1704.
VIII. Phebe, b. 19th December, 1706.
IX. David, b. 28th September, 1708.

JOSEPH KENDALL, b. at Woburn, 17th December, 1688; m. (firstly) Susanna, surname unknown, who d. 23d December, 1727; m. (secondly) Mercy, surname unknown, who d. 6th March, 1789, aged 83; he lived in the Shawshine District of Woburn, now the town of Burlington and d. 3d October, 1743.

ISSUE BY FIRST MARRIAGE

I. Jonathan, b. 29th October, 1718; d. before 3d October, 1743.
II. JOSHUA, b. 7th March, 1720, of whom later.
III. Mary, b. 6th January, 1723; m. 1746, Ignatius MARION, son of Isaac and Rebekah (KNIGHT) MARION of Boston, and a descendant of John MARION of Watertown, 1640, who was Selectman of Boston in 1693.

ISSUE BY SECOND MARRIAGE

I. Susanna, d. 2d August, 1807; m. Amos REED.
II. Joseph, b. 9th July, 1730; a soldier in the Revolution; m. three times.
III. Oliver, b. 10th August, 1734.
IV. Jacob, b. 9th October, 1738; m. 1761, Keziah JOHNSON, and a descendant of Maj. William JOHNSON, Assistant in the Colonial Government and Major in the Militia, son of Capt. Edward JOHNSON, Soldier,

Explorer and the first Historian of the colony. After the death of Jacob KENDALL, his widow *m.* 1779, Amos WYMAN and again in 1799, Ebenezer RICHARDSON as his seventh wife.

v. Esther, *b.* 25th November, 1740.
vi. Sarah, *b.* 5th March, 1743; *m.* 1762, Capt. Reuben KIMBALL, a Revolutionary soldier, son of Richard and Susanna (BALCH) KIMBALL and of the sixth generation of the old family founded in America by Richard KIMBALL.

JOSHUA KENDALL, *b.* 7th March, 1720; *m.* (firstly) 1745, Esther BUCK, dau. of John and Priscilla BUCK of Woburn and gr. gr. gd. dau. of William BUCK of Cambridge, who came to New England in the ship *Increase* in 1635; *m.* (secondly) 2d May, 1753, Susanna JOHNSON; he lived in the present town of Burlington, then part of Woburn and was a soldier in the Revolution; *d.* 9th February, 1810, in his ninetieth year.

ISSUE BY FIRST MARRIAGE

I. Joshua, *b.* 9th February, 1746; sesttled in East Sudbury; *m.* 6th December, 1770, Mary RUTTER, dau. of Joseph and Mary RUTTER; he was a Corporal in Colonel PIERCE's Regiment at the battle of Lexington.
II. Jonathan, *b.* 4th June, 1749; *d.* in infancy.
III. JONATHAN, *b.* 1st September, 1751, of whom later.

ISSUE BY SECOND MARRIAGE

I. Susanna, *b.* 25th January, 1754.
II. Benjamin, *b.* 16th March, 1756; *m.* 1780, Elizabeth DEAN.
III. Oliver, *b.* 14th November, 1759.
IV. Rebecca, *b.* 5th February, 1763.
V. Joel, *b.* 16th December, 1766.
VI. Daniel, *b.* 8th August, 1771.
VII. William, *b.* 14th July, 1774; *m.* 1797, Ruth SKELTON.

JONATHAN KENDALL, *b.* at Woburn, 1st September, 1751; *d.* 15th February, 1796; he was a Fifer in the Woburn Company in the Revolution; *m.* 1st December, 1774, Joanna BROOKS, dau. of Isaac and Joanna (HOLDEN) BROOKS of Woburn, she was of the sixth generation of the family founded by Henry BROOKS who settled at Concord, Massachusetts, in 1639, and soon after became one of the first settlers of Woburn.

ISSUE

I. Isaac, *b.* 19th February, 1777; *m.* 1805, Lucy SABELLS of Boston and was the father of Isaac KENDALL of Charlestown, Massachusetts, who *m.* Nancy BRADFORD, a descendant of Governor William BRADFORD, who came on the *Mayflower*.

COLONIAL FAMILIES OF THE UNITED STATES

II. Joanna, *b.* 9th May, 1779.
III. LOAMMI, *b.* 12th June, 1781, of whom later.
IV. Sally, *b.* 12th April, 1783.

LOAMMI KENDALL, *b.* 12th June, 1781; lived at Charlestown, Massachusetts, where he was an eminent Freemason; *m.* 23d July, 1808, Nancy L. ROBERTS.

ISSUE

I. Eliza B., *b.* 9th July, 1809; *m.* 1827, William TUFTS, son of Nathan and Deborah (FROTHINGHAM) TUFTS, Secretary of the Massachusetts Mutual Insurance Company.

ISSUE

1. William Clark TUFTS, *b.* 11th September, 1829.
2. Helen E. TUFTS, *m.* Charles T. CROCKER, son of Alvah CROCKER who was first President of the Fitchburg Railroad and a Manufacturer and Capitalist of Fitchburg, Massachusetts.
3. Emma TUFTS, *b.* 15th December, 1848; *m.* James ADAMS, Jr., third Mayor of Charlestown and President of the Warren Institution for Savings.

II. Loammi, *b.* 23d December, 1810.
III. ISAAC, *b.* 19th September, 1812, of whom later.
IV. Mary Ann, *b.* 14th December, 1814; *d.* 12th May, 1876.

ISAAC KENDALL, *b.* 19th September, 1812; a wealthy shipping merchant of Charlestown, Massachusetts; *m.* 1853, Elizabeth Bishop BEAL, dau. of William and Dolly (WHITNEY) BEAL of Boston. She was of the seventh generation of the family of John BEAL of Hingham, Norfolk, England and Hingham, Massachusetts. Her father, William BEALS, was for many years, publisher of the *Boston Post* and was son of Joshua BEAL, a Revolutionary soldier. Dolly WHITNEY was daughter of Silas WHITNEY who was in Colonel BROOK'S Regiment at the battle of White Plains, and gd. daughter of Sergt. Daniel WHITNEY, also a Revolutionary soldier. The WHITNEY family, long prominent in Herefordshire, England, was founded in America in 1636, by John WHITNEY, one of the first settlers of Watertown, Massachusetts.

ISSUE

I. Mary Elizabeth, *m.* 14th October, 1880, Rev. Samuel Clark BUSHNELL of Madison, Connecticut, and Arlington, Massachusetts, son of Cornelius Scranton BUSHNELL, who made possible the building of the warship *Monitor* and was part owner of her at the time of her fight with the *Merrimac*.

ISSUE

1. Alice Kendall BUSHNELL, *b.* June, 1887.
2. Samuel Kendall BUSHNELL, *b.* 29th May, 1892.

II. WILLIAM BEALS, *b.* 5th January, 1857, the subject of this memoir.
III. Alice Louise, *m.* 4th June, 1891, Rev. Daniel Hoffman MARTIN, A.B., of the College of the City of New York, 1881, graduate of Union Theological Seminary 1884 and D.D. Ursinus College, 1896, son of Abraham and Katherine (HOFFMAN) MARTIN.

ISSUE

1. Elizabeth Kendall MARTIN, *d.* in infancy.
2. Katherine Kendall MARTIN, *b.* June, 1894.
3. Anna Louise MARTIN, *b.* April, 1896.

Arms.—Gules a fesse chequy or and azure between three eagles displayed of the second.
Crest.—An eagle displayed or.
Motto.—Virtus depressa resurget.
Residenze.—41 West Eleventh Street, New York City.
Clubs.—Players, Westchester Country, Racquet.

Livingston

JOHN HENRY LIVINGSTON of Clermont, New York; b. at Oak Hill, Columbia County, New York; 8th July, 1848; graduated at Columbia, 1869; LL.B., 1871; admitted to the Bar, 1871.

Lineage

REVEREND ALEXANDER LIVINGSTON who d. 1597, was a son of James LIVINGSTON, killed at the Battle of Pinkie, 1547, who was the second son of William, third Lord Livingston of Callendar, who m. circa 1500, Agnes HEPBURN. He was one of the very earliest ministers of the Reformed Church in Scotland; presented by William, sixth Lord Livingston, to the Rectory of Monyabroch (now Kilsyth) County, Stirling, August, 1560, m. Barbara LIVINGSTON. (See "Livingstons of Livingston Manor" by E. B. Livingston, pages 3-6, and 13; as well as "Select Biographies," Volume I, page 130, printed for the Wodrow Society in 1845 at Edinburgh.

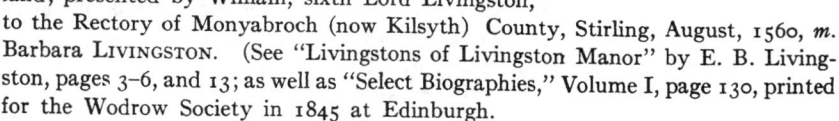

ISSUE

1. WILLIAM, b. 1576, of whom below.

WILLIAM LIVINGSTON, b. 1576; d. before October, 1641; graduated at Glasgow, University, 1595; instituted to the Rectory of Monyabroch, 15th July, 1599; deprived for opposing the Restoration of Episcopacy, 1613, but was soon after, 1st October, 1613, appointed minister at Lanark; m. Agnes LIVINGSTON, who d. 1617, dau. of Alexander LIVINGSTON of Falkirk.

ISSUE BY FIRST MARRIAGE

1. JOHN, b. at Monyabroch (Kilsyth) Scotland, 21st June, 1603, of whom below.

REV. JOHN LIVINGSTON, b. at Monyabroch (Kilsyth) Scotland, 21st June, 1603; d. at Rotterdam, Holland, between 14th and 21st August, 1672; graduated at the University of Glasgow, 1621; licensed to preach, 1625; ordained, 1630; instituted as Minister at Ancrum, 1648; one of three Delegates sent by the "Committee of Estates" to Breda to treat with Charles II as to his restoration, etc.; m. at Edinburgh, 23d June, 1635, Janet FLEMING, dau. of Bartholomew and Marion (HAMILTON) FLEMING of that well known family, of which the head at that time was the Earl of Wigton, who together with his son Lord FLEMING was present at their wedding.

ISSUE

I. John, b. in Ireland, 30th June, 1636; d. 8th January, 1639.
II. William, b. at Lanark, 7th January, 1638; Clerk to the Sessions, Edinburgh; m. 23d December, 1663, Ann VEITCH, was buried in Grey-Friars Burial Ground, 12th June, 1700.
III. Bartholomew, b. 3d September, 1639; d. 24th September, 1641.
IV. Agnes, b. 20th September, 1640; d. 17th October, 1641.
V. Marion, b. 10th October, 1642; m. 28th September, 1658, Rev. John SCOTT, Minister at Hawick, d. in July, 1661 or 1667 (?).
VI. Janet, b. 28th September, 1643; m. Andrew RUSSELL, of Rotterdam, d. in August, 1696.
VII. John, b. 20th August, 1644; d. October, 1645.
VIII. Agnes, b. 18th August, 1645.
IX. James, b. 22d September, 1646; m. twice; buried 4th June, 1700, had issue. He was the father of Robert LIVINGSTON who is usually known as "The Nephew" to distinguish him from Robert LIVINGSTON, his uncle and the first Lord of the Manor of Livingston.
X. Joanna, b. September, 1647; d. October, 1648.
XI. Barbara, b. 21st June, 1648; m. ———— MILLER; had issue.
XII. John, b. 29th June, 1652; d. 12th October, 1652.
XIII. Andrew, b. August, 1653; d. February, 1655.
XIV. ROBERT, b. 13th December, 1654, of whom later.
XV. Elizabeth, b. 10th December, 1657; d. 31st October, 1666.

HON. ROBERT LIVINGSTON of Albany, New York; b. 13th December, 1654, at Ancrum, Edinburgh, North Britain; d. 1st October, 1728; emigrated to America, 1673; settled first at Charlestown, Massachusetts, and afterwards, in 1674, at Albany, New York, where he soon became prominent, holding numerous official positions, being Member of the Colonial Assembly, 1709–1725, and Speaker from 1718; having gradually acquired the Indian title to a large tract of land on the east side of the Hudson River, he obtained a patent from Governor Thomas DONGAN in 1686, which was confirmed by Royal Charter in 1715, erecting the manor and lordship of Livingston, with advowdson and other manorial rights; m. 9th July, 1679, Alida (SCHUYLER) VAN RENSSELAER, dau. of Philip Pieterse SCHUYLER and widow of the Rev. Nicholas VAN RENSSELAER.

ISSUE

I. John, b. 26th April, 1680, Colonel; d. 19th February, 1720; m. (firstly) Mary WINTHROP, dau. of Fitz John WINTHROP, Governor of Connecticut, 1698–1707; m. (secondly) Elizabeth KNIGHT, dau. of a Mrs. Sarah KNIGHT.
II. Margaret, b. 5th December, 1681; m. 20th December, 1700, Colonel VETCH, first English Governor of Annapolis Royal; d. June, 1758.
III. Joanna Philippina, b. 1st February, 1684; d. 24th January, 1689–1690.

IV. PHILIP, b. 9th July, 1686, of whom later.
V. Robert, b. 24th July, 1688, first Proprietor of Clermont; m. 11th November, 1717, Margaret HOWARDEN of New York; d. 27th June, 1775.

ISSUE

1. Robert R., b. in New York, August, 1718; d. 9th December, 1775; Judge of the Admiralty Court, 1760; Justice of New York Supreme Court, 1763; Member of the Provincial Assembly, 1759–1768; m. 8th December, 1742, Margaret BEEKMAN, dau. of Col. Henry BEEKMAN.

ISSUE

1^1. Janet, b. 27th August, 1743; d. 6th November, 1828; m. 24th July, 1773, Gen. Richard MONTGOMERY who was killed at the storming of Quebec, 31st December, 1775.
2^1. Catherine, b. 20th February, 1845; d. 29th April, 1752.
3^1. Robert R., b. in New York, 27th November, 1746; one of the most distinguished men of his day in America; admitted to the Bar, 1773; Member of the Continental Congress of 1775–1776–1779–1780–1784; one of the Committee of Five appointed to draw up the Declaration of Independence; Member of the Provincial Congress, 1775–1777; Chancellor of the State of New York, 1777–1801; Secretary of Foreign Affairs, 1781–1783; Member of the New York Convention of 1788; Minister to France, 1801–1803; Negotiator of the Louisiana Purchase; m. 9th September, 1770, Mary STEVENS, dau. of John STEVENS of Hunterdon, New Jersey; d. at Clermont, 26th February, 1813.

ISSUE

1^2. Elizabeth Stevens, b. 5th May, 1780; d. 10th June, 1829; m. 20th November, 1799, Edward Philip LIVINGSTON, Lieutenant-Governor of New York, 1830, State Senator, and gd. son of Philip LIVINGSTON, one of the Signers of the Declaration of Independence; had issue.
2^2. Margaret Maria, b. 11th April, 1783; d. 8th March, 1818; m. 10th July, 1799, Robert L. LIVINGSTON; had issue.

4^1. Margaret, b. 6th January, 1749; d. at Rhinebeck, New York, 19th March, 1823; m. 22d February, 1779, Dr. Thomas TILLOTSON of Maryland, Surgeon-General, Northern Department, Continental Army.
5^1. Henry Beekman, b. 9th November, 1750; Colonel 4th New York Regiment, Continental Army; d. 5th November, 1831; m. 11th March, 1781, Anne Hume SHIPPEN, a dau. of Dr. William SHIPPEN.

336   COLONIAL FAMILIES OF THE UNITED STATES

6^1. Catherine, *b.* 14th October, 1752; *d.* 14th July, 1849; *m.* 30th June, 1793, Rev. Freeborn GARRETSON.

7^1. John R., of Massena, Dutchess County, New York; *b.* 13th February, 1755; *d.* 25th September, 1851; *m.* (firstly) 1779, Margaret SHEAFFE, who *d.* 1784; *m.* (secondly) 30th May, 1789, Eliza McEVERS, dau. of Charles McEVERS of New York.

8^1. Gertrude, *b.* 16th April, 1757; *m.* 11th May, 1779, Gen. Morgan LEWIS, Governor of the State of New York, 1804; *d.* 9th March, 1833.

9^1. Joanna, *b.* 14th September, 1759; *d.s.p.* 1st March, 1829; *m.* Peter R. LIVINGSTON, Speaker of New York Assembly, 1823, President of the Senate, 1828.

10^1. Alida, *b.* 24th December, 1761; *d.* 24th December, 1822; *m.* 19th January, 1785, Gen. John ARMSTRONG, United States Minister to France, 1804–1810, who *d.* 1st April, 1843.

11^1. Edward, *b.* 28th May, 1764; *d.* 23d May, 1836; at Montgomery Place, Dutchess County, New York; Member of Congress, 1795–1801; United States Attorney, New York, and Mayor, New York City, 1801; moved to New Orleans, 1803; Member of Congress 1822–1829; United States Secretary of State, 1831; Minister to France, 1833; *m.* (firstly) 10th April, 1788, Mary McEVERS, dau. of Charles McEVERS, *d.* 13th March, 1801; *m.* (secondly) 3d June, 1805, Louise (DE CASTERA) DE LASSY, dau. of Jean D'Avezac DE CASTERA of New Orleans, and widow of Capt. Moreau DE LASSY.

VI. Gilbert, *b.* 3d March, 1690; *d.* 25th April, 1746; *m.* 22d December, 1711; Cornelia BEEKMAN, *b.* 18th June, 1693; *d.* 24th June, 1742, dau. of Henry BEEKMAN; had issue.

VII. William, *b.* 17th March, 1692; *d.* 5th November, 1692.

VIII. Johanna, *b.* 10th December 1694; *m.* Cornelius Gerrit VAN HORNE.

IX. Catherine, *b.* 22d May, 1698; *d.* 6th December, 1699.

PHILIP LIVINGSTON of Albany, New York; *b.* there 9th of July, 1686; *d.* at New York, 4th February, 1749; second Lord of the Manor of Livingston; Secretary for Indian Affairs, 1722; Clerk of the County of Albany, 1721–1749; Member of the Provincial Council, 1724–1749; *m.* 19th September, 1707, Catherine VAN BRUGH, dau. of Peter VAN BRUGH.

ISSUE

I. Robert, third Lord of the Manor of Livingston; *b.* 16th December, 1708; *d.* 27th November, 1790; Member of the House of Assembly, 1737–1759; *m.* (firstly) Mary TONG, *b.* 3d June, 1711, *d.* 30th May, 1765, dau. of Walter TONG, and had issue; *m.* (secondly) Gertrude (VAN RENSSELAER) SCHUYLER, *b.* 1st October, 1714, *d.* 1790, dau. of Kiliaen VAN RENSSELAER and widow of Adoniah SCHUYLER.

II. Peter Van Brugh of New York City, *bapt.* 3d November, 1710; *d.* 1793; graduated at Yale, 1731; Member of the Committee of One Hundred, 1775; Member and first President of Provincial Congress, 1775; *m.* November, 1739, Mary ALEXANDER, *b.* 16th October, 1721, *d.* 27th September, 1769, sister of William ALEXANDER, Lord Stirling. They had 12 children. (See page 549 of "The Livingstons of Livingston Manor."

III. Peter, *bapt.* 20th April, 1712; *d.* young.

IV. John, *bapt.* at Albany, 11th April, 1714; *d.* 1778; *m.* 3d December, 1742, Catherine DE PEYSTER, dau. of Abraham DE PEYSTER; had issue.

V. PHILIP, *b.* 15th January, 1716, of whom later.

VI. Henry, *bapt.* 5th April, 1719; *d.s.p.* in Jamaica, West Indies, 1772.

VII. Sarah, *bapt.* 2d May, 1721; *d.* October, 1722.

VIII. William, *b.* 8th November, 1723; *d.* 25th July, 1790; graduate of Yale, 1741; Member of the Provincial Assembly, 1759–1761; Governor of New Jersey, 1776–1790, LL.D., 1788; *m.* circa 1745, Susannah FRENCH, *bapt.* 19th June, 1723, *d.* 17th July, 1789.

IX. Sarah, *bapt.* 7th November, 1725; *d.* March, 1805; *m.* 1st March, 1748, William ALEXANDER, Lord Stirling; had issue.

X. Alida, *bapt.* 18th July, 1728; *d.* February, 1790; *m.* (firstly) 26th September, 1750, Henry HANSEN; *m.* (secondly) 26th September, 1766, Col. Martin HOFFMAN; had issue.

XI. Catherine, *bapt.* 15th April, 1733; *m.* 18th April, 1759, John L. LAWRENCE.

PHILIP LIVINGSTON of New York City, *b.* 15th January, 1716; *d.* 12th June, 1778; graduated at Yale, 1737; Alderman of New York, 1754–1763; Member of the Provincial Assembly, 1759–1769; Speaker, 1768; Signer of the Declaration of Independence, 1776; State Senator, 1777; *m.* 14th April, 1740, Christina TEN BROECK, dau. of Col. Dirck TEN BROECK, *b.* 30th December, 1718, *d.* 29th June, 1801.

ISSUE

I. PHILIP PHILIP, *b.* 28th May, 1741 of whom later.

II. Dirck, or Richard, *b.* 6th June, 1743; *d.* unmarried.

III. Catherine, *bapt.* 25th August, 1745; *d.* 17th April, 1810; *m.* (firstly) 23d January, 1764, Stephen VAN RENSSELAER; *m.* (secondly) 19th July, 1775, Dominie Eilardus WESTERLO.

IV. Margaret, *bapt.* 26th October, 1747; *d.* 17th January, 1830; *m.* 30th July, 1776, Thomas JONES, M.D.

V. Peter Van Brugh, *bapt.* 13th March, 1751; *d.* unmarried in Jamaica, West Indies.

VI. Sarah, *b.* 7th December, 1752; *d.* 29th December, 1814; *m.* 26th November, 1775, her cousin, Rev. John Henry LIVINGSTON, D.D., President of Queen's College, New Jersey, *b.* 30th May, 1746, *d.* 20th January, 1825.

338 COLONIAL FAMILIES OF THE UNITED STATES

VII. Abraham, *bapt.* 3d July, 1754; *d.* unmarried in 1782; Commissary to the American Army during the War of Independence.
VIII. Alida, *bapt.* 3d August, 1757; *d.* unmarried.
IX. Henry Philip, Captain in Washington's Life Guards; *bapt.* 26th March, 1760; *d.* unmarried.

PHILIP PHILIP LIVINGSTON, *b.* at Albany, New York, 28th May, 1741; *d.* 2d November, 1787; settled in Jamaica, West Indies, before 1768; *m.* 29th June, 1768, Sarah JOHNSON, *b.* 23d March, 1749, *d.* 6th November, 1802, dau. of Thomas JOHNSON, of St. Elizabeth Parish, Jamaica, West Indies; had issue.

ISSUE

I. Philip Henry, *b.* 30th October, 1769; *d.* December, 1831; *m.* 8th May, 1788, Maria LIVINGSTON, dau. of Walter LIVINGSTON of Teviotdale, Columbia County, New York, *d.* August, 1828.
II. George, *b.* 14th October, 1771.
III. Catherine, *b.* 13th October, 1772; *d.* 20th March, 1819; *m.* 13th October, 1796, John SANDERS of New York, who *d.* in Jamaica, West Indies, December, 1818.
IV. Christina, *b.* 26th September, 1774; *d.* 24th August, 1841; *m.* 29th March, 1797, John N. McCOMB.
V. Sarah, *b.* 29th February, 1776; *d.* 12th April, 1797.
VI. Henry, *b.* 13th May, 1777; *d.* young.
VII. EDWARD PHILIP, *b.* 24th November, 1779, of whom later.
VIII. Jasper Hall, *b.* 3d December, 1780; *d.* 9th August, 1835; *m.* 14th July, 1802, Eliza LIVINGSTON, *b.* 15th February, 1786, *d.* 25th October, 1860, dau. of Col. Henry Brockholst LIVINGSTON, Judge of the Supreme Court of the United States.
IX. Washington, *b.* 6th July, 1783; *d.* in infancy.
X. Maria Margaret, *b.* 30th December, 1787; *d.* 3d September, 1791.

EDWARD PHILIP LIVINGSTON of New York; *b.* in Jamaica, West Indies, 24th November, 1779; *d.* 3d November, 1843; Lieutenant-Governor of New York, 1830; *m.* 20th November, 1799, his cousin Elizabeth Stevens LIVINGSTON, *b.* 5th May, 1780, *d.* 10th June, 1829, eldest dau. of Robert R. LIVINGSTON of Clermont, Chancellor of New York.

ISSUE

I. Robert Clermont, *b.* 10th June, 1802; *d.* July, 1802.
II. Mary, *b.* 20th August, 1804; *d.* 3d April, 1819.
III. Robert Clermont, *b.* 27th September, 1806; *d.* April, 1811.
IV. Margaret, *b.* 17th August, 1808; *d.* 28th April, 1874; *m.* 4th October, 1827, David Augustus CLARKSON, son of Thomas Sheatfield and Elizabeth (VAN HORNE) CLARKSON, *b.* 6th September, 1793, *d.* 24th November, 1850; had issue.

COLONIAL FAMILIES OF THE UNITED STATES

v. Edward, *b.* 11th October, 1810; *d.* March, 1815.
vi. Catherine (twin), *b.* 10th October, 1813; *d.* June 1815.
vii. Elizabeth (twin), *b.* 10th October, 1813; *d.* 25th January, 1896; *m.* January, 1833, Edward Hunter LUDLOW, son of Gabriel Ver Planck and Elizabeth (HUNTER) LUDLOW, *b.* 3d August, 1810, *d.* 27th November, 1884; had issue.
viii. Emma, *b.* 29th September, 1815; *d.* 24th July, 1828.
ix. CLERMONT, *b.* 4th September, 1817; *d.* 4th November, 1895; of whom later.
x. Robert Edward of Northwood, Columbia County, New York; *b.* 23d May, 1820; *d.* 20th January, 1889; *m.* 19th December, 1854, Susan Maria Clarkson DE PEYSTER, dau. of Capt. James Ferguson and Susan Maria (CLARKSON) DE PEYSTER.

ISSUE

1. Catherine Goodhue.
2. Robert R., of Northwood, New York; *b.* 8th February, 1858; *d.* 16th April, 1899; *m.* 15th April, 1884, Mary TAILER, dau. of Edward N. TAILER of New York.

ISSUE

1¹. Robert Reginald, *b.* 4th August, 1888.
2¹. Laura Suffern, *m.* 6th September, 1914, Howland Shippen DAVIS, son of Howland and Anna (SHIPPEN) DAVIS of New York.

3. Edward de Peyster, *b.* 6th March, 1861.
4. Goodhue, *m.* 8th April, 1896, Louisa ROBB, dau. of James Hampden ROBB of New York.

xi. Mary, *b.* 23d June, 1823; *d.* 17th November, 1898; *m.* 17th June, 1849, Levinus CLARKSON, son of Levinus and Ann Mary (VAN HORNE) CLARKSON, *b.* 30th August, 1813; *d.* 14th August, 1861; had issue.

CLERMONT LIVINGSTON of Clermont, New York; *b.* 4th September, 1817; *d.* 4th November, 1895; *m.* (firstly 8th October, 1844, Cornelia LIVINGSTON, *b.* 29th February, 1824, *d.* 21st September, 1851, dau. of Herman LIVINGSTON and Sarah (HALLETT) LIVINGSTON, of Oak Hill, New York.

ISSUE

i. Mary, *b.* 14th August, 1845; *d.* 26th July, 1876; *m.* 7th September, 1864, Frederick DE PEYSTER, *b.* 13th December, 1842, *d.* 30th October, 1874, son of Gen. John Watts and Estelle (LIVINGSTON) DE PEYSTER.
ii. JOHN HENRY, *b.* 8th July, 1848, the subject of this memoir.

Residence.—Clermont (Post Office Tivoli-on-Hudson), New York.

Arms.—Quarterly, first and fourth argent, three cinquefoils gules, within a double treasure flory counter flory vert; second and third sable a bend between six billets, or.

Crest.—A demi-Hercules wreathed about the head and middle, holding in the dexter hand a club erect, and in the sinister a serpent all proper.

Motto.—Si Je Puis.

Club.—University, New York.

Societies.—Cincinnati, Colonial Wars, President of the Order of Colonial Lords of Manors in America, New York Branch Sons of the Revolution, St. Nicholas.

Lyman

GEORGE ALEXANDER LYMAN of Claremont, California; *b.* 26th June, 1838, in Winchester, New Hampshire; *m.* 13th February, 1865, Mary Eliza JONES, *b.* 31st August, 1839, dau. of James A. and Margaret JONES of Lee Center, Illinois.

ISSUE

I. James Alexander, M.A. Beloit; Ph.D., Johns Hopkins; *b.* 17th October 1866, Instructor at one time of chemistry in Portland Academy, Portland, Oregon; now Professor of Physics and Chemistry in Pomona College, Claremont, California; *m.* 7th June, 1897, Ethel Anna SKINNER of Portland, Oregon, dau. of Porter N. and Florence SKINNER of Portland, Oregon.

ISSUE

1. Mary Ethel, *b.* 8th July, 1899.
2. Ida Grace, *b.* 14th April, 1902.
3. George Porter, *b.* 26th May, 1905.

II. George Richard, B.A., Beloit; Ph.D., Harvard; *b.* 1st December 1871; for ten years Professor of Botany, Dartmouth College, Hanover, New Hampshire; now Pathological Inspector, United States, Department of Agriculture Washington, D. C.; *m.* 23d June, 1903, Frances Ellen BADGER, dau. of Warren H. and Emma BADGER of Dixon, Illinois.

ISSUE

1. Mavis Katherine, *b.* 15th October, 1907.

GEORGE ALEXANDER LYMAN, *b.* 26th June, 1838, in Winchester, New Hampshire; was educated in the Northfield Institute, Northfield, Massachusetts; went to Illinois with his parents in 1856; after the Civil War he took up the work of newspaper editor and publisher in Amboy, Illinois, retiring from the business in 1914, and is now living in Claremont, California; he served the City of Amboy as postmaster for sixteen years; was one of the founders of the Baronial Order of Runnemede.

Lineage

WODIN, or ODIN (Roman Othinus), King of North Europe in the third century, about 225 A.D.; *m.* Frea or Frigga. Their son named
  BELDEG, or BALDER, *m.* Nama, daughter of Gewan, and had
  BRENDIUS, or BRANDS, who was father of
  FORDIGARUS, or FROETHGAR, who was father of
  WIGGER, who had
  GEWESIUS or GEWISCH, who had

Effa, or Esta, who had
Effa, who had
Eliseus, who had
Cerdic, first king of West Saxons, died A.D. 534, and had
Kenric, or Cynric, crowned 514, d. 560, and had
Cheanlin, crowned 560, and had
Cuthwin, killed in battle with Britons 584, and had
Cuth, who had
Chelwald, who had
Kenred, who had
Ingels, or Ingeld, who had
Eoppa or Offa, who had
Easa, who had
Alkmund, or Athemuna, who had
Egbert, who m. Redbeurga, and had
Ethelwulf, d. 858; m. Osburga, dau. of Oslac the Thane, and they were the parents of
Alfred the Great, King of England; m. Ethelbith, dau. of Earl Ethelran, and had
Edward the Elder, King of England, who m. Edgine, dau. of Earl Sigellane, and had
Princess Edgina (widow of Charles III, King of France), who m. (secondly) Henry, third Count of Vermandois and Troyes, and had
Hubert, fourth Count of Vermandois and Tryoes, who m. Adelheid, dau. of Count de Valois, and had
Adela, Countess de Vermandois, m. Hugh, son of Henry I, King of France, and had
Lady Isabel de Vermandois, m. (firstly), Robert, first Baron re Bellemont, created Earl of Leicester and Mellent, and had
Robert, second Earl of Leicester, Lord Chief Justice of England, m. Lady Amicia de Waer, and had
Robert, third Earl of Leicester, Steward of England, d. 1196; m. Petronella, dau. of Hugh de Grentesmesmil, and had
Lady Margaret de Bellomont, who m. Saier de Quincy, created Earl of Winchester in 1207 and was one of the twenty-five barons who forced King John to sign Magna Charta in 1219, and had
Roger, second Earl of Winchester, Constable of Scotland, d. 1264, m. (firstly) Helen, dau. of Alan, Lord of Galloway, and had
Lady Elizabeth de Quincey, who m. Alexander, Baron Cumyn, second Earl Buchan, Son of Margery, Countess of Buchan and William, Baron Cumyn, son of Richard, Baron Cumyn, Judiciary of Scotland, A.D. 1178–1180, and his wife Lady Hexilda, gd. daughter of Donald Bane, King of Scots, and had
Lady Agnes Cumyn, m. Gilbert, Baron de Umfraville, and had
Gilbert, Baron de Umfraville, Governor of the castle of Forfar, and the terri-

COLONIAL FAMILIES OF THE UNITED STATES 343

tory of Angus; Earl of Angus in right of his wife, Matilda, Countess of Angus, whom he *m.* in 1243; he *d.* 1308, and had

ROBERT DE UMFRAVILLE, second Earl of Angus, who had by his wife, Lady ALIANORE

SIR THOMAS DE UMFREVILLE, of Harbottle, younger son, who *m.* Lady JOANE, dau. of Adam DE RODAM, and had

SIR THOMAS DE UMFRAVILLE, Lord of Riddlesdale and Kyme, who had by his wife, Lady AGNES

LADY JOANE DE UMFRAVILLE, who *m.* Sir William LAMBERT, of Owlton, Durham, and had

ROBERT LAMBERT of Owlton (or Owton), father of

HENRY LAMBERT, of Ongar, Essex, father of

ELIZABETH LAMBERT, who *m.* Thomas LYMAN, of Navistoke, Essex; *d.* 1509, and had

HENRY LYMAN, of Navistoke and High Ongar, who *m.* Alicia, dau. of Simon HYDE, of Wethersfield, Essex, and had

JOHN LYMAN, of High Ongar, *d.* 1587, at Navistoke, who had by his wife Margaret, dau. of William GIRARD of Beauchamps, Essex

HENRY LYMAN, of High Ongar, *m.* Philis SCOTT of Navistoke, and had

RICHARD LYMAN, Patriarch of the Lyman family in America; *b.* 1580 at High Ongar, England; removed to America in August, 1631; landed at Boston 11th November, 1631; became a settler in Charlestown, and with his wife, Sarah OSBORNE, joined the Church in what is now Roxbury, 15th October, 1635; he went with a party of about one hundred persons and became one of the first settlers of Hartford, Connecticut, and one of the original proprietors of the town; he *d.* in August, 1641, and his name is inscribed on a stone column now standing in the rear of the Center Church of Hartford, erected in memory of the first settlers of the city; *m.* Sarah OSBORNE, dau. of Roger OSBORNE, of Halstead, in Kent, England, and had

ISSUE (BORN AND BAPTIZED AT HIGH ONGAR)

I. William, buried at High Ongar, 28th August, 1615.
II. Phillis, *bapt.* 12th September, 1611; *m.* William HILLS.
III. Richard, *bapt.* 18th July, 1613; *d.* young.
IV. William, *bapt.* 8th September, 1616; *d.* November, 1616.
V. RICHARD, *bapt.* 24th February, 1617, of whom later.
VI. Sarah, *bapt.* 8th February, 1620.
VII. Anne, *bapt.* 12th April, 1621; *d.* young.
VIII. John, *bapt.* 1623.
IX. Robert, *bapt.* September, 1629; *m.* Hepzibah BASCOM, 15th November, 1662.

RICHARD LYMAN was *bapt.* 24th February, 1617; *d.* 3d June, 1662; residence Windsor, Connecticut; *m.* Hepzibah FORD, dau. of Thomas FORD of Windsor; removed to Northampton.

ISSUE

I. Hepzibah, *b.* in Windsor; *m.* 6th November, 1662, Joseph DEWEY.
II. Sarah, *m.* John MARSH, Jr., 1666.
III. Richard, *b.* in Windsor, Connecticut; removed from Northampton, Massachusetts, to Lebanon, Connecticut.
IV. Thomas, removed to Durham, Connecticut.
V. Eliza, *m.* Joshua POMEROY, 20th August, 1672.
VI. JOHN, settled in Hockanum, Hadley, Massachusetts, of whom later.
VII. Joanna, *b.* Northampton, 1658.
VIII. Hannah, *b.* 1660; *m.* Job POMEROY, 20th June, 1677.

JOHN LYMAN of Northampton, Massachusetts; *b.* 1655, in Windsor, Connecticut; *d.* 13th October, 1727, Northampton, Massachusetts; *m.* Abigail, surname unknown.

ISSUE

I. Abigail, *b.* 12th March, 1696; *d.* 15th April, 1696.
II. Abigail, *b.* 1st February, 1697; *d.* 20th April, 1742.
III. Nathan, *b.* 1st January, 1699; *d.* 11th April, 1700.
IV. James, *b.* 1700; *d.* 25th September, 1769.
V. Abner, *b.* February, 1701; *d.* 16th August, 1746.
VI. CAPTAIN JOSHUA, *b.* 27th February, 1704, of whom later.
VII. Nathan, *b.* 5th May, 1706.

CAPTAIN JOSHUA LYMAN of Northampton, Massachusetts; *b.* 27th February, 1704; *d.* 1777, in Northfield; held a commission in the British Army; served upward of fourteen years in Colonial Wars; fourth in command at Fort Durmer under Captain KELLOGG, 1728–1740; Captain in Colonel WILLIAMS' Regiment, 1757; in Father RASLE'S War; *m.* 1st October, 1728, Sarah NARMON.

ISSUE

I. Simeon, *b.* 26th November, 1730.
II. John, *b.* 27th December, 1732.
III. Joshua, *b.* 10th March, 1734; *d.* 14th October, 1753.
IV. CAPTAIN SETH, *b.* 1st February, 1736, of whom later.
V. Mary, *b.* 22d September, 1738; *d.* 1st September, 1739.
VI. Sarah, *b.* 15th January, 1740.
VII. Mary, *b.* 15th August, 1742; *d.* 5th November, 1749.
VIII. James, *b.* 9th June, 1747.
IX. Esther, *b.* 12th June, 1752.

SETH LYMAN of Northfield, Massachusetts; *b.* there 1st February, 1736; *d.* there 14th October, 1817; enlisted as a private in Captain BURK'S Company, 1759; was in the Crown Point Expedition; promoted to Corporal; served as Sergeant during the Revolution; enlisted in Capt. Samuel MERRIMAN'S Company, Col. WRIGHT'S Regiment; took part in the battle of Saratoga, 1777; served in Colonel MERRIMAN'S Regiment; was present at the surrender of Burgoyne; *m.* 23d October, 1760, Eunice GRAVES, of Sunderland, Massachusetts.

ISSUE

I. TERTIUS, *b.* 2d November, 1761, of whom later.
II. Phineas, *b.* 13th November, 1763.
III. Lucy, *b.* 17th February, 1766; *d.* 6th December, 1852.
IV. Eunice, *d.* in infancy.
V. Seth, *b.* 8th September, 1772.
VI. Samuel, *b.* 28th March, 1775.
VII. Nancy, *b.* 17th August, 1777.
VIII. Aaron Graves, *b.* 2d December, 1780.
IX. Molly, *b.* 2d June, 1783.

TERTIUS LYMAN of Winchester, New Hampshire; *b.* 2d November, 1761, in Northfield; went from Northfield, Massachusetts, to Winchester, New Hampshire, and was one of the first settlers of that town; he served in the Revolutionary War during its last two years; *m.* (firstly) 10th April, 1787, Eunice HOUGHTON, *d.* 11th July, 1810; *m.* (secondly) 10th November, 1810, Hannah ALEXANDER.

ISSUE BY FIRST MARRIAGE

I. Freedom, *b.* 15th February, 1788.
II. Fanny, *b.* 5th February, 1790; *d.* 1847.
III. Eunice, *b.* 3d August, 1792; *d.* 1st August, 1794.
IV. Eunice, *b.* 20th August, 1795; *d.* 6th June, 1850.
V. Atta, *b.* 13th October, 1797; *d.* 7th July, 1852.
VI. Anson, *b.* 2d August, 1799; *d.* 5th June, 1855.
VII. TERTIUS ALEXANDER, *b.* 13th March, 1812, of whom below.

TERTIUS ALEXANDER LYMAN of Lee Center, Illinois; *b.* 13th March, 1812; *d.* 5th February, 1900; engaged in farming; he lived first in Winchester, New Hampshire, moving to Lee Center, Illinois, with his family March, 1856; *m.* 13th March, 1834, Sarah Pierce CODDING of Winchester, dau. of George and Abigail CODDING of Warwick, Massachusetts.

ISSUE

I. Sarah Alexander, *b.* 30th September, 1835; *m.* 22d March, 1865, Charles W. WILBER, Allen's Grove, Wisconsin; he *d.* 7th April, 1894, at Amboy, Illinois.
II. GEORGE ALEXANDER, *b.* 26th June, 1838, the subject of this memoir.
III. Levi Hall, *b.* 1st June, 1841; *d.* 3d September, 1900; *m.* Frances BRUCE of Allen's Grove, Wisconsin.

ISSUE

1. William.
2. Daisy.
3. Abbie.
4. Carrie.
5. Albert.

IV. Climea Osgood (twin), *b.* 24th June, 1843; *d.* 11th July, 1843.
V. Cyrus Osgood (twin), *b.* 24th June, 1843; *d.* 20th June, 1874; *m.* Jane EVITTS of Bradford, Illinois, who is still living.

ISSUE

1. Millie.
2. Mary.
3. Ruth.
4. Hannah.

Crest.—A demi-bull argent, attired and hoofed or, langued gules.
Motto.—Quod verum tutum.
Residence.—Claremont, California.
Societies.—Baronial Order of Runnemede, Colonial Wars, Sons of the American Revolution, Knights of the Globe.

Meirs

RICHARD WALN MEIRS, A.B.; *b.* 26th July, 1866, at Walnford, New Jersey; *d.* 20 April, 1917 at 1245 Walnut St., Philadelphia; *m.* 31st October, 1894, at Ravenhill School House Lane, Germantown, Pennsylvania, Anne Walker WEIGHTMAN, *b.* 28th April, 1871, dau. of William WEIGHTMAN, Jr., M.D., *b.* 30th October, 1846, *d.* 11th February, 1889, *m.* 18th November, 1868, Sabina Josephine D'INVILLIERS.

ISSUE

I. William Weightman, *b.* 18th September, 1895.
II. Anne Walker, *b.* 25th August, 1898.
III. Jarvis, *b.* 12th June, 1901.

Lineage (Meirs)

RICHARD WALN MEIRS, A.B., Princeton, 1888; President and Director Commercial Truck Company of America, Electric Securities Company, Pennsylvania Central Light and Power Company, Pennsylvania Power and Transmission Company, North Cambria Light and Power Company, Citizens Traction Company; Vice-President and Director Hudson Manhattan Railroad, Citizens Light and Power Company; Director Lewistown Reedsville Railroad, Winifred Coal Company, Winifred Railroad Company, Belmont Coal Company, Pennsylvania Hydro Electric Company; Manager Franklin Institute; Member First Troop Philadelphia Cavalry.

JOHN MEIRS, *b.* 29th September, 1796; *d.* 7th August, 1853; commissioned 1st April, 1824, Adjutant of the Monmouth Squadron, 3d Regiment Cavalry, Brigade of New Jersey; was a Member of the Society of Friends; *m.* 17th January, 1828, Lucretia Stockton GASKILL, *b.* 10th October, 1801, *d.* 9th September, 1875, he son of

APPOLLO MEIRS, 2d March, 1763; *d.* 3d May, 1855; *m.* 30th January, 1794, Unity SHINN, dau. of Thomas SHINN, *b.* 17th September, 1740, who *m.* Sarah VINACOMB, or VINICONE, *b.* 21st January, 1768, son of

DAVID MEIRS, *b.* 16th June, 1738; *d.* 14th September, 1816; *m.* Martha SWAIN, *b.* 26th July, 1736, *d.* 1st May, 1826, son of

CHRISTOPHER MIERS was the ancestor of the baron of the MIERS family of America.

Lineage (Waln)

RICHARD WALN of Burholme, in district called Bolling, West Riding of Yorkshire and his wife Jane, dau. of Edward RUDD, of Knowmeare, Yorkshire, were early converts to Quakerism, and belonged to Bolland Meeting, a branch of Settle Monthly Meeting, as early as 1654; in 1664 he sued at Whitwell Court for tithes and had a mare taken from him worth four pounds; he *d.* 7th April, 1659, and his widow, then of Slaidburn, *m.* 31st October, 1667, Robert BIRKET of Newton.

ISSUE

I. Richard, *d.* 26th March, 1698; came to Pennsylvania in 1682 and settled at Cheltenham Township, Philadelphia.
II. Ann, *b.* 15th August, 1654; *m.* circa 1681, James DILWORTH of Yorkshire, *d.* September, 1697; they came to Pennsylvania about the same time as Nicholas; his widow *m.* (secondly) Christopher SIBTHORP of Philadelphia.
III. NICHOLAS, *b.* circa, 1650, of whom later.

NICHOLAS WALN, *b.* circa 1650; *d.* 1721, at Burholme, West Riding of Yorkshire, England. Before his marriage he removed to Chapelcroft. On 7th June, 1682, Settle Monthly Meeting issued a joint certificate to him and family, and others, all more or less related by ties of blood, who intended removing to Pennsylvania. This party accompanied William PENN, Lord Proprietary of Pennsylvania on his first voyage to his Province and arrived on the *Welcome* at New Castle, Delaware River, Territories of Pennsylvania, 27th October, 1682. 21st and 22d April, Nicholas WALN bought of William PENN 1000 acres of land in Pennsylvania. He settled about 1st January, 1682–1683, on the Neshaminy in Middletown Township, where he erected his dwelling and in 1696 he removed to Philadelphia County. He was a Member of the First Assembly 12th March, 1682–1683; Represented Bucks County in the Assembly, 1687, 1689, 1692 and 1695; Member of the First Grand Jury, 25th October, 1683; Sheriff of Bucks County, 1685. Member of the Assembly from Philadelphia County, 1696–1697, 1700–1701, 1713–1715, 1717; was named as one of the Directors of Public Schools with James LOGAN, Isaac NORRIS, Edward SHIPPEN and others in 1711; he was practically the founder of Middletown Monthly Meeting; *m.* 1st October, 1673, at Slainmerow, Jane TURNER.

ISSUE

I. Jane, *b.* 16th July, 1675, in Yorkshire; *m.* 27th May, 1691, at "Neshamina," Samuel ALLEN, Jr. of Bucks County, Pennsylvania, son of Samuel ALLEN, who with his family came from England in the ship *Bristol Factor*, arriving at Chester, 11th December, 1681.
II. Margaret, *b.* 3d October, 1677, in Yorkshire; *d.* in infancy.
III. RICHARD, *b.* 6th June, 1678, in Yorkshire, of whom later.
IV. Margaret, *b.* 10th January, 1680–1681, in Yorkshire, England; *d.* before his father.
V. Hannah, *b.* 21st September, 1684, in Bucks County, Pennsylvania; *m.* (firstly) March, 1704, Thomas HODGES, *d.* 28th March, 1708, who had *m.* (firstly) her cousin, Jane DILWORTH; she *m.* (secondly) November, 1712, Benjamin SIMCOCK.
VI. Mary, *b.* 7th April, 1687, in Bucks County, Pennsylvania; *d.* 19th July, 1721; *m.* 1706, John SIMCOCK, brother of Benjamin. She was a minister of the Society of Friends.

VII. Ellen, *b.* 27th March, 1690, in Bucks County; *d.* unmarried 4th January, 1707.
VIII. Sarah, *b.* 9th June, 1692, in Bucks County; *m.* (firstly) 1711, Jacob SIMCOCK, *b.* 28th September, 1686; *d.* February, 1716–1717, leaving issue, brother of Benjamin and John; *m.* (secondly) 27th February, 1721–1722, Jonathan PALMER.
IX. John, *b.* 10th August, 1694, in Bucks County; *d.* 1720; *m.* 30th August, 1717, Jane MIFFLIN, *b.* 1696, dau. of John and Elizabeth (HARDY) MIFFLIN of Fountain Green, now (1916) part of Fairmount Park, Philadelphia, she gd. dau. of John MIFFLIN of Westminister, Wiltshire, England.
X. Elizabeth, *b.* 27th March, 1697, in Northern Liberties, Philadelphia; is supposed to have *m.* 24th April, 1719, James DUBERRY (properly DUBREE), *b.* 22d June, 1698, son of Jacob and Jane DUBREE.
XI. Nicholas, *b.* 24th March, 1698–1699, at Northern Liberties; *d.* there unmarried, 11th February, 1721–1722.
XII. William, *b.* 15th March, 1700–1701, at Northern Liberties; *m.* Ann HALL, dau. of Samuel and Mary HALL of Springfield, Chester County, Pennsylvania.

RICHARD WALN of Northern Liberties, Philadelphia, Pennsylvania; *b.* 6th June, 1678, at Burholme Parish of Slaidburn, West Riding of Yorkshire, England; *d.* 1756, at Norriton Township, Philadelphia; will dated 1st December, 1753; proved 16th June, 1756; *m.* prior to 30th September, 1706, Anne HEATH dau. of Robert HEATH.

ISSUE

I. Nicholas, *b.* 25th August, 1707; *d.* 3d September, 1707.
II. NICHOLAS, *b.* 19th March, 1709–1710, of whom later.
III. Jane, *b.* 6th August, 1711; *d.* 17th August, 1711.
IV. Jane, *b.* 20th February, 1712–1713; *d.* 4th October, 1714.
V. Anne, *b.* 16th February, 1714–1715; *m.* May, 1753, Jonathan MARIS, gd. son of George MARIS, Provincial Councillor.
VI. Richard, *d.* 5th June, 1717.
VII. Susanna, *b.* 9th June, 1719; *m.* November, 1739, Joseph LEWIS.
VIII. Robert, *b.* 21st March, 1720–1721; *m.* Rebecca COFFIN.
IX. Joseph, *b.* 18th December, 1722; *d.* 1760; *m.* 31st December, 1747, Susannah PAUL, dau. of James PAUL.
X. Mary, *b.* 16th August, 1724; *m.* Joseph BROWN.

NICHOLAS WALN of Northern Liberties, Philadelphia; *b.* 19th March, 1709–1710; *d.* August, 1744; will dated 16th August; probabed 3d August, 1744; *m.* 23d May, 1734, Mary SHOEMAKER, *d.* 1756, dau. of George and Rebecca (DILWORTH) SHOEMAKER, the youngest dau. of James and Anne (WALN) DILWORTH.

ISSUE

I. Ann, *d.* unmarried.
II. RICHARD, *b.* circa, 1737, of whom later.
III. Rebecca, *m.* Abraham HOWELL.
IV. Nicholas, *b.* 14th November, 1742; *d.* 29th September, 1813; *m.* 22d May, 1771, Sarah RICHARDSON, *b.* 11th October, 1746, *d.* 13th April, 1825, only child of Joseph and Sarah (MORRIS) RICHARDSON and gd. dau. of Anthony and Mary (CODDINGTON) MORRIS.

RICHARD WALN of Walnford, New Jersey, and Philadelphia, Pennsylvania, Gentleman; *b.* circa 1737; *d.* 23d May, 1809; was engaged in mercantile pursuits in Philadelphia and acquired considerable wealth; removed in 1774 to Monmouth County, New Jersey, where he purchased a large tract of land and built his mansion; the estate he named "Walnford;" after the Revolution he returned to Philadelphia; *m.* 4th December, 1760, Elizabeth ARMITT, *d.* 1790, dau. of Joseph ARMITT in Philadelphia, merchant, head of an old Burlington County, New Jersey, family.

ISSUE

I. Joseph, *b.* 1761; *d.* either 10th September or 9th October, 1824; *m.* 12th February, 1801, Elizabeth STOKES, dau. of John STOKES.
II. Mary, *d.* 1844; *m.* 1786, Thomas WISTER, *b.* 1764, *d.* 1851, son of Richard and Sarah (WYATT) WISTER.
III. Elizabeth, *b.* circa 1767; *d.* unmarried, 22d December, 1837, in Philadelphia.
IV. Hannah, *m.* John RYERS; had issue.
V. Richard, *d.* young.
VI. NICHOLAS, *b.* 28th November, 1763, of whom later.
VII. Jacob Shoemaker, *b.* 1776, at Walnford, New Jersey; *d.* 4th April, 1850; *m.* 5th August, 1804, Sarah MORRIS, *b.* 2d September, 1788, *d.* 18th May, 1862, dau. of Benjamin Wister and Mary (WELLS) MORRIS.

NICHOLAS WALN of Walnford, Monmouth County, New Jersey; *b.* 28th November, 1763; *d.* 6th April, 1848, at Walnford; *m.* 11th April, 1799, at Upper Springfield Meeting, Sarah RIDGWAY, *b.* 8th November, 1779, in Salem, New Jersey, *d.* 28th August, 1872, at Walnford, dau. of John and Elizabeth (WRIGHT) RIDGWAY of Burlington County, New Jersey. He son of John and Phoebe (BELLANGEE) RIDGWAY; son of Thomas and Ann (PHARO) RIDGWAY of Burlington County, New Jersey, the son of Richard and Elizabeth (CHAMBERLAIN) RIDGWAY of England, among the first English settlers on the West Side of the Delaware River.

ISSUE

I. RICHARD, *b.* 12th November, 1802, of whom later.
II. Elizabeth, *b.* 21st January, 1800; *d.* 22nd December, 1821; age twenty-one years; *m.* 7th June, 1821, Richard BRUERE.
III. Joseph, *b.* 20th May, 1805; *d.* November, 1872; *m.* and had issue.

COLONIAL FAMILIES OF THE UNITED STATES 351

IV. John Ridgway, b. 8th February, 1808; m. Maria KIRBY.
V. Nicholas, b. 23d September, 1810; d. 31st December, 1879; m. (firstly) Unity TILTON; m. (secondly) Mary KIRBY, d. 6th August, 1907.
VI. Sarah, b. 6th July, 1816; d. 15th March, 1907, at Walnford; m. 1855, Jacob HENDRICKSON.

RICHARD WALN of Walnford, New Jersey; b. 12th November, 1802; d. 30th June, 1873, at Mt. Holly, New Jersey; m. (firstly) Mary Ann ALLEN, b. 2d December, 1807, at Ocean County, New Jersey, d. 3d May, 1840, at Ocean County, New Jersey, dau. of Riley and Sarah (WARREN) ALLEN; m. (secondly) Caroline MOUNT.

ISSUE BY FIRST MARRIAGE

I. Nicholas, b. 28th December, 1837; d. 5th April, 1915; m. 17th November, 1870, Ada ALLMENDINGER of Philadelphia, d. 27th May, 1907.
II. ELIZABETH, b. 4th September, 1838, of whom later.

ISSUE BY SECOND MARRIAGE

I. Anna, b. 1855; m. Judge Benajah P. WILLS, of Mt. Holly, New Jersey.

ISSUE

1. Mabel WILLS.
2. Richard Waln Wills.

ELIZABETH WALN, b. 4th September, 1838, at New Egypt, New Jersey; m. 12th February, 1862, John Gaskill MEIRS, b. 16th September, 1839, d. 4th September, 1909, son of John and Lucretia (GASKILL) MEIRS of Monmouth County, New Jersey. He a member of the Society of Friends, son of John MEIRS, Esquire, commissioned 1st April, 1824, Adjutant of the Monmouth Squadron, Third Regiment Cavalry, Brigade of Militia of New Jersey.

ISSUE

I. Sarah MEIRS, b. 31st March, 1863; d. 7th July, 1865.
II. Mary Ann MEIRS, b. 6th August, 1864; d. 1st July, 1865.
III. RICHARD WALN MEIRS, b. 26th July, 1866, the subject of this memoir.
IV. Job Hillman Gaskill MEIRS, b. 23d May, 1868; d. 11th September, 1894, adopted by his uncle Job Hillman GASKILL for whom he was named and by act of Assembly dropped the surname MEIRS, leaving his name the same as that of his uncle and adopted father; m. 12th February, 1891, his cousin, Helen MEIRS, dau. of Collin Butterworth MEIRS and his wife Louisa BUTTERWORTH, who were also cousins.
V. John MEIRS, b. 29th April, 1870; Member of Camden Bar, New Jersey; m. January, 1908, Sarah (HENSHAW) BRIGHT.

COLONIAL FAMILIES OF THE UNITED STATES

ISSUE

1. Elizabeth Waln, *b.* 12th July, 1913.
2. John, *b.* 7th October, 1914.

VI. Mary Ann MEIRS, *b.* 27th February, 1872; unmarried.
VII. Fanny Campbell MEIRS, *b.* 22d August, 1873; *d.* unmarried 9th January, 1897.
VIII. Lucretia Stockton MEIRS, *b.* 27th July, 1876; unmarried.
IX. Elizabeth Waln MEIRS, *b.* 1st November, 1877; unmarried.
X. David Allen MEIRS, *b.* 10th December, 1879; unmarried.

Residences.—1724 Walnut Street, Philadelphia; "Ravenhill," School Lane, Germantown, Pennsylvania, and Walnford, Monmouth County, New Jersey.

Clubs.—University, Racquet, Pen and Pencil, Princeton, Corinthian Yacht, Huntington Valley Country, Philadelphia Country Club, in Philadelphia, Metropolitan, Princeton and Grolier, in New York, Nassau and Cottage Clubs of Princeton.

Societies.—Colonial Wars, Welcome of Pennsylvania, Pennsylvania Historical and Genealogical Society, Academy of Fine Arts and Horticultural Society.

Miller

CHARLES KINGSBURY MILLER, of Chicago, Illinois; *b.* 15th April, 1850, in Lodi, Seneca County, New York; *m.* 31st December, 1879, Matilda (SMITH) WADE of Cincinnati, Ohio, dau. of William SMITH, *b.* 1812, in Belfast, Ireland, *m.* October, 1847, at Cincinnati, Ohio, Sarah Letitia BEATTY, *b.* in Enniskillen, Ireland.

ISSUE

I. Arlowe Kingsbury, *b.* 7th December, 1881; *d.* 20th April, 1903.
II. Loris Almy, *b.* 15th May, 1884; graduated Harvard, 1906; *m.* 6th April, 1910, Madeleine TINKHAM, of Boston, Massachusetts.

ISSUE
1. Kathleen Bennett, *b.* 3d November, 1910.
2. Eleanor Frances, *b.* 5th December, 1911.

CHARLES KINGSBURY MILLER was educated at Crean's private school and the public schools of Chicago; was engaged in the newspaper advertising business as Charles K. MILLER and Company, till 1890 when he retired; in 1894 he began active patriotic work to secure legislation to protect the national flag from desecration. To this end, for a number of years he wrote and published flag literature, which was extensively circulated throughout the United States to aid the efforts of patriotic societies and organizations in securing flag legislation. While engaged in this patriotic work Charles Kingsbury MILLER received autograph letters from five Presidents of the United States approving the movement. Forty states have now enacted flag laws. Author: "Excerpts from an Egyptian Manuscript," under nom de plume K. ESRYER. Life Member Society Colonial Wars, Sons of the American Revolution, Holland Society of Chicago, Huguenot Society of America, New York; American Geographical Society, New York; National Geographic Society, Washington, D. C.; Union League and Press Clubs of Chicago.

Lineage

WILLIAM ALMY gentleman (vide marriage license 1626) of South Kilworth, *b.* probably at Dunton-Bassett, in Leicestershire, England, the earliest known home of the Almey's—removed to Lynn, Massachusetts, Sandwich, and Portsmouth, Rhode Island; *b.* 1601, *d.* 28th February, 1676; will proved 23d April, 1677; *m.* in 1626 Audrey BARLOWE, of Lutterworth; *b.* 1603, *d.* 1676; he was in New England prior to 1631; in 1635 having been home to England he returned to New England, in the ship *Abigail;* Freeman, 1655; Juryman, 1656; Commissioner, 1656–1657, 1663; Foreman of Grand Jury. William's father Christopher Almey, gentleman (vide will, 2d October, 1624), *b.* 1575; *d.* 4th October, 1624 at South Kilworth.

354 COLONIAL FAMILIES OF THE UNITED STATES

Roberte ALMEY, husbandman, of Dunton—will 11th December, 1579. Proved 8th February, 1581, was ancestor.

ISSUE

I. Ann, *b.* 1627; *d.* 17th May, 1709; *m.* John GREEN, *b.* 1620, *d.* 27th November, 1708.
II. CHRISTOPHER, *b.* 1632, of whom later.
III. John, *d.* 1st October, 1676; 24th July, 1667, Lieutenant of Troop of Horse; served as Captain in King Philip's War, 1676; *m.* Mary COLE, dau. of James and Mary COLE, she *m.* (secondly) 1677, John POCOCKE.
IV. Job, *d.* 1684; Deputy, 1670; Committee to treat with Indians, 7th May, 1673; Assistant, 1673–1675; *m.* Mary UNTHANK, *d.* 1724, dau. of Christopher and Susanna UNTHANK.
V. Catherine, *m.* Bartholomew WEST.

CHRISTOPHER ALMY, *b.* 1632; *d.* 30th January, 1713; will proved 9th February, 1713, disposing of a considerable estate; Freeman, 1658; in 1667 bought land with others of the Indians at Monmouth, New Jersey, where he lived some years, returning to Rhode Island before 1680, however; in 1690 he was Deputy to the General Court from Portsmouth, Rhode Island, and the same year chosen Assistant; 27th February, 1690, chosen and elected Governor but refused to serve for reasons satisfactory to the Assembly; this was the first election for Governor since the deposition of ANDROS; 24th August, 1693, Messenger from Rhode Island to England, delivered the address from Rhode Island and his own petition to Queen Mary; he bought lands in Pocasset (Tiverton) from the Indian Sachems; he was at the time a "Plymouth Colonist" and identified with Freetown, which included Fall River; *m.* 9th July, 1661, Elizabeth CORNELL, who *d.* 1708, dau. of Thomas and Rebecca CORNELL of Hertford, England. Thomas CORNELL was an Ensign, 1642–1644.

ISSUE

I. Sarah, *b.* 17th April, 1662; *d.* 1708; *m.* (firstly) Richard CADMAN, *d.* 1695; *m.* (secondly) Jonathan MERIKEN; issue by both marriages.
II. Elizabeth, *b.* 29th ———, 1663; *d.* 1712; *m.* (firstly) John MORRIS; *m.* (secondly) John LEONARD, son of Henry and Mary LEONARD; issue by second marriage.
III. WILLIAM, *b.* 27th October, 1665, of whom later.
IV. Ann, *b.* 29th March, 1667; *m.* (firstly) Richard DURFEE, *d.* 1700, son of Thomas DURFEE; *m.* (secondly) Benjamin JEFFERSON.
V. Christopher, of Newport, Rhode Island; *b.* 26th December, 1669; *m.* (firstly) 16th April, 1690, Joanna SLOCUM, *b.* 9th October, 1672; *m.* (secondly) Mary, surname unknown, *b.* March, 1670; *d.* 15th September, 1759; issue by both marriages.
VI. Rebecca, *b.* 26th January, 1671; *d.* 1708; *m.* 28th April, 1692, John TOWNSEND, son of Thomas TOWNSEND.

COLONIAL FAMILIES OF THE UNITED STATES 355

VII. John, *b.* April, 1673; *d.* same year.
VIII. Job, *b.* 10th October, 1675; *d.* 2d December, 1743; Freeman, 1708; 4th May, 1709, appointed on a special committee to assist the Governor for advice to manage affairs, etc.; Deputy 1709, 1716-1720, 1725-1726; Captain, 1726.
IX. A child, *b.* 1676; *d.* young.

WILLIAM ALMY of Tiverton, Rhode Island; *b.* 27th October, 1665; *d.* 6th July, 1747; will proved 29th April, 1747; 2d March, 1692, was an inhabitant at organization of Connecticut; *m.* (firstly) Deborah COOK, dau. of John and Mary (BORDEN) COOK; *m.* (secondly) Hope BORDEN, *b.* 3d March, 1685, *d.* 1762, dau. of John and Mary BORDEN; no issue by second marriage. The first BORDENS came over from Normandy with William the Conqueror and for services rendered received estates in Kent, England, settled there ever since and were a powerful family.

ISSUE BY FIRST MARRIAGE

I. Mary, *b.* 7th August, 1689.
II. John, *b.* 10th October, 1692; served as Captain in King Philip's War and was one of those who fell a victim to the treachery of the Indians.
III. JOB, *b.* 28th April, 1696, in Tiverton Rhode Island, of whom later.
IV. Elizabeth, *b.* 14th November, 1697.
V. Samuel, *b.* 15th April, 1701.
VI. Deborah, *b.* 27th July, 1703.
VII. Rebecca, *b.* 14th October, 1704.
VIII. Joseph (twin), *b.* 3d October, 1707.
IX. William (twin), *b.* 3d October, 1707.

COLONEL JOB ALMY of Newport, Rhode Island; *b.* 28th April, 1696; was appointed 4th May, 1709, on a special council to assist the Governor in the management of the expedition against Canada; between the years 1709 and 1726, he was Deputy from Newport to the General Assembly; the "Peasefield" was his property when the battle of Pease (pea) field was fought and is still in the possession of an ALMY; he like his father, bought land of the Sachems; *m.* wife's name is not known.

ISSUE

I. Samuel, *b.* 20th September, 1725; in Dartmouth, Mass.—removed to Cambridge, New York; will proved 7th February, 1806.

ISSUE

I. THOMAS, *b.* 13th March, 1747; in Dartmouth, Mass.—removed, first to Cambridge, New York, afterward to Sharon, N. Y.; will proved 22d May, 1828.

ISSUE

I. SAMUEL, *b.* 8th March, 1778, at Dartmouth, Mass.—removed first to Cambridge, New York, of whom below.

CAPTAIN SAMUEL ALMY of Dartmouth, Cambridge, New York, and Farmerville; *b.* 8th March, 1778; *d.* 14th August, 1825; was one of the first settlers of Cayuga; now Seneca County, locating between Seneca and Cayuga Lakes; was one of the founders of the town of Farmville, now called Interlaken; in the War of 1812, was an Ensign in the 128th Regiment, Light Infantry, State of New York, and was promoted a Captain in the same Regiment; *m.* 1st November, 1801, Jane RAPPLEYE, *b.* 19th February, 1780, Penns Neck, New Jersey, *d.* 2d February, 1862, dau. of Jacobus RAPPLEYE, of New Brunswick, New Jersey, *b.* 1743, *d.* 27th October, 1827, a descendant of Colonel Gaspard Colet DE RAPELJE, who served in the French Army under Francis I and Henry II.

ISSUE

I. Ira, *b.* 15th September, 1802; *d.* 12th November, 1884.
II. Silvester, *b.* 1804; *d.* 22d October, 1842.
III. Milton Genoa, *b.* 4th October, 1806; *d.* 2d February, 1882.
IV. Lusally, *b.* 24th February, 1808; *d.* 3d January, 1835.
V. Clarinda, *b.* 26th January, 1814; *d.* 13th April, 1878.
VI. Calista D., *b.* 11th May, 1816; *d.* 6th November, 1858.
VII. James G., *b.* 9th January, 1818; *d.* 13th February, 1870.
VIII. POLLY ANN, *b.* 16th September, 1820, of whom below.

POLLY ANN ALMY, *b.* 16th September, 1820; *d.* 6th March, 1911; one of the founders of the Woman's Christian Temperance Union; *m.* 29th October, 1845, Youngs Woodhull MILLER, of Monroe, New York, *b.* 14th September, 1816, *d.* 10th December, 1892, son of Austin Joseph MILLER.

ISSUE

I. James Almy MILLER, *b.* 29th January, 1847; *d.* 9th October, 1899.
II. CHARLES KINGSBURY MILLER, *b.* 15th April, 1850; the subject of this memoir.
III. Jennie Eva MILLER, *b.* 17th December, 1854.
IV. Roy Paul MILLER, *b.* 8th May, 1861; *d.* 17th February, 1864.

Arms.—Gules within a bordure or, a tower triple turreted, two keys crossed in base argent.

Crest.—A standard, lance, sword and shield conjoined, within the shield a crusader's cross, or.

Residence.—1432 North State Parkway, Chicago, Illinois.

Clubs.—Union League of New York, Union League of Chicago, Press of Chicago, Athletic of Washington, D. C.

Societies.—Colonial Wars, Sons of the American Revolution, Holland Society of Chicago, Huguenot Society of America, American Geographical Society of New York, National Geographic Society, New England Society of Chicago, American Flag Association of New York, Order of Founders and Patriots of America and War of 1812.

Minot

JOSEPH GRAFTON MINOT, *b.* 13th January, 1858; *m.* 10th June, 1890, Honora Elizabeth Temple WINTHROP, dau. of Thomas Lindall WINTHROP of Boston.

ISSUE

I. Joseph Grafton Winthrop, *b.* 17th October, 1892.

Lineage

JOHN MINOT of Springwell, in the Parish of Little Chesterford, County Essex; will proved at Colchester 18th December, 1542; descended from Thomas Minot, Secretary to the Abbot of Walden about 1400; *m.* wife's name unknown.

ISSUE

I. George.
II. ROBERT, *d.* 1559, of whom later.
III. William.

ROBERT MINOT was buried at Little Chesterford, 14th December, 1559; will proved 7th January, 1560; *m.* Ellen, surname unknown, buried at Little Chesterford, 7th February, 1595.

ISSUE

I. JOHN, of whom later.
II. Anne.
III. Katherine.
IV. Margaret.

JOHN MINOT of Saffron Walden; *m.* Anne, surname unknown.

ISSUE

I. Margaret, *bapt.* 5th September, 1585.
II. Mary, *bapt.* 5th May, 1588.
III. John, *bapt.* 29th March, 1590.
IV. GEORGE, *bapt.* 20th November, 1592, of whom later.
V. William, *bapt.* 1596.

GEORGE MINOT of Dorchester, Massachusetts; *bapt.* 20th November, 1592, in England; *d.* 24th December, 1671; emigrated to America, 1630, and settled in Dorchester, Massachusetts; admitted Freeman, 1634; Deputy to General Court, 1636; *m.* Martha, surname unknown, *d.* 23d December, 1657.

ISSUE

I. George, *bapt.* at Saffron Walden, 11th July, 1624; *d.* in infancy.
II. JOHN, *b.* 2d April, 1626, of whom later.
III. James, *b.* 31st December, 1628; *d.* 30th March, 1676; left issue; *m.* (firstly) 9th December, 1653, Hannah STOUGHTON, dau. of Col. Israel STOUGHTON; *m.* (secondly) 21st May, 1673, Hephzibah CORLETE, dau. of Elijah CORLETE.
IV. Stephen, *b.* 2d May, 1631; *d.* 16th February, 1672; *m.* 10th November, 1654, Truecrosse DAVENPORT, dau. of Capt. Richard DAVENPORT; left issue.
V. Samuel, *b.* 18th December, 1635; *d.* 8th December, 1690; *m.* 23d June, 1670, Hannah HOWARD, dau. of Robert HOWARD.

JOHN MINOT of Dorchester, Massachusetts; *b.* 2d April, 1626; *d.* 12th August, 1669; Freeman, 1665; *m.* (firstly) 19th May, 1647, Lydia BUTLER, *d.* 25th January 1667, dau. of Nicholas BUTLER, *m.* (secondly) the widow of John BIGGS, dau. of John BASSETT.

ISSUE BY FIRST MARRIAGE

I. JOHN, *b.* 22d January, 1648, of whom later.
II. James, of Concord, *b.* 14th September, 1653; *d.* 20th September, 1735; graduated at Harvard, 1675; Captain of Militia, 1684; Deputy, 1700–1701; *m.* Rebecca WHEELER, dau. of Capt. Timothy WHEELER; had issue.
III. Martha, *b.* 22d September, 1657; *d.* unmarried, 23d November, 1678.
IV. Stephen, *b.* 10th August, 1662; *d.* November, 1732; Justice of the Peace; Colonel of Militia; *m.* 1st December, 1686, Mercy CLARK, dau. of Capt. Christopher CLARK; left issue.
V. Samuel, *b.* 3d July, 1665; *m.* Hannah JONES, dau. of ——— JONES; had issue.

JOHN MINOT of Dorchester; *b.* 22d January, 1648; served in Mount Hope Campaign, King Philip's War, 1675; *m.* 11th March, 1670, Elizabeth BRECK, *d.* 6th April, 1691, dau. of Edward BRECK.

ISSUE

I. JOHN, 1672, of whom later.
II. Josiah, *b.* 25th December, 1674; *d.* in infancy.
III. Israel, *b.* 23d August, 1676.
IV. Josiah, *b.* 27th August, 1677.
V. Jerusha, *b.* 28th January, 1679; *m.* 18th January, 1706, Zabdiel BOYLSTON.
VI. George, *b.* 16th February, 1682.

JOHN MINOT of Dorchester; *b.* 10th October, 1672; *m.* (firstly) 21st May, 1696, Mary BAKER, *d.* 15th February, 1717, dau. of John BAKER; *m.* (secondly) Hannah ENDICOTT, who *d.s.p.*, dau. of ——— ENDICOTT.

ISSUE

I. Elizabeth, *b.* 24th February, 1697; *d.* in infancy.
II. Elizabeth, *b.* 6th June, 1699; *d.* in infancy.
III. John, *b.* 1st June, 1701; *d.* in infancy.
IV. GEORGE, of whom later.
V. Mary, *b.* 28th December, 1705; *d.* in infancy.
VI. Mary, *b.* 9th March, 1708; *m.* 18th March, 1730, Oliver WISWALL.
VII. Elizabeth, *b.* 23d February, 1711; *m.* 27th January, 1729, Thomas WYER.

GEORGE MINOT of Dorchester; *b.* 2d November, 1703; *d.* 10th November, 1744; Cornet of Horse, 1st Massachusetts Regiment, 1741; *m.* 24th December, 1729, Abigail FENNO, dau. of Benjamin FENNO.

ISSUE

I. JOHN, *b.* 9th November, 1730, of whom later.
II. Jerusha, *b.* 9th January, 1734; *m.* Col. Lemuel ROBINSON.
III. Abigail, *b.* 8th January, 1737.
IV. Samuel, *b.* 13th March, 1742.

JOHN MINOT of Dorchester; *b.* 9th November, 1730; *d.* 25th January, 1805; Lieutenant of Militia; *m.* Martha BLAKE, *d.* 13th August, 1797, dau. of Nathaniel BLAKE.

ISSUE

I. Elizabeth, *b.* 4th December, 1753; *m.* 30th April, 1775, William SUMNER.
II. GEORGE, *b.* 1755, of whom later.
III. Martha, *b.* 8th August, 1760; *m.* 17th December, 1781, Lemuel CRANE.
IV. John, *b.* 7th August, 1764; *d.* 21st January, 1774.
V. Hannah, *b.* January, 1767; *m.* 7th March, 1797, Joseph WILD.
VI. Abigail, *b.* 31st May, 1769; *m.* 18th December, 1794, Joseph PIERCE.
VII. Nathaniel, *b.* 12th July, 1773; *m.* (firstly) Rachel WILD; *m.* (secondly) Elizabeth BAILEY, *d.* 5th February, 1855; leaving issue.

GEORGE MINOT of Dorchester; *b.* 27th November, 1755; *d.* 14th September, 1826; Matross (artillery man) in Colonel ROBINSON's Regiment, in the Revolutionary War; *m.* 29th October, 1778, Eunice BILLINGS, *d.* 18th December, 1849, dau. of Oliver BILLINGS.

ISSUE

I. John, *b.* 9th May, 1779; *d.* in infancy.
II. George (twin), *b.* 28th April, 1781; *d.* in infancy.
III. Eunice (twin), *b.* 28th April, 1781; *m.* Essa GLOVER.
IV. JOHN, *b.* 16th November, 1783, of whom later.
V. Sophia, *b.* 2d September, 1787; *m.* Daniel TALBOT.

VI. Martha, b. 2d August, 1789; m. Caleb WILSON; d. 17th August, 1874.
VII. Elizabeth, b. 11th July, 1793.
VIII. George, b. 6th May, 1796.
IX. Oliver Billings, b. 12th January, 1802; d. in infancy.
X. Mary Davenport, b. 27th August, 1803; d. unmarried, 30th December, 1848.

JOHN MINOT, b. 16th November, 1783; d. 5th March, 1861; m. 27th November, 1806, Calla SMITH, d. 2d October, 1851, dau. of Joseph SMITH.

ISSUE

I. John Oliver Billings, b. 16th December, 1807; d. 10th March, 1880.
II. Elizabeth, b. 13th June, 1809; d. 17th December, 1814.
III. Henry Dearborn, b. 4th November, 1811; d. 20th May, 1816.
IV. Elizabeth Augusta, b. 24th September, 1816; d. 25th December, 1896; m. Dr. Benjamin H. WEST.
V. CHARLES HENRY, b. 11th January, 1819, of whom later.
VI. Caroline Augusta, b. 10th March, 1824; d. in infancy.

CHARLES HENRY MINOT, b. 11th January, 1819; m. 28th January, 1857, Maria Josephine GRAFTON, d. 12th July, 1893, dau. of Maj. Joseph GRAFTON, U. S. A., Surveyor of the Port of Boston, and, by her had issue.

ISSUE

I. JOSEPH GRAFTON, b. 13th January, 1858, the subject of this memoir.
II. Grace Josephine, v. 19th September, 1859; m. 12th May, 1886, Francis Inman AMORY.
III. Charles Henry, b. 9th November, 1862; d. 30th November, 1887.

Residence.—301 Berkeley Street, Boston, Massachusetts.
Arms.—Azure, two chevronels dancette argent, in chief a label of three points gules.
Crest.—A cross and three stars gules.
Motto.—Ad astra per aspera.

Morrison

SAMUEL TURNER MORRISON of Iowa City, Iowa; *b.* there 14th July, 1878; *m.* there, 20th January, 1910, Hazel Adelaide FRISBIE, *b.* there 10th November, 1892, dau. of Albert Butler and Anna (WEAVER) FRISBIE.

ISSUE

I. Cora Adelaide, *b.* 23d October, 1910.
II. William Frisbie, *b.* 31st July, 1914.

SAMUEL TURNER MORRISON was educated at State University of Iowa; Director of the Commercial Savings Bank; Treasurer of the Iowa Improvement Company; Graduate State University of Iowa; Secretary and Treasurer STEVENS-MORRISON Investment Company; Director Mississippi Valley Electric Company.

Lineage

JOHN S. MORRISON, *b.* in Londonderry, Ireland, 1760; *d.* 31st January, 1844, at Tremont, Illinois; came circa 1792 from Londonderry or Derry, Ireland and settled in Franklin County, Pennsylvania; *m.* Ann GILFILLAN, *d.* 8th August, 1828, in Franklin County, Pennsylvania, a relative of Alexander T. STEWART, the New York Merchant.

ISSUE

I. Andrew, *b.* 22d June, 1791, in Ireland.
II. Elizabeth, *b.* 16th September, 1793; *d.* 23d August, 1840; *m.* 26th August, 1830, James F. HENDERSON of Wyoming, Illinois, who *d.* 9th February, 1881.
III. Nancy, *b.* 27th September, 1795; *m*, 1st April, 1816, Isaac WHITE of Illinois.
IV. James Gilfillan, *b.* 20th June, 1797; *d.* November, 1850.
V. JOHN HUSTON, *b.* 19th May, 1799, of whom later.

JOHN HUSTON MORRISON of Iowa City; *b.* 19th May, 1799; *d.* 3d May, 1869; *m.* 10th January, 1825, at Chambersburg, Pennsylvania, Isabella Work DICKEY, *b.* 30th October, 1807, *d.* 8th December, 1879, dau. of John DICKEY, *b.* 1782; *d.* 1855, and Isabella WORK.

ISSUE

I. Rev. Theodore Nevin of Chicago, Illinois; *b.* London, Franklin Company, Pennsylvania, 5th November, 1825; *d.* 30th March, 1889; *m.* Anna Eliza HOWLAND, *b.* 1827, *d.* 31st December, 1890.

II. John Crawford of Albia, Iowa; *b.* Indiana County, Pennsylvania, 19th September, 1830; *d.* Albia, Iowa, August, 1907; *m.* 6th June, 1865, Ella A. SWAN.
III. Anna Belle, *b.* Indiana County, Pennsylvania, 16th August, 1832; *m.* David YOUNG of Illinois, who *d.* in Iowa.
IV. James Work, *b.* Pekin, Illinois, 2d January, 1836; *d.* 14th September, 1902; *m.* Hannah Caroline STEWART, *b.* Owego, New York, *d.* 9th February, 1865.
V. WILLIAM ANDREW, *b.* 10th March, 1838, in Tremont, Illinois, of whom later.
VI. Martha Elizabeth, *b.* 9th May, 1840, in Tremont, Illinois; *m.* James L. FEELEY.
VII. Susan Pauline, *b.* 9th October, 1843, in Tremont, Illinois; *m.* A. J. CASSADAY.

WILLIAM ANDREW MORRISON of Iowa City, Iowa; *b.* 10th March, 1838, at Tremont, Illinos; *d.* 29th May, 1900, at Iowa City, Iowa; *m.* 3d November, 1863, at Burlington, Iowa, Elizabeth Francanna JONES, *b.* 20th January, 1838, in Springfield, Ohio.

ISSUE

I. Wesley Jones, M.D., *b.* 29th November, 1870, at Iowa City, Iowa; *m.* 17th January, 1900, Mary THOMAS, dau. of John M. and ——— (CONGER) THOMAS.

ISSUE

1. Elizabeth, *b.* 2d September, 1905.
2. John, *b.* 4th September, 1907.

II. Cora Belle, resides at Iowa City, Iowa; Member Colonial Dames of America.
III. SAMUEL TURNER, *b.* 14th July, 1878, the subject of this memoir.
IV. William Francis, *b.* 26th February, 1881; Major of the United States Field Artillery; *m.* 7th November, 1905, Bessie TAYLOR.

ISSUE

1. Virginia, *b.* 6th September, 1906.

Arms.—Or, on a cross sable five fleur-de-lis of the field.
Crest.—A cubit arm in armour holding a branch of oak all proper.
Residence.—Iowa City, Iowa.
Clubs.—University, Elks.
Societies.—Colonial Wars, Sons of the American Revolution.

Maternal Lineage

Burgess

COLONEL WILLIAM BURGESS, *b.* 1662; *d.* 24th January, 1686; came from Truro, Cornwell County, Wales; settled in Virginia, then South River, Maryland, Anne Arundel County; Member of the Assembly, 1681-1682; Member of the Council, 1682-1686; Colonel of Foot; Justice of the High Provincial Court; General of all Military Forces of the Province of Maryland; his landed estate comprised some 10,000 acres of land; *m.* (firstly) Elizabeth ROBINS, dau. of Edward ROBINS; *m.* (secondly) Mrs. Richard EWEN; *m.* (thirdly) Ursula GORDON.

ISSUE

I. CAPTAIN EDWARD, of whom later.
II. George, was High Sheriff; *m.* Catherine STOCKETT, widow, and removed to County Devon, England.
III. William.
IV. John, *d.* young.
V. Joseph, *d.* young.
VI. Benjamin, sold his estate and went to England.
VII. Charles of Westphalla; *m.* a dau. of Capt. Henry HANSLAP; had issue.
VIII. Elizabeth.
IX. Susannah, *m.* Maj. Nicholas SEWALL.
X. Anne.

CAPTAIN EDWARD BURGESS came from Virginia with his father; was Commissioner for Opening the Port of Londontown; Justice of the Provincial Court and Captain of the Foote; he was the Executor and heir of George PUDDINGTON who came to Virginia in the *Sea Flower* in 1622; *m.* Sarah CHEW, dau. of Samuel CHEW, the son of John of Chestertown.

ISSUE

I. Samuel, *m.* Elizabeth DURBIN.
II. John, *m.* (firstly) Jane MACKLEFRESH; *m.* (secondly) 1733, Elizabeth SPARROW.
III. Margaret, *m.* ———— WARE.
IV. Elizabeth, *m.* ———— NICHOLSON.
V. Anne, *m.* ———— WHITE.
VI. SARAH, of whom later.
VII. Susannah, *m.* ———— RICHARDSON.

SARAH BURGESS of MARYLAND; *m.* 1709, Benjamin GAITHER of Gaither Fancy, Howard County, Maryland.

COLONIAL FAMILIES OF THE UNITED STATES

ISSUE
I. Benjamin GAITHER, *d.* unmarried.
II. JOHN GAITHER, *b.* 1767, of whom later.
III. Edward GAITHER, *m.* Eleanor WHITTLE.
IV. Samuel GAITHER, Attorney; *d.* unmarried.
V. Henry GAITHER.
VI. William GAITHER.
VII. Elizabeth GAITHER, *m.* ——— DAVIS.
VIII. Anne GAITHER, *m.* ——— HAMMOND.
IX. Sarah GAITHER.
X. Mary GAITHER, *m.* ——— LONG.
XI. Cassandra GAITHER, *m.* ——— LINTHICUM.

JOHN GAITHER of "Bite the Biter" Howard County, Maryland; *m.* Agnes ROGERS, dau. of Capt. John ROGERS of Prince George County, Maryland.

ISSUE
I. Evan GAITHER.
II. Vachel GAITHER, was a Captain in the Revolution.
III. Zachariah GAITHER, *m.* Sarah WARFIELD, dau. of Edward and Rachel (RIGGS) WARFIELD.
IV. John Rogers GAITHER.
V. Mary GAITHER, *m.* Seth WARFIELD.
VI. SARAH GAITHER, of whom later.
VII. Susannah GAITHER, *m.* Nathan WATERS.
VIII. Agnes GAITHER.

SARAH GAITHER of South River, Maryland; *m.* Richard WARFIELD, of "Brandy," near Millersville, Maryland.

ISSUE
I. Launcelot WARFIELD.
II. Mary WARFIELD.
III. Richard WARFIELD, Jr.
IV. ELIZABETH WARFIELD, *b.* 1747, of whom later.

ELIZABETH WARFIELD, *m.* 15th April, 1762, Col. Charles WARFIELD, of Carroll County, Maryland.

ISSUE
I. Alexander WARFIELD.
II. Mary WARFIELD.
III. Elizabeth WARFIELD.
IV. Rezin WARFIELD.
V. Anne WARFIELD, *b.* 17th March, 1779; *m.* 15th December, 1796, Rev. Dr. Joshua JONES, whose son Wesley JONES, *m.* Margaret James POOLE,

COLONIAL FAMILIES OF THE UNITED STATES 365

whose dau. Elizabeth Francanna JONES, *m.* William Andrew MORRISON, whose son Samuel Turner MORRISON is the subject of this memoir.
VI. Elizah WARFIELD.
VII. Launcelot WARFIELD.
VIII. David WARFIELD.
IX. Dennis WARFIELD.
X. Rev. Charles WARFIELD.

Arms (BURGESS).—Or a fesse chequy, or, and gules, in chief, three crosses, crosslet fitchie of the last.

Warfield

CAPTAIN RICHARD WARFIELD came from Berkshire, England, and settled near Annapolis in 1662, west of Crownsville, Anne Arundel County, Maryland; d. 1703–1704; in 1696 was one of the Vestry of St. Ann's Church; he was Captain of Anne Arundel Militia, 1689; signed an address to King William, 1689, as "Military Officer;" was a large landowner, his estate reaching back to the beautiful sheet of water, Round Bay of the Severn; *m.* in 1670, Elinor BROWNE, heiress of Capt. John BROWNE of London, England, who with his brother, Capt. Peregreen BROWNE ran two of the best equipped merchant transports between London and Annapolis.

ISSUE

I. Richard, *m.* (firstly) Marion CALDWELL; *m.* (secondly) Sarah GAMBRILL.
II. Elinor.
III. John, *m.* 1696, Ruth GANTHER.
IV. Alexander.
V. Benjamin.
VI. Rachel, *m.* ——— YATES.

RICHARD WARFIELD, *b.* 1676; *d.* 1755; Burgess for Anne Arundel County, Maryland, 1716–1717; Justice of Anne Arundel County, 1714–1715, 1718–1719, 1722, 1732–1737; Presiding Justice, 1735–1737; Vestryman of St. Anne's Parish, 1710–1729; *m.* circa 1700, Ruth CRUTCHLEY, dau. of Thomas and Margaret (BALDWIN) CRUTCHLEY.

ISSUE

I. ALEXANDER, of whom later.
II. Ruth, *m.* Joseph HALL.
III. Rachel, *m.* Robert DAVIDGE.
IV. Lydia, *m.* (firstly) Dr. Samuel STRINGER; *m.* (secondly) Col. Charles RIDGLEY of Hampton.

ALEXANDER WARFIELD of Warfield's Contrivance, Howard County, Maryland; *d.* 1773; *m.* Dinah DAVIDGE, 3d December, 1723.

ISSUE

I. Joshua (Dr.)
II. Azel.
III. Rezin.
IV. Philemon (Capt.), m. Assantha WATERS.
V. CHARLES (Colonel), of whom later; b. 30th August, 1738; d. 23d June, 1790.
VI. Sophia, m. ——— SIMPSON.
VII. Dinah, m. ——— WOODWARD.
VIII. Sarah, m. ——— PRICE.
IX. Ann, m. (firstly) ——— MARRIOTT; (secondly) ——— COALE.
X. Basil.
XI. Davidge.

COLONEL CHARLES WARFIELD, m. 15th April, 1762, Elizabeth WARFIELD; removed to Sams Creek near Carroll County, Maryland.

ISSUE

I. Alexander.
II. Mary.
III. Sarah.
IV. Elizabeth.
V. Rezin.
VI. Rezin.
VII. Anne, b. 17th March, 1774; m. 15th December, 1796, Rev. Dr. Joshua JONES, their son, Wesley JONES, m. Margaret James POOLE, their dau. Elizabeth Francanna JONES, m. William Andrew MORRISON.

ISSUE

1. Wesley Jones MORRISON, M.D.; b. 29th November, 1870; m. 17th January, 1900, Mary THOMAS, dau. of John THOMAS.

ISSUE

1[1]. Elizabeth MORRISON, b. 2d September, 1905.
2[1]. John MORRISON, b. 4th September, 1907.

2. Cora Belle MORRISON.
3. Samuel Turner MORRISON, b. 14th July, 1878; m. 20th January, 1910, Hazel A. FRISBIE.

ISSUE

1[1]. Cora A. MORRISON, b. 23d October, 1910.
2[1]. William F. MORRISON, b. 31st July, 1914.

4. William Francis MORRISON, b. 26th February, 1881, Major of United States Field Artillery; m. 7th November, 1905, Bessie TAYLOR, dau. of Col. Sydney W. TAYLOR.

ISSUE

1^1. Virginia MORRISON, b. 6th September, 1906.

VIII. Elizah.
IX. Launcelot.
X. David.
XI. Dennis.
XII. Charles (Rev.).

Hanson

JOHN HANSON, b. 1630; d. 1714; he was a Justice of the Peace for Charles County, Maryland, 1694-1696; his son

SAMUEL HANSON, b. 1685; d. 1740; Burgess Charles County, 1716-1717, 1728-1731; Commissary Charles County, 1734; m. Elizabeth STORY; their son

SAMUEL HANSON, b. 1716; d. 1794; was Justice and County Commissioner Charles County, 1755-1775, and High Sheriff, 1774.

Hutchins

FRANCIS HUTCHINS lived in Calvert County, Maryland; he m. Elizabeth BURRAGE, dau. of John BURRAGE and Margaret, surname unknown; he was a Member of the Maryland House of Assembly, 1694; Justice of Calvert County, 1679-1698; Burgess for Calvert County, 1682-1684, 1694-1697; d. 1698; Mary HUTCHINS m. Samuel THOMAS.

Richardson

WILLIAM RICHARDSON came to Virginia in the *Paul* of London in 1634; removed to Maryland in 1666; became a Member of the Lower House of the Assembly, 1676-1683; Member of the Maryland General Assembly, 1678-1684; d. 1697; m. Elizabeth EWEN, widow of Richard TALBOT.

Rogers

MAJOR JOHN ROGERS lived in Prince George County, Maryland; he was a Member of the Conventions of Maryland, 1774-1776; Council of Safety, 1775; Major Lower Battalion of Prince George County, Maryland; d. 1789.

Thomas

LIEUTENANT PHILIP THOMAS came from Bristol, England, in 1651; he m. Sarah HARRISON; Member of the High Commission governing Maryland, 1656; one of those who in 1659 surrendered the government to Lord Baltimore, Lieutenant Provincial Forces of Maryland before 1656.

Wynne

DOCTOR THOMAS WYNNE, Speaker of the First Provincial Assembly of Pennsylvania, 1682–1683, having accompanied William PENN to America in the *Welcome;* Judge of the Supreme Court, 1686–1690; President of Assembly, 1687–1688; *m.* Martha BUTTALL.

Mould

JOHANNES C. MOULD of Montgomery, New York; b. there 3d February, 1783, in the Mould Homestead; d. there March, 1870; m. 17th June 1815, Mary SHAFER, b. 1798, d. 29th January, 1861.

ISSUE

I. Christopher, b. 16th May, 1816; d. 23d May, ——; m. 11th December, 1843.
II. Catharina, b. 23d February, 1818; d. 13th August, 1818.
III. Daniel, b. 6th June, 1819; d. 12th March, 1902.
IV. Moses, b. 6th October, 1821; d. 14th August, 1877.
V. Mary, b. 17th July, 1826; d. 1899; m. 27th March, 1845, Thomas WAIT of Montgomery, New York, b. 27th January, 1821, d. 1903, son of Samuel and Mary (WELCH) WAIT of Banwell, Somersetshire, England, who came to America in 1821 and settled in Montgomery, New York.

ISSUE

1. Thomas WAIT, d. in infancy.
2. Thomas WAIT, d. in infancy.
3. Martha WAIT, b. 10th January, 1847; m. 1872 (?).
4. Charles D. WAIT, b. 18th October, 1848; m. 1897 (?).
5. Mary E. WAIT, b. 10th October, 1850; m. 1885 (?).
6. George W. WAIT, b. 7th November, 1852; d. 18th August, 1911; m. 1897 (?).
7. Alida WAIT, b. 15th March, 1856; m. 1880.
8. Effie WAIT, b. 25th February, 1858; m. 1883 (?).
9. Wesley WAIT, D.D.S., of Newburgh, New York; b. 15th May, 1861; is patentee of the fan used in the New York concentrating air to the axis of motion; also the inventor of the electric sockets used on incandescent lamps which he sold to Thomas A. EDISON in 1885; the inventor also for a device for interlocking steel girders, eliminating the use of rivets; is the author of a treatise entitled "Basic Laws of the Universe or the Unit of Universal Existence," m. (firstly) Emily S. RAWLINS, dau. of Gen. John A. RAWLINS; m. (secondly) 1905, Anne E. KNAPP, dau. of Samuel Trevor KNAPP.

ISSUE

1^1. Lucille Rawlins WAIT, b. 25th February, 1887; m. 7th June, 1906, John S. BULL.

ISSUE

1^2. Stephen BULL, b. 19th January, 1907.
2^2. J. A. Rawlins BULL, b. 25th July, 1908.
3^2. William BULL, b. 24th October, 1912.
4^2. Richard W. BULL, b. 31st July, 1914.

10. Augustus WAIT, b. 1863; d. 1868.
11. Annie WAIT, b. 15th April, 1868; unmarried.

VI. Eva, b. 4th March, 1824; d. 11th May, 1891.
VII. Martha, b. 7th February, 1827; d. 1846.
VII. Jessie, b. 19th December, 1831; d. 26th September, 1911.
IX. Herman, b. 24th April, 1834; d. 1843.
X. William S., b. 8th January, 1837.
XI. John C., b. 8th October, 1839; m. 16th March, 1908.
XII. Anna, b. 27th April, 1842; d. 23d August, 1914.

Arms (WAIT).—Argent a chevron between three bugle horns stringed sable, garnished or.
Crest.—A bugle horn stringed sable garnished or.
Motto.—Pro aris et focis.

Lineage (Mould)

This surname appears in Colonial documents spelled variously MOUL, MAUL, MOUWL and MOYL. In the original Dutch MOUL signifies "mouth." For a century and a half the name has been spelled MOULD. According to the records of the Holland Society, Christoffel MOUL is the progenitor of the MOULD family in America. He was a son of Johannes MOUL of Leyden, Holland. That the family was of distinguished station is evidenced by the family crest which is thus described by FAIRBAIRN, "demi-lion rampant, gardant, or." Christoffel MOUL sailed for America on the ship *Friendship*, commanded by Captain HEYDT, which reached Esopus (now Kingston, New York), in 1710. Here he lived until 1732. In 1715 he enlisted under Captain WITTAKER in Col. John RUTSEN's Regiment and was frequently called upon to defend life and property from the incursions of the Indians. In 1732 Christoffel MOUL removed to that part of Wallkill precinct now embraced in the town of Montgomery, Orange County, New York, where the family have resided for many generations. He became an Elder of the First Dutch Reformed Church of Montgomery in 1736. He served in Capt. John BYARD's Company of Militia, enlisting in 1738; m. Anna Juliana SERVIN, SEVRING, SERGIN or ZARINS as variously spelt.

ISSUE

I. Diewertjen, *b.* 12th September, 1712; *m.* 14th January, 1733, Andries DEKKER.

ISSUE

1. Phillipus DEKKER, *bapt.* 26th March, 1735.
2. Annaatje J. DEKKER, *b.* 3d May, 1737.

II. Margriet, *b.* 19th September, 1714; *bapt.* 22d October, 1734; *m.* Benjamin CONSTAYSEL (CONSTABLE).

ISSUE

1. Phillipus, *b.* 7th October, 1740.
2. Marretje B., *b.* 17th May, 1743.
3. Christoffel, *b.* 20th May, 1745.
4. Marretje, *b.* 23d May, 1749.
5. Benjamin (twin), *b.* 19th January, 1751.
6. Deborah (twin), *b.* 19th January, 1751.
7. Johannes, *b.* 24th October, 1754.

III. Anna Catryna, *b.* 3d November, 1717; *bapt.* in Montgomery, 23d May, 1736; *m.* Henrich WELLER.

ISSUE

1. Anna Juliana WELLER, *b.* 7th October, 1740.
2. Wilhelimne WELLER, *b.* 20th May, 1745.
3. Phillipus WELLER, *b.* 1st August, 1747.
4. Lea WELLER, *b.* 28th March, 1751.
5. Catherina WELLER, *b.* 16th May, 1753.

IV. JOHANNES, *b.* 31st July, 1720, of whom later.

V. Phillipus, *b.* 12th October, 1722; *m.* Susanna HUI (HUEY).

ISSUE

1. Antje, *b.* 15th October, 1751.
2. Catharina, *b.* 24th October, 1754; said to have *m.* Isaac ROOSA.
3. Robert, *b.* 27th August, 1757; *m.* Jane STEWART.
4. James, *b.* 8th January, 1761.
5. Philip (not authentic).

VI. Marretje, *b.* 16th July, 1734; *m.* Jan MAKLIN.

ISSUE

1. Anna MAKLIN, *b.* 15th October, 1751.
2. Maria MAKLIN, *b.* 18th November, 1753.

VII. Annanje, *b.* 17th April, 1726; *m.* Johannes or John KAMPFORT (COMFORT).

ISSUE

1. Hanna KAMPFORT, *bapt.* 30th April, 1751.
2. Rachel KAMPFORT, *bapt.* 1st January, 1754.
3. Mary KAMPFORT, *bapt.* 2d February, 1756.
4. Sarah KAMPFORT, *bapt.* 14th November, 1765.
5. Deborah KAMPFORT, *bapt.* 30th April, 1768.

VIII. Elizabeth, *b.* 25th September, 1727; *m.* William COMFORT.

ISSUE

1. William COMFORT, *b.* 13th January, 1754.
2. Elizabeth COMFORT, *b.* 5th May, 1759.
3. Susanna COMFORT, *b.* 2d May, 1761.
4. Jopia COMFORT, *b.* 4th November, 1769.

JOHANNES MOULD, *b.* 31st July, 1720, in Kingston; *d.* 15th March, 1804; was a Sergeant in Captain New KIRK's Company of Militia in 1756 for guarding the Western frontier; served during the War of the Revolution in Colonel McCLANGHRY's Regiment; *m.* 6th September, 1743, Maria Catharina MENGES, *b.* 7th April, 1746, *d.* 26th May, 1806.

ISSUE

I. CHRISTOFFEL, *b.* 20th May, 1745, of whom later.
II. Antje, *b.* 7th April, 1746; *m.* Abraham DICKERSON.

ISSUE

1. Molly DICKERSON, *b.* 31st October, 1767.
2. Antje DICKERSON, *b.* 10th January, 1772.
3. Elenora DICKERSON, *b.* 8th October, 1775.
4. Adam DICKERSON, *b.* 4th April, 1779.

III. Johannes, *b.* 31st May, 1756; served during the War of the Revolution in Colonel McCLANGHRY'S REGIMENT; *m.* 8th May, 1777, Maria LAW.
IV. Eva, *b.* 4th February, 1761; *m.* Johannes MILLER, *b.* May, 1756.

CHRISTOFFEL MOULD, *b.* in the town of Montgomery, New York, 20th May, 1745; served in the Colonial Wars in both Ulster and Orange County Militia and during the War of the Revolution in Colonel McCLANGHRY's Regiment; *m.* 23d March, 1773, Rubina DICKERSON.

ISSUE

I. Johannes, *b.* 10th April, 1774; *bapt.* 2d May, 1774; *d.* young.
II. Eleanora (date of birth illegible).
III. Wilhelm, *b.* 7th April, 1777.

COLONIAL FAMILIES OF THE UNITED STATES

    IV. Maria, *b.* 25th October, 1778.
    V. Elizabeth, *bapt.* 13th May, 1781.
    VI. JOHANNES C., *b.* 3d February, 1783, the subject of this memoir.
    VII. Philip, *b.* 28th June, 1785.
    VIII. Eva, *b.* 16th September, 1787.
    IX. Anne, *b.* 10th November, 1789.
    X. Caty (Katie), *b.* 3d February, 1792.

Arms (MOULD).—Sable two bars wavy argent, in chief a lion passant guardant of the last.

Crest.—A demi-lion rampant guardant or.

Penrose

BOIES PENROSE, Senator, A.B.; *b.* at Philadelphia, 1st November, 1860; graduated with honors at Harvard University, 1881; A.B., 1881; admitted to the Bar of Philadelphia, and practiced in Philadelphia, 1883; Member of the House of Representatives, 1884-1886, Member of the State Senate, 1887-1890; President pro tem, 1889 and 1891; United States Senator, Pennsylvania, three terms, 1897-1915; Chairman Republican State Committee, 1903-1905; Member Republican National Committee 1904, 1908; Delegate Republican National Committee, 1900, 1904 and 1908. Author: "History of the City Government of Philadelphia."

Lineage

BARTHOLOMEW PENROSE, son of Bartholomew PENROSE of St. Stephens' Parish, Bristol; *bapt.* 21st January, 1674; *d.* November, 1711; emigrated to America and settled in Philadelphia circa 1700; *m.* 1703, Esther LEECH, dau. of Tobias Leech, of Philadelphia (formerly of Cheltenham County, Gloucester), England.

ISSUE

I. Dorothy, *b.* 1703; *d.* 11th August, 1764.
II. Sarah, *b.* 1705; *d.* 28th April, 1777; *m.* Richard MATHER.
III. Bartholomew, *b.* 1708; *m.* 21st May, 1737, Mary KIRLL, dau. of John KIRLL; had issue.
IV. THOMAS, *b.* 1709, of whom later.

THOMAS PENROSE of Philadelphia; *b.* 1709; *d.* 1757; *m.* 21st October, 1731, Sarah COATS, dau. of John COATS, of Philadelphia, she *m.* (secondly) Capt. Lester FALKNER, and *m.* (thirdly) Anthony DUCHÉ.

ISSUE

I. Bartholomew, *d.* young.
II. Thomas, *b.* 22d January, 1734; *d.* 28th November, 1815; *m.* 7th July, 1757, Ann DOWDING, dau. of Joseph DOWDING; left issue.
III. John, *d.* young.
IV. JAMES, *b.* 23d February, 1738, of whom later.
V. Samuel, *b.* 11th November, 1742; *d.* 1796; left issue; *m.* (firstly) 30th April, 1766, Ann FLEESON, dau. of Plunket FLEESON; *m.* (secondly) 30th September, 1780, Sarah MOULDER.
VI. Bartholomew, *d.* in infancy.

COLONIAL FAMILIES OF THE UNITED STATES 375

VII. Isaac, b. 1st March, 1747; d. 16th January, 1784; left issue; m. (firstly) Cassandra HALL, of Maryland, who d. 1781; m. (secondly) Ann, surname not given.
VIII. Benjamin, d. young.
IX. Jonathan, b. 10th July, 1752; m. 8th November, 1775, Ann ROWAN, dau. of John ROWAN; had isssue.

JAMES PENROSE of Philadelphia; b. there, 23d February, 1738; d. 7th September, 1771; m. 1766, Sarah BIDDLE, who d. 24th October, 1794, dau. of John BIDDLE, of Philadelphia, she m. (secondly) 15th August, 1776, John SHAW.

ISSUE

I. John, d. in infancy.
II. CLEMENT BIDDLE, b. 20th February, 1771, of whom later.

CLEMENT BIDDLE PENROSE of Philadelphia; b. there 20th February, 1771; one of the three Commissioners for the Territory ceded by France to the United States; m. 1st August, 1796, Anne Howard BINGHAM, dau. of Maj. Charles BINGHAM.

ISSUE

I. CHARLES BINGHAM, b. 6th October, 1798, of whom later.
II. Clement Biddle, b. 30th September, 1802; m. 3d June, 1830, Anne WILLIAMSON, dau. of Joseph Biddle WILLIAMSON of New Orleans.
III. James Wilkinson, Major in United States Army; b. 1808; m. 1st January, 1849, Mary Ann HOFFMAN, dau. of Gen. William HOFFMAN, of the United States Army.
IV. Howard.
V. Ann, d. 1832.
VI. Mary, d. 1886.
VII. Sarah Tillier, d. 15th December, 1821.

CHARLES BINGHAM PENROSE, b. at Frankford, Philadelphia, 6th October, 1798; d. 1857, admitted to the Bar, in Philadelphia, 9th May, 1821; Member of the Senate of Pennsylvania, 1833–1842; Speaker of the Senate; Solicitor to the Treasury, 1841; m. 16th March, 1824, Valeria Fullerton BIDDLE, dau. of William McFunn BIDDLE.

ISSUE

I. William McFunn, Colonel 6th Regiment, United States Army; b. 29th March, 1825; d. 2d September, 1872; m. July, 1858, Valeria MERCHANT, dau. of Gen. Charles MERCHANT.

ISSUE

1. Sarah Merchant.
2. Valeria Biddle.
3. Ellen Williams.
4. Virginia Merchant.

II. RICHARD ALEXANDER FULLERTON, b. 24th March, 1827, of whom later.
III. Sarah Clementina, m. September, 1854, William Sergeant BLIGHT.

ISSUE

1. Charles Penrose BLIGHT, b. 8th October, 1855; d. unmarried, 4th July, 1895.
2. William Sergeant BLIGHT, b. 7th March, 1858, of the Philadelphia Bar; m. 6th December, 1890, Cornelia Taylor BLIGHT, dau. of Isaac Oliver BLIGHT.
3. Elihu Spencer BLIGHT, b. 11th November, 1860; graduated at the University of Pennsylvania, 1881.
4. Lydia Spencer BLIGHT, b. 26th April, 1863; m. 7th December, 1886, John F. HAGEMAN, of New Jersey, who d. 1st July, 1893.

IV. Clement Biddle, b. 27th October, 1832; Member of the Philadelphia Bar and Judge of the Orphans' Court; m. 30th September, 1857, Mary LINNARD, dau. of Stephen Beasley LINNARD.

ISSUE

1. Emily Linnard, b. 17th October, 1858.
2. Valeria Fullerton, b. 29th October, 1860.
3. Charles Bingham, d. young.
4. Stephen Beasley Linnard, B.A., S.D., D.D.; b. 20th December, 1864; President of Whitman College, Walla Walla, Washington; was graduated B.A., William College, 1885; B.D., Yale, 1890; given honorary degree D.D. by Ripon and Williams, 1905; Pastor Congregational Church of Daylon, Washington, 1890–1894; President of Whitman College, Walla Walla, Washington, 1894—; President of Pacific Coast Theological Conference; President of Association of Colleges and Universities of the Pacific Northwest; Secretary-Treasurer of the Northwestern Educational Foundation; m. 17th June, 1896, in Hartford, Connecticut, Mary Deming SHIPMAN, b. 27th July, 1868, dau. of the Hon. Nathaniel SHIPMAN, who m. 25th May, 1859, Carline ROBINSON.

ISSUE

1^1. Mary Deming, b. 26th March, 1898.
2^1. Frances Shipman, b. 16th February, 1900.
3^1. Clement Biddle, b. 14th November, 1902.
4^1. Nathaniel Shipman, b. 14th November, 1902.
5^1. Virginia, b. 9th September, 1904.
6^1. Stephen Beasley Linnard, b. 19th March, 1904.

COLONIAL FAMILIES OF THE UNITED STATES

5. Helen, *m.* 17th October, 1901, Thomas Leiper HODGE.
6. Elizabeth Colegate, *m.* 3d February, 1891, Rev. Henry Everston COBB, D.D.

ISSUE

1^1. Dorothy Penrose COBB, *b.* 31st October, 1892.
2^1. Oliver Ellsworth COBB, *b.* 3d February, 1895.
3^1. Emily Linnard COBB, *b.* 22d June, 1899.
4^1. Clement Biddle Penrose COBB, *b.* 16th September, 1900.

7. Lydia Baird, *b.* 22d September, 1871.
8. Mary Clementina, *b.* 16th April, 1875.

v. Charles Bingham, *b.* 29th August, 1838; *m.* 29th December, 1870, Clara ANDAIRESE, dau. of Dr. James Wheeler ANDAIRESE.

ISSUE

1. Charles Bingham, *b.* 25th March, 1872.
2. Clement Andairese, of Baltimore, Maryland; *b.* 2d January, 1874; graduated M.D., Johns Hopkins University.

RICHARD ALEXANDER FULLERTON PENROSE, *b.* at Carlisle, Pennsylvania, 24th March, 1827; graduated at the University of Pennsylvania, M.D., 1849; Dickinson College, LL.D., 1872; Member of the College of Physicians, Philadelphia, and one of the Founders of the University Hospital; *m.* 28th September, 1858, Sarah Hannah BOIES, dau. of Jeremiah Smith Hubbard BOIES, of Cecil County, Maryland.

ISSUE

I. Boies, *d.* in infancy.
II. BOIES, *b.* 1st November, 1860, the subject of this memoir.
III. Charles Bingham, *b.* 1st February, 1862; A.B., Harvard, 1881; A.M., Ph.D., 1884; M.D., University of Pennsylvania, 1884 (LL.D., 1909); Resident Physician, Pennsylvania Hospital, 1885–1886; Out-Patient Surgeon to same; Surgeon to Gynecean Hospital, from its foundation, 1887; Surgeon German Hospital, 1890; Professor of Gynecology, University of Pennsylvania, 1893–1899; retired; President Pennsylvania Board Game Commissioners; Members Advisory Board Pennsylvania State Department of Health; Member College of Physicians of Philadelphia, American Philosophical Society, Academy Natural Sciences (Member of Council); Fellow American Association for the Advancement of Science; President Zoological Society, Philadelphia; Member Philadelphia Club. Author: "Text Book of Diseases of Women" (six editions); contributor to medical publications and to scientific journals on mathematics and physical subjects; Director

Philadelphia Saving Fund Society. Residence, 1720 Spruce Street, Philadelphia, Pennsylvania; *m.* 17th November, 1892, Katherine DREXEL of New York, dau. of Joseph W. DREXEL.

ISSUE

1. Charles Bingham, *d.* in infancy.
2. Sarah Hannah Boies, *b.* 23d June, 1896.
3. Boies, *b.* 20th November, 1902.

IV. Richard Alexander Fullerton, *b.* 17th December, 1863; Geologist, Mining Engineer, A.B., Harvard, 1884; A.M., Ph.D., 1886; unmarried; Geologist in charge survey of Eastern Texas, for Texas Geological Survey, 1888; appointed 1889 by Geological Survey of Arkansas to make detailed reports on the manganese and iron ore regions of Arkansas; Professor Economical Geology, at Leland Stanford, Jr. University, 1893; Special Geologist United States Geological Survey, 1894, to examine and report on gold districts of Cripple Creek, Colorado; Member Board of Managers Philadelphia, Germantown and Norristown Railway Company; Director Ridge Avenue Passenger Railway Company of Philadelphia; Trustee University of Pennsylvania; Associate Editor *Journal of Geology;* Member American Philosophical Society; Fellow Royal Geographical Society, American Association for the Advancement of Science, Geological Society of America, Colorado Scientific Society; Member American Institute Mining Engineers; Mining and Metallurgical Society of America, Geological Society, Washington, Academy of Natural Sciences, Philadelphia, Washington Academy Sciences. Author: "The Nature and Origin of Deposits of Phosphate of Lime," 1888; "Geology of the Gulf Tertiary of Texas," 1889; "Manganese: Its Uses, Ores, Deposits," 1890; "The Iron Deposits of Arkansas," 1892; also other reports, papers, and articles on economical geology. Residence, 1331 Spruce Street, Philadelphia, Pennsylvania.

V. Spencer, Mining Engineer; *b.* Philadelphia, 2d November, 1865; A.B., Harvard, 1886; a founder, Secretary and Director of Utah Copper Company; a pioneer in Cripple Creek, Colorado, Mining District, and still identified with several of its mines; Secretary and Director United States Sugar and Land Company, Beaver Land and Irrigation Company; Director Ray Consolidated Copper Company, Chino Copper Company, First National Bank (Colorado Springs, Colorado), Cripple Creek Central Railroad, Beaver, Penrose and Northern Railway, Grand Junction and Grand River Valley Railway, Colorado; on staff of Governor PEABODY of Colorado, 1903–1904; Republican, Member of the following Clubs, Philadelphia, Union League, Philadelphia Country, Racquet (Philadelphia), University, Union League

COLONIAL FAMILIES OF THE UNITED STATES

(New York), Denver, Denver Country (Denver), El Paso, Cheyenne Mountain, (Colorado Springs), Alta (Salt Lake City), Yondotega (Detroit), Travelers (Paris, France). Residence, Colorado Springs; *m.* 26th April, 1906, Mrs. Julie Villiers (LEWIS) MCMILLAN, of Detroit.

VI. Francis Boies, *b.* 2d August, 1867; *d.* at El Paso, Texas, 8th June, 1901.

Residence.—1331 Spruce Street, Philadelphia, Pennsylvania.
Arms.—Argent, three bends sable each charged with as many roses as of the field.
Crest—A trout Naiant or.

Presby

FRANK HENRY PRESBY of Montclair, New Jersey; *b.* 2d October, 1856, at Newark, New Jersey; *m.* there 5th December, 1895, Harriet Myers COOK, *b.* 16th July, 1875, dau. of William Halsey COOK, *b.* 3d October, 1839, *m.* 12th October, 1869, to Ida M. TAYLOR, who *d.* 14th December, 1875.

ISSUE

I. Dorothea, *b.* 15th September, 1896; *d.* 1 May, 1899.
II. Mildred, *b.* 17th April, 1899.
III. Betsey Flint, *b.* 2nd February, 1905.

FRANK HENRY PRESBY was educated at the public schools of Newark, New Jersey; was for twenty-four years with the Clark Estates, New York, fourteen years as agent and manager.

Lineage

JOSEPH PRESBY also known as PRESBURY of Bradford, New Hampshire, *b.* 1753; *d.* 11th October, 1827; served in Capt. Isaac BALDWIN'S Company in Col. John STARKE's 1st New Hampshire Regiment, Revolutionary War; he entered the service 23d April, 1773, and served three months and sixteen days; was in service 26th September, 1776, in Col. Thomas TASH's Regiment; *m.* Hannah CAMPBELL.

ISSUE AMONG OTHERS

I. JESSE CAMPBELL, *b.* 1796, of whom later.

JESSE CAMPBELL PRESBY of Bradford, New Hampshire; *b.* 22d February, 1796; *d.* 1851; *m.* 1821, Betsy Walton FLINT, *b.* 8th August, 1798, *d.* 1821, dau. of Deacon Simeon FLINT, *b.* 24th June, 1775, at North Reading, Massachusetts, *d.* 3d July, 1857, in Stripton, Canada, *m.* 25th September, 1795, Betsy POPE, *b.* 13th August, 1777, in Danvers, Massachusetts. Simeon FLINT was the fifth son of Lieut. Benjamin FLINT, who served in the French and Indian Wars, he being the son of Captain Thomas FLINT, who served in King Philip's War and in the expedition in 1675 against the Narragansetts, in which he was wounded. Betsey POPE, was dau. of Ebenezer and Annie (PUTNAM) POPE, who was *m.* 17th July, 1757; Ebenezer POPE was the son of Joseph POPE, *b.* Salem Village, 16th June, 1687, *d.* there 13th September, 1755, *m.* 7th February, 1715, Mehitable PUTNAM, *b.* there 20th July, 1695. She was the daughter of John PUTNAM, III, of Salem Village, *b.* 14th July, 1667, *m.* Hannah, surname not given. John PUTNAM was the son of Captain PUTNAM, *bapt.* in Astons Abbots, England, 27th May, 1627, *d.* April, 1710, in Salem Village, was Corporal, 1672; served in the troops raised at Salem and Lynn for King Philip's War, Commissioned Lieutenant, 7th October, 1678; Captain, 1687; Deputy to the General Court, 1679–1692. He *m.* 3d September, 1652, Rebecca PRINCE. Capt. John PUTNAM was the son of John PUTNAM, the emigrant, *bapt.* at Wingrove Bucks,

17th January, 1579, d. 30th October, 1662, in Salem, Massachusetts; admitted to the Church in Salem in 1647, m. Priscilla GOULD. His ancestry runs as follows: Nicholas,[11] John,[10] Richard,[9] Henry,[8] Nicholas[7] (of the Record of 1574), William,[6] Henry,[5] William,[4] Robert,[3] Sir Roger,[2] Sir Roger,[1] and Thomas PUTNAM.

ISSUE AMONG OTHERS

I. WILLIAM JOSEPH HENRY, b. 1825, of whom later.

WILLIAM JOSEPH HENRY PRESBY of Newark, New Jersey; b. 22d October, 1825, in Sherbrooke Canada; d. 23d January, 1870; m. 25th December, 1855, Elizabeth Ann HUSK, b. in Denville, New Jersey, d. 5th February, 1913, at Montclair, gd. dau. of Jonathan HUSK, who served as a private in Capt. Yelles MEADE's Company, 1st New Jersey Regiment, Revolutionary War; 1st New Jersey Regiment and was discharged 5th March, 1779.

ISSUE

I. FRANK HENRY, b. 2d October, 1856, the subject of this memoir.

Residence.—95 Upper Mountain Avenue, Montclair, New Jersey.
Clubs.—Montclair, Montclair Golf, Montclair Athletic, Drug and Chemical Club of New York.
Societies.—Colonial Wars, Sons of American Revolution, New Jersey Historical.

Price

BRIGADIER-GENERAL BUTLER DELAPLAINE PRICE, U. S. A., of Philadelphia, Pennsylvania; *b.* 27th May, 1845, at Philadelphia; *m.* 18th October, 1866, at Philadelphia, Clara Agnes GILLMORE, dau. of James Clarkson and Elizabeth Ann (DUNLAP) GILLMORE.

ISSUE

I. Elizabeth Senter, *b.* 4th September, 1867; *m.* 17th August, 1899, Carver HOWLAND (see "Colonial Families," volume IV, pages 221-23).

ISSUE

1. Jeanette HOWLAND, *b.* 6th May, 1902.

II. Gillmore Delaplaine, *b.* 7th March, 1870; *m.* 11th June, 1902, Elizabeth Arnold WHALING.

ISSUE

1. Mary Gwynne, *b.* 16th March, 1903.
2. Barbara, *b.* 29th July, 1907; *d.* 6th September, 1909.

III. Ethel Huntt, *b.* 7th April, 1876; *d.* 19th April, 1884.

BUTLER DELAPLAINE PRICE entered the Volunteer Service of the United States as Second Lieutenant of the 2d Pennsylvania Cavalry, 6th December, 1861; promoted to First Lieutenant, 1863; Captain, 1864; Honorably mustered out of Volunteer Service, 5th January, 1865; served in the Cavalry Corps, Army of the Potomac; appointed Second Lieutenant, 4th United States Infantry, 11th May, 1866; First Lieutenant, 25th November, 1873; Regimental Adjutant, 1881-1886; Captain, 17th September, 1886; Major, 2d March, 1899; Lieutenant Colonel, 1st United States Infantry, 5th March, 1901; transferred to 4th United States Infantry, 23d July, 1901; Colonel, 16th United States Infantry, 18th October, 1902; retired at his own request after forty-two years service, 26th December, 1905; Brigadier General, United States Army, Retired, 26th December, 1905; participated in campaign of Army of the Potomac (except Wilderness), 1862-1865; served on the Plains for twenty-three years in all, participating in Indian campaigns, 1867-1879; served in the Cuban campaign of 1898 against Santiago de Cuba, participating in battles of El Caney, San Juan and Capture of Santiago; sailed on United States Transport *Grant* for the Philippines in January, 1899 (by Suez Canal), reached Manila 7th March, took part in various campaigns on islands until 25th December, 1901; commanded Brigade at the Military Manoeuvers at Manassas, September, 1904; commanded all Regular Troops at the St. Louis Exposition, November, 1904, to January, 1905; commanded a Brigade at Fort William McKinley, Philippine Islands, from 26th January, 1905, to the latter part of August or first part of September.

COLONIAL FAMILIES OF THE UNITED STATES

Lineage

The PRICE family is descended from Patriarch Jonathan PRICE, a native of Wales, *b.* 1699; he settled in Philadelphia; *m.* 8th February, 1731, Mary CHANDLER, dau. of John and Elizabeth (———) CHANDLER of Philadelphia.

ISSUE

I. JOHN, of whom later.
II. Mary, *m.* ——— ASHTON.
III. Susannah, *m.* ——— AYRES.

JOHN PRICE of Philadelphia; *m.* 29th December, 1760, Hannah DELAPLAINE, dau. of James DELAPLAINE, son of Patrician Emigrant DELAPLAINE of France and Holland, who founded the family name in Pennsylvania.

ISSUE

I. CHANDLER, *b.* 22d February, 1766, of whom later.

CHANDLER PRICE of Philadelphia; *b.* 22d February, 1766; *d.* 27th December, 1827; *m.* 8th March, 1800, Ellen MATLACK, *b.* 17th November, 1780 *d.* 28th March 1862 dau. of Titus and Sarah (RENSHAW) MATLACK.

ISSUE

I. Sarah *b.* 6th March 1801; *d.* April 1877.
II. Ellen Matlack *b.* 23 April 1804; *d.* 7th January 1894.
III. Elizabeth *b.* 30th March 1806; *d.* 3d October 1867.
IV. RICHARD BUTLER of whom later.
V. Chandler *b.* 22d January 1810; *d.* 3d April 1813.

RICHARD BUTLER PRICE of Philadelphia Pennsylvania; *b.* 15th December 1807; *d.* 15h July, 1876; *m.* 25th October, 1841, Elizabeth Senter HUNTT, *b.* 1815, *d.* 9th January, 1883, dau. of Clement Smith and Sarah Ann (SENTER) HUNTT of Virginia, Purser, United States Navy. Sarah Ann (SENTER) HUNTT, *b.* 1798, *d.* January, 1884, dau. of Dr. Isaac and Eliza (ARNOLD) SENTER of Rhode Island. Dr. SENTER was *b.* 1753, at Londerry, New Hampshire, *d.* at Newport, Rhode Island, 10th December, 1799. It was while pursuing his studies with Dr. MOFFATT, a Scotch physician, that he received news of the battle of Lexington, 19th April, 1775. He joined the Rhode Island troops as Surgeon and marched to Cambridge; was with General ARNOLD at the assault upon Quebec, where he was captured and held for some time as a prisoner; retired from the Army in 1779 and resumed the practice of medicine at Pawtucket; later served several terms as a Representative to the General Assembly; in 1780 was appointed Surgeon and Physician General and removed to Newport; was an able writer and contributor to European journals; was a Fellow of the London, England and Massachusetts Medical Societies; he was a member of the Society of the Cincinnati and for many years President of the Rhode Island Society.

ISSUE OF RICHARD BUTLER AND ELIZABETH SENTER (HUNTT) PRICE

I. Fannie Maria, *b.* 19th April, 1843; *d.* 12th January, 1845.
II. BUTLER DELAPLAINE, *b.* 27th May, 1845, the subject of this memoir.
III. Ella Virginia, *b.* 15th January, 1848; *d.* 21st November, 1851.
IV. Chandler, *b.* 16th May, 1851; *d.* 7th November, 1861.

Residence.—"The Cairo," Washington, D. C.
Clubs.—Army and Navy.
Societies.—Loyal Legion, Sons of the American Revolution, Army of the Potomac (Life Member), Army and Navy Union, Foreign Wars, Military Order of the Caraboa, National Geographic Society, Newport Historical Society (Newport, Rhode Island).

Roach

WALTER THOMAS ROACH, *b.* 5th November, 1870, in Philadelphia; *m.* 17th January, 1899, at Media, Pennsylvania, Mary Fisher STELLWAGEN, *b.* 28th February, 1871, in Philadelphia, dau. of Thomas Cook STELLWAGEN, M.D., of "Belair," Media, Pennsylvania, *b.* 24th July, 1841; son of Captain Henry S. STELLWAGEN, U. S. Navy and Mary Ann COOK, *m.* 5th March, 1868, Annie Eliza CARPENTER, *b.* 13th March, 1843, *d.* 6th October, 1907, dau. of Francis G. CARPENTER and Mary Blake RISBROUGH.

Lineage

The founder of this branch of the American family was Isaac ROACH, I; *b.* in Scotland circa 1710; he was sailing master of a British fleet sent from England in 1740 to determine the boundary line between Delaware and Maryland; he settled at Rehoboth, Delaware, in the same year; *m.* in England circa 1730.

ISSUE

1. ISAAC, *b.* 1748, in Rehoboth, Delaware, of whom below.

ISAAC ROACH, II, *b.* 1748, at Rehoboth, Delaware, but shortly after removed to Philadelphia where he resided in the old district of Southwark until his death in August, 1818; he was Treasurer of the Society for the Relief of Distressed and Decayed Pilots; he held a Captain's commission in the Colonial Navy under the Navy Board and Pennsylvania Committee of Safety for the Defense of the Delaware River and Bay from 23d October, 1775, and remained in the service until 23d August, 1784; he commanded the armed boats *Delaware, Congress, Wirt, Chatham, Franklin* and *Hancock*. His record is referred to in "Journal of Isaac ROACH," printed in *Pennsylvania Historical Society Magazine* in 1893, page 129, and his commissions were held successively under the proprietary of Pennsylvania from Benjamin FRANKLIN, George WASHINGTON, John ADAMS, JEFFERSON and MADISON, and, with the exception of a few years, he remained in Government Service until his death. His services are mentioned in the Minutes of the Naval Board on pages 128, 153, 264, 267, 275, 294, 305, 756 and 761, Volume 1, in Library of Historical Society of Pennsylvania and other Libraries. He filled the grade of First and Second Lieutenant of various armed boats before promotion to the Captaincy and took part in the defense of Fort Mifflin on the Delaware. He was an officer on board the *Charming Sally*, a brig assisting the *Hyder Ali* in the capture of the British ship *General Monk* in Delaware Bay and was badly wounded in that engagement. The *Charming Sally* was captured by the British and recaptured by Captain ROACH. Captain ROACH was one of a Committee in 1779 formed to dispense Provisions during the scarcity of food during and following the War. He was also one of a Committee afterwards termed the "Patriotic Society" which was formed after the British occupancy of Philadelphia to denounce Toryism and British sympathizers, a part of which sympathy was manifested by the holding of the fête known as the "Meschianza" for the entertainment of British officers then in Philadelphia. Captain ROACH commanded the pilot boat *Federal Pilots* during the Land and Water Pageant at Philadelphia 4th July, 1788. He *m.* 25th January, 1775, at St. Paul's Church on South Third Street, Philadelphia, Martha SCANLAN, dau. of William SCANLAN of Dublin, Ireland; he *d.* in 1818 and was buried at St. Peter's, Third and Pine Streets, Philadelphia.

ISSUE

I. George Washington, *d.* unmarried.
II. ISAAC, III, *b.* in Philadelphia 24th February, 1786, of whom later.
III. A daughter, *d.* in early youth.
IV. A daughter, *d.* in early youth.

ISAAC ROACH, III, of Philadelphia, Pennsylvania; born there 24th Feb., 1786; *d.* 30th December, 1848; was buried in family vault at St. Peter's, Third and Pine Streets, Philadelphia; served with distinction in the War of 1812; he was first commissioned as Lieutenant, 2d Regiment Artillery, under Lieut.-Col. Winfield SCOTT; later Adjutant, 2d Regiment Artillery, under Col. George IZARD; was a prisoner of War in Quebec, finally making his escape with two companions but after facing the hardships and rigors of a Canadian winter, was recaptured by troops in pursuit. He was a volunteer and second in command of the attacking party led by Lieutenant ELLIOTT of the United States Navy in two small boats which captured the British vessels of war *Detroit* and *Caledonian* under the British guns at Fort Erie, a feat described by Henry CLAY in his speech on the new army bill in 1813 as one which "whether placed on maritime or land account, for judgment, skill and courage has never been surpassed." He resigned from the Army, by brevet; 1st April, 1824, Major ROACH served as Guardian of the Poor; Commissioner of the Almshouse Purchase; Manager of Christ Church Hospital; Member of the Select Council of Philadelphia and Board of Health; Treasurer of the United States Mint at Philadelphia, and was elected Mayor of Philadelphia, in 1838; he was also a Vestryman of St. Peter's, Third and Pine Streets, for many years; *m.* 4th October, 1819, Mary HUDDELL, dau. of Joseph and Rebecca (ALLEN) HUDDELL, descendant from Nathaniel ALLEN, *b.* in Somersetshire, England, and landed at Chester, Pennsylvania, December, 1681, from Bristol, England, in the ship *Bristol Factor*, Roger DREW, Master; he was one of Penn's Commissioners to found a colony, his commission from William PENN bears date, London, 25th October, 1681; Nathaniel ALLEN was one of the first Grand Jury which assembled in Pennsylvania.

ISSUE

I. William, *b.* 18th July, 1820, in Fort Columbus, Governor's Island, New York; *d.* 7th October, 1821.
II. JOSEPH HUDDELL, *b.* 17th April, 1822, of whom later.

III. Thomas Randall, *b.* 10th October, 1823; *d.* 11th April, 1875; unmarried.
IV. Rebecca Huddell, *b.* 26th April, 1825; *d.* 1888; *m.* Samuel COOPER; no issue.
V. Isaac (twin), *b.* 8th July, 1827; *d.* 26th July, 1827.
VI. Allen (twin), *b.* 8th July, 1827; *d.* 30th July, 1827.

JOSEPH HUDDELL ROACH of Philadelphia, Pennsylvania; *b.* 17th April, 1822, in Philadelphia; *d.* 16th May, 1876; was a Vestryman at old St. Peter's Church; a member of Capt. John CADWALADER's Artillery Company in 1844, and a member of the old Schuylkill Skating Club, Social Art (afterwards Rittenhouse Club); *m.* 15th April, 1846, Eliza Walter JONES, dau. of Walter Moore and Maria (HOLTON) JONES of Philadelphia. Walter Moore JONES was a descendant from Rhys JONES, *b.* in Llamorganshire, Wales, who arrived with his wife Hannah, and son, Richard, as one of the colony which landed at Upland, near Chester, in 1684. He held no office; his family by marriage was connected with notable families of the colonies; his gd. son, Rhys JONES, *m.* Amy COCK, gd. dau. of Judge COCK, one of PENN's Justices, at Chester, also one of the Councillors to Governor MARKHAM. Maria HOLTON was the dau. of Robert HOLTON of "Mulberry Fields," Park Hall, St. Mary's County, Maryland, and Mary WISEMAN, dau. of Henry WISEMAN, who was one of the Councillors of Governor Leonard CALVERT, son of the first Lord Baltimore and settled in St. Mary's County, Maryland, in 1634. Henry WISEMAN came of an old Essex County family and was the son of Sir Thomas WISEMAN, Knight, of Rivenhall, and was one of that party of gentlemen adventurers, who arrived in Maryland on the ships *The Ark* and *The Dove*, to found the colony under the land grants of the Crown to George CALVERT, first Lord Baltimore. Maria HOLTON *m.* (secondly) Joseph R. CHANDLER of Massachusetts and Philadelphia, United States Minister to Naples, Member of Congress, etc.

ISSUE

I. JOSEPH CHANDLER, *b.* 13th March, 1847, of whom later.
II. Mary Huddell, *b.* 7th November, 1848; *d.* 23d August, 1912; *m.* 5th June, 1879, Pierce ARCHER, II, *b.* 25th September, 1838, *d.* 1st December, 1913, son of Pierce ARCHER.

ISSUE

1. Nina Roach ARCHER, *b.* 7th June, 1880; *m.* 21st May, 1901, Arthur Primrose BAUGH, *b.* 26th April, 1879, son of William Maddon and Harriet (THOMPSON) BAUGH of Philadelphia.

ISSUE

1^1. Arthur Primrose BAUGH, Jr., *b.* 9th June, 1902.
2^1. Pierce Archer BAUGH, *b.* 6th February, 1905.
3^1. Nina BAUGH, *b.* 18th March, 1907.
4^1. Mary Archer BAUGH, *b.* 18th September, 1909.

2. Pierce ARCHER, III, b. 1st January, 1882; m. 9th June, 1910, Dorothy Kingston HOFFMAN, b. 3d November, 1886, dau. of John White and Florence Kingston (McCAY) HOFFMAN.

ISSUE

1¹. Pierce ARCHER, Jr., IV, b. 10th February, 1912.
2¹. John Hoffman ARCHER, b. 29th July, 1913.
3¹. Harriet Kingston ARCHER, v. 8th April, 1916.

JOSEPH CHANDLER ROACH of Philadelphia, Pennsylvania; b. there 13th March, 1847; d. there 7th May, 1888; was a Graduate of Seton Hall College, Pennsylvania, and was in business as a Merchant; he was one of the founders of the Riverton, New Jersey, and Chesapeake Bay Yacht Clubs. He m., 4th January, 1870, Mary Zema THOMAS of Philadelphia, b. 27th April, 1847, dau. of John Gallaher THOMAS (b. Hunterstown, Adams Co., Pa. 18th October 1818, m. 19th May, 1846, d. 8th January 1849) of Emmitsburg, Md. and Philadelphia and Josephine BEYLLE, dau. of Joseph Beylle BAILLY, who m. about 1800 Marie Madeleine Therese Luise LE MAISTRE b. Fort Dauphin, St. Domingo, 1781, d. in Philadelphia 1872, dau. of Louis LE MAISTRE, Captain of Dragoons and Commandant of Limonade Parish, St. Anne, St. Domingo, son of Jean Pierre LE MAISTRE, Seneschal Judge Civil and Criminal of Cap, St. Domingo, and Marie Madeleine LE COISTEUX. Louis LE MAISTRE m. 1780 Marie Madeleine Pierre DE MONTENEGRO, dau. of Jacques Bruno Thomas DE MONTENEGRO, Captain of Militia and native of Seville in Spain and Marie Madeleine LE MAISTRE. Joseph Beylle BAILLY was the son of Jean Silvain BAILLY, son of James and Cecilia (GUICHON) BAILLY. He Curator of the Royal Gallery of Paintings under Louis XVI. Jean Silvain BAILLY was the first President of the National Assembly, first Mayor of Paris and was a pupil and associate of LACAILLE, the great astronomer. BAILLY was elected a member of the Academy of Sciences, 1763; a Member of the French Academy, 1783; a Member of the Academy of Inscriptions and Belles Lettres, 1785; he was guillotined 12th November, 1793, by order of the Revolutionary Tribunal on account of his loyalty to Queen Marie Antoinette.

ISSUE

I. WALTER THOMAS, b. 5th November, 1870, the subject of this memoir
II. Joseph HUDDELL, b. 18th January, 1873; m. 27th April, 1898, Alice Morgan BANKSON, b. 3d April, 1875, dau. of John Palmer BANKSON, b. 5th December, 1834, d. 27th December, 1876, m. Anne Catherine, dau. of Morgan ASH. John Palmer BANKSON was Captain of Company F, 118th (Corn Exchange) Regiment, Pennsylvania Volunteers; in 1863 Assistant Inspector-General of 1st Brigade, 1st Division, 5th Army Corps; the same year acting Assistant Inspector, 1st Division, 5th Corps, on Major-General GRIFFIN's Staff; Brigadier-General, National Guard of Pennsylvania, 1869; Major-General, National Guard, 1876; was elected a member of the Schuylkill Fishing Company of the State in Schuylkill, 25th March, 1870.

ISSUE

1. Joseph Huddell, Jr., *b.* 3d February, 1899.
2. Katherine Bankson, *b.* 30th April, 1900.
3. Alice Margaret, *b.* 30th January, 1902; *d.* 3d February, 1906.
4. Isaac, IV, *b.* 17th March, 1906.
5. Thomas Bankson, *b.* 22d June, 1907.
6. Walter Thomas, II, *b.* 21st November, 1910.

III. Mary Edith, *b.* 7th April, 1874; *m.* (firstly) 27th October, 1897, George Edward CURTIS; *m.* (secondly) 3d November, 1909, Dr. Fielding Otis LEWIS, *b.* 20th August, 1878, graduated June, 1906, Jefferson Medical College, Philadelphia; Assistant Laryngologist and Assistant in Otology at Jefferson Medical College Hospital; Laryngologist to the Philadelphia General Hospital; Laryngologist to the State Hospital for Feeble Minded and Epileptics at Spring City, Pennsylvania; Member American Medical Association, Pennsylvania State Medical Association, Philadelphia County Medical Society, Philadelphia Laryngological Society, American Laryngological, Otological and Rhinological Society, Racquet Club; son of James Fielding LEWIS, M.D., and Sarah OVERBY of Hubbardsville, Henderson County, Kentucky.

ISSUE BY FIRST MARRIAGE

1. George Edward CURTIS, Jr., *b.* 20th January, 1900; *d.* 24th August, 1900.

ISSUE BY SECOND MARRIAGE

1. Mary Edith LEWIS, *b.* 12th October, 1911.

Residence.—"Blue Hill Farm," Media, Delaware County, Pennsylvania.
Motto.—Mon Dieu est ma roche.
Clubs.—Rittenhouse, Rose Tree Hunt.
Societies.—Historical Society of Pennsylvania.

Robbins

REV. FRANCIS LE BARON ROBBINS, A.B., D.D., of Greenfield, Massachusetts; formerly of Philadelphia, Pa.; *b.* 2d May, 1830; *m.* 14th October, 1874, Lucy Morton HARTPENCE, *b.* 13th October, 1856, at Nashville, Tennessee, dau. of Rev. Alexander and Martha (MORTON) HARTPENCE and niece of Hon. Levi P. MORTON.

ISSUE

I. Eleanor Hartpence, *b.* 4th July, 1875; *d.* 4th April, 1878.
II. Howard Chandler, B.A., D.D., of 209 Madison Avenue, New York City; *b.* 11th December, 1876, in Philadelphia, Pennsylvania; B.A., Yale College, 1899; B.D., Episcopal Theological School, Cambridge, 1903; D.D. Williams College, 1916; ordained Deacon, 1903, by the Rt. Rev. William LAWRENCE, Bishop of Massachusetts; Priest, 1904, by the Rt. Rev. Edwin S. LINES, Bishop of Newark; Curate, St. Peter's, Morristown, New Jersey, 1903-1905; Rector, St. Paul's, Englewood, New Jersey, 1905-1911; Rector, Church of the Incarnation, New York, since 1911; Dean elect of the Cathedral of St. John the Devine, New York; Chaplain of the Society of Colonial Wars in the State of New York, since 1914; Member of the National Institute of Social Sciences, Member of the Elihu Club, New Haven, and Yale Club, New York, and of the following societies, Phi Beta Kappa, Chi Delta Theta, Sons of the Revolution, Colonial Wars, Mayflower Descendants; *m.* 30th April, 1907, Englewood, New Jersey, Mary Louise BAYLES, *b.* 9th May, 1879, dau. of Robert and Martha (SMITH) BAYLES.
III. Helen Morton, *b.* 4th November, 1878; *d.* 28th May, 1891.
IV. Margaret Bradford, *b.* 11th September, 1881; *m.* 1909, Hon. Dana MALONE, *b.* Arcade, New York, 8th October, 1857; son of James C. and Mary E. MALONE, received public school education; student, Harvard Law School; admitted to bar, 1881; Trial Justice, Franklin County, Massachusetts, 1890-1906; Member Massachusetts House of Representatives, 1893, 1894 (Chairman Judiciary Committee); Senate, 1895-1896 (Chairman Judiciary Committee); Member Republican State Committee, 1897-1905; District Attorney, Northwestern District of Massachusetts, 1902-1905; Attorney-General of Massachusetts, 1906-1910; resumed practice January, 1911; Director of First National Bank, Greenfield; Trustee and Member of Investment Committee, Franklin Savings Institution, Greenfield; Episcopalian, and is a member of the Algonquin, Brookline Country, and Harvard Clubs. Residence, Greenfield, Massachusetts.

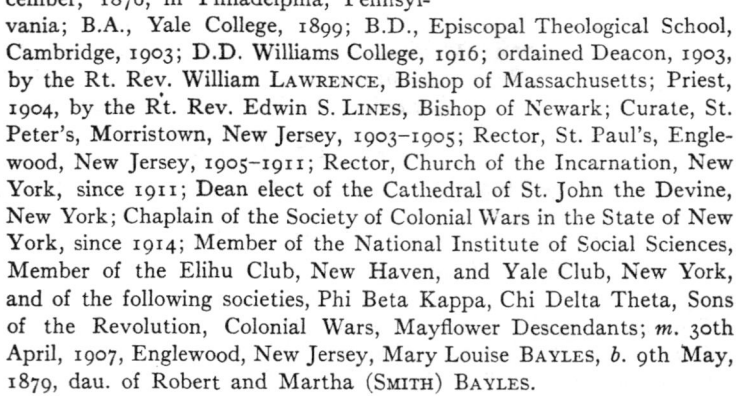

ISSUE

1. Helen MALONE.
2. Frances MALONE.
3. Dana Bradford MALONE.

V. Mary Alice, *b.* 19th December, 1882.
VI. Francis Le Baron, *b.* 3d May, 1884, at Geneva, Switzerland; A.B., LL.B., A.B., Williams College, 1906; LL.B., Harvard, 1910; member of the firm of Winthrop and Stimson, attorneys at law 32 Liberty Street, New York City; *m.* 18th June, 1910, Frances Cleveland LAMONT, dau. of the late Col. Daniel Scott and Juliet (KINNEY) LAMONT of New York City. Col. Daniel Scott LAMONT was Secretary of War during President CLEVELAND'S second administration. Francis Le Baron ROBBINS, Jr., is a member of Harvard (Williams), Meadow Brook, Williams, Huntington Country and Church Clubs, Society of Mayflower Descendants and Society of the Colonial Wars.

ISSUE

1. Elizabeth Bradford, *b.* 15th January, 1915.

VII. Dorothea Le Baron, *b.* 16th November, 1889.

REV. FRANCIS LE BARON ROBBINS, graduated at Williams College; A.B., 1854; D.D., Union College; ordained to the Presbyterian Ministry, 1860; Pastor of Green Hill Presbyterian Church, Philadelphia, 1860–1867; Founder and Pastor Oxford Presbyterian Church, Philadelphia, 1869–1883; Founder and Pastor Beacon Presbyterian Church, Philadelphia, 1886, an institutional church established in the midst of 100,000 working people in Kensington, Philadelphia. Residence, Greenfield, Massachusetts.

Lineage

RICHARD ROBBINS, *b.* in England; came to America in 1639; settled first at Charlestown, Massachusetts, and soon after at Cambridge; shared in the division of the Church Lands, 1652, receiving 80 acres; in 1678 he gave deeds to his sons, Samuel, 36 acres; Nathaniel, 34; to dau. Rebecca and her husband, John WOODWARD, 30 acres; *m.* Rebecca, surname not given.

ISSUE

I. John, *bapt.* 31st May, 1640.
II. Samuel, *b.* 22d May, 1643.
III. NATHANIEL, *b.* 1649, of whom later.
IV. Rebecca, *m.* John WOODWARD.

NATHANIEL ROBBINS of Cambridge; *b.* there 1649; *d.* there 1719; *m.* 7th August, 1669, Mary BRAZIER.

ISSUE AMONG OTHERS

I. Mercy, *b.* 30th November, 1676.
II. NATHANIEL, *b.* 28th February, 1678, of whom later.

NATHANIEL ROBBINS of Cambridge, Massachusetts; *b.* there 28th February 1678; *d.* there 26th January, 1761; *m.* 1695, Hannah CHANDLER, dau. of William CHANDLER, who *m.* Mary DANE, dau. of Dr. John DANE.

ISSUE AMONG OTHERS

I. PHILEMON, *b.* 19th September, 1709, of whom later.

REV. PHILEMON ROBBINS of Branford, Connecticut; *b.* 19th September, 1709, at Cambridge; *d.* 13th August, 1781, in Branford; Graduate of Harvard College, 1729; was a Pastor greatly beloved by his people; a memorial tablet to him has been placed at the right of the pulpit in the Congregational Church of Branford to keep alive the memory of his work and worth; *m.* (firstly) 24th December, 1735, Hannah FOOTE, *d.* 16th June, 1776, dau. of Dr. Isaac FOOTE and his wife Rebecca DICKERMAN, dau. of Lieut. Abraham DICKERMAN; *m.* (secondly) 28th October, 1778, Mrs. Jane MILLS, who *d.* 30th July, 1788.

ISSUE BY FIRST MARRIAGE

I. Philemon, *b.* 1st November, 1736; *d.* 6th September, 1757.
II. Chandler, *b.* 19th August, 1738; *m.* Jane PRINCE.
III. AMMI RUHAMAH, *b.* 25th August, 1740, of whom later.
IV. Hannah, *b.* 1st September, 1742; *d.* 11th November, 1747.
V. Rebecca, *b.* 27th July, 1744; *d.* 7th February, 1751.
VI. Irene, *b.* 16th November, 1746; *d.* 6th January, 1800; *m.* George D. THOMPSON.
VII. Sarah, *b.* 11th January, 1749; *m.* Rev. Peter STARR.
VIII. Hannah Rebecca, *b.* 18th April, 1751; *d.* 9th February, 1799; *m.* (firstly) Rev. John KEEP; *m.* (secondly) Hon. Jahleel WOODBRIDGE.
IX. Rebecca Hannah, *b.* 7th April, 1753; *d.* 1st September, 1789; *m.* Dr. William M. GOULD.

REV. AMMI RUHAMAH ROBBINS of Norfolk, Connecticut; *b.* 25th August, 1740, in Branford, Connecticut; *d.* 31st October, 1813, in Norfolk; Graduate of Yale College, 1760; was installed Minister at Congregational Church at Norfolk, 28th October, 1761; settled as Minister there fifty-two years; Chaplain in Revolutionary Army; Trustee of William College for seventeen years; studied theology with Dr. BELLAMY and for many years had a large number of students with him fitting for college; *m.* 16th May, 1762, Elizabeth LE BARON, dau. of Dr. Lazarus LE BARON and his wife Lydia BRADFORD, dau. of David BRADFORD, who was grandson of Governor William BRADFORD.

COLONIAL FAMILIES OF THE UNITED STATES

ISSUE

I. Philemon, *b.* 18th March, 1763; *d.* 20th March, 1763.
II. Philemon, *b.* 28th March, 1764; *d.* 26th September, 1766.
III. Elizabeth, *b.* 5th January, 1766; *d.* 9th January, 1766.
IV. Mara, *b.* 8th January, 1767; *d.* 9th January, 1767.
V. Ammi Ruhamah, *b.* January, 1768; *m.* Salome ROBBINS.
VI. Elizabeth, *b.* 8th January, 1770; *d.* 6th October, 1815; *m.* (firstly) 1789, Grove LAWRENCE; *m.* (secondly) 16th May, 1811, Roswell GRANT.
VII. Nathaniel, *b.* 18th June, 1772; *d.* 19th February, 1814; was twice married.
VIII. Francis LeBaron, *b.* 9th March, 1775; *d.* young.
IX. Thomas, *b.* 11th August, 1777; *d.* 13th September, 1856.
X. Sarah, *b.* 29th August, 1779; *m.* Joseph BATTELL.
XI. James Watson, *b.* 19th April, 1782; *m.* Maria EGGLESTON.
XII. SAMUEL, *b.* 29th August, 1784, of whom later.
XIII. Francis Le Baron, *b.* 30th December, 1787; *d.* April, 1850; *m.* (firstly) Priscilla (LE BARON) ALDEN; *m.* (secondly) Hannah S. COOK.

SAMUEL ROBBINS of Woodbury, Connecticut, and Camillus, New York; *b.* 29th August, 1784, in Norfolk, Connecticut; *d.* 6th April, 1860, in Penn Yan, New York; *m.* 27th May, 1817, Fanny OSBORNE, daughter of Jeremiah and Anna (SHERWOOD) OSBORNE and sister of Hon. Thomas Burr OSBORNE, Judge of Fairfax County. Jeremiah OSBORNE served as a soldier throughout the Revolutionary War, later a Member of the Legislature of Western Connecticut.

ISSUE

I. Mary Sherwood, *b.* 25th July, 1818; *m.* 3d September, 1846, Rev. James H. KASSON.
II. Frances, *b.* 20th September, 1820; *d.* 26th March, 1886; *m.* 16th September, 1847, Rev. William Wiltshire ROBINSON.
III. Samuel, *b.* 2d September, 1822; *d.* 8th June, 1869; *m.* 29th June, 1858, Elizabeth M. OLIVER.
IV. Susan, *b.* 31st December, 1825; *d.* 31st August, 1873; *m.* 15th September, 1853, Rev. Charles LITTLE.
V. Thomas Burr, *b.* 4th January, 1828; was one of the largest coal operators in Western Pennsylvania; *m.* (firstly) 25th May, 1850, Alice BROCKWAY; *m.* (secondly) 17th September, 1861, Mary Ann Haight WELLS, dau. of Hon. Henry WELLS of the Supreme Court of New York and gd. dau. of Dr. WELLES of General WASHINGTON's Staff.

ISSUE BY FIRST MARRIAGE

1. William, *b.* 11th January, 1852; *m.* 13th September, 1877, Rose BIGNAL.
2. Francis Le Baron, *b.* 3d September, 1855; *m.* 18th May, 1882, Helen GILL.
3. Edward, *b.* 26th August, 1857; *d.* 11th June, 1860.

ISSUE BY SECOND MARRIAGE

1. Henry Welles, *b.* 31st July, 1870; *m.* 6th June, 1894, Elizabeth Kemp RUTTON.

ISSUE

1¹. Thomas.

2. Bertine, *b.* 2d July, 1873; *d.* 9th March, 1874.

VI. FRANCIS LE BARON, *b.* 2d May, 1830, the subject of this memoir.
VII. Sarah Elizabeth, *b.* 21st February, 1835; *d.* 13th April, 1896; *m.* 25th August, 1864, Rev. James M. ANDERSON.

ISSUE

1. Jessie Milan ANDERSON, *b.* 6th May, 1865; *m.* 1896, Robert S. CHASE.

ISSUE

1¹. Elizabeth Le Baron CHASE, *b.* 13th April, 1903.

2. Elizabeth Marshall ANDERSON, *b.* 22d August, 1866.
3. Agnes S. ANDERSON, *b.* 6th October, 1868.
4. Robbins Battell ANDERSON, *b.* 15th June, 1877; *m.* 1st November, 1910, Mary MORRIS.

ISSUE

1¹. Elizabeth ANDERSON, *b.* August, 1911.
2¹. Jean ANDERSON, *b.* November, 1912.

Arms.—Gules two fleurs de lis; each divided paleways and fastened to the side of the escutcheon, the points following each other or.
Crest.—A talbot's head or.
Residence.—Greenfield, Massachusetts.

Robertson

EWING WELCH ROBERTSON, M.D., of Cleveland, Ohio; *b.* 15th March, 1831, at Dansville, New York; *d.* 7th November, 1907; *m.* 22d January, 1857, Elizabeth White CRANDALL, *b.* 12th May, 1836, at Almond, New York, *d.* 2d April, 1914, Cleveland, Ohio, dau. of Col. David and Serena (WHITE) CRANDALL.

ISSUE

I. Addie Crandall, *b.* 10th September, 1859; *d.* 23d August, 1886; *m.* 1882, Rudolph Philip GERLACH of Cleveland, Ohio.

II. Mary D., Daughter American Revolution; *b.* at Wellsville, New York; *m.* 22d December, 1891, William Wright NICOLA, of Cleveland, Ohio, and Pittsburgh, Pennsylvania, *d.* 9th January, 1906, son of Felix and Mary Wright NICOLA.

ISSUE

1. Elizabeth Mary NICOLA, *b.* 3d July, 1897, at Cleveland, Ohio, Daughter American Revolution; graduate of Laurel School, Cleveland, 1915, and Holton Arms School, Washington, D. C., 1916.

III. Lou E., *b.* at Cleveland, Ohio; Daughter American Revolution; *m.* 28th October, 1908, George Albert STANLEY of Cleveland, Ohio, and Long Island, New York, son of Joseph and Eliza (BRAGG) STANLEY

ISSUE

1. Constance Robertson STANLEY, *b.* 27th November, 1909, at Cleveland, Ohio.
2. George Albert STANLEY, Jr., *b.* 2d October, 1911, at Cleveland, Ohio.

EWING WELCH ROBERTSON, M.D., attended Alfred University; graduated at the University of Michigan, 1854; during the Civil War he served as a Surgeon in the Union Army; located at Carver Hospital and Army Square Hospital, Washington, Convalescent Camp, Virginia, and Union Hospital, Memphis, Tennessee.

Lineage

The ROBERTSONs are descended from the ancient Earls of Athol, descended from Duncan, Chief of the Clan ROBERTSON, who with great courage apprehended the murderers of James I, King of Scotland; James II bestowed upon his family for their Crest a hand supporting a regal crown, and for their motto, "Virtutes Gloria Merces." The first of the family in America was ROBERT ROBERTSON, *b.* in Scotland, 1628,

396 COLONIAL FAMILIES OF THE UNITED STATES

who settled in Newburyport, Massachusetts, and *m.* there Mary SILVER, their son
DANIEL ROBERTSON of Coventry, Connecticut; *b.* 9th October, 1667; served in the Colonial Wars; *m.* 24th January, 1719, Lydia STRONG, their son
Daniel ROBERTSON, II, *b.* 21st October, 1721; *d.* 6th February, 1793, of Coventry, Connecticut; was an Ensign in the Colonial Wars in 1759 and served in Captain Buell's Company, during the Lexington Alarm; *m.* 21st November, 1755, Susannah ROBERTSON, their son
DANIEL ROBERTSON, III, *b.* 6th January, 1761; served in the War of 1812; *m.* 10th April, 1796, Amelia JANES, their son
NATHAN ROBERTSON, *b.* 1800; *d.* 1854; *m.* 1828, Mathilda (TOWNSEND) JONES, dau. of Major and Sarah (TOWNSEND) JONES, their son
EWING WELCH ROBERTSON, *b.* 15th March, 1831, the subject of this memoir.

Reed

The REEDS, spelt variously REID, READE, READ, are descendants of the Princes of Northumberland. The family is a noble one and many of the name are gentlemen of Coat Armour. Thomas REED, Esq., of Barton Court, County of Berks, England, *b.* circa 1490, was living in 1575; *m.* Ann HOO, dau. of Thomas HOO, Esq., of "The Hoo," County of Hertford, England. Barton Court was the scene of a battle between Loyalists and Parliamentarians, his son
THOMAS REED, II, was clerk of The Green Cloth; *m.* Mary STONEHOUSE of Little Peckham, County of Kent, his son
SIR THOMAS REED, III, *m.* Mary BROCKET, dau. of Sir John BROCKET of Brocket Hall, Hertfordshire, his son
SIR THOMAS REED, IV, of Brocket Hall, *m.* Mary CORNWALL, dau. of Thomas CORNWALL, Lord of Stropshire, his son
WILLIAM REED, gd. son of the Lord of Stropshire, *b.* at Brocket Hall, 1587, was the oldest of the Puritans by the name of REED. He sailed from London on the ship *Defence*, July, 1635, with his wife, who was Mabel KENDALL, gd. dau. of Henry SACHERELL of Radcliffe, England, arriving at Boston, Massachusetts, October, 1635. He settled at Woburn, Massachusetts. He returned to England where he *d.* at Prestwich Lodge, New Castle upon Tynne in 1656. He was a brother of Col. Thomas READE, who was a famous Indian fighter. His will, which made Oliver CROMWELL, Executor, was recorded in Middlesex Probate Office, 16th December, 1661. He left one of the largest estates in New England at that time, his son
GEORGE REED, *b.* at Brocket Hall, Hertfordshire in 1629; *d.* 21st February, 1706, came to New England with his parents in the ship *Defence* and settled at Woburn where he became a large landowner; the farm on which he lived is now owned by Nathan BLANCHARD, Esq., in what is now Burlington; *m.* 4th August, 1651, Elizabeth GENNISON of Watertown, his son
CAPTAIN WILLIAM REED, *b.* 22d September, 1662, was a prominent citizen of Lexington, Massachusetts, and represented the town at General Court; Treasury

Volume 122-123 contains entries showing Capt. William REED and his company were paid for military services during the Colonial Wars; m. 24th May, 1686, Abigail KENDALL. Both he and his wife are buried in the old Lexington graveyard, his son MAJOR BENJAMIN REED, b. 22d October, 1696; d. 13th July, 1789; served during Colonial Wars, being Major in Col. William BRATTLE's regiment of Massachusetts Militia; was a Representative in the General Assembly for ten years; m. Rebecca STONE, b. 1696; she was of the STONE family, first settlers of Cambridge and a descendant of Isaac STEARNS who settled near Watertown, Massachusetts, near Mount Auburn, who came over in 1630 in the ship with Governor WINTHROP and Sir Richard SALTONSTALL, bringing the Massachusetts Charter. Sarah STEARNS, dau. of Isaac STEARNS, descendant of the STEARNS family of Nottinghamshire, whose coat of arms can be seen in the old STEARNS homestead near Mount Auburn, Watertown, and is the same as that borne by the Archbishop of Yorke, a descendant of the STEARNS of Nottinghamshire, m. Deacon Samuel STONE, the first, son of Gregory STONE, Representative for Cambridge in 1638. Rebecca STONE was dau. of Deacon Samuel STONE, III, who in 1638 was the largest landowner of Cambridge, Massachusetts, his dau.

ABIGAIL REED, b. 16th May, 1720; m. 11th November, 1737, Deacon John MUZZEY, of Lexington. The MUZZEYS were descendants of a noble French family, his dau.

ABIGAIL MUZZEY, b. 16th May, 1739; m. 30th December, 1756, Thomas WHITE of Spencer, Massachusetts, gd. son of Col. Joseph BUCKMINSTER, Sr.

White

From Ancestry of JOSEPH NELSON WHITE, Marchmont, Winchendon, Massachusetts.

ROBERTUS WHITE, mentioned as Robert WHYTE DE ALNEWYK, in the Knights Fees of Yorkshire, 31st Edward I, 1303, as of Aghton. Hartill, Wapentake Aghton is the present Egton in North Riding; in Chaper House, Westminster; Willelmus White, living in Yorkshire, England, in 1339, m. Katharine WHITE, his son

WILLELMUS WHITE, living in Yorkshire, England, in 1339, his son

ADAM WHITE, of Yorke, 1365, his son

JOHANNIS WHITE, of Yorke, 1390, his son

JOHANNIS WHITE, JR., Alderman and Grosiour of Yorke; living in 1394, his son

WILLIAM WHITE, of Yorke, Chamberlain, in 1408; Member of Parliament in 1491-1504; Lord Mayor of London in 1496; d. 1504, his son

JOHN WHITE, silversmith, moved to London where he m. in 1543, Johanna LYDDEN, his son

THOMAS WHITE, m. 28th November, 1567, Agnes WRIGHT, of Fewston, Yorkshire, his son

WALTER WHITE of Fewston, Yorkshire, d. 13th March, 1629; buried in St. Michael's Parish Church, Fewston, built in 1234; m. 3d April, 1593, Janet SAUNDERS, dau. of William and Agnes SAUNDERS, his son

WALTER WHITE, *bapt.* 18th October, 1600, in the old church at Fewston, Yorkshire; *m.* 4th April, 1635, Margaret EARLY of Berkshire, his son

THOMAS WHITE of Charlestown, Massachusetts; *b.* 28th January, 1636, at Midgeham, Berkshire, England; *d.* 30th September, 1716; came to Boston on the ship *Annabel*, 8th May, 1660, locating at Charlestown. Thomas WHITE was a man of affairs, of business ability and sterling qualities; he served during King Philip's War; he is buried in the historic old Phipps Street Burying Ground at Charlestown; *m.* 17th November, 1663, Mary FROTHINGHAM, dau. of William and the noted Ann FROTHINGHAM, a descendant of Sir Peter FROTHINGHAM of Kent, England. Frothingham Hall was standing in 1844. He came from Holderness, Yorkshire, in John WINTHROP's Company, bringing the Massachusetts Charter, his son

THOMAS WHITE, Jr., of Charlestown; *b.* 15th October, 1664; *m.* 4th January, 1684, Sarah RAND, dau. of Thomas RAND, Sergeant, she died 1st April, 1749; her grave stone still stands in the old Phipps Street burying ground at Charlestown, his son

LIEUTENANT JOHN WHITE, *b.* at Charlestown, 22d August, 1695; *d.* at Spencer, Massachusetts, 26th August, 1778. He was commissioned Lieutenant and was associated with Col. Joseph BUCKMINSTER, Jr., during the French and Indian War. Colonel BUCKMINSTER, Senr., was representative to General Court from 1709 to 1733; Captain of Grenadiers in Sir Charles HOBBY's Regiment at the time of the expedition to Port Royal, and Colonel during Colonial Wars in the service of the King of England; Colonel BUCKMINSTER, Sr., *b.* 31st July, 1666; *d.* 1747; *m.* Martha SHARPE, dau. of Lieut. John SHARPE who was killed during King Philip's War at Sudbury fight with the Indians, April, 1676. He was the son of Joseph BUCKMINSTER, I, of Muddy Brook, now Brookline, Massachusetts, *d.* 20th November, 1668; *m.* Elizabeth CLARKE, dau. of Hugh CLARKE, Member of Ancient and Honorable Artillery Company in 1666. Colonel BUCKMINSTER was a descendant of John BUCKMINSTER of Petersborough, Northamptonshire, England. Lieut. John WHITE *m.* Sybilla BUCKMINSTER, *b.* 1705, dau. of Col. Joseph BUCKMINSTER, Sr., of Framingham, Massachusetts, his son

THOMAS WHITE, *b.* at Framingham, Massachusetts, 17th July, 1731; *d.* at Spencer, 25th February, 1822; *m.* 30th December, 1756, Abigail MUZZEY, dau. of Deacon John and Rebecca Reed MUZZEY, of Lexington, Massachusetts, his son

JOEL WHITE, *b.* at Spencer, Massachusetts, 3d May, 1766; was a pioneer of Western New York, locating in Alleghany County, when Indians still occupied that territory; *m.* Abigail CUTTING, *b.* 27th October, 1774, dau. of Silas CUTTING, of Royalston, Massachusetts, who was killed after three years service in the Revolutionary War. She was of the CUTTING, PEABODY and WARREN families of Watertown, Massachusetts, his dau.

SERENA WHITE, *b.* at Almond, New York, 3d October, 1795; *d.* 9th June, 1862; *m.* Col. David CRANDALL of Rhode Island, *b.* 18th January, 1789, *d.* 6th November, 1853, son of Carey CRANDALL. He served a short time in War of 1812. Governor CLINTON appointed him Colonel of 1st Regiment of Militia in Alleghany County, New York. Serena WHITE was a cousin of Joseph WHITE, one of the first cotton manufacturers of New England, who was gd. father of Joseph Nelson WHITE of Winchenden, Massachusetts, her dau.

ELIZABETH WHITE CRANDALL, *b.* at Almond, New York, 12th May, 1836; *d.* at Cleveland, Ohio, 2d April, 1914; attended Alfred University and graduated from Leicester Academy, Leicester, Massachusetts, 1853; *m.* 22d January, 1857, Ewing Welch ROBERTSON, M.D., the subject of this memoir.

Arms.—Gules three wolves heads erased argent, armed and langued azure lying on a compartment under the arms, a man in chains.
Crest.—A dexter arm and hand, erect, holding a regal crown all proper.
Motto.—Virtutis gloria merces.

Rothrock

JOHN ROTHROCK of Richmond, Missouri; *b.* 10th September, 1846, at Camden, where the family resided for two years on their way to California; *d.* 14th January, 1886; *m.* 30th November, 1869, at Richmond, Missouri, Alice HUDGINS, *b.* 7th March, 1847, *d.* 7th January, 1901, dau. of William Blake and Mary Frances (WIRT) HUDGINS.

ISSUE

I. Aileen, *b.* 12th September, 1870; *m.* 31st July, 1886, Louis WILLIAMS, *b.* 1865, son of John and Elizabeth WILLIAMS.

ISSUE

1. Maud Rothrock WILLIAMS, *b.* 19th September, 1890; graduated in Class 1908, Virginia College for Women, Roanoke, Virginia.

II. Allen, *b.* 11th September, 1873; *d.* March, 1874.
III. Francis Blake, M.D., of Colorado Springs, Colorado; *b.* 20th August, 1875; *m.* 23d February, 1910, Nancy EWING, *d.* 12th August, 1913, dau. of Joel EWING, of Memphis, Missouri.

ISSUE

1. Francis Blake, *b.* 12th September, 1911; *d.* 12th September, 1911.
2. Nancy Alice, *b.* 12th August, 1913.

JOHN ROTHROCK was one of the prominent business men of southwest Missouri; eh was educated in Richmond, Missouri, at the old Richmond College that went out of existence in June, 1915, after a life of over sixty years.

Lineage

ABRAHAM ROTHROCK of the Pflatz, Germany, was the father of four sons, all of whom are accredited with coming to America and settling there.

ISSUE

I. Ludwig, no date of arrival given.
II. George, *b.* 1710; no date of arrival given; *m.* wife's name un-known.

ISSUE

1. Philip, *b.* 1757, in Bucks County, Pennsylvania; *d.* 13th October, 1851; settled in Mifflin County, near McVeytown, Pennsylvania; *m.* circa 1797, Martha LOBAUGH, *b.* 5th April, 1777, *d.* 22d January, 1858, dau. of Abraham and Mary LOBAUGH.

COLONIAL FAMILIES OF THE UNITED STATES 401

ISSUE

1¹. Abraham, b. 19th April, 1806; d. 9th September, 1894; m. 11th May, 1837, Phebe Brinton TRIMBLE of Delaware County, Pennsylvania, b. 10th March, 1810, d. 14th September, 1894, dau. of Joseph and Jane H. (BRINTON) TRIMBLE.

ISSUE

1². Joseph Trimble, M.D., of West Chester, Pennsylvania. (See "Who's Who in America.")

III. Johaannes, came to Pennsylvania, 29th September, 1733.
IV. PHILIP, b. 8th December, 1713, of whom below.

PHILIP ROTHROCK was a Moravian Preacher of York, Pennsylvania; b. 8th December, 1713, in Pflatz, one hour's ride from Worms, Germany; d. 23d February, 1803, at his home in York. Came to Pennsylvania in 1733 and settled first on the Skippack in Philadelphia County, later removed to York, Pennsylvania. The later years of his life were spent in Manchester Township, York County, Pennsylvania. He was one of the founders of the Moravian Church at that place as well as being interested in the Moravian Congregations throughout Pennsylvania. While not a soldier during the American Revolution he was active in the politics of the time, having served as Commissioner recruiting soldiers for the Army. He gave information with regard to various political occurrences and discovered a plot of the Tories against the town of York in 1778. In 1774 he served as Judge of Elections held in York, was united by Brother SPANGENBERG of the Moravian Congregation in marriage 22d March, 1740, to Catherine KUNTZ, b. 20th March, 1720, in Rothenbach, near Gunnstadt in the Pflatz and came to America in 1726. She was received in the Moravian Congregation 11th June, 1756, during Brother Peter's Visitation, she d. 10th November, 1777; he m. (secondly) 21st September, 1781, Mrs. Eleanore (MAQUINET) GALATIN, widow, b. 14th August, 1724, in Schwarzenau, Witgensteen, who d.s.p.

ISSUE BY FIRST MARRIAGE

I. Jacob, of York, Pennsylvania; b. 25th May, 1741; m. 21st April, 1765, Barbara WELLER, b. 16th April, 1746. In December, 1782, the family removed to Baltimore, Maryland.

ISSUE

1. Eva Elizabeth, b. 1st March, 1766.
2. Catherine, b. 12th December, 1767; d. 1768, buried in Moravian Cemetery.
3. Eva, b. 5th August, 1769.
4. George, b. 28th April, 1771.

COLONIAL FAMILIES OF THE UNITED STATES

5. Catherine, *b.* 17th November, 1772.
6. Jacob, *b.* 21st September, 1774.
7. Susanna, *b.* 24th November, 1776; *d.* same year.
8. John, *b.* 27th April, 1778.
9. Maria, *b.* 31st July, 1780.

II. Anne Maria, *b.* 25th September, 1742; *d.* in infancy.
III. JOHN, *b.* 18th February, 1744, of whom later.
IV. Catherine, *b.* 30th September, 1745; *d.* in infancy.
V. Peter (twin), *b.* 22d October, 1748; settled in North Carolina.
VI. Philip (twin), *b.* 22d October, 1748; settled in North Carolina.
VII. George, *b.* 29th October, 1748; resided in Baltimore, Md.
VIII. Valentine, *b.* 31st August, 1750; *d.* in infancy.
IX. Valentine, II, *b.* 17th October, 1751; settled in North Carolina.
X. Benjamin, *b.* 9th November, 1753.
XI. Joseph, *b.* 11th May, 1755.
XII. Catherine, *b.* 18th May, 1757.
XIII. Ann Maria, *b.* 1st March, 1759.
XIV. Frederick, *b.* 30th September, 1760.

LIEUTENANT JOHN ROTHROCK of York, Pennsylvania; *b.* 18th February, 1744; *d.* 28th August, 1805; was a printer by trade during the First Continental Congress in York; he had charge of printing the Continental Currency; he served as Lieutenant throughout the American Revolution; he was very active in the Moravian Church; *m.* (firstly) 1st May, 1767, Dorothy GUMP, *b.* 11th October, 1749, *d.* 18th December, 1775; *m.* (secondly) 5th November, 1776, Salome Charity WORLEY, *b.* 20th February, 1759, in York, Pennsylvania, *d.* 1st March, 1828, dau. of Daniel and Maria WORLEY.

ISSUE

I. Elizabeth, *b.* 16th September, 1778.
II. Ann Maria, *b.* 17th February, 1780.
III. GEORGE, *b.* 24th May, 1781, of whom later.
IV. James, *b.* 22d May, 1782.
V. Charity, *b.* 17th September, 1783; *m.* 1802, George TEST, son of George and Margaret (WOGAN) TEST of York, Pennsylvania.

ISSUE

1. Maria TEST, *m.* Ezekiel BUCKINGHAM.

ISSUE

1^1. John BUCKINGHAM, *b.* 5th May, 1832; *m.* 1850, Rebecca McGINLEY.

ISSUE

1². Maria Catherine BUCKINGHAM, *b.* 7th April, 1852; *d.* 14th July, 1911; *m.* W. F. EICHAR.
2². William Andrew BUCKINGHAM of Baltimore, Maryland; *b.* 18th March, 1853; *m.* Grace V. LOUCKS.
3². Henry BUCKINGHAM, *b.* 23d August, 1858; resides at 123 East Market Street, York, Pennsylvania.
4². Rebecca Elizabeth BUCKINGHAM, *b.* 11th February, 1864; *m.* 29th April, 1891, Dr. John H. YEAGLEY, of York, Pennsylvania.

VI. Susanna, *b.* 20th April, 1785.
VII. William, *b.* 23d September, 1786.
VIII. Philip Jacob, *b.* 10th February, 1788; *d.* 1st August, 1847, in Williamsport, Pennsylvania; *m.* in York, Pennsylvania, Sarah YOST, *b.* 31st July, 1795, *d.* 27th January, 1885, in Williamsport.

ISSUE

1. George, *b.* 19th November, 1827; *d.* 3d March, 1912, in Williamsport, Pennsylvania.

ISSUE

1¹. Boyd P., Curator State Museum, Harrisburg, Pennsylvania.

IX. Rebecca, *b.* 23d March, 1789.
X. Joseph, *b.* 11th November, 1790; murdered in 1802 and his body thrown in Codorus River, York, Pennsylvania.
XI. Henry R., *b.* 5th January, 1792, in York, Pennsylvania; *d.* 8th August, 1872, in Bellefonte, Pennsylvania; *m.* 26th September, 1826, Nancy RAMSEY, of Muncy, Pennsylvania.

ISSUE

1. Joseph, *b.* 2d July, 1827; *d.* in infancy.
2. Thomas, *b.* 19th March, 1829; *d.* 27th November, 1901; *m.* 1851, Elizabeth JOSLYN, *b.* 1834, *d.* 1st January, 1903.

1¹. Oscar, *b.* 7th June, 1854; *d.* 12th April, 1898; *m.* 5th March, 1887, Anna Belle Crawford SEYMOUR, *b.* 31st May, 1860.

ISSUE

1². Donald, *b.* 26th August, 1888, Ulster Park, New York.
2². Wilfred Leester, *b.* 1889.
3². Olivia, *b.* 1890.

3. David, *b.* 19th September, 1831; *d.* 20th December, 1906, in Bellefonte, Pennsylvania.
4. Ann Elita, *b.* 24th September, 1839; *d.* 1914; ———— LONG, of Bellefonte, Pennsylvania.
5. John, of Longmont, Colorado; *b.* 3d March, 1834.
6. Henry, *b.* 16th September, 1843.

XII. Thomas, *b.* 17th July, 1792.
XIII. Susan, *b.* 9th December, 1796.

GEORGE ROTHROCK of York, Pennsylvania; *b.* 24th May, 1783; *d.* 8th August 1851; removed to Bellefonte, Centre County, Pennsylvania, served in the War of 1812, as a private in the York County Militia; *m.* (firstly) 1800, Isabella TEST, dau. of George and Margaret (WOGAN) TEST. George TEST was one of the four founders in 1782 of the Methodist Church in York, Pennsylvania; *m.* (secondly) Mrs. Prudence (PURDUE) THOMAS, widow.

ISSUE BY FIRST MARRIAGE

I. William, Philipsburg, Pennsylvania; *m.* Matilda, surname unknown.

ISSUE

1. Jennie.
2. Isabella, *m.* Downes RHODES.
3. Margaret. 4. George. 5. Clifford.
6. Ada, *m.* Robert BUCKLER.

II. Wilson, *b.* 1829; *d.* 1911; *m.* Anna, surname unknown.

ISSUE

1. Mary, *b.* 1860; *m.* John Henry DUNBAR.
2. Margaret. 4. Jessie. 6. John. 8. George.
3. Isabella. 5. Elizabeth. 7. Henry. 9. Alexander.

III. HENRY, *b.* 7th August, 1813, of whom later.
IV. Jacob, *b.* Bellefonte, Pennsylvania; *m.* Adeline, surname unknown.
V. Alexander, *d.* Camden, Missouri; *m.* Ellen, surname unknown.
VI. Mary, *b.* 1830; *d.* Philadelphia, Pennsylvania; *m.* Henry WEAVER of Philadelphia, Pennsylvania.
VII. Margaret.
VIII. Charity.

ISSUE BY SECOND MARRIAGE

I. Huling Herbert, of Lock Haven, Pennsylvania; *m.* wife's name not known.

ISSUE

1^1. James Huling.

COLONIAL FAMILIES OF THE UNITED STATES 405

HENRY ROTHROCK of Richmond, Ray County, Missouri; *b.* 7th August, 1813, in York, Pennsylvania; *d.* 13th March, 1884; *m.* (firstly) 1835, Mary YOUNG, dau. of Jacob YOUNG, she *d.* in the winter of 1849 of cholera while crossing the Colorado Plains, where she was buried; *m.* (secondly) 4th July, 1853, Elizabeth (RIFFE) GILLY, widow of Edward GILLY.

ISSUE BY FIRST MARRIAGE

I. William, *b.* 11th February, 1837; unmarried.
II. Andrew, *b.* 1st November, 1838; *d.* in infancy.
III. Isabella, *b.* 12th February, 1840; *d.* 1912; *m.* Nathan WARNER.
IV. Russell, *b.* 5th February, 1842; *d.* in infancy.
V. George Test, *b.* 12th December, 1843; killed in 1864 while serving in Federal Army during Civil War; unmarried.
VI. John, *b.* 10th September, 1846, the subject of this memoir.
VII. Wilson, *b.* 20th January, 1849; *d.* unmarried, June, 1915, in Omaha, Nebraska.

ISSUE BY SECOND MARRIAGE

I. Mollie, *b.* 16th June, 1854; *m.* 1874, William MILLIGAN, of Richmond Missouri.

ISSUE

1. Kate MILLIGAN, *b.* 1878.
2. James Russell MILLIGAN, *b.* 1882.
3. LeRoy Jacob MILLIGAN, *b.* 1892.
4. Maud MILLIGAN, *b.* February, 1880.
5. Maurice MILLIGAN, *b.* 1885; *m.* 30th November, 1911, Susan Isabel McDONALD, dau. of J. Allen McDONALD, of Richmond, Missouri.
6. Eugene MILLIGAN, *b.* 15th March, 1890; *d.* 8th July, 1912.

ISSUE

1[1]. Susan Isabel MILLIGAN, *b.* 27th August, 1912.

II. Jacob, *b.* 23d December, 1855; unmarried, of Richmond, Missouri.
III. Charles, *b.* 18th December, 1858; *d.* in infancy.

Rush

CAPTAIN RICHARD RUSH, U.S.N. (Retired), of Washington, D. C.; *b*. 28th February, 1848; *m*. 10th July, 1873, Ella Mary DAY, second daughter of Edgar Burr DAY, of Catskill-on-Hudson.

ISSUE

I. Richard, *b*. 28th September, 1875; *d*. 21st November, 1875.
II. Ella Day, *b*. 1st November, 1876; *m*. 23d September, 1905, William SPENCER MURRAY, of Annapolis, Maryland.

Lineage

JOHN RUSH, the founder of this family, was *b*. in England, 1620; *d*. 1699, at Byberry, Pennsylvania; commanded a troop of horse in Cromwell's Army; he embraced the principles of the Quakers in 1660; emigrated to Pennsylvania, 1683, with seven children and several grandchildren and settled at Byberry, thirteen miles from Philadelphia; in 1691 he and his whole family became Keithians and in 1697 most of them became BAPTISTS; his sword was in possession of Jacob RUSH and his watch in possession of Gen. William DARK of Virginia, but later both were deposited in Independence Hall in Philadelphia; *m*. 8th June, 1648, at Horton County, Oxford, Susanna LUCAS.

ISSUE

I. Elizabeth, *b*. 16th June, 1649; *m*. in London, 27th May, 1680, Richard COLLET, by whom she had issue; emigrated with her husband to Pennsylvania, 1682, and settled at Byberry.
II. WILLIAM, *b*. 21st July, 1652, of whom later.
III. Thomas, *b*. 7th November, 1654; *d*. 18th June, 1676, in London, England.
IV. Susanna, *b*. 26th December, 1656; *m*. John HART in England and had issue.
V. John, *b*. 1st May, 1660.
VI. Francis, *b*. 8th April, 1662; *d*. unmarried.
VII. James, *b*. 21st July, 1664; buried at Banbury, 24th January, 1671.
VIII. Joseph, *b*. 26th October, 1666; *d*. in infancy.
IX. Edward, *b*. 27th September, 1670; *d.s.p.*
X. Jane, *b*. 27th December, 1673–1674; *m*. John DARKE, and had issue.

WILLIAM RUSH of Byberry, Pennsylvania; *b*. 21st July, 1652, in England; *d*. at Byberry, Pennsylvania, 1688; *m*. (firstly) in England, Aurelia, surname not given, she *d*. 1683; *m*. (secondly) wife's name not given.

COLONIAL FAMILIES OF THE UNITED STATES 407

ISSUE BY FIRST MARRIAGE

I. Susanna, *b.* 1675; *m.* (firstly) John WEBSTER; *m.* (secondly) ———— GILBERT.
II. Elizabeth, *b.* 1677; *d.s.p.; m.* Timothy STEVENSON, who afterward *m.* Rachel, the widow of his brother-in-law, James RUSH.
III. James, *b.* 1679, of whom below.

JAMES RUSH of Byberry, Pennsylvania; *b.* 1679; *d.* 16th March, 1727, at Byberry, Pennsylvania; *m.* Rachel PEART.

ISSUE

I. JOHN, *b.* 1712, of whom later.
II. Elizabeth, *b.* 1714; *m.* Edward PARRY.
III. William, *b.* 1716; *m.* Mary WILLIAMS; had issue.
IV. Rachel, *b.* 1718; *d.* in infancy.
V. Joseph, *b.* 1720; *d.* unmarried.
VI. James, *b.* 25th March, 1723; *d.* unmarried.
VII. Thomas, *b.* 1724; *d.* unmarried.
VIII. Ann, *m.* John ASHMEAD.
IX. Aurelia, *d.* in infancy.

JOHN RUSH, *b.* at Byberry, Pennsylvania, 1712; *d.* 26th July, 1751; *m.* Susanna HALL, *d.* 2d July, 1795, dau. of Joseph HALL of Tacony.

ISSUE

I. James, *b.* 1739; *d.* young.
II. Rachel, *b.* 1741; *d.* 1798; *m.* (firstly) Angus BOYCE; *m.* (secondly) Joseph MONTGOMERY.
III. Rebecca, *b.* 1743; *d.* 1793; *m.* Thomas STAMPER; left issue.
IV. BENJAMIN, *b.* 24th December, 1745, of whom later.
V. Jacob, *b.* 24th November, 1747; *d.* 5th January, 1820; Judge of the High Court of Errors and Appeals of Pennsylvania, 1784–1806; President of the Court of Common Pleas of Philadelphia, 1806–1820; *m.* Mary RENCH.
VI. Stevenson, *d.* in infancy.
VII. John, *d.* in infancy.

BENJAMIN RUSH, M.D., of Philadelphia, Patriot; *b.* 24th December, 1745; *d.* 19th April, 1813; graduated at the University of Edinburgh, 1768; returned to America and settled in Philadelphia, 1769, where he became Medical Professor in the University of Pennsylvania; Member of Provincial Conference of Pennsylvania, and later of Congress; signed the Declaration of Independence, 4th July, 1776; *m.* 11th January, 1776, Julia STOCKTON, who *d.* 7th July, 1848, eldest dau. of Hon. Richard STOCKTON.

ISSUE

I. John, b. 17th July, 1777; an officer in the United States Army; d. unmarried 9th August, 1837.
II. Anne Emily, b. 1st January, 1779; d. 27th April, 1850; leaving issue; m. 12th March, 1799, Ross CUTHBERT of Canada.
III. RICHARD, b. 29th August, 1780, of whom later.
IV. Susanna, b. 7th January, 1782; d. in infancy.
V. Elizabeth, b. 14th February, 1783; d. in infancy.
VI. Mary, b. 16th May, 1784; d. 2d November, 1849; m. Thomas MANNERS; left issue.
VII. James, b. 15th March, 1786; d.s.p. 26th May, 1869; m. 19th October, 1819, Phoebe Ann RIDGWAY, dau. of Jacob RIDGWAY.
VIII. William, b. 8th November, 1787; d. in infancy.
IX. Benjamin, b. 3d July, 1789; d. in infancy.
X. Benjamin, b. 18th February, 1791; d. unmarried, 17th December, 1824.
XI. Julia, b. 22d November, 1792; d.s.p. 19th April, 1860; m. 17th June, 1820, Henry J. WILLIAMS.
XII. Samuel, b. 1st August, 1795; d. 24th November, 1859; leaving issue; m. Nancy WILMER.
XIII. William, b. 11th May, 1801; d. 20th November, 1864; leaving issue; m. 18th July, 1827, Elizabeth Fox ROBERTS, dau. of Hugh ROBERTS.

RICHARD RUSH of Philadelphia, Pennsylvania; b. there, 29th August, 1780; d. 30th July, 1859; admitted to the Bar of Philadelphia, 1800; Attorney General of Pennsylvania, 1811; Comptroller of the United States Treasury, 1811; United States Attorney-General, 1814–1817; Minister to the Court of St. James, 1817–1825; Secretary of the United States Treasury, 1825–1829; Minister to France, 1847–1849; m. 29th August, 1809, Catherine E. MURRAY, d. 24th March, 1854, dau. of Dr. James MURRAY (see MURRAY, Volume II, "Colonial Families").

ISSUE

I. Benjamin, b. 23d January, 1811; d. 30th June, 1877; admitted to the Bar of Philadelphia, 1833; Secretary of United States Legation in London, 1837–1841; m. 24th April, 1849, Elizabeth M. SIMPSON, dau. of Dr. William SIMPSON, of Pittsburgh, Pennsylvania.

ISSUE

1. William Simpson, b. 28th January, 1851; d. unmarried, 2d June, 1869.
2. Catherine Eliza Murray, b. 21st December, 1853; m. 24th April, 1895, William Masters CAMAC.
3. Mary Theresa de Leelen, b. 11th February, 1855; m. 30th April, 1890, Rev. Richard Lewis HOWELL, d. 24th May, 1903.

II. JAMES MURRAY, b. 10th July, 1813, of whom later.
III. Richard, b. 11th March, 1815; d. 29th October, 1826.

COLONIAL FAMILIES OF THE UNITED STATES

IV. Sarah Maynadier, *b.* 17th September, 1817; *d.* in infancy.
V. Julia, *b.* 11th November, 1818; *d.* in infancy.
VI. Anna Maria, *b.* 23d April, 1820; *d.* unmarried, 25th December, 1887.
VII. Sarah Catherine, *b.* 29th June, 1823; *d.* unmarried, 17th July, 1905.
VIII. Richard Henry, *b.* 14th January, 1825; *d.* 17th October, 1893; left issue; *m.* (firstly) 4th February, 1851, Sarah Anna BLIGHT; *m.* (secondly) 11th December, 1856, Susan Bowdoin YERBY, dau. of Dr. George YERBY.
IX. Julia Stockton, *b.* 21st July, 1826; *d.* 20th January, 1858; left issue; *m.* 1st June, 1854, John CALVERT.

JAMES MURRAY RUSH of Philadelphia; *b.* 10th July, 1813; *d.* there 7th February, 1872; *m.* (firstly) 28th January, 1847, Eugenia Frances (HIESTER) SHEAFF, dau. of John HIESTER, of Reading, Pennsylvania, and widow of William SHEAFF; *m.* (secondly) 29th November, 1853, Elizabeth DENNIS, *d.* 16th May, 1856, dau. of Lyttleton Upshur DENNIS, and widow of Lyttleton DENNIS.

ISSUE BY FIRST MARRIAGE

1. RICHARD, *b.* 28th February, 1848, the subject of this memoir.

ISSUE BY SECOND MARRIAGE

1. Elizabeth Murray, *b.* 26th January, 1856; *m.* 20th April, 1882, John Biddle PORTER of the United States Army.

ISSUE

1. Margaretta Biddle PORTER, *b.* 13th June, 1883.
2. Catherine Rush PORTER, *b.* 27th January, 1885.
3. Elizabeth Murray PORTER, *b.* 3d September, 1893.

Residences.—1831 Jefferson Place, Washington, D. C., and "The Elms," Catskill-on-Hudson, New York.
Arms (RUSH of England).—Gules on a fesse or, between three horses courant argent as many annulets azure.
Crest.—A wolf's head erased ermine.
Motto.—Omnia Deo Pendant.

Saltonstall

RICHARD MIDDLECOTT SALTONSTALL, *b.* 28th October, 1859; *m.* 17th October, 1891, Eleanor BROOKS, dau. of Peter C. BROOKS of West Medford.

ISSUE

I. Leverett, *b.* 1st September, 1892.
II. Eleanor, *b.* 19th October, 1894.
III. Muriel Gurdon, *b.* 26th March, 1896.
IV. Richard, *b.* 23d July, 1897.

RICHARD MIDDLECOTT SALTONSTALL graduated at Harvard College, 1880, and is a member of the Suffolk Bar.

Lineage

GILBERT SALTONSTALL of Rookes Hall, in the Parish of Halifax, County York, Buried at Halifax, 29th December, 1598, was son of Richard SALTONSTALL, whose family had been seated in Halifax for more than two centuries; *m.* Isabel, name not given, and had issue.

ISSUE

I. SAMUEL, *d.* 1613, of whom later.
II. Richard (Sir), of the Manor of Moorhall, County Northampton; *d.* 17th March, 1601, M.P. for the City of London, 1586; Sheriff of London, 1588; Lord Mayor, 1597–1598; Knighted, 1598, Master of the Skinners Company, 1593, 1595, and 1599; *m.* Susanna POYNTZ, dau. of Thomas POYNTZ, of North Okenden; had issue.
III. Mary, *m.* Francis SAVILE, son of Henry Savile, of Lupsett, High Sheriff of County York, 1567, and brother of Sir George Savile, First Baronet of Thornhill.

SAMUEL SALTONSTALL of Rookes and Huntwicke, County York; *d.* 8th January, 1613; will proved 22d July, 1613; *m.* (firstly) Anne RAMSDEN, dau. of John RAMSDEN of Longley; *m.* (secondly) Elizabeth OGDEN, dau. of Thomas OGDEN.

ISSUE BY FIRST MARRIAGE

I. RICHARD, *bapt.* 4th April, 1586, of whom later.
II. Gilbert, *d.* in the lifetime of his father.

ISSUE BY SECOND MARRIAGE

I. Samuel, of Rogerthorpe, *m.* Barbara RUDSTON, dau. of Walter RUDSTON, of Hayton.

COLONIAL FAMILIES OF THE UNITED STATES

  II. John.
  III. Thomas, of Grainge Hall, York.
  IV. George, of Kingston-upon-Hull.
  V. Anne.
  VI. Elizabeth, *m.* 1623, Henry BUNNY.
  VII. Mary, *d.* 1622; *m.* John BATEMAN.
  VIII. Margaret, *m.* Henry GAMBLE.
  IX. Barbara, *m.* Christopher RASBY, of Smeaton, County York.

SIR RICHARD SALTONSTALL of Huntwicke, County York; *bapt.* at Halifax, 4th April, 1586; *d.* circa 1658; Lord of the Manor of Ledsham, near Leeds; Justice of the Peace, and Treasurer for Lame Soldiers, 1605; Knighted, 1616; emigrated to New England with Governor WINTHROP in the *Arbella*, 1630, having been appointed First Assistant, 1629; commenced the settlement of Watertown, 1630; returned to England, 1631; earnestly he befriended America in England by thought and deed and was active with the Lords Brooke and Say and Seale and other Puritans in the settlement of Connecticut; Ambassador to Holland, 1644; *m.* (firstly) Grace KAYE, dau. of Robert KAYE, Esq., of Woodsome, County York; *m.* (secondly) Elizabeth WEST, sister of Sir Thomas WEST, third Lord De la Warr, Governor of Virginia, 1610; *m.* (thirdly) Martha WILFRED.

ISSUE BY FIRST MARRIAGE

  I. RICHARD, *b.* at Woodsome, County York, 1610, of whom later.
  II. Robert, emigrated to New England, 1630; *d.* unmarried, 1650; settled at Watertown, and afterwards at Boston; Member of Artillery Company, 1638.
  III. Samuel, resided at Watertown; *d.* unmarried, 21st January, 1696.
  IV. Henry (M.D.), Member of Artillery Company, 1639; graduated at Harvard College, 1642; returned to England.
  V. Rosamond ⎫ Went to New England with their father, 1630, and re-
  VI. Grace   ⎭ turned with him to England, 1631.

RICHARD SALTONSTALL of Ipswich, Massachusetts; *b.* at Woodsome, County York, 1610; *d.* at Hulme, County Lancaster, England, 29th April, 1694, at the home of his son-in-law, Sir Edward MOSELEY; matriculated at Emmanuel College, Cambridge, 1627; accompanied his father to New England, 1630; admitted Freeman, 18th October, 1631; returned with his father to England, 1631, but went again to America in 1635 in the *Susan and Ellen*, and settled in Ipswich, Massachusetts, where he became Deputy to the General Court, 1635–1637; and Assistant 1637–1649; 1664 and 1680–1683; in 1641 was Sergeant-Major under ENDICOTT of the Essex Regiment; *m.* in England, June, 1633, Muriel GURDON, dau. of Brampton GURDON, of Assington, County Suffolk, the distinguished patriot and member of Parliament, and returned to England again in 1649 on account of his wife's health; again coming to America about 1664.

COLONIAL FAMILIES OF THE UNITED STATES

ISSUE

I. Muriel, *b.* in England, 1634; *m.* Sir Edward MOSELEY, of Hulme, County Lancaster, who *d.* 1695; leaving issue.
II. Richard, citizen of London; *d.s.p.* 1666.
III. NATHANIEL, *b.* at Ipswich, circa 1632, of whom later.
IV. Abigail, *m.* Thomas HARLEY, of Hinsham Court, County Hereford.
V. Elizabeth, *m.* Hercules HORSEY; had issue.

COLONEL NATHANIEL SALTONSTALL, *b.* circa 1639, at Ipswich, Massachusetts; *d.* 21st May, 1707; graduated at Harvard College, 1659; admitted Freeman, 1665; Representative, 1666; Town Clerk of Haverhill, 1669–1671; Colonel of Essex Regiment, 1679–1686, and was in command of the troops sent against Governor ANDROS in 1680; Assistant, 1679–1686, and 1689–1692; Member of the Council, Judge of Oyer and Terminer Court, 1692; when he refused to participate in the monstrous trials for witchery, leaving his seat to be occupied by Jonathan CORWAN, brother of the Sheriff that was called upon to hang so many innocent victims; *m.* 28th December, 1663, Elizabeth WARD, *d.* 29th April, 1714, dau. of Rev. John WARD, of Haverhill.

ISSUE

I. Gurdon, *b.* 27th March, 1666, at Haverhill, Massachusetts; *d.* 20th September, 1724; graduated at Harvard College, 1684; settled at New London, Connecticut, 1691; the distinguished minister of New London and Governor of Connecticut 1708–1724; *m.* (firstly) Jerusha RICHARDS, *d.* 25th July, 1697, dau. of James RICHARDS; *m.* (secondly) Elizabeth ROSEWELL, *d.* 12th September, 1710, dau. and sole heir of William ROSEWELL of Branford; *m.* (thirdly) Mary (WHITTINGHAM) CLARKE, *d.s.p.*, 23d January, 1730, dau. of William WHITTINGHAM and widow of William CLARKE of Boston.
II. Elizabeth, *b.* 17th September, 1668; *d.* 8th July, 1726; *m.* (firstly) Rev. John DENISON, who *d.* 1689, and had issue; *m.* (secondly) Rev. Roland COTTON of Sandwich, and had issue.
III. RICHARD, *b.* 25th April, 1672, of whom later.
IV. Nathaniel, *b.* 5th September, 1674; graduated at Harvard College, 1695; Tutor and Librarian, 1697–1701; *m.* Dorothy FRIZEL, *d.s.p.* 1739, at Woburn, widow of John FRIZEL of Boston.
V. John, *b.* 14th August, 1678; *d.* in infancy.

RICHARD SALTONSTALL, *b.* 25th April, 1672; *d.* 22d April, 1714; graduated at Harvard, 1695; Representative from Haverhill, 1600; Major, 1704; afterwards Colonel; *m.* 25th March, 1702, Mehitabel WAINWRIGHT, dau. of Capt. Simon WAINWRIGHT of Haverhill.

COLONIAL FAMILIES OF THE UNITED STATES

ISSUE

I. RICHARD, *b.* 24th June, 1703, of whom later.
II. Ward, *b.* 21st May, 1705; *d.* in infancy.
III. Nathaniel, *b.* 3d June, 1706; graduated at Harvard College, 1727.
IV. Elizabeth, *b.* 5th June, 1707; *d.* young.

RICHARD SALTONSTALL, *b.* at Haverhill, Massachusetts, 24th June, 1703; *d.* 20th October, 1756; graduated at Harvard College, 1722; Colonel, 1726; Representative from Haverhill, 1727; Judge of Superior Court, 1736-1756; *m.* (firstly) June, 1726, Abigail WALDRON, *d.* 16th March, 1735; *m.* (secondly) Mary JEKYLL, *d.s.p.*, dau. of John JEKYLL, Collector of Customs at Boston; *m.* (thirdly) Mary COOKE.

ISSUE BY SECOND MARRIAGE

I. Abigail, *b.* 5th October, 1728; *m.* Col. George WATSON of Plymouth.
II. Elizabeth, *b.* 5th June, 1730; *d.* young.
III. Richard, *b.* 5th April, 1732; graduated at Harvard College, 1751; Representative from Haverhill, 1761-1769; Colonel of Essex Regiment, 1754; served to end of French War, 1760; High Sheriff of Essex; *d.* unmarried, in London, 6th October, 1785.
IV. William, *b.* 2d November, 1733; *d.* in infancy.
V. William, *b.* 17th October, 1734; *d.* young.

ISSUE BY THIRD MARRIAGE

I. NATHANIEL, *b.* 10th February, 1746, of whom later.
II. Mary, *b.* 4th September, 1749; *d.* 24th December, 1791; *m.* Rev. Moses BADGER, *d.* 1792 at Providence, Rhode Island.
III. Middlecott Cooke, *b.* 24th January, 1752; *d.* in infancy.
IV. Leverett, *b.* 25th December, 1754; Captain in the British Army; *d.* 20th December, 1782, at New York.

NATHANIEL SALTONSTALL of Haverhill, Massachusetts; *b.* 10th February, 1746; *d.* 15th May, 1815; graduated at Harford College, 1766; *m.* 21st October, 1780, Anna WHITE, *d.* 21st October, 1841, dau. of Samuel WHITE, of Haverhill.

ISSUE

I. Mary Cooke, *b.* 20th September, 1781; *d.* 7th August, 1817; *m.* 9th October, 1806, Hon. John VARNUM, *d.* 23d July, 1836; had issue.
II. LEVERETT, *b.* 13th June, 1783, of whom later.
III. Nathaniel, *b.* 1st October, 1784; *d.* 19th October, 1838; *m.* 30th November, 1820, Caroline SANDERS, *d.* 1st March, 1882, youngest dau. of Thomas SANDERS.
IV. Sarah, *b.* 5th November, 1790; *d.* 25th July, 1870; *m.* 16th June, 1816, Isaac R. HOWE of Haverhill; had issue.

v. Richard, of Baltimore; b. 16th June, 1794; d. 1834; graduated at Harvard College, 1813; m. 24th October, 1822, Margaret Ann SAVAGE, of Virginia, d. 1st November, 1834; had issue.
vi. Matilda, b. 9th December, 1796; d. 21st May, 1831; m. 16th June, 1825, Fisher HOWE of New York, d. 7th November, 1871.

LEVERETT SALTONSTALL, b. 13th June, 1783; d. 8th May, 1845; graduated at Harvard College, 1802; LL.D., 1838; Speaker of Massachusetts House of Representatives; President of the State Senate; First Mayor of Salem, 1836–1838; Representative in Congress, 1838–1843; m. 7th March, 1811, Mary Elizabeth SANDERS, d. 11th January, 1858, dau. of Thomas SANDERS, of Salem.

ISSUE

I. Anne Elizabeth, b. 16th February, 1812; d. unmarried, 10th July, 1881.
II. Caroline, b. 2d September, 1815; d. unmarried, 23d February, 1883.
III. Richard Gurdon, b. 29th June, 1820; d. in infancy.
IV. Lucy Sanders, b. 10th February, 1822; d. 24th December, 1890; m. 30th June, 1847, John Francis TUCKERMAN, M.D.
V. LEVERETT, b. 16th March, 1825, of whom later.

LEVERETT SALTONSTALL, b. at Salem, 16th March, 1825; graduated at Harvard College, 1844; A.M., LL.B., 1847; Overseer of Harvard University for eighteen years; m. 19th October, 1854, Rose S. LEE, dau. of John Clarke LEE, of Salem.

ISSUE

I. Leverett, b. 3d November, 1855; d. young.
II. RICHARD MIDDLECOTT, b. 28th October, 1859, the subject of this memoir.
III. Rose Lee, b. 17th June, 1861; d. 28th February, 1891; m. 6th November, 1884, George Webb WEST, M.D.

1. George Saltonstall WEST, b. 26th June, 1887.
2. Alice Lee WEST, b. 26th October, 1885; m. Hallam L. MORRIS.

IV. Mary Elizabeth, b. 17th October, 1862; m. (firstly) 30th June, 1884, Louis Agassiz SHAW, d. 3d July, 1891; m. (secondly) John CURTIS, d. 15th April, 1895.

ISSUE BY FIRST MARRIAGE

1. Quincy Adams SHAW, b. 21st May, 1885; m. Madeline MITCHELL.

V. Philip Leverett, b. 4th May, 1867; graduated at Harvard College, 1889; m. 18th June, 1890, Frances Ann Fitch SHERWOOD.

COLONIAL FAMILIES OF THE UNITED STATES

ISSUE

1. Katharine, *b.* 10th April, 1891.
2. Rose Lee, *b.* 27th May, 1892.
3. Frances Sherwood, *b.* 11th October, 1893.
4. Philip Leverett, *b.* 30th August, 1899.
5. Mary, *b.* 24th February, 1901.
6. Nathaniel, *b.* 24th April, 1903.

VI. Endicott Peabody, *b.* 25th December, 1872; graduated at Harvard College, 1894; *m.* 2d November, 1898, Elizabeth Baldwin DUPEC, dau. of William R. DUPEC.

ISSUE

1. Elizabeth, *b.* 26th July, 1900.

Residence.—Chestnut Hill, Newton, Massachusetts.
Arms.—Or, a bend between two eaglets displayed, sable.
Crest.—Out of a ducal coronet or, a pelican's head azure, vulning its breast gules.

Sanderson

LUCIEN SANDERSON of New Haven, Connecticut; *b.* in Bernardstown, Massachusetts, 3d July, 1859; *m.* in New Britain, Connecticut, 11th June, 1889, Clara Noyes SHERWIN, *b.* 15th January, 1863, dau. of William F. SHERWIN, *b.* in Backland, Massachusetts, 14th March, 1826, *d.* in Boston, 14th April, 1888, *m.* Mary A. HOWES, *b.* in Ashfield, Massachusetts, 11th June, 1828, *d.* in East Haven, Connecticut, 25th October, 1903.

ISSUE

I. Marie, *b.* 22d February, 1897.
II. Helen, *b.* 1st February, 1903.

LUCIEN SANDERSON is active in all public matters but declines to have any civil or political office; is a member of the New Haven Chamber of Commerce; second Vice-President of Orange Bank and Trust Company, Orange, Connecticut; Presient of Sanderson Fertilizer and Chemical Company of New Haven, Connecticut.

Lineage

The immigrant ancestor of this family was Edward SANDERSON of Watertown, Massachusetts, *b.* in England. He was a brother of Robert SANDERSON, who was associated with John HULL in the minting of the "Pine Tree Shilling," *m.* 15th October, 1645, Mary EGGLESTON.

ISSUE

I. JONATHAN, *b.* 16th September, 1646, of whom later.
II. Esther, *bapt.* 20th March, 1687.

JONATHAN SANDERSON of Watertown, Massachusetts; *b.* in Watertown, 16th September, 1646; *d.* 3d September, 1735; was Constable, 1695; Selectman and Deacon for many years; *m.* 24th October, 1669, Abial BARTLETT, *b.* 28th May, 1651, *d.* 13th September, 1723, younger dau. of Ensign Thomas BARTLETT of Watertown who came in 1630, commissioned Ensign 1639, *m.* Hannah, surname unknown.

ISSUE

I. JONATHAN (twin), *b.* 28th October, 1675, of whom later.
II. Abial (twin), *b.* 28th October, 1675.
III. Thomas, *b.* 10th March, 1676.
IV. John, *b.* 25th March, 1677.
V. Benjamin, *b.* 28th May, 1679.
VI. Samuel, *b.* 28th May, 1681.
VII. Edward, *b.* 3d March, 1684.
VIII. Hannah, *bapt.* 31st May, 1689.

COLONIAL FAMILIES OF THE UNITED STATES

JONATHAN SANDERSON, *b.* in Cambridge, 28th October, 1675; *m.* 14th July, 1699, Abigail FISKE.

ISSUE AMONG OTHERS

1. NATHANIEL, *b.* 30th May, 1713, of whom later.

NATHANIEL SANDERSON, *b.* at Watertown, 30th May, 1713; *m.* 4th October, 1739, Mary DRURY, of Framingham.

ISSUE

1. JONATHAN, *b.* September, 1740, of whom later.

JONATHAN SANDERSON *b.* September, 1740; served during the Revolution in Colonel DIKE's Regiment, also that of Col. Arthur SPARKAWS; *m.* 8th March 1768, Mary CURTISS.

ISSUE

1. JOHN, *b.* 21st May, 1769, of whom later.

JOHN SANDERSON, *b.* 21st May, 1769; *m.* 8th January, 1812, Lydia MORTON.

ISSUE

1. JOHN, *b.* 10th July, 1814, of whom later.

JOHN SANDERSON, *b.* 10th July, 1814; *m.* 29th October, 1840, Mary OSGOOD.

ISSUE AMONG OTHERS

1. LUCIEN, *b.* 3d June, 1859, the subject of this memoir.

Crest.—On a mount vert a talbot sable, eared or, spotted gold.
Motto.—Sans Dieu Rien.
Residence.—New Haven, Connecticut.
Clubs.—Union League and New Haven Automobile.
Societies.—Founders and Patriots.

Skinner

LEVIN PHILLIPS SKINNER, deceased, of Cambridge, Dorchester County, Maryland; *b.* 10th August, 1835; *d.* 20th November, 1912, at Baltimore, Maryland; *m.* 7th November, 1859, Mary Eugenia WILLIS.

ISSUE

I. Evelena Colston, *m.* George Whitefield WOOLFORD, son of John S. B. and Mary (REES) WOOLFORD of Woolford, Maryland.

ISSUE

1. Mildred Rees WOOLFORD, *m.* P. Watson WEBB.

ISSUE

1¹. Virginia WEBB.

2. Mabel WOOLFORD. *m.* Richard HARDING
3. Miles Hogan WOOLFORD.

II. William Woolford of Kensington, Maryland; *b.* 28th March, 1874; *m.* 24th August, 1899, Georgeanna MITCHELL, dau. of John and Rebecca (MITCHELL) MITCHELL.

ISSUE

1. Eugenia Woolford, *b.* 20th November, 1904.

III. Maud Eugenia, *b.* 5th March, 1876; *m.* 28th June, 1899, by Rev. Thomas Carter PAGE at Christ Protestant Episcopal Church, Cambridge, Maryland, Robert Eugene TUBMAN of "Glasgow," Dorchester County, Maryland.

ISSUE

1. Dorothy Keene TUBMAN, *b.* 23d September, 1901; *d.* 6th October, 1902.
2. Mary Keene TUBMAN, *b.* 24th May, 1904.
3. Elizabeth Willis TUBMAN, *b.* 28th July, 1907.

IV. Levin Phillips of Cambridge, Maryland; *b.* 14th September, 1878; *m.* 25th June, 1913, Mildred Lee WRIGHT, dau. of Joseph O. and Margaret (LEE) WRIGHT of Cambridge, Maryland.

ISSUE

1. Mildred Lee, *b.* 29th December, 1914.

Lineage

THOMAS SKINNER, d. previous to 10th February, 1675; one of the Gentlemen Justices of Dorchester County, Maryland; came from the Colony of Virginia previous to 20th October, 1669, as on that date he proved his right to 150 acres of land for transportation, of Elizabeth, his wife, John, his son, and William MERCHANT, his servant, from Virginia; was commissioned Gentleman Justice, 16th October, 1761, and also served as such in 1674 and 1675; m. Elizabeth, surname not given, who m. (secondly) prior to January, 1678, Henry BECKWITH of Dorchester county.

ISSUE

I. Thomas, removed to Talbot County, before 1678; will proved 6th November, 1707; m. Mary, surname unknown.

ISSUE

1. Martin, d. unmarried, will proved 7th May, 1711.
2. Elizabeth.
3. Ann, m. Thomas ENNALLS.
4. Mary.

II. John.
III. WILLIAM, b. circa, 1669, of whom later.
IV. Mary (probably), who m. Moses LE COMPTE.

WILLIAM SKINNER, Gentleman, of Broad Creek, Talbot County, Maryland; b. circa 1669; d. intestate prior to 24th May, 1744; Justice of the Peace, 18th September, 1718, and November, 1719; m. (firstly) circa, 1695, Hester (LECOMPTE) Fox, dau. of Anthony and Hester (DOTTANDO) LECOMPTE, a French Huguenot who came to Maryland before 1655 and first settled in Calvert County where on 7th of February, 1665, "Antoine LECOMPTE assigned 200 acres of land to Ishmael WRIGHT." He returned to London for bride, as there is recorded as follows: St. Hellen's Parish Register Bishopsgate, London, page 156, June 11, 1661 "Anthony LECOMPTE of the Parishe of Macke neere Callis in France and Esther Dottando of Deepe in France, weare mared." He was one of His Lordship's Justices of the Peace of Dorchester County from 1669 to 1671. William SKINNER, m. (secondly) Elizabeth COLSTON, widow of James COLSTON of Talbot County.

ISSUE BY FIRST MARRIAGE

I. William, Jr., b. 1698; d. 1743; m. Sarah, surname not known.

ISSUE

1. Sarah, b. 8th December, 1734.
2. William.
3. Esther.

4. Mary, m. ——— HOPKINS.
5. Elizabeth.

II. PHILEMON, b. 2d December, 1701; bapt. 3d May, 1702, of whom later.

ISSUE BY SECOND MARRIAGE

I. Thomas, will probated 5th July, 1768, of Dorchester County.
II. Samuel.
III. Mordecai, of Dorchester County.
IV. Esther, m. John LEEDS.

PHILEMON SKINNER of Talbot County, Maryland; b. 2d December, 1701; bapt. 3d March, 1702; d. between 28th April, 1761, and 1st December, 1762; Constable Mill Hundred, 1761; m. after 1724, Lucy HAMBLETON, dau. of William and Margaret (SHERWOOD) HAMBLETON, b. 1683, she the dau. of Hugh and Mary SHERWOOD. Hugh SHERWOOD was a Vestryman of St. Michael's Parish, a Justice of the Peace of Talbot County, 1696–1698; and a Member of the Assembly, 1690.

ISSUE

I. WILLIAM, b. 1741, of whom later.
II. John, d. in Talbot County; will proved 23d January, 1816.
III. Ruth, m. ——— LAMDEN.
IV. Rachel, m. ——— GRAHAM.
V. A daughter, m. ——— EAGAN.

WILLIAM SKINNER of Talbot County, Maryland, took the "Oath of Fidelity," March, 1778; b. 1741; d. 20th February, 1813; m. (firstly) Elizabeth JONES, d. June, 1829; m. (secondly) Elizabeth (FOOKES) STEWART, b. 5th October, 1756, dau. of Joseph and Mary (KIRK) FOOKES and widow of John Travillian STEWART.

ISSUE BY FIRST MARRIAGE

I. THOMAS, b. 2d February, 1772, of whom later.

ISSUE BY SECOND MARRIAGE

I. Polly Hambleton, b. 6th October, 1782; m. Eggleston BROWN.

ISSUE

1. Eliza BROWN.
2. Ann BROWN.
3. Thomas E. BROWN.
4. William James BROWN.
5. Margaret Anne BROWN, m. ——— MOWBRAY.
6. Mary Skinner BROWN, m. ——— SMITH.
7. John Wesley BROWN.

II. James Fookes, *b.* 5th September, 1784; *m.* Nancy PATTISON.

ISSUE

1. Emily, *m.* ———— BRANNOCK.
2. Joseph.
3. Levin, *m.* Susie PHILLIPS.
4. Adeline, *m.* ———— BRANNOCK.
5. Elizabeth.
6. Mary, *m.* Rev. John BAIN.
7. Samuel.
8. Sally Ann, *m.* ———— THOMAS.

III. Zachariah, *b.* 13th March, 1787; *m.* Hannah Bond JONES, dau. of Lieut.-Col. John and Cassandra (FELL) JONES, *b.* 1765, of Dorchester County Maryland, served in the Revolutionary War, the son of Col. Thomas Jones of the Revolutionary Army.

ISSUE

1. William, *b.* 1810; *m.* 7th November, 1833, Eliza SAULSBURY.

ISSUE

1^1. Katharine, *m.* Jackson HOLLAND.
2^1. William James, *m.* Victoria JONES.
3^1. Thomas, *b.* 22d March, 1842; *d.* 26th August, 1907; *m.* Mary Florence STANSBURY, *b.* 1844, *d.* 8th August, 1876, dau. of James STANSBURY and Elleanor FOREMAN.

ISSUE

1^2. Laurice Edward, *b.* 24th June, 1868; educated Baltimore City College, University of Maryland; Lawyer; LL.B., University of Maryland, 1890; *m.* 18th January, 1893, Nettie Esther HOWSER, dau. of Gassaway Sellman HOWSER and Cecelia BRAMWELL of Maryland.

ISSUE

1^3. William Howser, *b.* 2d November, 1895.
2^3. Maurice Edward, *b.* 10th March, 1901.
3^3. Robert Stansbury, *b.* 10th March, 1901.

2^2. Ferdinand Stansbury, *b.* 27th January, 1871; *d.* June, 1911.

4^1. John, *m.* Carrie, surname unknown.
5^1. Hannah Elizabeth.

6^1. Cora.
7^1. Eliza, *m.* Charles ASKEW.
8^1. Jennie, *m.* Emmitt DOWNS.

2. John Jones, *b.* 6th September, 1813; *d.* 17th February, 1888; *m.* (firstly) 16th October, 1839, Emaline JONES; *m.* (secondly) 9th October, 1856, Marguerretta M. TEAL.

ISSUE BY FIRST MARRIAGE

1^1. John O., Major in United States Army, Retired; Superintendent of Columbia Hospital, Washington, D. C.; *m.* ———— BAILEY.
2^1. Mary Frances, *d.* February, 1903; *m.* David Webster CULPEPPER.

ISSUE

1^2. Fannie CULPEPPER.
2^2. Charles CULPEPPER.
3^2. Hattie CULPEPPER, *m.* August, 1893, Charles B. DAVIS.
4^2. Bessie CULPEPPER, *m.* Henry GILLIS.

3^1. Emma Virginia, *m.* (firstly) 12th May, 1869, Benjamin Whitely WOOLFORD, *d.* 16th August, 1871; *m.* (secondly) 6th November, 1885, Rev. W. F. HAYES.

ISSUE BY FIRST MARRIAGE

1^2. Benjamin Whitely WOOLFORD, *m.* 18th December, 1895, Ida Stengle HOOPER, dau. of W. R. and Elizabeth HOOPER.

ISSUE BY SECOND MARRIAGE OF JOHN JONES AND MARGUERRETTA (TEAL) SKINNER

1^1. Eugenia, *d.* aged 17 years.
2^1. Milton Ellis, *b.* 16th January, 1863; *m.* 12th May, 1898, Jessie PARKER.

ISSUE

1^2. Jessie Parker Skinner, *b.* 17th March, 1902.

3^1. Edgar Martin, *b.* 16th August, 1866; *m.* 13th October, 1896, Mattie MITCHELL.

ISSUE

1^2. Shirley Eugenia, *b.* 7th May, 1898.
2^2. Emily Margaret, *b.* 13th December, 1902.
3^2. Edgar Martin, *b.* 6th August, 1910.

3. Thomas, *b.* 29th November, 1815; *m.* (firstly) ———— JONES; *m.* (secondly) ———— BUSEY.

4. Cassandra Jones, *b.* 2d October, 1817; *d.* 30th September, 1820.
5. James Aquilla, *b.* 15th November, 1820; *d.* circa 1906; *m.* (firstly) Cassandra WOOLFORD; *m.* (secondly) Jane FREEMAN.
6. Washington Hammond, *b.* 7th May, 1822; *m.* Emma MUSSELMAN; *d.* 25th February, 1901.
7. Zachariah H., *b.* 5th July, 1825.
8. Mary Elizabeth, *b.* 20th October, 1827; *d.* 29th May, 1831.
9. Alexander Summerfield, *b.* 26th December, 1829; *m.* Sarah A. HURTY, *d.* 25th April, 1908.
10. Richard Standley, *b.* 25th May, 1832; *d.* 29th June, 1832.

IV. Margaret, *b.* 23d January, 1790; *m.* Thomas GOSLIN.
V. William, *b.* 6th February, 1792; *m.* 29th November, 1814, Beckie PATTISON.

ISSUE

1. Jeremiah Pattison.
2. James.
3. George W., *d.* unmarried.
4. Anne E.
5. William H., *b.* 3d July, 1823; *d.* 9th April, 1891; *m.* 26th April, 1854, Martha Ann WILSON, *b.* 21st June, 1830.

ISSUE

1^1. Harry G., *b.* 17th December, 1858; *m.* Gertrude THOMPSON.

ISSUE

1^2. Ella, *m.* J. Reese PITCHER.
2^2. Annie, *m.* Colin STEWART.
3^2. Mattie, unmarried.
4^2. Mary (Mollie), *m.* J. Fred GRAFFLIN.
5^2. Howard, *d.* unmarried.
6^2. Birdie, *m.* ——— ENSOR.

6. Margaret E.
7. Caroline P.
8. Mary R.

VI. Sarah, *b.* 1st March, 1794; *m.* Mimos CONWAY or CONAWAY.
VII. Ann, *b.* 27th June, 1797; *m.* Samuel PATTISON.
VIII. Elizabeth, *b.* 20th November, 1800; *d.s.p.* 7th August, 1825; *m.* 23d January, 1825, Stephen HURST, *b.* 1794, will dated 19th October, 1847, will proved 29th January, 1873 (according to family MSS. he died 23d October, 1846), he *m.* (secondly) 29th January, 1829, Ann JONES and had issue.

THOMAS SKINNER of Cambridge, Maryland; *b.* 2d February, 1772; *d.* 3d December, 1813; *m.* 16th February, 1800, Sarah LEE, *d.* 4th September, 1815, aged 38 years.

ISSUE

I. Mary, *b.* 6th January, 1801; *m.* 9th October, 1817, Andrew MARSHALL.
II. William, *b.* 7th December, 1802.
III. Margaret, *b.* 7th April, 1805; *d.* unmarried, 30th May, 1875.
IV. ZACHARIAH, *b.* 30th May, 1807, of whom later.
V. Philemon, *b.* 14th October, 1809.
VI. Susan, *b.* 25th August, 1811.
VII. Joseph (twin), *b.* 18th December, 1813; *d.* in infancy.
VIII. Benjamin (twin), *b.* 18th December, 1813; *d.* in infancy.

ZACHARIAH SKINNER of Dorchester County, Maryland; *b.* 30th May, 1807; *d.* 10th April, 1883; *m.* 25th February, 1830, Susan Ann PHILLIPS.

ISSUE

I. Thomas Richard, *b.* 1st July, 1831; *d.* 15th September, 1815.
II. LEVIN PHILLIPS, *b.* 11th August, 1834, the subject of this memoir.
III. Henry White, *b.* 28th June, 1838; *d.* 28th July, 1838.
IV. William Henry, *b.* 20th October, 1839.

Arms.—Sable a chevron or, between three griffins heads, erased argent.
Crest.—A griffin's head erased argent, holding in the mouth a dexter gauntlet or.
Motto.—Nunquam non paratus.

Spencer

MATTHEW LYLE SPENCER, A.B., A.M., Ph.D., of Appleton, Wisconsin; *b.* 7th July, 1881, at Batesville, Mississippi; *m.* 22d December, 1908, at Spartanburg, South Carolina, Lois HILL, dau. of Rufus Sadler and Emma (McMULLAN) HILL of Hartwell, Georgia.

ISSUE

I. Manly Lyle, *b.* 10th May, 1911.

MATTHEW LYLE SPENCER, College Professor; A.B., Kentucky Wesleyan College, 1903; A.M., 1904; A.M., Northwestern University, 1905; Ph.D., University of Chicago, 1910; Instructor and Professor of English, Kentucky Wesleyan College, 1901–1904; Assistant Professor of English, Wofford College, 1907–1910; Professor of English, Woman's College of Alabama, 1910–1911; Professor of English, Lawrence College, since 1911; Fellow, University of Chicago, 1905–1907, 1909–1910; Editor, Simms's "Yemassee;" Author: "Corpus Christi Pageants in England," "Practical English Punctuation," "News Writing," etc.

Lineage

The ancestor of this family was Col. Thomas SPENCER of Charlotte County Virginia; *d.* 1793; *m.* Eliza Julia FLOURNOY, *b.* 5th December, 1721.

ISSUE

I. Mary, *b.* 20th October, 1742; *m.* ——— SPEED.
II. Sion, *b.* 12th April, 1744.
III. John, *b.* 16th December, 1745, of whom later.
IV. Elizabeth Julia, *b.* 18th June, 1747; *m.* ——— SPEED.
V. Ann, *b.* 13th July, 1749.
VI. Thomas, *m.* Lucy WATKINS.
VII. Martha Owen, *m.* ——— HALLOWAY.
VIII. Samuel F.
IX. Judith, *m.* Martin PEARCE.
X. Gideon, *m.* Catherine CLEMENTS.

CAPTAIN JOHN SPENCER of Charlotte County, Virginia; *b.* 16th December, 1745; *d.* 1828; *m.* 1765, Sally WATKINS, *b.* 1748, dau. of Thomas WATKINS, of Powhatan County, Virginia, and his wife, *née* ANDERSON.

ISSUE

I. Frances A., *b.* 1766; *m.* 1788, Jesse WINFREY, *b.* 1764, *d.* 1810.
II. THOMAS COLE, of whom later.
III. Jane, *m.* (firstly) Allen WARREN; *m.* (secondly) ———— YARBROUGH.
IV. Elizabeth Julia, *m.* Dr. TODD, of Georgia.
V. Henry, Colonel, *m.* Sallie W. BOULDIN.

CAPTAIN THOMAS COLE SPENCER of Charlotte County, Virginia; *b.* 1774; *d.* 1860; *m.* (firstly) 1796, Frances PEARCE, of New Jersey, *d.* 1817; *m.* (secondly) Mary SPAULDING.

ISSUE

I. Sally W., *m.* Robert A. SMITH.
II. Harriet G., *b.* 1800; *m.* 1834, William MATTHEWS.
III. Matilda Cole, *m.* 1839, James H. WILSON.
IV. Elvira H.
V. Jane P., *m.* Samuel HALLOWAY, of Kentucky.
VI. Martha F., *m.* 1844, Thomas HORACY.
VII. John James Robertson, *b.* 1806; *m.* 1829, Eliza W. BOULDIN.
VIII. Henry Martyn, *m.* Clementine S. REID.
IX. MATTHEW LYLE, *b.* 6th May, 1809, of whom later.
X. Thomas Cole, Rev., *b.* 1811; *m.* 1830, Eliza W. FENNELL.

MATTHEW LYLE SPENCER of Lunenburg County, Virginia; *b.* 6th May, 1809; *d.* 28th December, 1887; *m.* 3d April, 1838, Louisa Stokes NEAL, *b.* 15th January, 1817, *d.* 1874.

ISSUE

I. Mary Frances, *m.* Dr. Walter Hugh DRANE of Georgia.
II. Thomas James.
III. Susan Rives, *m.* Edward WALSH of Mississippi.
IV. Sarah Watkins, *d.* in infancy.
V. Colin Stokes.
VI. Samuel Graham.
VII. Elizabeth Williams, *m.* Thomas McGEHEE of Georgia.
VIII. Lelia Matilda, *d.* in infancy.
IX. Louisa Virginia, *m.* Lucus Polk JONES.
X. FLOURNOY POINDEXTER, of whom later.
XI. Colie Pierce, *m.* Hiram Walter DRANE.
XII. Matthew Lyle.
XIII. Ada Catherine, *m.* Rev. Junius Wayne ALLEN.
XIV. Jessie, *d.* in childhood.

FLOURNOY POINDEXTER SPENCER of Batesville, Mississippi; *b.* 2d April, 1857; *d.* 14th December, 1904; *m.* 10th February, 1880, Alice Eleanor MANES, *b.* 14th January, 1863, dau. of Henry MANES of Thomasville, Georgia.

COLONIAL FAMILIES OF THE UNITED STATES

ISSUE

I. MATTHEW LYLE, *b.* 7th July, 1881, the subject of this memoir.
II. Eleanor Elizabeth, *b.* 31st December, 1883; *d.* 10th October, 1911; *m.* Cokie V. SPRINKLE, of Indiana.

ISSUE

1. Eleanor Elizabeth SPRINKLE.

III. Flournoy Poindexter, *b.* 28th September, 1885; unmarried.
IV. Leslie Louise, *b.* 30th December, 1887, *m.* Frederick BYRD of Georgia.

Arms (SPENCER of Virginia).—Quarterly or and gules, in the second and third a fret of the first, over all on a bend sable three fleur-de-lis argent.
Motto.—Dieu defend le droit.
Residence.—Appleton, Wisconsin.
Clubs.—Riverview Country and Milwaukee Press.
Societies.—Sons of the American Revolution, Kappa Alpha, Tau Kappa Alpha, Wisconsin Academy of Sciences, Arts and Letters, Modern Language Association of America, Fellow Royal Society of Arts and Sciences, England.

Stockton

MAJOR RICHARD STOCKTON, JR., of Bordentown, New Jersey; b. 9th January, 1888, at Rotterdam, Holland; m. 24th July, 1907, at Camden, New Jersey, Helen Beryl GOVE, b. 22d December, 1887, at Trenton.

ISSUE

I. Richard Finch, b. 23d September, 1908.
II. Jack Potter, II, b. 22d March, 1910.
III. Robert Field, b. 14th October, 1915.
IV. Helen Clemence Carolyn, b. 15th January, 1917.

RICHARD STOCKTON, JR. (see "Who's Who in America," 1916–1917), Gold Medalist, Military Service Institution of the United States, 1912; Gold Medalist, Military Service Institution of the United States, 1915; Gold Medalist, Military Service Institution of the United States, 1916; Reeve Memorial Prize Essayist, Military Service Institution of the United States, 1915; American Cross of Honor, awarded 1914, for valor. Author of "Peace Insurance;" co-author of "Troops on Riot Duty;" author of "The Guardsman's Handbook (eight editions) and a frequent contributor to the service publications and various periodicals. (*Infantry Journal, Collier's Weekly, North American Review, Outlook*, etc.) Lecturer on Military Subjects. Appointed by the War Department as one of a board of officers to write the "Manual for Officers of the National Guard and Volunteers of the United States" now in preparation. Expert Rifleman, 1910–1916. Long Distance Expert (a New Jersey designation instituted in 1913), 1913–1916; Coach Bordentown Military Institute Rifle Team (Military School Champions of the United States, 1913–1914), since 1913· Private, Company A., Corps of Cadets, National Guard of New Jersey, 18th September, 1901; Corporal, Company A, Corps of Cadets, National Guard of New Jersey, 19th June, 1903; transferred to Company B., 19th June, 1903; Sergeant, Company B, Corps of Cadets, National Guard of New Jersey, 18th September, 1903; Company Quartermaster Sergeant and Acting Battalion Quartermaster, Corps of Cadets, New Jersey, 31st May, 1904; Orderly Sergeant, Corps of Cadets, 2d Brigade, New Jersey, by detail, July, 1904; Second Lieutenant, Company A, Corps of Cadets, New Jersey, 22d September, 1904. Discharged graduation, 20th September, 1905; Second Lieutenant, Battalion Quartermaster and Commander, 3d Infantry, New Jersey, 22d May, 1906; resigned 1st September, 1907 (left the State). Private, Company E, 2d Infantry, New Jersey, 26th May, 1910; First Lieutenant, Company E, 2d Infantry, New Jersey, 23d June, 1910; Captain, Company E, 2d Infantry, New Jersey, 11th May, 1911. Assigned Regimental Quartermaster, 12th February, 1912; assigned to command Supply Company, 2d Infantry, New Jersey, 5th January, 1915; Assigned Assistant Inspector of Small

Arms Practice, February, 1915. Resigned 6th September, 1916. Major, Infantry, Officers' Reserve Corps, United States Army, 26th October, 1916; Instructor in Military Science, Bordentown Military Institute since 1911; Trustee, American Defense Society since 1915; Board of Governors, American Cross of Honor since 1915; Associate Editor, *American Defence* (monthly) since 1916. Major STOCKTON is an ardent advocate of adequate preparedness. Since 1907, he has worked for absolute Federal control of the National Guard. In December, 1915, before the officers of his regiment (then 2d New Jersey Infantry) and prominent guests, he made a speech attacking the militia system and the political appointments of high offices. Though aimed at inefficiency in general, this was construed as an attack on Brigadier-General SADLER, the Adjutant-General of New Jersey. Major (then Captain) STOCKTON was asked to resign but refused, stating that he could be removed only by sentence of a court martial. No court was ordered, and friends claimed that this indicated that Major STOCKTON's position is correct. He received high praise for his attitude from the foremost military authorities and highest officers in the country, it being an article on the subject which won for him the Gold Medal of the Military Service Institution for the second time. Major STOCKTON believes that the citizen soldiery, be it called National Guard or any other name will never be efficient until it is controlled entirely by the United States, rather than State Governments. He has prepared plans showing how this may be accomplished practically and legally. In 1916 Major STOCKTON made a complete investigation of the mobilization and concentration of the Army and National Guard on the Mexican border, being sent by the Mayor's Committee on National Defense of New York City. He covered the entire border in the course of his inspection of the troops. At the time of going to press, July 12th, 1917, Major Stockton was in active service in the war with Germany.

Lineage

The ancestor of this family was Richard STOCKTON, Lieutenant of Horse; *b.* in England, circa 1630; *d.* in Flushing, Long Island, September, 1707, Probably gd. son of Randall STOCKTON of London and gr. gd. son of John STOCKTON of Keddington, Cheshire County, England, and a descendant of Sir John STOCKTON, Lord Mayor of London, 1470-1471. Came to America with son Richard, settled first in Flushing, Long Island, prior to 8th November, 1656. Removed to Oneanickon, New Jersey, 1694 and bought 2000 acres of land; commissioned Lieutenant of Horse, 22d April, 1665; *m.* in England in 1652 Abigail, surname not known (see "The Stockton Family," by Thomas Coates STOCKTON, M.D., of San Diego, California, published by The Carnahan Press, Washington, D. C., 1911.

ISSUE

I. RICHARD, *b.* in London, England, probably 1654, of whom later.
II. John, *b.* 1674; *d.* 29th March, 1747; *m.* (firstly) Mary LEEDS, dau. of Daniel LEEDS, Surveyor General of West New Jersey; *m.* (secondly) Ann OGBORN, widow of John OGBORN.

III. Job, *m.* Ann PETTY, sister of William PETTY.
IV. Abigail, *m.* Jacob RIDGEWAY, Sr. of Burlington County, New Jersey.
V. Mary, *m.* (firstly) Thomas SHINN, son of John SHINN; *m.* (secondly) Silas CRISPEN, son of Rear Admiral William CRISPEN of the Royal Navy.
VI. Sarah, *m.* (firstly) Benjamin JONES of Burlington County, New Jersey; *m.* (secondly) 1706, William VEMCOMB.
VII. Hannah, *m.* Philip PHILLIPS.
VIII. Elizabeth, *m.* William BUDD, son of William and Ann BUDD.

RICHARD STOCKTON of Princeton, New Jersey; *b.* in London, England, probably 1654; *d.* 1709, at Princeton. He accompanied his father from England to Long Island 1656. In 1701, purchased from William PENN an estate of 6000 acres which included the entire present borough of Princeton, where he settled in August, 1695; built "Morven" which has been the family homestead for over 215 years (1701-1916) and which is now occupied by his gr., gr., gr., gd. son Bayard STOCKTON; *m.* 8th November, 1691, Susannah Witham ROBINSON, *b.* 29th November, 1668, *d.* April, 1749, dau. of Robert and Ann WITHAM and widow of Thomas ROBINSON.

ISSUE

I. Richard, *b.* 1693; *m.* Esther SMITH, Long Island, New York, 1707 (?).
II. Samuel, *b.* 1695; *d.* 1739; *m.* (firstly) Ann DOUGHTY, dau. of Jacob and Amy DOUGHTY, *m.* (secondly) Rachel STOUT, dau. of Col. Joseph and Ruth STOUT.
III. Joseph, *b.* 1697; *d.* 15th March, 1770; *m.* Elizabeth DOUGHTY, sister of brother's wife.
IV. Robert, *b.* 1699; *d.* 1745; *m.* Rebecca PHILLIPS, March, 1740.
V. JOHN, *b.* 8th August, 1701, of whom later.
VI. Thomas.

HON. JOHN STOCKTON of Princeton, New Jersey; *b.* 8th August, 1701; *d.* there 1787; Chief Judge of the Court of Common Pleas of Somerset County, New Jersey; was instrumental in securing at Princeton, the "College of New Jersey" (Princeton University); together with Thomas LEONARD, Esq., and John HORNER, Esq., John STOCKTON laid the corner stone of the "College of New Jersey;" he with the same two men gave the necessary bonds to secure the land for the College; *m.* 21st February, 1729, Abigail PHILLIPS, *b.* 9th August, 1708, dau. of Philip and Hannah (STOCKTON) PHILLIPS.

ISSUE

I. RICHARD, *b.* 3d October, 1720, of whom later.
II. Sarah, *b.* 19th June, 1732; *d.* 1736.
III. John, *b.* 4th August, 1734; *d.* 1736.
IV. Hannah, *b.* 21st July, 1736; *m.* Hon. Elias BOUDINOT, President of Continental Congress, 21st April, 1763.

COLONIAL FAMILIES OF THE UNITED STATES

v. Abigail, *b.* 13th November, 1738; *m.* Capt. Samuel PINTARD, British Army.
vi. Susanna, *b.* 2d January, 1742; *m.* Lewis PINTARD, brother of Capt. Samuel PINTARD.
vii. John, *b.* 22d February, 1744; *m.* Mary HIBBETS, widow of James NELSON and dau. of ——— HIBBETS.
viii. Philip, *b.* 11th July, 1746; *d.* 12th January, 1792; *m.* 13th April, 1767, Catharine CUMMING dau. of Robert and Mary Noble CUMMING, and sister of Gen. John Noble CUMMING.
ix. Rebecca, *b.* 5th July, 1748.
x. Samuel William, *b.* 4th February, 1751.

HON. RICHARD STOCKTON, "The Signer," of "Morven," Princeton, New Jersey; *b.* 3d October, 1730; *d.* 28th February, 1781, at "Morven;" studied under Rev. Samuel FINLEY; attended West Nottingham Academy; was graduated in the first class from the College of New Jersey, Princeton, New Jersey; A.B., 1748; A.M., 1751. Studied law under Judge David OGDEN of Newark, New Jersey; admitted to the bar, 1754; became Counsellor, 1758; Member of the King's Council, New Jersey, 1768–1774. While in Scotland and England, 1766–1767, secured Dr. John WITHERSPOON to act as President of Princeton College, for which he received a vote of thanks from the trustees. Made Judge of the Provincial Supreme Court, 1774; Member of the Continental Congress at Philadelphia, 1776–1777, and one of the Signers of the Declaration of Independence, 4th July, 1776. Was made a prisoner of War by the British while serving as Inspector of the Northern Army, 30th November, 1776 and so mistreated that Congress passed resolutions directing General WASHINGTON to threaten the British with reprisals. Part of "Morven" his estate and valuable library, was destroyed by the British; was appointed Chief Justice of New Jersey, but declined; died in his fifty-first year, his health having broken down under the treatment he received from his British captors. Was a Trustee of the College of New Jersey, 1757–1781; serving as Secretary, 1757–1765, and received the degree of Sergeant at Law in 1763. Published an "Expedient for the Settlement of American Dispute," addressed to Lord DARTMOUTH, 12th December, 1774; *m.* Annis BOUDINOT, *d.* 6th February, 1801, dau. of Elias and Catherine (WILLIAMS) BOUDINOT and sister of Dr. Elias BOUDINOT. She is the author of a poem addressed to General WASHINGTON after the surrender of Yorktown and "Welcome Mighty Chief, Once More" and various periodical contributions.

ISSUE

i. RICHARD, "The Duke," *b.* 17th August, 1764, of whom later.
ii. Lucius Horatio, *d.* 26th March, 1835; *m.* ——— MILNOR (probably Sarah).
iii. Julia, *m.* April, 1777, Dr. Benjamin RUSH, Signer of Declaration of Independence.

IV. Susan, d. 2d October, 1821; m. Alexander CUTHBERT of Canada.
V. Mary, b. 17th April, 1761; d. 18th March, 1846; m. Rev. Andrew HUNTER.
VI. Abigail, m. Robert FIELD of Burlington County, New Jersey.

HON. RICHARD STOCKTON, "The Duke," of Princeton, New Jersey; b. 17th April, 1764, at "Morven;" d. 7th March, 1828; Lawyer; graduated from the College of New Jersey, Princeton; A.B., 1779; A.M., 1782; studied law under his uncle Dr. Elias BOUDINOT; admitted to the Bar, 1784, and commenced practice at Princeton. Presidential Elector on the WASHINGTON and ADAMS ticket, 1792 and 1801; elected by the Federalists as United States Senator from New Jersey to fill vacancy caused by resignation of Frederick FREYLINGHUYSEN, 1796–1799, when he declined re-election. Member of Congress (House of Representatives), 1813–1815; was again Presidential Elector in 1801 on the ADAMS and PINCKNEY and a member of the State Legislature, 1813–1815. Was made Trustee of the College of New Jersey, 1791–1828, and received the honorary degree of LL.D. from Queen's (now Rutgers) College, New Brunswick, New Jersey, 1815, and from Union College, Schenectady, New York, 1816; m. Mary FIELD, b. 10th October, 1776, d. 25th December, 1837, dau. of Robert and Mary (PEALE) FIELD and sister of Robert FIELD who m. Abigail STOCKTON, sister of "The Duke."

ISSUE

I. Mary F., b. 1790; d. 9th August, 1865; m. William HARRISON.
II. Richard, b. 1791.
III. Julia, b. 1793; m. John RHINELANDER.
IV. ROBERT FIELD, "The Commodore;" b. 20th August, 1795; d. 7th October, 1866, of whom later.
V. Horatio, b. 1797.
VI. Caroline, b. 1799.
VII. Samuel Witham, b. 1801.
VIII. William Bradford, b. 1802, d.s.p.
IX. Annis, b. 1804.

HON. ROBERT FIELD STOCKTON, A.M., "The Commodore," of Princeton, New Jersey; b. there 20th August, 1795; d. there 7th October, 1866 (see "Life of Commodore STOCKTON," published by Derby and Jackson, New York, 1856); Midshipman, United States Navy, 18th September, 1811; served on Frigate *President*, under Commodore ROGERS; active service in the War of 1812; participated in the defense of Baltimore, June, 1814, being promoted for his gallantry; on 9th September, 1814, gained the name of "Fighting Bob," and said to be the original man with that nickname; served as Aide to the Secretary of the Navy. During War of the Barbary Powers, he served first as Junior Lieutenant on the *Guerrier*, Commodore DECATUR's flagship and subsequently as First Lieutenant on the schooner *Spitfire*, taking part in the capture of the Algerian frigate *Mishoun*, 17th June, 1815, and of the brig, *Estecio* a few days following. In 1816, he again cruised in the Mediterreanean as Seventh Lieutenant on the *Washington,* Commodore CHAUNCEY's Squadron; was promoted Second Lieutenant and subsequently First Lieutenant of the *Erie,* returning to the United States in 1812; was transferred soon after to the command of the schooner *Alligston* and under the auspices of the American Colonization Society, visited the west coast of Africa where, in 1822, he founded a Colony at Mesurado, which became in 1847 the Republic of Liberia. He subsequently captured the Portuguese Letter of Marque *Marrianna Flora* and the French slaver *Jeune Eugenie.* This latter case was taken to Court and Captain STOCKTON, defended by Daniel WEBSTER, won the case. Thus he was the first to establish the right of a warship to capture slave vessels under a foreign flag. Was ordered to the West Indies to check the depredations of the pirates and surveyed the Southern Coasts, 1823-1824; during which time he married. Obtained leave of absence from 1826-1838 and made his home in Princeton, New Jersey, where he established a newspaper to which he contributed editorials, stating that his support of President ADAMS would be based upon the latter's "good behavior in office," an independent attitude which he continued to maintain throughout his career. Was a delegate to the Democratic State Convention, 1826; was the Founder and first President of the New Jersey Colonization Society and the chief promoter of the Delaware and Raritan Canal, visiting Europe to obtain a loan for the completion; he served as executive officer of the flagship *Ohio,* Mediterranean Squadron, Commodore Isaac HULL, 8th December, 1838-1839, bearing official dispatches to Great Britain where he investigated the improvements in naval architecture; was promoted Port Captain, 1839. Supported Gen. William Henry HARRISON for the Presidency, 1840, and declined the portfolio of the Navy offered by President TYLER, 1841. He was one of the first commanders to apply steam to naval purposes; building in 1842-1844, the famous sloop of war *Princeton* of which he was placed in command. On the trial down the Potomac River, 28th February, 1844, through the accidental explosion of one of the guns, opposite Mount Vernon, Able P. UPSHUR, Secretary of State, Thomas W. GILMER, Secretary of the Navy and David GARDINER, father-in-law of President TYLER were killed as well as several of the crew, while Captain STOCKTON, and others were severely injured. A court of inquiry showed that this gun was fired at the order of the Secretary of the Navy, contrary to Captain STOCKTON's desires. Captain STOCKTON was completely acquitted of all blame. Later on in the same year, he was appointed to carry the annexation resolutions to the Government of Texas, and sailed in the *Princeton.* Was promoted Commander-in-Chief of the Pacific Squadron, October, 1845, and sailed in the frigate *Conyers* with Mr. TEN EYCK, commissioner, from Norfolk, Virginia, around Cape Horn to the Sandwich Island and finally to Monterey, California, of which place Commodore John D. SLOAT, U. S. N., had taken possession of, 7th July, 1846. Commodore STOCKTON took command by proclamation of the entire American force on the Pacific Coast and in coöperation with Col. John C. FREMONT, captured Los Angeles, 13th August, 1846; assumed office as the first American Governor of California (military), appointing Colonel FRE-

MONT, Commander of the military forces; recaptured San Diego, San Gabriel and Le Mesa; Maj.-Gen. S. W. KEARNEY was later second in command. Commodore STOCKTON returned to San Diego 17th January, 1847, after having successfully negotiated with Mexico for the ceding of California to the United States, which act was formally ratified by the treaty of 2d February, 1848. Upon his return to New Jersey, he received the thanks of the State Legislature and was tendered a reception. He resigned from the Navy, 28th May, 1850. Was elected to the United States Senate from New Jersey to the Thirty-second Congress for the full term, 1851–1857, but resigned 20th January, 1853; was President of the Delaware and Raritan Canal, 1853–1866; was a Delegate to the Peace Congress at Washington, D. C., 13th February, 1861; received the honorary degree of A.M. from the College of New Jersey, 1851; the city of Stockton, California, the torpedo boat and the destroyer *Stockton*, were named in the Commodore's honor; a memorial window in memory of Commodore STOCKTON and of Admirals SLOAT and FARRAGUT was placed in St. Peter's Chapel, Mare Island Navy Yard, California, in 1902; *m.* 1823, Harriet Maria POTTER, who *d.* 1862, dau. of John POTTER of Charleston, South Carolina.

ISSUE

I. Richard, *b.* 22d January, 1824; *d.* 5th April, 1876; *m.* (firstly) Caroline Bayard DODD; *m.* (secondly) Susan B. DODD.
II. JOHN POTTER, "The Senator;" *b.* 2d August, 1826, of whom later.
III. Catherine Elizabeth, *m.* William Armstrong DODD.
IV. Mary, *b.* 1830; *m.* Rear Admiral John C. HOWELL.
V. Robert Field, *b.* 22d January, 1832; *d.* 5th May, 1898; *m.* Anna Margaretta POTTER.
VI. Harriet Maria, *b.* 1834.
VII. Caroline, *m.* Capt. William Rawle BROWN of the United States Navy.
VIII. Julia, *b.* 1837; *m.* Edward M. HOPKINS.
IX. Annis, *m.* 21st February, 1865, Franklin Davenport HOWELL.

HON. JOHN POTTER STOCKTON, A.B., A.M., LL.B., "The Senator," of Princeton, New Jersey; *b.* 2d August, 1826; *d.* 22d January, 1900, in New York City; graduated at the College of New Jersey; A.B., 1843; A.M., 1846. Attorney at Law, 1847; Counsellor, 1850; revised the "Proceedings and Practice" of Courts of New Jersey and was State Reporter to the court of Chancery. United States Minister to Italy, 1857–1861; elected United States Senator from New Jersey, 1865; by a plurality of the Legislature; took his seat 4th March, 1866, but election contested and unseated 27th March by a vote of 23 to 25, notwithstanding the unanimous vote of the Committee on the Judiciary in favor of the validity of his election. Was a Delegate at large to all the Democratic conventions from 1864 to the close of his life. As Chairman of the New Jersey delegation at the Chicago Convention, 29th August, 1864, he presented the name of George B. MCCLELLAN as candidate for

President of the United States. Received the honorary degree of LL.D. from the Princeton University in 1882. Author of "Equity Reports," three volumes, 1856–1858. United States Senator from New Jersey, 1869, for full term of six years expiring 4th March, 1875. He was a Member of the Committee on Foreign Affairs, the Navy Appropriations, etc., and was instrumental in first establishing life saving stations on the Atlantic Coast. Attorney-General of New Jersey, 1877, for twenty years; *m.* Sara MARKS, *b.* New Orleans, 1829, *d.* 29th September, 1887, dau. of Albert I. MARKS, *b.* London, April, 1815, *d.* Princeton, June, 1850.

ISSUE

I. Robert Field, *b.* 5th January, 1847; *d.* 20th October, 1891.
II. John Potter, *b.* 1852.
III. Saidee, *b.* 5th November, 1853; *d.* 2d January, 1868.
IV. RICHARD, *b.* 4th June, 1858, of whom later.
V. Julia, *b.* Rome, Italy, 27th May, 1860; *d.* 8th November, 1905, Richard C. ST. JOHN.

HON. RICHARD STOCKTON of Trenton, New Jersey; *b.* 4th June, 1858; Consul to Rotterdam, 1885–1888; Charge d'Affairs at The Hague, 1888; awarded Gold Medal by Congress for life saving, 31st July, 1879; awarded American Cross of Honor; Member of Board of Governors, American Cross of Honor; first to secure "Dollar Gas" in New Jersey; Member of firm of TAYLOR, SMITH and HARD, Members of New York Stock Exchange; Commissioner of Charities and Corrections, State of New Jersey, since 1915; Alternate Delegate at Large, Democratic Convention at St. Louis, 1916; Elector Wilson-Marshall ticket, 1916; *m.* Clemence Eliza FINCH, *b.* 22d February, 1864, dau. of George Ralsey and Ellen (CHAPMAN) FINCH of St. Paul, Minnesota.

ISSUE

I. RICHARD, *b.* 9th January, 1888; the subject of this memoir.
II. George Finch, *b.* 27th May, 1890; *d.* 11th November, 1891.
III. Jack Potter, *b.* 29th September, 1891, in Princeton, New Jersey; *m.* Louise HAINES dau. of Henry A. HAINES of Elizabeth, New Jersey.

ISSUE

1. Henry Haines, *b.* 29th February, 1916.

IV. Violet, *b.* 5th August, 1894; *m.* 18th September, 1915, Charles Ashley VOORHEES.
V. Ellen Rosemary, *b.* 26th February, 1900.

Arms.—Gules, a chevron vaire, argent and azure between three mullets, or.
Crest.—A lion rampant, supporting an Ionic pillar.
Motto.—Omnia Deo Pendent.
Residence.—Bordentown, New Jersey.

Clubs.—Army and Navy, New York City; New Jersey State Rifle Association, Sea Girt.

Societies.—Colonial Wars; Sons of the American Revolution; Society of the War of 1812; Military Order of Foreign Wars; Union Society of the Civil War; United Military Order of America; Army League; Military Service Institute of the United States; United States Infantry Association; National Security League, American Defense Society.

Tilghman

RICHARD TILGHMAN of St. Davids Pennsylvania; *b.* at Philadelphia, Pennsylvania, 25th January, 1865; *m.* 1889, Gabriela DE POTESTAD, dau. of the Marquis Luis DE POTESTAD-FORNARI and Gabriela CHAPMAN, his wife of Philadelphia.

ISSUE

I. Gabriela.
II. Richard, *b.* 1893.

Lineage

RICHARD TILGHMAN of Holloway Court, Snodland, Kent, was living circa 1450; *m.* Dionysia, surname unknown.

ISSUE

I. THOMAS, of whom later.
II. William, of London, in his will, dated 15th September, 1493, and proved in 1494, leaves a bequest for masses for the souls of his deceased parents, Richard and Dyonisia.

THOMAS TILGHMAN, of Holloway Court; *m.* Joan, surname unknown.

ISSUE

I. WILLIAM, of whom later.
II. Ralph.
III. John.

WILLIAM TILGHMAN of Holloway Court; *d.* 27th August, 1541; will proved 22d November, 1541; a momument was erected to him in Snodgrass Church, giving the date of his death and the names of his two wives; *m.* (firstly) Isabel AVERY; *m.* (secondly) Joan AMHERST.

ISSUE BY FIRST MARRIAGE

I. RICHARD, *d.* 1518, of whom below.

RICHARD TILGHMAN of Snodland; *d.* 1518; his will was proved 12th November, 1518; *m.* Julyan PORDAGE, dau. of William PORDAGE.

ISSUE

I. WILLIAM, *b.* 1518, of whom below.

438 COLONIAL FAMILIES OF THE UNITED STATES

WILLIAM TILGHMAN of Holloway Court, Snodland, Kent; *b.* 1518; was buried 24th February, 1594; will proved 24th April, 1594; Cornet First Troop Philadelphia City Cavalry; Captain 2d Troop Philadelphia City Cavalry; *m.* (firstly) Mary BERE, dau. of John BERE of Rochester; *m.* (secondly) Joan AMIAS, who *d.s.p.*, and was buried 20th September, 1563, dau. of Andrew AMIAS; *m.* (thirdly) 11th August, 1567, Dorothy REYNOLDS, who *d.s.p.* and was buried 21st November, 1572; *m.* (fourthly) circa 1575, Susanna WHETENHALL, dau. of Thomas WHETENHALL, of Hextall's Court, East Peckham, Kent, and Dorothy FANE his wife. Susanna WHETENHALL through her gd. mother, Alice BIRKLEY, wife of George WHETENHALL, whose mother, Elizabeth NEVILLE, wife of Thomas BERKELEY, was a dau. of Sir George NEVILLE, Baron Abergavenny, who *d.* 1492, was a lineal descendant of Edward III.

ISSUE BY FIRST MARRIAGE

I. Joan, *b.* 15th December, 1540.
II. Edward of Holloway Court; *b.* 15th April, 1542. buried 23d December, 1611; *m.* Margaret BREWER, of Ditton, who was buried 23d October, 1613.

ISSUE

1. Francis, *m.* 15th June, 1615, Margery SPRACKLING, dau. of Sir Adam SPRACKLING of Ellington on Thanet. He inherited Holloway Court which he sold in the reign of James I.

III. Henry, *b.* 11th January, 1543 or 1544.
IV. Dorothy, *b.* 4th February, 1545.

ISSUE BY FOURTH MARRIAGE

I. Whetenhall, *b.* 25th July, 1576; *m.* Ellen RENCHING, dau. of Richard and Susan (HONEYWOOD) RENCHING, and had issue.
II. Dorothy, *b.* 11th January, 1578; *d.* 18th September, 1605; left issue; *m.* Thomas ST. NICHOLAS, who was *b.* 1567, *d.* 1626, was *bapt.* 10th April, 1584, of Ashe, County Kent.
III. OSWALD, *b.* 4th October, 1579, of whom later.
IV. Charles, *b.* 13th October, 1582; buried 25th May, 1608.
V. Lambard, *b.* 10th April, 1584; *d.* young.
VI. Lambard, *bapt.* 18th August, 1586; *d.* in infancy.

OSWALD TILGHMAN of London, England; *b.* 4th October, 1579; *bapt.* 11th October, 1851; *d.* 1628; his will was proved 22d January, 1628; Member of the Grocers' Company of London; *m.* (firstly) 13th January, 1612, Abigail TAYLER, then twenty-six years old, dau. of Rev. Francis TAYLER, Vicar of Godalming, Surrey; *m.* (secondly) 15th November, 1626, Elizabeth PACKNAM, who *d.s.p.*

COLONIAL FAMILIES OF THE UNITED STATES

ISSUE BY FIRST MARRIAGE

RICHARD TILGHMAN of London, England; *b* 3d September, 1626; *d*. 7th January, 1676; his will was proved 6th March, 1675-1676; an eminent Surgeon in London, and one of the petitioners for the life of Charles I; emigrated to America, with his family in 1661, in the ship *Elizabeth and Mary* and settled at the "Hermitage" in Maryland; commissioned High Sheriff of Talbot County; 1st May, 1669, and served until 17th June, 1671; *m*. in England, Mary FOXLEY, who survived him and *d*. between 1699 and 1700.

ISSUE

I. Samuel, *b*. 11th December, 1650; *d*. young.
II. Mary, *b*. February, 1655; *m*. Matthew WARD, *d*. 1677, of Talbot County

ISSUE

1. Matthew Tilghman WARD, *b*. 1677; *d.s.p.* 25th May, 1741; Speaker of the Maryland Assembly, 1716-1718; Chief Justice of the Provincial Court, 1729-1732; Member of Council, 1719-1741; at the time of his death President; Major-General, Commanding the Eastern Shore Militia, 1739; *m*. (firstly) Mabel MURPHY, widow of Capt. James MURPHY; *m*. (secondly) Margaret LLOYD, dau. of Capt. Philemon LLOYD.

III. William, *b*. 16th February, 1658; *d*. unmarried, 1682.
IV. Rebecca, *d*. 1725; *m*. 1681, Simon WILMER of Kent County, who *d*. 1699; had issue.
V. Deborah, *b*. 12th March, 1666.
VI. RICHARD, of whom later.

COLONEL RICHARD TILGHMAN of the "Hermitage," Talbot County, Maryland; *b*. 23d February, 1672; *d*. 23d January, 1738; will proved 14th March, 1738; represented Talbot County, in the Maryland Assembly, 1698-1702; Member of Council, 1711-1738; Chancellor of the Province, 1722; *m*. 7th January, 1700, Anna Maria LLOYD, *b*. 1676, *d*. December, 1748, dau. of Col. Philemon LLOYD, of Talbot County, and Henrietta Maria (NEALE) BENNETT; she dau. of Capt. James NEALE and widow of Richard BENNETT, Sr.

ISSUE

I. Mary, *b*. 23d August, 1702; *d*. 10th January, 1736; *m*. 12th October, 1721, James EARLE.
II. Philemon, *b*. 1704; *d*. young.
III. Richard, Colonel, of the "Hermitage," Queen Anne County; *b*. 28th April, 1705; *d*. 29th September, 1768; Just'ce of the Provincial Court o: Maryland, 1746-1766 and was of the Quorum of that body from 1754; *m*. Susanna FRISBY, *b*. 19th June, 1718, dau. of Peregrine and

Elizabeth (SEWALL) FRISBY, she dau. of Maj. Nicholas SEWALL; had issue.

IV. Henrietta Maria, b. 18th August, 1707; d. 7th November, 1771; m. (firstly) 22d April, 1731, George ROBINS; m. (secondly) 1747, William GOLDSBOROUGH; had issue.

V. Anna Maria, b. 15th November, 1709; d. 30th August, 1763; m. (firstly) William HEMSLEY; m. (secondly) Col. Robert LLOYD; had issue.

VI. William of Groces, Talbot County; b. 22d September, 1711; d. 1782; one of the Justices of Queen Anne County, 1734-1736, 1737-1739, 1743-1745, 1747-1751, and 1754-1760; Presiding Justice of Queen Anne County from 1755-1760; Member of the Assembly from Queen Anne County, 1734-1738; m. 2d August, 1736, his cousin, Margaret LLOYD, b. 16th February, 1714, dau. of James and Ann (GRUNDY) LLOYD; had issue.

VII. EDWARD, b. 3d July, 1713, of whom later.

VIII. James, Lawyer; b. 6th December, 1716; d. 24th August, 1793; Member of Maryland Assembly, 1762-1763; removed to Philadelphia in 1763; Member of Council there; Secretary of the Pennsylvania Land Office 1st January, 1769; returned to Maryland and settled in Chestertown, 1777; m. Anna FRANCIS, dau. of Tench FRANCIS of Fansley, Talbot County; had issue.

IX. Matthew of Bayside, Talbot County; b. 17th February, 1718; d. 4th May, 1790; Captain of a troop of horse, 1741; commissioned 1741 one of the Justices of Talbot County from that time until 1775; one of the Quorum from 1749; Presiding Justice of Talbot County from 1769; Member of the Maryland Assembly, 1751-1774; Speaker of the House, 1773-1774; President of the Maryland Convention, 1774-1776; and headed every delegation sent by the Convention to Congress; Member of Congress, 1774-1777; Senator from Talbot County, 1777-1781; he takes high rank as a Statesman; m. 6th April, 1741 Anna LLOYD, b. 13th February, 1723, d. 15th March, 1794.

ISSUE

1. Margaret, b. 13th January, 1742; d. 14th March, 1817; m. 23d June, 1763, Charles CARROLL, Barrister, b. 22d March, 1723, d. 23d March, 1783; had two children, twins, who d. in infancy.
2. Matthew Ward, b. 1743; d. 17th March, 1753.
3. Richard, Major; b. 28th January, 1746; d. 28th May, 1805; m. (firstly) his cousin, Margaret TILGHMAN, b. 24th December, 1744, d. 24th December, 1779, dau. of William TILGHMAN of Grasse; m. (secondly) Mary TILGHMAN, b. 8th September, 1762, d. 18th October, 1793, dau. of Col. Edward TILGHMAN of Wye.
4. Lloyd, b. 27th July, 1749; d. 1811; m. 22d January, 1785, Henrietta Maria TILGHMAN, b. 22d February, 1763, d. 2d March, 1796, dau. of his uncle James TILGHMAN.

COLONIAL FAMILIES OF THE UNITED STATES

5. Anna Maria, b. 17th July, 1755; d. 17th January, 1843; m. 1783, her cousin, Col. Tench TILGHMAN, who carried the news of Cornwallis' surrender, from Yorktown to the Congress in Philadelphia.

COLONEL EDWARD TILGHMAN of Wye, Queen Anne County; b. 3d July, 1713; d. 9th October, 1786, High Sheriff of Queen Anne County, from 5th November, 1739, to 5th November, 1742; one of the Justices of the County, 1743-1749; Member of Assembly, 1746-1771; Speaker of the House, 1770-1771; in 1765 was a Member of the Stamp Act Congress and one of the committee who drew up the remonstrance to Parliament; m. (firstly) Anna Maria TURBUTT, dau. of Maj. William TURBUTT, of Queen Anne County; m. (secondly) 1749, Elizabeth CHEW, b. 25th November, 1720, dau. of Samuel and Elizabeth (GALLOWAY) CHEW of Dover; m. (thirdly) 25th May, 1759, Juliana CARROLL, dau. of Dominick and Mary (SEWALL) CARROLL of Cecil County, she dau. of Maj. Nicholas SEWALL.

ISSUE BY FIRST MARRIAGE

I. Anna Maria, m. Bennet CHEW.

ISSUE BY SECOND MARRIAGE

I. R'chard.
II. EDWARD, b. 11th February, 1751, of whom later.
III. Benjamin.
IV. Elizabeth, m. her cousin, Richard TILGHMAN, of the "Hermitage," son of Richard TILGHMAN; had issue.
V. Anna Maria, m. (firstly) Charles GOLDSBOROUGH, b. 1744, d. 1774; m. (secondly) Rt. Rev. Robert SMITH, Bishop of South Carolina, who d. 28th October, 1801; had issue.

ISSUE BY THIRD MARRIAGE

I. Matthew, b. 5th June, 1760; Member of the Legislature for Kent County, 1789, 1793-1794; Speaker of the House, 1794; m. 1788, Sarah SMYTH dau. of Thomas SMYTH, of Chestertown; had issue.
II. Benjamin, b. December, 1764.
III. Mary, m. her cousin, Richard TILGHMAN, son of Matthew TILGHMAN.
IV. Susanna, m. Richard Ireland JONES.

EDWARD TILGHMAN of Philadelphia; b. 11th February, 1751; d. 1st November, 1815; m. 26th May, 1774, Elizabeth CHEW, dau. of Benjamin CHEW, Chief Justice of Pennsylvania, 1774.

ISSUE

I. Elizabeth, m. 24th January, 1804, William COOKE, of Baltimore; had issue.
II. Edward, b. 27th February, 1779; d. 1826; m. Rebecca WALN; had issue.
III. BENJAMIN, b. 1st January, 1785, of whom later.
IV. Mary Anna, m. 1817, William RAWLE, of Philadelphia, who m. (secondly) Emily CADWALADER, dau. of Gen. Thomas CADWALADER; had issue.

BENJAMIN TILGHMAN of Philadelphia; *b.* 1st January, 1785; *d.* 1850; *m.* Anna Maria McMURTRIE, dau. of William McMURTRIE, of Philadelphia.

ISSUE

I. Edward.
II. William McMurtrie, *m.* Katherine INGERSOLL; had issue.
III. Benjamin Chew.
IV. RICHARD ALBERT, *b.* 1824, of whom later.
V. Anna Maria.
VI. Emily, *d.* unmarried 3d June, 1830.

RICHARD ALBERT TILGHMAN of Philadelphia, Pennsylvania; *b.* 1824; *d.* 1899; *m.* 1860, Susan Price TOLAND, dau. of Robert TOLAND.

ISSUE

I. Benjamin Chew.
II. RICHARD, *b.* 25th January, 1865, the subject of this memoir.
III. Edith.
IV. Susan.
V. Agnes.
VI. Angela.

Arms.—Per fesse sable, and argent, a lion rampant-regardant, double queued, counterchanged, crowned, or.
Crest.—A demi-lion issuant, statant, sable, crowned, or.
Residence.—St. Davids, Pennsylvania.

Trippe

CHARLES WHITE TRIPPE of New York City; b. at New York City, 8th June, 1872; m. 27th November, 1895, Lucy Adeline TERRY, b. 29th October, 1872, dau. of Juan T. TERRY.

ISSUE

I. Charles White, Jr., b. 30th August, 1896: d. 23rd August, 1899.
II. Juan Terry, b. 27th June, 1899.
III. Katherine Louise, b. 5th September, 1900.

CHARLES WHITE TRIPPE was educated at Columbia University in the Class of 1894, and upon leaving College immediately associated himself with the Engineering Corps at the Chicago Worlds Fair of 1892. At the completion of this he became a Sanitary Engineering Expert of the New York City Board of Health. In 1901 he became a member of the Banking House of SCHUYLER, CHADWICK and STOUT and in 1906 formed the Banking House of TRIPPE and Company, and joined the New York Stock Exchange, becoming the board member of his firm.

Lineage

The TRIPPES lived in Kent County, England, as far back as the Norman Conquest. The name is found in the "Doomsday Book" in the titles of lands, A.D. 1234. Nicholas TRIPPE gave Lamplands, County Kent, to Elham Church. The first record we have of this family in Maryland is in 1663 when Lieutenant Henry, the immigrant and our direct ancestor, b. Canterbury, England, 1632; d. in Dorchester County, Maryland, March, 1698, who had fought in Flanders under the Prince of Orange, afterwards William III of England, brought with him to the Province of Maryland, three of his troopers and by Royal Grant took up land in Dorchester County; Representative in Maryland Assembly, 1671–1675, 1661–1682, 1692–1693; one of the Committee of Twenty for regulating affairs in Maryland, 1690; Justice and County Commissioner, 1669–1681, 1685–1694; Captain of Foot, 1676; Major of Horse, 1689; Thomas TRIPPE his brother is mentioned by James, Duke of York, afterwards James II, in his Autobiography Nairn papers as aiding him to escape from St. James Palace after the beheading of Charles I. Col. Henry TRIPPE m. (firstly) in 1665 Francis BROOKE, widow of Michael BROOKE of St. Leonard's Creek, Calvert County, Maryland; m. (secondly) Lady Elizabeth TRIPPE who survived him and by whom he had four sons and one daughter. He settled in Maryland in 1663, and on 9th November, 1670, he bought of John EDMONDSON a tract of land called Sark on the south side of Choptank River near its mouth originally patented to Francis ARMSTRONG, added this land to what had been given by Royal Grant in 1663 and it became the family seat in Dorchester County, and so remained until recently, known as Todds Point.

ISSUE BY SECOND MARRIAGE

I. Henry, d. 1744; Captain Dorchester County Militia; m. Susannah HERRON.
II. John, moved to Bath County, Kentucky.
III. Edward, m. Susan (SHERWOOD) HAMBLETON, who d. 1755, dau. of Hugh and Mary SHERWOOD and widow of Philemon HAMBLETON.
IV. WILLIAM, d. 24th April, 1770, of whom later.
V. Henrietta, m. 25th November, 1746, John CARSLAKE.

WILLIAM TRIPPE of Dorchester County, Maryland; d. 24th April, 1770; m. Jean TATE.

ISSUE

I. Henrietta, m. ———— HUGHES.
II. Elizabeth, m. Edward NOEL of Castle Haven.

ISSUE

1. Elizabeth NOEL, m. Rev. James KEMP, Protestant Episcopal Bishop of Maryland.
2. Sarah NOEL, m. Captain Cox of the United States Navy.

ISSUE

1¹. A son, Lieutenant Cox, of the United States Navy; m. a sister of Capt. James LAWRENCE, United States Frigate *Chesapeake*.

III. WILLIAM, of whom later.
IV. Edward of Dorchester County; m. Sarah (NOEL) BYUS, dau. of Edward NOEL of Castle Haven, and widow of Joseph BYUS.

ISSUE

1. James of Cambridge, Maryland; d. 1812; m. (firstly) Elizabeth PENNELL who d.s.p.; m. (secondly) Mary PENNELL who d. 1812.

ISSUE

1¹. Joseph Everett, b. at Cambridge, Maryland, 18th July, 1805; d. Baltimore, Maryland, 28th December, 1882; m. 30th May, 1837, Sarah Patterson CROSS of Cecil County, Maryland, dau. of ———— CROSS and Rachel WALLACE, his wife.

ISSUE

1². Andrew Cross, b. 29th November, 1839; m. 7th November, 1872, Caroline Augusta MCCONKY, dau. of James and Mary Dawes (GRAFTON) MCCONKY.
2². Mary Pennell, d.s.p. 11th September, 1904; m. William BELL.

COLONIAL FAMILIES OF THE UNITED STATES

3². Rachel Elizabeth, unmarried.
4². Joseph Everett, b. 6th May, 1845; m. Frances HOLLIDAY, dau. of Daniel HOLLIDAY.

v. John, b. 17th April, 1711; was a Captain of Cavalry in the French and Indian Wars; m. 1745, Elizabeth NOEL, b. 25th April, 1729, d. 24th April, 1778.

ISSUE

1. Amelia, m. Col. James WOOLFORD of Dorchester County.
2. William, m. his cousin, Mary NOEL.

ISSUE

1¹. Margaret, m. Capt. Jesse HUGHES of Somerset County, Maryland.
2¹. Eliza, m. James PRICE of Talbot County, Maryland.
3¹. John, Lieutenant in United States Navy, distinguished himself at Tripoli, 1804, and had a sword and gold medal voted him by Congress, and a sword by the State of Maryland; d. 9th July, 1810; in command of the United States Brigantine *Vixen;* n 1910 the United States Navy Department commemorated her name on the Destroyer, *U. S. S. Trippe.*

3. Edward, b. 29th June, 1771; d. 2d February, 1836; m. (firstly) 25th February, 1794, Elizabeth BARNEY, dau. of Moses and Sarah (BOND) BARNEY; m. (secondly) Ann Tolly TOWSON, dau. of Gen. William TOWSON of Baltimore County, she d.s.p.; m. (thirdly) his cousin, Sarah E. TRIPPE, dau. of Richard TRIPPE, and left one son.

ISSUE

1¹. Edward Richard, M.D., of Easton, Maryland.

4. Henrietta, b. 16th April, 1774; m. Col. William BIRCKHEAD.
5. Levin, killed at sea, in command of the Privateer *Isabella.*
6. Frances, m. John Elder GIST, of Baltimore County.
7. May, m. (firstly) Maj. Peter WEBB; m. (secondly) Dr. Samuel DICKINSON of Talbot County.

vi. Jean.

WILLIAM TRIPPE, b. circa 1720; d. 1st June, 1777; bought Tenneys Point on Tread Avon, from Elizabeth SKILLINGTON, and in 1775 bought Avonville formerly called Marshy Point and Canterbury Manor, from Nicholas GOLDSBOROUGH and made :t his family seat; m. (firstly) 21st April, 1744, Elizabeth GIBSON, widow of Jacob GIBSON, who d. leaving one son; m. (secondly) 21st January, 1760, Elizabeth SKIN-

NER of Talbot County, who *d.* 9th May, 1811, aged 75 years and had five children (Talbot Wills No. 3, folio 5, Will dated 30th May, 1777 and probated 12th August, 1777).

ISSUE BY SECOND MARRIAGE

I. James.
II. RICHARD, *b.* 30th June, 1763, of whom later.
III. John.
IV. Edward.
V. Mary.

RICHARD TRIPPE, *b.* 30th June, 1763; *d.* 16th January, 1849; *m.* (firstly) 5th January, 1794, Harriet EDMONDSON, *b.* 5th January, 1774, *d.* 13th December, 18—, and had issue; *m.* (secondly) Mary ENNALLS, dau. of Col. Joseph ENNALLS, who was on George Washington's Staff, and Sarah HERON, of Dorchester County, she *d.* 14th October, 1836, aged 56 years, and is buried at Avonville; had issue.

ISSUE BY FIRST MARRIAGE

I. William, *b.* 25th November, 1794; *d.* 11th September, 1816.

ISSUE BY SECOND MARRIAGE

I. Sarah Elizabeth.
II. Mary Suzannah.
III. Richard John.
IV. Edward Thomas, *b.* 14th February, 1808; *d.* 23d September, 1842; *m.* 30th November, 1841, Catherine D. BOWIE.

ISSUE

1. Richard, *m.* Sophie Kerr THOMAS, dau. of ex-Governor Philip Francis THOMAS.

V. JOSEPH ENNALLS, *b.* 6th March, 1810, of whom later.
VI. William James.
VII. Mary Harriett.
VIII. Robert H.
IX. Margaret Helen.
X. Nicolas Hammond.

JOSEPH ENNALLS TRIPPE, *b.* 6th March, 1810; *d.* October, 1894; *m.* 6th November, 1832, Elizabeth H. DARROW of New York City.

ISSUE

I. Mary Caroline.
II. Sarah Elizabeth.
III. Richard Henry.

IV. Caroline Ennalls.
V. FREDERICK WRIGHT, *b.* 6th July, 1839, of whom later.
VI. Joseph Ennalls.
VII. William Henderson.

FREDERICK WRIGHT TRIPPE, *b.* 6th July, 1839; *d.* 22d August, 1891; as First Lieutenant in the New Jersey Militia he served in the Civil War of 1861; *m.* Mary Louise WHITE of New York City.

ISSUE

I. Frederick Louis, *b.* 8th April, 1871.
II. CHARLES WHITE, *b.* 8th June, 1872, the subject of th's memoir.
III. Julian, *b.* 21st June, 1876.

Arms.—Gules a chevron between three nags heads erased or, bridled sable.
Crest.—An eagle's head gules, issuing out of rays or.
Motto.—Ready and True.
Residences.—163 East 78th Street, New York City; "Chadeline," Greenwich, Connecticut.
Clubs.—Columbia University, Calumet, Blind Brook Apawamis Club, New York Athletic Club.
Societies.—Colonial Wars, Sons of Veterans.

Tubman

ROBERT EUGENE TUBMAN of Baltimore, Maryland; *b.* 12th June, 1875, at "Glasgow" near Cambridge, Maryland; *m.* 28th June, 1899, Maud Eugenia SKINNER, dau. of Levin Philip and Mary Eugenia (WILLIS) SKINNER (see Skinner Family, p. 418).

ISSUE

I. Dorothy Keene, *b.* 23d September, 1901; *d.* 6th October, 1902.
II. Mary Keene, *b.* 24th May, 1904.
III. Elizabeth Willis, *b.* 28th July, 1907.

ROBERT EUGENE TUBMAN was educated in Cambridge, Maryland; moved to Baltimore in 1896; after traveling commercially several years, engaged in the wholesale Boot and Shoe business in Baltimore City under the name of The Robert E. Tubman Company, also President of the Shoe and Leather Board of Trade and Director of the National Bank of Baltimore, and the Credit Men's Association.

Lineage

JUSTICE RICHARD TUBMAN of Dorchester County, Maryland; will dated 6th April, 1719; probated 13th January, 1727; removed from the western shore, Calvert County, Maryland, subsequent to 9th December, 1669, and the family have been seated in Dorchester County ever since. On 30th September, 1670, he was awarded land due for military service against the Indians; he was awarded by the Assembly of 1678, 600 pounds of Tobacco for services in an expedition against the Nanticoke Indians; on 16th October, 1694, the name of Richard TUBMAN appears on a list of Commissioners and Justices appointed for Dorchester County and in the group of men marked "Justices" on 8th June, 1699, it was ordered by the Council that Richard TUBMAN's name appear on the list of Gentlemen Justices of Dorchester County. His landed holdings approximated at 1000 acres; his first landed holdings he named "St. Giles Field," indicating he probably came from St. Giles Parish, London; *m.* Eleanor, surname unknown.

ISSUE

1. RICHARD, II, probably only child, of whom later.

LIEUTENANT RICHARD TUBMAN, II, of Dorchester County, Maryland; he was a large landowner; was First Lieutenant in the first company formed in Dorchester County called (The Bucks Company) of which his brother-in-law Justice Benjamin KEENE was Captain, and so enrolled 30th November, 1775; *m.* Sarah KEENE, dau. of Benjamin KEENE, Sr., and gd. daughter of Capt. John KEENE of the Colonial Militia.

COLONIAL FAMILIES OF THE UNITED STATES 449

ISSUE

I. Mary, m. Thomas KEENE, son of Richard and Sussannah (POLLARD) KEENE.

ISSUE

1. William Billingsley KEENE, was the founder of the Medical and Chirurgical Society of Baltimore in 1779.

II. RICHARD, III, of whom later.
III. John, d. 5th November, 1774; m. Rachel, surname not given.

ISSUE

1. Richard, m. 24th July, 1794, Elizabeth TRAVERS.

RICHARD TUBMAN, III, Planter of Dorchester County, Maryland, took the oath of Fidelity 24th January, 1778; d 1818; m. (firstly) Nancy ———; m. (secondly); no issue by second marriage.

ISSUE BY FIRST MARRIAGE

1. Richard, IV, m. 11th August, 1808, Susan KEENE, sister of Mary G. KEENE TUBMAN.
II. DR. ROBERT FRANCIS, b. 7th May, 1791, of whom later.

ROBERT FRANCIS TUBMAN, M.D., of Glasgow, Cambridge, Dorchester County; b. 7th May, 1791; d. 24th December, 1864; Graduate of the University of Pennsylvania and practiced his profession in the county for many years; he acquired the fine old estate known as "Glasgow," in 1842; m. (firstly) 7th December, 1815, Dorothy STAPLEFORT, gd. dau. of Raymond STAPLEFORT, d. 22d February, 1829; m. (secondly) 2d May, 1830, Mary Gaither KEENE, b. 22d January, 1811; d. 31st March, 1876, dau. of Benjamin, Jr. and Ann (GAITHER) KEENE; no issue by first marriage.

ISSUE BY SECOND MARRIAGE

1. Benjamin Gaither Keene, b. 12th September, 1831; d. 22d March, 1879; m. 23d October, 1855, Margaret Jane THOMSON of Frederick, Maryland.

ISSUE

1. William Billingsley Keene, b. 8th January, 1857; m. 1896, Roberta KEEN, dau. of John and Harriet Anne (CRIGHTON) KEEN.
2. Benjamin Lynn Lacklin, b. 5th December, 1858; drowned 17th September, 1869.

II. Samuel Alexander, b. 17th October, 1833; d. 20th May, 1897, in Westminster, Maryland; m. 17th April, 1866, Nannie HAMMOND, dau. of Henry HAMMOND and Fannie Jackson BIAYS.

ISSUE

1. Henry Francis, *b.* 27th February, 1868; *d.* 31st January, 1888.
2. Samuel Alexander, Jr., *b.* 17th August, 1870; *m.* 19th June, 1895, Mary Imogene BERRY, dau. of John Benton Nathaniel BERRY and Rosalie Eugenia BERRY.

ISSUE

1^1. Rosalie Eugenia Berry, *b.* 8th June, 1896.
2^1. Samuel Alexander, III, *b.* 13th January, 1898.

3. Clarence Eugene, *b.* 9th April, 1875; *m.* 22d April, 1903, Marie Regina POWER, dau. of Vincent W. and Emma (JACOBS) POWER.

ISSUE

1^1. Frances Ann, *b.* 2d April, 1904.
2^1. Eugene Power, *b.* 21st January, 1906.
3^1. Robert Keene, *b.* 26th January, 1908.
4^1. Vincent Alexander, *b.* 18th February, 1910.
5^1. Henry Harrison, *b.* 23d December, 1912.
6^1. Richard Hammond, *b.* 14th October, 1914.

III. Maria Ann, *b.* 5th August, 1834; *d.* May, 1910; *m.* 3d June, 1862, Dr. J. Haines McCULLOUGH of Cecil County, Maryland.

IV. Julia Louisa, *b.* 29th May, 1835; *d.* 8th January, 1895; *m.* 15th November, 1866, William Daingerfield RENNOLDS, *b.* 1840, *d.* 30th January, 1896, son of Dr. Henry Starkley RENNOLDS of the United States Navy.

ISSUE

1. Elizabeth RENNOLDS, *b.* 1869; *m.* (firstly) 10th October, 1894, T. Walter HEDIAN; *m.* (secondly) William BRISTOL.

ISSUE

1^1. William BRISTOL, Jr., *b.* 1908.

V. Eugene Francis, *b.* 31st March, 1836; *d.* 19th June, 1900; *m.* April, 1867, Carrie COSKERY, dau. of Dr. Felix Stanistan and Eliza (HARDY) COSKERY.

ISSUE

1. Francis Joseph, *b.* October, 1867; *m.* September, 1900, Gladys HALLEY.

ISSUE

1^1. Frances Halley, *b.* 1902.

COLONIAL FAMILIES OF THE UNITED STATES 451

VI. Mary Henrietta, *b.* 27th December, 1844; *d.* 7th February, 1893; *m.* 3d May, 1864, Robert E. WATERS, son of Robert Custis WATERS and Matilda BROUGHTON.

ISSUE

1. Robert Francis Tubman WATERS, *b.* 20th January, 1865; *d.* 25th January, 1865.
2. Leon Wilson WATERS, *b.* 8th June, 1866.
3. Carlos WATERS, *b.* 1878.
4. Marguerite WATERS, *b.* 1880.

VII. Robert Francis, *b.* 26th December, 1847; *d.* 4th April, 1848.
VIII. ROBERT CONSTANTINE, *b.* 2d February, 1851, of whom below.

ROBERT CONSTANTINE TUBMAN of "Glasgow," Dorchester County, Maryland; *b.* 2d February, 1851; *m.* 24th August, 1872, E. Nellie COVEY of Caroline County, Maryland, dau. of Mitchel and Martha (NEALE) COVEY.

ISSUE

I. Martha Mary, *b.* 17th May, 1873; *m.* 1905, Dr. William T. SEABURY, of Connecticut.
II. ROBERT EUGENE, *b.* 12th June, 1875, the subject of this memoir.
III. Granville Lloyd, *b.* 30th December, 1884; *m.* 6th October, 1909, Mary Naomi WILLIS, dau. of William W. WILLIS.

ISSUE

1. Ellen Louise, *b.* 12th February, 1911.
2. Granville Lloyd, *b.* 30th December, 1912.

IV. Julian Le Roy, *b.* 9th August, 1887; *m.* 1911, Mary RILIE (?).

ISSUE

1. Julia Keene, *b.* May, 1913.

V. Nellie Lucille, *b.* 12th August, 1896.

Residence.—1615 St. Paul Street, Baltimore, Maryland.
Clubs.—Baltimore Country, Merchants.
Societies.—Maryland Historical.

Venable

FRANCIS PRESTON VENABLE, A.M., Ph.D., LL.D., of Chapel Hill, North Carolina; *b.* in Prince Edward County, Virginia, 17th November, 1856; *m.* 3d November, 1884, Sally Charlton MANNING, dau. of John MANNING, of Chapel Hill, North Carolina.

ISSUE

I. Louis Manning, *b.* 19th October, 1885.
II. Cantey McDowell, *b.* 27th February, 1887.
III. Charles Scott (twin), *b.* 3d September, 1891.
IV. John Manning (twin), *b.* 3d September, 1891.
V. Frances Preston, *b.* 28th October, 1903.

FRANCIS PRESTON VENABLE graduated at the University of Virginia, 1879; studied at Bonn, 1879–1880; A.M., Ph.D., Gottingen, 1881; Berlin, 1889; Sc.D., Lafayette 1904; LL.D., University of Pennsylvania, University of Alabama, University of South Carolina, Jefferson Medical College; Professor of Chemistry, 1880–1900; President, 1900–1914, University of North Carolina; President of Southern Educational Association, 1903; American Chemical Society, 1905; Southern Association of Schools and Colleges, 1909; Fellow Chemical Society of London, American Association for the Advancement of Science; Member Deutsche Chemische Gesellschaft, American Philosophical Society. Author of "Manual of Qualitative Analysis," 1883; "Short History of Chemistry," 1894; "Development of Periodic Law," 1896; "Inorganic Chemistry According to the Periodic Law" (with James Lewis Howe, q.v.) 1898; "Study of the Atom," 1904.

Lineage

The ancestor of this family was Abraham VENABLE who emigrated from England to Virginia about 1680; *m.* Elizabeth (LEWIS) NIX, dau. of Hugh LEWIS, and widow of John NIX.

ISSUE

I. Joseph, settled at Snow Hill, Maryland.
II. ABRAHAM, *b.* 22d March, 1700, of whom below.

ABRAHAM VENABLE of Prince Edward County, Virginia; *b.* 22d March, 1700; *d.* 16th December, 1768; *m.* Martha Davis, *b.* 14th July, 1702, *d.* 13th January, 1765, dau. of Nathaniel DAVIS of Hanover County.

ISSUE

1. Abraham, *b.* 9th February, 1725; *d.* 20th March, 1778; of Prince Edward County, Virginia; *m.* Elizabeth MICHAUX, *b.* 1731, *d.* 1801, dau. of Jacob MICHAUX of Cumberland County; had issue.

COLONIAL FAMILIES OF THE UNITED STATES 453

II. Hugh Lewis of Louisa County, Virginia; *m*. Mary MARTIN, dau. of William MARTIN of Albemarle County, Virginia; had issue.
III. Charles, *m*. Elizabeth SMITH, dau. of Robert SMITH of Port Royal, Virginia; had issue.
IV. NATHANIEL, *b*. 1st November, 1733, of whom later.
V. James, *m*. Judith MORTON, dau. of Joseph MORTON; had issue.
VI. William, *d*. 12th March, 1772; *m*. Ann CLARK, dau. of Isaac CLARK of Louisa County, Virginia; had issue.
VII. John, *m*. Agnes MOORMAN, dau. of Charles MOORMAN of Louisa County, Virginia; had issue.
VIII. Anne, *m*. Philip KING, of Cumberland County, Virginia.
IX. Elizabeth, *m*. Josiah MORTON, of Charlotte County, Virginia.
X. Mary, *m*. (firstly) Charles MOREMAN, of Campbell County, Virginia; *m*. (secondly) ———— STRANGE, of Breckenridge County, Kentucky.

NATHANIEL VENABLE of Slate Hill, Prince Edward County, Virginia; *b*. 1st November, 1733; *d*. 27th December, 1804; *m*. 29th March, 1755, Elizabeth WOODSON, *d*. 29th September, 1791, dau. of Richard WOODSON.

ISSUE

I. SAMUEL WOODSON, *b*. 19th November, 1756, of whom later.
II. Abraham B., *b*. 20th November, 1758; *d*. at Richmond, Virginia, 26th December, 1811; graduated at Princeton College, New Jersey, 1780; Member of Congress from Virginia, 1791-1799; United States Senator, 1803-1804.
III. Ann, *b*. 18th November, 1760; *d*. 1826; *m*. Thomas WATKINS.
IV. Richard N., *b*. 16th January, 1763; *m*. Mary MORTON, dau. of Col. William L. MORTON; had issue.
V. Martha, *b*. May, 1765; *m*. her cousin Nathaniel VENABLE.
VI. Ann, *b*. 6th November, 1767; *d*. 1768.
VII. Ann, *b*. 9th December, 1768; *m*. James DANIEL; had issue.
VIII. Agnes, *b*. 15th April, 1771; *d*. unmarried, 1802.
IX. Mary, *b*. 16th June, 1773.
X. Nathaniel E. (?), *b*. 13th February, 1776; *d.s.p.* 1801.
XI. Frances, *b*. 18th April, 1778; *d*. unmarried, 1799.
XII. William L., *b*. March, 1780; *m*. Frances W. NAUTZ; had issue.
XIII. Thomas, *b*. 4th November, 1782; *d*. unmarried.
XIV. Elizabeth, *b*. 21st November, 1784; *m*. Dr. Goodrich WILSON; had issue.

SAMUEL WOODSON VENABLE of Prince Edward County, Virginia; *b*. 19th November, 1756; *m*. 15th August, 1781, Mary S. CARRINGTON, dau. of Judge Paul CARRINGTON.

ISSUE

I. NATHANIEL E., of whom later.
II. Paul Carrington, M.D.; *m.* (firstly) the widow of ———— DAVIS, who *d.s.p.*; *m.* (secondly) Emily CARRINGTON.

ISSUE

1. George Carrington, M.D.; *m.* Margaret MOSELEY.
2. Sally Tucker, *m.* William G. VENABLE.
3. Mary C., *m.* F. Edward HUGHES.
4. Emily.
5. Margaret.
6. Louisa J., *m.* 27th April, 1864, Rev. Bennett W. MOSELEY.
7. Anna.

III. Samuel Woodson, *m.* Jane REID of Lexington, Virginia.

ISSUE

1. Andrew Reid, served in Confederate States Army with the rank of Major of Cavalry.
2. Mary Carrington, *m.* James MCNUTT.
3. Margaret Ann.
4. Jane Reid.
5. Louisa, *m.* Dr. William MCNUTT.

IV. Abraham Woodson of Granville, North Carolina; *b.* 17th October, 1799; *d.* 24th February, 1876; admitted to the Bar, 1821; removed to Granville County, North Carolina, 1828; Representative in the United States Congress, 1846–1853; *m.* Isabella Alston BROWN, *d.* 14th April, 1876, dau. of Dr. Thomas BROWN of Lanark, Scotland, and Granville, North Carolina.

ISSUE

1. Thomas Brown, Lieutenant-Colonel in the Confederate States Army; *m.* Cordelia KINGSBURY; had issue.

ISSUE

1^1. Abraham W. 2^1. Thomas. 3^1. Isabella.

2. Samuel Frederick, M.D., Major in the Confederate States Army.
3. Mary Grace, *m.* Richard V. DANIEL; had issue.
4. Martha Daniel, *m.* (firstly) Samuel V. MORTON; *m.* (secondly) Alexander HAMILTON.
5. Isabella Brown, *m.* Rev. Taylor MARTIN of North Carolina.
6. Elizabeth W., *m.* William Morton WATKINS; had issue.

COLONIAL FAMILIES OF THE UNITED STATES

v. Margaret Read, *b*. 20th October, 1802; *d*. 31st May, 1857; *m*. Nicholas CABELL of Nelson County; had issue.
vi. Anne, *m*. Isaac READ.
vii. Mary C., *m*. William L. WOMACK.
viii. Clementina, *m*. Rev. William S. REID, D.D., of Lynchburg.
ix. Henningham, *m*. Rev. Robert ANDERSON.
x. Agnes, *m*. Capt. Henry E. WATKINS, of Prince Edward County, Virginia.
xi. Mildred C., *m*. Charles SHEPPERSON.

NATHANIEL E. VENABLE of Prince Edward County, Virginia; *d*. 21st September, 1846; *m*. Mary Embry SCOTT, dau. of Col. Charles SCOTT of Halifiax County.

ISSUE

i. Samuel Woodson, *m*. Elizabeth Thornton CARRINGTON; had issue.
ii. CHARLES SCOTT, *b*. 19th April, 1827, of whom later.
iii. Nathaniel W., M.D.; *m*. Tennessee MARR; had issue.
iv. Paul Carrington, *d*. April, 1915; had issue.
v. Mary P., *m*. Thomas Frederick VENABLE; had issue.
vi. Agnes Catherine, *m*. (firstly) Nathaniel A. VENABLE; *m*. (secondly) Albert G. MCGEEHEE.
vii. Sarah Scott, *d*. 12th April, 1873; unmarried.
viii. Elizabeth G., *m*. William Fontaine CARRINGTON, M.D.; had issue.
ix. Frances J., *m*. Alexander CARRINGTON.

LIEUTENANT-COLONEL CHARLES SCOTT VENABLE, LL.D.; *b*. in Prince Edward County, Virginia, 19th April, 1827; *d*. 11th August, 1900; Captain of Engineers in the Confederate States Army, 1861; Lieutenant-Colonel and Aide-de-Campe to Gen. Robert E. LEE, 1862–1865; taking part in all the important engagements of the Army of Northern Virginia; LL.D., of the University of Virginia, 1868; *m*. (firstly) Margaret Cantey McDOWELL, *b*. 26th March, 1836, *d*. 15th January, 1874; *m*. (secondly) Mary M. (SOUTHALL) BROWN, dau. of Hon. Valentine Wood SOUTHALL, and widow of Col. J. Thompson BROWN, of the Confederate States Army.

ISSUE BY FIRST MARRIAGE

i. FRANCIS PRESTON, *b*. 17th November, 1856, the subject of this memoir.

ISSUE BY SECOND MARRIAGE

i. Charles.

Residence.—Chapel Hill, North Carolina.
Arms.—Azure two bars argent.
Crest.—A wyvern passant gules, issuing from a weir argent.
Motto.—Venabulis vinco.
Clubs.—Δ. K. E.: Φ. B. K.
Societies.—American Association for the Advancement of Science, American Philosophical Society, American Chemical Society, London Chemical Society, German Chemical Society.

Voorhees

CAPTAIN GEORGE VAN WICKLE VOORHEES of Somerville, New Jersey; *b.* 11th May, 1876, at New Brunswick, New Jersey; *m.* 24th October, 1906, at Somerville, New Jersey, Ethel Margaret FEINDELL, *b.* 28th August, 1881, dau. of John Theodore FEINDELL, *b.* 7th August, 1855, who *m.* 17th November, 1880, Sarah Agnes GARRETSON, *b.* 8th July, 1853, *d.* 21st March, 1893.

GEORGE VAN WICKLE VOORHEES was educated at Rutgers Preparatory School; D.D.S., University of Pennsylvania; elected Captain of Company M, 2d Infantry, National Guard of New Jersey, 29th March, 1915.

Lineage

COERT ALBERTS of Voor-Hees who resided in front of the village of Hees near the town of Ruinen, Province of Drenthe, in the Netherlands. The name is derived from *voor*, before or in front of, and Hees, the village above mentioned.

STEVEN COERTE VAN VOOR HEES of Voor Hees, Drenthe, Holland; *b.* there 1600; *d.* 16th February, 1684, at Flat Lands, Long Island; emigrated from Holland in April, 1660, in the ship *Bontekoe* ("Spotted Cow") with his wife and children; purchased a farm at Flat Lands, 29th November, 1660; was a Magistrate of Flat Lands in 1664, and on a patent, 1667; *m.* (firstly) in Holland, name unknown; *m.* (secondly) on Long Island, Willempie Roeloffse SEUBERING, *b.* 1619, *d.* 1690, dau. of Reolof SEUBERING.

ISSUE

I. Hendrickjen Stevense, *m.* Jan KIERS.
II. Merghin Stevense, *d.* 28th October, 1702, N. S.; *m.* (firstly) ———— ROELOFS; *m.* (secondly) Remmelt WILLEMSE.
III. COERT, of whom later.
IV. Lucas Stevense, *b.* 1650; *d.* 1713; was a Member of Flatlands Dutch Church in 1677 and Elder in 1711; Magistrate in 1680; at Flatland, Long Island, *m.* (firstly) Catherine Hansen VAN NOSTRAND, dau. of Hans VAN NOORTSTRAND and Jannecken Gertitse VAN LOON; *m.* (secondly) 26th January, 1689, Jannetje Minnes, dau. of Minne Johannis and Rensie FADDANS; *m.* (thirdly) circa 1703, Catherine VAN DYCK.

ISSUE BY FIRST MARRIAGE

I. Jan Lucasse, *bapt.* 19th February, 1675; had fifteen brothers and sisters; *m.* (firstly) 10th October, 1699, Anna VAN DUYCKHUYSEN, dau. of Jan Teunissen VAN DUYCKHUYSEN and Achia (or Agatha) STOOT-

COLONIAL FAMILIES OF THE UNITED STATES 457

HOFF, *bapt.* 7th April, 1677, *d.* 5th January, 1702; *m.* (secondly) 5th March, 1704, Mayke R. SCHENCK, dau. of Capt. Roelof Martense SCHENCK, and Annatie PIETERS, *b.* 14th January, 1684, *d.* 25th November, 1736; (thirdly) 25th January, 1737, Jannetje REMSEN, dau. of Jacob REMSEN and Gertrude VANDERBILT, *bapt.* 27th July, 1701, *d.* 24th August, 1747.

ISSUE

1¹. Petrus, of New Brunswick, New Jersey; son of Jan Lucasse and Mayke R. (SCHENCK) VAN VOORHEES, *b.* 6th January, 1712, at Flatland; *d.* circa 3d April, 1751; had thirteen brothers and sisters; *m.* Mary, surname unknown.

ISSUE

1². Peter, *b.* 1750; *d.* 10th October, 1823; was a soldier in the Revolutionary War; had four brothers and sisters; *m.* 15th February, 1775, Elizabeth Tallman STEVENSON, *b.* 15th November, 1756, *d.* 11th January, 1824.

ISSUE

1ᶜ. John P., *b.* 5th June, 1783; *d.* 15th May, 1863; was a Lieutenant in the 3d New Jersey Cavalry, War of 1812; had five brothers and sisters; *m.* (firstly) 26th April, 1804, Catherine VOORHEES, *b.* 26th February, 1785, *d.* 13th June, 1835, dau. of John G. VOORHEES; *m.* (secondly) 21st November, 1840, Gitty Jane VOORHEES, *b.* 15th May, 1814, *d.* 29th April, 1876, dau. of Peter L. and Eva (VAN VOORHIES) VOORHEES of Somerset County, New Jersey.

v. Jan Stevense, *b.* 1652; will proved 20th November, 1735; *m.* (firstly) Cornelia Reiniers WIZZEL-PENNING, dau. of Reinier WIZZEL-PENNING and Jannetje SNEDIKER; *m.* (secondly) 8th October, 1680, Femmetje Aukes VAN NUYSE, dau. of Auke Janse VAN NUYSE and Magdalena PIETERSE, *bapt.* 12th March, 1662.
vi. Albert Stevense, *m.* (firstly) Barrentje WILLEMSE; *m.* (secondly) 24th April, 1681, Tilletje Reiniers WIZZEL-PENNING, dau. of Reinier WIZZEL-PENNING and Jannetje SNEDIKER; *m.* (thirdly) Helena VAN DER SCHURE.
vii. Altje Stevense, *b.* 1656; *m.* 1673, Barrent Jurianz RYDER.
viii. Jannetje Stevense, *m.* (firstly) Jan Martense SCHENCK, *d.* 1689; *m.* (secondly) 29th February, 1690, Alexander SYMPSON.
ix. Hendrickje Stevense, *m.* (firstly) Jan KIERSTEAD; *m.* (secondly) Albert Albertse TERHUNE, *bapt.* 13th August, 1651, will dated 3d February, 1704.

x. Abraham Stevense, *m.* Altje, dau. of Jacobus Gerritsen STRYCKER and Ida HUYBRECHTS.

CAPTAIN COERT STEVENSE VAN VOORHEES of Flat Lands, Long Islands; *b.* at Hees, near Ruinen, Holland, 1637; *d.* circa 1702, Flat Lalnds, Long Island; was a Deacon of the Dutch Church of Flat Lands, 1677; Magistrate in 1664 and 1673; commissioned by Lieut.-Gov. Jacob LEISLER, Captain of Militia, 27th December, 1689; Member of the General Assembly held in City Hall, New Amsterdam on 10th April, 1664; Representative of Flatlands in the Provincial Assembly of 19th March, 1664; Delegate to the Convention held in New Orange to confer with Governor COLVE on 26th March, 1674; commissioned by the Director General and Council for the office of Schepens of New Amesfoort, Flatlands, 20th March, 1664; *m.* prior to 1664, Marretje Gerritse VAN COUWENHOVEN, *bapt.* 10th April, 1644, at Long Island, *d.* there between 1702 and 1709, dau. of Gerrit Wolfertse VAN COUWENHOVEN and Aeltie Lambertse COOL.

ISSUE

I. STEVEN COERTE, of whom later.
II. Marretje Coerte, *m.* 11th December, 1681, Jacob REMSEN.
III. Albert Coerte, *m.* (firstly) Sara Willemse CORNELL; *m.* (secondly) 15th May, 1743, Willemtje SUYDAM; *m.* (thirdly) 1st December, 1744, Ida VANDERBILT.
IV. Gerrit Coerte, *d.* circa, 1703; *m.* (firstly) Mensie JANSE; *m.* (secondly) 26th April, 1685, Willemtje PIETERS.
V. Altje Coerte, *d.* 12th November, 1746; *m.* (firstly) Johannes WILLEMSE; *m.* (secondly) 16th April, 1687, Joost Rutgertse VAN BRUNT.
VI. Neeltje Coert, *b.* 30th June, 1676; *d.* 4th August, 1750; *m.* Garret R. SCHENCK of Monmouth, New Jersey.
VII. Cornelis Coerte, *bapt.* 23d January, 1678; *m.* Antie REMSEN.
VIII. Annatie Coerte, *bapt.* 5th December, 1680; *m.* Jan RAPALJE, of Brooklyn, Long Island.
IX. Johannes Coerte, *b.* 20th April, 1683; *d.* 16th October, 1757; *m.* (firstly) Barbara VAN DYCK, dau. of Achaias VAN DYCK and Jannetje LAMBERTS; *m.* (secondly) 2d May, 1744, Sarah VAN VLEIT.

STEVEN COERTE VAN VOORHEES of Flatlands, Long Island; *b.* circa 1667; *d.* there 16th February, 1723; *m.* Agatha JANSE of Long Island; his name appears on a True List of Officers and Soldiers belonging to the Regiment of Militia in Kings County, New York, 1715.

ISSUE

I. Coert, *bapt.* 15th November, 1694, at Brooklyn, New York; *m.* Grietje, dau. of Garret Pieterse WYCKOFF of Flatlands, Long Islands, and Catherine NEVIUS.

COLONIAL FAMILIES OF THE UNITED STATES 459

II. JOHN, of whom later.
III. Antie, *m*. Rem. Gerretse VAN NOSTRAND.
IV. Lucresy, *m*. Nicholas WILLIAMSON of Gravesend, Long Island.
V. Altje, *m*. 17th October, 1708, Albert TERHUNE, son of Jan Albertse TERHUNE and Annatie Roelofse SCHENCK,*bapt*. 13th April, 1684,*d*. 1721.
VI. Sara, *m*. Jacobus GERRITSEN.
VII. Maria, *m*. Jacob REMSEN.

JOHN VAN VOORHIES of Gravesend, Long Island, *m*. ——— SEYTIE.

ISSUE

I. STEPHEN J., *b*. February, 1739, of whom later.
II. John, *m*. Jannetje RYDER, *b*. 1753; *d*. 30th December, 1835.
III. Jacobus, will proved 22d September, 1817; *m*. Geertie or Charity SUYDAM.

STEPHEN J. VAN VOORHIES of Gravesend, Long Island; *b*. February, 1739; *d*. there 23d May, 1816; *m*. there 31st May, 1767, Phebe RYDER, *b*. 22d January, 1749, on Long Island, *d*. there 25th March, 1816; his name appears on the Militia Roll of Gravesend, of 1761; he served as private in New York Militia in the Revolution.

ISSUE

I. Seytie, *b*. 27th August, 1769; *d*. 1st June, 1827; *m*. 9th December, 1789, Abraham EMMONS.
II. Jacobus, *b*. 20th October, 1771; *d*. 1812; *m*. 7th August, 1804, Phebe JOHNSON, *b*. 5th March, 1783, *d*. 1st March, 1874.
III. Jane, *b*. 4th April, 1773; *d*. 17th September, 1831; *m*. 4th April, 1797, George SUYDAM.
IV. EVA, *b*. 10th September, 1778, of whom later.
V. John S., *b*. 8th October, 1780; *d*. 23d February, 1862; *m*. 26th August, 1804, Adrianna VOORHEES, *b*. 22d August, 1787, *d*. 2d June, 1854.
VI. Stephen, *b*. 12th May, 1783; *d*. 6th July, 1783.
VII. Stephen, *b*. 16th January, 1785; *d*. 8th September, 1785.
VIII. Stephen S., *b*. 25th July, 1787; *d*. 12th February, 1872; *m*. 15th May, 1808, Catherine VAN BRUNT, *b*. 15th August, 1785; *d*. 20th June, 1856.

EVA VAN VOORHIES, *b*. 10th September, 1778, in Gravesend, Long Island; *d*. 2d May, 1858, Somerset County, New Jersey; *m*. 21st August, 1804, Peter L. VOORHEES, *b*. 2d February, 1781, in Somerset County, New Jersey, *d*. there 17th March, 1847; Peter L. VOORHEES was the son of Lucas VOORHEES, who was in the Revolution in the Somerset County, New Jersey Militia, and was wounded at the Battle of Monmouth, 28th June, 1778; Lucas VOORHEES was the son of Abraham VAN VOORHEES who also served in the Somerset County Militia, Revolutionary War.

ISSUE

I. Johannah, *b.* 3d November, 1805; *d.* October, 1862; *m.* Minna CORTELYOU.
II. Phebe, *b.* 30th August, 1807; *d.* 1813.
III. Elizabeth, *b.* 30th August, 1807; *d.* 1813.
IV. Stephen, *b.* 3d February, 1810; *d.* 1813.
V. Syche Ann, *b.* 3d January, 1812; *d.* 1813.
VI. GITTY JANE, of whom later.
VII. Stephen S., *b.* 16th September, 1816; *m.* 28th May, 1845, Hannah C. CORWIN.
VIII. John, *b.* 21st December, 1818; *d.* 7th January, 1832.
IX. Phebe Ann, *b.* 23d February, 1821; *m.* William MESEROLE.

GITTY JANE VOORHEES of New Brunswick, New Jersey; *b.* 14th May, 1814, in Somerset County, New Jersey; *d.* 29th April, 1876, in New Brunswick; *m.* 21st November, 1846, as his second wife, John P. VOORHEES of New Brunswick, New Jersey, *b.* there 5th June, 1783, *d.* there 15th May, 1863, and who had served as Second Lieutenant in Capt. James C. VAN DYKE'S Troop of Horse Artillery (doing duty as Cavalry) 3d New Jersey, War of 1812.

ISSUE BY SECOND MARRIAGE

I. Stephen, *b.* 5th February, 1844; *d.* 1st June, 1864, at Battle of Cold Harbor, Virginia, was in 14th New Jersey.
II. Matilda Ackerman, *b.* 28th May, 1846; *d.* 21st April, 1872; *m.* 3d May, 1865, Henry V. L. SENKER.
III. ARCHIBALD CRAIG, *b.* 1st March, 1851, of whom later.

ARCHIBALD CRAIG VOORHEES of New Brunswick, New Jersey; *b.* there 1st March, 1851; *d.* there 26th November, 1910; *m.* 11th August, 1875, Annie Elizabeth COLE, *b.* 4th July, 1851, at Old Bridge, New Jersey, dau. of James Longstreet COLE. A. Craig VOORHEES served as Private, Corporal, Sergeant, First Sergeant and elected Captain of Company D, 3d New Jersey (now Company H.), 2d New Jersey National Guard.

ISSUE

I. GEORGE VAN WICKLE, *b.* 11th May, 1876, the subject of this memoir.
II. Edward Craig, *b.* 12th June, 1878; Graduate of Stevens Institute of Technology, Drexel Institute, Philadelphia, and School of Mines, University of Paris.

Arms.—Quarterly first and fourth gules a towerd' or, opened of the field, second and third Argent, a tree eradicated vert.
Crest.—A tower d' or.
Motto.—Virtus castellum meum.

COLONIAL FAMILIES OF THE UNITED STATES 461

Residence.—108 Mountain Avenue, Somerville, New Jersey.

Clubs.—Somerville Country, Bachelor of Somerville, University of Pennsylvania Club of New York City.

Societies.—Society of Colonial Wars; Sons of the American Revolution; Society of the War of 1812; Union Lodge No. 19, Free and Accepted Masons; Keystone Chapter No. 25, Royal Arch Masons; Temple Commandery No. 18, Knights Templar; Salaam Temple, Ancient and Accepted Order of the Nobles of the Mystic Shrine; Past Exalted Ruler of Somerville Lodge No. 1068, Benevolent and Protective Order of Elks.

Warren

NATHAN WARREN of Waltham, Massachusetts; *b.* there 11th February, 1838; *m.* 18th January, 1883, at Springfield, Massachusetts, Charlotte Elizabeth BACON, *b.* 16th June, 1855, dau. of Francis Bond and Charlotte (HARE) BACON of Springfield.

ISSUE

I. Richard, *b.* 15th August, 1887.
II. Margaret, *b.* 8th October, 1892.

NATHAN WARREN during the Civil War served, 1862–1863, as a Corporal in the 45th Massachusetts Volunteers; in service military capacity in Department of Gulf, 1864; in War Department at Washington, 1865; a Member of the Massachusetts Legislature, 1880–1881; for more than twenty years Chairman of Board of Trustees of the Public Library of Waltham; was President of the Boston Underwriters Association from 1893 to 1894; Vice-President Waltham Savings Bank; President Massachusetts Society Sons of the American Revolution, 1910–1911; Treasurer General National Society Sons of the American Revolution, 1903–1905.

Lineage

JOHN WARREN of Watertown, Massachusetts; *b.* in England, 1585; *d.* 13th December, 1667; came to New England from Nayland, England, on the fleet with Sir Richard SALTONSTALL in 1630 and settled at Watertown; admitted Freeman 18th May, 1631; was Selectman, 1636–1640, and held good estates in land in Watertown; *m.* in England Margaret, surname unknown, who *d.* 6th November, 1662.

ISSUE

I. John, *b.* in England, 1622; *d.* 1703; was a Captain; *m.* 11th July, 1667, Michal (JENNISON) BLOISE, dau. of Robert JENNISON and widow of Richard BLOISE.
II. Mary, (twin) *b.* in England; *m.* 30th October, 1642, John BIGELOW.
III. DANIEL, (twin) *b.* in England, 1628, of whom later.
IV. Elizabeth, *m.* circa 1654, James KNAPP.

DANIEL WARREN of Watertown, *b.* in England 5th February, 1627–1682; took the oath of fidelity, 1652; was Selectman for twelve years between 1680 and 1698; Member of Watertown Train Band, 1653, in Capt. Nathaniel DAVENPORT'S Company; King Philip's War, Great Swamp Fight, 19th December, 1675; in Sudbury Fight, 1675; *m.* 10th December, 1650, Mary BARRON, eldest dau. of Ellis and Grace BARRON.

ISSUE

I. Mary, *b.* 29th November, 1651; *m.* (firstly) 29th May, 1668, John CHILD; *m.* (secondly) 13th April, 1677, Nathaniel FISK.
II. Daniel, *b.* 6th October, 1653.

COLONIAL FAMILIES OF THE UNITED STATES 463

III. Hannah, *m.* 24th September, 1675, David MEAD.
IV. Sarah, *b.* 4th July, 1658.
V. Elizabeth, *b.* 17th September, 1660; *m.* 6th December, 1681, Jonathan TAINTER.
VI. Susanna, *b.* 26th December, 1663; *d.* under fifteen years.
VII. JOHN, *b.* 5th March, 1666, of whom later.
VIII. Joshua, *b.* 4th July, 1668.
IX. Grace, *b.* 14th March, 1672; *m.* 20th January, 1691, Joseph MORSE.

ENSIGN JOHN WARREN of Weston, Massachusetts; *b.* 5th March, 1665-1666; *d.* July, 1703; *m.* Mary BROWN, *b.* 1662, dau. of Jonathan BROWN.

ISSUE

I. JOHN, *b.* 15th March, 1684-1685, of whom later.
II. Daniel.

JOHN WARREN of Weston, Massachusetts; *b.* there 15th March, 1684-1685; *d.* 25th March, 1745; *m.* 1708, Abigail LIVERMORE, *d.* October, 1743, dau. of Samuel LIVERMORE.

ISSUE

I. Sarah, *b.* 1705.
II. Mary, *b.* 1710.
III. Ann, *b.* 1712.
IV. John, *b.* 1713.
V. Josiah, *b.* 1715.
VI. Isaac, *b.* 1717.
VII. ELISHA, *b.* 13th April, 1718, of whom later.
VIII. Ebenezer, *b.* 1719.
IX. Abigail, *b.* 1720; *d.* 1737.
X. Abijah, *b.* 1721; *d.* 1737.
XI. Prudence, *b.* 1724.
XII. Beulah, *b.* 1725.
XIII. Lydia, *b.* 1728.

ELISHA WARREN of Weston, Massachusetts; *b.* 13th April, 1718; *d.* 1795; *m.* Sarah ABBOTT, *b.* November, 1718, dau. of Nehemiah ABBOTT.

ISSUE

I. Nehemiah, *b.* 23d January, 1746.
II. Amos, *b.* 23d October, 1748.
III. Micah, *b.* 3d August, 1750.
IV. Sarah, *b.* 3d May, 1752.
V. Abijah, *b.* August, 1754.
VI. Abigail, *b.* 28th February, 1756.

VII. Isaac (twin), b. 30th July, 1758.
VIII. Abigail (twin), b. 30th July, 1758.
IX. NATHAN, b. 5th February, 1761, of whom later.

NATHAN WARREN of Weston, Massachusetts; b. 5th February, 1761; d. 26th July, 1843; m. 19th November, 1786, Betsey SMITH, b. 1765, d. 1804, dau. of Samuel SMITH.

ISSUE

I. Sarah, b. 30th January, 1788; d. 1865.
II. Cyrus, b. 28th November, 1789; d. 1866.
III. Anne, b. 25th February, 1792; d. 1852.
IV. Nathan, b. 18th August, 1794; d. 1884.
V. NEHEMIAH, b. 8th September, 1796, of whom later.
VI. Eliza, b. 15th July, 1798; d. 1833.
VII. Abigail, b. 9th June, 1800; d. 1869.
VIII. Samuel, b. 26th April, 1802; d. 1867.
IX. Mary, b. 11th April, 1804; d. December, 1878.

NEHEMIAH WARREN of Waltham, Massachusetts; b. 8th September, 1796, at Weston, Massachusetts; d. 7th March, 1885; m. 11th May, 1830, Sally WYMAN, b. 21st November, 1794; d. 9th February, 1887, dau. of Benjamin WYMAN of Woburn, Massachusetts.

ISSUE

I. John Benjamin, b. 3d April, 1831; d. 1861; m. 1860, Frances M. VILES.
II. Ellen Elizabeth, b. 30th April, 1833; m. 1860, Emory W. LANE.
III. Sarah Boynton, b. 17th August, 1835; m. 1862, George W. WARREN.
IV. NATHAN, b. 11th February, 1838, the subject of this memoir.

Arms.—Gules a lion rampant argent; a chief chequey or and azure.
Crest.—Out of a ducal coronet a demi-wivern, wings expanded.
Motto.—Pro Patria mori.
Residence.—50 Weston Street, Waltham, Massachusetts.
Clubs.—Massachusetts, Middlesex, Albemarle Golf.
Societies.—Colonial Wars, Sons of the American Revolution, Boston Chamber of Commerce, Good Government Association, New England Historic-Genealogical Society.

Whipple

BRIGADIER-GENERAL CHARLES HENRY WHIPPLE, U. S. A., retired, of Los Angeles, California; *b.* 12th June, 1849, at Adams, New York; *m.* 5th December, 1871, at Cincinnati, Ohio, Evelyn Elizabeth McLEAN, *b.* 5th July, 1851, dau. of Gen. Nathaniel Collins McLEAN, *b.* 2d February, 1818, *d.* 4th January, 1905, *m.* 5th September, 1838, Caroline Thew BURNET, *b.* 26th August, 1820, *d.* 15th April, 1856, and gd. dau. of Justice John McLEAN of the United States Supreme Court.

ISSUE

I. Charles Henry, *b.* 18th November, 1872; First Lieutenant, United States Army, retired; *m.* (firstly) 12th March, 1900, Aida Mae BULGER; *m.* (secondly) 25th June, 1907, Mrs. Mary Goodridge GOULD, dau. of William M. and Caroline (WILCOX) GOODRIDGE.

II. Henry Benjamin, *b.* 4th August, 1874; General Manager New York Dock Company; *m.* 17th January, 1900, Katherine Nelson MEADE, *b.* 29th January, 1876, dau. of Rev. Philip Nelson and Sara Jane (RANNELLS) MEADE.

III. Nathaniel McLean, *b.* 25th September, 1875; *d.* 23d December, 1902, unmarried.

CHARLES HENRY WHIPPLE was educated at St. Paul's School, Concord, New Hampshire; from 1871 to 1881 Cashier Citizens' National Bank of Faribault, Minnesota; 18th February, 1881, appointed Major and Paymaster, promoted Lieutenant-Colonel and Colonel in the Pay Department of the United States Army; appointed Paymaster-General of the Army with rank of Brigadier-General 1st January, 1908; retired 15th February, 1912.

Lineage

CAPTAIN JOHN WHIPPLE of Providence, Rhode Island; *b.* in England, 1617; *d.* 16th May, 1685; was in Dorchester, Massachusetts, 1632; came in the second immigration from England; deputy to Rhode Island General Court 1666–1677; *m.* in Dorchester, 1639, Sarah, surname unknown.

ISSUE

I. John, *b.* 1640; *d.* 15th December, 1700; *m.* (firstly) Mary OLNEY; *m.* (secondly) Rebecca SCOTT.
II. Sarah, *b.* 1642; *d.* 1687; *m.* John SMITH.
III. Samuel, *b.* 1644; *d.* 12th March, 1711; *m.* Mary HARRIS.
IV. Eleazer, *b.* 1646; *d.* 25th August, 1719; *m.* Alice ANGELL.

v. Mary, b. 1648; d. 1698; m. Epenetus OLNEY.
vi. William, b. 1652; d. 9th March, 1712; m. Mary ———.
vii. Benjamin, b. 1654; d. 11th March, 1704; m. Ruth MATTHEWSON.
viii. DAVID, b. 28th September, 1656, of whom later.
ix. Abigail, b. 1660; d. 19th August, 1725; m. (firstly) Stephen DEXTER; m. (secondly) Maj. William HOPKINS.
x. Joseph, b. 1662; d. 28th August, 1746; m. Alice SMITH.
xi. Jonathan, b. 1664; d. 8th September, 1721; m. (firstly) Margaret ANGELL; m. (secondly) Anna surname unknown.

DAVID WHIPPLE of Attleborough, Massachusetts; b. 28th September, 1656, at Dorchester, Massachusetts; d. 18th December, 1710, at Rehoboth, Rhode Island; was Ensign at the time of his death; m. (firstly) 15th May, 1675, Sarah HEARNDEN; m. (secondly) 11th November, 1677, Hannah TOWER, b. 17th July, 1652, d. November, 1722, dau. of John and Margaret (IBROOK) TOWER.

ISSUE BY FIRST MARRIAGE

i. David, b. 1676, at Hingham, Massachusetts; d. young.

ISSUE BY SECOND MARRIAGE

i. Israel, b. 16th August, 1678; drowned 13th June, 1720; m. Mary WILMARTH.
ii. Deborah, b. 12th September, 1681; m. ——— TOWER, of Attleboro.
iii. JEREMIAH, of whom later.
iv. William, b. 27th May, 1685; m. Mary surname unknown.
v. Sarah, b. 18th November, 1687; m. ——— RAZEE.
vi. Hannah, b. 9th January, 1690.
vii. Abigail, b. 20th October, 1692.

JEREMIAH WHIPPLE of Cumberland, Rhode Island; b. 26th June, 1683; d. 14th May, 1721; was Ensign of 6th Company of 2d Regiment Rhode Island Troops; m. 22d November, 1711, Deborah BUCKLIN, of Rehoboth, b. 15th May, 1692, dau. of Joseph BUCKLIN.

ISSUE

i. Hannah, b. 14th July, 1712.
ii. DAVID, b. 1st May, 1714, of whom later.
iii. Jeremiah, b. 5th March, 1716; d. aged 82 years; m. Hannah BROWN.
iv. Amy, b. 21st May, 1718; d. 27th April, 1721.
v. Sarah, b. 8th December, 1720; m. John DEXTER of Cumberland, Rhode Island.

DAVID WHIPPLE of Cumberland, Rhode Island; b. 1st May, 1714; d. 6th October, 1766; Representative to Rhode Island General Assembly from Cumberland, 1756–1757; m. 7th July, 1737, Martha READ, b. 4th November, 1715, dau. of Thomas READ.

COLONIAL FAMILIES OF THE UNITED STATES

ISSUE

I. Simon, *b.* 28th September, 1738; *m.* ——— MILLER.
II. David, *b.* 14th July, 1740; *d.* young.
III. George, *b.* 11th July, 1742; *m.* Sarah COREY.
IV. Otis, *b.* 19th August, 1744; *m.* Mary ARNOLD.
V. Cynthia, *b.* 17th August, 1746; *m.* Isaac BRAYTON.
VI. Lydia, *b.* 7th September, 1748; *m.* Zebedee ARNOLD.
VII. Amy, *b.* 2d November, 1750; *m.* Joseph BUCKLIN.
VIII. Jonathan, *b.* 8th September, 1752; *m.* Mary JENNISON.
IX. BENJAMIN, of whom later.
X. Joseph, *b.* 21st March, 1761; *d.* 18th July, 1762.

BENJAMIN WHIPPLE of Albany, New York; *b.* 17th November, 1754, at Cumberland, Rhode Island; *d.* 30th April, 1819; seaman under Capt. Abraham WHIPPLE and was captured and confined on the British Prison-Ship *Jersey*; *m.* 8th January, 1783, Susanna HALL, *b.* 14th January, 1762, of Wrentham, Massachusetts, *d.* 13th May, 1840, dau. of John HALL of Wrentham.

ISSUE

I. Nancy, *b.* 8th December, 1784; *d.* 27th August, 1856; *m.* Cyrus TROWBRIDGE.
II. Susanna, *b.* 10th January, 1787; *d.* April, 1818; *m.* Otis WHIPPLE.
III. Esther, *b.* 5th February, 1789; *d.* 3d February, 1828.
IV. George, *b.* 28th March, 1791; *d.* 22d July, 1796.
V. Cynthia, *b.* 3d February, 1793; *d.* 14th July, 1847; *m.* Timothy GLADDING.
VI. JOHN HALL, *b.* 22d September, 1795, of whom later.
VII. Martha, *b.* 29th September, 1798; *d.* 6th October, 1799.
VIII. Benjamin Brayton, *b.* 23d November, 1800; *d.* 2d April, 1835; *m.* Sally BAKER.
IX. Ann Frances, *b.* 3d February, 1803; *d.* December, 1875; *m.* Hon. Elias RANSOM.
X. Rev. George, *b.* 4th June, 1805; *d.* 6th October, 1876; *m.* 2d April, 1840, Alice Bridge WEBSTER, niece of Daniel WEBSTER.

JOHN HALL WHIPPLE of Adams, New York; *b.* 22d September, 1795, at Albany, New York; *d.* 15th December, 1859, at Adams; *m.* 25th September, 1820, Elizabeth WAGER, *b.* 21st December, 1798, *d.* 21st March, 1870, dau. of Hon. Henry WAGER of Westernville, New York; was one of the electors of Thomas JEFFERSON.

ISSUE

I. HENRY BENJAMIN, *b.* 15th February, 1822, of whom later.
II. Sarah Brayton, *b.* 29th January, 1824; *d.* 20th March, 1885; *m.* Hiram SALISBURY.

III. Susan Letitia, b. 3d January, 1826; d. 28th November, 1894; m. Zaccheus HILL.
IV. John, b. 1st April, 1828; d. 21st March, 1879; unmarried.
V. Rev. George Brayton, b. 26th June, 1830; d. 19th July, 1888; m. Mary J. MILLS.
VI. Francis Ransom, 1835-1850.
VII. David Wager, b. 1839; d. 1840.

RIGHT REVEREND HENRY BENJAMIN WHIPPLE, Bishop of Minnesota; b. 15th February, 1822, at Adams, New York; d. 16th September, 1901, at Faribault, Minnesota; was educated in private schools in the State of New York. At the age of ten years was placed in Professor's AVERY'S private school in Clinton, New York, and next in School under Rev. Dr. BOYD and Dr. COVERT. Was Division Inspector with rank of Colonel on Staff of Maj.-Gen. John GORSE, New York State Militia. Received his theological training under Rev. Dr. W. D. WILSON later of Cornell University. 26th August, 1849, was ordained Deacon by Bishop DELANCEY in Trinity Church, Geneva, New York. The following February ordained Priest in Christ Church, Sackett's Harbor, and immediately thereafter called to Zion Church, Rome, New York. In 1856 was called to establish the first Protestant Episcopal Church in Chicago, Illinois. Among his parishoners were Generals BURNSIDE and MCCLELLAN. Erected the Church of the Holy Communion, which was destroyed at the time of the great Chicago fire, 13th October, 1859; was consecrated first Bishop of Minnesota at St. James Church, Richmond, Virginia, at the session of the General Convention. It was through his unselfish efforts that the Diòcese of the State of Maryland has the finest diocesan library in the United States. He was loyal and fearless in protecting the rights of the Indians in Minnesota, against unlawful aggressions on the part of unscrupulous whites. He stood preëminently as the most rational, just and enlightened man who had any dealing with Indian affairs and for his sincerity and directness the Indians gave him the name of "Straight Tongue." He gave clear warning of the Indian massacre that occurred in 1862. Was appointed on many commissions by different Presidents of the United States. In 1871 an English Bishopric was offered him by the Archbishop of Canterbury and the Bishop of Winchester and by the King and Synod of the Sandwich Islands. In 1873 he was elected one of the Trustees of the great Peabody Fund for educational work in the South. In 1888 by request of the Archbishop of Canterbury, Bishop Whipple preached the opening sermon of the Lambeth Conference at Lambeth Palace, London. From the Universities of Oxford, Cambridge and Durham he received the honorary degrees of D.D. and LL.D., and D.D. from Hobart College. On 3d June, 1897, by a request of the preceding year, he preached in Salisbury Cathedral at the great service in commemoration of the thirteen hundredth anniversary of the baptism of King Ethelbert, the first Christian Saxon king, with a congregation of seven thousand persons, a procession of seven hundred bishops and vested clergy and fourteen hundred choristers. The same year he preached one of the special sermons before Oxford and the "Ramsden Sermon" before Cambridge, which, by request of the S. P. G., was published for circulation. He also preached the opening sermon after the restoration of the wonderful old Cathedral Church of St. Saviour's, London, vibrant with history, and in the Ladye Chapel, in which Bishop GARDNER held court and condemned to be burned at the stake the Bishop of St. David's, Bishop FARRAR of Worcester, John ROGERS and five priests. It was said by many of the one hundred and fifty bishops present at this service that Bishop WHIPPLE seemed to have reached the zenith of impassioned out pouring of spiritual truths, striking the keynote of everything most needed in the Christianization of the world. In August, 1897, Bishop Whipple preached the Tennyson memorial sermon in the Poet's parish church at Freshwater, Isle of Wight, at the time of the unveiling, by the Archbishop of Canterbury and the Dean of Westminster, of the memorial erected by the poet's friends in America and England—the Iona cross, which stands a beacon for sailors on the summit of the downs. He was Chaplain General of the Society of Colonial Wars and Sons of the American Revolution; *m.* (firstly) 5th October, 1842, Cornelia WRIGHT, *b.* 10th November, 1816, *d.* 16th July, 1890, dau. of Benjamin and Sarah (WARD) WRIGHT of the families of PELL and WARD of New York; *m.* (secondly) 22d October, 1896, Evangeline (MARRS) SIMPSON only dau. of Francis and Jane (VAN POELIEN) MARRS of Massachusetts, and widow of Michael SIMPSON.

ISSUE BY FIRST MARRIAGE

I. Sarah Elizabeth, *b.* 2d August, 1843; *m.* Charles A. FARNUM of Philadelphia.
II. Cornelia Ward, *b.* 26th August, 1845; *d.* 21st May, 1884; *m.* (firstly) William Wilkins DAVIS; *m.* (secondly) Dr. Francis M. ROSE.
III. Jane Whiting, *b.* 10th March, 1847; *m.* Henry A. SCANDRETT of Faribault, Minnesota.
IV. CHARLES HENRY, *b.* 12th June, 1849, the subject of this memoir.
V. Frances Ransom, *b.* 5th June, 1853; *m.* (firstly) Frank G. CRAW; *m.* (secondly) Freedom W. JACKSON of Cleveland, Ohio.
VI. John Hall, *b.* 16th March, 1857; *d.* 6th August, 1878; unmarried.

Arms.—Sable on a chevron between three swans heads erased argent, as many crescents of the field.
Crest.—An elephant passant ermine.
Residence.—Los Angeles, California.
Clubs.—California Club, Los Angeles, California, Athenian Club, Oakland, California.
Societies.—Colonial Wars, New York State Society of the Cinncinnati, Loyal Legion of the United States, Sons of the American Revolution, War of 1812, Military Order of the Caraboa.

White

JOSEPH NELSON WHITE of Winchendon Springs, Massachusetts; b. there 4th October, 1851; m. 14th September, 1875, Annie EVANS, dau. of Seth and Winifred Miller (BROWN) EVANS of Cincinnati. He son of David and Rachel (BURNET) EVANS, who was son of Benjamin and Hannah EVANS. Benjamin EVANS emigrated to Pennsylvania in 1696, d. 1747.

ISSUE

I. Winifred Evans, b. 12th July, 1876.
II. Nelson Davis, b. 19th October, 1878.
III. Joseph Nelson, b. 2d August, 1881.
IV. Madeleine Evans, b. 26th March, 1887.
V. Rachel Burnet, b. 9th June, 1892.

JOSEPH NELSON WHITE was educated at Winchendon Academy and Highland Military Academy, Worcester, Massachusetts; graduated from the latter in 1867, being second in the class; in 1868 attended the Institute of Technology, Boston; in 1869 entered into the employ of his father; in 1877 he with his brother Zadoc bought the Jaffrey Mills; Director of the Safety Fund National Bank of Fitchburg, 1879; in 1885 bought the Cheshire Mill plant at East Jaffrey, New Hampshire. In 1887 he built Marchmont on an estate of about 500 acres; was a member of the Ancient and Honorable Artillery Company, Boston, Massachus etts, from 1885 to 1896 and resigned on last date: he spent several years writing the genealogy of the WHITE family, which publication has been accepted by the British Museum and by the best historical societies in this country; during the past thirty years he has travelled extensively in Europe and America; for thirty-five years has been general manager of NELSON D. WHITE & SONS and WHITE, Brother, who own and operate seven manufacturing plants and do business in all parts of the world, with a combined capital of about two millions of dollars. 1888, Vice-President of the Winchendon Savings Bank; appointed postmaster 6th April, 1889, by President CLEVELAND; 5th July, 1898, unanimously elected a Member of the School Board and chosen Secretary; Trustee of the Murdock Fund; 1901, Director in the Monadnock National Bank of Jaffrey, New Hampshire. Has been President of the Murdock Fund since 1903. Is a large owner in sugar plantations in the Hawaiian Islands; in 1914 established the Annie Evans White Memorial of $50,000 the interest of which is to be used for the needy poor of Winchendon. On 8th February, 1914, he erected the Corinthian Column at Riverside Cemetery to the memory of his wife; is a large owner in the Fitchburg Yarn Company of Fitchburg, Massachusetts, and was one of the Directors in the Parkhill Manufacturing Company, manufacturers of fine ginghams.

Residence.—"Marchmont," Winchendon Springs, Massachusetts.
Societies.—Ancient and Honorable Artillery Company, 1885–1896.

Lineage

The WHITE family is a very old one, and the name appears among the people of many countries. The branch of which the subject of this memoir is a member first comes to our attention in picturesque old Yorkshire, England, in the thirteenth century. There the family lived in the shadow of the grand York Cathedral. and in it they worshipped more than five hundred years ago. The beautiful Fountains Abbey was a joy to them, as its ruins are to the WHITES today.

WILLELMI WHITE (WHITE) frater Nicholas de Ebor in Kirkby's Inquest for Yorkshire, taken 5 Edward I, 1277, as of Hebden, Staincliffe, Wapentake. It is not known if he was any relation to Robertus WHITE who is mentioned in the Knight's Fees or Yorkshire, 31st Edward I., 1303, as of Aghton, Hartill Wapentake, but, if as has been asserted, and is almost certain, that the Inquest, which Adams KIRKBY, Treasure, held concerning the tenures in capite, was made in 35 instead of 5 Edward I, or in 1306, it is just possible that these two WHITES, who held land in Yorkshire by tenure in capite about the same time, and very close to each other, were related in some way. This KIRKBY's Inquest or Quest is sa:d to be in the nature of Domeday, and is of great importance as showing the landed proprietors at the time. When the lands of the conquered English were divided amongst the vassals of the Norman invaders, the obligation was imposed upon them of supplying the crown with a certain number of Knights, specified in the infeoffment. These knights had allotments of land from the King's immediate tenants, and held of their several lords by homage, fealty, and so forth. Their lands were called Fees, and composed the barony of the king's vassals. Aghton is, of course, the present Egton in North Riding. The name appeared next in Yorkshire with Willemus WHITE, b. 1339, who was made a freeman, 12 Edward III, 1339, when he is described as of Killum, the present Kilham, in East Riding, Yorkshire. What relationship there existed between him and the two WHITES previously mentioned is not known, inasmuch as the other two were designated as WHITE in capital letters, and consequently, indicating a surname and William was not so designated but by being called "LE WHITE" evidently was so called on account of a light complexion, or for some similar reason, and hence might be designated as the progenitor of his branch, he was not related to the two other WHITES, as there surely was no reason whatever why he, if a descendant, should be called "LE WHITE," instead of WHITE, as the two other, Robertus and Willelmi, of earlier date. (List of Freemen of York, 12 Edward III.) The above datum as referring to Willemus LE WHITE is useful, as proving his residence in the city of Kilham at this period; it also shows that he was desirous to trade within the jurisdiction of the city or borough, for which purpose he was compelled to obtain the freedom of the city. This freedom could be obtained in four ways: by servitude, i.e., apprenticeship to a freeman; by patrimony; i.e., being the child of a freeman born after the parent's admission to his freedom, or by purchase or gift of the city. That the freemanship was obtained, in this case, neither by servitude nor patrimony, in which case the name of the parent of the child would appear, would seem to prove that Willemus "LE WHITE" had purchased or received the freedomship as a gift by the city or borough, which would indicate that he was one of the earliest settlers there. He probably came from Lincolnshire, Parish of Thoresby, after having crossed the river Humber, and drifted north, as his son Petrus WHITE "rendered homage to the Archbishop of York for land held in York of the see." "Item eisdem die et anno (May 31st, 1369). Petrus WHYT fecit eidem patri consimile hom. pro terris quas tenet in Camp de Caldon." He was referred to as a brother of ADAM WHITE "a walker" who became freeman of York in 1365, "son of Willemus WHITE and brother of Petrus of Thoresby Parish. He had two sons:

    I. Ricardus, who was "a perpetus Vicarius . . . de Blida" and made his will which was probated 10th July, 1393.
    II. JOHANNIS, of whom later.

JOHANNIS WHITE was a slaymaker, "became freeman in 1390," son of Adam WHITE, freeman in 38 Edward III, "when his name is spelled WHYT," and had son called Johannis WHIT, "Jr.," who was also a slaymaker.

    I. JOHANNIS, JR., IV, of whom later.
    II. Roberto, who was of Tykill, the present Tikill, and is mentioned in the will of Johannis Shakespere DE DONCASTER as executor, proved 29th November, 1433.

JOHANNIS WHITE, JR., a "slaymaker" in 1394, when he became a freeman; he is mentioned in the will of William MERING of Newark, as executor, 1449.

ISSUE

    I. WILLIAM, of whom later.
    II. Nicholas, a boucher; Freeman in 1451; *m.* and left descendants.
    III. John, who had son Georgius, who left descendants.
    IV. Bartholomew, who had a Dispensation from the Archbishop of York as "scutifer" to *m.* Alice, dau. of Thomas SHOLDAM, of Martham, "scutifer;" related in third degree; citing dispensation of Nicholas V, dated 5th August, 1449.

WILLIAM WHITE, who, on his admission as freeman, 30 Henry VI (1451), is called "fil Johannis WHITE slaymaker;" he studied first for the priesthood, but soon gave that up and became a merchant in York, and a man of great prominence; a Chamberlain in 1408; Sheriff in 1481–1482; Member of Parliament in 1491, and in 1504; was Lord Mayor in 1496; he died in February, 1504–1505, and in his testament and will, which was proved 27th February, that year, "to be beried in the qwere of Saynt John Bapte in my Parish Kyrk . . . . for my funeral expenses and my eythen day 20 . . . . mentions wife Agnes, and sons Robert and William. He is mentioned in the will of Robert JOHNSON, Alderman of York, dated 20th January, 1496, proved 14th March, 1497-1498, "William WHYTE, alderman, my huge rynge of golde whiche that John KEISTER made in the year that I was Maire." The wife, Agnes BARKER, mentioned in William WHITE's will, was his second wife, and he married her the year before he died, receiving from the Archbishop of York a license to the Curate of St. Michael's Ousebridge, York, to marry "William WHITE, Parish of St. John, Merchant, and Agnes BARKER, Parish of St. Michael. Banns once." He had no children with this wife, and the name of the first wife is not known.

ISSUE BY FIRST MARRIAGE

I. William, settled in St. Michael in Huggin Lane; m. Alice WOOD, of St. Michael ad Baldum, obtaining a license 22d January, 1520.
II. ROBERT, of whom later.

ROBERT WHITE or Robertus WHYTE, Merchant, fil Willelmi WHYTE, Merchant as he is called, when he became freeman 10 Henry VIII (1518). He is mentioned, as Roberto Whyte DE ALNEWYK, in will of Thomas ASKWYK of Alnwyck, 5th August, 1503. John MARSHALL, previously mentioned, made his will 15th December, proved 31st July, 1526-1527, as of York, Merchant, and in this he mentions Robert WHITE's childer, to ichow of his sones xxs., and ichow of his goughtours x s., also referring to Robert WHITE's father William WHITE, sone of John WHITE, Alderman and Grosiour of Yorke. He m. Ketherine WHITE, dau. of Davy WHITE, who received "a smoke" in will of Agnes CONSTABLE of Witherwick, proved 16th November, 1522. She also received "a silver spoone" in will of Kath. HENRISON's will of 13th May, 1541, proved 13th July, 1545, of Kingston upon Hull. In the reference to the "Testaments" I have, to escape repetition, used the word "will" but it should be understood, that until 32 Henry VIII (1540) no man, however rich in lands, had power to make his "will" and leave away a single acre from his heir. His "testament" dealing solely with his money, and other personal property, he could make; at his death, the document was proved, and a certificate or "probate act" was annexed to the parchment transcript of the will. All "testaments" here referred to were registered at York. Robert WHITE and Katherine, his wife, had issue:

I. Alexander, who is mentioned as to receive x s. or the worth of it . . . . in "testament" of Thomas MASON, Alderman of York, proved 9th April, 1529.
II. JOHN, of whom later.
III. Katherine, m. Martin SNOW, and had issue.
IV. Margaret, m. Samuel THOMAS, but had no issue.

JOHN WHITE was a silversmith and moved to London to practice his trade, as appears, when he married, as son of Robert and Katherine his wife, of York, 8th February, 1543-1544, Johanna LYDDEN, now of Parish Whittsam, Diocese of Canterbury, late of Cavood, Yorkshire, dau. of ———— LYDDEN and Johanna his wife.

ISSUE

I. Johannis, who was buried in St. Martins in the Field, 3d November, 1553.
II. Anne, *m.* in that parish, Robertus CUDD, 29th October, 1564; she *d.* 18th November, 1565, "dau. of John WHITE and Johanna his wife, and sister of Johannis WHITE, deceased."
III. THOMAS, of whom later.
IV. Gabriel, *m.* Anne WEBBE, widow, 26th November, 1571.
V. Andree, *m.* and had a son, John, *bapt.* 28th January, 1609.

THOMAS WHITE *m.* as per General License of 28th November, 1567, Agnes WRIGHT, spinster, of the City of London, Parish of St. Ethelburgh; she was dau. of Walter WRIGHT and Elizabeth, his wife, of St. Michael Parish, Fewston, Yorkshire. THOMAS WHITE, late of London, son of John WHITE and Johanna, his wife, of Longe Sandall, Yorkshire, husbandman, made his will 15th June, 1597, proved 27th May, 44 Elizabeth (1601), but administration was not granted until 24th March, 1602, to "his son William," of Long Sandall, Tuotion, Doncaster.

ISSUE

I. William, who had administration granted to him, as son of Thomas, 24th March, 1602, at Long Sandall, Tuotion, Doncaster, Yorkshire, to which place his father had removed.
II. Ralph, *m.* Ellen WRIGHT, dau. of Martin WRIGHT, of Fewston, Yorkshire, to which place he removed, and where his children were baptized.

ISSUE

1. Ralph, *bapt.* 15th August, 1596.

ISSUE

1¹. Ellen, *bapt.* 6th May, 1627.
2¹. John, *bapt.* 15th April, 1639.
3¹. Walter, *bapt.* 15th April, 1639.
4¹. Margaret, *bapt.* 25th June, 1645.
5¹. Child, buried 25th June, 1645.

2. Agnes, *bapt.* 10th June, 1599.

III. WALTER, of whom later.

WALTER WHITE was buried in St. Michael Parish, Fewston, Yorkshire, 13th March, 1629; *m.* Janet SAUNDERS, dau. of William SAUNDERS and Agnes, his wife, 3d April, 1593.

ISSUE

I. William, *bapt.* after 20th July, 1594; buried 19th March, 1633.
II. WALTER, *bapt.* 19th October, 1600, of whom later.

COLONIAL FAMILIES OF THE UNITED STATES

III. Agnes, *bapt.* December, 1604, "before the 13th."
IV. Dorothy, *bapt.* 30th December, 1610, Fewston Register.
V. Mary, buried 23d April, 1598.
VI. Child, buried between June and July, 1599.
VII. Child, buried 10th January, 1610.

WALTER WHITE, *bapt.* 19th October, 1600, in St. Michael Parish, Fewston, Yorkshire, *m.* (firstly) 4th April, 1635, Margaret EARLY, who *d.* 1645, a widow, of Midgeham, Berkshire, aged 27 years, consequently *b.* 1608; *m.* (secondly) 7th October, 1645, at St. Michael, Fewston, Yorkshire, Mary BROWNE, who *d.s.p.*

ISSUE BY FIRST MARRIAGE

1. THOMAS, *b.* 28th January, 1636, of whom later.

THOMAS WHITE, *b.* 28th January, 1636, in Midgeham, Berkshire County, England; *bapt.* 28th August, 1642, in St. Michael's Church, Fewston, Yorkshire, England. He was the only child of Walter and Margaret (EARLY) WHITE, who were *m.* 4th April, 1635. He emigrated to New England on the ship *Annabel*, Martin HARMON, master, 8th May, 1660, from London. The parentage of Thomas WHITE, the date of his departure from England, and in fact anything relating to him before his marriage to Mary FROTHINGHAM have been matters of conjecture, until the discovery of the passenger list of the ship *Annabel* in the British Museum. This paper was probably in the Custom House in Boston until the Revolutionary War, and taken to England at that time by officers of the Crown. "There cannot be the slightest doubt that the Thomas WHITE of St. Michael, Fewston, Yorkshire, *b.* 1636, the emigrant, Thomas WHITE, on "Annabel" also *b.* 1636, as he was aged 24 when he emigrated in 1660, and the Thomas WHITE of Charlestown, Massachusetts, who was 80 years old when he *d.*, 30th September, 1716, and consequently, *b.* also in 1636, were one and the same person, and this so much more so as no data indicate that he ever married or died in England, which would surely have been the case if he remained, while the other members of the family are all accounted for; we do not know of any other Thomas WHITE of the New World who was *b.* in 1636 than the man of Charlestown; and although every data referring to any one by the name of WHITE has been copied in Great Britain down to 1700, there is no Thomas WHITE, *b.* in 1636, who is not accounted for, by marriage or death. All this makes it as clear as we possibly can make any data bearing upon the connections between the emigrants and the foreign ancestry, that the three persons, of same name and same age, one of which neither married nor died in England, were the same person; this so much more so as the fact that Thomas WHITE *m.* a Yorkshire woman, and so comparatively near as Holderness, where many intermarriages took place. All emigration lists from the very first, the Oblata Rolls, which begin I John are in the British Museum, although not indexed. Fewston, Yorkshire, England, had been for many years the family locality. Thomas WHITE spent the first twenty-three years of his life in Midgeham, Berkshire, his mother's home, and in Fewston. In deeds signed by himself and his wife he is designated as "yeoman" a distinction of eminent respectability. Thomas WHITE *m.* Mary FROTHINGHAM, the youngest child and favored dau. of William FROTHINGHAM. 17th November, 1663, when he was about 27 years of age. Mary FROTHINGHAM was *b.* 1st April, 1638. William FROTHINGHAM, her father, came from Holderness, Yorkshire, England, in John WINTHROP's first company Thomas WHITE's name appears in the list of freeman of Charlestown, 23d May, 1666. He was admitted to the Church 22d March, 1668; he was a soldier in King Philip's War, and served in Captain SYLL's Company, 30th November, 1675; he received for service performed one pound, four shillings, nine pence; he was also a member of Capt. John CUTLER's company of Charlestown, 24th July, 1676. Nathaniel FROTHINGHAM, Andrew STIMPSON, Thomas RAND and Peter FROTHINGHAM were members of the same company (see Bodge's "Soldiers in King Philip's War," second edition). Thomas WHITE was a man of affairs and of business ability and sterling integrity, he *d.* in Charlestown, 30th September, 1716, in his eightieth year, as per the gravestone in the old "Phipps St. burying ground." Administration was taken on his estate 7th January, 1717.

ISSUE

I. THOMAS, *b.* 15th October, 1664, of whom later.
II. William, *b.* 12th September, 1667.
III. Samuel, *b.* 24th October, 1669.
IV. Elizabeth, *b.* 28th February, 1671.

THOMAS WHITE of Charlestown, Massachusetts; *b.* there 15th October, 1664; *d.* probably 14th August, 1748; owned the Church Covenant 6th December, 1686; *m.* 4th January, 1684, Sarah RAND, *b.* circa 1666, *d.* 7th April, 1749, dau. of Sergeant Thomas and Sarah (EDENDEN) RAND, he son of Robert and Alice (*b.* 1596) (SHARP) RAND. Sarah EDENDEN was the dau. of Edmund and Elizabeth (WHITMAN) EDENDEN.

ISSUE

I. Thomas, *b.* 18th December, 1685.
II. Samuel, *b.* 4th June, 1690.
III. Sarah, *b.* no record; *m.* ———— KENDALL.
IV. JOHN, *b.* 22d August, 1695, of whom later.
V. Hannah, *b.* 25th August, 1698; *m.* ———— HESSING.
VI. Mary, *b.* 30th June, 1701; *m.* ———— MANNING.
VII. Rebecca, *b.* 1st December, 1704; *d.* 1721.
VIII. Abigail, *b.* 2d June, 1708.

LIEUTENANT JOHN WHITE of Spencer, Massachusetts; *b.* 22d August, 1695, in Charlestown, Massachusetts; *d.* 26th August, 1778, in Charlestown; left Charlestown when a young man and went to Framingham; he was commissioned Lieutenant and was associated with Col. Joseph BUCKMINSTER, Jr., during the French and

Indian Wars; in 1748 he removed with his family to Leicester; he was chosen 14th May, 1754, as Sealer of Weights and Measures and the following year Assessor and Selectman; he was at one time a slave holder; *m.* 24th July, 1728, Sybilla BUCKMINSTER, dau. of Col. Joseph, BUCKMINSTER, Sr., of Framingham.

ISSUE

I. John, *b.* 17th October, 1728; *d.* 18th September, 1803; *m.* 1759, Silence BALDWIN.
II. THOMAS, *b.* 17th July, 1731, of whom later.
III. Rebecca, *b.* 5th February, 1736.
IV. Sarah, *b.* 22d January, 1737.
V. Sybilla, *b.* 29th October, 1741.
VI. Rand, *b.* 15th October, 1751; served in the Lexington Alarm 19th April 1775; *m.* Mehitable RICE.

THOMAS WHITE, farmer and blacksmith, of Spencer, Massachusetts; *b.* 17th July, 1731, in Framingham, Massachusetts; *d.* 25th February, 1822; was a farmer and blacksmith; had landed estate comprising 500 acres; during the Revolution he was drafted into the Continental Army but his oldest son Thomas went as his substitute; he was the genealogist of his family; he claimed descent from four nations, the WHITES from England, the BUCKMINSTERS from Scotland, the MUZZEYS from France and the REEDS from Denmark; *m.* 30th December, 1756, Abigail MUZZEY, *b.* circa 1739, *d.* 11th September, 1811, dau. of Deacon John and Rebecca (REED) MUZZEY.

ISSUE

I. THOMAS, *b.* 24th November, 1757, of whom later.
II. Thaddeus, *b.* 16th July, 1759; served during the entire war in the Continental Army.
III. Abigail, *b.* 3d May, 1761.
IV. Mary, *b.* 11th November, 1762.
V. Benjamin, *b.* 8th August, 1764.
VI. Joel, *b.* 3d May, 1766.
VII. Sibillab, *b.* 13th February, 1768; *m.* ———— LAMBS.
VIII. Nancy, *b.* 25th May, 1769; *m.* ———— MASON.
IX. Jonab, *b.* 20th April, 1771.
X. Elizabeth (Betsey), *b.* 1st July, 1774; *m.* Joseph MASON.
XI. Amasa, *b.* 6th February, 1776.
XII. John Bradshaw, *b.* 1st February, 1778.
XIII. Mollie, *b.* 2d September, 1782.

THOMAS WHITE of Royalston, Massachusetts; *b.* 24th November, 1757, in Spencer, Massachusetts; *d.* 21st July, 1849, at Boyleston; enlisted 17th May, 1776, in Capt. John CARRIEL's Company, Col. Josiah WHITNEY's Regiment; re-enlisted 1st August, 1776; enlisted 27th July, 1777, Capt. David PROUTY's Company, Colonel

CUSHING's Regiment; re-enlisted 8th July, 1779, same Company, Colonel DENNY's Regiment; enlisted 19th October, 1779, in Capt. Joseph RICHARDSON's Company, Col. Samuel DENNY's Regiment; was at Ticonderoga, Bennington; saw service with WASHINGTON's army in New Jersey; *m.* 2d September, 1784, Hannah ESTABROOK, *b.* 1762, *d.* 25th July, 1830, aged 68 years, dau. of Ebenezer and Ruth ESTABROOK of Royalton, gd. dau. of Col. Joseph and Submit (LORING) ESTABROOK of Royalton.

ISSUE

I. Polly, *b.* 23d May, 1786.
II. Nancy, *b.* 15th October, 1789; *m.* ——— STILES of Boylston.
III. JOSEPH, *b.* 24th January, 1792, of whom later.
IV. Hannah, *b.* February, 1794.
V. Thomas, *b.* 5th June, 1796.
VI. Ebenezer, *b.* 13th July, 1798.

DEACON JOSEPH WHITE, Cotton Manufacturer, of West Boyleston, Massachusetts; *b.* 24th January, 1792, in Royalston, Massachusetts; *d.* 9th October, 1864; he was in the cotton business for more than fifty years and was one of the first cotton and wire manufacturers of New England; in politics he was a Whig and strong tariff man; he predicted the Civil War and after the States seceded he was a strong supporter of the Government; was Justice of the Peace and Trial Justice; was one of the founders of Worcester Academy and one of its trustees; was President of Nelson Mills Corporation; *m.* 30th January, 1817, Matilda DAVIS of Paxton, Massachusetts, *d.* 9th November, 1864.

ISSUE

I. NELSON DAVIS, *b.* 24th July, 1818, of whom later.
II. Persis Arminda, *b.* 11th January, 1820; *m.* Dr. Josiah ABBOTT.
III. Windsor Newton, *b.* 4th March, 1823.
IV. Hannah Mandana, *b.* 27th June, 1825.
V. Joseph Estabrook, *b.* 19th June, 1831.
VI. Francis Wayland, *b.* 26th October, 1834.

NELSON DAVIS WHITE, Cotton Manufacturer of Winchendon, Massachusetts; b. 24th July, 1818, in West Boyleston, Massachusetts; *d.* 2d March, 1889, in New York; was an ardent supporter of the Government during the Civil War; Member of the Massachusetts Legislature, 1861; was a Selectman of Winchendon; Vice-President of the Savings Bank; Director in the National; President of the Hampden Cotton Mills of Holyoke, Massachusetts; Director in the Boston, Barre and Gardner Railroad Company; *m.* December, 1847, in Buckfield, Maine, Julia Davis LONG, *d.* 31st October, 1882, dau. of Zadoc and Julia (TEMPLE) LONG.

COLONIAL FAMILIES OF THE UNITED STATES

ISSUE

I. Julia Matilda, *b.* 15th June, 1849.
II. JOSEPH NELSON, *b.* 4th October, 1851, the subject of this memoir.
III. Zadoc Long, *b.* 29th December, 1854.
IV. Percival Wayland, *b.* 25th December, 1857.
V. Allan Temple, *b.* 27th June, 1860.
VI. Charles Davis, *b.* 12th November, 1861.
VII. Nellie Mandana, *b.* 8th April, 1873.

Buckminster

According to tradition the American ancestors of this family was Thomas BUCK-MINSTER who lived in Brookline and came from Wales before 1640; *m.* Johanna, surname unknown, who after his death *m.* Edwin GARFIELD; his son

JOSEPH BUCKMINSTER, *m.* Elizabeth CLARKE, dau. of Huth and Elizabeth CLARKE who lived in Watertown and afterwards Roxbury, their son

COLONEL JOSEPH BUCKMINSTER, *b.* 2d August, 1710, was Captain of a Company of Grenadiers in the Port Royal Expedition; was in command 22d April, 1756; was ordered by Governor SHERLEY to raise 50 men out of his Regiment for the Crown Point Expedition; in 1702 he removed to Framingham; *m.* Martha SHARP, dau. of Lieut. John and Martha (VOSE) SHARP, he son of Robert SHARP of Braintree, 1642. She dau. of Robert and Sarah VOSE, said to have come from Lancashire, England, and settled on a farm that part of Dorchester, now Milton, their dau. Sybilla BUCKMINSTER *m.* Lieut. John WHITE, *b.* 22d August, 1695, *d.* 26th August, 1778, their son

THOMAS WHITE, *b.* 17th July, 1731; *d.* 25th February, 1822; *m.* 30th December, 1756, Abigail MUZZEY, *b.* circa 1739, their son

THOMAS WHITE, *b.* 24th November, 1767; *d.* 21st July, 1849; *m.* 2d September, 1784, Hannah ESTABROOK, *b.* 1762, *d.* 25th July, 1830, their son

DEACON JOSEPH WHITE, *b.* 24th January, 1792; *d.* 9th October, 1864; *m.* 30th January, 1817, Matilda DAVIS, *d.* 9th October, 1864, their son

NELSON DAVIS WHITE, *b.* 24th July, 1818; *d.* 2d March, 1889; *m.* December, 1847, Julia Davis LONG, *d.* 31st October, 1882, their son

JOSEPH NELSON WHITE, *b.* 4th October, 1851, the subject of this memoir.

Muzzey

The MUZZEYS were early in Lexington and were for a century and a half among the leading influential founders of that place.

ROBERT MUZZEY was freeman of Ipswich in 1634, his son

BENJAMIN MUZZEY, *m.* Alice DEXTER, *b.* in England, dau. of Richard DEXTER of Boston, 1642, and Charlestown, 1644, gd. dau. of the Rev. Samuel DEXTER of Malden, their son

BENJAMIN MUZZEY, Jr., of Cambridge Farms was a large land owner and tax payer; member of committees, an assessor and tithing man; *m.* Sarah, surname unknown, their son

JOHN MUZZEY of Lexington, opened the first public house there; was on the school committee; was Selectman and Assessor and a land owner in Templeton also; m. Elizabeth BRADSHAW, dau. of John and Mary BRADSHAW, and gd. dau. of Humphrey and Patience (BOWERS) BRADSHAW. Patience BRADSHAW was the dau. of George and Barberie BOWERS, their son

DEACON JOHN MUZZEY of Spencer, was Town Clerk, Selectman, Assessor, and a Representative; Member of the General Court; was appointed a Justice of the Peace by Governor HUTCHINSON; m. Rebecca REED, dau. of Benjamin and Rebecca (STONE) REED, son of William and Abigail (KENDALL) REED, he son of George REED, the son of William and Mabel (KENDALL) (?) REED, who came to New England from London in the ship *Defense* in 1635. Rebecca STONE was the dau. of Samuel and Dorcas (JONES) STONE. Samuel JONES (?) was the son of Samuel and Sarah (STEARNS) JONES, she the dau. of Isaac and Mary STEARNS. The Coat of Arms of the STEARNS family was: Or, a chevron between three crosses, flag sable. Crest: A cock starling ppr. Deacon John and Rebecca (REED) MUZZEY had issue, their dau.

ABIGAIL MUZZEY, b. circa 1739; m. 30th December, 1756, Thomas WHITE, b. 17th July, 1731, their son

DEACON JOSEPH WHITE, b. 24th January, 1792; m. 30th January, 1817, Matilda DAVIS, their son

NELSON DAVIS WHITE, b. 24th July, 1818; m. December, 1847, Julia Davis LONG; their son

JOSEPH NELSON WHITE, b. 4th October, 1851, the subject of this memoir.

Estabrook

REV. JOHN ESTABROOK of Lexington, Massachusetts, came from England in 1660 with two brothers, one of which settled in Concord and the other in Swanzey. John entered Harvard College in 1664; m. name unknown; his son

CAPTAIN JOSEPH ESTABROOK, b. 1669; d. 23d November, 1773, in Lexington; was Captain of the local military company; m. (firstly) 31st December, 1689, Millicent WOODHOUSE, dau. of Henry WOODHOUSE of London, England, and of Concord; m. (secondly) 25th August, 1693, Mrs. Hannah LORING of Hingham. His son by his first marriage was

CAPTAIN JOSEPH ESTABROOK, JR., was Captain of the local military company; Deacon of the church and filled almost every important office in the town; d. 19th August, 1740; m. (firstly) 8th July, 1713, Submit LORING, his step-sister, who d. 31st March, 1718; m. (secondly) 26th March, 1719, Hannah BOWERMAN, dau. of Joseph and Phoebe BOWERMAN, their son

EBENEZER ESTABROOK, b. 21st September, 1740; was Selectman 1784, 1786, 1788, 1791, 1794, 1798 and 1803; m. 13th December, 1759, Ruth REED, b. 7th November, 1741, dau. of Capt. Isaac and Rebecca REED, their dau.

HANNAH ESTABROOK, b. 1762; d. 25th July, 1830; m. 2d September, 1784, Thomas WHITE of Royalston, their son

COLONIAL FAMILIES OF THE UNITED STATES 481

JOSEPH WHITE, b. 24th January, 1792; d. 9th October, 1864; m. Matilda DAVIS, their son
NELSON DAVIS WHITE, b. 24th July, 1818; d. 9th October, m. Julia Davis LONG, their son
JOSEPH NELSON WHITE, b. 4th October, 1851, the subject of this memoir.

Mrs. Annie (Evans) White's Ancestry

The EVANS family were Quakers.
WILLIAM EVANS, emigrant to Pennsylvania in 1696, d. 1747 (gravestone).
OWEN EVANS, lived in Pennsylvania, b. in Pennsylvania, 1699; d. 1754.
THOMAS EVANS, b. 23d July, 1737; d. 13th March, 1810.
BENJAMIN EVANS, b. in Pennsylvania, 12th October, 1760; moved to South Carolina and m. Hannah ————; moved to Waynesville, Warren County, Ohio, 1803; d. 10th July, 1830.

ISSUE

I. DAVID, of whom below.

DAVID EVANS, b. in South Carolina, 30th June, 1793; d. in Waynesville, Ohio, 17th November, 1861; m. in Miami meeting 2d June, 1813, Rachel BURNET, dau. of John and Rebecca BURNET, b. 18th October, 1794; d. May, 1885, in her ninety-first year.

ISSUE

I. John EVANS, b. 9th March, 1814.
II. Joel EVANS, b. 25th January, 1816.
III. SETH EVANS, b. 21st October, 1817, of whom later.
IV. Evan EVANS, b. 1st July, 1820; d. 21st October, 1821.
V. Owen EVANS, b. 17th August, 1821; d. 29th January, 1823.
VI. Rebecca EVANS, b. 15th August, 1823; d. 25th December, 1845.
VII. Benjamin EVANS, b. 16th December, 1824.
VIII. Mary EVANS, b. 27th July, 1826; d. 9th April, 1850.
IX. Hannah EVANS, b. 3d April, 1829; d. 14th November, 1889.
X. Ann EVANS, b. 1st May, 1831.
XI. Jason EVANS, b. 31st March, 1833.

SETH EVANS, b. 21st October, 1817; d. 13th December, 1890; he went to Cincinnati when he was twenty-eight years old, and became one of the leading and successful business men of the city; m. 25th October, 1848, Winifred Miller BROWN, their dau.
Annie EVANS, m. 14th September, 1875, JOSEPH NELSON WHITE, the subject of this memoir.

Ancestry of Julia Davis (Long) White

THOMAS CLARKE one of the Pilgrims; came to Plymouth, Massachusetts, in the *Ann* in 1625; *d.* 24th March, 1697; his gravestone still stands on Burial Hill in Plymouth; he lived in Plymouth and *m.* Susannah RING; his son

JAMES CLARK, *b.* 1636, and lived in Plymouth; *m.* in 1657 to Abigail LOTHROP, *b.* 1639, dau. of Rev. John LOTHROP, who came over in the *Griffin* in 1635, and was the first minister in Barnstable, where his house still stands, being used as a public library; his son

THOMAS CLARK, *b.* and lived in Plymouth; called "Silver headed Thomas" because, scalped by Indians when a boy, he wore a silver plate; *m.* (secondly) Elizabeth CROW; his son

JOSIAH CLARK, *b.* 1690, and lived in Plymouth; *m.* Thankful TUPPER; their son

ISRAEL CLARK, *b.* 1720, and lived in Plymouth; *m.* Deborah POPE, of Sandwich, Massachusetts, their dau.

THANKFUL CLARK, *b.* 1750, and lived in Plymouth; *m.* 1770, Miles LONG, who came to Plymouth from North Carolina, their son

THOMAS LONG, *b.* August, 1771; lived in Plymouth and Middleboro, Massachusetts, and moved to Buckfield, Maine, in 1806, *d.* there 16th October, 1861; *m.* 8th November, 1795, Bathsheba CHURCHILL, their son

ZADOC LONG, *b.* in Middleboro, Massachusetts, 28th July, 1800; lived in Buckfield, Maine; *d.* at Winchendon, Massachusetts, 3d February, 1873; *m.* 31st August, 1824, at New Gloucester, Maine, to Julia Temple DAVIS.

ISSUE

I. JULIA DAVIS LONG, of whom later.
II. Persis Seaver LONG, *b.* 14th February, 1828; *d.* 27th April, 1893; *m.* ———— BARTLETT.
III. Zadoc LONG, Jr., *b.* 26th April, 1834; *d.* 14th September, 1866.
IV. John Davis LONG, *b.* 27th October, 1838; *m.* 13th September, 1870.

JULIA DAVIS LONG, *b.* 26th April, 1834; *d.* 31st October, 1882; *m.* December, 1847, Nelson Davis WHITE, their son

JOSEPH NELSON WHITE, *b.* 4th October, 1851, the subject of this memoir.

Ancestry of Matilda (Davis) White

DOLOR DAVIS, *b.* circa 1600 in Kent, England; came to Boston with Simon WILLARD in May, 1634; settled in Cambridge, then in Duxbury about 1640, then in Barnstable in 1643, where he *d.* 1673, having meantime lived in Concord from 1655 to 1666, where his sons settled; *m.* circa 1624 Margarey WILLARD, *b.* 1602, dau. of Richard WILLARD, of Horsemondon, Kent. She was sister of Major Simon WILLARD, of Concord, where she *d.* between 1655 and 1666, their son

SAMUEL DAVIS, *m.* 11th January, 1665, at Lynn, Massachusetts, Mary MEADS or MEADOWS, who *d.* 3d October, 1710, their son

LIEUTENANT SIMON DAVIS, b. 9th August, 1683; d. at Holden, 16th February, 1763, and buried there; m. 1713, Dorothy, surname unknown, who d. at Holden, 21st July, 1776, and is there buried; their son
SIMON DAVIS, b. 17th May, 1714; lived at Rutland and d. 9th April, 1754; m. Hannah GATES, of Stowe, who d. 7th January, 1761, aged 46 years; their son
DEACON DAVID DAVIS, b. 1740; lived in Paxton; m. 22d November, 1764, Abigail BROWN; their son
SIMON DAVIS, b. 2d September, 1765, at Paxton; lived at Paxton, West Boylston, and Falmouth, Maine; d. at Falmouth (now Deering) 17th March, 1810; his gravestone is there; m. (firstly) 25th February, 1789, Persis NEWTON.

ISSUE

I. Matilda DAVIS, m. 30th January, 1817, Joseph WHITE, their son Nelson Davis WHITE, b. 24th July, 1818; m. December, 1847, Julia Temple LONG; their son JOSEPH NELSON WHITE, b. 4th October, 1851, the subject of this memoir.
II. Persis DAVIS, m. Isaac GROSS.
III. Julia Temple DAVIS, b. at Falmouth, Maine, 17th February, 1797; d. in Buckfield, Maine, 19th September, 1869, and there buried; m. 31st August, 1824, Zadoc LONG; moved to New Gloucester, where her mother married, 19th August, 1813, a third husband, Capt. David NELSON of that town.

Frothingham

WILLIAM FROTHINGHAM came from Holderness, Yorkshire, England, and became an inhabitant of Charlestown, Massachusetts, in 1630; d. 10th October, 1651. He came with about eight hundred others in John WINTHROP's fleet who located at Salem, Charlestown, Cambridge, Boston, etc. In the church in Boston his name with that of his wife Anna are Nos. 74 and 75. 19th October, 1630 he desired admission as Freeman and was sworn 6th March, 1632. Seized of land in the neighborhood of Eden Street next to Bunker's, and the same is now occupied in part by his descendants. Wife's name was Anna, surname unknown. A rough sketch of a stone now standing in Charlestown burying ground bears the following inscription: "Anne FROTHINGHAM, Aged 87 Years, Died ye 28 of July, 1674." The presumption is she was the widow of William FROTHINGHAM. No authentic history of the family back of William FROTHINGHAM excepting the general fact that he belonged to the Holderness family of FROTHINGHAM, Kent, whose son Robert FROTHINGHAM m. Elizabeth HANSARD, dau. of ———— HANSARD of County Lincoln, 21 Henry VII, whose son Peter HANSARD of South Frothingham in Holderness made his will 21st July, 33 Henry VIII, whose son Edmund FROTHINGHAM was living in 1584 and whose son Edward FROTHINGHAM, had three children: I. Christopher, b. 1572; II. Francis; III. Michael, the first of whom was aged 12 in 1584.

ISSUE

I. Berthia, *b.* 7th February, 1631.
II. John, *b.* 10th August, 1633.
III. Elizabeth, *b.* 15th March, 1635.
IV. Peter, *b.* 15th April, *bapt.* 17th April, 1636; *d.* 12th December, 1688; Freeman 1668; *m.* 14th March, 1665, Mary LORDEN.
V. MARY, *b.* 1st April, *bapt.* 8th April, 1638, of whom later.
VI. Nathaniel, *b.* 16th April; *bapt.* 26th April, 1640; *d.* 12th December, 1688; Freeman, 1671.
VII. Stephen, *b.* 11th November, 1641; *bapt.* same month.
VIII. Hannah, *b.* 29th January, 1643; *m.* 5th July, 1665, Joseph KETTLE.
IX. Joseph, *b.* 1st December, 1645; *d.* soon.
X. Samuel, *d.* 25th May, 1683; Freeman, 1671; *m.* 1668, Ruth GEORGE, dau. of John GEORGE.
XI. William (perhaps).

MARY FROTHINGHAM, *b.* 1st April; *bapt.* 8th April, 1638; *m.* 17th November 1663, Thomas WHITE, *b.* 28th January, 1636; their son

THOMAS WHITE, *b.* 15th October, 1664; *m.* 4th January, 1684, Sarah RAND; their son

LIEUTENANT JOHN WHITE, *b.* 22d August, 1695; *m.* 24th July, 1728, Sybilla BUCKMINSTER; their son

THOMAS WHITE, *b.* 17th July, 1731; *d.* 25th February, 1822; *m.* 30th December 1756, Abigail MUZZEY, *b.* circa 1739; their son

THOMAS WHITE, *b.* 24th November, 1767; *d.* 21st July, 1849; *m.* 2d September, 1784, Hannah ESTABROOK, *b.* 1762, *d.* 25th July, 1830; their son

DEACON JOSEPH WHITE, *b.* 24th January, 1792; *d.* 9th October, 1864; *m.* 30th January, 1817, Matilda DAVIS, *d.* 9th October, 1864; their son

NELSON DAVIS WHITE, *b.* 24th July, 1818; *d.* 2d March, 1889; *m.* December 1847, Julia Davis LONG, *d.* 31st October, 1882; their son

JOSEPH NELSON WHITE, *b.* 4th October, 1851, the subject of this memoir.

Arms.—(Frothingham) Azure a bend between six mullets or.
Crest.—On a torce a buck trippant ppr. armed gules.
Motto.—Servabo Fidem.

White

WILLIAM GARDNER WHITE of St. Paul, Minnesota; *b.* in South Hadley, Massachusetts, 30th September, 1854; *m.* 22d May, 1878, Carolyn Elizabeth HALL.

Lineage

ELDER JOHN WHITE of Cambridge and Hadley, Massachusetts, and Hartford, Connecticut; *d.* December, 1683; will dated 17th December, 1683; one of the original proprietors of Hartford; removed to Hadley, 1659, and went back to Hartford before 1675, and was prominent in affairs of both towns; Freeman 4th March, 1633; came in the *Lion* from London, England; arrived at Boston, 16th September, 1632, and settled in Cambridge (then called Newtown); Deputy from Hadley, 1664 and 1669; representative in General Assembly; *m.* in England Mary ———.

ISSUE

I. Mary, *b.* in England; *m.* Jonathan GILBERT.
II. NATHANIEL, *b.* 1629, of whom later.
III. Lieutenant Daniel, *d.* 27th July, 1713; took oath of allegiance 8th February, 1669; Freeman, 1690; *m.* 1st November, 1661, Sarah CROW, *b.* before 1646, *d.* 1719, dau. of John CROW.

ISSUE

1. Sarah, *b.* 14th October, 1662.
2. Mary, *b.* 1664; *d.* young.
3. Mary, *b.* 5th or 25th August, 1665; *m.* (firstly) ——— WELLS; *m.* (secondly) after 1713, ——— BARNARD.
4. Elizabeth, *b.* 13th November, 1668.
5. Daniel, *b.* 4th July, 1671.
6. Hannah, *b.* 4th July, 1674; *d.* young.
7. Esther, *d.* 1675.
8. John, *b.* 16th November, 1676; *d.* young.
9. Esther, again.
10. Hannah, *d.* September, 1679.
11. Esther, again.
12. Mehitable, *b.* 14th March, 1683.

IV. Sarah, *m.* (firstly) Stephen TAYLOR; *m.* (secondly) 15th October, 1666, husband's name unknown; *m.* (thirdly) February, 1679, Walter HICKSON, and had issue by each.
V. Jacob, *b.* at Hartford, 9th October, 1645.

CAPTAIN NATHANIEL WHITE of Meriden, Connecticut; *b.* probably in England, 1629; *d.* 27th August, 1711; resided in Middletown, Haddam and Meriden, Connecticut; was of the Grand Jury, 1662; Ensign of Middletown Farm Band, 1664; Lieutenant, 1677; Captain, 1699; Commissioner of Middletown, Haddam and Meriden, 1699, and many years thereafter; Deputy for one hundred and fourteen different times between 1659 and 1710, serving fifty-one years continuously between 1661 and 1710; *m.* (firstly) Elizabeth surname unknown *b.* 1625, *d.* 1690; *m.* (secondly) Martha (COIT) MOULD, *b.* probably 1644, *d.* 14th April, 1730, widow of Hugh MOULD and dau. of John COIT.

ISSUE BY FIRST MARRIAGE

I. NATHANIEL, *b.* 7th July, 1652, of whom later.
II. Elizabeth, *b.* 7th March, 1655.
III. John, *b.* 9th April, 1657.
IV. Mary, *b.* 7th April, 1659.
V. Daniel, *b.* 23d February, 1662.
VI. Sarah, *b.* 22d January, 1664.
VII. Jacob, *b.* 10th May, 1665.
VIII. Joseph, *b.* 20th February, 1667.

DEACON NATHANIEL WHITE of Hadley, Massachusetts; *b.* 7th July, 1652; *d.* 15th February, 1742; served in third Indian War and took part in the Deerfield Meadow Fight, 29th February, 1704; *m.* Elizabeth SAVAGE, *b.* 3d June, 1655, *d.* 30th January, 1742.

ISSUE AMONG OTHERS

I. Joseph, *b.* 28th February, 1687.

DEACON JOSEPH WHITE of Hadley, Massachusetts; *b.* 28th February, 1687; *d.* before 1770; served in Regiment commanded by Col. Benj. GOLDTHWART, which was sent to reinforce the Colonial Forces at Lake George, 1756; *m.* Abigail CROFT, *b.* 29th September, 1688; *d.* 15th November, 1770.

ISSUE AMONG OTHERS

I. JOSIAH, *b.* 1729.

DEACON JOSIAH WHITE of South Hadley, Massachusetts; *b.* 1729; *d.* 29th March, 1809; served as a Member of the South Hadley Company, commanded by Capt. Samuel SMITH, which marched to the relief of Fort William Henry, 1757; *m.* Mary SMITH, *b.* 3d March, 1733, *d.* 21st September, 1818.

ISSUE AMONG OTHERS

I. ELDAD, *b.* 31st March, 1768, of whom below.

ELDAD WHITE, *b.* 31st March, 1768; *d.* 11th April, 1823; *m.* Hannah Day, *b.* 7th March, 1769, *d.* 15th March, 1851.

COLONIAL FAMILIES OF THE UNITED STATES

ISSUE AMONG OTHERS

I. CYRUS, *b.* 21st October, 1795, of whom below.

CYRUS WHITE, *b.* 21st October, 1795; *d.* 1876; *m.* Rebecca WHITE, *b.* 15th May, 1805, *d.* 15th July, 1843.

ISSUE AMONG OTHERS

I. William, *b.* 30th June, 1829, of whom below.

WILLIAM WHITE of South Hadley, Massachusetts; *b.* 30th June, 1829; *d.* 31st December, 1892; *m.* Amanda PRESTON, *b.* 30th August, 1830.

ISSUE

I. WILLIAM GARDNER, *b.* 30th September, 1854, the subject of this memoir.

Arms.—Argent, a chevron gules, between three popinjays vert, beaked, legged and collared gules, within a bordure azure charged with eight bezants.

Crest.—Between two wings argent, a popinjay's head vert, collared gules, holding in the beak a rose gules, slipped and leaved of the second.

Motto.—Virtus omnia vincit.

Residence.—767 Goodrich Avenue, St. Paul, Minnesota.

Societies.—Colonial Wars.

Whitman

CHARLES SEYMOUR WHITMAN, b. 28th August, 1868, at Sprague, Connecticut; m. 22d December, 1908, at New York City, Olive HITCHCOCK, dau. of Oliver Nelson and Josephine (LLOYD) HITCHCOCK.

ISSUE

I. Olive, b. 28th October, 1910, New York City.
II. Charles Seymour, Jr., b. 11th March, 1915, at Albany, New York.

CHARLES SEYMOUR WHITMAN, A.B., Amherset College, 1890; A.M., Williams College, 1904; LL.B., New York University, 1894; LL.D., from Amherst and from New York University 1913; LL.D., Williams, 1916, engaged in the practice of Law after graduation; was assistant corporation counsel, New York City, 1901–1903; President of the City Magistrates' Court, New York City, 1904–1907, and Judge of the Court of General Sessions by appointing of Governor HUGHES, 1907; District Attorney New York County from 1st January, 1910 to 1914; elected 3d November, 1914, Governor of the State of New York; reëlected 7th November, 1916. Governor WHITMAN comes of a long line of distinguished ancestors, among whom are three Colonial Governors, namely, Governor John HAYNES of Massachusetts and Connecticut, Governor George WYLLYS of Connecticut, and Governor John WEBSTER of Connecticut. He descends also from the well-known BULKELEY family of Connecticut and from the SEYMOURS who fought so well first for the Colonies and later for the States. Those of his ancestors who were not soldiers, were either prominent men of letters or members of the governing bodies in town or colony, wealthy landowners or ministers.

Lineage

JOHN WHITMAN, the emigrant ancestor of nearly all of the WHITMAN name in America, was one of the earliest settlers of Weymouth, Massachusetts. He came probably from Holt, Norfolk, England, though the family name appears also in Chesham, County Bucks. He was made a Freeman of Weymouth in December 1638, and became Deacon of the Church there on 13th March, 1638–1639; he was a town officer in 1643, and in 1646, was commissioned one of three to "end small causes;" from 14th May, 1645, till the 16th March, 1680, he was Ensign of the Military Company in Weymouth; on 19th March, 1648, he sold land in Braintree, and acknowledged this sale 26th November, 1656; his will was dated 9th March, 1685, and proved 19th March, 1692–1693; in it he makes bequests to his sons, John, Abijah, Zechariah; daughters Sarah JOANES, Mary PRATT, Judah, wife of Philip KING, Elizabeth GREEN; grandchildren, Joseph and Elizabeth GREEN and the chil-

COLONIAL FAMILIES OF THE UNITED STATES 489

dren of deceased daughter Hannah FRENCH; he *d.* 13th November, 1692, aged about 90 years; he *m.* probably Ruth ———.

ISSUE

I. Thomas, *b.* about 1629; *d.* 1712; *m.* 22d November, 1656, Abigail BYRAM, dau. of Ensign Nicholas and Martha (SHAW) BYRAM; all their children but John were born at Brodgewater (Bridgewater ?).

ISSUE

1. John, *b.* 5th September, 1658; *d.* 28th July, 1728; *m.* Hannah PRATT.
2. Ebenezer, *b.* about 1673; *d.* 1713; *m.* Abigail BURNHAM.
3. Nicholas, *b.* 1675; *d.* 6th August, 1746; *m.* (firstly) Sarah VINING; *m.* (secondly) Mary CARY; *m.* (thirdly) Mary CONANT.
4. Susanna, *m.* Benjamin WHITE.
5. Mary, *m.* probably Seth LEACH.
6. Naomi, *m.* William SHAW.
7. Hannah, *m.* David LEACH.

II. John, *d.* 1st February, 1713; *m.* (firstly) 19th October, 1662, Ruth REED, probably dau. of William REED, *d.s.p.* 1662; *m.* (secondly) Abigail HOLLIS. The following list of children is drawn from two sources: one the Weymouth Vital Records, the other a list compiled fifty years ago by Judge WHITMAN.

ISSUE

1. Ruth, *b.* 1663–1665.
2. Mary, *b.* 1666; *m.* Capt. John TORREY.
3. John, *b.* 22d June, 1668; *m.* Dorothy PRATT.
4. Ebenezer, *b.* 1670; *m.* Deborah RICHARDS.
5. Experience, *b.* 1673.
6. Samuel, *b.* 1673 (?); *m.* (firstly) Mary RICHARDS; *m.* (secondly) Elizabeth TURNER.

III. Sarah, *d.* 11th June, 1718; aged about 65 years; *m.* about 1653, Abraham JONES, son of Thomas Jones "the tailor" of Bull; *b.* 1629, *d.* 25th January, 1718.

ISSUE

1. Thomas JONES, *b.* about 1656–1657.
2. Abraham JONES, *b.* 1659.
3. Joseph JONES, *d.* 1769; *m.* Lydia ———.
4. Benjamin JONES, *b.* 1668; *d.* 27th December, 1748; *m.* Elizabeth ———; *b.* 1668, *d.* 13th September, 1748.
5. Deacon John JONES, *b.* 1669; *m.* (firstly), Sarah ———; *m.* (secondly) (perhaps) Abigail ———.

6. Ephraim JONES, *d.* 27th January, 1752; *m.* (firstly) 13th January, 1708, Mary SPEAR; *m.* (secondly) 5th April, 1714, Mary ADAMS; *m.* (thirdly) 10th April, 1735, Hannah COPELAND.
7. Josiah JONES.
8. Sarah JONES, before her father's will was drawn in 1718, *m.* Mordecaia LINCOLN, the gr. gr. gr. gd. father of Abraham LINCOLN (see Abraham LINCOLN, Vol. III, "Colonial Families").

IV. Mary, *b.* 1634, *d.s.p.* 10th July, 1716; *m.* 22d November, 1656, John PRATT.
V. Hannah, *b.* 24th August, 1641; *d.* before her father's will was drawn in 1685; *m.* 19th September, 1660, Capt. Stephen FRENCH.

ISSUE

1. Mary FRENCH, *b.* 11th May, 1662; *d.* before 1718; *m.* William BADLAM.
2. Stephen FRENCH, *b.* 1st June, 1664; *d.* 23d January, 1742; *m.* Abigail BEAL.
3. Samuel FRENCH, *b.* 5th May, 1668.
4. Hannah FRENCH, *b.* 19th April, 1670, probably *d.* unmarried.
5. Elizabeth FRENCH, *b.* 29th April, 1674, probably *d.* unmarried.

VI. REVEREND ZECHARIAH, *b.* 1644, of whom below.
VII. Abiah, *b.* Weymouth about 1646; *d.* 28th January, 1727–1728, in his eighty-second year; *m.* Mary FORD, who *d.* 15th March, 1715, dau. of Andrew FORD.

ISSUE

1. Elizabeth, *b.* 1673; *d.* before 1722; *m.* Timothy COOPER.
2. Lydia, *b.* 1678; *d.* 1750; *m.* Capt. John THOMAS.
3. John, *b.* 1681; *d.* 1758; *m.* (firstly) 25th March, 1713, Rebecca MANLEY.
4. Mary, *b.* 14th October, 1683; *d.* after husband's will was drawn 1757 *m.* John DAILEY.
5. Zachary, *b.* 2d January, 1685; *d.s.p.*
6. Eleanor, *b.* 3d September, 1688; *m.* (pub. 10th September, 1714) William TURNER.
7. Abiah, *b.* 30th November, 1690; *d.* 30th January, 1770, aged 80 years; *m.* (firstly) 28th October, 1715, Ruth PITTEE; *m.* (secondly) 3d May 1739, Sarah REED.

VIII. Elizabeth, *d.* 2d February, 1720; *m.* May, 1657, Joseph GREEN.

ISSUE

1. Joseph GREEN, *b.* 2d or 28th April, 1658; *m.* (firstly) Ann ————; *m.* (secondly) his intention was published three times with three different women; which one he married, or whether all three, is not certain.

COLONIAL FAMILIES OF THE UNITED STATES

2. John GREEN, b. 16th or 22d July, 1661; d. 1734; m. Patience ———.
3. Elizabeth GREEN, b. 5th April, 1664; m. John GURNEY.
4. Mary GREEN, b. 15th August, 1667.
5. Zachary GREEN, b. 7th April, 1671.

IX. Judith, b. (probably youngest dau.); m. prior to 1672, Philip KING, of Weymouth, who d. in 1710, some time before his wife.

ISSUE

1. Mary KING, m. John LEONARD.
2. Elizabeth KING, m. 17th December, 1696, John HALL.
3. Experience KING, b. 1678; d. 1752; m. 2d June, 1703, Nicholas WHITE.
4. Hannah KING, m. (perhaps firstly) John ALDEN; perhaps secondly, Jonathan PADDLEFORD.
5. Lydia KING, m. Nathaniel ROGERS, sixth in descent from John ROGERS the Martyr, according to the family tradition.
6. Judith KING, m. 8th January, 1712-1713, Ebenezer WILLIAMS.
7. John KING, b. 1681; d. 1741; m. 1st February, 1699-1700, Alice DEAN.
8. Abigail KING, m. about 1700, Jonathan PADDLEFORD (Philip KING's will and the Weymouth town records disagree about which of these two girls married Jonathan PADDLEFORD.

REV. ZECHARIAH WHITMAN, b. 1644; d. at Hull, Massachusetts, 5th November, 1726; graduated from Harvard in 1668 and was ordained 13th September, 1670; he was first minister at Point Alderton, Nantasket or Hull; Freeman, May-1673; he owned considerably property, some at Milford, Connecticut, by inheritance, and some at Stow, Massachusetts, on the Assabet River, through his wife; he was a "good scholar and penman and wrote most of the wills and legal documents in Hull;" his records and family papers, which were destroyed by fire about 1780, were kept first by his son the Reverend Samuel, and later by his grandson, the Rev. Elnathan WHITMAN of Hartford; m. at Roxbury, 26th October, 1671, Sarah ALCOCK, bapt. at Roxbury, 26th August, 1650, d. at Hull, 3d April, 1715, dau. of Dr. John ALCOCK, of Roxbury.

ISSUE

I. Zechariah, b. 1672; d. 1752; m. (firstly) Sarah TREAT; m. (secondly) Damaris CARMEN.
II. John, b. 1674; d. 22d February, 1684; the stone over his grave, put up first by his father, is the oldest in the Hull graveyard.
III. Joanna, m. Ephraim or John HUNT.
IV. REVEREND SAMUEL, b. 1676-1677, of whom later.
V. Sarah, d. 29th September, 1784, at Hull; m. (firstly) ——— COCKS; m. (secondly) Lieut. Robert GOULD, Sr., as his third wife; she d. without issue.

vi. Elizabeth, *d.* 19th November, 1708, at Hull.
vii. John (again), 1688; *d.* 3d August, 1772; *m.* (firstly) widow Mary GRAVES; *m.* (secondly) Dorcas (GREEN) CHITTY, widow.
viii. Mary, *m.* Nathaniel JACOBS, of Hull.
ix. Eunice, *b.* 10th April, 1696; *d.* 5th October, 1734.

REV. SAMUEL WHITMAN, *b.* 1676–1677; *d.* 31st July, 1751, at Farmington, Connecticut; graduated from Harvard in 1696; he is said to have tutored there for a short time; later he taught the Grammar School at Salem, Massachusetts; he was ordained 10th December, 1706, and removed to Farmington, where he was minister till his death; he ranked among the foremost literary men of New England; in 1726, and for twenty years thereafter, he was a Fellow of Yale; *m.* at Hartford 19th March, 1707, Sarah STODDARD, *b.* at Northampton, Massachusetts, 1st April, 1686, *d.* at Farmington, 10th September, 1755, dau. of Rev. Solomon and Esther (WARHAM) STODDARD.

ISSUE

i. Rev. Elnathan, *b.* at Farmington, 12th January, 1709; *d.* 4th March, 1777; *m.* Abigail STANLEY.
ii. Solomon, *b.* 20th April, 1710; *d.* 13th September, 1803; *m.* Susanna COLE.
iii. Eunice, *b.* 24th February, 1712; *d.* 2d February, 1777; *m.* Col. John STRONG.
iv. JOHN, *b.* 22d December, 1713, of whom below.
v. Dr. Samuel, *b.* 13th January, 1716; *d.* unmarried 4th December, 1751.
vi. Sarah, *b.* 12th March, 1718; *d.* 24th March, 1805; *m.* Rev. John TRUMBULL.
vii. Elizabeth, *b.* 17th January, 1721; *d.s.p.* 27th December, 1795; *m.* Rev. Thomas STRONG.

DEACON JOHN WHITMAN, *b.* at Farmington, 22d December, 1713; *d.* at West Hartford, 10th July, 1800; *m.* (firstly) Abigail PANTRY, *bapt.* at West Hartford, 12th March, 1712; *d.* at West Hartford, 19th February, 1765, dau. of John and Mary (NORTON) PANTRY; *m.* (secondly) 24th January, 1768, Hannah WELLS, dau. of Ebenezer and Rachel (SKINNER) WELLS, *b.* 4th November, 1728, *d.* 28th October, 1802; John WHITMAN was deacon in the West Hartford Church for nearly half a century. He resided on the PANTRY farm in that town; all his children were by the first marriage.

ISSUE

i. Abigail, *b.* 12th November, 1739; *d.* 12th March, 1758; *m.* Ebenezer WELLS.
ii. JOHN, *b.* 11th February, 1741, of whom below.
iii. Lucy, *b.* 10th January, 1745; *d.* 4th May, 1810; *m.* Capt. Charles SEYMOUR. This couple are also the ancestors of Charles Seymour WHITMAN, the subject of this sketch.

COLONIAL FAMILIES OF THE UNITED STATES

IV. Sarah, *b.* 27th February, 1747; *d.* 16th November, 1834; *m.* (firstly) Thomas Hart HOOKER; *m.* (secondly) Capt. Seth COLLINS.

V. Eleanor, *b.* July, 1752; *d.* young.

VI. Captain Samuel, *b.* 29th July, 1753; *d.* 7th February, 1810; *m.* Abigail ABBOTT.

VII. Eleanor (again), *b.* 20th July, 1755; *d.* 20th November, 1827; *m.* Ebenezer FAXON.

JOHN WHITMAN, *b.* at West Hartford, 11th February, 1741; *d.* there, 22d Septemper, 1813; was a farmer in West Hartford and built a house there which was occupied by his descendants; *m.* (firstly) at Bloomfield, Connecticut, 6th December, 1764, Anne SKINNER, *b.* at Bloomfield, 28th November, 1741, *d.* 28th November, 1806, dau. of Timothy and Ruth (COLTON) SKINNER; *m.* (secondly) 28th October, 1807, Eleanor (MONTAGUE) PRATT.

ISSUE

I. James, *b.* 2d September, 1765; *d.* 17th April, 1833; *m.* Abigail BUTLER.

II. Dr. Timothy, *b.* 13th April, 1768; *d.* 30th May, 1830; *m.* Laura SEYMOUR.

III. JOHN PANTRY, *b.* 26th November, 1770, of whom below.

IV. Anna, *b.* 23d May, 1774; *d.* 11th April, 1845; *m.* Timothy BALCH.

V. Lucy, *b.* 1776; *d.s.p.* August, 1796.

VI. Eunice, *b.* 1778; *d.* young.

VII. Eunice (again), *b.* 1779–1780; *d.* 8th May, 1846; *m.* Lemuel HURLBUT, Jr.

VIII. Ruth, *b.* 28th September, 1784; *d.* 11th February, 1858; *m.* Asahel THOMPSON.

JOHN PANTRY WHITMAN, *b.* at West Hartford, 20th November, 1770; *d.* at Williamstown, Massachusetts, 18th March, 1834; removed from West Hartford to Williamstown, where he and his brother Dr. Timothy were connected in business together they gave fifteen hundred dollars to Williams College in 1827, and in 1842, the widow Lucy WHITMAN gave one thousand dollars to the same College; *m.* at West Hartford, 26th June, 1796, his cousin Lucy SEYMOUR, dau. of Capt. Charles and Lucy (WHITMAN) SEYMOUR, *b.* at West Hartford, 23d December, 1768, *d.* at Williamstown, 1st February, 1853.

ISSUE

I. SEYMOUR, *b.* 15th August, 1805, of whom below.

II. Lucy Skinner, *b.* 5th March, 1808; *d.s.p.* 13th July, 1831; *m.* Dr. Henry LYMAN.

SEYMOUR WHITMAN, *b.* at Williamstown, 15th August, 1805; *d.* there 11th March 1856; was a merchant of Williamstown; in 1858, his homestead was sold to Williams College, as a residence for its Presidents; *m.* at Granville, New York, 28th January, 1833, Anna Maria BULKELEY, *b.* at Granville, New York, 21st September, 1806, *d.* at Hoosac Falls, New York, 9th April, 1886, dau. of Charles and Lucy (BEMAN) BULKELEY.

ISSUE

I. REV. JOHN SEYMOUR, *b.* 7th November, 1833, of whom later.
II. Lucy Beman, *b.* 25th July, 1835; *m.* Rev. John TATLOCK.
III. Charles Addison, *b.* 10th October, 1837; *d.* young.
IV. Charles Addison (again), *b.* 26th March, 1840; *d.* young.
V. Frances A., *b.* 1841; *m.* Professor Hans C. G. VON JAGERMANN.

REV. JOHN SEYMOUR WHITMAN, *b.* at Williamstown, 7th November, 1833; *d.* in New York City 28th February, 1909; graduated from Williams College in 1854, and from Union Theological Seminary in 1860; had churches at Lyndon, Vermont; Charlemont, Massachusetts; Sprague, Connecticut; Rochester, Minnesota; Chatham, Ohio; and Canfield; *m.* at Auburn, New York, 13th June, 1860, Lillie ARNE, *b.* at Auburn, 29th April, 1833, *d.* at New York City, 6th March, 1904, dau. of Dr. David ARNE.

ISSUE

I. John Munroe, *b.* Rochester, Minnesota, 22d November, 1861; *d.* in New York City 1st September, 1902.
II. Mary Eva, *b.* Williamstown, Massachusetts, 30th November, 1862; *d.* Auburn, New York, 21st July, 1863.
III. Maria Louise, *b.* Sprague, Connecticut, 30th October, 1866.
IV. CHARLES SEYMOUR, *b.* 28th August, 1868, the subject of this memoir.

Arms.—Per Fesse, or and sable a maunch counterchanged.
Crest.—On the stump of a tree a buck.
Motto.—Per ardus surgo.
Residence.—Executive Mansion, Albany, New York.
Societies.—Society of Colonial Wars, Sons of the American Revolution, Order of Runnemede.
Clubs.—(New York) University, City, Union League, Century Association, Alpha Delta Phi, Sleepy Hollow, Ardsley, Aero, Republican, West Side Republican, etc.; Mason; Business Association; President Anti-Policy Society of New York; Trustee of New York Skin and Cancer Hospital.

Whitney

JOSEPH CUTLER WHITNEY, A.B., of Boston, Massachusetts; b. 7th December, 1856; m. 9th November, 1882, Georgina HAYWARD, m. dau. of George and Anne (UPTON) HAYWARD, M.D. Dr. HAYWARD was of Harvard University, 1842, and was gd. son of Lemuel HAYWARD, A. M., Harvard University, 1768; M.D. 1808, Surgeon of the Massachusetts Colony Army, 1775.

ISSUE

I. Henry Lawrence, b. 13th January, 1886.
II. George Hayward, b. 31st January, 1892.
III. Robert Upton, b. 6th November, 1895.

JOSEPH CUTLER WHITNEY graduated at Harvard University, A.B., 1878; Trustee of the Milton Public Library; Selectman of the Town of Milton; Surveyor of Highways; Overseer of the Poor, 1894–96.

Lineage

The ancestor of this family was John WHITNEY of Ilseworth, County Middlesex b. 1592; bapt. at St. Margaret's, Westminster, 20th July, 1592; d. 1st June, 1673; son of Thomas WHITNEY of Lambeth Marsh, who was possibly a descendant of the family of WHITNEY of Whitney County, Hereford; member of the Merchant Taylor's Company, London; emigrated to America, April, 1635, and settled in Watertown, Massachusetts; Town Clerk, 1655; m. (firstly) Elinor, surname not given, d. 11th May, 1659; m. (secondly) 29th September, 1659, Judah CLEMENT, who d.s.p. prior to 1673.

ISSUE

I. Mary, b. 23d May, 1619; d. in infancy.
II. John, b. 1621; d. 12th October, 1662; m. 1642, Ruth REYNOLDS, leaving issue, from whom descended Eli WHITNEY, b. 1765, d. 1825, the inventor of the Cotton Gin.
III. Richard, b. 1624; m. 1651, Martha COLDHAM, and had issue, from whom descended the Hon. William Collins WHITNEY, Secretary of the Navy, 1885, and the Professors Dwight WHITNEY of Yale College.
IV. Nathaniel, b. 1627; d. in infancy.
V. THOMAS, b. 1629, of whom later.
VI. Jonathan, b. 1634; m. 1656, Lydia JONES, dau. of Lewis JONES, d. 1702; had issue.
VII. Joshua, b. 15th July, 1635; d. 7th August, 1719; m. (firstly) Lydia, surname not given; m. (secondly) Mary, surname not given; m. (thirdly) Abigail TARBALL; left issue.

VIII. Caleb, d. 1640.
IX. Benjamin, b. 6th June, 1643; d. 1723; m. (firstly) Jane, surname not given; m. (secondly) Mary POOR; had issue.

THOMAS WHITNEY of Watertown, Massachusetts; b. 1629; d. 20th September, 1719; m. 11th January, 1655, Mary KENDALL.

ISSUE

I. THOMAS, b. 24th August, 1656, of whom later.
II. John, b. 9th May, 1659; d. in infancy.
III. John, d. in infancy.
IV. Eleazer (twin), b. 7th April, 1662; m. 11th April, 1687, Dorothy ROSS; dau. of James ROSS; had issue.
V. Elnathan (twin), b. 7th April, 1662, d.s.p.
VI. Mary, b. 22d December, 1663; d. in infancy.
VII. Bezaleel, b. 16th September, 1665.
VIII. Sarah, b. 23d March, 1667; m. Charles CHADWICK.
IX. Isaiah, b. 16th September, 1671; d. 1711; m. Sarah WOODWARD, dau. of George WOODWARD.
X. Mary, d. in infancy.
XI. Martha, b. 30th January, 1674; d. unmarried.

THOMAS WHITNEY of Watertown, Massachusetts; b. 24th August, 1656; d. 12th April, 1742; m. 29th January, 1679, Elizabeth LAWRENCE, d. 8th February, 1742.

ISSUE

I. Thomas, b. 17th September, 1681; m. 26th July, 1704, Mary BAKER; had issue.
II. Elizabeth, b. 16th February, 1683.
III. Mary, b. 13th January, 1686.
IV. BENJAMIN, b. 7th October, 1687, of whom later.
V. Nathan, m. 18th November, 1719, Mary HOLMAN, dau. of Jeremiah HOLMAN; had issue.
VI. Susanna.
VII. Abigail, m. 1724, John RAND.

BENJAMIN WHITNEY of Marlborough and Boston, Massachusetts; b. 7th October, 1687; d. 24th October, 1737; m. (firstly) 7th February, 1710, Sarah BARRETT, d. 15th February, 1730, dau. of John BARRETT; m. (secondly) 1730, Abigail BRIDGE, d. 1st August, 1767, dau. of Matthew BRIDGE.

ISSUE

I. Deborah, b. 7th November, 1711; m. Joseph WHEELER; had issue.
II. Barrett, b. 22d September, 1715; m. 1737, Elizabeth ADAMS.

COLONIAL FAMILIES OF THE UNITED STATES 497

III. David, b. 21st January, 1717; m. Mercy, surname not given.
IV. Persis, b. 10th January, 1719; m. Nathan GOODALE; had issue.
V. Solomon, b. 20th January, 1721; d. 1758; m. 5th October, 1749, Elizabeth SMITH; had issue.
VI. Sarah, b. 13th July, 1723; m. Abraham JOSLIN; had issue.
VII. Timothy, b. 6th July, 1725; d. in infancy.
VIII. Dinah, b. 12th July, 1727; m. 1756, Elijah LIVERMORE; had issue.
IX. Job, b. 22d October, 1729; graduated at Harvard, 1758; d. unmarried, 13th June, 1761.

ISSUE BY SECOND MARRIAGE

I. Abigail, b. 13th May, 1731; d.s.p. May, 1793; m. Samuel AUSTIN.
II. Benjamin, b. 9th May, 1732; d. unmarried 22d March, 1751.
III. George, b. 27th March, 1733; d. unmarried 26th December, 1751.
IV. SAMUEL, b. 5th September, 1734, of whom later.
V. Anna, b. 27th October, 1736; d.s.p. 2d January, 1762; m. 22d December, 1761, William BOWES.

SAMUEL WHITNEY of Boston, and Concord, Massachusetts, and Castine, Maine; b. 5th September, 1734; d. 29th May, 1808; m. 20th October, 1757, Abigail CUTLER, d. 2d July, 1813, dau. of David CUTLER.

ISSUE

I. Samuel, b. 15th July, 1759; d. unmarried, 1783.
II. David, b. 14th August, 1761; d. 17th September, 1818; m. (1) July, 1786, Betsy DERBY; left issue.
III. Benjamin, b. 11th April, 1763; d. unmarried, 1784.
IV. Anna, b. 30th July, 1764; d. 1788; m. 13th September, 1787, James ADAMS.
V. George, b. 22d September, 1765; d. 1805; leaving issue.
VI. James, b. 1st December, 1766; d. unmarried, 1796.
VII. Abigail, b. 22d April, 1768; d. unmarried 4th June, 1808.
VIII. Samuel Austin (twin), b. 19th January, 1769; d. 15th October, 1846; m. 28th July, 1801, Ruth PERKINS, d. 15th September, 1849, dau. of John PERKINS; had issue.
IX. Lydia (twin), b. 19th January, 1769; d. 1771.
X. JOSEPH, b. 27th September, 1771, of whom later.
XI. William, b. 13th November, 1772; d. unmarried, 1809.
XII. John, b. 19th December, 1773; d. unmarried, 1803.
XIII. Cyrus, b. 24th December, 1774; m. 28th December, 1795, Mary BREWER; had issue.
XIV. Sarah, b. 2d February, 1776; m. 5th May, 1808, David HOWE; had issue.
XV. Polly, b. 14th September, 1777; d. in infancy.
XVI Eben, b. 17th March, 1780; m. 27th August, 1807, Bathsheba HESTON. dau. of Col. Thomas HESTON; had issue.

XVII. Henry, *b.* 29th January, 1783; *d.* 27th April, 1837; *m.* Lucy PERKINS, dau. of John PERKINS; had issue.

JOSEPH WHITNEY of Boston, Massachusetts; *b.* 27th September, 1771; *m.* 24th September, 1793, Sallie COLLINS, who *d.* 22d September, 1799, dau. of Elizah COLLINS. He *d.* in Boston 24th June, 1812.

ISSUE

I. JOSEPH, *b.* 11th June, 1796, of whom below.

JOSEPH WHITNEY of Boston, Massachusetts; *b.* 11th June, 1796, *d.* 11th September, 1869; *m.* 23d July, 1822, Elizabeth PRATT, *d.* 5th January, 1890, dau. of John PRATT.

ISSUE

I. Caroline Elizabeth, *b.* 25th October, 1825; *d.* 24th April, 1908; *m.* 28th November, 1847, Hezron Ayers JOHNSON; had issue.
II. HENRY AUSTIN, *b.* 6th October, 1826, of whom later.
III. Sarah Josephine, *b.* 18th January, 1837; *d.* 25th March, 1842.

HENRY AUSTIN WHITNEY, A.M., of Boston, Massachusetts, *b.* there 6th October, 1826; *d.* there 21st February, 1889; graduated A.M. Harvard, 1846; President Boston and Providence Railroad; *m.* 3d March, 1852, Fanny LAWRENCE, *d.* at Boston, 28th January, 1883, dau. of William LAWRENCE.

I. Henry Lawrence, *b.* 27th October, 1853; *d.* young.
I. JOSEPH CUTLER, *b.* 7th December, 1856, the subject of this memoir.
III. Ellerton Pratt, *b.* 21st August, 1858; *m.* 5th June, 1901, Cushman SARGENT.
IV. Elizabeth, *b.* 23d March, 1860; *d.* 19th February, 1903; *m.* 30th October, 1884, James Jackson MINOT, M.D.; had issue.
V. Constance, *b.* 11th May, 1865; *m.* 11th September, 1890, Franz Edward ZORRAHN.

Arms.—Paly of six or and gules, a chief vert.
Crest.—A bull's head couped sable armed argent the points gules.
Motto.—Fortiter sustine.
Residence.—232 Marlboro Street, Boston, Massachusetts, "The Elms," Milton, Massachusetts.
Clubs.—Tennis and Racquet, Hoosic-Whisick, Exchange, Ponkapog (of Providence) and Country.

Wolcott

ROGER WOLCOTT, A.B., LL.B., of Milton, Massachusetts; *b.* 25th July, 1877; was educated at private schools; graduated at Harvard, A.B., 1899; LL.B., 1902.

Lineage

HENRY WOLCOTT, *bapt.* at Lydeard, St. Lawrence, County Somerset, 6th December, 1578; *d.* 30th May, 1655; son of John WOLCOTT, yeoman, of Tolland, County, Somerset; emigrated to America, March, 1630; settled in Windsor, Connecticut; Member First Assembly, Connecticut Colony, 1637; Member Connecticut House of Magistrates, 1638–1655; *m.* 19th January, 1606, Elizabeth SAUNDERS, *d.* 7th July, 1655, dau. of Thomas SAUNDERS of Lydeard, St. Lawrence.

ISSUE

I. John, *b.* 1607; *d.s.p.* in England.
II. Henry, *b.* 21st January, 1611; *d.* 12th July, 1680; *m.* 18th November, 1641, Sarah NEWBERRY; had issue.
III. George, *d.* 11th February, 1662; *m.* Elizabeth TREAT; had issue.
IV. Christopher, *d.s.p.*; 7th September, 1662.
V. SIMON, *b.* 11th September, 1624, of whom later.
VI. Anna, *m.* 16th October, 1646, Matthew GRISWOLD.
VII. Mary, *d.* 16th September, 1689; *m.* 25th June, 1646, Job DRAKE.

SIMON WOLCOTT of Windsor, Connecticut; *b.* 11th September, 1624; *d.* 11th September, 1687; Captain Simsbury Trainband, 1673; Townsman of Simsbury, 1674; *m.* (firstly) 19th March, 1657 Joanna COOK, *d.s.p.* 27th April, 1657, dau. of Aaron COOK; *m.* (secondly) 17th October, 1661, Martha PITKIN, *d.* 13th October, 1719.

ISSUE

I. Elizabeth, *b.* 19th August, 1662; *m.* 10th December, 1680, Daniel COOLEY.
II. Martha, *b.* 17th May, 1664; *m.* 6th January, 1686, Thomas ALLYN.
III. Simon, *b.* 24th June, 1666; *d.* 28th October, 1732; *m.* 5th December, 1689, Sarah CHESTER, dau. of Capt. John CHESTER; had issue.
IV. Joanna, *b.* 30th June, 1668; *m.* 2d September, 1690, John COLTON.
V. Henry, *b.* 20th May, 1670; *d.* November, 1746; *m.* (firstly) 1st April, 1696, Jane ALLYN, dau. of Thomas ALLYN; *m.* (secondly) Rachel TALCOTT; *m.* (thirdly) Hannah WOLCOTT, widow of John WOLCOTT.
VI. Christopher, *d.* in infancy.

VII. William, b. 6th November, 1676; d. 26th January, 1749; m. 5th November, 1706, Abiah HAWLEY; had issue.
VIII. ROGER, b. 4th January, 1679, of whom later.
IX. Mary, d. in infancy.

GOVERNOR ROGER WOLCOTT of Windsor, Connecticut; b. 4th January, 1679; d. 17th May, 1767; Representative to the General Assembly, 1709; Justice of the Peace, 1710; Councillor, 1714; Judge of County Court, 1721; Judge of Superior Court, 1732; Deputy Governor of Connecticut, 1741; Chief Justice, 1741; Major-General and second in command in Sir William PEPPERELL'S expedition which captured Louisbourg, 1745; Governor of Connecticut, 1750–1754; m. 3d December, 1702, Sarah DRAKE, d. 21st January, 1747, dau. of Job DRAKE.

ISSUE

I. Roger, b. 14th September, 1704; Major; Judge of Superior Court; m. (firstly) Marah NEWBERRY, dau. of Capt. Benjamin NEWBERRY; m. (secondly) Eunice (COLTON) ELY, d. 19th October, 1759, widow of John ELY and dau. of John COLTON; had issue.
II. Elizabeth, b. 10th April, 1706; m. Roger NEWBERRY.
III. Alexander, b. 20th January, 1708; d. 8th October, 1711.
IV. Samuel, b. 9th January, 1710; d. 27th December, 1717.
V. Alexander, b. 7th January, 1712; d. 25th March, 1795; graduated at Yale, 1731; M.D.; m. (firstly) Lydia ATWATER; m. (secondly) Mary ALLYN; m. (thirdly) Mary RICHARDS; had issue.
VI. Sarah, d. in infancy.
VII. Sarah, b. 31st January, 1715; d. unmarried, 5th January, 1735.
VIII. Hephzibah, b. 23d June, 1717; m. John STRONG.
IX. Josiah, b. 6th February, 1719; d.s.p. 29th January, 1802.
X. Erastus, b. 8th February, 1721; d. 10th May, 1722.
XI. Epaphras, b. 8th February, 1721; d. 3d April, 1733.
XII. Erastus, b. 21st September, 1722; Speaker of General Assembly; Judge of Probate; Chief Justice of County Court; Brigadier-General of Connecticut Troops, 1777; m. 10th February, 1746, Jerusha WOLCOTT, dau. of John WOLCOTT, he d. 14th September, 1793; had issue.
XIII. Ursula, b. 30th October, 1724; d. 5th April, 1788.
XIV. OLIVER, b. 20th November, 1726, of whom later.
XV. Mariann, b. 1st January, 1729; m. Thomas WILLIAMS.

GOVERNOR OLIVER WOLCOTT of Litchfield, Connecticut; b. 20th November, 1726; d. 1st December, 1797; graduated at Yale, 1747; M.D.; State Representative; Councillor; Chief Judge of Court of Common Pleas; Judge of Probate, 1774; Major-General of Militia; Member of Congress, 1775; signer of the Declaration of Independence, 1776; Lieutenant-Governor of Connecticut, 1786–1796; Governor 1796–1797; m. 21st January, 1755; Laura COLLINS d. 19th April, 1794, dau. of Capt. Daniel COLLINS.

COLONIAL FAMILIES OF THE UNITED STATES 501

ISSUE

I. Oliver, *d.* in infancy.
II. Oliver (Governor), *b.* 11th January, 1760; *d.* 1st June, 1833, leaving issue; graduated at Yale, 1778, LL.D.; Comptroller of United States Treasury, 1791; Secretary of Treasury, 1795-1810; Circuit Judge, 1801; Governor of Connecticut, 1817-1827; *m.* (firstly) June, 1785, Elizabeth STOUGHTON, dau. of Capt. John STOUGHTON.
III. Laura, *b.* 15th December, 1761; *m.* William MOSELEY.
IV. Mary Ann, *b.* 16th February, 1765; *d.* 1805; *m.* 13th October, 1789, Chauncey GOODRICH, Member of Congress, 1794-1801; United States Senator, 1807-1813.
V. FREDERICK, *b.* 2d November, 1767, of whom later.

FREDERICK WOLCOTT of Litchfield, Connecticut; *b.* 2d November, 1767; *d.* 25th May, 1837; graduated at Yale, 1786; Clerk of Court of Common Pleas, 1793; Clerk of Superior Court, Litchfield County, 1798-1836; State Senator, 1810-1823; Judge of Probate, 1796-1837; *m.* (firstly) 12th October, 1800, Elizabeth HUNTINGTON, *d.* 2d April, 1812, dau. of Col. Joshua HUNTINGTON; *m.* (secondly) 21st June, 1815, Sally Worthington (GOODRICH) COOKE; *d.* 14th Septmber, 1842, dau. of Rev. Samuel GOODRICH, and widow of Amos COOKE.

ISSUE BY FIRST MARRIAGE

I. Mary Ann Goodrich, *b.* 9th August, 1801; *m.* Asa WHITEHEAD.
II. Hannah Huntington, *b.* 14th January, 1803; *m.* Rev. Frederick FREEMAN.
III. JOSHUA HUNTINGTON, *b.* 29th August, 1804, of whom later.
IV. Elizabeth, *b.* 6th March, 1806; *d.* 15th October, 1875; *m.* John P. JACKSON.
V. Frederick Henry, *b.* 19th August, 1808; *m.* (firstly) Abby Woolsey HOWLAND dau. of Gardiner G. HOWLAND; *m.* (secondly) Sarah Elizabeth Chase MERCHANT, dau. of Gen. Charles S. MERCHANT; had issue.
VI. Laura Maria, *b.* 14th August, 1811; *m.* Robert G. RANKIN.

ISSUE BY SECOND MARRIAGE

I. Charles Moseley, *b.* 20th November, 1816; *m.* (firstly) Mary E. GOODRICH, dau. of Samuel GOODRICH; *m.* (secondly) Catherine RANKIN, dau. of Henry RANKIN; had issue.
II. Chauncey Goodrich, *d.* in infancy.
III. Henry Griswold, *b.* 4th November, 1820; *d.s.p.* 8th May, 1852; United States Consul at Shanghai, China.
IV. Mary Frances, *b.* 9th July, 1823; *m.* Theodore FROTHINGHAM.

JOSHUA HUNTINGHAM WOLCOTT of Boston, Massachusetts; *b.* 29th August, 1804; *d.* 6th January, 1891; *m.* (firstly) 12th November, 1844, Cornelia FROTHINGHAM, *d.* 1st June, 1850, dau. of Samuel FROTHINGHAM; *m.* (secondly) 12th November, 1851, Harriet FROTHINGHAM.

ISSUE BY FIRST MARRIAGE

1. Huntington Frothingham, b. 4th February, 1846; Second Lieutenant 2d Regiment, Massachusetts Cavalry, United States Volunteers; d.s.p. 10th June, 1865.

ISSUE BY SECOND MARRIAGE

1. ROGER, b. 13th July, 1847, of whom later.

HON. ROGER WOLCOTT of Boston, Massachusetts; b. there 13th July, 1847; d. there 21st December, 1900; Governor of the State of Massachusetts; graduated at Harvard University, 1870; Chief Marshal on the two hundred and fiftieth anniversary of the founding of Harvard College, 1886; m. 2d September, 1874, Edith PRESCOTT, dau. of William G. PRESCOTT, gd. dau. of William Hickling PRESCOTT, the historian, and gr. gr. gd. dau. of Col. William PRESCOTT, Commander of American troops at Battle of Bunker Hill.

ISSUE

I. Huntington Frothingham, b. 29th November, 1875; d. 19th February, 1877.
II. ROGER, b. 25th July, 1877, the subject of this memoir.
III. William Prescott, b. 1st May, 1880.
IV. Samuel Huntington, b. 9th November, 1881; m. Hannah STEVENSON, 19th June, 1907, at Milton, Massachusetts, dau. of Robert Hooper and Carolyn (JAMES) YOUNG STEVENSON of Boston.

ISSUE

1. Edith Prescott, b. 4th September, 1908, at Milton, Massachusetts.
2. Samuel Huntington, b. 31st August, 1910, at Milton, Massachusetts.
3. Robert Stevenson, b. 3d February, 1914, at Milton.

V. Cornelia Frothingham, b. 3d February, 1885; m. 18th April, 1911, at Boston, Rev. Samuel Smith DRURY, son of Samuel Smith DRURY, M.D., of Bristol, Rhode Island, and Anna Wheeler Goodwin DRURY of Sutton, Massachusetts.

ISSUE

1. Samuel Smith DRURY, b. 29th December, 1911, at Milton, Massachusetts.
2. Roger Wolcott DRURY, b. 3d March, 1914, at Brookline, Massachusetts.

VI. Oliver, b. 7th April, 1891.

Arms.—Argent, a chevron between three chess rooks, sable.
Crest.—A bull's head erased, argent, armed or, ducally gorged of the last.
Motto.—Nullius addictus jurare in verba magistri.
Residence.—Milton, Massachusetts.

Wolfe

FLAVIUS JOSEPHUS WOLFE of Mauckport, Harrison County, Indiana; b. 8th December, 1831; d. 27th September, 1912; m. 25th February, 1861, Amanda Louise BURTON, b. 25th February, 1839, dau. of Isom and Mary (ALEXANDER) BURTON.

ISSUE

I. Blanche Martin, b. 5th January, 1862; m. 2d December, 1890, James R. COOK, Attorney at Law, of Mt. Vernon, Kentucky, b. 25th January, 1862, son of Milton J. and Sallie (BAUGH) COOK.

ISSUE

1. Lucien Russell COOK, b. 13th February, 1892; d. 13th February, 1904.
2. Jessamine Bertha COOK, b. 21st May, 1895.

II. Bertha Frances of Washington, D. C.; b. 29th January, 1864, on Buck Creek, Harrison County, Indiana; Graduate of Mitchell, Indiana High School; holds degrees of B.S. and B.A. from Southern Indiana Normal College and degrees of M.A. from George Washington University; held the chair of English in Western Normal College at Bushnell, Illinois, and Southern Indiana Normal College; is an elocutionist, being a pupil of Virgil Alonzo PINKLEY, of Cincinnati College of Music; is a writer of short stories; Founder and Regent of Wendell Wolfe Chapter, Daughters of the American Revolution of Washington, D. C., named in honor of her ancestor, Capt. George Wendell WOLFE, Member College Women's Club, of Washington, D. C.; Historian of League of American Pen Women; Past Matron of Order of the Eastern Star, Member of Columbian Women and Indiana Society of Washington, D. C.

III. Iras Louise, b. 31st October, 1865; d. 12th February, 1889; m. 30th March, 1887, Rev. William Clifford MONROE.

ISSUE

1. Vincent Wolfe MONROE, b. 29th January, 1889.

IV. Elmer Burton, b. 12th April, 1869; d. 26th May, 1899.
V. Flavius Josephus, Jr., b. 3d March, 1875; m. 4th June, 1895, Jessie BASS, b. 1876, dau. of Aaron and Jennie (TOLLIVER) BASS.

ISSUE

1. Roscoe Burton, b. 10th March, 1896.
2. Clara Louise, b. 17th February, 1898.

Lineage

The founder of this family was Capt. George Wendell WOLFE, of Germany; *b.* 1720; *d.* 1816; emigrated to America circa 1768 and settled in Northumberland County, Pennsylvania, in the Valley of the Susquehanna on Little Turtle Creek; commanded the 5th Company of Northumberland County, Pennsylvania, Associators in the Revolutionary War; was a Member of the first Grand Jury in Northumberland County, Pennsylvania, April 1772; *m.* Ann Elizabeth REID.

ISSUE

I. Michael.
II. Jacob.
III. *JOHN, of whom later.
IV. Andrew.
V. Peter.
VI. Joseph.
VII. Henry.

JOHN WOLFE of Pickaway Plains, Ohio; *m.* in Pennsylvania, Mary Ann AURAND (or AURANDTS) dau. of John AURAND.

ISSUE

I. GEORGE WASHINGTON, of whom later.
II. Jacob.
III. Philip.
IV. Margaret.
V. John Henry.

GEORGE WASHINGTON WOLFE of Jefferson County, Kentucky; *m.* Mary Margaret CONRAD, dau. of George CONRAD, of Pennsylvania.

ISSUE

I. PETER, *b.* 5th May, 1799; *d.* 16th August, 1868; of whom later.
II. John, *m.* Mary MILLER.
III. Samuel, *m.* (firstly) Elizabeth BURFORD; *m.* (secondly) Elizabeth STEPHENSON.
IV. Henry, *m.* Sophia ZILLHART.
V. George, I, *m.* (firstly) Eliza TRESSENRIDER; *m.* (secondly) Mahitable MITCHELL.
VI. Elizabeth, John HUBBARD.
VII. Susan, *m.* George A. MOTTWEILER.
VIII. Margaret, *m.* Henry BONEBRAKE.
IX. Sarah (twin), *m.* John JOHNSON.
X. David (twin), *m.* (firstly) Mary UTZ; *m.* (secondly) Margaret EDLEMAN.

PETER WOLFE of Harrison County, Indiana; *b.* 5th May, 1799; *d.* 16th August, 1868; *m.* (firstly) 28th November, 1824, Nancy HAGGERDAY, *b.* 4th August, 1802, *d.* 5th October, 1826; *m.* (secondly) 6th June, 1830, Salome WELKER, *b.* 9th August, 1810, *d.* 13th June, 1890, dau. of Daniel and Nancy (REAGAN) WELKER.

COLONIAL FAMILIES OF THE UNITED STATES

ISSUE BY FIRST MARRIAGE

I. Lucinda Ann, *b.* 1st November, 1825; *d.* 1912; *m.* 1845, Dr. John WOODWARD.

ISSUE BY SECOND MARRIAGE

I. FLAVIUS JOSEPHUS, *b.* 8th December, 1831, the subject of this memoir.
II. Nancy Margaret, *b.* 30th September, 1834; 1911; *m.* Jeremiah BEARD.

ISSUE

1. Ada BEARD, *m.* Alonzo SENTNEY.
2. Olive BEARD, *m.* Lindsey JACKSON.
3. Clay Wolfe BEARD, *m.* Pauline TARKINGTON.

III. Marcus Aurelius, *b.* 18th October, 1837; *m.* 1860, Lucy Frances BEARD.

ISSUE

1. Frank Beard, *b.* June, 1861; *m.* Belle DOBBINS.

ISSUE

 1^1. Lee B. 2^1. Ray. 3^1. Ann Marie.

 2. Clay, *b.* ——— 1865.

IV. Leonidas Oliver Perry, M.D., *b.* 16th March, 1841; *d.* 1911, **unmarried**.

Index

A

Abbott, Abel, 5
Abigail, 493
Ada Frances, 6
Amy Ann, 6
Ann, 5
Ann Eliza (Hunt), 6
Anne, 4
Anne (Hance), 6
Anne (Newbold), 5
Anne (Rickey), 6
Anne (Satterthwaite), 4
Arthur Brenton, 3
Catherine (Moyer), 6
Charles, 5
Charles Conrad, 3, 7
Charles Shewell, 7
David, 5
Edith, 6
Elizabeth, 4, 5, 6
Elizabeth (Hastings), 4
Elizabeth W. (Longstreth), 5
Ephraim Olden, 6
Francis, 6
Francis L., 7
George, 5, 6
George B., 6
Hannah, 6
Helen Shewell (Keim), 7
Helena (Laurie), 5
Howard, 5
Jane, 4
Jennie (Fine), 7
John, 4, 5, 6
John Rickey, 6
Joseph, 5, 6
Joseph de Benneville, 7
Joseph Gardner, 6
Josiah, 478
Julia Boggs, 3
Julia Boggs (Olden), 3
Julia C. (Shewell), 6
Lucie (Laurie), 5
Lucy, 6
Margery (Smith), 5

Abbott—*Continued*
Maria Olden, 3
Marmaduke, 5
Martha (Ellis), 6
Mary, 4, 5
Mary G., 6
Nehemiah, 463
Persis Arminda, 478
Rachel, 4
Rebecca, 5
Rebecca (Comfort), 6
Rebecca (Harrison), 6
Rebecca (Holloway), 5
Rebecca (Howard), 5
Rebecca F. (Pitfield), 5
Richard Mauleverer, 3
Samuel, 4, 5,
Sarah, 4, 463
Sarah Ann (Jones), 5
Susan, 6
Susan (Conrad), 6
Susan S. (Stokes), 5
Susanna, 6
Susannah (Bullock), 5
Thomas, 6
Timothy, 4, 5, 6
William, 5
Abell, George, 197
Jennie (Webb), 197
John L., 200
Margaret, 189, 194
Matilda, 200
Susanna (Duke), 200
Thomas, 200
Abernathy, Gabriella (Smith) Poague, 292
Joseph, 292
Ackers, Elizabeth, 52
Ackerson, Ann, 225
Ackincloss, Mary (Fillis), 32
Ackley, Gideon, 162
Hannah, 162
Adams, Abigail, 313
Alice, 10
Anna (Whitney), 497

Adams—*Continued*
Anne, 9, 10
Anzie, 130
Bessie Innes, 12
Bethia, 321
Bowler, 8
David, 119
Ebenezer, 8, 10, 11, 14
Edward, 311
Elizabeth, 294, 496
Elizabeth (———), 311
Elizabeth (Johnson), 119
Elizabeth (Fauntleroy), Cocke, 9
Elizabeth (Griffin), 9
Elizabeth (Paine), 311
Elizabeth (Southall), 10
Elizabeth Innes, 11
Elizabeth Pressin, 9
Ellen Green (Williams), 11
Emma (Tufts), 331
Esther (Sparhawk), 311
George William, 11
Gilmer Speed, 8, 12
Hannah (Webb), 321
Hannah W. (Woodward), 11
Henrietta Catherine (Bickley), 11
Henry, 311
Innes Callaway, 11
Israel, 24
James, 331, 497
James Innes, 11
James P., 119
Jane Ruffin (Robertson), 11
Jessie St. John, 12
John, 10, 11, 293, 321, 311
Jonathan, 311
Joseph, 311
Kate, 11
Katherine Elizabeth (Innes), 10, 11
Lettie Reed (Robinson), 8
Linnie, 119
Lucy Ness, 11

507

INDEX

Adams—*Continued*
Lucy W. (Thornton), 11
Margaret (Calvert), 293
Margaret (Winston), 10
Maria (Gilmer), 11
Mariah, 294
Martha Bell (Speed), 11, 17
Mary, 311, 312, 321, 490
Mary (———), 311
Mary (Blackmore), 311
Mary (Selden), 11
Mary (Webb), 321
Mary Griffin, 11
Peter, 311, 321
Rebecca, 311
Rebecca (Atkinson), 24
Rebecca (Graves), 311
Richard, 8, 9, 10, 11
Samuel, 311, 321.
Samuel G., 11
Samuel Griffin, 10, 11
Sarah, 9, 10, 14
Sarah (Mowisin), 10
Sarah (Travers), 10
Sarah Travers Daniel (Hay), 10
Susan, 21
Susanna, 311
Tabitha, 8, 9
Tabitha (Cocke), 8
Thomas, 8, 11, 17, 311
Thomas Bowler, 10
Ursula, 311
William, 8, 10
William Preston Robert, 11
Adamson, Hannah M., 107
Aiken, Eusebia (Alexander), 21
James, 21
Akers, Agnes (Bryan), 106
John, 106
Mary, 106
Alberts, Coert, 456
Albin, Margaret Ella, 256
Alcock, John, 491
Sarah, 299, 491
Alden, Hannah (King), 491
John, 55, 266, 491
Priscilla, 266
Priscilla (Le Baron), 393
Alexander, Abigail, 19, 20
Abigail (Rockwood), 20
Abigail (Searle), 19
Amos, 20

Alexander—*Continued*
Anna, 20
Asa, 20
Azubah (Wright), 20
Betsey L. (Swan), 20
Calvert Page, 22
Carrie Adeline, 21
Charles Winthrop, 18
Daniel, 19
Donald Briggs, 18
Eben Roy, 22
Ebenezer, 19, 20, 21
Elias, 20
Elisha, 20
Elizabeth, 19
Elizabeth Blake (Wood), 18
Emery, 21
Eunice (Scott), 21
Eusebia, 21
George, 19
Hannah, 345
Hannah (Allen), 19
Harriet Bethiah (Briggs), 18
Harriet Bradford, 18
Harriet Sherman (Burchsted), 21
Henry Foster, 21
Hollis Williams, 22
John, 18, 19, 20
John Hollis, 22
Joseph, 19
Lucretia, 20
Mabel, 22
Margaret (Mattoon), 19
Marion Louise, 18
Mary, 19, 20, 337, 503
Mary (Bond), 20
Mary Brown, 21
Mehitabel (Buck), 20
Merab Ann, 21
Nancy (Wilson), 21
Nathaniel, 19
Octavia, 21
Oliver Brown, 21
Polly (Pratt), 20
Reuben, 20
Rhoda (Scott), 21
Rosemary (Conroy), 22
Ruth (———), 20
Samuel, 19
Sarah, 19
Sarah (Foster), 20
Sarah (Gaylord), 19

Alexander—*Continued*
Sarah (Howe), 20
Sarah (Livingston), 337
Simeon, 20
Solomon, 20
Susan (Adams), 21
Susanna (Sage), 19
Thaddeus, 20
Thankful, 19, 20
Thankful (Alexander), 20
Thankful (Ashley), 20
Thomas, 19, 20
Whittaker Howland, 21
Willard Huntington, 21
Willard Scott, 21
William, 337
Winthrop, 18, 22
Allen, ———, 300
Ada Catherine (Spencer), 426
Anna Maria (Dunton) Gemmill, 204
Elizabeth (Allyn), 223
Elizabeth (Rush), 206
Hannah, 19
Jane (Waln), 348
John, 214
Junius Wayne, 426
Lucy Anna, 296
Mary Ann, 351
Mary McElroy, 13
Nathaniel, 386
Rebecca, 386
Riley, 351
Samuel, 348
Sarah (Warren), 351
William, 206
William Henry, 204
Allerton, Isaac, 18
Allison, Rebecca, 225
Allmendinger, Ada, 351
Allston, Amy Frances, 200
Elizabeth, 230
Allyn, Elizabeth, 223
Jane, 499
Martha (Wolcott), 499
Mary, 500
Thomas, 499
Almey, Roberte, 354
Almy, Ann, 354
Audry (Barlow), 353
Calista, 356
Catherine, 354
Christopher, 354

INDEX 509

Almy—*Continued*
Clarinda, 356
Deborah, 355
Deborah (Cook), 355
Elizabeth, 354, 355
Elizabeth (Cornell), 354
Ira, 356
James G., 356
Jane (Rappleye), 356
Joanna (Slocum), 354
Job, 354, 355
John, 354, 355
Joseph, 355
Lusally, 356
Mary, 355
Mary (———), 354
Mary (Cole), 354
Mary (Unthank), 354
Milton Genoa, 356
Polly Ann, 356
Rebecca, 354, 355
Samuel, 355, 356
Sarah, 354
Silvester, 356
Thomas, 355
William, 353, 354, 355
Alston, Jane, 116
Joseph John, 154
Louisa Dandridge (Thomas), 154
Sarah Joseph, 154
Alton, Ann M. (Jacobs), 301
John N., 301
Ambler, Deborah, 174
Hannah, 174
Ames, Adelaide, 325
James Furman, 325
Margaretta Nataline (Kelton), 325
Mary Jane (Kirk), 325
Sarah J., 55
Thales L., 325
Amherst, Joan, 437
Amias, Andrew, 438
Joan, 438
Amory, Francis Inman, 360
Grace Josephine (Minot), 360
Anchor, Thomas, 188
Anderson, ———, 425
Agnes S., 394
Ann, 95
Charles, 154
Elizabeth, 394

Anderson—*Continued*
Elizabeth Marshall, 394
Henningham (Venable), 455
James M., 394
Jean, 394
Jessie Milan, 394
Louise Ellen, 100
Mary (Morris), 394
Peter, 100
Robbins Battell, 394
Robert, 455
Sarah (Claiborne), 154
Sarah Elizabeth, 394
Andrews, Edmund, 62
Edmund Lathrop, 62
Edward Wyllys, 62
Ethel (Baker), 62
Frances Ethel, 62
Frank Baker, 62
Jane, 76
Andross, Edmund, 64
Angell, Alice, 465
Margaret, 466
Apperson, ———, 13
Martha (Speed), 13
Archer, Dorothy Kingston (Hoffman), 388
Harriet Kingston, 388
John Hoffman, 388
Mary Huddell (Price), 387
Nina Roach, 387
Pierce, 387, 388
Armistead, Elizabeth (Stanley), 296
Mary Bowles, 286
Mary Walker, 296
Walter Keith, 296
Armitt, Elizabeth, 350
Joseph, 350
Armstrong, ———, 202
Alida (Livingston), 336
Charles, 70
John, 336
Lucretia (Knapp), 70
Mary (Dent), 202
Mary Ogier, 257
Millia, 172
Arne, David, 494
Lillie, 494
Arnold, Ann, 69
Dorothy, 299
Eliza, 383
Elsie (Howe), 69

Arnold—*Continued*
Guy Perry, 69
John, 69
Lucretia (Baker), 69
Martha, 190
Mary, 467
Nancy Long, 69
Samuel Baker, 69
Silvanus, 69
Zebedee, 467
Arthur, John, 73, 82
Olive, 73, 82
Arundel, Anne, 288
Thomas, 288
Ash, Anne Catherine, 388
Morgan, 388
Ashley, Abner, 148
Lydia (Churchill), 148
Thankful, 20
Ashlock, Delia, 71
Ashmead, Ann (Rush), 407
John, 407
Ashton, ———, 383
Mary (Price), 383
Askew, Charles, 422
Eliza (Skinner), 422
Askins, Anne, 294
Askwyk, Thomas, 473
Aslett, John, 306
Rebecca, 306
Rebecca (Ayer), 306
Atcheson, Eleanor, 310
Atherton, Anna, 181
Atkinson, Abigail, 24, 25, 26
Abigail (Bailey), 26
Adeline (Reed), 26
Alice Tucker, 23
Amos, 26
Ann (Bates), 26
Anna, 25, 26
Anna (Bailey), 26
Anna (Knowlton), 26
Anna G. (Sawyer), 26
Anna Greenleaf, 28
Anne, 28
Caroline Heath, 28
Caroline Penniman, 28
Catherine (Bartlett), 26
Charles, 26
Charles Follen, 27
Charles Heath, 28
Charlotte (Swasey), 26
Deacon Ichabod, 25

INDEX

Atkinson—*Continued*
Deborah (Knight), 24
Edward, 28
Edward William, 28
Eliot Heath, 23
Eliza (Rider), 26
Elizabeth, 24, 25, 27, 85
Elizabeth (Greenleaf), 24
Elizabeth (Staigg), 27
Elizabeth Bispham (Page), 23
Elizabeth Parsons, 28
Ellen Forbes (Russell), 28
Emiline (Little), 26
Emily Cabot, 27
Eunice, 25, 26
Frances (Farrington), 26
Francis Parkman, 27
George, 26, 27, 28
George Henry, 26
Hannah, 25, 26
Hannah (Hale), 25
Harry Morell, 27
Henry, 23, 28
Henry Morell, 27
Henry Russell, 28
Humphrey, 25
James Sawyer, 27
John, 23, 24, 25
Joseph, 24, 25, 26
Joshua T., 26
Josiah L., 26
Judith, 25, 26
Judith (Worth), 25
Lincoln, 28
Lydia, 25
Lydia (Little), 25
Lydia (Stickney), 25
Margaret, 24
Marian, 27
Mary, 24, 25, 27
Mary (Peters), 27
Mary (Pike), 24
Mary (Merrill), 26
Mary (Wheelright), Lyde, 23
Mary Caroline (Heath), 28
Mary Forbes, 28
Mary Heath, 28
Mary Peters, 27
Matthias, 26
Miriam, 26
Mittie Harmon (Jackson), 28

Atkinson—*Continued*
Moses, 25, 26
Moses L., 26
Nancy (Bates), 26
Nancy (Little), 26
Nathaniel, 24
Priscilla (Bailey), 25
Rebecca, 24
Richard Staigg, 27
Robert Whitman, 23, 28
Samuel, 24, 25
Samuel Greenleaf, 23
Sara, 24, 25
Sara (Myrick), 24
Sarah, 25, 26
Sarah (Hale), 25, 26
Sarah (Morris), 24
Sarah Cabot (Parkman), 27
Silas, 25
Simeon, 25
Stephen, 26
Susan, 27
Susanna, 25
Theodore, 23, 24, 25
Thomas, 24
William, 26, 28
William Parsons, 27
Atwater, Annah (Clark) Clark, 159
Lydia, 500
Stephen, 159
Audubon, Eliza (Bachman), 141
John W., 141
Maria (Bachman), 141
Victor G., 141
Aurand, John, 504
Mary Ann, 504
Austin, Abigail (Whitney), 497
Anna, 220
Anne (Goodrich), 220
Benjamin, 220
Goodrich, 220
Moses, 220
Samuel, 497
Avery, Abigail, 31, 32
Ann, 32
Benjamin Park, 38
Charles Russell, 33, 38
Deborah, 32
Deborah (Lothrop), 32
Deborah Palmer, 33
Ebenezer, 31

Avery—*Continued*
Elisha, 32
Elisha Lothrop, 33
Elizabeth, 31, 32
Elizabeth Draper, 33
Elizabeth (Lane), 31
Elizabeth (White), 31
Ellen Waters, 34, 38
Emma (Putnam), 32
Emma Park, 38
Emma Parke, 34
Ephraim, 31
Fannie Falconer, 34, 38
Frances, 30
Hannah, 31
Hannah (Platt?), 32
Hannah Ann (Park), 33
Hannah Platt, 33
Hannah Stanton, 33, 38
Henry Ogden, 34, 38
Isabel, 437
Jane (Gunning), 33
Job, 32
John, 31, 32, 250
John William, 33
Jonathan, 31
Joseph Platt, 33
Lydia (Healey), 31
Margaret (———), 30
Mary, 31, 32
Mary (Deming), 32
Mary (Fillis), Ackincloss, 32
Mary (Lane), 31
Mary (Rotch), 32
Mary (Woodmansey), Tapping, 30
Mary A. (Fuller), 33
Mary Ann (Ogden), 34, 38
Mary Henrietta, 34, 38
Mary Rebecca, 38
Mary Rebecca Halsey, 33
Mehitable (Hinckley), Worden, 31
Rachel, 31
Richard, 30
Robert, 30, 31, 32
Ruth, 32
Ruth (Knowles), 32
Ruth (Little), 31
Ruth (Smith), 32
Samuel, 32
Samuel P., 38

INDEX

Avery—*Continued*
Samuel Putnam, 30, 33, 34, 38
Sarah (Coit), 33
Sarah (Fairchild), 33
Sarah Elizabeth (Betsey), 33
Septimus, 32
Stephen, 33
Susan Jane, 33, 38
Thomas, 30
William, 30
William Deacon, 31
Ayer, Hannah, 306
John, 306
Rebecca, 306
Aylett, Elizabeth (Henry), 244
Philip, 244
Ayres, ———, 383
Susannah (Price), 383

B

Bachman, Eliza, 141
Lynch Helen, 141
Maria, 141
Backus, Hannah, 97
John, 97
Mary (Bingham), 97
Sarah (Bingham), 98
Whiting, 98
William, 97
Bacon, ———, 51
Abigail, 42, 44
Abigail (———), 41
Abigail (Cady), 149
Abigail (Farwell) Richardson, 44
Abigail (Kelly), 54
Abigail (Lovejoy), 44
Abigail (Taylor), 43
Agnes, 50
Agnes (———), 50
Agnes (Cockfield), 50
Alice, 42, 51
Alice (———), 41, 49, 51
Alice (Leach), 53
Alvan, 54, 55
Amanda, 54
Amos, 149
Anna (Fay), 54
Anne, 50
Annie P. (Sargent), 55
Asa, 53, 54
Barbara, 41

Bacon—*Continued*
Barbaro, 50
Benjamin, 43
Caroline Frances, 45
Charles Edward, 55
Charles Francis, 40, 47
Charlotte (Hare), 462
Charlotte Elizabeth, 462
Cicily (Hoo), 49
Columbus, 44
Daniel, 41, 51, 52, 53, 54
David, 43, 54
Della (Grow) Nichols, 54
Dorothy (Bradbury), 54
Dow (———), 40
Ebenezer, 44, 53
Ebenezer Farwell, 44, 45
Edmund, 50
Eleanor (Edwards), 54
Elihu, 54
Elizabeth, 41, 42, 50, 51, 53
Elizabeth (Ackers), 52
Elizabeth (Bacon), 51
Elizabeth (Comins), 54
Elizabeth (Crofts), 50
Elizabeth (Giles), 43
Elizabeth (Hancock) Wyman, 43
Elizabeth (Knight), 42
Elizabeth (Wylie), 41, 50
Elvira (McLaughlin), 45
Emily Jane, 47
Evelina, 45
Evelina Maria, 47
Frances, 44
Francis Bond, 462
Gertrude S. (Barnes), 45
Grace (Blowerses), 41, 50
Grumbaldus, 40
Hannah, 52
Hannah (Fales), 52
Hannah (Lovejoy), 44
Helen M. (Watson), 45
Helena (Gedding), 49
Helena (Tillott), 49
Henry, 49, 50
Henry McCobb, 55
Hepisbah (Boutelle), 53
Horace, 54, 55
Horace Baldwin, 55
Horace Sargent, 48, 55
Huldah, 53
Isaac, 41

Bacon—*Continued*
Jacob, 42, 52
James, 44, 52
Jane (Faunce), 45
Jarib, 53
Joane (———), 50
John, 40, 41, 42, 49, 50, 51, 52, 53, 54, 149
John Hancock, 45
Jonathan, 43, 54
Joseph, 43, 44
Joshua, 43
Josiah, 43
Judith (Wyman), 43
Julia (Bardwell), 49
Julia A., 45
Liday, 44
Lois (Fisk), 54
Lucy, 54
Lydia, 42, 43
Lydia (Dewing), 52
Malvina (Meng) Harrison, 48
Margaret (———), 40, 50
Margaret Burnett, 55
Margarey (Thorpe), 49
Martha, 52
Mary, 42, 43, 44, 50, 52, 54
Mary (———), 42, 43, 51, 52, 53
Mary (Baldwin), 53
Mary (Comins), 55
Mary (Fisher), 52
Mary (Haines), Noyes, 42
Mary (Olds), 53
Mary (Read), 41
Mary (Reed), 51
Mary (Richardson), 42, 51
Mary (Whitney), 52
Mary (Wood), 52
Mary A. (Maxwell), 55
Mary Angeline, 47
Mary Baldwin, 55
Mary Elizabeth, 55
Mary Emery (Coffin), 55
Mary Roads (Stickney), 44
Michael, 41, 42, 50, 51
Nathaniel, 43
Polly (Jones), 53
Rachel, 41
Rebecca, 52
Rebecca (Hall), 52
Rebecca (Taylor), 43

INDEX

Bacon—*Continued*
Richard, 41, 50
Robert, 50
Roger, 49
Rose, 41, 50, 51
Rufus, 53
Ruth, 43
Ruth (Warriner), 54
Samuel 43, 52
Samuel Adams, 45
Sarah, 41, 42, 44, 51, 52, 53, 55
Sarah (Churchill), 149
Sarah (Davis), 43
Sarah (Milliken), 54
Sarah (Richardson), 42
Sarah Elizabeth (Sargent), 55
Solomon, 43
Stephen, 52
Stephen Sargent, 48
Susan Nancy (Clark), 55
Susanna, 52
Susanna (Spencer), 41
Thomas, 41, 50, 52, 53
William, 41, 44, 50
Badger, Emma, 341
Frances Ellen, 341
Mary (Saltonstall), 413
Moses, 413
Worren H., 341
Badlam, Mary (French), 490
William, 490
Bagby, Agnes (Bryan) Akers, 106
Reuben B., 106
Bailey, Abigail, 26
Ann, 123, 316
Anna, 26
Elizabeth, 359
Hellen, 291
John, 83, 291
Mary (Bartlet), 83
Mary (Newsome), 291
Priscilla, 25
Sarah, 291
Theresa Lucretia, 222
Bailly, Cecilia (Guichon), 388
James, 388
Jean Silvain, 388
Joseph Beylle, 388
Bain, John, 421
Mary (Skinner), 421

Baird, Absalom, 58, 59, 60, 61
Alexander, 60
Andrew Todd, 60
Ann, 59
Anna Maria, 59
Annie (Nelson), 60
Catharine, 59, 60
Catherine (M'Clean), 58
Clara (Wilson), 60
Cornelia Wyntje, 57
Cornelia Wyntje (Smith), 61
David Wilson, 59
DuBois, 59
Ellen, 60
George, 59
George Brown, 59
Harriet Newell (Gilfillan), 59
Harriet Steele (Clark), 59
Jane, 59, 60
Jane (Wilson), 59
Jane Wilson, 60
John, 58, 59
John Absolom, 57
John M'Culloch, 59
John Mitchell, 60
Laura Rebecca (Updegraff), 59
Louisa Todd, 60
Margaretta Montgomery (M'Culloch), 59
Maria, 60
Martha, 59
Minnie (Dawley), 57
Nancy (McCullough), 60
Nancy (Mitchell), 60
Read M'Culloch. 59
Sarah, 13, 59, 60
Sarah Wilson, 60
Susan, 60
Susan Campbell, 59
Susanna Harlan (Brown), 58
Thomas, 59
Thomas Harlan, 60
William, 57, 59, 60, 61
William Jourdan Bates, 60
Baker, Aaron Y., 68
Abell, 78
Abigail, 63
Alice (Dayton), 63
Ann, 69
Ann (Topping), 63
Anne (O'Connor), 71
Azariah C., 67

Baker—*Continued*
Benjamin Franklin, 68
Betsey, 66
Caroline, 69, 78
Catalyntje (Schellinger), 224
Catharine (Hammond), 68
Catherine (Paddock), 71
Catherine(Schellinger),63,64
Caty, 66, 67
Daniel, 63, 64
Deborah (Avery), 32
Delia (Ashlock), 71
Delilah (Brown), 70
Dorothy, 70
Dugald Cameron, 69
Edwin, 69
Eliza, 67, 70
Eliza (Nichols), 70
Eliza (Warner), 62
Eliza Ogden, 71
Elizabeth, 66, 67, 68, 69
Elizabeth (Chandler), 67
Elizabeth (Ford), 68
Elizabeth (Osborn), 64
Elizabeth D., 69
Emily, 69
Emily Alice, 68
Esther, 66
Ethel, 62
Eunice, 67
Eunice (Conger), 67
Fanny, 67, 70
Fanny (Wheeler), 70
Fanny E., 69
Fanny Grace, 71
Florence, 71
Frances (Downe), 62
Frances (Fleet), 71
Frances J., 69
Frank, 62, 70
Franklin, 68
George E., 69
Gertrude Gretchen, 71
Grattan Henry, 71
Hannah, 63, 66, 224
Harriet (Kennedy), 67
Helen, 70
Irene, 67
Jacob, 66
Jane Elizabeth (Heinly), 71
Jean, 70
Jefferson, 67
Jeremiah, 64

INDEX

Baker—*Continued*
  Job, 70
  John, 64, 69, 358
  John H., 68
  Jonathan, 63, 66
  Joseph, 32, 67
  Julia Dennison, 69
  Julianna, 68
  Kate, 68
  Katharine, 63
  Keturah (Gosslee), 62
  Lavinia (McCormick), 69
  Louisa (Tunnicliff), 67
  Lucretia, 69
  Margaret Helen, 71
  Maria (Dorsey), 68
  Martha (Goodsell), 66
  Mary, 63, 67, 71, 358
  Mary (Baker), 67
  Mary (Barker), 66
  Mary (Brundage), 68
  Mary (Eaton), 69
  Mary Papillon Barker, 68
  Matilda (Blair), 69
  Mercy, 64, 66
  Mercy (Schellinger), 65
  Micah, 64
  Nathaniel, 63, 64, 224
  Nora, 62
  Patience Hatch (Graves), 71
  Paul, 70
  Peter, 66
  Ralph W., 71
  Richard, 67, 69, 70
  Richard Guy, 71
  Richard Selden, 71
  Richard Ward, 71
  Robert Anderson, 70
  Roxanna (Kingsley), 68
  Ruth, 67
  Sally, 467
  Samuel, 62, 64, 66, 67, 68, 69
  Sarah, 68
  Sarah (Boyd), 69
  Sarah (Morris), 66
  Sarah (Post), 63
  Seneca, 67
  Silas Wheeler, 70
  Sophia, 67, 68
  Susannah, 63
  Thomas, 62, 63, 64, 224
  Thomas Corwin, 69
  Thomas J., 67

Baker—*Continued*
  Thomas Jefferson, 69
  Trpyhena, 68
  William, 67
  William F., 69
  William Fleet, 71
  William Pitt, 66
  Zack, 69
Bakon, Agnes, 40
  Anne, 40
  Elizabeth, 40
  Henry, 40
  Johan (———), 40
  John, 40
  Mary, 40
  Thomas, 40
Balch, Anna (Jay), 303
  Anna (Whitman), 493
  Lewis P. W., 303
  Mary, 313
  Susanna, 330
  Timothy, 493
Baldwin, Abigail (Burr), 53
  Anna (Bissell), 201
  Anna Bissell, 201
  Bridget (Goodwin), 148
  David, 53, 148
  Hannah, 66
  Jehiel, 148
  Joseph, 201
  Lois (Churchill), 148
  Margaret, 103, 365
  Martha, 148
  Mary, 53
  Silence, 477
Ball, Elias, 231
  Mary How (Wilson), 231
Ballard, Anson, 157
  Harriet (Story), 157
  Lena Amanda, 157
  Lydia, 76
  Rachel, 223
Ballet, ———, 51
  Rose (Bacon), 51
Bancker, Adrian, 267
Bancroft, Alice (Bacon), 42
  Jane, 42
  John, 42
  Thomas, 42
Banks, Mary, 288
Bankson, Alice Morgan, 388
  Anne Catherine (Ash), 388
  John Palmer, 388

Banyer, Goldsborough, 303
Barclay, Andrew, 303
  Ann Margaret, 303
Barde, Elizabeth, 102
  John Louis, 102
Bardwell, Julia, 49
Barker, Agnes, 473
  Edward, 66
  Hannah (Baldwin), 66
  Mary, 66
Barlow, Audry, 353
  Louisa Shaw, 302
Barnard, ———, 485
  Mary (White) Wells, 485
Barnes, Abigail, 147
  Gertrude S., 45
  Polly, 218
  Rebecca, 318
Barney, Candace, 68
  Elizabeth, 445
  Moses, 445
  Sarah (Bond), 445
Barret, Abraham Hite, 273
  Amanda, 277
  Ann (Ferrel), 274
  Ann (Ludwell), 274
  Anne (Lee), 275
  Anne E. (Rodes), 276
  Brooks (Burke), 276
  Clifton Rodes, 277
  Daniel Thompkins, 277
  Dorothea (Payne), 274
  Edgar Lee, 277
  Elizabeth, 276
  Elizabeth (Lewis), 275
  Elizabeth (Lowry), 275
  Ella (Johnson), 276
  Francis, 275
  George Arthur, 277
  George Twyman, 277
  Henrie, 277
  Henry Owsley, 276
  John, 272, 275, 276
  John Garnett, 277
  John McKenzie, 277
  Leah Ethel, 277
  Lura A. (Barret), 277
  Margarette (Brown), 275
  Maria (McKenzie), 277
  Maria Elizabeth, 276
  Martha America (Pattie), 272, 276
  Mary Edith, 277

INDEX

Barret—*Continued*
Mary Elizabeth (Goodloe), 275
Mary Walker, 276
Mary Walker (Wood), 272, 275
Mary Washington, 277
Mason Brown, 276
Nancy (Dangerfield), 274
Penelope (Gilbert), 273
Robert, 273, 274, 275
Rosa Johnson (Robinson), 276
Rosa Robinson, 276
Thomas L., 273
Virginia, 277
William, 274
William Francis, 275, 276
William Goodloe, 276
Zachariah Wood, 277
Barrett, John, 496
Sarah, 496
Barritt, Hannah Platt (Avery), 33
Stephen, 33
Barron, Ellis, 462
Grace, 462
Mary, 462
Bartlet, Abigail, 83, 84
Abigail (———), 83
Abigail (Staples), 85
Alice, 83, 85
Anne, 82
Bertha (Miriam), 85
Christopher, 82
Dorcas, 85
Dorcas (Moulton), 85
Dorcas (Phillips), 83
Dorothy, 83
Elizabeth, 84
Elizabeth (Atkinson), 85
Elizabeth (Bartlet), 84
Elizabeth (Titcomb), 83
Gideon, 83
Hannah, 83, 85
Hannah (Emery), 83
Heard John, 85
James, 85
Joan, 82
John, 82, 83
Josiah, 84
Lucretia, 85
Mary, 83, 84, 85

Bartlet—*Continued*
Mary (Rust), 83
Meribah (Littlefield), 83
Nathan, 83, 84, 85
Nathaniel, 83
Phebe, 84
Rebecca, 83, 84
Richard, 82, 83
Samuel, 83
Sarah, 83, 85
Sarah (Merrill), 83
Sarah (Shapleigh), 85
Seth, 83
Shuah, 84, 85
Shuah (Heard), 84
Thomas, 82, 83
Tirza (Titcomb), 83
Bartlett, ———, 482
Abial, 416
Abigail, 74
Abigail (———), 74
Abigail (Burbank), 86
Agnes Vernon, 80
Albert Joseph, 78
Alfred Henry, 78
Alice Wheaton, 79
Amos Pettengill, 77
Anna (Pettengill), 76
Anna Frances, 77
Anne, 74
Caroline (Baker), 78
Caroline A. (Goodwin), 86
Caroline Elizabeth (Rice), 72
Catherine, 26
Charles Edward, 87
Christopher, 74
Clarissa (Walker), 76
Clementin (Raitt), 87
Daniel, 74, 76
Donald, 80
Dorcas (Phillips), 74
Doris Jeannette, 79
Dorothy, Hinman, 72
Edmund Benton, 77
Edwin Julius, 72, 79
Edwin Rice, 72
Eleanor (Pettengill), 76
Elizabeth, 86
Elizabeth (Titcomb), 74
Elizabeth Mehitable, 87
Elizabeth S., 86
Ellen Motley, 78

Bartlett—*Continued*
Emily D. (Shorey), 86
Esther Adelaide (Pitkin), 79
Ezra, 75
Fanny (Gordon), 79
Gordon, 79
Grace Greenleaf, 78
Grace Isabel, 87
Hannah, 74, 76, 249, 327, 416
Hannah (Colcord), 76
Hannah (Emery), 74
Hannah (Herbert), 75
Hannah (Webster), 75
Harriet Buck, 77
Harriet Greenleaf (Crane), 78
Harriet Mary (Buck), 77
Harriette Louise, 72
Helen, 78
Henry Bancroft, 79
Ichabod, 76
James, 76, 85, 86
James W., 86, 87
Jane (Andrews), 76
Jean (McRae), 87
Joanna, 73
John, 73, 74
John Foster, 72
John Hill, 86
John Howard, 87
Joseph, 75, 76, 78
Josiah, 75, 76
Justin S., 86
Laura (Bradlee), 78
Laura Amelia (Benton), 77
Laura Bradlee, 79
Levi, 75
Levi James, 78
Lois, 75
Lois (Hill), 85
Lucinda, 86
Lucy (Knowlton), 86
Lydia (Ballard), 76
Lydia F. (Worster), 86
Marian, 75
Margaret (Motley), 78
Margaret (Woodman), 74
Margaret Jaffrey (Porter), 72
Mary, 75
Mary (———), 74
Mary (Bartlett), 75

INDEX

Bartlett—*Continued*
  Mary (Hoyt), 74
  Mary (Ordway), 74
  Mary (Rust), 74
  Mary Bacon (Learned), 79
  Mary E. (Moulton), 87
  Mary Ellen, 77
  Mary Wentworth, 77, 78
  Mary Wentworth (Campbell), 77
  Mehitable (Emery), 86
  Nannette Marie (Huston), 77
  Nathan, 86
  Norman Williams, 77
  Persis Seaver (Long), 482
  Peter, 76
  Phebe (Burbank), 86
  Ralph Sylvester, 81, 84, 87
  Rebecca, 74
  Rhoda, 75
  Richard, 73, 74
  Richard Learned, 79
  Robert Learned, 79
  Rolla Willis, 87
  Samuel, 74, 75
  Samuel Colcord, 72, 76, 77, 78, 79
  Sarah, 76, 86
  Sarah C., 78
  Sarah Maria, 77
  Sarah Maria (Rogers), 76
  Shuah, 86
  Simeon, 75
  Stephen, 75
  Susan Lord (Pitkin), 79
  Susannah, 76
  Sylvester, 84, 86
  Thomas, 74, 75, 327, 416
  Tirza (Titcomb), 74
  Virginia, 78
  Virginia Louise (Millard), 77
  William, 86
  William Alfred, 79
  William Henry, 77, 78
  William Pitkin, 79
Barttelot, Adam, 72
  Assoline (Stopham), 82
  Edmund, 73, 82
  Edmund of Ernly, 73
  Elizabeth (Gates), 73, 82
  Elizabeth (Gore), 73
  George, 73

Barttelot—*Continued*
  Joan (De Lewknor), 73, 82
  Joan (De Stopham), 73
  John, 72, 73, 82
  Nigel, 81
  Olive (Arthur), 73, 82
  Petronilla (———), 82
  Richard, 73, 82
  Thomas, 73, 82
  Walter, 81
  Walter Balfour, 73
  Barttelot de Stopham, William, 72, 82
Bascom, Hepzibah, 343
Bass, Aaron, 503
  Jennie (Tolliver), 503
  Jessie, 503
Basset, Ruth, 329
Bassett, John, 358
Bastians, Hachim, 223
Bateman, John, 411
  Mary (Saltonstall), 411
Bates, Ann, 26
  Celia, 170
  Hannah, 170
  Jonathan, 175
  Mary Ann, 175
  Nancy, 26
  Sarah (Davenport), 175
Battaile, Maria, 144
Battell, Joseph, 393
  Sarah (Robbins), 393
Baugh, Arthur Primrose, 387
  Harriet (Thompson), 387
  Mary Archer, 387
  Nina, 387
  Nina Roach (Archer), 387
  Pierce Archer, 387
  Sallie, 503
  William Maddon, 387
Baugher, Lillian Bevan, 143
Bayard, Anna Maria, 302
  Balthazer, 302
Bayles, Martha (Smith), 390
  Mary Louise, 390
  Robert, 390
Bayley, George, 291
  Isaac, 74, 83
  Rebecca (Bartlet), 83
  Rebecca (Bartlett), 74
Beal, Abigail, 490
  Dolly (Whitney), 331
  Elizabeth Bishop, 331

Beal—*Continued*
  Hannah, 186
  John, 331
  Joshua, 331
  Mary, 264
  William, 331
Beale, ———, 198
  Catherine (Duke), 198
  John, 263
  Nazareth (Hobart) Turner, 263
Beall, Mary, 279
  Ninian, 279
Beard, Ada, 505
  Clay Wolfe, 505
  Jeremiah, 505
  Lucy Frances, 505
  Nancy Margaret (Wolfe), 505
  Olive, 505
  Pauline (Tarkington), 505
Beaseley, Elizabeth Marshall, 131
Beatty, Sarah Letitia, 353
Beaumont, Rebecca, 158
  William, 158
Bebe, Alfred, 160
  Sarah (Clark), 160
Beckley, ———, 179
  Catherine, 179
  John, 179
Beckwith, Henry, 419
  Matthew, 214
Beddingfield, Alice (Gibbes), 229
  Thomas, 229
Bedon, Elizabeth, 229
  Julia Davie, 285
  Richard Stobo, 285
Beebe, John, 214
  Thomas, 214
Beecher, Edith (Cromwell) Gist, Williams, 236
  Hulda, 147
  John, 236
Beekman, Cornelia, 336
  Henry, 335, 336
  Margaret, 335
Beff, Christina, 134
Behre, Florence, 285
Belden, Elizabeth, 147
  Lydia, 147

INDEX

Belding, Dorothy (Willard), 180
  Hannah, 180
  John, 180
Bell, Anna Elizabeth, 118
  David, 16, 240
  Frances M., 294
  Judith (Cary), 240
  Judith Cary, 240
  Martha (Fry), 16
  Mary Pennell (Trippe), 444
  Prudence, 174
  William, 444
Bellangee, Phoebe, 350
Bellingham, Alan, 151
  Grace, 151
Beman, Lucy, 494
Benedict, Abigail, 175
  Isaac, 175
Benison, Mary, 230
Benjamin, Daniel, 313
  Elizabeth (Browne), 313
Bennett, David, 169
  Elizabeth, 169
  Henrietta Maria (Neale), 439
  Mary, 169
  Phebe, 219
  Richard, 439
Bent, John, 214
Benton, Laura Amelia, 77
Bere, John, 438
  Mary, 438
Berkeley, Elizabeth (Neville), 438
  Thomas, 438
Berkheimer, Ida, 256
Bernard, Catharine Frances, 155
Berry, John Benton Nathaniel, 450
  Mary Imogene, 450
  Rosalie Eugenia, 450
Bertrand, Ann Frances (Johnson), 310
  John, 9
  Lucien, 310
  Mary Anne, 9
Betts, Aaron, 89
  Abijah, 89
  Amanda E., 90
  Amos, 90
  Amy Ellen, 91
  Caroline A. (Dewey), 90

Betts—*Continued*
  Charles Dewey, 90
  Comstock, 89
  Daniel, 88, 89, 90
  Deborah, 89
  Deborah (Taylor), 89
  Elijah, 89
  Elizabeth, 89
  Ellen (Porter), 91
  Emily, 90
  Enoch, 90
  Fanny Johnston, 91
  Frances Julia, 90
  Frederic J., 90
  George Frederic, 90
  Georgina, 91
  Hannah, 88, 89
  Hannah (Paxson), 110
  James, 88
  Jesse, 89, 110
  Joel, 89
  John, 88, 110
  Josiah, 89
  Julia, 90
  Juliana, 90
  Lydia, 89, 90
  Maria Caroline, 90
  Mary, 88, 89, 91
  Mary (Taylor), 89
  Nathan Comstock, 90
  Preserved, 89
  Rachel (Bye), 110
  Rebecca, 89
  Reuben, 89
  Ruth, 89
  Samuel, 88
  Samuel Comstock, 89
  Samuel Rosseter, 90
  Samuel Rossiter, 88, 91
  Sarah, 88, 89
  Sarah (Comstock), 89
  Sarah (Rosseter), 90
  Sarah Maria, 90
  Stephen, 88
  Thomas, 88
  Timothy, 89
  Uriah, 89, 90
  Zachariah, 110
  Zebulon, 90
Bewicke, Calverley, 282
Beylle, Joseph, 388
  Josephine, 388

Beylle—*Continued*
  Marie Madelaine Luise Therese (Le Maistre), 388
Biays, Fannie Jackson, 449
Bickley, Henrietta Catherine, 11
Bicknell, (Sarah), 135
Biddle, Abigail, 94
  Abigail (Heap), 93
  Adele, 95
  Agnes, 95
  Ann, 95
  Ann (Anderson), 95
  Ann (Mullanphy), 94
  Anna H. (Stokes), 94
  Anthony, 96
  Charles, 94, 95
  Charles John, 95
  Circe (Deronceray), 94
  Cordelia (Bradley), 96
  Craig, 95, 96
  Edith, 95
  Edward, 94, 95, 96
  Eliza (Bradish), 94
  Elizabeth, 93
  Elizabeth (Ross), 94
  Elizabeth B. (Hopkinson) Keating, 94
  Emily (Drexel), 96
  Emma (Mather), 95
  Esther, 92
  Frances, 95
  Frances (Marks), 93
  Hannah (Shepard), 94
  James, 93, 94, 95
  Jane, 95
  Jane Josephine (Sarmiento) Craig, 95
  Jane Margaret (Craig), 95
  Joanna Wharton, 92
  John, 93, 94, 375
  Joseph, 93
  Laura (Whelen), 96
  Lilian Howard (Lee), 96
  Lilian Lee, 96
  Livingston, 96
  Lydia, 94
  Lydia (Howard), 93
  Lydia (Wardell), 93
  Mary, 94, 95
  Mary (Scull), 93
  Meta Craig, 95
  Meta Craig (Biddle), 95

INDEX

Biddle—*Continued*
  Mildred, 95
  Nicholas, 92, 94, 95, 96
  Penelope, 93
  Richard, 95
  Sarah, 93, 375
  Sarah (Kemp), 92
  Sarah (Lippincott), 92
  Sarah (Owen), 93
  Sarah (Rogers), 93
  Thomas, 94
  Valeria, Fullerton, 375
  William, 92, 93
  William McFunn, 375
  William Shepard, 94
  Winthrop Lee, 96
Bidwell, Polly, 98
Bigbee, Archibald, 293
  Lydia (Calvert), 293
Bigelow, John, 462
  Mary, 462
Biggs, John, 358
Bignal, Rose, 393
Bignall, Ann, 13
Bigod, Hugh, 4
  Roger, 4
Biles, Anne (Abbott), 4
  Jonathan, 4
Billings, Eunice, 359
  Oliver, 359
Billington, Harriet (Johnson), 311
  Thomas, 311
Bingham, ——— (Maynard), 98
  Aaron, 98
  Abel, 97
  Abigail (Foote), 98
  Abigail (Scott), 97
  Ann (Huntington), 97
  Ann Howard, 375
  Betsey (Rash), 98
  Caroline, 98
  Charles, 375
  Cyrus, 98
  Deborah, 97
  Edward, 98
  Eleazer, 98
  Elizabeth (Manning), 97
  Elizabeth (Odell), 97
  Esther, 98
  Esther (Loomis), 98
  Ezra, 98

Bingham—*Continued*
  Faith (Ripley), 97
  Fanny (White), 98
  Flavel, 98
  Hannah, 98
  Hannah (Backus), 97
  Hannah (Daggett), 98
  Harvey, 98
  Howard Henry Charles, 99
  Jerusha (Sprague), 98
  Joel Foote, 98
  Jonathan, 97
  Joseph, 97
  Josiah, 98
  Lucille (Rutherfurd), 97
  Miriam, 98
  Miriam (Phelps), 98
  Mary, 97, 98
  Mary (Kingsbury), 98
  Mary (Rudd), 97
  Nathaniel, 97
  Polly (Bidwell), 98
  Polly (Wales), 98
  Rachel (Huntington), 97
  Rebecca, 98
  Rebecca (Bishop), 98
  Rutherfurd, 97
  Samuel, 97
  Sarah, 98
  Sarah (Lobdell), 97
  Sarah (Long), 98
  Silas, 98
  Stephen, 97, 98
  Susan (Grew), 99
  Tabitha, 98
  Theodore Alfred, 97, 99
  Thomas, 97
  William, 98
Birch, ———, 291
  Henrietta (Calvert), 291
Birckhead, Henrietta (Trippe), 445
  William, 445
Bird, Mark, 102
  Thomas, 214
Birket, Jane (Rudd) Waln, 347
  Robert, 347
Birkley, Alice, 438
Bishop, Audrey, 326
  Maitland Lathrop, 326
  Marjory Stevens (Kendall), 326

Bishop—*Continued*
  Rebecca, 98
  Sarah, 174
Bispham, Josephine Augusta, 23
Bissell, Anna, 201
  John, 214
Bisset, Catharine, 138
Black, Ada Frances (Abbott), 6
  Alfred L., 6
Blackmore, Mary, 311
Blackshaw, Elizabeth (Bye), 110
  Nehemiah, 110
  Randall. 110
Blair, Eliza Violet (Gist), 240
  Francis P., 240
  Matilda, 69
  Montgomery, 240
Blake, Charlotte, 283
  Daniel, 283
  Margaret (Izard), 283
  Martha, 359
  Nathaniel, 283, 359
Blakiston, Mary (Calvert), 288
  William, 288
Blanchard, James, 54
  Lucy (Bacon), 54
  Moses, 54
Bland, ———, 10
  Louise Christine, 246
  Mary, 275
Bledsoe, Jesse, 240
  Sarah Howard (Gist), 240
Blight, Charles Penrose, 376
  Cornelia Taylor, 376
  Cornelia Taylor (Blight), 376
  Elihu Spencer, 376
  Isaac Oliver, 376
  Lydia Spencer, 376
  Sarah Anna, 409
  Sarah Clementina, 376
  William Sergeant, 376
Bliss, Thomas, 214
Blodgett, Ruth, 328
  Ruth (Eggleden), 328
  Samuel, 328
Bloise, Michal (Jennison), 462
  Richard, 462
Blowerses, Grace, 41, 50

INDEX

Boaak, James, 164
  Mehetable (Corwin), 164
Boardman, Daniel, 147
  Elizabeth, 307
  Hannah (Wright), 147
  Martha, 147
  Samuel, 147
  Sarah, 147
Boarman, Anne, 289
Bobo, Lucy R., 271
Boggs, Maria Brenton, 3
Boies, Jeremiah Smith Hubbard, 377
  Sarah Hannah, 377
Bolton, Thomas, 273
Bon Coeur, George Bunker, 133
  William, 133
Bond, Grace (Coolidge), 313
  Henry, 20
  John, 237
  Jonas, 313
  Mary, 20
  Mary (Cutting), 20
  Ruth, 237
  Sarah, 313, 445
  Thomas, 94
Bone, Joseph, 107
  Rachel (Bryan), 107
Bonebrake, Henry, 504
  Margaret (Wolfe), 504
Bonneau, Floride, 126, 130
Bonney, Abigal (Genung), 225
  Jethro, 225
  Nancy, 225
Booker, Maria Louisa, 8
  Nancy, 269
Borden, Mary, 355
Boswell, Joseph, 240
  Judith Cary (Gist), 240
Bosworth, Beatrix (———), 260
  Benjamin, 260
  Bridget, 299
  Hannah, 299
  Hulda, 299
  Nathaniel, 299
Boudinot, Annis, 431
  Catherine (Williams), 431
  Elias, 430, 431, 432
  Hannah (Stockton), 430
Bouldin, Eliza W., 426
  Sallie W., 426
Bourchiers, Joane, 297

Boutelle, Hepisbah, 53
Bowerman, Hannah, 480
  Joseph, 480
  Phoebe, 480
Bowers, Barberie, 480
  George, 480
  Patience, 480
Bowes, Anna (Whitney), 497
  William, 497
Bowie, Catherine D., 446
  John, 207
Bowler, Anne, 8
  Thomas, 8
Bowling, Edgar Simeon, 156
  Josephine Claiborne (McIlwaine), 156
Bowman, Caroline, 134
  Marietta Gridley, 18
Bowyer, Luke, 243
Boyce, Angus, 407
  Cora Mae, 146
  Joseph C., 146
  Lydia Ida (Langdon), 146
  Rachel (Rush), 407
Boyd, Lucy Waller, 270
  Sarah, 69
Boyer, Mary (Henry), 243
Boyle, Emeline (Gist), 237
  Joseph, 237
Boylston, Jerusha (Minot), 358
  Zabdiel, 358
Bradbury, Dorothy, 54
  Dorothy (Clark), 54
  Joseph, 54
Bradford, David, 392
  Lydia, 392
  Nancy, 330
  William, 18, 251, 330, 392
Bradish, Eliza, 94
Bradlee, Laura, 78
  Nehemiah, 78
Bradley, Cordelia, 96
  Mary Susan (Waddill) Shepherd, 113
  Priscilla, 113
  Samuel, 217
  Sarah, 217
  William Joseph, 113
Bradshaw, Elizabeth, 480
  Humphrey, 480
  John, 480
  Mary, 480

Bradshaw—*Continued*
  Patience (Bowers), 480
Bragg, Edward, 214
  Eliza, 395
  Margaret, 294
Bramwell, Cecelia, 421
  Elizabeth (———), 278
  George, 278
Branch, Anne Harris, 117
  James Read, 117
  Martha Louise (Patteson), 117
Brannock, ———, 421
  Adeline (Skinner), 421
  Emily (Skinner), 421
Brant, Joseph, 190
Brantingham, Esther E., 257
Brattan, Molly, 316
Bray, Sarah (Dandridge) Claiborne, 152
  Thomas, 152
Brayne, Anne Butler, 244
Brayton, Cynthia (Whipple), 467
  Isaac, 467
Brazier, Mary, 391
Breck, Edward, 358
  Elizabeth, 358
Breckinridge, James D., 16
  Lucy Fry (Speed), 16
Brent, Anne, 289, 297
  Anne (Calvert), 289
  Elizabeth (Reed), 289, 297
  Fulke, 289
  Giles, 289
  Henry, 289
  Margaret, 289
  Richard, 289, 297
Brereton, Jane (Claiborne), 152
  Thomas, 152
Brewer, David, 53
  Margaret, 438
  Mary, 497
Brewster, James, 162
  Love, 35
  Rebecca Daggett, 162
  Sarah, 35
  Sarah (Collier), 35
  William, 18, 263, 323
Brice, Hannah (Bryant) Isaac, 280
  Richard, 280

INDEX

Bridge, Abigail, 496
  Anna, 312, 318
  Anna (Danforth), 312, 315
  Elizabeth, 312
  Elizabeth (———), 312
  John, 312
  Martha, 312
  Mathew, 312, 315
  Matthew, 312, 496
  Samuel, 312
  Sarah, 312
  Thomas, 312
Briggs, Harriet Bethiah, 18
  Joseph, 100
  Mary Ann (Dilingham), 18
  William Henry, 18
Brigham, Anne, 168
Bright, Sarah (Henshaw), 351
Briles, Rachel, 252
Briles-Whisenhurst, Rachel, 253
Brinton, Jane H., 401
Bristol, Elizabeth (Rennolds), 450
  William, 450
Brocket, John, 396
  Mary, 396
Brockett, Hannah, 184
Brockway, Alice, 393
Bronson, Maria (Mattison), 309
  Maria Cornelia, 309
  Nelson, 309
  Sarah, 181
Brooke, ——— (Moore), 101
  A. Louise (Clingan), 103
  Ann, 101, 102, 199
  Ann (Evans), 101
  Ann (Grant), 101
  Anna, 101
  Anne (Calvert), 289
  Baker, 289
  Charles, 103, 289
  Edward, 102, 103
  Eleanor, 101
  Elizabeth (Barde), 102
  Elizabeth Barde, 102
  Elizabeth Muhlenberg, 100
  Frances, 101
  Francis, 443
  George, 100, 101, 102, 103
  Hanna (Evans), 101
  James, 100, 101
  John, 100, 101
  Leonard, 289

Brooke—*Continued*
  Louise Ellen (Anderson), 100
  Lucile Stewart (Polk), 100
  Maria Teresa, 103
  Mary, 289
  Mary Baldwin (Irwin), 103
  Mary Baldwin Irwin, 103
  Matthew, 100, 101, 102
  Michael, 443
  Mildred Crew, 252
  Reese, 101
  Sarah, 101, 102
  Sarah (Reese), 101
  Thomas, 101, 102
  Thomas Snowden, 252
  William, 101
Brooks, Eleanor, 410
  Eunice, 327
  Henry, 330
  Isaac, 98, 330
  Joanna, 330
  Joanna (Holden), 330
  John, 328
  Peter C., 410
  Tabitha (Bingham), 98
Broughton, Abigail (Raynor), 328
  Charlotte, 283
  John, 328
  Mary (Izard) Izard, 283
  Matilda, 450
  Thomas, 283
Brown, Abigail, 483
  Abigail (Adams), 313
  Abraham, 68
  Ann, 420
  Anna Dorinda, 170
  Anne Wildes, 46
  Asa, 70
  Caroline (Stockton), 434
  Catherine, 134
  Content, 190
  Deborah, 164
  Delilah, 70
  Ebenezer, 313
  Eggleston, 420
  Eliza, 420
  Elizabeth (Smith), 296
  Enoch, 296
  George, 58, 124
  Grace, 313
  Hannah, 190, 313, 314, 318, 466

Brown—*Continued*
  Hannah (Bartlet), 83
  Hannah (Douglas), 190
  Hannah (Pease), 313
  Isaac, 313
  Isabella Alston, 454
  J. Thompson, 455
  J(ames?), 190
  John Wesley, 420
  Jonas, 314
  Jonathan, 190, 463
  Joseph, 279, 349
  Josiah, 314
  Lucretia (Gray), 68
  Lucy (Douglas), 190
  Margaret, 136
  Margaret Anne, 420
  Margarette, 275
  Martha (Calhoun), 124
  Mary, 463
  Mary (Balch), 313
  Mary (Fessenden), 313
  Mary (Waln), 349
  Mary M. (Southall), 455
  Mary Skinner, 420
  Minnie, 149
  N., 250
  Nathaniel, 83
  Polly Hambleton (Skinner), 420
  Prudence, 190
  Samuel, 313
  Sarah, 313, 314
  Sarah (Bond), 313
  Susanna, 313
  Susanna (Harlan), 58
  Susanna Harlan, 58
  Thankful, 314
  Thomas, 454
  Thomas E., 420
  William, 313
  William James, 420
  William Rawle, 434
  Winifred Miller, 470, 481
Browne, Abraham, 312, 313
  Abram, 313
  Benjamin, 313
  Ebenezer, 313
  Elinor, 365
  Elizabeth, 313
  Hannah, 313
  John, 365
  Jonathan, 313

Browne—*Continued*
  Lydia, 313
  Lydia (———), 312
  Mary, 153, 199, 475
  Mary (Shattuck), 313
  Nathaniel, 199
  Patience, 313
  Peregreen, 365
  Samuel, 313
  Sarah, 313
  William, 313
  William Burnett, 153
Bruce, Charles, 246
  Frances, 345
Bruen, Alexander M., 303
  Sarah Louisa (Jay), 303
Bruere, Elizabeth (Waln), 350
  Richard, 350
Brummal, Josiah, 270
  Mary Chastain (Hundley), 270
Brundage, Cornelius Y., 69
  Frances J. (Baker), 69
  Mary, 68
Brush, Betty, 164
Bryan, Agnes, 106
  Alanson, 106, 107
  Albert, 107
  Andrew Alanson, 107
  Andrew Morrison, 106
  Ann (Parker), 107
  Arthur Channing, 107
  Austin, 107
  Beedy, 107
  Catherine, 106, 143
  Catherine (Evans), 106
  Catherine M. (Pearson), 107
  Charles Fremont, 107
  Clarence W., 108
  Clarissa, 106
  Cynthia, 106
  David, 106
  Dennis, 107
  Easter (Mendenhall), 107
  Eliza (Legaré) 143
  Elizabeth, 106
  Elizabeth Jane (Letson), 104
  Elizabeth M. (Cobb), 107
  Elma Alfretta, 107
  Ernest Edwin, 107
  Francis, 104, 105
  Frederick Homer, 107

Bryan—*Continued*
  Gertrude Leo (Parkhurst), 108
  Hannah M. (Adamson), 107
  Harriet (Harner), 107
  James, 105, 106
  James Johnson, 107
  Jane, 106
  Jesse, 105
  John, 104, 106, 142
  John Andrew, 105
  John Mendenhall, 107
  Lillian (———), 107
  Lillian Augustine, 107
  Margaret, 104, 105, 106
  Margaret (———), 105
  Margaret (Kirk), 107
  Margaret (Watson), 105
  Margaret A. (Victor), 107
  Margaret Swinton, 143
  Martha (Strode), 105
  Mary, 106
  Mary (Akers), 106
  Mary (Johnson), 106
  Mary (Morrison), 105
  Mary Elizabeth (Job), 107
  Mildred (Johnson), 106
  Morgan, 104, 105
  Morrison, 106
  Morrison Gabriel, 107
  Neri, 107
  Peyton (Short), 106
  Rachel, 107
  Rebecca (———), 106
  Rhoda, 107
  Rhoda (Johnson), 106
  Ruth May (Goss), 104
  Sarah (Mendenhall), 107
  Sarah (Moorman), 107
  Sedellia (Martin), 107
  Sitnah Ann (Pearson), 107
  Tacy Jane (Smith), 107
  Talitha, 107
  Walter Emmett, 108
  William, 104, 105, 106
  William Akers, 106
  William Alanson, 104, 107
  William Albert, 107
  William Smith, 104, 105
Bryant, Hannah, 280
  Richard, 280
Buck, Blanch E. (Staples), 47

Buck—*Continued*
  Elizabeth (Churchill), 20, 146
  Emily Jane, 47
  Emily Jane (Bacon), 47
  Enoch, 179
  Esther, 330
  George Faunce, 47
  Harriet Mary, 77
  Henry, 20, 146
  Ira D., 77
  Lizzie, 47
  Mary (Kirby), 179
  Mehitabel, 20
  Samuel Dutton, 47
  Sarah, 179
  Thomas Barnes, 47
Buckingham, Ezekiel, 402
  Grace V. (Loucks), 403
  Henry, 403
  John, 402
  Maria (Test), 402
  Maria Catherine, 403
  Rebecca (McGinley), 402
  Rebecca Elizabeth, 403
  William Andrew, 403
Buckler, Ada (Rothrock), 404
  Robert, 404
Buckley, Daniel, 102
  Thomas, 102
Bucklin, Amy (Whipple), 467
  Deborah, 466
  Joseph, 466, 467
Buckmaster, Damaris, 260
Buckminster, Elizabeth (Clarke), 398, 479
  Johanna (———), 479
  John, 398
  Joseph, 397, 398, 476, 477, 479
  Martha (Sharp), 479
  Martha (Sharpe), 398
  Sybilla, 398, 477, 479, 484
  Thomas, 479
Buckwater, Sarah (Webb), 321
  Zachariah, 321
Budd, Ann, 430
  Elizabeth (Stockton), 430
  William, 430
Bulger, Aida Mae, 465
Bulkeley, Anna Maria, 493
  Charles, 494
  Lucy (Beman), 494

INDEX 521

Bull, Hannah, 159
  J. A. Rawlins, 370
  John S., 370
  Lucille Rawlins (Wait), 370
  Richard W., 370
  Stephen, 370
  William, 370
Bulla, Elizabeth (Hoover), 253
  William, 253
Buller, Jane, 152
Bullitt, Ann (Fry), 16
  William C., 16
Bullock, Elizabeth (Wright), 5
  Joseph, 5
  Susannah, 5
Bump, Alice, 310
Bunny, Elizabeth (Saltonstall), 411
  Henry, 411
Burbank, Abigail, 86
  Phebe, 86
Burchard, Josiah, 89
  Sarah (Betts), 89
Burchsted, Benjamin, 21
  Harriet Sherman, 21
Burford, Elizabeth, 504
Burgess, Anne, 363
  Beedy, 106
  Benjamin, 363
  Catherine (Stockett), 363
  Charles, 363
  Cynthia (Bryan), 106
  Edward, 363
  Elizabeth, 363
  Elizabeth (Durbin), 363
  Elizabeth (Robins), 363
  Elizabeth (Sparrow), 363
  George, 363
  Jane (Macklefresh), 363
  John, 363
  Joseph, 363
  Margaret, 363
  Richard (Ewen), Mrs., 363
  Samuel, 363
  Sarah, 363
  Sarah (Chew), 363
  Susannah, 363
  Ursula (Gordon), 363
  William, 363
Burke, Brooks, 276
Burkett(?), Sarah, 254
Burks, Elizabeth, 115

Burnap, Abner, 98
  Sarah (Bingham), 98
Burnell, Francis, 153
  Martha, 153
Burnet, Caroline Thew, 465
  John, 481
  Rachel, 470, 481
  Rebecca, 481
Burnham, Abigail, 489
  Hannah (Deming), 180
  Peter, 180
Burns, Frances, 70
Burr, Aaron, 246
  Abigail, 53
  Jane (Abbott), 4
  Joseph, 4
Burrage, Elizabeth, 367
  John, 367
  Margaret (———), 367
Burrill, Mercy, 265
Burroughs, Catharine Helen (Churchill), 149
  Eliza T. (Dent), 202
  George, 149
  John, 149
  John Amory, 202
Burt, Armistead, 129
  Mary Catherine (Calhoun), 129
Burton, Amanda Louise, 503
  Isom, 503
  Lewis William, 48
  Mary (Alexander), 503
Burwell, Alice (———), 314
  Elizabeth, 290, 314
  Ephraim, 314
  John, 314
  Joseph, 314
  Mary, 314, 319
  Nathan, 314
  Samuel, 314, 319
  Sarah, 314
  Sarah (Fenn), 314
  Zarachiah, 314
Busey, ———, 422
Bushnell, Alice Kendall, 331
  Cornelius Scranton, 331
  Mary, 188, 194
  Mary Elizabeth (Kendall), 331
  Samuel Clark, 331
  Samuel Kendall, 331

Buswell, Alexander Thorn, 271
  Alice Thorne, 272
  Claiborne Watkins, 272
  Virginia (Hundley), 271
  Walter Hundley, 272
Butler, Abigail, 493
  Elizabeth (Churchill), 147
  Frances (Talbot), 289
  James, 261, 289
  Jane (Jackson), 230
  Lydia, 358
  M. C., 119
  Miriam, 261
  Nicholas, 354
  Richard, 147
Buttall, Martha, 368
Butterworth, John F., 303
  Louisa, 351
  Maria (Jay), 303
Bye, Abigail (Kinsey), 111
  Albert, 111
  Alva May (Taylor), 112
  Amos, 111
  Andrew Moore, 112
  Ann, 110
  Anne, 111
  Arthur Edwin, 109, 112
  Benjamin Tilghman, 111
  Caroline (Speakman), 112
  Charles Paxson, 111
  Colin Taggart, 112
  Deborah, 110, 111
  Deborah (Paxson), 111
  Elizabeth, 110
  Enoch, 110, 111
  Enoch Mortimer, 111
  Geertruide Margarethe Jacoba (Van Eeghen), 109
  Hezekiah, 110, 111
  Isabel (Pyle), 112
  Jemina, 111
  John, 109, 110
  Jonas, 110
  Jonathan, 111
  Maria Catherine (Heldring), 109
  Margaret, 109
  Margaret Taylor, 112
  Martha, 110
  Martha (———), 110
  Mary, 110
  Mary (Ingham), 110
  Mary Anne (Woolens), 111

INDEX

Bye—*Continued*
Mary Elizabeth (Coleman), 111
Nathaniel, 110
Ottho Gerhard Heldring-Bye, 109
Phoebe Pusy (Passmore), 111
Pusey Passmore, 112
Rachel, 110
Ranulph de Bayeux, 109
Raymond Taylor, 112
Rosalie Paxson, 112
Ruth Anna, 112
Samuel, 110
Samuel Kinsey, 111
Sarah, 110
Sarah (Kinsey), 111
Sarah (Pearson), 110
Sarah (Pettit), 111
Susan (Gatchell), 111
Thomas, 109
William Thompson, 111
Byllange, Edward, 92
Byram, Abigail, 489
Martha (Shaw), 489
Nicholas, 489
Byrd, Frederick 427
Leslie Louise (Spencer), 427
Mary, 226
Byus, Joseph, 444
Sarah (Noel), 444

C

Cabell, Abraham Joseph, 116
Adah (Wymond), 117
Agnes Bell, 117
Agnes C. (Coles), 116
Agnes Sarah Bell (Gamble), 116
Anna Elizabeth (Bell), 118
Anna Maria (Wilcox), 116
Anne, 114
Anne Harris (Branch), 117
Anthony, 114
Arthur Grattan, 117
Ballard Hartwell, 113
Bridget, 114
Catherine Anne, 116
Christopher, 114
Edward Carrington, 116, 117
Elizabeth, 114, 115, 116
Elizabeth (Burks), 115

Cabell—*Continued*
Elizabeth (Cabell), 116
Elizabeth (Fowell), 114
Elizabeth Caskie, 117
Elizabeth Hannah, 116
Elvira, 245
Emma Catherine, 116
George, 114, 115, 116, 245
Hannah (Carrington), 115
Henry Coalter, 116
Henry Landon, 117
Isa (Carrington), 117
James Branch, 113, 118
James Caskie, 117
Jane (Alston), 116
Joanna, 114
John, 114, 115
John Bell, 118
John Grattan, 116
John Lottier, 118
Joseph, 115
Joseph Carrington, 116
Louisa Elizabeth, 116
Margaret, 245
Margaret (Jordan), 115, 116
Margaret (Meredith), 115
Margaret (Venable), 116
Margaret Constance, 117
Margaret Read (Venable), 455
Margaret Sophia (Caskie), 117
Mary, 115
Mary (———), 114
Mary (Carter), 116
Mary (Hopkins), 115
Mary (Prestwood), 114
Mary Anne, 116
Maude Crenshaw (Morgan), 118
Nannie (Enders), 117
Nicholas, 114, 115, 116, 445
Nicholas Carrington, 116
Paulina, 245
Paulina (Jordan), 115
Priscilla (Bradley), 113
Rachel (Hooper), 114
Richard, 113, 114
Robert Gamble, 116, 117, 118
Samuel, 113, 114
Sarah, 115
Susan, 114

Cabell—*Continued*
Susanna (Wyatt), 116
Susannah (Peter), 113
Thomasin (———), 113
William, 114, 115, 116, 245
William H., 116, 117
William Wirt, 116
William Wymond, 117
Cadman, Richard, 354
Sarah (Almy), 354
Cadwalader, Mary Anna (Tilghman), 441
Thomas, 441
Cady, Abigail, 149
Sarah (Boardman), 147
Cain, Harriet Chisolm, 231
John Calhoun, 231
Caldwell, Alfred, 69
Ann, 59
Hannah (Ker) Van Wyck, 316
James, 59
James E., 316
John, 128
Marion, 365
Martha, 128
Martha (Baird), 59
Calhoun, Agnes, 125
Agnes (Long), 123
Alexander, 125
Andrew, 119, 125, 128
Andrew Pickens, 130, 131
Ann, 124
Anna Maria, 130
Anne, 125
Anne (Gist), 237
Anzie (Adams), 130
Benjamin, 126, 128
Benjamin Alfred, 129
Benjamin P., 130
Caroline, 126, 128
Catherine, 122, 123, 124, 125, 126, 127, 129
Catherine (Calhoun), 123
Catherine (Montgomery), 122, 123
Catherine Jenne De Groffenreid, 129
Creighton Lee, 131
David Adams, 119
Duff Green, 131
Edward, 129
Edward Boiseau, 127

INDEX 523

Calhoun—*Continued*
Eliza, 124
Elizabeth, 124
Elizabeth Marshall (Beaseley), 131
Elizabeh Mary, 124
Ephraim, 125
Eugenia, 129
Esther, 125
Ezekiel, 122, 125, 126, 127
Florence, 127
Florence C., 128
Floride (Bonneau), 126, 130
Floride (Lee), 131
Floride Bonneau, 126, 127, 130
Floride Bonneau (Calhoun), 126, 130
Frances (Darricourt), 124
Frances (Hamilton), 125
Frances E. (Lee), 128
Frances Josette, 124
Francis Augustus, 129
George McDuffie, 128, 129
George Williams, 131
Harriet, 125
Henry Davis, 127
J. Christopher, 128
James, 119, 122, 123, 128, 130, 237
James Edward, 119, 127, 131
James F., 128
James Lawrence, 128, 129
James Martin, 128
James Montgomery, 125
Jane, 124, 129
Jane (Orr), 128
Jane Hamilton, 125
Jean, 127
Jean (Ewing), 126
John, 126
John Alfred, 128
John C., 123, 128, 130
John Caldwell, 119, 126. 128, 129, 130, 131
John Ewing, 124, 126, 130
John Joseph, 124
Joseph, 123, 124, 125
Joseph Selden, 124
Julia (Peterman), 130
Julia Johnson, 119
Kate Kirby (Putnam), 130

Calhoun—*Continued*
Kitty, 125
Kitty (Johnson), 125
Levi (Casey), 123
Linnie (Adams), 119
Louise, 124
Lucrecia, 120
Lucretia Ann, 129
Ludlow, 129
Margaret, 120, 124
Margaret (Cloud), 130
Margaret Green, 131
Margaret Maria, 131
Margaret Maria (Green), 130
Maria (Simkins), 127
Martha, 124, 129, 131
Martha (Caldwell), 128
Martha Cornelia, 130
Martha J., 128
Martha Maria, 126, 127
Martha Maria (Davis), 126
Mary, 124, 125, 127, 129
Mary (Falconer), 122
Mary (Speed), 124
Mary Catherine, 129
Mary Elizabeth, 125
Mary Lucretia, 132
Nancy (De Groffenreid), 129
Olga (Dininy), 119
Patrick, 120, 122, 125, 127, 128, 129, 130, 131
Patsey (Moseley), 123
Rachel, 125
Rebecca, 124, 125, 127
Rebecca (Tonnyhill), 125
Samuel, 124
Sarah, 125, 128, 129
Sarah C. (Norwood), 127
Sarah Caldwell (Martin), 128
Sarah Caroline, 128
Sarah Louise, 127
Sarah Porter (Williams), 131
Susan, 126
Susan (Pickens), 128
Susan Wilkinson, 128
Tescharner, 129
Thomas, 129
Thomas Smith, 124
Warren Davis, 127
William, 122, 123, 124, 125, 129

Calhoun—*Continued*
William Henry, 128
William Lowndes, 130
William P., 125
William Ransom, 126
William Sheridan, 127
Willie Norwood, 127
Callaway, Elizabeth, 10
James, 10
Katherine Elizabeth, 10, 11
Calvert, Amand Carr, 296
Anna Maria, 296, 297
Anne, 288, 289, 290, 291, 293
Anne (Arundel), 288
Anne (Askins), 294
Anne (Boarman), 289
Anne (Brent), 289, 297
Anne (Crupper), 290
Anne (Jennings) Norman, 294
Anne (Nottley), 290
Anne (Wolseley), 289
Anne (Wynne), 287
Anne Beck, 294
Anne Beck (Calvert), 294
Anne Strother, 295
Barbara (Doane), 290
Benjamin Franklin, 291
Caldwell Carr, 296
Catherine, 294
Catherine (Salvage), 296
Cecilius, 288, 289, 290, 291, 294, 295
Charles, 288, 289, 290
Delia, 292
Dorothy, 288
Edward, 296
Elizabeth, 288, 290, 291, 294, 295, 296
Elizabeth (Harrison), 290
Elizabeth (Lord), 290
Elizabeth (Stone), 289
Elizabeth Lovell, 297
Elizabeth Lovell (Carr), 296
Francis, 288
Gabriel, 291
George, 48, 287, 288, 290, 291, 293, 294, 296
George Washington, 291
Gettie, 292
Grace, 288
Grace (Crossland), 287
Hannah, 292, 295

524 INDEX

Calvert—*Continued*
Helen, 288
Hellen (Bailey), 291
Henrietta, 291
Henry, 288
James Lockhart, 295
Jane, 293, 295
Jane (Lowe) Sewall, 288
Jane (Sewell), 289
Jeremiah, 295
Jeremiah Strother, 295
John, 287, 288, 289, 290, 291, 294, 409
John Strother, 291, 296
Joseph Carr, 296
Julia Stockton (Rush), 409
Katherine, 295
Katherine (Marsham), 289
Katherine Kennerley, 296
Landon Ralls, 297
Leonard, 197, 287, 288, 289, 297
Lucy, 296
Lydia, 293, 294
Lydia Beck, 296
Lydia Beck (Ralls), 291, 293
Margaret, 293
Margaret (Charleton), 288
Mariah, 295
Martha, 296
Mary, 287, 288, 293, 295, 296
Mary (Banks), 288
Mary (Darnall), 288
Mary (Howson), 290
Mary (Strother) Deatherage, 290
Mary Elizabeth (Ferguson), 291
Mary Frances (Jenkins), 296
Mary Landon Armistead (Rosser), 296
Mary Rosser, 297
Mary Wade (Strother), 295
Matilda, 295
Nancy Beck, 291
Nancy Beck (Calvert), 291
Olivia Jane, 296
Patsy, 296
Philip, 289
Priscilla, 295
Priscilla (Smither), 295
Ralls, 293, 295, 296
Richard, 290

Calvert—*Continued*
Robert Singleton, 296
Samuel Ralls, 291
Sarah, 290, 291, 293, 295
Sarah (Bailey), 291
Sarah Anne, 291
Sarah Anne (Calvert), 291
Sarah Katherine, 48
Thomas, 290
William, 289, 290
William Launcelot, 295
Willie Anne (Woods), 291
Ziba, 291
Camac, Catherine Eliza Murray (Rush), 408
William Masters, 408
Cameron, Agnus, 68
Alexander, 127
Mary Pappilon Barker (Baker), 68
Camp, Anna, 148
Campbell, ———, 60
Anna (McCarthy), 316
Duncan, 54
Elizabeth (Henry), 243
Hannah, 380
James, 316
John, 152
Josephine (Rabineau), 324
Josephine Parmly, 324
Katherine (Claiborne), 152
Mary Wentworth, 77
Mary Wentworth (Williams), 77
Olivia, 54
Robert, 244
Sarah (Isaac), 281
Sarah Butler (Henry), 244
Susan (Baird), 60
Thomas, 244
William, 53, 243, 281
William M., 77
William Shaw, 324
Canby, Brenton Arthur, 3
Edward, 3
Joseph, 3
Joseph Olden, 3
Joseph Paxson, 3
Margery (Paxson), 3
Maria Olden (Abbott), 3
Pease, 3
Capen, Elizabeth, 266
John, 266

Capp, Alfred, 136
Allen, 136
Anna (Faber), 134
Anthony, 134
Barbara, 134
Caroline (Bowman), 134
Catherine, 134
Catherine (Brown), 134
Charles, 136
Charles Singer, 135
Christina (Beff), 134
Christopher, 134, 135
Dean, 134
Edward Payson, 136
Elizabeth (Zimmerman), 134
Emma, 134
Emma (Dean), 134
Estelle, 136
George, 134
George Frederick, 133
George Michael, 133
George S., 135
George Thomas, 135
Henry M., 134
Ida Estelle (Stitt), 136
Jacob, 134
John, 134, 135
John A., 135
John Andreas, 134
John Charles, 133, 135
John Frederick, 133
John George, 133
John Michael, 134
John Singer, 136
Joseph, 134
Lillian, 136
Lillian E. (Stillwell), 135
Louise Thayer, 137
Margaret (———), 134
Margaret (Brown), 136
Mary, 134
Mary (Michener), 136
Mary Ann, 135
Michael, 134
Miriam, 136
Ninian, 134
Peter, 134
Sabina, 134
Sallie (Seltzer), 134
Samuel, 135, 136
Samuel M., 136
Sarah (Bicknell), 135
Sarah (Chamberlain), 135

INDEX

Capp—*Continued*
Sarah (Singer), 135
Sarah Elizabeth, 135
Sarah Emma, 136
Seth Bunker, 133, 137
Susan, 134
Susanna, 130
Thomas H., 135
Valentine, 134
William Edgar, 136
William Musser, 133, 136
Capron, Ruth E., 149
Carlisle, Esther, 206
Carman, Cecil, 238
  Charles, 238
  Damaris, 491
  Prudence, 238
Carnac, Margaret, 216
Carpenter, Alexander, 248
  Ann Eliza, 385
  Francis G., 385
  Mary Blake (Risbrough), 385
  Polly, 310
Carr, ———, 127
  Cabel, 167
  Chloe, 150
  Delia (Strother), 296
  Elizabeth Lovell, 296
  Grace Mabel, 259
  Joseph, 296
  Mary (Calhoun), 127
Carrington, Alexander, 455
  Anne (Adams), 10
  Anne (Mayo), 115
  Benjamin, 116
  Elizabeth G. (Venable), 455
  Elizabeth Thornton, 455
  Emily, 454
  Emma Catherine (Cabell), 116
  George, 115
  Hannah, 115
  Henry, 116
  Isa, 117
  Louisa Elizabeth, 116
  Mary Anne (Cabell), 116
  Mary S., 453
  Mayo, 10
  Paul, 453
  Paul S., 116
  William Fontaine, 455

Carroll, Charles, 440
  Dominick, 441
  Eliza (Isaac), 281
  Hannah, 169
  John, 169, 281
  Juliana, 441
  Margaret (Tilghman), 440
  Mary (Sewall), 441
  Rebecca, 169
  Sarah C., 301
  Sarah Crosby, 167, 170, 301
  Wyman, 167, 170, 301
Carslake, Henrietta (Trippe), 444
  John, 444
Carter, Barzillai, 160
  Christopher, 115
  Cinderilla, 160
  Eunice (Brooks), 327
  James W., 245
  Laura Helen (Henry), 245
  Mary, 116
  Mary (Cabell), 115
  Mary (Crary), 160
  Naomi, 159
  Samuel, 327
  Thomas, 328
Cary, Archibald, 240
  Judith, 240
  Mary, 489
Case, Albert, 160
  Henry, 163
  Luther R., 301
  Martha (Corwin), 163
  Mary (Clark), 160
  Sarah C. (Jacobs), 301
Casey, Levi, 123
Caskie, Elizabeth (Pinchman), 117
  James, 117
  Margaret Sophia, 117
Cassaday, A. J., 362
  Susan Pauline (Morrison), 362
Catef, Joseph, 75
  Marian (Bartlett), 75
Cattell, Benjamin, 238
  Mary (McCall), 238
Caulkins, Sarah, 188
Chadwick, Charles, 496
  Sarah (Whitney), 496

Chaffin, John, 270
  Martha Louisa (Hundley), 270
Chambard, ———, 67
  Irene (Baker), 67
Chamberlain, Charles, 135
  Elizabeth, 350
  Sarah, 135
Chamberlayne, Elizabeth Claiborne Mann, 155
  Elizabeth Weldon Claiborne (Mann), 155
  Lewis Parke, 155
  Mary Gibson, 155
Chamberlin, Benjamin, 317
  Leah (Eaton), 317
Chamblin, Olivia Jane, 296
  William, 296
Champlin, Charles Davenport, 68
  Emily Alice (Baker), 68
Champney, Margaret, 228
  Richard, 228
Chandler, Elizabeth, 67
  Elizabeth (———), 383
  Elizabeth (Douglas), 188, 194
  Hannah, 392
  John, 188, 194, 383
  Joseph R., 387
  Maria (Holton) Roach, 387
  Mary, 383
  Mary (Dane), 392
  Sarah, 223
  William, 392
Chany, Ann, 280
Chapin, Marion Orinda (Cummings), 185
  Marvin, 185
Chaplin, Joseph, 300
  Martha, 142
  Sarah (Jacob) Mason, 300
Chapline, Isaac, 287
  John, 287
  Mary, 287
  Mary (?) (Calvert), 287
  Mary (Hopper), 287
  William, 287
Chapman, Abigail, 37
  Ellen, 435
  Gabriela, 437
  William, 37
Chappel, Amanda, 165

INDEX

Chappell, ———, 130
  George, 215
Charleton, Margaret, 288
Chase, Elizabeth Le Baron, 394
  Jessie Milan (Anderson), 394
  Robert S., 394
  Salmon P., 249
Chastaigner, Alexandre Thesee, 282
  Magdalene Elizabeth, 282
Cheeseman, Josephine, 195
Chester, John, 499
  Sarah, 499
Chew, Anna Maria (Tilghman), 441
  Benjamin, 441
  Bennet, 441
  Elizabeth, 441
  Elizabeth (Galloway), 441
  John, 363
  Samuel, 363, 441
  Sarah, 363
Child, John, 462
  Mary (Warren), 462
Childs, Alice Eliza (Gibbes), 234
  David A., 234
  Mary Eugenia (Gibbes), 234
  William G., 234
Chisolm, ——— (Lodge), 142
  Alexander, 139, 140, 142
  Alexander Hext, 142
  Alexander Robert, 140
  Alexina Pauline, 142
  Alfred de Jouve, 141
  Angus, 139
  Ann, 140
  Archibald, 139
  Benjamin Ogden, 143
  Caroline E. (Moodie), 141
  Caspar A., 141
  Catherine (Bryan), 143
  Catherine (Macrae), 140
  Catherine Bryan, 143
  Christina, 140, 142
  Colin, 139, 140
  Edith (Lawrence), 142
  Elizabeth (Rhoades), 143
  Elizabeth Prioleau, 142
  Emily Providence, 141
  Evelyn Z., 141
  Felicia O. (Hall), 141

Chisolm—*Continued*
  Francis Miles, 143
  George, 140, 141, 142
  George Edings, 142, 143
  Harriet Emily (Schutt), 141
  Harriet S., 143
  Helen (Garnett), 144
  Henry Lewis, 141
  Jabez, 241
  James Julius, 143, 144
  Janet (Fraser), 140
  Janet (Mackenzie) MacDonald, 139
  Jessie Edings, 142
  John, 139, 241
  John A., 241
  John Bachman, 141
  John Ban, 140
  John Julian, 141, 143
  John Rogers, 142
  Julia, 143
  Katherine A. (Reed), 141
  Katherine Imogen, 143
  Katherine Prioleau, 141
  Lillian Bevan (Baugher), 143
  Lynch Helen (Bachman), 141
  M. Elizabeth (Steele), 143
  Margaret Elizabeth (Edings), 140
  Margaret Swinton (Bryan), 143
  Margaret Willing, 142
  Marianne (Porcher), 140
  Martha (Chaplin), 142
  Mary Bellinger (Gregg), 141
  Mary (Grant), 139
  Mary (Gregg), 141
  Mary Ann (Rogers), 142
  Mary Edings, 143
  Mary Fredericka, 142
  Mary Maria, 142
  Nannie (Miles), 141
  Octavia (De Saussure), 141
  Octavius, 142
  Paul Hamilton, 144
  Providence Hext, 142
  Providence Hext (Prioleau), 140
  Robert George, 141
  Robert Trail, 140, 141, 143
  Samuel Prioleau, 142

Chisolm—*Continued*
  Sarah, 231
  Sarah G. (Maxwell), 140
  Sarah Maynard (Edings), 142
  Sarah Parteous (Cuthbert) Dana, 142
  Susan Matilda Harriet, 140
  Thomas, 140
  Thomas Hanscome, 142
  Virginia (Tweed), 144
  William, 140
  William Augustus Muhlenberg, 142
  William Bachman, 141
  William Edings, 142, 144
  William Garnett, 138, 144
  William Gregg, 141
  William S., 142
Chisolme, Alexander, 140
  Ann, 140
  Christina, 140
  Judith, 140
  Judith (Radcliffe), 140
Chittenden, William, 214
Chitty, Dorcas (Green), 492
Choate, Sally, 218
Christian, Anne (Henry), 243
  George William, 243
Church, ———, 33
  Elizabeth, 264
  Elizabeth Draper (Avery), 33
  Mary (Churchill), 146
  Samuel, 146
Churchill, ——— (Randall), 149
  Abiah (Wildman), 147
  Abigail (Barnes), 147
  Abigail (Webster), 148
  Achsah Eadie, 149
  Alice P. (Martinie), 149
  Alvin, 148
  Amy (Styles), 148
  Anice, 148
  Ann, 147
  Anna (Camp), 148
  Arthur Chester, 146
  Bathsheba, 482
  Benjamin, 147
  Benjamin Franklin, 150
  Caleb Washington, 149
  Caroline (Eadie), 150

INDEX 527

Churchill—*Continued*
Carrie, 150
Carrie (Churchill), 150
Catharine (Merry), 149
Catharine Helen, 149
Catherine (Watson), 149
Charles, 147
Chauncey, 149
Chloe (Carr), 150
Chloe Irene, 149
Cora Mae (Boyce), 146
David, 147
Delphine (Roe), 149
Dinah, 147
Doris May, 150
Dorothy (———), 147
Eadie, 150
Edith, 150
Electa, 148
Eliza (Pratt), 149
Elizabeth, 20, 146, 147
Elizabeth (Belden), 147
Elizabeth (Culver), 148
Elizabeth (Dyer), 148
Elizabeth (Foote), 146
Eunice (Culver), 148
Ezekiel, 148
Florence Hermia, 146
Giles, 147
Gladys Erminie, 150
Hannah, 146, 147
Helen (Dowd), 149
Herman, 146, 150
Hulda (Beecher), 147
Irena, 149
Irving Lester, 146
James, 150
Jason Merry, 150
Jennie E. (French), 150
Jerusha (Gaylord), 147
Jesse, 147
Joab, 148
John, 148
John Wesley, 149
Jonathan, 147, 179
Joseph, 147, 148
Josiah, 146
Jotham, 149
La Fayette Marion, 149
Leo, 150
Lois, 148
Lydia, 148
Lydia (Belden), 147

Churchill—*Continued*
Lydia (Dickerman), 147
Martha, 148
Martha (Baldwin), 148
Martha (Boardman), 147
Martha Asenath, 149
Mary, 146, 147
Mary (———), 147
Mary (House), 148
Mary (Hurlburt), 147
Mary Sarah (Crosley), 150
Minnie (Brown), 149
Muriel Jean, 150
Nathaniel, 147
Olive, 149
Olive Clarinda, 149
Oliver Clinton, 149
Ruth (Tryon), 147
Sally (Seeley), 148
Samuel, 147, 148
Sarah, 147, 149
Sarah (Boardman) Cady 147
Sarah (Buck) Deming, 179
Sarah (Deming), 147
Sarah Erminie (Woodworth), 150
Silas, 148
Sylvanus Amos, 149, 150
Sylvanus Woodworth, 150
Sylvester, 148, 149
Sylvina, 148
Thankful, 148
Thankful (Hewit) Seager, 147
Theodosia (House), 148
William, 147, 148
Claiborne, ——— (Hayward), 154
——— (Scott), 153
Alan dictus, 151
Ann (Fox), 153
Anna Augusta, 154
Anne, 153
Anne Augusta, 155
Annie Leslie (Watson), 154
Augustine, 153
Bernard, 153
Buller, 153
Donald Fraser, 156
Elizabeth, 152, 154
Elizabeth (———), 152
Elizabeth Weldon, 155

Claiborne—*Continued*
Herbert, 153
Jane, 152
Jane (Buller), 152
Jane (Cole), 153
Jeanne (Roblot), 151
John Greggory, 154
John Herbert, 151, 154, 155
Katherine, 152
Leonard, 152, 153
Lucy Herbert, 154
Maria, 154
Marie Louise, 151
Marie Louise (Claiborne), 151
Martha (———), 152
Martha (Burnell), 153
Martha (Jones), 153
Martha (Ravenscroft) Poythress, 153
Martha Jane, 154
Mary, 152, 153
Mary (Browne), 153
Mary (Gregory), 154
Mary (Herbert), 153
Mary (Ruffin), 153
Mary (Whitehead), 153
Mary E. (Weldon), 154
Mary Louisa, 154
Nathaniel, 153
Patsy (Ruffin), 154
Richard, 154
Robert Watson, 156
Sarah, 154
Sarah (Dandridge), 152
Sarah Joseph (Alston), 154
Sarah Joseph Alston, 155
Susanna, 153
Thomas, 152, 153
Ursula, 152
Weldon, 154
William, 152, 153
William Charles Cole, 151
Clapp, Nicholas, 214
Clark, Abigail, 158
Abigail (Lothrop), 482
Ada, 160
Alice, 157
Alice (Cummings), 157
Andrew, 159
Ann, 453
Annah, 159
Annah (Clark), 159

INDEX

Clark—*Continued*
Asa, 159
Beaumont, 159
Benjamin, 160
Bethsheba (Pratt), 159
Betsy, 159
Christopher, 159, 358
Cinderilla (Carter), 160
Daniel, 159
Deborah (Pope), 482
Delia M. (Taylor), 160
Diadama (Coleman), 160
Diana, 160
Dorothy, 54
Elizabeth, 158, 159, 160
Elizabeth (Crow), 482
Elizabeth (Williams), 159
Eunice Amelia (Wheeler), 160
Ezra, 159, 160
Fanny, 160
George, 159
Hannah (Bull), 159
Harriet Steele, 59
Henry, 160
Hester, 159, 164
Irene, 159
Isaac, 453
Israel, 482
James, 158, 482
James Freeman, 14
Jane (Turner), 159
Jesse, 159
John, 157, 158, 159, 160
John Cummings, 157
Joseph, 59, 158
Josiah, 482
Leda Amanda (Ballard), 157
Lydia, 219
Lydia (Grenell), 158
Lydia (Mallory), 159
Mary, 159, 160, 328
Mary (Coley), 157
Mary (Kirtland), 158
Mary (Minor), 158
Mary (Pratt), 159
Mary (Vrenne), 159
Mary (Ward) Fletcher, 157
Mary A., 310
Mary Elizabeth (Bacon), 55
Mary H., 233
Mercy, 358
Miriam (Bingham), 98

Clark—*Continued*
Naomi (Carter), 159
Nathaniel, 158, 159
Norman, 160
Orlando Elmer, 157, 158, 160
Paul, 159
Penniah (Nott), 159
Peter, 159
Phoebe, 159
Phoebe (Nott), 158
Polly (De Wolf), 160
Rebecca, 158
Rebecca (Beaumont), 158
Rebecca (Parker), 158
Rufus, 160
Saidee Matthews (Coyne), 39
Samuel, 158
Samuel E., 55
Samuel Wellman, 39
Sarah, 158, 159, 160
Sarah (Jones), 158, 159
Sarah (Wheeler), 159
Susan Nancy, 55
Susanna, 253
Susannah (Ring), 482
Temperance, 158
Thankful, 482
Thankful (Pratt), 159
Thankful (Tupper), 482
Tilden Ballard, 157
William, 98, 159
Clarke, Elizabeth, 280, 398, 479
George Rogers, 244
Hugh, 398
Huth, 479
Mary (Whittingham), 412
Thomas, 482
William, 412
Clarkson, Ann Mary (Van Horne), 339
David Augustus, 338
Elizabeth (Van Horne), 338
Levinus, 339
Margaret (Livingston), 338
Mary Rutherfurd, 304
Matthew, 304
Susan Maria, 339
Susan Matilda, 304
Thomas Sheatfield, 338
Clay, Henry, 240
Cleburne, Alan dictus, 151

Cleland, Annie (Young), 273
Robert Ray, 273
William G., 273
Clement, Joseph, 25
Judah, 495
Sarah (Atkinson), 25
Clements, Catherine, 425
Clemson, Anna Calhoun, 131
Anna Maria (Calhoun), 130
Floride, 131
Thomas G., 130
Cliborne, Agnes (Lowther), 152
Elizabeth (Curwen), 151
Grace (Bellingham), 151
John, 151
Robert, 152
Rowland, 151
Thomas, 152
William, 152
Cliburne, Edmund, 151
Richard, 151
Clifford, James, 279
Clingan, A. Louise, 103
Charles M., 103
Maria Teresa (Brooke), 103
Cloud, Margaret, 130
Mary, 294
Clough, A. J., 45
Clover, John, 44
Clymer, Elizabeth Barde (Brooke), 102
Heister, 102
Coale, ———, 366
Ann (Warfield) Marriott, 366
Elizabeth (Atkinson), 27
G. O. G., 27
Marian, 27
Coats, John, 374
Sarah, 374
Cobb, Clement Biddle Penrose, 377
Dorothy Penrose, 377
Elizabeth Colegate (Penrose), 377
Elizabeth M., 107
Emily Linnard, 377
Henry Everton, 377
Julianna (Baker), 68
Oliver Ellsworth, 377
Zenas, 68

INDEX

Cochran, Catherine (Rush), 207
Jane, 16
John, 207, 217
Sarah (Fulton), 217
Cochrane, Caroline (Toney), 286
John, 286
Cock, Amy, 387
Cocke, Anne (Claiborne), 153
Bowler, 9
Elizabeth (Fauntleroy), 9
John, 154
Lucy Herbert (Claiborne), 154
Richard, 8, 153
Tabitha, 8
Tabitha (Fry), 9
Cockey, John, 238
Susan, 238
Cockfield, Agnes, 50
Cocks, ———, 491
Sarah (Whitman), 491
Codding, Abigail, 345
George, 345
Sarah Pierce, 345
Coddington, Mary, 350
Coe, Elmore Frank, 209
Mary Louise, 209
Cofer, Fannie Poindexter (Spears), 272
James Madison, 272
Coffin, Daniel, 84
Dorcas (Bartlet), 85
Edmund, 55, 84
Mary (Atkinson), 25
Mary Emery, 55
Moses, 25
Nathan, 85
Nathaniel, 84
Rebecca, 349
Sara (Atkinson), 24
Shuah (Bartlet), 84
Stephen, 24
Tristam, 55
Cogswell, Edward, 215
Coit, David, 33
John, 486
Martha, 486
Sarah, 33
Sarah (Chandler), 223
Colby, Ichabod, 76
Jane, 76

Colcord, Hannah, 76
Mehitable (Ladd), 76
Samuel B., 76
Coldham, Martha, 495
Cole, Annie Elizabeth, 460
Catherine (Bryan), 106
Elizabeth, 41
Hannah, 190
James, 354
James Longstreet, 460
Jane, 153
Marinda, 225
Mary, 354
Robert, 25
Samuel, 106
Susanna, 492
Susanna (Atkinson), 25
William, 153
Coleman, Diadama, 160
John, 111
Mary Elizabeth, 111
Coles, Agnes C., 116
Coley, Mary, 157
Collet, Elizabeth (Rush), 205, 406
Richard, 205, 406
Collier, Jane, 35
Sarah, 35
William, 35
Collins, Ann (Abbott), 5
Daniel, 500
Laura, 500
Paulina, 225
Sarah (Whitman) Hooker, 493
Seth, 493
Thomas, 5
Colman, Elizabeth Williams (Hobard or Hubbard), 266
James, 266
Colston, Elizabeth, 419
James, 419
Colton, Electa, 181
Eunice, 500
Joanna (Wolcott), 499
John, 499, 500
Ruth, 493
Theophilus, 250
Combs, Elizabeth (Abbott), 6
Ezekiel, 6
Comey, Elizabeth, 327
Comfort, Elizabeth, 372
Elizabeth (Moul), 372

Comfort—*Continued*
Jopia, 372
Rebecca, 6
Susannah, 372
William, 372
Comins, Barnabas, 54
Elizabeth, 54
Mary, 55
Mary (Bacon), 54
Mary (Patker), 54
Reuben, 54
Comstock, Elisha, 175
Harriet (Davenport), 175
Samuel, 89
Sarah, 89
Conant, Anna (Alexander), 20
Ezra, 20
Mary, 489
Cone, Daniel, 161
Elizabeth (Warner), 161
Hannah (Ackley), 162
Hannah (Bingham), 98
Harriet Elizabeth (Uhlhorn), 161
James, 161
James Brewster, 161, 162
John, 98
Joseph Warren, 162
Leslie (Dillingham), 22
Mehitable (Spencer), 161
Mehitable (Swan), 162
Nathaniel, 161
Rebecca Daggett (Brewster) 162
Sarah Hungerford), 161
Sylvanus, 161
William H., 22
William Russell, 162
Conger, ———, 362
Eunice, 67
Conklin, Katharene, 34, 38
Conkling, Jeremiah, 223
Mary (Gardiner), 223
Conrad, Catherine (Capp), 134
Elizabeth (Abbott), 5, 6
George, 504
John, 134
Mary Margaret, 504
Solomon White, 5, 6
Susan, 6
Conroy, Rosemary, 22
Constable, Agnes, 473

INDEX

Constaysel, Benjamin, 371
  Christoffel, 371
  Deborah, 371
  Johannes, 371
  Margriet (Moul), 371
  Marretje, 371
  Phillipus, 371
Converse, Edward, 185
  Hannah, 185
  Israel, 185
  James, 53
  Joshua, 322
  Sarah (Webb), 310
  Susanna, 170
Conway, Mimos, 423
  Sarah (Skinner), 423
Cook, Aaron, 499
  Blanche Martin (Wolfe), 503
  Deborah, 355
  Hannah S., 393
  Harriet Myers, 380
  James R., 503
  Jessamine Bertha, 503
  Joanna, 499
  John, 355
  Lucien Russell, 503
  Mary, 230
  Mary (Borden), 355
  Mary Ann, 385
  Milton J., 503
  Sallie (Baugh), 503
  William Halsey, 380
Cooke, Amos, 501
  Elizabeth (Tilghman), 441
  Mary, 413
  Sally Worthington (Goodrich), 501
  William, 441
Cool, Aeltie Lambertse, 458
Cooley, Daniel, 499
  Elizabeth (Wolcott), 499
  Obadiah, 53
Coolidge, Grace, 313
Cooper, Elizabeth (Whitman), 490
  Hannah, 300
  John M., 295
  Lucy, 300
  Lydia Beck (Kaylor), 295
  Rebecca Huddell (Price), 387
  Samuel, 387

Cooper—*Continued*
  Timothy, 490
  William, 100
Copeland, Desire, 265
  Hannah, 490
  John, 265
  Lawrence, 265
  Samuel, 265
Corbet, Mary, 217
Corbin, Henry, 9
  Mary Elizabeth, 295
  Winifred, 9
Corcoran, Ella N. (Miles), 255
  T., 255
Corey, Sarah, 467
Corlete, Hephzibah, 358
Cornell, Charles Russell, 33
  Elizabeth, 354
  Hannah Stanton (Avery), 33
  Rebecca, 354
  Sara Willemse, 458
  Thomas, 354
Cornwall, Mary, 396
  Thomas, 396
Cortelyou, Minna, 460
Corwin, Abigail, 164
  Amanda (Chappel), 165
  Annie M. (Garretson), 165
  Benjamin, 164, 165
  Betty (Brush), 164
  Charles Edward, 163, 166
  David, 164
  Deborah (Brown), 164
  Deborah (Wells), 164
  Edward Calwell, 165
  Edward Tanjore, 166
  Eliza, 165
  Eliza Ann (Kelly), 165
  Elizabeth, 164, 165
  Elizabeth (Goldsmith), 164
  Elizabeth (Wickham), 165
  Ellen Gibb (Kingsley), 163
  Euphemia Kipp, 166
  Francis Huntington, 166
  Gabriel, 165
  George, 164
  George Brainard, 166
  George S., 166
  Hannah, 163
  Hannah (Reeves), 164
  Hannah C., 460
  Henry Wisner, 165
  Hester, 164

Corwin—*Continued*
  Hester (Clark), 164
  James, 164, 165
  James H., 165
  James Horton, 165
  John, 163, 164, 165
  Laura, 165
  Leah (Johnson), 164
  Leah Margaret, 166
  Leah Margaret (Corwin), 166
  Lewis B., 165
  Margaret (Morton?), 163
  Maria, 165
  Martha, 163
  Martha (Stuart), 165
  Martin Luther, 164
  Matthias, 163, 164
  Mary, 163
  Mary (———), 163, 164
  Mary (Garland), 165
  Mary (Glover), 163
  Mary (Simvall), 165
  Mary Ann (Shuart), 165
  Mary Esther (Kipp), 166
  Mehetable, 165
  Mehetable (Horton), 164
  Moses, 165
  Olivia (Gladen), 165
  Rebecca, 163
  Rebecca Jane (Newman), 164
  Samuel, 164
  Sarah, 163, 164
  Sarah (———), 164
  Sarah (Hubbard), 164
  Sarah L. (Sinnerd), 165
  Theophilus, 163
  William, 164
  William Owen, 165
Coskery, Carrie, 450
  Eliza (Hardy), 450
  Felix (Stanistan), 450
Coslet, Sarah, 216
Cotton, Elizabeth (Saltonstall), Denison, 412
  John, 168
  Prudence (Wade), Crosby 168
  Roland, 412
  Seaborn, 168
  Verlinda Spriggs, 289
Cotrell, Emeline, 150

INDEX

Cottman, Joseph, 200
  Sarah Jane (Hobbs), 200
Councell, Catherine Carroll, 200
  George Montgomery, 200
  Henrietta (Price), 200
Coventry, Mary, 229
  Thomas, 229
Covey, E. Nellie, 450
  Martha (Neale), 451
  Mitchel, 451
Cox, ———, 444
  Arthur John, 226
  Frederick Gardiner, 226
  Louisa Catherine, 226
  Sarah (Noel), 444
  Sarah Eliza (Hershier), 226
  Sarah Elizabeth, 226
  Thomas Gardiner, 226
  Thomas Jefferson, 226
Coxe, Anne (Calvert), 291
  David J., 291
Coyne, Anne Augusta, 39
  Bertha Park, 39
  Charles Russell, 39
  Fanny C. (Waters), 39
  Hannah Anne (Park) Avery, 38
  Jane (Goodale), 39
  Jane Augusta, 39
  John Nicholas, 38, 39
  Maie Park, 39
  Pauline Mary (Hemingway), 39
  Saidee Matthews, 39
  Sallie Johnson (Matthews), 39
  William Henry Harrison, 39
Craig, Jane Josephine (Sarmiento), 95
  Jane Margaret, 95
  John, 95
  John C., 95
  Margaret, 95, 315
Craighead, ———, 128
  Alexander, 128
Crandall, Carey, 398
  Charles, 176
  Clarence, 176
  David, 395, 398
  Elizabeth White, 395, 399
  Mary Vere (Davenport), 176

Crandall—*Continued*
  Roland, 176
  Serena (White), 395, 398
Crane, Harriet Greenleaf, 78
  Lemuel, 359
  Martha (Minot), 359
Crary, Mary, 160
Craver, George, 295
  Jane (Calvert), 295
Craw, Frances Ransom (Whipple), 469
  Frank G., 469
Crawford, Catherine (Nelson), 317
  Joseph, 317
  Leah, 317, 320
  Lucretia, 316
Crew, Elizabeth, 111
Crighton, Harriet Anne, 449
Crispen, Mary (Stockton)
  Shinn, 430
  Silas, 430
  William, 430
Crissey, John, 174
  Martha (Davenport), 174
Crocker, Adeline H., 300
  Alvah, 331
  Charles T., 331
  Elizabeth Priolean (Chisholm), 142
  Helen E. (Tufts), 331
  Samuel E., 142
Croft, Abigail, 486
Crofts, Elizabeth, 50
Cromwell, Edith, 235
  John, 236
  Oliver, 122, 235
  Richard, 235, 236
  Violetta (Gist), 240
  William, 236, 240
Crosby, Alison, 168
  Anne (Brigham), 168
  Anne (Wright), 168
  Annie Dorinda Brown, 170
  Anthony, 168
  Attaresta (Dike), 170
  Betty, 170
  Celia (Bates), 170
  Elijah, 170
  Elizabeth, 169
  Elizabeth (Bennett), 169
  George S., 301
  George Stephen, 167, 171

Crosby—*Continued*
  Hannah, 170
  Hannah (Bates), 170
  Hannah (Carroll), 169
  Henry, 21
  Hephsibah (Pearson), 169
  Jane, 169
  Jane (Sotheron), 168
  John, 171
  Jonathan, 168, 169
  Mabel (Dillingham), 21
  Mary B., 301
  Mary Bailey (Jacobs), 167
  Mary Larned, 167
  Nathaniel, 169
  Pearson, 170
  Polly (Green), 170
  Prudence (———), 168
  Prudence (Wade), 168
  Richard, 169
  Sarah, 167, 170, 301
  Sarah Carroll, 167
  Simon, 168
  Stephen, 167, 169, 170
  Susan Mason (Larned), 170
  Susanna (Johnson), 170
  Sybil, 170
  Talcott, 170
  Thomas, 168
  William, 168
Crosley, Emeline (Cotrell), 150
  Fred, 150
  Mary Sarah, 150
Cross, ———, 444
  Miriam (Atkinson), 26
  Rachel (Wallace), 444
  Ralph, 26
  Robert, 214
  Sarah Patterson, 444
Crossland, Grace, 287
  Joanna, 287
  Thomas, 287
Crotty, Gertrude, 172
  Millia (Armstrong), 172
  William, 172
Crow, Deborah, 32
  Elizabeth, 482
  John, 485
  Sarah, 485
Crupper, Anne, 290
Crutchley, Margaret (Baldwin), 365

Crutchley—*Continued*
  Ruth, 365
  Thomas, 365
Cudd, Anne (White), 474
  Robertus, 474
Culcheth, Anne, 229
Culpepper, Bessie, 422
  Charles, 422
  David Webster, 422
  Fannie, 422
  Hattie, 422
  Mary Frances (Skinner), 422
Culver, Elizabeth, 148
  Eunice, 148
Cumming, Catharine, 431
  John Noble, 431
  Mary Noble, 431
  Robert, 431
Cummings, ———— (Moore), 185
  Abigail (Parkhurst), 184
  Abraham, 184
  Alice, 157
  Ann, 183, 184
  Asa, 185
  Benjamin, 184
  Bera, 185
  Betty, 184
  Charlotte Converse, 185, 186
  Deborah, 185
  Deborah (Kendall), 185
  Ebenezer, 184
  Edwin, 185
  Eleazer, 184
  Elizabeth, 183, 184
  Elizabeth (Kinsley), 184
  Elizabeth (Shedd), 184
  Fanny, 185
  Hannah, 184, 185
  Hannah (Converse), 185
  Hannah (Kendall), 185
  Hannah (Marsh), 185
  Isaac, 183, 184
  James, 157, 184, 185
  Jane, 185
  Jane (————), 184
  Jerahameal, 184, 185
  John, 183, 184, 185
  Joseph, 185
  Josephine (Harris), 185
  Laura, 185
  Leonard, 184, 185
  Lot (Dixon), 186

Cummings—*Continued*
  Louisa (Gill), 185
  Lucinda, 185
  Lydia, 184
  Lydia (Spencer), 185
  Marion Orinda, 185
  Mary, 184
  Nathaniel, 184
  Polly, 185
  Priscilla (Warner), 183
  Rachel, 185
  Samuel, 184
  Sarah, 184
  Sarah (Howlett), 183
  Sarah (Wright), 184
  Silas, 185
  Solon, 185
  Susan (White), 185
  Theron, 185
  William, 184
Cuningham, Elizabeth (Ross), 324
  John Welsh, 324
  Margaretta Ross, 324
Currier, ————, 75
Curtin, Andrew G., 95
Curtis, Abigail, 265
  Elizabeth (Hoover), 254
  George Edward, 389
  Henry, 265
  John, 265, 414
  Mary, 179
  Mary Edith (Roach), 389
  Mary Elizabeth (Saltonstall) Shaw, 414
  Samuel, 19
  Sarah (Alexander), 19
  Theophilus, 265
Curtiss, Mary, 417
Curwen, Elizabeth, 151
  Thomas, 151
Cushing, Daniel, 298
  Elizabeth (Jacob) Thaxter, 298
  Matthew, 298
  Sarah (Jacob), 298
Cuthbert, Alexander, 432
  Anne Emily (Rush), 408
  Ross, 408
  Sarah Porteous, 142
  Susan (Stockton), 432
Cutler, Abigail, 497
  David, 497

Cutter, Sarah, 35
Cutting, Abigail, 398
  Mary, 20
  Silas, 398
Cutts, Hannah (Bartlet), 85
  Richard, 85
  Robert, 85

D

Dabney, Mary, 243
  Susannah, 290, 295
Daggett, Hannah, 98
Dailey, John, 490
  Mary (Whitman), 490
Dana, Sarah Porteous (Cuthbert), 142
Dandridge, Dorothea (Spotswood), 244
  Dorothea Spotswood, 244
  Nathaniel West, 244
  Sarah, 152
  Unity (West), 244
Dane, John, 392
  Mary, 392
Danforth, Anna, 312, 314, 315
  Elizabeth (————), 314
  Elizabeth (Poulter), 315
  Jonathan, 315
  Mary (Withington), 314
  Nicholas, 314
  Samuel, 315
  Thomas, 314
Dangerfield, Nancy, 274
Daniel, Alice (Gibbes), 229
  Ann (Venable), 453
  James, 453
  John, 229
  Mary Grace (Venable), 454
  Richard V., 454
Daniels, Clarissa, 221
  Elizabeth Hannah (Cabell), 116
  John, 214
  William, 116
Dark, William, 205
Darke, Jane (Rush), 206, 406
  John, 206, 406
Darnall, Mary, 288
Darone, Ruth E., 256
Darricourt, Frances, 124
Darrow, Elizabeth H., 446
Dart, Daniel, 188
  Elizabeth (Douglas), 188

# INDEX

Davenport, Abigail, 173
  Abigail (Benedict), 175
  Abigail (Pierson), 173
  Abraham, 173
  Amzi Benedict, 175
  Charles Benedict, 172, 176
  Deborah (Ambler), 174
  Deodate, 173, 174
  Dorothy, 176
  Eleazer, 174
  Elizabeth, 173, 174, 175
  Elizabeth (Huntington), 174
  Elizabeth (Jones), 174
  Elizabeth (Morris) Maltby, 173
  Elizabeth (Wolley), 172
  Farwell, 176
  Flora Dwight (Luefkin), 175
  Frances Gardiner, 176
  G. C., 172
  Gertrude (Crotty), 172
  Gould, 174
  Hannah (Ambler), 174
  Hannah (Wilson), 175
  Harriet, 175
  Henry Benedict, 175
  Henry Joralemon, 175
  Hezekiah, 174, 175
  Isaac Gould, 175
  James, 175
  James Pierpont, 175
  Jane Joralemon, 172
  Jane Joralemon (Dimon), 175
  John, 172, 174
  John Gaylord, 175
  John William, 175
  Joseph, 173, 174
  Josiah, 174
  Julia Ann, 175
  Julius, 175
  Lemoine (Farwell), 175
  Lewis Benedict, 175
  Lydia (Raymond), 174
  Lydia (Woodward), 173
  Margery, 176
  Martha, 173, 174
  Martha (Warren), 175
  Mary, 173
  Mary (Webb), 174
  Mary Ann (Bates), 175
  Mary Jane, 175
  Mary Vere, 176

Davenport—*Continued*
  Maurice, 175
  Millia Crotty, 172
  Nathan, 174
  Persis, 300
  Pierrepont, 176
  Prudence (Bell), 174
  Ralph, 174
  Rhoda, 174
  Richard, 358
  Ruth (Ketchams), 174
  Sarah, 173, 174, 175
  Sarah (Bishop), 174
  Silas, 174
  Stephen, 174
  Thaddeus, 174
  Theodora, 173, 175
  Theodora (Davenport), 175
  Theodore, 175
  Truecrosse, 358
  William, 175
  William Edwards, 176
Davidge, Dinah, 365
  Rachel (Warfield), 365
  Robert, 365
Davidson, John, 202
Davis, ———, 115, 310, 454, 364
  Abigail (Brown), 483
  Anna (Shippen), 339
  B. O., 17
  Charles B., 422
  Clarinda, 149
  Cornelia Ward (Whipple), 469
  David, 101, 483
  Dolor, 482
  Dorothy (———), 483
  Eleanor (Brooke), 101
  Elizabeth (Cabell), 115
  Elizabeth (Gaither), 364
  Hannah (Gates), 483
  Harriet (Calhoun), 125
  Hattie (Culpepper), 422
  Howland, 339
  Howland Shippen, 339
  Jefferson, 121, 290
  Joseph, 43
  Julia Temple, 482, 483
  Margarey (Willard), 482
  Martha, 452
  Martha Maria, 126
  Mary, 256
  Mary (Meads), 482

Davis—*Continued*
  Matilda, 478, 479, 480, 481, 483, 484
  Miller, 253
  Nathaniel, 452
  Persis, 483
  Persis (Newton), 483
  Rachel (Hoover), 253
  Reuben, 54
  Sally (Johnson), 310
  Samuel, 482
  Sarah, 43
  Sarah (Patten), 43
  Simon, 483
  Susan Fry (Speed), 17
  Thomas, 125
  William Ransom, 126
  William Wilkins, 469
Davison, Jane (Bryan), 106
  John, 106
Dawkins, Joseph, 198
  Mary, 198
  Mary (Hall), 198
Dawley, Minnie, 57
  Olive Pratt, 57
Dawson, Helen, 271
  J. A., 271
  Mary Silvia (Hundley), 271
  Sarah (Jay), 304
  William, 304
Day, Edgar Burr, 406
  Ella Mary, 406
  Hannah, 486
Dayton, Alice, 63
  Alice (Wilton), 63
  Ralph, 63
D'Albini, William, 4
De Alnewyk, Roberto Whyte, 473
De Barttelot, Adam, 73, 81, 82
De Beauchamp, Elizabeth, 297
De Beaufort, Joane Plantagenet, 297
De Bohun, Henry, 133
De Busli, Roger, 260
De Castera, Jean d'Avezac, 336
  Louise, 336
De Chisolme, Alexander, 138, 139
  Anne (De Lauder), 138
  Catherine, 139
  Catherine (Bisset), 138

INDEX

De Chisolme—*Continued*
  Emma (De Vipount), 138
  John, 138
  Margaret (De L'Aird), 139
  Margaret (Haliburton), 138
  Margaret (Mackintosh), 139
  Marion (Douglas), 138
  Muriel, 138
  Richard, 138
  Robert, 138
  Thomas, 139
  Wiland, 139
De Clare, Gilbert, 4
  Richard 4,
De Crossland, Roger, 287
De Doncaster, Johannis
  Shakespere, 472
De Groffenreid, Catherine
  Jenne, 129
  Lucretia Ann (Calhoun)
  Townes, 129
  Nancy, 129
  Tescharner, 129
De Halis, Agnes, 49
  Roger, 49
D'Invilliers, Sabina Josephine, 347
De Koven, Frances Russell, 187
De Kype, Roeloff, 166
De Lacie, John, 4
De L'Aird, Margaret, 139
De La Mater, Caroline, 204
  John, 204
De Lancey, Alice, 283
  Peter, 283
De Langley, Abbot, 49
De Lanvallie, William, 3
De Lassy, Louise (De Castera), 336
  Moreau, 336
De Lauder, Anne, 138
De Lewknor, Joan, 73, 82
  John, 73, 82
De Malahide, Talbot, 288
De Montenegro, Jacques
  Bruno Thomas, 388
  Marie Madeleine (Le Maistre), 388
  Marie Madeleine Pierre, 388
De Mowbray, William, 4
De Nagell, E., 119
  Julia Johnson (Calhoun), 119

De Neville, Anne (Stafford), 297
  Elizabeth (De Beauchamp), 297
  George, 297
  Henry, 297
  Joane (Bourchiers), 297
  Joane Plantagenet (De
  Beaufort), 297
  Margaret, 297
  Ralph, 297
  Richard, 297
De Peyster, Abraham, 337
  Catherine, 337
  Estelle (Livingston), 339
  Frederick, 339
  James Ferguson, 339
  John Watts, 339
  Mary (Livingston), 339
  Susan Maria (Clarkson), 339
  Susan Maria Clarkson, 339
De Potestad, Gabriela, 437
De Potestad-Fornari, Gabriela
  (Chapman), 437
  Luis, 437
De Quincy, Saise, 4
De Rapelje, Gaspard Colet, 356
De Roos, Robert, 4
De Saussure, Henry Wm., 141
  Octavia, 141
De Stopham, Joan, 73
  John, 73, 82
De Vere, Robert, 4
De Vipount, Emma, 138
  William, 138
De Warrene, Edmund, 40
  Henry, 40
  John, 40
  Ran(d)ulf, 40, 49
  Robert, 40
  Robert John, 40
  Roger, 40
  Rudueph, 40
  Thomas, 40
  William, 40, 49
De Wolf, Polly, 160
Dean, Alice, 491
  Elizabeth, 330
  Emma, 134
  Phebe A., 301
Deas, Anne (Izard), 284
  William Allen, 284

Deatherage, Mary (Maddox), 293
  Mary (Strother), 290
  William, 290, 293
Deatherage-Calvert, Mary
  (Strother), 290
Decorne, Frances, 206
Deering, Mary Wentworth
  (Bartlett), 77
  William Case, 77
Dekker, Andries, 371
  Annaatje, 371
  Diewertjen, 371
  Phillipus, 371
Deland, Diana (Clark), 160
  Elisha, 160
Delaplaine, Hannah, 383
Deming, —————— (Diggins), 181
  —————— (Ware), 180
  Alonzo Decalvis, 181
  Anna (Kilbourn), 180
  Anne, 181
  Anne (Deming), 181
  Anson Harrington, 181
  Asenath (Scoville), 180
  Caroline Matilda, 182
  Catherine (Beckley) Dewey, 179
  Charlotte Louise (Northrop) 181
  David, 179
  Dinah (Churchill), 147
  Dorothy, 180
  Ebenezer, 179
  Edna, 181
  Electa (Colton), 181
  Elihu Goodsell, 181
  Eliza (Goodsell), 181
  Elizabeth, 180
  Elizabeth (—————), 180
  Elizabeth (Gilbert), 179
  Elizabeth Ives, 99
  Elsa Louise, 178
  Ephraim, 180
  Eri Jerome, 181
  Esther (—————), 181
  Ezekiel, 180
  Frederick, 180, 181
  Hannah, 180
  Hannah (Beldig), n180
  Hannah (Goodrich), 180
  Hannah (Lusk), 180
  Hannah Keith (Judson), **182**

INDEX

Deming—*Continued*
  Honor (Treat), 178
  Honour, 179, 180
  Jacob, 147
  Janna, 180
  Jedediah, 181
  John, 178, 179
  Jonathan, 179
  Josiah, 180
  Judson Keith, 178, 182
  Keith Worthington, 178
  Laura Sophia (Herrick), 181
  Lucretia, 180
  Lucy Willard, 181
  Lydia, 180
  Lyman, 181
  Mabel (———), 181
  Martha, 179
  Mary, 32, 179
  Mary (———), 179
  Mary (Curtis), 179
  Mary (Mygatt), 179
  Mary Colebrook (Worthington), 178
  Mary Goodsell, 182
  Mercy, 179
  Nelson Jerome, 182
  Prudence, 180
  Prudence (Steele), 180
  Rachel, 179
  Rebecca (Treat), 179
  Roger, 181
  Samuel, 179
  Sarah, 147, 179, 181
  Sarah (———), 179
  Sarah (Buck), 179
  Sarah (Graves), 179
  Sarah (Jerome), 181
  Sarah Ann, 181
  Selah, 180, 181
  Stephen, 180
  Thankful (Tracy), 181
  Waitstill, 180
  William Morrison, 181
  Zama Eliza, 182
Denison, George, 194
  Elizabeth (Saltonstall), 412
  John, 412
  Sarah, 194
Dennett, John, 84
  Mary (Bartlet), 84
  Phebe (Bartlet), 84
  Thomas, 84

Dennis, Elizabeth, 409
  Lyttleton, 409
  Lyttleton Upshur, 409
Dennison, Irene (Clark), 159
  Joseph, 159
Denny, Archibald Marshall, 326
  Katherine Varnum, 326
  Katherine Varnum (Kendall), 326
  Kendall Whitney, 326
  William, 58
Dent, Abigail, 201
  Amy Frances (Allston), 200
  Anna, 201
  Charity, 202
  Christianna, 201
  Eliza T., 200
  Elizabeth (Edwards), 202
  Elizabeth Temperance (Mills), 200, 202
  George, 200, 201, 202
  Grace Arline, 200
  Hezekiah, 202
  John, 201, 202
  Lydia, 201, 202
  Martha, 200
  Mary, 200, 201
  Mary (———), 201
  Mary (Shercliffe), 201
  Mary Ann, 200, 202
  Peter, 201, 202
  Thomas, 200, 201, 202
  William, 202
Depew, Chauncey M., 121
Derby, Betsy, 497
Deronceray, Circe, 94
Devall, ———, 256
  Ella (Hoover), 256
Dewey, Caroline A., 90
  Catherine (Beckley), 179
  Daniel, 90, 179
  Hepzibah (Lyman), 344
  Joseph, 344
  Margaret, 263
Dewing, Jonathan, 52
  Lydia, 52
  Susanna (Bacon), 52
Dexter, Abigail (Whipple), 466
  Alice, 479
  John, 466
  Richard, 479
  Samuel, 479

Dexter—*Continued*
  Sarah (Whipple), 466
  Stephen, 466
Dickerman, Abraham, 392
  Lydia, 147
  Rebecca, 392
Dickerson, Abraham, 372
  Adam, 372
  Antje, 372
  Antje (Mould), 372
  Elenora, 372
  Molly, 372
  Rubina, 372
Dickey, Cornelia DeKoven, 187
  Frances Russell (De Koven), 187
  Hugh T., 187
  Isabella (Work), 361
  Isabella Work, 361
  John, 361
Dickinson, Elizabeth, 112
  Gideon, 26
  Judith (Atkinson), 26
  May (Trippe) Webb, 445
  Samuel, 445
Dike, Attaresta, 170
Dillingham, Alexander, 22
  Alveda (Greenwood), 22
  Edith, 22
  Frances (O'Rourke), 22
  Fred A., 21
  Leslie, 22
  Lottie, 324
  Mabel, 21
  Mary Ann, 18
  Paul, 22
  Sydney, 22
Dillon, Mary (Talbot), 289
  Robert, 289
Dilworth, Ann (Waln), 348
  Anne (Waln), 349
  James, 348, 349
  Jane, 348
  Rebecca, 349
Dimon, Jane Joralemon, 175
  John, 175
  Margaret (Joralemon), 175
Dininy, Olga, 119
Divers, George, 16
  Martha (Walker), 16
Dives, Margaret, 46

INDEX

Dix, Abigail, 35
  Edward, 35
  Jane, 35
Dixon, Hannah (Beal), 186
  J. Theron, 186
  John, 186
  Lot, 186
  Lucile Mast, 183
  Regina (Mast), 183
  Willis Milnor, 183, 186
Doane, Barbara, 290
  Isaiah, 204
  Maria (Dunton), 204
Dobbins, Belle, 505
Dodd, Caroline Bayard, 434
  Catherine Elizabeth (Stockton), 434
  Susan B., 434
  William Armstrong, 434
Donald, Agnes Helen, 79
Dorchester, Anthony, 215
Dorn, John H., 311
  Margaret Souder (Johnson), 311
Dorsey, Maria, 68
Dottando, Hester, 419
Doty, Abigail, 149, 150
Doughty, Amy, 430
  Ann, 430
  Elizabeth, 430
  Jacob, 430
Douglas, ——, (Mathews), 190
  —— (Travaissa), 190
  Abiah, 189, 194, 195
  Abiah (Hough), 188, 194
  Abigail (Starr), 195
  Alanson, 190, 191
  Alfred, 195
  Ann, 187, 188, 189, 194
  Ann (Mattle), 187, 194
  Ann (Sutherland), 191
  Ann Grace (Page), 193
  Anna Sutherland, 192
  Anne, 193
  Anne (Page), 326
  Asa, 189
  Benajah, 189, 190
  Caleb, 194
  Caroline H. (Whitehead), 190
  Charles Selden, 191
  Charlotte, 190

Douglas—*Continued*
  Charlotte Cornelia Dickinson (Ferris), 191
  Clifton Alden, 136
  Content, 190
  Cornelia De Koven (Dickey), 187
  Earl, 195
  Elizabeth, 188, 194, 195
  Elizabeth (Williams), 190
  Erskine, 195
  Eunice, 195
  George, 190, 195
  George Henry, 191
  George William, 187, 191
  Grace Josephine, 193
  Hannah, 189, 190
  Hannah (Brown), 190
  Hannah (Cole), 190
  Harriet, 190
  Harriet L. (Staple), 191
  Harry, 193, 195, 326
  James, 189
  Jerusha, 189
  John, 189, 190
  John Hancock, 190
  Jonathan, 190, 194, 195
  Josephine, 195
  Josephine (Cheeseman), 195
  Julia, 191
  Julia (Hempstead), 195
  Lucy, 190, 195
  Lucy (Way) Palmer, 195
  Lydia, 195
  Malcolm, 195
  Margaret, 194, 195
  Margaret (Abell), 189, 194
  Marion, 138, 193, 326
  Martha, 190
  Martha (Arnold), 190
  Martha (Gallup), 189
  Martha (Rathbone), 190
  Mary, 190
  Mary (——), 189
  Mary (Bushnell), 188, 194
  Mary (Hanover), 189
  Mary (Hempstead), 188, 194
  Mary (Warner), 191
  Mary Ann, 191
  Mary Hawley, 191
  Minerva, 190
  Miriam (Capp), 136
  Nathaniel, 190

Douglas—*Continued*
  Olive, 190
  Olive (Spaulding), 189
  Prudence (Brown), 190
  Rachel (Marsh), 189
  Rebecca, 189, 190, 194
  Rebecca (Wheeler), 189
  Rhoda (Hancock), 190
  Richard, 189, 194, 195
  Robert, 187, 188, 193, 194
  Samuel, 189, 194
  Sarah, 188, 189, 194, 195
  Sarah (Denison), 194
  Sarah (Olcott), 189
  Sarah (Proctor), 189
  Sarah (Robbins), 190
  Sarah A. (Hollister), 191
  Stephen Van Renssalaer, 190
  Sutherland, 191
  Thomas, 189
  Wheeler, 190
  William, 138, 187, 188, 189, 190, 193, 194, 195
  William Bradley, 191
Dow, Anne (Bakon), 40
Dowd, Helen, 149
  Richard, 149
Dowding, Ann (Penrose), 374
  Joseph, 374
Downe, Frances, 62
Downing, Dennis, 84
Downs, Emmitt, 422
  Jennie (Skinner), 422
Dozier, Harriet Hampton (Gibbes), 234
  John R., 234
Drake, Francis, 273
  Job, 499, 500
  Mary (Wolcott), 499
  Sarah, 500
Drane, Colie Pierce (Spencer), 426
  Hiram Walter, 426
  Mary Frances (Spencer), 426
  Walter Hugh, 426
Draper, Elizabeth (Avery), 32
  John, 32
Drayton, Charles, 126
Dresser, Joseph, 299
  Mercy (Jacob), 299
Drexel, Anthony J., 96
  Catharine, 378

INDEX

Drexel—*Continued*
Emily, 96
Joseph W., 378
Drury, Anna Wheeler Goodwin, 502
Cornelia Frothingham (Wolcott), 502
Ebenezer, 160
Hannah, 160
Hannah (Wooley), 160
John, 160
Luke, 54
Marian (Goodale), 160
Mary, 417
Roger Wolcott, 502
Samuel Smith, 502
Zedekiah, 160
DuBois, Catherine Helena (Jay), 304
Henry Augustus, 304
Dubree, Elizabeth (Waln), 349
Jacob, 349
James, 349
Jane, 349
Duché, Anthony, 374
Sarah (Coats) Penrose, Falkner, 374
Duff, William, 122
Dugans, Clara P., 235
Duke, Agnes Bernardette, 201
Andrew, 198, 199
Ann Eleanora, 200
Anna Bissell (Baldwin), 201
Basil, 198, 199
Benjamin, 199
Benjamin Hooper, 200
Betie Ann, 200
Catherine, 198
Catherine Carroll (Councell), 200
Charles Clarence, 201
Elisabeth Matilda, 200
Elizabeth, 198
Elizabeth Stuart (Hayden), 200
Esther (Parran), 199
George Dent, 200
Grace Arline (Dent), 200
James, 198, 199
James Roland, 200
James Thomas, 200
Jennie (Webb) Abell, 197

Duke—*Continued*
John, 198, 199, 200, 202
John Francis, 200
John Jenkins, 201
John Thomas, 200
Joseph, 198
Katherine Marie (Turner), 197
Leonard, 199
Lilian Paret (Turner), 201
Margaret (———), 198
Margaret Ann (Nuthall), 200
Margaret Martine, 200
Martha, 198, 199
Martha (———), 199
Martha (Dent), 200
Martha (Mackall), 198
Mary, 199
Mary (Browne) Wilson, 199
Mary (Dawkins), 198
Mary Ann (Dent), 200
Mary Mabel, 200
Mary Priscilla, 200
Mary Priscilla (Egerton), 199
Maud Francis, 201
Moses Parran, 199
Nannie (Hebb), 200
Richard, 197, 198, 199
Susanna, 200
Thomas, 197, 198
William, 198
William Bernard, 197, 200
Dulany, Anner Lee, 243
Bladen Tasker, 243
Jane Moss (Love), 243
Mary Bladen, 243
Dumont, Isaac, 160
Sarah (Clark) Bebe, 160
Dunbar, John Henry, 404
Mary, 230
Mary (Rothrock), 404
Duncan, William, 203
Dunlap, Ann, 382
Dunscomb, Euphemia, 303
Dunsten, Hannah, 55
Dunton, Abraham, 204
Amelia, 204
Anna, 204
Anna Maria, 204

Dunton—*Continued*
Anna Maria (McCarty), 204, 207
Anna Maria Gemmill, 208
Anna Maria Gordon (Gemmill), 205, 208
Anna Mary (Friberg), 204
Belle (Farr), 208
Bridget (Flanagan), 204, 207
Caroline (De La Mater), 204
Edna Drusilla (Hogan), 208
Elizabeth, 204, 205, 207, 208
Elizabeth Worrell, 205, 208
Emma, 208
Emma Drusilla (Hogan), 203
George, 204
Helen McClean, 203, 208
Helen Rowena (McClean), 203
Henry Hurd, 203, 208
Isaac, 204, 207, 208
Jacob, 203, 204, 205, 207, 208
James Gemmill, 205, 208
John, 204
Margaretha, 204
Maria, 204
Martha, 205, 207
Mary, 205, 207
Mary (Lillie), 208
Mary Simpson (Rush), 204
Sarah, 203
Stephen Morgan, 203, 208
Susan Ritchie, 208
Thomas, 203, 208
William, 203, 204
William Rush, 203, 205, 207, 208
Dupec, Elizabeth Baldwin, 415
William R., 415
Dupignac, Ebenezer R., 33
Sarah Elizabeth (Betsey), 33
Durbin, Elizabeth, 363
Durfee, Ann (Almy), 354
Richard, 354
Thomas, 354
Duyckinck, Mary, 302
Dwight, Michael, 31
Rachel (Avery), 31
Timothy, 51
Dyer, Elizabeth, 148

INDEX

E

Eadie, Abigail (Doty), 149, 150
  Achsah, 149
  Caroline, 150
  John, 149, 150
Eagan, ———, 420
Eager, William, 214
Eames, Margery, 298
Earle, Anne (Sorrell), 208
  Asphasio, 210
  Baylis, 210
  Bridget (———), 209
  Elizabeth (Price), 210
  Harriet (Harrison), 210
  Henry, 210
  Henry Montague, 209, 210
  James, 439
  John, 209
  Mary, 209
  Mary (———), 209
  Mary (Prince), 210
  Mary (Tilghman), 439
  Mary Louise (Coe), 209
  Phillis (———), 209
  Samuel, 209, 210
  Walter, 209
  William Edward, 210
Early, Margaret, 398, 475
Eastham, Susan, 292
Eastman, Ida Gardiner, 227
  Lauren Chase, 226
  Matilda E., 226
  Moses, 76
  Moses A., 226
  Nina Louise, 226
  Sarah Elizabeth (Gardiner), 226
  Susannah (Bartlett), 76
Eaton, Benjamin, 317
  Catherine (Little) Loup, 317
  Elizabeth, 317
  Grace, 328
  Jonas, 328
  Joseph, 328
  Leah, 317
  Mary, 69
  Rebekah (Kendall), 328
Edenden, Edmund, 476
  Elizabeth (Whitman), 476
  Sarah, 476
Edings, Margaret Elizabeth, 140

Edings—*Continued*
  Sarah (Evans), 142
  Sarah Maynard, 142
  William, 142
Edleman, Margaret, 504
Edmondson, Harriet, 446
Edmonston, Charles, 142
  Mary Maria (Chisholm), 142
Edwards, Alexander, 214
  Benjamin, 202
  Eleanor, 54
  Eliza, 221
  Elizabeth, 202
  John, 54
  Jonathan, 174, 305
  Josiah, 147
  Lucretia, 123, 130
  Mary (Churchill), 147
  Mary (Gardiner), 224
  Mary (Jay), 305
  Ninian, 123, 130
  Thomas, 224
Egerton, Mary Priscilla, 199
Eggleden, Ruth, 328
Eggleston, Maria, 393
  Mary, 416
Eichar, Maria Catherine (Buckingham), 403
  W. F., 403
Elder, Elizabeth, 236
  Jemima, 236
  John, 236
Elean, ———, 245
Elham, Mary, 228
  Richard, 228
Eliot, Francis, 264
  Mary, 264
Ellett, Bettie Thomas (Spears), 272
  Edwin Josiah, 272
  William Handley, 272
Elliott, Eliza Cathcart, 306
  Mary (Gibbes), 229
  Sarah (Jacob), 300
  Thomas, 229, 300
Ellis, Benjamin, 4
  Hannah, 218
  Jane, 251
  Joanna, 20
  John, 52
  Martha, 6
  Mary (Abbott), 4
  Richard, 218

Ellis—*Continued*
  Sarah, 218
  Sarah (Bacon), 52
Ely, Eunice (Colton), 500
  John, 500
Emerick, Charlotte, 225
Emerson, Abigail (Atkinson), 26
  Persis (Davenport), 300
  Robert, 26
  Sarah, 217, 300
  Simeon, 300
Emery, Abigail (Bartlet), 83
  Abigail (Bartlett), 74
  Andrew, 86
  Frank W., 235
  Hannah, 74, 83
  Hiram A., 86
  Hiram W., 86
  James, 84
  John, 74, 83
  Mary (Webster), 74
  Mehitable, 86
  Philomelia (Webber), 86
  Sarah (Bartlett), 86
  Shuah (Bartlett), 86
  William, 86
Emmons, Abraham, 459
  Seytic (Van Voorhies), 459
Emory, Mariana, 211
  Mariana Stoughton, 211
  Mariana Stoughton (Winder), 211
  Thomas, 211
Enders, Nannie, 117
Endicott, Hannah, 358
English, Anne Augusta (Claiborne) Lightfoot, 155
  Charles Albert, 155
  Margaret, 216
Ennalls, Ann (Skinner), 419
  Joseph, 446
  Mary, 446
  Sarah (Heron), 446
  Thomas, 419
Ensign, Elizabeth, 224
Ensor, ———, 423
  Birdie (Skinner), 423
Eppes, Richard, 8
  Tabitha (Adams), 8
Essinger, Phoebe, 324
Estabrook, Ebenezer, 477, 480
  Hannah, 478, 479, 480, 484

INDEX 539

Estabrook—*Continued*
Hannah (Bowerman), 480
Hannah (Loring), 480
John, 480
Joseph, 478, 480
Millicent (Woodhouse), 480
Submit (Loring), 477, 480
Ruth, 478
Ruth (Reed), 480
Estey, ———, 45
Julia A. (Bacon), 45
Evans, ———, 101
Ann, 207, 481
Anna (Brooke), 101
Annie, 470, 481
Benjamin, 470, 481
Catherine, 106
David, 470, 481
Evan, 481
George, 106
Hanna, 101
Hannah, 470, 481
Hannah (———), 481
Jason, 486
Joel, 481
John, 481
Mary, 481
Mary (Bryan), 106
Owen, 481
Rachel (Burnet), 470, 481
Rebecca, 481
Sarah, 142
Seth, 470, 481
Thomas, 481
William, 481
Winifred Miller (Brown), 470, 481
Eveleth, Sylvester, 215
Evitts, Jane, 346
Ewen, Elizabeth, 367
Richard (Mrs.), 363
Ewer, Albert, 69
Julia Dennison, 69
Ewing, Jean, 126

F

Faber, Anna, 134
Elizabeth, 134
Faddans, Jannetje Minnes, 456
Johannis, 456
Rensie, 456

Fairchild, Sarah, 33
Fairfield, Ann, 67
Baker, 67
Caty (Baker), 67
Christine, 67
Electa, 67
Eliza, 67
Emma, 67
John, 67
Kate, 67
Lure, 67
Rebecca, 67
Scott, 67
William, 67
Falconer, Mary, 122
Fales, Hannah, 52
Falkner, Lester, 374
Sarah (Coats) Penrose, 374
Fane, Dorothy, 438
Farewell, Eleazer, 184
Mary (Cummings), 184
Farley, Edwin P., 86
Elizabeth (Bartlett), 86
Elizabeth Carter, 284
James Parke, 284
Farmer, Dora Ellen, 257
Farnum, Charles A., 469
Sarah Elizabeth (Whipple), 469
Farr, Anna Maria Gemmill (Dunton), 208
Belle, 208
James McCullough, 208
Farrar, Jacob, 260
Mary, 260
Farree, Ann Elizabeth (Isaac), 281
John S., 281
Farrington, Frances, 26
Farwell, Abigail, 44
Isaac, 44
Lemoine, 175
Sarah, 44
Faunce, Asa, 45
Jane, 45
John, 248
Mercy, 248
Miriam, 45
Patience (Morton), 248
Fauntleroy, Catherine, 275
Elizabeth, 9
Faxon, Ebenezer, 493
Eleanor (Whitman), 493

Faxon—*Continued*
Elizabeth, 264
Richard, 264
Fay, Anna, 54
Daniel, 54
Feeley, James L., 362
Martha Elizabeth (Morrison), 362
Feindell, Ethel Margaret, 456
John Theodore, 456
Sarah Agnes (Garretson), 456
Fell, Cassandra, 421
Fenn, Sarah, 314
Fennell, Eliza W., 426
Fenno, Abigail, 359
Benjamin, 359
Fenwick, Elizabeth (Gibbes), 229
John, 229
Fenwicke, Edward, 283
Martha (Izard), 283
Ferguson, Betsey, 87
Elizabeth, 86
Emma Cabell (Henry), 245
James B., 245
Mary Elizabeth, 291
Shuah (Bartlet), 85
Stephen, 85
T. B., 127
Ferrel, Ann, 274
Ferris, Charlotte Cornelia Dickinson, 191
Orange, 191
Sophia (Rathbone), 191
Fessenden, Mary, 313
Field, Abigail (Stockton), 432
David Dudley, 193
Eleanor Kingland, 303
Harriet, 155
Hickson W., 303
Mary, 432
Mary (Peale), 432
Robert, 432
Fillis, Mary, 32
Finch, Clemence Eliza, 435
Ellen (Chapman), 435
George Ralsey, 435
Fine, Jennie, 7
Fisher, Mary, 52
Fisk, Lois, 54
Mary (Warren) Child, 462
Nathaniel, 462

INDEX

Fiske, Abigail, 417
  Abigail (Park), 35
  John, 35
  Martha, 35
Fite, Conrad, 237
  Pamela (Gist), 237
Fitz Eastman, Ann (Baker), 69
  Randolph, 69
Fitzrobert, John, 4
Flanagan, Bridget, 204, 207
Fleeson, Ann, 374
  Plunket, 374
Fleet, Albert S., 67
  Frances, 71
  Sophia (Baker), 67
  Sophia (Baker) Stearns, 68
  William, 68
Fleming, Bartholomew, 333
  Janet, 333
  Marion (Hamilton), 333
Fletcher, John, 157
  Mary (Ward), 157
Flint, Benjamin, 380
  Betsy (Pope), 380
  Betsy Walton, 380
  Simeon, 380
  Thomas, 380
Flournoy, Eliza Julia, 425
Fontaine, John, 244
  Peter, 244
Fookes, Elizabeth, 420
Foote, Abigail, 98
  Elizabeth, 146
  Hannah, 392
  Isaac, 392
  Joel, 98
  Nathaniel, 146
  Rebecca (Dickerman), 392
Ford, Andrew, 490
  Elizabeth, 68, 251
  Hepzibah, 343
  Mary, 490
  Noah Perry, 251
  Phoebe (Gurney), 251
  Sarah Williams, 248
  Thomas, 214, 343
Foreman, Elleanor, 421
Foster, Abigail (Alexander), 20
  Elizabeth Emmeline, 72
  Henry, 20
  Kezia, 307
  Sarah, 20

Foulke, Anzinetta (Miles), 255
  Morris Edkin, 255
Foutz, Margaret, 252
Fowel, Jacob, 44
Fowell, Elizabeth, 114
Fowler, Benonii, 280
  Drusilla (Isaac), 280
  Jeremiah, 280
  Joseph, 83
  Kezia (Isaac), 280
  Sarah (Bartlet), 83
Fox, Ann, 153
  Anne (West), 153
  Henry, 153
  Hester (Le Compte), 419
Foxley, Mary, 439
Foy, Andrew, 290
  Barbara (Doane) Calvert, 290
Francis, Anna, 440
  Tench, 440
Francois, Judith, 302
Franklin, Benjamin, 94
  Sophronia, 219
Fraser, Janet, 140
Freeman, Frederick, 501
  Hannah Huntington (Wolcott), 501
  Jane, 423
  John, 32
  Jonathan, 316
  Margaret Clark (Ker), 316
  Mercy, 32
Freer, Leon D., 271
  Martha, 230
French, Abigail (Beal), 490
  Alice, 183
  Elizabeth, 490
  Elizabeth (Cummings), 184
  Emily (Rice), 150
  Hannah, 490
  Hannah (Whitman), 489, 490
  Jason C., 150
  Jennie E., 150
  Joseph, 184
  Mary, 169, 490
  Samuel, 184, 490
  Sarah (Cummings), 184
  Stephen, 490
  Susannah, 337
Freshour, Mary, 166
Friberg, Anna Mary, 204

Fries, Jacob, 203, 204
Frisbie, Albert Butler, 361
  Anna (Weaver), 361
  Hazel A., 366
  Hazel Adelaide, 361
Frisby, Elizabeth (Sewall), 440
  Peregrine, 439
  Susanna, 439
Frizel, Dorothy, 412
Frost, Charles, 84
  Ellen Maria (Hubbard), 266
  George, 85
  Sarah (Bartlet), 85
  Sybilla, 261
  Rufus Smith, 266
Frothingham, Ann, 398
  Anne, 483
  Berthia, 484
  Christopher, 483
  Cornelia, 501
  Deborah, 331
  Edmund, 483
  Edward, 483
  Elizabeth, 484
  Elizabeth (Hansard), 483
  Francis, 483
  Hannah, 484
  Harriet, 501
  John, 484
  Joseph, 484
  Mary, 398, 475, 476, 484
  Mary (Lorden), 484
  Mary Frances (Wolcott), 501
  Michael, 483
  Nathaniel, 476, 484
  Peter, 398, 476, 484
  Robert, 483
  Ruth (George), 484
  Samuel, 484, 501
  Stephen, 484
  Theodore, 501
  William, 398, 476, 483, 484
Frueauf, J. F., 204
Fry, Ann, 16
  Christina (Capp), 134
  Elizabeth Speed (Smith), 16
  Henry, 15
  John, 9, 14, 16
  Joshua, 9, 14, 15, 16
  Lucy Gilmer, 11, 14, 16
  Martha, 16
  Martin, 134
  Mary Micou (Hill), 14

INDEX

Fry—*Continued*
Peachy (Walker), 9, 14, 16
Sally, 16
Sarah (Adams), 9
Susan, 16
Susan (Walker), 15
Tabitha, 9
Thomas Walker, 16
William A., 9
Fullam, Abigail (Nichols), 212
  Alexina (Seymour), 213
  Elisha, 212
  Francis, 212
  Jacob, 212
  Mariana Emory, 211
  Mariana Winder (Robinson), 211
  Nathan Seymour, 213
  Nelson, 212, 213
  Rhoda, 211
  Rhoda Ann (Stowitz), 213
  Sarah (Hagar), 212
  Sarah (Livermore), 212
  Tabitha (Whitney), 212
  William Freeland, 211, 213
Fuller, Esther 225
  Mary A., 33
  Sarah (Gardiner), 225
  W., 225
Fulton, Aaron, 219
  Andrew, 220
  Ann, 216
  Ann (Meredith), 216
  Ann (Wyer), 217
  Anne (Goodrich) Austin, 220
  Bennett D., 219
  Betsey (Heald), 219
  Caleb, 218
  Caroline (Nicholas), 218
  Clarissa (Daniels), 221
  Daniel, 218, 219
  David, 218
  Dorothy, 215
  Dorotie (———-), 215
  Eleazer Emerson, 218
  Elijah, 218, 219
  Elinor (Johnson), 216
  Elisha, 218
  Eliza (Edwards), 221
  Elizabeth, 216, 220
  Elizabeth (———), 215, 216, 217, 219
  Elizabeth (Ingraham), 217

Fulton—*Continued*
Elizabeth Harrison (Warner), 214
Elizabeth Hayden, 214
Eunice, 219, 220
Gaylord, 219
George, 215, 218
Hannah (———), 217
Hannah (Ellis), 218
Harriet D., 219
Harry, 219
Henry, 218
Hiram, 219
Hugh, 216
Ida Eleana (Lewis), 214
Irving Kent, 214
Isabel, 215
James, 216, 218
James Carnac, 216
Jane, 216
Janet, 216
Jennie (Taggart), 218
Jesse, 218, 219
Jesse Leroy, 219
John, 215, 216, 217, 218, 219, 220, 221
John A., 217
Lewis Edwards, 214
Lois (Vaughan), 219
Luke, 218
Lydia, 219
Lydia (Clark), 219
Margaret, 216, 219
Margaret (———) Mills, 217
Margaret (Carnac), 216
Margaret (English), 216
Margaret (Homer), 216
Martha (———), 219
Mary, 216, 324
Mary (———), 215
Mary (Corbet), 217
Mary (Humphrey), 219
Mary Ann, 216
Matthew, 215
Moses, 219
Nancy, 220
Nancy (Ann W.), 217
Nathan, 219
Paul, 216
Phebe (Bennett), 219
Philena (Hastings), 219
Polly (Barnes), 218
Polly (Jones), 219

Fulton—*Continued*
Polly (Orall), 217
Polly (Wood), 218
Richard, 215, 218
Robert, 214, 215, 216, 217, 218, 219
Rose Hinckley (Hayden), 214
Ruel, 219
Sally (Choate), 218
Samuel, 217, 218
Sarah, 217, 219, 220
Sarah (Bradley), 217
Sarah (Coslet), 216
Sarah (Ellis), 218
Sarah (Emerson), 217
Simeon, 218
Sophronia, 219
Sophronia (Franklin), 219
Stephen, 218
Susanne (Stewart), 220
Sylvia, 219
Thomas, 215, 216
William, 215, 216, 219, 220
William Edwards, 214, 221
William Goodrich, 221
William Hayden, 214
William Shirley. 214
Wells, 214

G

Gaines, Mary E., 245
  R. F., 245
Gaither, Agnes, 364
  Agnes (Rogers), 364
  Ann, 449
  Anne, 364
  Benjamin, 363, 364
  Cassandra, 364
  Edward, 364
  Eleanor (Whittle), 364
  Elizabeth, 364
  Evan, 364
  Henry, 364
  John, 364
  John Rogers, 364
  Mary, 364
  Samuel, 364
  Sarah, 364
  Sarah (Burgess), 363
  Sarah (Warfield), 364
  Susannah, 364
  Vachel, 364

INDEX

Gaither—*Continued*
　William, 364
　Zachariah, 364
Galatin, Eleanore (Maquinet), 401
Gale, Amos, 76
　Bartholomew, 42
　Ella L., 301
　Mary (Bacon), 42
　Sarah (Bartlett), 75
Gallagher, Sarah Elizabeth, 135
Gallaher, Mary Ann (Capp), 135
　Samuel Capp, 135
　Stephen, 135
　William, 135
Galloway, Elizabeth, 441
Gallup, Martha, 189
Gamble, Agnes Sarah Bell, 116
　Catharine (Grattan), 116
　Henry, 411
　Margaret (Saltonstall), 411
　Robert, 116
Gambrill, Sarah, 365
Gardiner, Abraham, 225
　Alanson, 225
　Alfred, 225
　Alvina, 225
　Ann (Ackerson), 225
　Catherine Larison (Marshall), 222
　Celesta (Richardson), 225
　Charlotte Margaret, 226
　Clarissa, 225
　David, 222, 223, 224
　Eleanor, 226
　Eleanor (Temple), 225
　Elinor (Grosbeck), 224
　Elizabeth, 223, 226
　Elizabeth (Allyn) Allen, 223
　Elizabeth (Ensign), 224
　Elizabeth (Hedges) Osborne, 223
　Esther (Fuller), 225
　Evaline, 310
　Franklin, 225
　George Schuyler, 222, 227
　Giles, 223
　Hannah, 224
　Hannah (Merry), 223
　Harriet, 225

Gardiner—*Continued*
　Henry, 224
　Howell, 224, 225
　James Lyon, 225
　Jemima (Howell) Stratton, 224
　Jeremiah, 224, 225
　John, 223, 224, 225
　Juliet, 222
　Keziah (Williams), 225
　Lion, 222, 223, 224
　Louisa Catherine (Henkel), 225
　Lyon, 226
　Margaret (Hench), 225
　Marilla Etta (Truesdell), 225
　Marinda (Cole), 225
　Martha (Young), 223
　Mary, 222, 223, 224
　Mary (King), 223
　Mary (Leringman), 223
　Mary (Parsons), 224
　Mary (Sanford), 224, 225
　Mary (Wilemsen), 223
　Mary Jeanette, 226
　Nancy (Bonney), 225
　Paulina (Collins), 225
　Phebe (Weed), 224
　Philip Stimson, 225
　Samuel, 224, 225
　Sanford, 225
　Sarah, 225
　Sarah (Chandler) Coit, 223
　Sarah (Hodge) Schuyler, 224
　Sarah Elizabeth, 226
　Silas Wright, 225
　Stephen Griffith, 225
　Stimson Brockway, 225
　Susan (Griffith), 225
　Rachel, 222
Gardner, Caroline Emma (Palmer), 46
　Charles Graham, 46
　Emily Beatrice, 46
　Ralph Graham, 46
Garfield, Benjamin, 328
　Edward, 215
　Edwin, 479
　Johanna (———) Buckminster, 479
　Rebecca, 328
Garland, Mary, 165

Garnett, Edgar Malcolm, 144
　Emily Dennis (Hayward), 144
　Grace Fenton (Mercer), 144
　Helen, 144
　James, 144
　James Mercer, 144
　John, 144, 273
　Maria (Battaile), 144
　Muscoe, 144
　Robert Selden, 144
Garretson, Annie M., 165
　Catherine (Livingston), 336
　Catherine Ann (Riker), 165
　Freeborn, 336
　John, 165
　Sarah Agnes, 456
Garrit, William, 36
Gaskill, Job Hillman, 351
　Lucretia, 351
　Lucretia Stockton, 347
Gason, Jane, 228
　Simon, 228
Gastlin, Elizabeth, 311
Gatchell, Henry, 111
　Susan, 111
Gates, Benjamin, 250
　Elizabeth, 73, 82
　Hannah, 483
　John, 73, 82
Gay, John, 52
　Rebecca (Bacon), 52
Gaylord, Elizabeth (Davenport), 173
　Elizabeth (Hull), 19
　Jerusha, 147
　Samuel, 19
　Sarah, 19
　William, 173
Geary, Ann (Douglas), 188, 194
　Nathaniel, 188, 194
Gedding, Helena, 49
Gemmill, Anna Maria (Dunton), 204
　Anna Maria Gordon, 205, 208
　James Ritchie, 204
Gennison, Elizabeth, 396
Genung, Abigail, 225
　George, ———, 75
　John, 484
　Ruth, 484

INDEX

Gerlach, Addie Crandall (Robertson), 395
Rudolph Philip, 395
Gerritsen, Jacobus, 459
Sara (Van Voorhees), 459
Gibb, Mary Hull, 163
Gibbes, Alexander Mason, 233
Alice, 229
Alice (Trewnwall), 228
Alice Eliza, 234
Allston, 231
Ann, 230
Ann (Wigg), 229
Ann Isabell, 231, 232
Ann Isabella (Mayrant), 231
Anne, 229, 231
Anne (Culcheth), 229
Anne (Uden), 228
Basil, 229
Benjamin, 231
Benjamin Taylor, 234
Bennet, 228
Calhoun Scott, 232
Caroline Elizabeth (Guignard), 232
Caroline S. (Scott), 232
Caroline S. (Thayer), 231
Caroline Scott, 232
Catherine Elizabeth, 230
Constantia, 230
Culcheth, 230
Daisy, 234
De Veaux, 234
Edmund, 228
Edwin, 231
Eliza, 231
Elizabeth, 229, 230, 232, 234
Elizabeth (Allston), 230
Elizabeth (Bedon), 229
Elizabeth (Haddrell), 230
Elizabeth (Hasell), 230
Elizabeth (Seay), 229
Elizabeth (Waller) Kilcreana, 234
Elizabeth (White), 230
Elizabeth P. (Hunt), 234
Ellen, 228
Ethel, 234
Eugenia (Talley), 234
Francis Guignard, 233
Frank Huger, 233
Hannah J. (Lamar), 232
Harriet, 231

Gibbes—*Continued*
Harriet Hampton, 234
Heloise (Weston), 233
Henry, 228, 230, 231
Hunter Allston, 234
James Guignard, 232, 234
James Hayward, 233
James Wilson, 231, 232
Jane, 229
Jane (Gason), 228
Jane (Jackson), Butler, 230
Jane (Turney), 228
Jane Mason, 233
Jenkin, 228
Jennie Guignard, 232
John, 228, 229, 230
Judith (Porter), 228
Lucy Elizabeth, 233
Margaret (Champney), 228
Marion Farrar, 232
Martha (Freer), 230
Mary, 229, 230
Mary (———), 229
Mary (Benison), 230
Mary (Cook), 230
Mary (Coventry), 229
Mary (Dunbar), 230
Mary (Elham), 228
Mary (How), 232
Mary (Woodward), 229
Mary Caroline, 232
Mary E. (McCullough), 234
Mary Eugenia, 234
Mary H. (Clark), 233
Mary How, 232
Mary Philip (Wilson), 230
Mary Susan, 231
Nathaniel, 233
Nicholas, 229
Robert, 229, 230
Robert W., 231
Robert Waller, 228, 234
Robert Wilson, 231, 232, 234
Sallie, 234
Samuel Wilson, 232
Sarah (Chisolm), 231
Sarah Eliza, 232
Sarah Postell, 231
Stephen, 228, 229
Susan K. (Hayward), 233
Susan Wilson, 231, 232
Thomas, 228, 229
Thomas Hasell, 234

Gibbes—*Continued*
Virginia Mason, 233
Wade Hampton, 233
Washington, 231
Washington Allston, 234
William, 228, 229, 230, 231
William Allston, 231
William Hasell, 230
William, Moultrie, 233
Gibson, Elizabeth, 445
Jacob, 445
Margaret (Bryan) Mitchell, 106
Patrick, 106
Giesler, Charles A., 46
Jennie C., 46
Margaret (Dives), 46
Gifford, Amelia, 256
Gilbert, ———, 206, 407
Arthur E., 309
Elizabeth, 179
Jonathan, 485
Josiah, 179
Maria Louise (Johnson), 309
Mary (White), 485
Penelope, 273
Susanna (Rush), 407
Susanna (Rush) Webster, 206
Gile, ———, 85
Alice (Bartlet), 85
Giles, Elizabeth, 43, 269
John, 43
William B., 269
Gilfillan, Ann, 361
Harriet Newell, 59
Gill, Helen, 393
Louisa, 185
Gilliam, Annie (Holmes) Henry, 246
Robert E., 246
Gillis, Bessie (Culpepper), 422
Henry, 422
Gilly, Edward, 405
Elizabeth (Riffe), 405
Gilman (?), Mary, 298
Gilmer, Francis Walker, 15
George, 15
Lucy (Walker), 15
Maria, 11
Thomas Walker, 16
Gillmore, Ann (Dunlap), 382
Clara Agnes, 382
James Clarkson, 382

INDEX

Girard, Margaret, 343
  William, 343
Gist, Anne, 237
  Anne Cary, 240
  Benjamin, 241
  Cecil, 237
  Cecil (Carman), 238
  Cecil Carman, 239
  Charles Wooster, 235
  Christopher, 235, 236, 239, 240
  Clara (Reinecker), 237
  Cornelius Howard, 237
  David, 239, 241
  Edith, 239
  Edith (Cromwell), 235
  Eliza Violet, 240
  Elizabeth, 237, 238
  Elizabeth (———), 241
  Elizabeth (Elder), 236
  Elizabeth Johnson, 241
  Ellen, 237, 238
  Emeline, 237
  Frances (Trippe), 237, 445
  George Reineker, 237
  Henry Cary, 240
  Independence, 239
  Jabez Chisolm, 241
  Jacob, 241
  James Black, 235, 242
  Jemima, 237, 239
  John, 237, 238
  John Elder, 237, 445
  Joseph, 236, 237, 241
  Joshua, 237, 239
  Joshua Howard, 237
  Judith Cary, 240
  Judith Cary (Bell), 240
  Kitty Malinda (Marrs), 241
  Laura Velma, 235
  Louisiana, 237
  Luella A. (Hatch), 235
  Maria Cecil, 240
  Mary (Howard), 236
  Mary (McCall) Cattell, 238
  Mary (Sterrett), 238
  Melville, 235
  Mordecai, 238
  Nancy, 240
  Nathaniel, 236, 239, 240, 241
  Owen, 237
  Pamela, 237
  Rachel, 239

Gist—*Continued*
  Richard, 236, 240
  Ruth, 237, 239
  Ruth (Bond), 237
  Sarah, 238, 239
  Sarah (Howard), 240
  Sarah Howard, 240
  Solomon, 241
  States, 239
  Susan (Cockey), 238
  Susannah, 239
  Thomas, 237, 238, 239, 240, 241
  Violetta, 238
  Violetta (Howard), 236
  William, 236, 237, 238, 240
  Zipporah, 236
  Zipporah (Murray), 236
Gladding, Cynthia (Whipple), 467
  Timothy, 467
Gladen, Olivia, 165
Glassford, Sarah (Little), 317
  William, 317
Glover, Charles, 163
  Essa, 359
  Eunice (Minot), 359
  Mary, 163
Goff, Eliza Cathcart (Elliott), 306
  Leah, 306
  Richard W. Petherbridge, 306
Goldsborough, Anna Maria (Tilghman), 441
  Charles, 441
  William, 440
Goldsmith, Elizabeth, 164
Gooch, Ursula (Claiborne), 152
  William, 152
Goodale, Jane, 39
  Marian, 160
  Nathan, 497
  Persis (Whitney), 497
Goode, John, 284
  Sallie, 284
Goodhue, Abigail (Bartlet), 83
  Samuel, 83
Goodloe, Mary Elizabeth, 275
Goodrich, Anne, 220
  Chauncey, 501
  Ephraim, 180
  Hannah, 180

Goodrich—*Continued*
  Hannah (Steele), 180
  Maria, 161
  Mary Ann (Wolcott), 501
  Mary E., 501
  Sally Worthington, 501
  Samuel, 501
  William, 214
Goodridge, Caroline (Wilcox), 465
  William, 465
Goodsell, Anna (Atherton), 181
  Elihu, 181
  Eliza, 181
  Martha, 66
  Martha (Davenport), 173
  Thomas, 173
Goodwin, ———, 25
  Bridget, 148
  Caroline A., 86
  Mary (Atkinson), 25
Gordon, Agnes Helen (Donald), 79
  Fanny, 79
  M. Lafayette, 79
  Ursula, 363
Gore, Richard, 73
Goslin, Margaret (Skinner), 423
  Thomas, 423
Goss, Rath May, 104
Gosslee, Keturah, 62
Gould, Martha, 173
  Mary Goodridge, 465
  Nancy, 301
  Nathan, 173
  Priscilla, 381
  Rebecca Hannah (Robbins), 392
  Robert, 491
  Sarah (Whitman) Cocks, 491
  William M., 392
Gove, Helen Beryl, 428
Grady, Henry W., 121
Grafflin, J. Fred, 423
  Mary (Skinner), 423
Grafton, Joseph, 360
  Maria Josephine, 360
  Mary Dawes, 444
Graham, ———, 420
  Rachel (Skinner), 420
Granger, David, 21
  Mary Brown (Alexander), 21

INDEX

Grant, Ann, 101
  Elizabeth (Robbins) Lawrence, 393
  Mary, 139
  Patrick, 139
  Roswell, 393
Grattan, Catharine, 116
Gratz, Benjamin, 240
  Maria Cecil (Gist), 240
Graves, Barnabas, 181
  Edna (Deming), 181
  Eunice, 345
  George, 179
  Mary, 492
  Patience Hatch, 71
  Rebecca, 311
  Sarah, 179
Gray, Candace (Barney), 68
  Daniel, 68
  Elizabeth, 68
  Eunice, 68
  Franklin, 68
  Harry, 68
  Jane, 68
  Jane (Stryker), 68
  Lauren, 68
  Levi, 68
  Lucretia, 68
  Lydia (Myrtle), 68
  Martha (Duke), 198
  Richard, 68
  Samuel Baker, 68
  Tryphena (Baker), 68
  William, 198
Grayson, Judith, 293
Greeley, Jonathan, 75
  Mary (Bartlett), 75
Green, Allen Jones, 284
  Ann (———), 490
  Ann (Almy), 354
  Ann (Marshall), 123
  Ann (Willis), 123
  Annie (Hunton), 222
  Annie Hunton, 222
  Caroline, 294
  Catherine (Calvert), 294
  Charles, 222
  Dorcas, 492
  Duff, 123, 130
  Edward Pendleton, 294
  Elizabeth, 488, 491
  George Gardiner, 222
  Gilbert, 222

Green—*Continued*
  Hannah (Kendall), 328
  Helen (Calvert), 288
  Henry, 294
  James William, 292
  John, 16, 123, 354, 491
  John Strother, 292
  Joseph, 170, 488, 490
  Lavinia (Jett), 292
  Lucretia (Edwards), 130
  Margaret Maria, 123, 130
  Mary, 491
  Mary Cadwallader, 284
  Mary Elizabeth, 294
  Mary Frances (Jett), 292
  Patience (———), 491
  Polly, 170
  Rachel (Gardiner), 222
  Robert, 122, 123
  Sally (Fry), 16
  Thomas, 288
  William, 122, 123, 128
  Zachary, 491
Greene, Abigail, 37
Greenleaf, Elizabeth, 24
Greenwood, Alveda, 22
  Phebe, 300
Gregg, Mary, 141
  Mary Bellinger, 141
Gregory, Ezra, 89
  Hannah (Betts), 89
  Mary, 154
  Roger, 154
Grenell, Lydia, 158
Greville, Elizabeth (Willoughby), 297
  Fulke, 297
  Katherine, 297
Grew, Elizabeth Ives (Deming), 99
  Harriet (Johnson), 99
  Henry, 99
  Henry Johnson, 99
  Susan, 99
Griffin, Cyrus, 9
  Elizabeth, 9
  Harriet (Douglas), 190
  Leroy, 9
  Mary Anne (Bertrand), 9
  Smith, 190
  Thomas, 9
Griffith, Henry, 225
  Mary (Gardiner), 224

Griffith—*Continued*
  Steven, 224
  Susan, 225
Griswold, Anna (Wolcott), 499
  Matthew, 499
Grosbeck, Elinor, 224
Gross, Isaac, 483
  Persis (Davis), 483
Grow, Della, 54
  Rebecca, 299
Grundy, Ann, 440
Grymes, ———, 293
  Catherine (Lindsay), 293
  Jane (Calvert), Maddox, Settle, 293
  Reynold, 293
Guest, Sarah, 271
Guichon, Cecilia, 388
Guignard, Caroline Elizabeth, 232
Guillaume, Louis, 67
  Mary (Baker), 67
Guldager, Carolina Magretha, 272
Gulick, Eliza (Baker), 67
  John G., 67
Gump, Dorothy, 402
Gundrum, John, 134
  Susanna (Capp), 134
Gunning, Jane, 33
Gurdon, Brampton, 411
  Muriel, 411
Gurney, Elizabeth (Green), 491
  John, 491
  Phoebe, 251

H

Hackett, Mary, 323
Haddrell, Elizabeth, 230
Hagar, Sarah, 212
Hageman, John F., 376
  Lydia Spencer (Blight), 376
Haggerday, Nancy, 504
Haines, Eliza, 42, 51
  Henry A., 435
  Louise, 435
  Mary, 42, 51
  Walter, 42, 51
Hale, Eunice, 180
  Gideon, 19
  Hannah, 25
  Sarah, 25, 26
  Thankful (Alexander), 19

INDEX

Haliburton, Catherine (Chisholme), 139
  Margaret, 138
  Walter, 138, 139
Hall, Ann, 349
  Carolyn Elizabeth, 485
  Cassandra, 375
  Elizabeth (King), 491
  Elizabeth D., 69
  Felicia O., 141
  James H., 69
  John, 467, 491
  Joseph, 365, 407
  Mary, 198, 349
  Rebecca, 52
  Ruth (Warfield), 365
  Samuel, 349
  Susanna, 407, 467
Hallett, Sarah, 339
Halley, Gladys, 450
Halliday, Walter, 214
Halloway, ———, 425
  Jane P. (Spencer), 426
  Martha Owen (Spencer), 425
  Samuel, 426
Hambleton, Lucy, 420
  Margaret (Sherwood), 420
  Philemon, 444
  Susan (Sherwood), 444
  William, 420
Hambrick, Mariah (Adams), 294
  Mariah (Calvert) Myers, 295
  Nimrod, 294, 295
Hamersley, Catherine Livingston (Hooker), 142
  James Hooker, 142
  John William, 142
  Margaret Willing (Chisolm), 142
Hamilton, Alexander, 454
  Andrew, 125
  Frances, 125
  Ian, 81
  Marion, 333
  Martha Daniel (Venable) Morton, 454
Hammond, ———, 364
  Anne (Gaither), 364
  Arthur W., 257
  Catharine, 68
  Fannie Jackson (Biays), 449

Hammond—*Continued*
  Henry, 449
  John, 168
  Mary Lillian (Hoover), 257
  Nannie, 449
  Prudence (Wade) Crosby, Cotton, 168
Hammonds, Benjamin, 314
  Sarah (Brown), 314
Hampton, Elizabeth, 210
  John Brewster, 32
  Ruth (Avery), 32
  Thomas, 273
Hance, Anne, 6
Hancock, Elizabeth, 43
  Mary (Prentice), 43
  Nathaniel, 43
  Rhoda, 190
Hane, Robert Y., 130
Hanover, Mary, 189
Hansard, ———, 483
  Elizabeth, 483
  Peter, 483
  Richard, 13
  Sarah (Speed), 13
Hanscom, Abigail (Bartlet), 84
  Moses, 84
Hansen, Alida (Livingston), 337
  Henry, 337
Hanslap, Henry, 363
Hanson, Elizabeth (Story), 367
  John, 367
  Samuel, 367
Hardesty, Rebecca (Hoover), 253
  Samuel, 253
Harding, Mabel (Woolford), 418
  Richard, 418
Hardy, Eliza, 450
  Elizabeth, 349
Hare, Charlotte, 462
  Elizabeth (Cabell), 116
  William B., 116
Hargrave, John, 255
  Mary Della (Miles), 255
  William H., 255
Harlan, Susanna, 58
Harley, Abigail (Saltonstall), 402
  Thomas, 412
Harlow, James, 250

Harmon, Caroline March, 28
Harner, Andrew, 107
  Harriet, 107
  Talitha (Bryan) Roberts, 107
Harrington, Mary (Browne) Warren, 313
  Samuel, 313
Harris, Handy, 125
  Josephine, 185
  Mary, 465
  Rachel (Calhoun), 125
  Walter, 215
Harrison, Benjamin, 12, 290
  Charles, 153
  Elizabeth, 290
  Elizabeth (Burwell), 290
  Elizabeth (Hampton), 210
  Ellwood Garrett, 48
  Harriet, 210
  James, 210
  Louise, 246
  Louise Christine (Bland), 246
  Lucy Gray (Henry), 246
  Mary (Claiborne), 153
  Mary F. (Stockton), 432
  Matthew Bland, 246
  Melvina (Meng), 48
  Rebecca, 6
  Robert Wiley, 246
  Sarah, 367
  William, 432
Hart, Anne Cary (Gist), 240
  John, 206, 406
  Nathaniel, 240
  Susanna (Rush), 206, 406
Hartpence, Alexander, 390
  Lucy Morton, 390
  Martha (Morton), 390
Harvey, Alvaretta, 257
  Charles Davis, 257
  Guy William, 257
  Hester Maria, 257
  Jerry E., 257
  Mary Jane (Hoover), 257
  Mary Ogier (Armstrong), 257
Harwood, Peter, 53
Hasell, Elizabeth, 230
Haskell, Abigail James (Hubbard), 267
  Simeon Dickenson, 267

INDEX

547

Hassell, Alice, 328
  Christopher, 328
  Richard, 328
Hastings, Courtland Ewart, 267
  Elizabeth, 4
  Florence Amelia (Hubbard), 267
  John, 4
  Philena, 219
Hatch, Charles Melzer, 235
  Clara P. (Dugans), 235
  James, 250
  Luella A., 235
Haven, Amy, 224
Haverstick, Alexander, 136
  Sarah Emma (Capp), 136
  Traff, 136
Hawkes, Adam, 214
Hawkins, John, 273
  Margaret, 12
Hawley, Abiah, 500
  Ezra, 68
  Kate (Baker), 68
Hay, Sarah Travers Daniel, 10
Hayden, Elizabeth Stuart, 200
  Rose Hinckley, 214
Hayes, Emma Virginia (Skinner) Woolford, 422
  Jack, 295
  Priscilla (Calvert), 295
  W. F., 422
Haynes, John, 488
Hayward, ———, 154
  Ann (Upton), 495
  Deborah, 265
  Emily Dennis, 144
  George, 495
  Georgina, 495
  Lemuel, 495
  Susan K., 233
Haywood, Persis, 328
Heald, Anna Maria (Hoover), 256
  Betsey, 219
  Franklin M., 256
Healey, Lydia, 31
Heap, Abigail, 93
Heard, John, 84
  Phebe (Littlefield), 84
  Shuah, 84
Hearnden, Sarah, 466

Heath, Albert, 221
  Anne, 349
  Caroline Penniman, 28
  Charles, 28
  Edward N., 221
  James M., 221
  Mary Caroline, 28
  Robert, 349
  William D., 221
Heaton, John, 291
  Sarah (Calvert), 291
Hebb, Nannie, 200
Hedges, Elizabeth, 223
Hedian, Elizabeth (Rennolds), 450
  T. Walter, 450
Heinly, Jane Elizabeth, 71
Heins, Sarah Postell (Gibbes), 231
  William F., 231
Heldring, Jan. Lodewijk, 109
  Maria Catherine, 109
Hele, Anne (Cabell), 114
  John, 114
Hellen, ———, 199
  Mary (Duke), 199
Hemingway, Gertrude, 39
  Pauline Mary, 39
  William, 39
Hempstead, Josiah, 195
  Julia, 195
  Mary, 188, 194, 195
  Robert, 188, 195
Hemsley, Anna Maria (Tilghman), 440
  William, 440
Hench, George, 225
  Margaret, 225
  Rebecca (Allison), 225
Henderson, Elizabeth (Morrison), 361
  James F., 361
Hendrickson, Jacob, 351
  Sarah (Waln), 351
Henkel, Charlotte (Emerick), 225
  Louisa Catherine, 225
  Philip M., 225
Henning, Fannie, 16
Henrison, Kath., 473
Henry, ——— (Elean), 245
  Alexander, 243
  Alexander Spotswood, 245

Henry—*Continued*
  Anne, 243, 244
  Anner Lee (Dulany), 243
  Annie (Holmes), 246
  Charles D., 258
  Dorothea Spotswood, 244
  Dorothea Spotswood (Dandridge), 244
  Edward, 244, 245
  Edward Winston, 245
  Elizabeth, 243, 244
  Elizabeth Watkins, 246
  Elvira (Cabell), 245
  Elvira Brice (McClelland), 245
  Elvira Bruce, 245
  Emma Cabell, 245
  Fayette, 245
  James, 245
  James Marshall, 246
  Jane, 243
  Jane (Youille), 245
  Jane Robertson, 245
  Jean (Robertson), 243
  John, 243, 244, 245, 247
  Laura Helen, 245
  Lou, 258
  Lucy, 243
  Lucy Gray, 246
  Lucy Gray (Marshall), 246
  Margaret Ann, 245
  Martha, 244
  Martha Catherine, 245
  Martha Catherine (Henry), 245
  Mary, 243
  Mary Bladen (Dulany), 243
  Mary E. (Gaines), 245
  Mary Gaines, 245
  Mitchell, 247
  Nathaniel, 245
  Patrick, 243, 245, 246, 268
  Paulina (Cabell), 245
  Richard, 245
  Robert Gaines, 245
  Sarah, 243
  Sarah (Scarborough), 245
  Sarah (Shelton), 244
  Sarah (Winston) Syme, 243
  Sarah Butler, 244
  Susanna, 243
  Thomas Stanhope, 245
  Virginia (Woodson), 245

INDEX

Henry—*Continued*
William, 243, 244
William Wirt, 243, 245, 246, 247
Henshaw, Sarah, 351
Hepburn, Agnes, 333
Herbert, Buller, 153
  Hannah, 75
  Mary, 153
  Richard, 75
Heron, Sarah, 446
Herrick, Alma (Hull), 181
  Henry, 214
  Jane Ripley (Hubbard), 266
  Laura Sophia, 181
  Moses Augustus, 266
  Samuel Bellows, 181
Herron, Susannah, 444
Hershier, Sarah Eliza, 226
Herter, Catharine, 197
  Ignatius, 197
Hessing, ———, 476
  Hannah (White), 476
Heston, Bathsheba, 497
  Thomas, 497
Heuple, Elizabeth, 226
Hewit, Thankful, 147
Heyward, Alice (Izard), 284
  Edward Barnwell, 285
  Joseph, 284
  Lucy Green (Izard), 285
Heywood, George, 215
Hibbets, Mary, 431
Hicks, Cornelia Baird, 57
  Cornelia Wyntje (Baird), 57
  William Whinnery, 57
Hickson, Sarah (White) Taylor, ———, 485
  Walter, 485
Hierlihys, Timothy, 99
Hiester, Eugenia Frances, 409
  John, 409
Higginbotham, Elvira Bruce (Henry), 245
  Jesse A., 245
Hill, ———, 75
  Abraham, 214
  Ann, 281
  Elizabeth (Ferguson), 86
  Emma (McMullan), 425
  John, 86
  Lois, 85, 425
  Mary (Bartlett), 75

Hill—*Continued*
  Mary Baldwin (Bacon), 55
  Mary Micou, 14
  Rodney D., 55
  Rufus Sadler, 425
  Susan Letitia (Whipple), 468
  Zaccheus, 468
Hillhouse, Frances Julia (Betts), 90
  William, 90
Hillman, James Frayer, 117
  Marguerite Cabell (Wright), 117
Hilton, Elizabeth, 206
  Joseph, 24
  Rebecca (Atkinson) Adams, 24
Hinchman, Bertha Laura (Hoover), 256
  Joe, 256
  Olive Mary (Hoover), 256
Hinckley, Hannah (Cummings), 185
  Joel, 185
  Mehitable, 31
  Thomas, 31, 323
Hinman, Dorothy, 72
  Frank H., 72
  Mary M. (Coleman), 72
Hiscox, Sarah, 37
Hitchcock, Josephine (Lloyd), 488
  Olive, 488
  Oliver Nelson, 488
Hobard (or Hubbard), Capen, 266
  Charles, 266
  Daniel, 266
  Elizabeth (Capen), 266
  Elizabeth Williams, 266
  Emeline, 266
  Sheldon, 266
  William, 266
Hobart, Aaron, 264
  Ann, 265
  Ann (Plomer), 264
  Benjamin, 265
  Caleb, 264, 265
  David, 263
  Deborah (Hayward), 265
  Elias, 264
  Elizabeth, 264
  Elizabeth (———), 263

Hobart—*Continued*
  Elizabeth (Church), 264
  Elizabeth (Faxon), 264
  Hannah, 264
  Isaac, 264
  Israel, 265
  James, 263
  Jane (———), 264
  John, 264
  Jonathan, 264
  Joshua, 264, 265
  Josiah, 264
  Lydia, 263
  Margaret (Dewey), 263
  Mary, 264
  Mary (Eliot), 264
  Mary (Beal) Stowell, 264
  Mehitable, 264
  Moses, 264
  Nathaniel, 264
  Nazareth, 263
  Nehemiah, 263
  Peter, 263, 265
  Rebecca, 263, 264
  Rebecca (Ibrook), 263
  Sarah, 263
  Susanna, 265
  Susannah (Newcomb), 265
  Thomas, 264
Hobart (or Hobard), Abigail, 266
  Abigail (Curtis), 265
  Benjamin, 266
  Charley, 266
  Daniel, 266
  Elisha, 266
  Hannah, 266
  Mercy (Burrill), 265
  Peter, 266
  Polly, 266
  Sally, 266
  Samuel, 265
  Thomas, 266
  William, 265
Hobart (or Hubbard), Benjamin, 265
  Daniel, 265
  Desire (Copeland), 265
  Elisha, 265
  Isaac, 265
  Joshua, 265
  Mercy, 265
  Peter, 265

INDEX 549

Hobart (or Hubbard)—Continued
  Rebecca, 265
  Susanna, 265
  William, 265
Hobbs, Joseph Cottman, 200
  Mary Mabel (Duke), 200
  Sarah Jane, 200
Hodge, Amy (Haven), 224
  Helen (Penrose), 377
  Reuben, 224
  Sarah, 224
  Sarah (Baird), 60
  Thomas Leiper, 377
  William, 60
Hodges, Elizabeth, 206
  Hannah (Waln), 348
  Jane (Dilworth), 348
  Thomas, 348
Hodsdon, ———, 85
  Lucretia (Bartlet), 85
Hoffman, Alida (Livingston) Hansen, 337
  Dorothy Kingston, 388
  Florence Kingston (McCay), 388
  John White, 388
  Katherine, 332
  Martin, 337
  Mary Ann, 375
  William, 375
Hogan, Edna Drusilla, 208
  Emma Drusilla, 203
  Hellen Ruhamah (McClean) 208
  Jonathan Elmer, 208
Hogg, Peter, 105
Holand, Mary Emily, 272
Holden, Donald Fraser (Claiborne), 156
  Joanna, 330
  Stephen West, 156
Holdrege, Annie Mumford (Hunt), 27
  Charles Francis, 27
  Emily Cabot (Atkinson), 27
  George Chandler, 27
  George W., 27
  Henry Atkinson, 27
Holland, Abiah (Douglas), 189
  Eleanor, 197
  Elizabeth (Park), 36
  Henry, 189

Holland—Continued
  Jackson, 421
  John, 36
  Katharine (Skinner), 421
Holliday, Daniel, 445
  Frances, 445
Hollingsworth, ———, 296
  Katherine Kennerley (Calvert), 296
Hollis, Abigail, 489
Hollister, Sarah A., 191
Holloway (Rebecca), 5
Holman, Jeremiah, 496
  Jonathan, 50
  Mary, 496
Holmes, Ann, 268
  Annie, 246
  Bartlett, 250
  Bradford, 250
  Bradford Reed, 251
  Caleb, 249, 250
  Edwin Bradford, 248, 251
  Edwin Pratt, 248
  Eleazer, 249, 250
  Elisha, 249
  Eliza Bonsall, 143
  Elizabeth, 249
  Esther, 250
  Frances, 248
  Francis B., 248
  Freeland S., 251
  Gamaliel, 250
  Hannah, 249
  Hannah (Sylvester), 249
  Harriet, 250
  Ichabod, 249
  James, 249
  Jerusha (Rawson), 249
  Job, 249, 250
  John, 248, 249
  Jonathan, 249, 250, 251
  Joshua, 249
  Judith (Tucker), 249
  Lemuel, 249
  Lewis Atwood, 251
  Lydia, 249, 250
  Mahala (Reed), 251
  Mahala R., 251
  Mary Frances, 248
  Mehitable (Stuart), 249
  Mercy, 249, 250, 251
  Molly, 249
  Nathaniel, 248, 249

Holmes—Continued
  Sally, 250
  Sarah, 249
  Sarah (———), 248
  Sarah Ellis, 251
  Sarah Frances (Pratt), 248
  Sullivan, 251
  Susan, 248
  Thomas, 248
  William, 250
  Zenas, 250
Holt, Eliza (Calhoun), 124
  James, 124
  William, 214
Holton, Eleazer, 19
  Maria, 387
  Mary (Wiseman), 387
  Robert, 387
  Sarah (Alexander), 19
Homer, Margaret, 216
Honeywood, Susan, 438
Hoo, Ann, 396
  Cicily, 49
  Thomas, 396
Hood, Ebenezer, 185
Hooker, Catherine Livingston, 142
  Sarah (Whitman), 493
  Thomas, 157
  Thomas Hart, 493
Hooper, Elizabeth, 422
  George, 114
  Ida Stengle, 422
  Rachel, 114
  W. R., 422
Hoops, Thomas, 15
Hoover, Abram, 254
  Absalom, 254
  Aldus Joel, 256
  Alfred, 254
  Alice M., 256
  Allan Henry, 258
  Allen, 256
  Amelia (Gifford), 256
  Andrew, 252, 253, 254
  Anna Maria, 256
  Arthur Eli, 257
  Benajah, 256
  Bertha A. (West), 256
  Bertha Laura, 256
  Catherine, 253, 254
  Catherine (Yount), 253
  Celia, 254

INDEX

Hoover—*Continued*
Charles E., 256
Clark, 255
Clyde, 256, 257
Cora, 256
Curtis (———), 254
David, 253, 254
Deborah, 254
Deborah (Tucker), 254
Delilah, 255
Dora Ellen (Farmer), 257
Eli, 255, 256
Elizabeth, 253, 254, 255
Elizabeth (Waymire), 253
Elizabeth A., 256
Ella, 256
Elva, 255
Enos, 254
Ensley, 254
Esther E. (Brantingham), 257
Eunice, 256
Frederick 253, 254, 256
George, 256
Gulielma (Ratliff), 253
H. Maria (Plummer), 257
Hannah (Leonard), 256
Hannah Martha, 257
Henry, 253, 254
Henry Davis, 257
Herbert Charles, 258
Herbert Clark, 257
Hulda Randall (Minthorn), 257
Ida (Berkheimer), 256
Ila, 257
Jacob, 253
Jennie M., 257
Jesse, 254
Jesse Clark, 257
John, 253, 254
John Farnum, 256
John Y., 255
Jonas, 252
Joseph, 253, 254, 257
Kate (———), 253
Lillian (Saunders), 256
Lillian B., 257
Lou (Henry), 258
Lydia (Vaughan), 253
Mahala, 254
Margaret (Foutz), 252
Margaret Ella (Albin), 256

Hoover—*Continued*
Mary, 253, 254, 258
Mary (Davis), 256
Mary (Jay), 255
Mary H., 255
Mary Jane, 257
Mary Lillian, 257
Michal (Yount), 254
Mildred Crew (Brooke), 252
Millicent (Winslow), 253
Noah, 254
Olive Mary, 256
Peter, 254
Pollie (———), 253
Rachel, 253
Rachel (Briles), 252
Rachel (Briles-Whisenhurst), 253
Rebecca, 253, 257
Rebecca (Yount), 254
Roy, 257
Ruth E. (Darone), 256
Samuel, 253
Sarah, 253, 255
Sarah (Burkett?), 254
Shubael, 254
Solomon Y., 255
Susan, 254
Susanna, 253
Susanna (Clark), 253
Susie, 255
Theodore Jesse, 252, 258
Vernon, 256
Walter, 256
William, 255
William (Sheets), 253
William E., 257
William Jason, 254
William L., 257
Hope, Theodore, 215
Hopkins, ———, 420
Abigail (Whipple) Dexter, 466
Edward M., 434
Julia (Stockton), 434
Mary, 115
Mary (Skinner), 420
William, 466
Hopkinson, Elizabeth B., 94
Hopper, Alice, 292
Mary, 287
Horacy, Martha F. (Spencer), 426
Thomas, 426

Hornsby, Joseph, 16
Mildred (Walker), 16
Horsey, Elizabeth (Saltonstall), 412
Hercules, 412
Horsley, Mary (Cabell), 115
William, 115
Horton, ——— (Wells), 164
Mehetable, 164
William, 164
Hosack, Catherine, 315
Simon, 315
Hough, Abiah, 188, 194
Edward, 188
Sarah (Caulkins), 188
William, 188, 193
Houghton, Aaron, 261
Abigail 261
Abigail (Merriam), 262
Achsa, 261
Amory B., 262
Beatrix, 261
Beatrix (———), 260
Benjamin, 261
Caleb, 261, 262
Charles Andrew Johnson, 259
Charlotte Johnson (Morris), 259
Cyrus, 261, 262
Damaris (Buckmaster), 260
Ebenezer, 261
Edward, 262
Eliza, 262
Eliza Adeline (Sawin), 262
Emily F., 262
Esther (Leffingwell), 261
Eunice, 261, 345
Experience (Pike), 261
Frederick 262
George B., 262
George Frederick, 262
Grace Mabel (Carr), 259
Harriet Cecil, 259
Hess Pringle, 259
John, 260
Jonas, 261
Lavina, 261
Lewis M., 262
Lucius Heywood, 262
Lucy (Wilder), 261
Martha S. (Osgood), 262
Mary, 261

INDEX 551

Houghton—*Continued*
Mary (Farrar), 260
Mary (Priest), 261
Mary (Taylor), 261
Mary Motte (Pringle), 259
Mary W., 262
Miriam (Butler), 261
Oliver, 261
Persis, 262
Ralph, 259, 260, 262
Richard, 259
Robert, 260, 261
Sarah, 261
Susanna (Sawyer), 262
Timothy, 260
William, 261
William Addison, 259, 262
William Joslin, 262
William Morris, 259
William Pringle, 259
House, John, 148
  Mary, 148
  Theodosia, 148
How, Ann Isabell, 231
  Mary, 232
  Thomas, 231, 232
Howard, Emily Providence (Chisholm), 141
  Hannah, 358
  Joanna (O'Carroll), 240
  John Eager, 236
  Joshua, 236, 240
  Judith, 310, 321
  Lydia, 93
  Mary, 236, 240
  Rebecca, 5
  Robert, 358
  Sarah, 240
  Stephen L., 141
  Violetta, 236, 240
Howarden, Margaret, 335
Howe, Abraham, 215
  David, 497
  Elsie, 69
  Fisher, 414
  Isaac R., 413
  Matilda (Saltonstall), 414
  Sarah 20
  Sarah (Saltonstall), 413
  Sarah (Whitney), 497
Howell, Abigail, 224
  Abraham, 350
  Annis (Stockton), 434

Howell—*Continued*
Arthur, 223
Edward, 223, 224
Elizabeth (Gardiner), 223
Franklin Davenport, 434
Henry, 179
Honour (Deming), 179
Jemima, 224
John C., 434
Mary (Stockton), 434
Mary Theresa de Leelen (Rush), 408
Rebecca (Waln), 350
Richard Lewis, 408
Howes, Mary A., 416
Howland, Abby Woolsey, 501
  Anna Eliza, 361
  Carver, 382
  Elizabeth Senter, 382
  Jeanette, 382
  John, 133
Howlett, Alice (French), 183
  Sarah, 183
  Thomas, 183
Howser, Cecelia (Bramwell), 421
  Gassaway Sellman, 421
  Nettie Esther, 421
Howson, Mary, 290
Hoyt, ———, 75
  Frances, 74
  John, 74
  Jonathan, 175
  Julia Ann (Davenport), 175
  Mary, 74
Hubbard, Abigail James, 261
  Alice (Bacon), 51
  Amelia Jane (Ripley), 263, 266
  Anthony, 42, 51
  Capen, 266
  Charles, 263, 266, 267
  Charles Dunlap, 263, 267
  Charles Pitcher, 263
  Elizabeth (Wolfe), 504
  Elizabeth Capen, 267
  Ellen Maria, 266
  Florence Amelia, 267
  Florence Hastings, 267
  Gertrude Robbins (Pitcher), 263
  Jane Ripley, 266
  John, 504

Hubbard—*Continued*
Martha Jane (Pack), 267
Sarah, 164
Sarah (Bacon), 42
Hubbell, Albert C., 309
  Cora, 309
  Mary (Lyon), 309
Huddell, Joseph, 386
  Mary, 386
  Rebecca (Allen), 386
Hudgins, Alice, 400
  Mary Frances (Wirt), 400
  William Blake, 400
Huested, Rhoda (Davenport), 174
  Thaddeus, 174
Huger, Daniel Elliot, 130
Huggett, ———, 221
  Lucy (Sackett), 221
  Mary, 221
Hughes, ———, 444
  F. Edward, 454
  Henrietta (Trippe), 444
  Jesse, 445
  Margaret (Trippe), 445
  Mary C. (Venable), 454
Hui (Huey), Susanna, 371
Hull, Alma, 181
  Elizabeth, 19
Hulst, Charlotte Margaret (Gardiner), 226
  George Duryee, 226
  Jeanette Gardiner, 226
  Magdalen Hulst (Stoolhoff), 226
Humphrey, Mary, 219
Hundley, Albert Roy, 272
  Ann, 268
  Ann (Holmes), 268
  Asa, 268
  Calhoun, 269
  Carolina Magretha (Guldager), 272
  Catherine, 268
  Cornelia (Jefferson), 269
  Dorothy, 271
  Edgar Archer, 272
  Elizabeth, 268, 270
  Elizabeth (Motley), 268
  Elizabeth Archer (Ogilby), 269
  Elizabeth Motley, 269
  Elner Eugene, 272

INDEX

Hundley—*Continued*
  Elner Musier, 272
  Eugene Russell, 271
  Frances Archer, 270
  Francis A., 269
  George Jefferson, 269
  Harriett Elizabeth, 271
  Harry Lee, 272
  Jefferson, 270
  Jincy Holmes, 268
  John Barret, 268, 273
  John Holmes, 269
  John Ogilby, 269, 272
  Josiah, 268, 269
  Josiah Brummal, 271
  Judith Farrer, 269
  Juliet Jefferson, 270
  Kate Taintor (Russell), 271
  Kate Thompson, 272
  Katherine Taintor, 271
  Lillie Elizabeth (Powers), 271
  Louisa, 268
  Lucile Pearce (Robinson) 268
  Lucy R. (Bobo), 271
  Lucy Waller (Boyd), 270
  Martha America (Barret), 276
  Martha America (Pattie) Barrett, 272
  Martha Louisa, 270
  Mary Chastain, 270
  Mary E., 273
  Mary Emily (Holand), 272
  Mary Holmes, 269
  Mary Silvia, 271
  Nancy (Booker), 269
  Nancy Holmes, 269
  Patrick Ogilby, 270
  Rebecca Porterfield, 272
  Richard Ogilby, 270, 272, 276
  Robert Garland, 270
  Samuel Holmes, 268
  Susanna Holmes, 269
  Sylvia, 268
  Virginia, 271, 273
  Waller Massie, 270
  William Holmes, 269
  William Patrick, 272
Hungerford, Sarah, 161
  Thomas, 161

Hunt, Ann Eliza, 6
  Annie Mumford, 27
  Elizabeth (Gibbes) Shepherd, 230
  Elizabeth P., 234
  Ephraim or John, 491
  Francis, 203
  Joanna (Whitman), 491
  Samuel, 230
  Sarah (Dunton), 203
Hunter, Andrew, 432
  Caroline Scott (Gibbes), 232
  Elizabeth, 339
  James E., 232
  Mary (Stockton), 432
  Susan Maria, 292
  William, 214
Huntington, Ann, 97
  Elizabeth, 174, 501
  Joshua, 501
  Rachel, 97
  Sarah (Clark), 158
  Simon, 158
Hunton, Annie, 222
Huntt, Clement Smith, 383
  Elizabeth Senter, 383, 384
  Sarah Ann (Senter), 383
Hurlbut, Eunice (Whitman), 493
  John, 179
  Lemuel, 493
  Mary, 147
  Mary (Deming), 179
Hurst, Ann (Jones), 423
  Elizabeth (Skinner), 423
  Stephen, 423
Hurty, Sarah A., 423
Husk, Elizabeth Ann, 381
  Jonathan, 381
Huston, James A., 77
  Nanette Marie, 77
Hutchins, Elizabeth (Burrage), 367
  Francis, 367
  Mary, 367
Hutchinson, Ann, 323
  Ann (Little), 317
  Chauncey, 317
  Martha (Corwin) Case, 163
  Thomas, 163
Hutton, ———, 125
  Agnes (Calhoun), 125
Huybrechts, Ida, 458

Hyde, Alicia, 343
  Samuel, 35

Ibrook, Margaret, 466
  Rebecca, 263
Ingersoll, Charles J., 95
  Katherine, 442
Ingham, Deborah (Bye), 110
  Jonas, 110
  Jonathan, 110
  Mary, 110
Inglis, Jean, 27
  Marian (Coale), 27
  Richard, 27
Ingraham, Elizabeth, 217
Innes, Ann, 11
  Henry, 10, 11
  James, 10
  Katherine Elizabeth, 10, 11
  Katherine Elizabeth (Callaway), 10
  Sarah, 11
Irvine, George, 206
  James, 206
  Mary (Rush), 206
Irwin, John Heister, 103
  Margaret (Baldwin), 103
  Mary Baldwin, 103
Isaac, Amy Phillips, 278
  Ann (Hill), 281
  Ann Elizabeth, 281
  Caroline, 281
  Drusilla, 280
  Eleanor Penny (Phillips), 278
  Eleanor Phillips, 278
  Eliza, 281
  Elizabeth (Clarke), 280
  Elizabeth (Moore), 280
  Elizabeth (Volz), 281
  George Washington, 281
  Hannah (Bryant), 280
  Harriet, 281
  Jemima, 280
  John H., 280
  Joseph, 279, 280
  Kezia, 280
  Maria (Peddaick) Rockey, 281
  Martha Ann, 281
  Martha B. (Ware), 281
  Mary, 280, 281

INDEX 553

Isaac—*Continued*
Mary Gertrude, 281
Mary Roach (Ware), 281
Mary Ware, 278
Rachel, 280
Randolph Moore, 278
Richard, 279, 280
Sarah, 280, 281
Sarah (Jacob), 280
Sarah (Pottenger), 279
Susan (Oliver), 281
Sutton, 280
Thomas Jefferson, 281
Uriah Randolph, 281
William Andrew Jackson, 281
William Moore, 278, 281
William Thomas, 278
Zedekiah Howard, 278
Zedekiah Moore, 281
Isacke, Edward, 279
Elizabeth, 279
Jane, 279
Joseph, 279
Margaret, 279
Rebecca, 279
Richard, 279
Sutton, 279
Isbell, Robert, 193
Iselin, Arthur, 303
Eleanor (Jay), 303
Israel, Ellena, 275
Izard, Alice, 284
Alice (De Lancey), 283
Alice De Lancey, 285
Alice Heyward, 285
Allen Cadwallader, 285
Anne, 283, 284
Annie, 282
Annie (Sale), 285
Benjamin, 282
Calverley (Bewicke), 282
Caroline, 284
Catherine, 283
Charles, 283
Charlotte, 283
Charlotte (Broughton), 283
Charlotte Georgina, 284
Claudia (Smith), 284
De Lancey, 285
Dorothy, 282
Dorothy (Smith), 282
Eliza Caroline, 284
Elizabeth, 283, 284

Izard—*Continued*
Elizabeth ———, 282
Elizabeth (Liddleton), 284
Elizabeth Carter (Farley) Shippen, 284
Emma Philadelphia (Middleton), 284
Florence (Behre), 285
George, 284, 285
Henrietta, 284
Henry, 283, 284, 285
Irene, 285
James Johnston, 285
John, 282, 283, 285
Josephine Bedon, 285
Julia Davie, 285
Julia Davie (Bedon), 285
Laura, 282
Laura (Lipscomb, 285
Lucy, 285
Lucy Green, 285
Magdalene Elizabeth (Chastaigner), 282
Margaret, 283
Margaret (Johnson), 283
Margaret Emma, 284
Martha, 283, 284
Mary, 283, 284
Mary (———), 282
Mary (Middleton), 282
Mary Cadwallader (Green), 284
Mary Fowler, 285
Mary Green, 285
Mattie Perry, 285
N. J. (Lyons), 282
Ralph, 282, 283, 284, 285
Roberta (Johnston), 285
Ruth, 285
Sallie (Goode), 284
Sarah Lyons, 282
Walter, 282, 283, 284, 285

J

Jackman, Elias, 24
Margaret (Atkinson), 24
Jackson, Andrew, 95
Anna Calvert, 297
Anna Maria (Calvert), 297
Anne Sophia, 297
Caroline Cochrane, 286
Caroline March (Harmon), 28

Jackson—*Continued*
Caroline Toney (Cochrane), 286
Churchill Calvert, 297
David, 324
Edward, 35, 297
Edward Calvert, 297
Elizabeth (Wolcott), 501
Elizabeth Melville, 286
Frances Ransom (Whipple) Craw, 469
Freedom W., 469
George Calvert, 297
Henry Melville, 286, 297
J., 250
James Churchill, 28
James Pace, 286
Jane, 230
John, 34
John P., 501
Josephine (Ross), 297
Lindsey, 505
Marguerite (Woods), 286
Marshall Parks, 297
Mary (Kelton), 324
Mittie Harmon, 28
Olive (Beard), 505
Olive Caldwell, 297
Rebecca (Lloyd), 286
Samuel Keerl, 297
Violet Lee (Pace), 286
Violet Pace, 286
William Congreve, 286, 297
Jacob, Alice (Westal), 280
Ann (Chany), 280
Benjamin, 280, 299
Deborah, 299
Dorothy (Arnold), 299
Elizabeth, 298
Elnathan, 299
Hannah, 298, 299
Hannah (Bosworth), 299
Hulda (Bosworth), 299
Jemima (Isaac), 280
John, 280, 298, 299
Joseph, 299
Josiah, 298
Margery (Eames), 298
Maria, 60
Mary, 298, 299
Mary (Russell), 298
Mercy, 299
Mercy (Whitman), 299

Jacob—*Continued*
  Mordecai, 280
  Nathaniel, 299
  Nicholas, 298
  Rebecca (———), 299
  Rebecca (Grow), 299
  Sarah, 280, 298
  Whitman, 299
Jacobs, ——— (Allen), 300
  Abel, 300
  Adeline H. (Crocker), 300
  Amasa, 300
  Ann M., 301
  Asa, 300
  Bela H., 301
  Betsy, 300
  Daisy Monell, 298
  Ella L. (Gale), 301
  Elmer Rand, 298
  Emma, 450
  Emma (Sabine), 300
  Emma A., 301
  Eunice (Joslin), 300
  Everett P., 301
  Frank W., 301
  Hannah (McLean), 300
  Harrie Kirtland, 298
  Harriet P. (Penhallow), 300
  Helen L., 301
  Hervey F., 301
  Hervey Wyman, 298
  Hiram, 300
  Ida (Pillsbury), 301
  Jerusha, 300
  Jesse, 300
  John, 300
  John R., 300
  Joseph, 83, 300
  Joseph Dresser, 167
  Lillian Julia, 298
  Louise (Martin), 300
  Lucy (Cooper), 300
  Lucy E., 301
  Luther Morse, 298, 301
  Luther William, 298
  Mary, 300
  Mary (Bartlet), 83
  Mary (Gilman?), 298
  Mary (Whitman), 492
  Mary B., 301
  Mary Bailey, 167
  Mercy, 300
  Nancy (Gould), 301

Jacobs—*Continued*
  Nathaniel, 492
  Nelson, 300
  Phebe (Greenwood), 300
  Phebe A. (Dean), 301
  Sarah, 300
  Sarah (Emerson), 300
  Sarah (Morse), 300
  Sarah (Plank), 300
  Sarah C., 301
  Sarah C. (Carroll), 301
  Sarah Crosby (Carroll), 167
  Sarah Elizabeth (Rand), 298
  Silas B., 301
  William, 300
  Wyman D., 301
James, Carolyn, 502
Janes, Amelia, 396
Jans, Anika, 136
Janse, Agatha, 458
  Mensie, 458
Jay, Alice, 305
  Alonzo, 255
  Ann, 302, 303
  Ann Margaret (Barclay), 303
  Anna, 303
  Anna Maria, 304, 305
  Anna Maria (Bayard), 302
  Anna Maricka, 302, 303
  Augusta, 303
  Augusta (McVickar), 303
  Augustus, 302, 304, 305
  Catherine Helena, 304
  Cornelia, 305
  De Lancey Kane, 304
  Delilah, 255
  Edith Van Cortlandt, 305
  Eleanor, 303
  Eleanor Kingland (Field), 303
  Eliza, 303
  Elizabeth Clarkson, 304
  Ellen, 255, 302
  Emily Astor (Kane), 304
  Euphemia (Dunscomb), 303
  Eve, 302
  Frances, 302
  Frederick, 303
  Harriette Arnold (Vinton), 305
  James, 302
  John, 67, 303, 304, 305

Jay—*Continued*
  John Clarkson, 305
  Josephine (Pearson), 304
  Judith, 302
  Judith (Francois), 302
  Julia (Post), 305
  Laura, 305
  Laura (Prime), 305
  Laura Prime, 305
  Louisa, 302
  Louisa Shaw (Barlow), 302
  Lucie (Oelrichs), 303
  Marguerite (Soleiac), 305
  Maria, 303
  Maria Arnold, 305
  Mary, 255, 302, 303, 305
  Mary (Duyckinck), 302
  Mary (Van Cortlandt), 302
  Mary Rutherfurd, 304, 305
  Mary Rutherfurd (Clarkson), 304
  Matilda Coster, 305
  Olive, 255
  Peter, 302
  Peter Augustus, 303, 304, 305
  Pierre, 302, 305
  Samuel, 255
  Sarah, 304, 305
  Sarah (Hoover), 255
  Sarah Livingston, 305
  Sarah Louise, 303
  Sarah Van Brugh (Livingston), 303
  Susan, 303
  Susan Alexander (McCook), 304
  Susan Matilda, 304
  William, 303
Jefferson, Ann (Almy) Durfee, 354
  Benjamin, 354
  Cornelia, 269
  John Garland, 269
  Peter, 14
  Thomas, 14, 15, 246, 269, 275
Jekyll, John, 413
  Mary, 413
Jenkins, Mary Frances, 296
Jennings, Ann, 294
Jennison, Mary, 467
  Michal, 462
  Robert, 214, 462

INDEX

Jerome, Asahel, 181
  Sarah, 181
  Sarah (Bronson), 181
Jeter, ———, 13
  Lucy (Speed), 13
Jett, Alice (Hopper), 292
  Eliza Lane, 292
  Ellen, 292
  Elvira, 292
  Hannah (Calvert), 292
  Hannah Calvert, 292
  Isabel (Roberts), 292
  James, 292
  John, 292
  Julia Anne (Lane), 292
  Lavinia, 292
  Mary Frances, 292
  William Armistead Lane, 292
Jewett, Elizabeth (Dixon), 183
  John, 183
Joanes, Sarah (Whitman), 488
Job, Mary Elizabeth, 107
Johnson, Alba Boardman, 306, 308
  Alfred, 26
  Alice (Bump), 310
  Alma Sara (Kemp), 308
  Ann Frances, 310
  Anna, 310, 322
  Anna (Atkinson), 26
  Anna (Kettle), 307
  Asa, 307
  Benjamin, 307
  Boardman, 307
  Caroline Elizabeth (Whitney), 498
  Catherine (Sprague), 307
  Charles Webb, 310
  Charles Williamson, 309, 310
  Charlotte Augusta, 259
  Christian, 324
  Clarissa (Bryan), 106
  Cora (Hubbell), 309
  David, 310, 322
  Diah, 170
  Dolly, 310, 322
  Edward, 329
  Eleanor (Atcheson), 310
  Eleanor B. (Peterson), 306
  Elihu, 309, 310, 322
  Elinor, 216
  Elizabeth, 119

Johnson—*Continued*
  Elizabeth (Boardman), 307
  Elizabeth (Gastlin), 311
  Elizabeth Ker, 309
  Elizabeth Little, 310
  Elizabeth Thomas (Reeves), 306
  Ella, 276
  Evaline (Gardiner), 310
  Fanny Johnston (Betts), 91
  Guy, 310, 322
  Hannah (Crosby), 170
  Harriet, 99, 311
  Harriet Livermore, 309
  Harriet Livermore (McCarthy), 310, 316
  Helen (Paxson), 306
  Henry Converse, 311
  Hepzibah (Page), 307
  Hezron Ayers, 498
  James Oran, 310
  Joel, 119
  John, 504
  Jonathan, 99
  Joshua Converse, 310, 322
  Jothan, 170
  Katherine (Calvert), 295
  Kezia (Foster), 307
  Keziah, 329
  Kitty, 125
  Leah, 164
  Leah (Goff), 306
  Louis Sterling, 311
  Louise Cotton, 309
  Lynch A., 106
  Margaret, 283
  Margaret Souder, 311
  Maria Cornelia (Bronson), 309
  Maria Louise, 309
  Mary, 106
  Mary (Stoddard), 91
  Mary A. (Clark), 310
  Mary Chapman, 310
  Mildred, 106
  Noah, 310, 322
  Oran, 310, 320, 322
  Phebe, 459
  Polly (Carpenter), 310
  Polly (Prentice), 310
  Rebecca (Aslett), 306
  Reeves Kemp, 306
  Rhoda, 106

Johnson—*Continued*
  Richard M., 119
  Robert, 283, 472
  Ruhamah, 42
  Ruth Anna, 306
  Sally, 322
  Samuel, 91
  Samuel Adams, 307
  Samuel Maxwell, 311
  Sarah, 310, 338
  Sarah (Lobdell), 310, 320
  Sarah (Webb) Converse, 310
  Sarah (Wolfe), 504
  Solomon, 215
  Susanna, 170, 330
  Susanna (Converse), 170
  Thomas, 295, 338
  Timothy, 306, 307
  William, 329
  William Henry, 310, 316
  William Lobdell, 309, 310
  Wolcott Howe, 91
Johnston, Roberta, 285
Jones, ———, 159, 257, 280, 422, 489
  Abraham, 489
  Amy (Cock), 387
  Ann, 423
  Anne (Warfield), 364, 366
  Benjamin, 430, 489
  Cassandra (Fell), 421
  Eliza Walter, 387
  Elizabeth, 174, 420
  Elizabeth (———), 489
  Elizabeth Francanna, 362, 365, 366
  Emaline, 422
  Ephraim, 490
  Frederick, 153
  Hannah, 358, 387
  Hannah (Copeland), 490
  Hannah Bond, 421
  James A., 341
  Jane (Owen), 325
  John, 421, 489
  Joseph, 489
  Joshua, 364, 366
  Josiah, 490
  Lewis, 495
  Lillian B. (Hoover), 257
  Louisa Virginia (Spencer), 426
  Lucus Polk, 426

INDEX

Jones—*Continued*
Lydia, 495
Lydia (———), 489
Margaret, 341
Margaret (Livingston), 337
Margaret James (Poole), 364, 366
Maria (Holton), 387
Martha, 153
Mary (Adams), 490
Mary (Clark), 159
Mary (Spear), 490
Mary Eliza, 341
Mathilda (Townsend), 396
Owen, 325
Phoebe Owen, 325
Polly, 53, 219
Rachel (Isaac), 280
Rebecca, 207
Rhys, 387
Richard, 387
Richard Ireland, 441
Sarah, 158, 159, 396, 490
Sarah (———), 489
Sarah (Stearns), 480
Sarah (Whitman), 489
Sarah Ann, 5
Susanna (Claiborne), 153
Susanna (Tilghman), 441
Thomas, 337, 421, 489
Victoria, 421
Walter Moore, 387
Wesley, 364, 366
Joralemon, Margaret, 175
Tuenis, 175
Jordan, Margaret, 115, 116
Paulina, 115
Josey, A. B., 285
Josephine Bedon (Izard), 285
Joslin, Abraham, 497
Eunice, 300
Sarah (Whitney), 497
Joslyn, Elizabeth, 403
Jost, Estelle (Capp), 136
Frederick, 136
Frederick W., 136
Gordon, 136
Judson, Frederick William, 182
Hannah Keith, 182
Lois (Keith), 182
Julian, Shubael, 254

K

Kamfort, Annaje, 371
Deborah, 372
Hanna, 372
John, 371
Mary, 372
Rachel, 372
Sarah, 372
Kane, Emily Astor, 304
Oliver De Lancey, 304
Kapp, Andreas, 133
Eva Marie, 133
George Frederick, 133
John Michael, 133
Kasson, James H., 393
Mary Sherwood (Robbins), 393
Kaye, Grace, 411
Robert, 411
Kaylor, George, 295
German, 295
Gideon, 295
Hannah, 295
James Calvert, 295
Jane Calvert, 295
John, 295
Josephus, 295
Lydia Beck, 295
Margaret Anne, 295
Mary Elizabeth (Corbin), 295
Mary Louise, 295
Robert, 295
Sarah (Calvert), 295
William, 295
Keating Elizabeth B. (Hopkinson), 94
Keats, Emma, 17
John, 17
Keen, Harriet Anne (Crighton), 449
John, 449
Roberta, 449
Keene, Ann (Gaither), 449
Benjamin, 448, 449
John, 448
Mary G., 449
Mary Gaither, 449
Richard, 449
Sarah, 448
Susan, 449
Sussannah (Pollard), 449

Keene—*Continued*
Thomas, 449
William Billingsley, 449
Keeney, William, 214
Keens, Joseph, 38
Mary, 38
Susanna Maria, 38
Keeny, John, 188, 194
Sarah (Douglas), 188, 194
Keep, Hannah Rebeccca (Robbins), 392
John, 392
Keim, Helen Shewell, 6
Keister, John, 473
Keith, Lois, 182
Kellogg, Amanda (Salisbury), 149
Chloe Irene (Churchill), 149
Cyrus, 149
Olive Clarinda (Churchill), 149
William A., 149
William S., 149
Kelly, Abigail, 54
Eliza Ann, 165
Joel, 54
Ruth (Wheelock), 54
Kelton, Agnes, 324
Agnes (Mackey), 324
Allen Cuningham, 324
Anna Campbell, 325
Anne Elizabeth, 324
Atlee Sanford, 325
Christian (Johnson), 324
David, 324
Edith Russell (Wills), 323
Francis, 324
George, 324
Henry Clay, 324
James, 323, 324
John, 324
John Cuningham, 324
John Cunningham Russell, 323
John Victor, 325
Joseph, 324
Josephine Campbell, 325
Josephine Parmly (Campbell), 324
Julia, 324
Lottie (Dillingham), 324
Margaret, 323
Margaret (Turner), 324

INDEX

Kelton—*Continued*
Margaretta, 324
Margaretta (———), 323
Margaretta Nataline, 325
Margaretta Ross (Cuningham), 324
Mary, 324
Mary (Fulton), 324
Mary (Hackett), 323
Mary Adelaide, 325
Phoebe (Essinger), 324
Phoebe Owen (Jones), 325
Rachel, 324
Robert, 324
Robert Hall Campbell, 323, 325
William Sutherland, 325
Kemp, Alma Sarah, 308
Elizabeth (Noel), 444
James, 444
Sarah, 92
Kendall, ———, 476
Abigail, 328, 396, 480
Abigail (Raynor) Broughton, 328
Alice (Hassell), 328
Alice (Hassell) Temple, 328
Alice Louise, 332
Amos, 329
Benjamin, 330
Daniel, 329, 330
David, 329
Deborah, 185
Deborah (Richardson), 329
Douglas, 193, 326
Ebenezer, 329
Elinor Whitney, 326
Eliza B., 331
Elizabeth, 328
Elizabeth (Comey), 327
Elizabeth (Dean), 330
Elizabeth Bishop (Beal), 331
Ephraim, 328
Esther, 329, 330
Esther (Buck), 330
Eunice (Brooks) Carter, 327
Francis, 327
Hannah, 185, 328
Hannah (Bartlett), 327
Hannah (Whittemore), 185
Hezekiah, 329
Isaac, 330, 331
Jacob, 328, 329, 330

Kendall—*Continued*
Joanna, 331
Joanna (Brooks), 330
Joel, 330
John, 185, 327, 329
Jonathan, 329, 330
Joseph, 329
Joshua, 329, 330
Kate Varnum (Whitney), 326
Katherine Varnum, 326
Keziah (Johnson), 329
Loammi, 331
Lucy (Sabells), 330
Mabel, 328, 396, 480
Marion (Douglas), 193, 326
Marjory Stevens, 326
Mary, 328, 329, 496
Mary (Locke), 328
Mary (Rutter), 330
Mary (Tidd), 327
Mary Ann, 331
Mary Elizabeth, 331
Mercy (———), 329
Nancy (Bradford), 330
Nancy L. (Roberts), 331
Nathan, 329
Oliver, 329, 330
Persis, 328
Persis (Haywood), 328
Phebe, 329
Rebecca, 330
Rebecca (Mixer), 328
Rebekah, 328
Ruth (Blodgett), 328
Ruth (Skelton), 330
Sally, 331
Samuel, 328
Sarah, 329, 330
Sarah (White), 476
Susanna, 329, 330
Susanna (———), 329
Susanna (Johnson), 330
Temple, 329
Thomas, 327, 328
William, 330
William Beals, 193, 326, 327, 332
William Floyd, 193, 326
Kennedy, Harriet, 67
John, 239
Sarah (Gist), 239
Kennison, Hugh, 86

Kennison—*Continued*
Myra A., 86
Sarah (Bartlett), 86
Ker, Anna (Livermore), 315, 319
Catherine, 315
Catherine (Loofbourow), 315
Catherine (Mattison), 315
Elizabeth, 310, 315, 316
Hannah, 315, 316
John, 315
Joseph, 315
Lydia, 315
Margaret, 315
Margaret (Craig), 315
Margaret Clark, 316
Mary, 315, 316
Nathan, 315, 319
Nathaniel, 315
Oliver Livermore, 315
Samuel, 315
Walter, 315
William, 315
Kerley, Joseph, 214
Ketchams, Ruth, 174
Kettle, Anna, 307
Hannah (Frothingham), 484
Joseph, 484
Key, Mary, 296
Kidder, Enoch, 43
Sarah (Davis) Bacon, 43
Kiers, Hendrickjen Stevense (Van Voor Hees), 456
Jan, 456
Kierstead, Hendrickje Stevense (Van Voor Hees), 457
Jan, 457
Kilbourn, Anna, 180
Ebenezer, 180
Eunice (Hale), 180
Kilcreana, Elizabeth (Waller), 234
R., 234
Kimball, Charles, 181
Mehitable, 76
Reuben, 330
Richard, 330
Sarah (Kendall), 330
Sarah Ann (Deming), 181
Susanna (Balch), 330
King, Abigail, 491
Alice (Dean), 491

INDEX

King—*Continued*
  Anne (Venable), 453
  Arvilla, 68
  Elizabeth, 491
  Experience, 491
  Hannah, 491
  John, 491
  Judah (Whitman), 488, 491
  Judith, 491
  Lydia, 491
  Mary, 223, 491
  Philip, 453, 488, 491
Kingsbury, Cordelia, 454
  Mary, 98
  Mary (Bacon), 52
  Nathaniel, 52
Kingsley, Ellen Gibb, 163
  Henry, 163
  Mary Hull (Gibb), 163
  Roxanna, 68
Kinney, Juliet, 391
Kinsey, Abigail, 111
  Benjamin, 111
  Elizabeth (Crew), 111
  Samuel, 111
  Sarah, 111
Kinsley, Elizabeth, 184
  Hannah (Brockett), 184
  Samuel, 184
Kip, ———, 136
Kipp, Mary (Freshour), 166
  Mary Esther, 166
  Nicholas, 166
Kirby, Maria, 351
  Mary, 179, 351
Kirk, Alice A., 107
  David, 260
  Margaret, 107
  Mary Jane, 325
Kirll, John, 374
  Mary, 374
Kirtland, Elizabeth Adeline, 298
  Mary, 158
Klein, J. A., 285
  Ruth (Izard), 285
Knapp, Ann (Baker), 69
  Anne E., 369
  Charles Maurice, 70
  Edward Young, 70
  Elisha, 20
  Elizabeth (Warren), 462
  Frances (Burns), 70

Knapp—*Continued*
  Hester Ann (Wooley), 70
  James, 462
  John, 35
  Lucretia, 70
  Lucretia (Alexander), 20
  Mary, 70
  Mary (Mudgett), 70
  Samuel Baker, 70
  Samuel Trevor, 369
  Sarah (Park), 35
  Sylvia (Mudgett), 70
  Thomas Jefferson, 70
  Zelotes, 69
Knight, Anna Mary (Miles), 255
  Deborah, 24
  Elizabeth, 42, 334
  John, 42
  Rebekah, 329
  Robert, 255
  Ruhamah (Johnson), 42
  Sarah, 334
Knowles, Mercy (Freeman), 32
  Ruth, 32
  Samuel, 32
Knowlton, Anna, 26
  Lucy, 86
Kockersperger, Elizabeth, 62
  Nora (Baker), 62
  Stephen Morris, 62
  William S., 62
Koenig, Regina, 183
Kuntz, Catherine, 401

L

Ladd, Mehitable, 76
Lakin, John, 42
  Mary (Bacon), 42
Lamar, Hannah J., 232
Lambert, Constance, 168
  Elizabeth, 343
Lamberts, Jannetje, 458
Lambis, Abijah, 53
Lambs, ———, 477
  Sibillah (White), 477
Lambson, Agnes (Kelton), 324
  Thomas, 324
Lamden, Ruth (Skinner), 420
Lamont, Daniel Scott, 391
  Frances Cleveland, 391
  Juliet (Kinney), 391

Lampman, Clark, 67
  Eunice (Baker), 67
Lane, Elizabeth, 31
  Ellen Elizabeth, 464
  Emory W., 464
  Job, 31
  John, 43, 264
  Julia Ann, 292
  Mary, 31
  Mary Newton, 291
  Mehitable (Hobart), 264
  Sarah, 31
Langdon, Lydia Ida, 146
Langmuir, Maud, 72
Lapham, Caroline (Baker), 69
  John, 69
Larabee, Sarah (Bacon), 55
  Seth L., 55
Larned, Anna Dorinda (Brown), 170
  Ellen D., 170
  George, 167, 170
  Susan Mason, 170
La Rue, Gertrude Lucile, 71
  Jane (Gray), 68
  Jonathan B., 68
Laskin, Hugh, 215
Latimer, Rebecca, 179
Laurence, Abigail, 36
  Lydia, 36
Laurie Garber, 92
  Helena, 5
  Lucie, 5
Law, Maria, 372
Lawrence, Edith, 142
  Catherine (Livingston), 337
  Elizabeth, 496
  Elizabeth (Robbins), 393
  Fanny, 498
  George, 313
  Grace, 313
  Grove, 393
  Henry Effingham, 142
  James, 444
  John L., 337
  Lydia (Underhill), 142
  William, 498
Lawson, John, 232
  Sarah Eliza (Gibbes), 232
Leach, Alice, 53
  David, 489
  Hannah (Whitman), 489

INDEX

559

Leach—*Continued*
  Mary (Whitman), 489
  Seth, 489
Learned, Ebenezer, 53
  Erastus, 79
  Mary Bacon, 79
Leavitt, Elizabeth (Atkinson), 24
  Mary (Hoover), 258
  Thomas, 24
  Van Ness, 258
  Van Ness Hoover, 258
Le Baron, Elizabeth, 392
  Lazarus, 392
  Lydia (Bradford), 392
  Priscilla, 393
Le Coisteux, Marie Madeleine, 388
Le Compte, Anthony, 419
  Hester, 419
  Hester (Dottando), 419
  Mary (Skinner), 419
  Moses, 419
Lee, Ann, 275
  Arthur, 275
  Charles O., 70
  DeWitt Rodgers, 70
  Eliza (Baker), 70
  Floride, 131
  Floride (Clemson), 131
  Frances E., 128
  Gideon, 131
  Harry, 275
  Henry, 244, 275
  John Clarke, 414
  John R., 96
  Lilian Howard, 96
  Lyman Charles, 70
  Margaret, 418
  Mary Rocelia, 70
  Richard Baker, 70, 275
  Roscoe Silas, 70
  Rose S., 414
  Sarah, 424
Leech, Esther, 374
  Tobias, 374
Leeds, Daniel, 429
  Esther (Skinner), 420
  John, 420
  Mary, 429
Leeke, Ebenezer, 63
  Hannah (Baird), 63

Leffingwell, Esther, 261
  Michael, 261
Legaré, Eliza, 143
  Eliza Catherine, 143
  Hugh Swinton, 143
  Mary (Swinton), 143
  Solomon, 143
Lekin, Lydia (Browne), 313
  William, 313
Le Maistre, Jean Pierre, 388
  Louis, 388
  Marie Madeleine, 388
  Marie Madeleine (Le Coisteux), 388
  Marie Madeleine Pierre (De Montenegro), 388
  Marie Madeleine Therese Luise, 388
Lemaster, Abby, 14
Leonard, Elizabeth (Almy) Morris, 354
  Hannah, 256
  Henry, 354
  John, 354, 491
  Mary, 354
  Mary (King), 491
Leonetti, Alexina Pauline (Chisholm), 142
  John B., 142
Leringman, Mary, 223
LeRoy, Elizabeth (Calhoun), 124
  James, 124
Letson, Augustus Franklin, 104
  Catherine Ellen (Webb), 104
  Elizabeth Jane, 104
Le White, Willemus, 471, 472
Lewis, Andrew, 15
  Catherine (Fauntleroy), 275
  Edward Cuffin, 214
  Edward H., 205, 207
  Elizabeth, 275, 452
  Fielding Otis, 389
  Gertrude (Livingston), 336
  Harriet Maria (Phippeney), 214
  Hugh, 452
  Ida Eleana, 214
  James Fielding, 389
  Joseph, 349
  Julie Villiers, 379
  Martha (Dunton), 205, 207

Lewis—*Continued*
  Martha Jane (Claiborne), 154
  Mary (Walker), 15
  Mary Edith, 389
  Mary Edith (Roach) Curtis, 389
  Merewether, 275
  Morgan, 336
  Nicholas, 15, 154
  Robert, 275
  Ruth (Gist), 239
  Sarah (Overby), 389
  Susanna (Waln), 349
  William, 239
Libby, George, 85
  Mary (Bartlet), 85
Liddleton, Elizabeth, 284
Lightfoot, Anne Augusta (Claiborne), 155
  Anne Claiborne, 155
  Harriet (Field), 155
  Helen Bernard, 155
  Helen Bertha (Quillian), 155
  Herbert Claiborne, 155
  John Bernard, 155
  Mary Waller (Mercer), 155
  Philip Howell, 155
Lillie, Mary, 208
Lincoln, Abraham, 206, 490
  Mordecaia, 490
  Rebecca, 206
  Sarah (Jones), 490
Lindsay, Anne (Calvert), 293
  Catherine, 293
  Catherine Washington (Sanford), 293
  George Waller, 293
  John Murray, 39
  Judith (Grayson), 293
  Maie Park (Coyne), 39
  Maria, 293
  Maria (Lindsay), 293
  Reuben, 16
  Sarah (Walker), 16
  Sarah Calvert, 293
  William, 293
  William Henry, 293
Link, Hannah (Calvert), 295
  Peter, 295
Linnard, Mary, 376
  Stephen Beasley, 376

INDEX

Linthicum, ———, 364
  Cassandra (Gaither), 364
Lippincott, Joanna (Wharton), 92
  Joshua Bertram, 92
  Sarah, 92
Lipscomb, Laura, 285
Lithgow, William, 44
Little, Abner, 26
  Ann, 316, 317
  Ann (Bailey), 316
  Ann (Warren), 32
  Catherine, 317
  Catherine (McIntyre), 137
  Charles, 393
  Emiline, 26
  Ephraim, 31
  Eunice (Atkinson), 25, 26
  John, 316, 317, 320
  Joshua, 25
  Leah (Crawford), 317, 320
  Lucretia (Crawford), 316
  Lydia, 25
  Mary, 317, 320
  Mary (Sturdevant), 31
  Molly (Brattan), 316
  Nancy, 26
  Nelly (Nelson), 316
  Ruth, 31
  Sarah, 317
  Stephen W., 24
  Susan (Robbins), 393
  Thomas, 32, 316
  William, 316
Littlefield, Dorcas, 85
  Meribah, 83
  Phebe, 84
Littleton, Nathaniel, 144
Livermore, Abigail, 318, 463
  Anna, 315, 318, 319
  Anna (Bridge), 318
  Daniel, 317, 318
  Dinah (Whitney), 497
  Edmund, 317
  Elijah, 318, 497
  Elizabeth, 317
  Grace, 318
  Grace (Sherman), 317
  Hannah, 317, 318
  Hannah (Brown), 314, 318
  Isaac, 318
  John, 317, 318
  Jonathan, 318

Livermore—*Continued*
  Lydia, 318
  Martha, 317
  Mathew, 318
  Mary, 317
  Nathaniel, 317, 318
  Rebecca, 318
  Rebecca (Barnes), 318
  Samuel, 314, 317, 318, 463
  Sarah, 212, 317, 318
  Thomas, 318
  William, 318
Livingston, Abraham, 338
  Agnes, 333, 334
  Agnes (Hepburn), 333
  Agnes (Livingston), 333
  Alexander, 333
  Alida, 336, 337, 338
  Alida (Schuyler) Van Rensselaer, 334
  Andrew, 334
  Ann (Veitch), 334
  Anne Hume (Shippen), 335
  Barbara, 333, 334
  Barbara (Livingson), 333
  Bartholomew, 334
  Catherine, 335, 336, 337, 338, 339
  Catherine (De Peyster), 337
  Catherine (Van Brugh), 336
  Catherine Goodhue, 339
  Christina, 338
  Christina (Ten Broeck), 337
  Clermont, 339
  Cornelia, 339
  Cornelia (Beekman), 336
  Cornelia (Livingston), 339
  Dirck, 337
  Edward, 336, 339
  Edward De Peyster, 339
  Edward Philip, 335, 338
  Eliza, 338
  Eliza (Livingston), 338
  Eliza (McEvers), 336
  Elizabeth, 334, 339
  Elizabeth (Knight), 334
  Elizabeth Stevens, 335, 338
  Elizabeth Stevens (Livingston), 335, 338
  Emma, 339
  Estelle, 339
  George, 338
  Gertrude, 336

Livingston—*Continued*
  Gertrude (Livingston), 336
  Gertrude (Van Rensselaer) Schuyler, 336
  Gilbert, 336
  Goodhue, 339
  Henry, 337, 338
  Henry Beekman, 335
  Henry Brockholst, 338
  Henry Philip, 338
  Herman, 339
  James, 333, 334
  Janet, 334, 335
  Janet (Fleming), 333
  Jasper Hall, 338
  Joanna, 334, 336
  Joanna Philippina, 334
  Johanna, 336
  John, 333, 334, 337
  John Henry, 333, 337, 339
  John R., 336
  Laura Suffern, 339
  Louisa (Robb), 339
  Louise (De Castera) De Lassy, 336
  Margaret, 334, 335, 337, 338
  Margaret (Beekman), 335
  Margaret (Howarden), 335
  Margaret (Sheaffe), 336
  Margaret Maria, 335
  Margaret Maria (Livingston), 335
  Maria, 338
  Maria (Livingston), 338
  Maria Margaret, 338
  Marion, 334
  Mary, 339
  Mary (Alexander), 337
  Mary (McEvers), 336
  Mary (Stevens), 335
  Mary (Tailer), 339
  Mary (Tong), 336
  Mary (Winthrop), 334
  Peter, 337
  Peter R., 336
  Peter Van Brugh, 337
  Philip, 335, 336, 337
  Philip Henry, 338
  Philip Philip, 337, 338
  Robert, 334, 335, 336
  Robert Clermont, 338
  Robert Edward, 339
  Robert L., 335

INDEX

Livingston—*Continued*
Robert R., 335, 338, 339
Robert Reginald, 339
Sarah, 337, 338
Sarah (Hallett), 339
Sarah (Johnson), 338
Sarah (Livingston), 337
Sarah Van Brugh, 303
Susan Maria Clarkson (De Peyster), 339
Susannah (French), 337
Walter, 338
Washington, 338
William, 303, 333, 334, 336, 337
Lloyd, Ann (Grundy), 440
Anna, 440
Anna Maria, 439
Anna Maria (Tilghman) Hemsley, 440
Eliza Armistead (Selden), 286
Henrietta Maria (Neale) Bennett, 439
James, 440
John, 286
Josephine, 488
Margaret, 439, 440
Philemon, 439
Rebecca, 286
Robert, 440
Lobaugh, Abraham, 400
Martha, 400
Mary, 400
Lobdell, ——— (Venable), 320
Abijah, 317, 320
Abraham, 320
Ann, 319
Caleb, 319
Charles Sidney, 320
Daniel, 320
Ebenezer, 319
Elizabeth, 319
Elizabeth (Lockwood), 320
Elizabeth (Sherwood), 320
Hannah, 319, 320
Henry Milton, 320
Huldah, 320
Isaac, 320
Jacob, 319
James, 320
James Alexander, 320
John, 320

Lobdell—*Continued*
John Little, 320
Joshua, 314, 319, 320
Mary, 319, 320
Mary (Burwell), 314, 319
Mary (Little), 317, 320
Mary (Reynolds), 319
Persis (Pierce), 319
Rachel, 320
Rebecca, 319, 320
Samuel, 319
Sarah, 97, 310, 319, 320
Sarah (Scott), 320
Simon, 319, 320
Susannah, 319
William S., 320
Locke, Mary, 328
Mary (Clark), 328
Samuel, 328
William, 328
Lockhart, Talitha (Bryan), 107
William, 107
Lockwood, Elizabeth, 320
Lodge, ———, 142
Long, ———, 364, 404
Agnes, 123
Ann Elita (Rothrock), 404
Bathsheba (Churchill), 482
John Davis, 482
Julia (Temple), 478
Julia Davis, 478, 479, 480, 481, 482, 484
Julia Temple, 483
Julia Temple (Davis), 482, 483
Mary (Gaither), 364
Miles, 482
Robert, 214
Sarah, 98
Persis Seaver, 482
Thankful (Clark), 482
Thomas, 482
Zadoc, 478, 482, 483
Longstreth, Elizabeth W., 5
Loofbourow, Catherine, 315
Loomis, Esther, 98
Israel, 98
Rebecca (Bingham), 98
Lord, ———, 84
Elizabeth, 290
Mary (Bartlet), 84
Lorden, Mary, 484

Loring, Hannah, 480
Hannah (Jacob), 298
Submit, 477, 480
Thomas, 298
Lothrop, Abigail, 482
Abigail (Avery), 32
Deborah, 32
Deborah (Crow), 32
Elisha, 32
John, 482
Samuel, 32
Lottier, Agnes Bell (Cabell), 117
John D., 117
Loucks, Grace V., 403
Loughery, Esther (Rush), 207
John, 207
Lounsbury, Monmouth, 174
Sarah (Davenport), 174
Loup, Catherine (Little), 317
Joseph, 317
Love, Esther (Calhoun), 125
Jane Moss, 243
William, 125
Lovejoy, Abigail, 44
Emma (Dunton), 208
Hannah, 44
Wallace Williams, 208
Lowe, Jane, 288
Lowry, Elizabeth, 275
Lowther Agnes, 152
Richard, 152
Lucas, Nicholas, 92
Susanna, 406
Ludlow, Edward Hunter, 339
Elizabeth (Hunter), 339
Elizabeth (Livingston), 339
Gabriel Ver Planck, 339
Ludwell, Ann, 274
Luefkin, A. D., 175
Flora Dwight, 175
Lusk, Hannah, 180
Isabel, 180
Thomas, 180
Lux, George, 94
Lydden, ———, 473
Johanna, 397, 473
Lyde, ———, 23
Mary (Wheelwright), 23
Lydell, George, 152
Lydick, D, 204
Elizabeth (Dunton), 204

INDEX

Lyman, Aaron Graves, 345
  Abbie, 346
  Abigail, 344
  Abigail (———), 344
  Abner, 344
  Albert, 346
  Alicia (Hyde), 343
  Anne, 343
  Anson, 345
  Atta, 345
  Carolina, 55
  Carrie, 346
  Climea Osgood, 346
  Cyrus Osgood, 346
  Daisy, 346
  Dorothy Bacon, 55
  Edward, 55
  Eliza, 344
  Elizabeth (Lambert), 343
  Esther, 344
  Ethel Anna (Skinner), 341
  Eunice, 345
  Eunice (Graves), 345
  Eunice (Houghton), 345
  Fanny, 345
  Frances (Bruce), 345
  Frances Ellen (Badger), 341
  Freedom, 345
  George Alexander, 341, 345
  George Porter, 341
  George Richard, 341
  Hannah, 344, 346
  Hannah (Alexander), 345
  Henry, 343, 493
  Hepzibah, 344
  Hepzibah (Bascom), 343
  Hepzibah (Ford), 343
  Ida Grace, 341
  James, 344
  James Alexander, 341
  Jane (Evitts), 346
  Joanna, 344
  John, 343, 344
  Joshua, 344
  Levy Hall, 345
  Lucy, 345
  Lucy Skinner (Whitman), 493
  Margaret (Girard), 343
  Margaret Burnett, 55
  Mary, 344, 346
  Mary Eliza (Jones), 341
  Mary Ethel, 341

Lyman—*Continued*
  Mavis Katherine, 341
  Millie, 346
  Molly, 345
  Nancy, 345
  Nathan, 344
  Philis, 343
  Philis (Scott), 343
  Phineas, 99, 345
  Pomeroy Joshua, 344
  Ralph B., 55
  Richard, 343, 344
  Robert, 343
  Ruth, 346
  Samuel, 345
  Sarah, 343, 344
  Sarah (Narmon), 344
  Sarah (Osborne), 343
  Sarah Alexander, 345
  Sarah Pierce (Codding), 345
  Seth, 344, 345
  Simeon, 344
  Tertius, 345
  Tertius Alexander, 345
  Thomas, 343, 344
  William, 343, 346
Lynde, Rebecca (Clark), 158
  Samuel, 158
Lyon, Mary, 309
Lyons, Elizabeth Watkins (Henry), 246
  Henningham, 246
  James, 246
  Mary Morrison (Maben), 246
  N. J., 282
  William Henry, 246
  William Wirt Henry, 246

M

McCall, Ann (Yates), 238
  George, 238
  James, 127
  Mary, 238
McCalls, James, 125
McCarthy, Ann Catherine, 316
  Anna, 316
  Catherine Hosack, 316
  Charles, 316
  Elizabeth (Ker), 310, 316
  Elizabeth Van Wyck, 316
  Hannah Caldwell, 316
  Harriet Livermore, 310, 316

McCarthy—*Continued*
  John, 310, 316
  Margaret Ker, 316
  Maria Eleanor, 316
  William, 316
McCarty, Anna Maria, 204, 207
McCay, Florence Kingston, 388
McClean, Catherine, 58
  Helen Rowena, 203
  Hellen Ruhannah, 208
McClelland, Elvira Brice, 245
  Margaret (Cabell), 245
  Thomas S., 245
  Thomas Stanhope, 245
McClenachan, Elyah, 324
  Rachel (Kelton), 324
McClung, James, 67
  Ruth (Baker), 67
McClure, Andrew, 237, 238
  Samuel, 294
  Sarah (Gist), 237, 238
  Virginia Emma (Smith), 294
McComb, Christina (Livingston), 338
  John N., 338
McConky, Caroline Augusta, 444
  James, 444
  Mary Dawes (Grafton), 444
McCook, Susan Alexander, 304
McCormick, Edward, 292
  Ellen (Jett), 292
  Lavinia, 69
McCulloch, Margaretta Montgomery, 59
McCullough, J. Haines, 450
  Maria Ann (Tubman), 450
  Mary E., 234
  Nancy, 60
McDonald, J. Allen, 405
  Susan Isabelle, 405
McDonough, Brice, 71
  Gertrude Gretchen (Baker), 71
McDowell, Margaret Cantey, 455
McEvers, Charles, 336
  Eliza, 336
  Mary, 336
McFunn, Lydia (Biddle), 94
  William, 94

INDEX

McGee, Elizabeth (Gist), 237
  Ramsey, 237
McGeehee, Agnes Catherine (Venable) Venable, 455
  Albert G., 455
McGehee, Elizabeth Williams (Spencer), 426
  Thomas, 426
McGinley, Rebecca, 402
McIlwaine, Anne Claiborne, 156
  Edgar Simeon (Bowling), 156
  Elizabeth Herbert, 156
  Hibernia, 156
  Isabella Louisa (Martin), 156
  Isabella Martin, 156
  Joseph Alston Claiborne, 156
  Lucy Atkinson, 156
  Lucy Atkinson (Pryor), 155
  Robert Dunn, 155
  Sarah Joseph Alston (Claiborne), 155
  William Baird, 155, 156
McIntyre, Catherine, 317
McKelvey, James, 124
  Jane (Cahoun), 124
McKenzie, Maria, 277
McKewn, Andrew, 241
  Elizabeth Johnson (Gist), 241
McLane, Catherine (Hoover), 253
  John, 253
McLaughlin, Elvira, 45
McLean, Caroline Thew (Burnet), 465
  Evelyn Elizabeth, 465
  Hannah, 300
  John, 465
  Nathaniel Collins, 465
McMillan, Julie Villiers (Lewis), 379
McMullan, Emma, 425
McMurtrie, Anna Maria, 442
  William, 442
McNeill, Nancy Long (Baker), 69
  Stanfield Pinkhard, 69
McNutt, James, 454
McRae, Jean, 87
McVickar, Augusta, 303
  John, 303

McWithy, Marshall, 255
  Sarah Jane (Miles), 255
Maben, Mary Morrison, 246
MacDonald, Aeneas, 139
  Janes (Mackenzie), 139
Mackall, Ann (Brooke). 199
  Barbara (Smith), 198
  Benjamin, 198
  James, 199
  John, 199
  Martha, 198
  Martha (Duke), 199
Mackenzie, Alexander, 139
  Elizabeth (Stewart), 139
  Janet, 139
  Kenneth, 139
Mackey, Agnes, 324
  David, 324
Mackhoe, Daniel, 161
Mackie, Ann (Chisholm), 140
  Mungo, 140
Mackintosh, Lauchlan, 139
  Margaret, 139
Macklefresh, Jane, 363
Macrae, Catherine, 140
Maddox, Jane, 293
  Jane (Calvert), 293
  John, 293
  Mary, 293
  Sarah, 293
Madison, Susanna (Hery), 243
  Thomas, 243
Mahler, Charles Frederick, 309
  Frederick E., 309
  Harriet Livermore, 309
Mainwaring, Oliver, 214
Makin, Grace, 317
Maklin, Anna, 371
  Jan, 371
  Maria, 371
Marretje (Moul), 371
Malet, William, 4
Mallory, Lydia, 159
Malone, Dana, 390
  Dana Bradford, 391
  Frances, 391
  Helen, 391
  James C., 390
  Margaret Bradford (Robbins), 390
  Mary E., 390

Maltby, Elizabeth (Morris), 173
  Sarah (Davenport), 173
  William, 173
Manes, Alice Eleanor, 426
  Henry, 426
Manigault, Gabriel, 283
  Margaret (Izard), 283
Manley, Rebecca, 490
Mann, Bernard, 155
  Catharine Frances (Bernard), 155
  David Meade Bernard, 155
  Elizabeth Weldon (Claiborne), 155
  Elizabeth Weldon Claiborne, 155
  John, 155
  John Herbert Claiborne, 155
Manners, Mary (Rush), 408
  Thomas, 408
Manning, ———, 476
  Elizabeth, 97
  J. L., 126
  John, 452
  Mary (White), 476
  Sally Charlton, 452
Mapes, Jabez, 163
  Jacob, 163
  Mary (Corwin), 163
Maquinet, Eleanore, 401
Margison, Alvina (Gardiner), 225
  Cornelius, 225
Marion, Ignatius, 329
  John, 329
  Mary (Kendall), 329
  Rebekah (Knight), 329
Maris, Anne (Waln), 349
  George, 349
  Jonathan, 349
Marks, Albert I., 435
  Frances, 93
  Sara, 435
Marlow, Benjamin, 281
  Eliza (Isaac) Carroll, 281
  Mary (Isaac), 281
Marr, Tennessee, 455
Marriot, Ann (Warfield), 366
Marriott, ———, 366
Marrs, Evangeline, 469
  Francis, 469

Marrs—*Continued*
Jane (Van Poelien), 469
Katy Malinda, 241
Marsh, Hannah, 185
  John, 344
  Rachel, 189
  Sarah (Lyman), 344
Marshall, Alice (Adams), 10
  Andrew, 424
  Ann, 123
  Ann (Bailey), 123
  Catherine Larison, 222
  Charles Boss, 222
  Elizabeth Edmunds (Watkins), 246
  Frances Josette (Calhoun), 124
  Grace, 193
  Humphrey, 123
  J. W., 124
  James Pulliam, 246
  John, 123, 473
  Lucy Gray, 246
  Markham, 123
  Mary (Skinner), 424
  Theresa Lucretia (Bailey), 222
  William, 10
Marsham, Anne (Calvert) Brooke Brent, 289
  Katherine, 289
  Richard, 289
Martin, Abraham, 332
  Alice Louise (Kendall), 332
  Anna Louise, 331
  Bridget (Cabell), 114
  Daniel Hoffman, 331
  Elizabeth Kendall, 329
  Isabella Brown (Venable), 454
  Isabella Louisa, 156
  Katherine (Hoffman), 332
  Katherine Kendall, 331
  Louise, 300
  Mary, 453
  Sarah Caldwell, 128
  Sedellia, 107
  Taylor, 454
  Thomas, 114
  William, 453
Martinie, Alice P., 149
  David, 149
  Mary (Triplet), 149

Marvin, Matthew, 215
Mascraft, Hannah (Carroll), Crosby, 169
  Jacob, 169
Mason, ———, 477
  Alex, 300
  Elizabeth (White), 477
  Joseph, 477
  Nancy (White), 477
  Sarah (Jacob), 300
  Thomas, 473
Massey, Mary Elizabeth (Calhoun), 125
  Nathan, 125
Massie, Elizabeth (Adams), 294
  John W., 294
  Lewis Davis, 294
  Margaret (Bragg), 294
  Margaret Elizabeth, 294, 296
  Mary (Cloud), 294
  Mary Virginia, 294
  Thomas Bernard, 294
Mast, John, 183
  Regina, 183
  Regina (Koenig), 183
Mateer, S., 136
Mather, Elizabeth (Davenport), 173
  Emma, 95
  Richard, 374
  Sarah (Penrose), 374
  Warham, 173
Mathews, ———, 190
  Catherine (Calvert) Green, 294
  Elvira, 294
  George Washington, 294
  Henry, 294
  Hiram, 294
  Jacob, 294
  Rufus, 294
Matlack, Ellen, 383
  Sarah (Renshaw), 383
  Titus, 383
Matthews, Anne (Calhoun), 125
  Caleb B., 39
  Elizabeth (Calvert), 288
  Harriet G. (Spencer), 426
  Isaac, 125
  Mary (Myers), 39

Matthews—*Continued*
Sallie Johnson, 39
Samuel, 288
William, 426
Matthewson, Ruth, 466
Mattison, Catherine, 315
Mattle, Ann, 187, 194
  Thomas, 187, 194
Mattoon, Margaret, 19
Mauleverer, Anne, 4
  Anne (Pierson), 4
  Edmund, 4
  Richard, 4
Maury, Elizabeth (Walker), 16
  James, 275
  Matthew, 16
Maxwell, James, 55
  Mary A., 55
  Nancy, 55
  Sarah G., 140
Maynard, ———, 98
Mayo, Anne, 115
Mayrant, Ann Isabel, 231
Mead, David, 463
  Elizabeth (Betts), 89
  Hannah (Warren), 463
  Zachariah, 89
Meade, Katherine Nelson, 465
  Philip Nelson, 465
  Sara Jane (Rannells), 465
Meads, Mary, 482
Meder, John, 203, 204
Meigs, John, 214
Meirs, Anne Walker, 347
  Anne Walker (Weightman), 347
  Appollo, 347
  Christopher, 347
  Collin Butterworth, 351
  David, 347
  David Allen, 352
  Elizabeth Waln, 352
  Fanny Campbell, 352
  Helen, 351
  Jarvis, 347
  Job Hillman Gaskill, 351
  John, 347, 351, 352
  John Gaskill, 351
  John Waln, 352
  Louisa (Butterworth), 351
  Lucretia (Gaskill), 351
  Lucretia Stockton, 352

INDEX

Meirs—*Continued*
Lucretia Stockton (Gaskill), 347
Martha (Swain), 347
Mary Ann, 352
Richard Waln, 347, 351
Sabina Josephine (D'Invilliers), 347
Sarah, 351
Sarah (Henshaw) Bright, 351
Unity (Shinn), 347
William Weightman, 347
Melyn, Cornelia, 65, 224
Cornelis, 65, 66, 224
Mendenhall, Easter, 107
Sarah, 107
Meng, Charles Henry, 48
Malvina, 48
Sarah Katherine (Calvert), 48
Menges, Maria Catharina, 372
Menough, John, 323
Margaret (Kelton), 323
Mercer, Grace Fenton, 144
Hugh, 94
James, 144
Mary Waller, 155
Merchant, Charles, 375
Charles S., 501
Sarah Elizabeth Chase, 501
Valeria, 375
Meredith, Ann, 216
David, 206
Jane (Henry), 243
Margaret, 115
Samuel, 243
Sarah (Aurelia), 206
Meriken, Jonathan, 354
Sarah (Almy) Cadman, 354
Mering, William, 472
Meriwether, Nicholas, 15
Thomas, 105
Merriam, Abigail, 262
Merrill, Mary, 26
Sarah, 83
Merritt, George, 191
Julia (Douglas), 191
Merry, Benjamin, 149
Catharine, 149
Clarinda (Davis), 149
Cornelius, 223
Hannah, 223

Merry—*Continued*
John, 149, 223
Mary, 149
Puah, 223
Rachel (Ballard), 223
Walter, 188
Meserole, Phebe Ann, 460
William, 460
Metcalf, James W., 90
Maria Caroline (Betts), 90
Michaux, Elizabeth, 452
Jacob, 452
Michener, Mary, 136
Middleton, Arthur, 282, 284
Emma Philadelphia, 284
Henry, 140
Margaret Emma (Izard), 284
Mary, 282
Mary (Izard), 284
Nathaniel Russell, 284
Oliver Hering, 140
Susan Matilda Harriet (Chisholm), 140
Thomas, 284
Mifflin, Elizabeth (Hardy), 349
Jane, 349
John, 349
Miles, Anna Mary, 255
Anzinetta M., 255
Eliza A. E. (Reeve), 255
Elizabeth (Hoover), 255
Ella N., 255
Enoch P., 255
Jesse E., 255
Mary Della, 255
Mary H. (Hoover), 255
Nannie, 141
Rebecca E., 255
S. Emma, 255
Sabina Iowa, 255
Sarah Jane, 255
William, 255
Wm. Porcher, 141
Millard, Anderson, 77
Virginia Louise, 77
Miller, ———, 334, 467
Arlowe Kingsbury, 353
Austin Joseph, 356
Barbara (Livingston), 334
Charles Kingsbury, 353, 356
Eleanor Frances, 353
Elizabeth, 36

Miller—*Continued*
Eva (Mould), 372
James Almy, 356
Jennie Eva, 356
Johannes, 372
Kathleen Bennett, 353
Loris Almy, 353
Madeleine (Tinkham), 353
Margaret Ann (Henry), 245
Mary, 504
Mary Ann (Douglas), 191
Matilda (Smith) Wade, 353
Roy Paul, 356
Samuel, 191
William A., 245
Youngs Woodhull, 356
Milligan, Eugene, 405
James Russell, 405
Kate, 405
Le Roy Jacob, 405
Maud, 405
Maurice, 405
Susan Isabel, 405
Susan Isabel (McDonald), 405
William, 405
Milliken, John Mulberry, 54
Sarah, 54
Sarah (Simonton), 54
Mills, Elizabeth Temperance, 200, 202
Jane, 392
John, 217
Margaret (———), 217
Mary J., 468
Milnor, ———, 431
Milton, John, 12
Minor, Mary, 158
Minot, Abigail, 359
Abigail (Fenno), 359
Anne, 357
Anne (———), 357
Calla (Smith), 360
Caroline Augusta, 360
Charles Henry, 360
Elizabeth, 359, 360
Elizabeth (Bailey), 359
Elizabeth (Breck), 358
Elizabeth (Whitney), 498
Elizabeth Augusta, 360
Ellen (———), 357
Eunice, 359
Eunice (Billings), 359

566 INDEX

Minot—*Continued*
George, 357, 358, 359, 360
Grace Josephine, 360
Hannah, 359
Hannah (Endicott), 358
Hannah (Howard), 358
Hannah (Jones), 358
Hannah (Stoughton), 358
Henry Dearborn, 360
Hephzibah (Corlete), 358
Honora Elizabeth Temple
    (Winthrop), 357
Israel, 358
James, 358
James Jackson, 498
Jerusha, 358, 359
John, 357, 358, 359, 360
John Oliver Billings, 360
Joseph Grafton, 357, 360
Joseph Grafton Winthrop, 357
Josiah, 358
Katherine, 357
Lydia (Butler), 358
Margaret, 357
Maria Josephine (Grafton), 360
Martha, 358, 359, 360
Martha (———), 357
Martha (Blake), 359
Mary, 357, 359
Mary (Baker), 358
Mary Davenport, 360
Mercy (Clark), 358
Nathaniel, 359
Oliver Billings, 360
Rachel (Wild), 359
Rebecca (Wheeler), 358
Robert, 357
Samuel, 358, 359
Sophia, 359
Stephen, 358
Thomas, 357
Truecrosse (Davenport), 358
William, 357
Minthorn, Hulda Randall, 257
Miriam, Bertha, 85
Mitchell, A. R., 233
    Ann (Baird), 59
    Daniel, 106
    Elizabeth (Bye), 110
    George, 110
    Georgeanna, 418

Mitchell—*Continued*
Harriet Couturier (Thomas), 233
John, 60, 211, 418
Madeline, 414
Mahitabel, 504
Margaret (Bryan), 106
Maria (Jacob), 60
Mattie, 422
Nancy, 60
Rebecca, 418
Rebecca (Mitchell), 418
Sarah, 211
Zachariah S., 59
Mixer, Isaac, 214, 328
Rebecca, 328
Rebecca (Garfield), 328
Molineux, Jane, 266
Monroe, Iras Louise (Wolfe), 503
James, 95
Vincent Wolfe, 503
William Clifford, 503
Montague, Eleanor, 493
Richard, 215
Montfort, Henrie (Barret), 277
John Barret, 277
Richard, 277
Montgomery, Catherine, 122, 123
Elizabeth (Gibbes), 234
Janet (Livingston), 335
Joseph, 407
Rachel (Rush) Boyce, 407
Richard, 335
W. S., 234
Moodie, Caroline E., 141
Moody, ———, 75
Abigail (Atkinson), 25
Joshua, 25
Samuel, 179
Sarah (Deming), 179
Moore, ———, 101, 185
Bernard, 15
Elizabeth, 15, 280
George, 281
Hester (———), 280
John, 214
Judith, 111
Thomas, 280
Zedekiah, 281
Moorhead, John, 216

Moorman, Agnes, 453
Charles, 453
Sarah, 107
Moreman, Charles, 453
Mary (Venable), 453
Morgan, Jemina, 236
John, 179
Maude Crenshaw, 118
Rachel (Deming), 179
Thomas, 236
Morris, Alice Lee (West), 414
Ann (Innes), 11
Anthony, 350
Benjamin Wister, 350
Charlotte Augusta (Johnson), 259
Charlotte Johnson, 259
DeWitt Clinton, 259
Elizabeth, 173
Elizabeth (Almy), 354
Hallam L., 414
John, 11, 173, 354
Mary, 394
Mary (Coddington), 350
Mary (Wells), 350
Nicholas, 289
Sarah, 24, 66, 350
Susan (Talbot), 289
Morrison, Andrew, 361
Ann (Gilfillan), 361
Anna Belle, 362
Anna Eliza (Howland), 361
Bessie (Taylor), 362, 367
Cora A., 366
Cora Adelaide, 361
Cora Belle, 362, 366
Elizabeth, 361, 362, 366
Elizabeth Francanna (Jones), 362, 366
Ella A. (Swan), 362
Hannah Caroline (Stewart), 362
Hazel A. (Frisbie), 366
Hazel Adelaide (Frisbie), 361
Isabella Work (Dickey), 361
James Gilfillan, 361
James Work, 362
John, 362, 366
John Crawford, 362
John Huston, 361
John S., 361
Martha Elizabeth, 362

INDEX

Morrison—*Continued*
Mary, 105
Mary (Thomas), 362, 366
Nancy, 361
Samuel Turner, 361, 362, 365, 366
Susan Pauline, 362
Theodore Nevin, 361
Virginia, 362, 367
Wesley Jones, 362, 366
William Andrew, 362, 365, 366
William F., 366
William Francis, 362, 367
William Frisbie, 361
Morse, Elizabeth (Park), 36
Grace (Warren), 463
John, 36
Joseph, 463
Sarah, 300
Morton, Elizabeth (Venable), 453
George, 248
Joseph, 453
Josiah, 453
Judith, 453
Levi P., 390
Lydia, 417
Margaret, 163
Martha, 390
Martha Daniel (Venable), 454
Mary, 453
Patience, 248
Samuel V., 454
William L., 453
Moseley, Bennett W., 454
Edward, 412
Laura (Wolcott), 501
Louisa J. (Venable), 454
Margaret, 454
Muriel (Saltonstall), 412
Patsey, 123
William, 123, 501
Motley, Elizabeth, 268
Margaret, 78
Robert, 78
Mottweiler, George A., 504
Susan (Wolfe), 504
Moul, Anna Catryna, 371
Anna Juliana (Servin), 370
Annanje, 371
Antje, 371

Moul—*Continued*
Catharina, 371
Christoffel, 370
Diewertjen, 371
Elizabeth, 372
James, 371
Jane (Stewart), 371
Johannes, 371
Margriet, 371
Marretje, 371
Philip, 371
Phillipus, 371
Robert, 371
Susanna (Hui), 371
Mould, Anna, 370
Anne, 373
Antje, 372
Catharine, 369
Caty, 373
Christoffel, 372
Christopher, 369
Daniel, 369
Eleanora, 372
Elizabeth, 373
Eva, 370, 372, 373
Herman, 370
Hugh, 486
Jessie, 370
Johannes, 372, 373
Johannes C., 369
John C., 370
Maria, 373
Maria (Law), 372
Maria Catharina (Menges), 372
Martha, 370
Martha (Coit), 486
Mary, 369
Mary (Shafer), 369
Moses, 369
Philip, 373
Rubina (Dickerson), 372
Wilhelm, 372
William S., 370
Moulder, Sara, 374
Moulton, Dorcas, 85
Mary E., 87
Mount, Caroline, 351
Mowbray, ———, 420
Margaret Anne (Brown), 420
Mowisin, Sarah, 10
Moyer, Catherine, 6

Mudge, Mary (Alexander), 19
Micah, 19
Mudgett, Mary, 70
Sylvia, 70
Muhlenberg, Frederick Augustus, 142
Mary Ann C., 142
William Augustus, 142, 143
Mullanphy, Ann, 94
Mumford, Agnes, 197
Eleanor (Holland), 197
Mary Bassett, 112
William, 197
Munier, F. S., 276
Maria Elizabeth (Barret), 276
Munro, Eve (Jay), 302
Harry, 302
Murckland, Margaret Burnett (Bacon) Lyman, 55
Walter E., 55
Murphy, James, 439
Mabel, 439
Murray, Catherine E., 408
Ella Day (Rush), 406
James, 236, 408
Jemina (Morgan), 236
William Spencer, 406
Zipporah, 236
Musier, Catherine Elkins, 271
John, 271
Sarah (Guest), 271
Musselman, Emma, 423
Musser, George, 133
Mussey, Joseph, 25
Lydia (Stickney) Atkinson, 25
Muzzey, Abigail, 397, 398, 477, 479, 480, 484
Abigail (Reed), 397
Alice (Dexter), 479
Benjamin, 479
Elizabeth (Bradshaw), 480
John, 397, 398, 477, 480
Rebecca Reed, 398, 477, 480
Robert, 479
Sarah (———), 479
Myers, Jacob, 295
Mariah (Calvert), 295
Mary, 39
Mygatt, Ann, 179
Joseph, 179
Mary, 179

INDEX

Mynne, Anne, 287
  Elizabeth (Wroth), 288
  George, 288
Myrick, Sara, 24
Myrtle, Lydia, 68

N

Narmon, Sarah, 344
Nautz, Frances W., 453
Neal, Elizabeth, 286
  Louisa Stokes, 426
Neale, Elizabeth (Calvert), 290
  Henrietta Maria, 439
  James, 290, 439
  Martha, 451
  Mary (Brooke), 289
  Raphael, 289
Neely, Eunice (Gray), 68
  James, 68
Nelson, Annie, 60
  Catherine, 317
  David, 483
  James, 431
  John, 60
  Mary (Hibbets), 431
  Mary Jane, 292
  Nelly, 316
  Thomas, 275
Neville, Elizabeth, 438
  George, 438
Nevius, Catherine, 458
Newberry, Benjamin, 500
  Elizabeth (Wolcott), 500
  Marah, 500
  Roger, 500
  Sarah, 499
Newbold, Anne, 5
Newcomb, Francis, 265
  Peter, 265
  Susannah, 265
Newell, ———, 310
  Sally (Johnson) Davis, 310
  Thomas, 214
Newman, Mary (Hoover), 253
  Patience, 31
  Rebecca Jane, 164
  Thomas, 253
Newport, Christopher, 144
Newsome, Mary, 291
Newton, Persis, 483
Nicholas, Caroline, 218

Nichols, Abigail, 212
  Annie Dorinda Brown (Crosby), 170
  Della (Grow), 54
  Edgar Crosby, 171
  Eliza, 70
  Frank Herbert, 171
  Jonathan, 170
  Susan Georgiana, 171
Nicholls, Jane, 278
Nicholson, ———, 363
  Elizabeth (Burgess), 363
Nicklin, Catharine Thornton (Pendleton), 291
  Elizabeth (Calvert), 291, 296
  Jacob Richards, 292
  John Bailey, 291
  Joseph, 291, 296
  Joseph Marshall, 291
  Levi Orme Connor, 292
  Margaretta (Shriver), 292
  Martha Ann, 292
  Martha Anne, 296
  Mary Jane (Nelson), 292
  Mary Newton (Lane), 291
  Susan (Eastham), 292
  Susan Maria (Hunter), 292
  William Henry Harrison, 292
Nicola, Elizabeth Mary, 395
  Felix, 395
  Mary D. (Robertson), 395
  Mary Wright, 395
  William Wright, 395
Ninegret, George, 37
Nix, Elizabeth (Lewis), 452
  John, 452
Noble, Alexander, 126, 127, 128
  Catherine (Calhoun), 126, 127
  Daniel, 91
  Ezekiel Pickens, 129
  John, 126, 127
  Mary, 91
  Mary (Calhoun), 127
  Mary A., 91
  Sarah (Calhoun), 129
  Susan Wilkinson (Calhoun), 128
Noel, Edward, 444
  Elizabeth, 444, 445
  Elizabeth (Trippe), 444

Noel—*Continued*
  Mary, 445
  Sarah, 444
Nolan, Charles, 68
  Sophia (Fleet), 68
Norman, Anne (Jennings), 294
Norris, Patrick, 125
  Rachel (Calhoun), 125
North, John, 215
Northrop, Charlotte Louise, 181
  Harmon, 181
  Israel, 181
  Joseph, 182
  Lucy Willard (Denning), 181
  Mary Goodsell (Deming), 182
  Sarah (Wooster), 181
Norton, Charlotte, 150
  Mary, 492
  Thomas, 214
Norwood, Sarah C., 127
Nott, John, 159
  Penniah, 159
  Phoebe, 158
Nottley, Ann, 290
  Thomas, 290
Noyes, ———, 26
  Anna (Atkinson), 26
  Mary (Haines), 42, 51
  Thomas, 42, 51
Nuthall, Margaret Ann, 200
  Matilda (Abell), 200
  William, 200

O

O'Carroll, Joanna, 240
O'Connor, Anne, 71
Odell, Elizabeth, 97
Oelrichs, Lucie, 303
Ogborn, Ann, 429
  John, 429
Ogden, Elizabeth, 410
  Henry Aaron, 34, 38
  Katharene (Conklin), 34, 38
  Mary Ann, 34, 38
  Thomas, 410
Ogilby, Elizabeth Archer, 269
Olcott, Sarah, 189
Olden, Amy, 6
  Job Gardner, 3
  Julia Boggs, 3
  Maria Brenton (Boggs), 3

INDEX

Olds, Mary, 53
Oliver, Elizabeth M., 393
  Susan, 281
Olney, Mary, 465
Orall, Polly, 217
Orcut, James, 299
  Mary (Jacob), 299
Ordway, Hannah (Bartlett), 74
  John, 74
  Mary, 74
O'Rourke, Frances, 22
Orr, Jane, 128
Osborn, Elizabeth, 64
  Joseph, 64
Osborne, Anna (Sherwood), 393
  Elizabeth (Hedges), 223
  Fanny, 393
  Jeremiah, 393
  Mary, 5
  Roger, 343
  Sarah, 343
  Thomas Burr, 393
Osgood, Martha S., 262
  Mary, 417
Osman, Abraham, 163
  Jacob, 163
  Rebecca (Corwin), 163
  Sarah (Corwin), 163
Otis, John, 298
  Mary (Jacob), 298
Overby, Sarah, 389
Owen, Bethia, 165
  Jane, 325
  Owen, 93
  Sarah, 93
Oyer, Fanny (Clark), 160
  Peter D., 160

P

Pace, Elizabeth (Neal), 286
  James Baker, 286
  Violet Lee, 286
Pack, Joseph Sayre, 267
  Martha Jane, 267
Packer, William F., 111
Packman, Elizabeth, 438
Paddleford, Abigail (King), 491
  Hannah (King) Alden, 491
  Jonathan, 491
Paddock, Catherine, 71
Page, Ann Grace, 193
  Anne, 326

Page—*Continued*
  Byrd Alston, 154
  Edward Augustus, 23
  Elizabeth (Bryan), 106
  Elizabeth Bispham, 23
  Grace (Marshall), 193
  Hepzibah, 307
  Herbert Claiborne, 154
  Herbert H., 154
  John, 106
  Josephine Augusta (Bispham), 23
  Kingman, 326
  Kingman Fogg, 193
  Mary Louisa (Claiborne), 154
  Matthew, 155
  Randolph Rosewell, 155
  Weldon Bathurst, 154
Paige, William, 53
Paine, Elizabeth, 311
  Evelina (Bacon), 45
  Henry, 45
  Horner H., 185
  Laura (Cummings), 185
Palmer, Anne Wildes (Brown), 46
  Annie G., 46
  Caroline Emma, 46
  Caroline Frances (Bacon), 45
  Charles James, 45
  Edward Francis, 46
  Edward James Barnes, 45
  Florence Mary, 47
  Frederick Tobey, 46
  George Monroe, 46
  Helen E., 45
  James Monroe, 45
  Jennie C. (Giesler), 46
  Jennie Carolyn, 46
  Jonathan, 45, 349
  Lucy (Way), 195
  Marion Prescott, 46
  Martha (Prescott), 45
  Mary E. (Primmer), 46
  Samuel, 195
  Sarah (Waln) Simcock, 349
  William Lincoln, 46
Pancoast, Joseph, 5
  Rebecca (Abbott), 5
Pantry, Abigail, 492
  John, 492
  Mary (Norton), 492

Park, Abigail, 35, 36
  Abigail (Chapman), 37
  Abigail (Dix), 35
  Abigail (Greene), 37
  Abigail (Laurence), 36
  Ann, 37
  Anne (Spring), 36
  Benjamin, 33, 36, 37, 38
  Deliverance, 36
  Edward, 35
  Elizabeth, 35, 36
  Elizabeth (Miller), 36
  Hannah Ann, 33
  Hannah Anne, 38
  Henry, 37
  Isabel, 35
  John, 35, 36, 37
  Jonathan, 36
  Jonathan Greene, 37
  Joseph, 36, 37
  Lydia (Laurence), 36
  Martha (Fiske), 35
  Mary, 36, 37
  Rebecca, 35
  Richard, 35
  Samuel, 37
  Sarah, 35
  Sarah (Collier) Brewster, 35
  Sarah (Cutter), 35
  Sarah (Hiscox), 37
  Solomon, 36
  Susanna Maria, 38
  Susanna Maria (Keens), 38
  Thomas, 35, 36, 37
Parker, Ann, 107
  Catherine (Calhoun), 125
  Edwin, 129
  Elizabeth (Clark) Pratt, 158
  Eugenia (Calhoun), 129
  Jessie, 422
  John W., 125
  Jonathan, 32
  Joseph, 98
  Mary (Bingham), 98
  Rebecca, 158
  Ruth (Avery), 32
  William, 158
Parkhurst, Abigail, 184
  Betty (Cummings), 184
  George, 313
  Gertrude Leo, 108
  Joel, 184
  Sarah (Browne), 313

Parkman, Sarah Cabot, 27
Parran, Esther, 199
  John, 199
Parry, Edward, 407
  Elizabeth (Rush), 407
Parshall, Elizabeth (Gardiner), 223
  James, 223
Parsons, Hannah (Baker), 224
  Joseph, 215
  Mary, 224
  Samuel, 224
Passano, Edward Boteler, 278
  Edward Magruder, 278
  Eleanor Phillips (Isaac), 278
  Howard Isaac, 278
  William Moore, 278
Passmore, Andrew, 111
  Judith (Moore), 111
  Phoebe Pusey, 111
Patten, Sarah, 43
Patter, Hannah (Livermore), 318
  Nathaniel, 318
Patterson, Elizabeth (Baker), 69
  John G., 69
  Robert, 95
Patteson, Martha Louise, 117
Pattie, Martha America, 272
Pattison, Ann (Skinner), 423
  Beckie, 423
  Nancy, 421
  Samuel, 423
Patker, Mary, 54
Paul, James, 349
  Susannah, 349
Paxson, Benjamin, 111
  Deborah, 111
  Deborah (Taylor), 111
  Hannah, 110
  Helen, 306
  Margery, 3
Payne, Dorothea, 274
Peach, Joseph, 280
  Mary (Isaac), 280
Peale, Mary, 432
Pearce, Eliza, 268
  Frances, 426
  Judith (Spencer), 425
  Martin, 425
Pearson, ———, 111
  Catherine M., 107

Pearson—*Continued*
  Grace (Vipont), 110
  Hephsibah, 169
  Jemina (Bye), 111
  Josephine, 304
  Judith (Atkinson), 25
  Mary (French), 169
  Sarah, 110
  Silas, 25
  Sitnah Ann, 107
  Stephen, 169
  Thomas, 110
Peart, Rachel, 206, 407
Pease, Ann (Dixon), 183
  Hannah, 313
  John, 183
Peasley, Anne (Calvert), 288
  William, 288
Peay, Austin, 16
  Peachy Walker (Speed), 16
Peddaick, Maria, 281
Peirce, Elizabeth (Cole), 41
  Lydia (Bacon), 42
  Rachel (Bacon), 41
  Samuel, 42
  Thomas, 41
Pellew, Edward, 303
  Eliza (Jay), 303
  George, 303
  Henry Edward, 303
Pemberton, ———, 255
  Albert H., 257
  Delilah (Jay), 255
  Hannah Mabel, 257
  Hannah Martha (Hoover), 257
  Roland Leigh, 257
Pendleton, Ann (Park), 37
  Catharine Thornton, 291
  Peleg, 37
Penhallow, Harriet R., 300
Penn, William, 92, 100
Pennell, Elizabeth, 444
  Mary, 444
Penny, Alexander, 278
  Amy, 278
  Elizabeth (———), 278
  Henry, 278
  John, 164
  Sarah (Corwin), 164
  Susan Ford, 278
Perkins, Eleanor, 72

Perkins—*Continued*
  Harriette Louise (Bartlett), 72
  John, 497, 498
  Lucy, 498
  Moses Bradstreet, 72
  Richard Bartlett, 72
  Ruth, 497
Penrose, Ann, 375
  Ann (———), 375
  Ann (Dowding), 374
  Ann (Fleeson), 374
  Ann (Rowan), 375
  Anne (Williamson), 375
  Anne Howard (Bingham), 375
  Bartholomew, 374
  Benjamin, 375
  Boies, 374, 377, 378
  Cassandra (Hall), 375
  Charles Bingham, 375, 376, 377, 378
  Clement Andairese, 177
  Clement Biddle, 375
  Dorothy, 374
  Elizabeth Colegate, 377
  Ellen Williams, 375
  Emily Linnard, 376
  Esther (Leech), 374
  Frances Shipmen, 376
  Francis Boies, 379
  Helen, 377
  Howard, 375
  Isaac, 375
  James, 374, 375
  James Wilkinson, 375
  John, 374, 375
  Jonathan, 375
  Julie Villiers (Lewis) McMillan, 379
  Katherine (Drexel), 378
  Lydia Baird, 377
  Mary, 375
  Mary (Krill), 374
  Mary (Linnard), 376
  Mary Ann (Hoffman), 375
  Mary Clementina, 377
  Mary Deming, 376
  Mary Deming (Shipman), 376
  Nathaniel Shipman, 376
  Richard Alexander Fullerton, 376, 377, 378

INDEX

Penrose—*Continued*
Samuel, 374
Sarah, 374
Sarah (Biddle), 375
Sarah (Coats), 374
Sarah (Moulder), 374
Sarah Clementina, 376
Sarah Hannah (Boies), 377
Sarah Hannah Boies, 378
Sarah Merchant, 375
Sarah Tillier, 375
Spencer, 378
Stephen Beasley Linnard, 376
Thomas, 374
Valeria (Merchant), 375
Valeria Biddle, 375
Valeria Fullerton, 376
Valeria Fullerton (Biddle), 375
Virginia, 376
Virginia Merchant, 375
William McFunn, 375
Pepper, Elijah, 291
Elizabeth (Calvert), 291
Pepperrell, William, 19, 85, 161
Perrin, Ann (Calhoun), 124
William, 124
Peter, John, 113
Susannah, 113
Peterman, Julia, 130
Peters, Mary, 27
Mary Jane (Thompson), 27
Richard, 27
Peterson, Eleanor B., 306
Elizabeth (Claiborne), 154
Thomas, 154
Pettengill, Amos, 76
Anna, 76
Benjamin, 76
Charlotte (True), 76
Eleanor, 76
Mehitable (Kimball), 76
Pettingell, Cutting, 25
Judith (Atkinson), 25
Pettit, Charity, 111
Sarah, 111
William, 111
Petty, Ann, 430
William, 430
Pharo, Ann, 350
Phelps, Ichabod, 161

Phelps—*Continued*
Miriam, 98
William, 214
Phillips, Abigail, 430
Amy (Penny), 278
Catherine (———), 278
Dorcas, 74, 83
Eleanor Penny, 278
Hannah (Stockton), 430
James, 278
Jane (Nicholls), 278
Peter, 278
Philip, 430
Rebecca, 430
Susan, 17
Susan Ann, 424
Susie, 421
Thomas, 278
Phippeney, Harriet Maria, 214
Pickens, Andrew, 127
Susan, 128
Pierce, Abigail (Minot), 359
Abijah, 314
Elizabeth, 319
Elizabeth (Kendall) Winship, 328
Joseph, 328, 359
Judith, 43
Persis, 319
Thankful (Brown), 314
Thomas, 319
Pierpont, Abigail (Davenport), 173
Hannah (Livermore) Patter, 318
James, 173
Robert, 318
Pierrepont, Anna Maria (Jay), 304
Henry Evelyn, 304
Pierson, Abigail, 173
Abraham, 173
Anne, 4
Pieters, Annatie, 457
Gerrit Coerte (Van Voorhees), 458
Pieterse, Magdalena, 457
Pike, Experience, 261
Mary, 24
Sybilla (Frost), 261
William, 261
Pillsbury, Ida, 301

Pilsbury, Elizabeth (Atkinson), 25
Samuel, 25
Pinchman, Elizabeth, 117
Pinckney, Charles Cotesworth, 284
Pintard, Abigail (Stockton), 431
Lewis, 431
Samuel, 431
Susanna (Stockton), 431
Pitcher, Ella (Skinner), 423
Gertrude Robbins, 263
J. Reese, 423
William Robinson, 263
Pitfield, Rebecca F., 5
Pitkin, Esther Adelaide, 79
John Jay, 79
Martha, 499
Susan Jeannette, 79
Susan Lord, 79
Pittee, Ruth, 490
Plank, Hannah (Cooper), 300
Robert, 300
Sarah, 300
Plantagenet, John, 297
Katherine (Roet) Swynford, 297
Platt (?), Hannah, 32
Plomer, Ann, 264
Plummer, H. Maria, 257
Plumstead, Clement, 93
Sarah (Biddle) Righton, 93
Poague, Gabriella (Smither), 292
Irving, 292
Pococke, John, 354
Poindexter, Edwin W., 270
Frances Archer (Hundley), 270
Polk, Lucile Stewart, 100
William Plunket Stewart, 100
Pollard, George, 11
Mary Griffin (Adams), 11
Sussannah, 449
Pollock, Atcheson, 292
Hannah Calvert (Jett), 292
Pomeroy, Eliza (Lyman), 344
Hannah, (Lyman), 344
Job, 344
Poole, Margaret James, 364, 366

INDEX

Poor, Mary, 496
Pope, Annie (Putnam), 380
  Betsy, 380
  Deborah, 482
  Ebenezer, 380
  Joseph, 380
  Mehitable (Putnam), 380
Porcher, Marianne, 140
Pordage, William, 437
Porter, Alexander J., 72
  Amy Agnes Sheffield, 91
  Amy Ellen (Betts), 91
  Catherine Rush, 409
  Constance Elaine, 91
  Elizabeth Murray, 409
  Elizabeth Murray (Rush), 409
  Ellen, 91
  John Addison, 91
  John Biddle, 409
  Josephine Earl, 91
  Josephine Earl (Sheffield), 91
  Judith, 228
  Margaret Jaffrey, 72
  Margaretta Biddle, 409
  Mary (Noble), 91
  Mary A. (Noble), 91
  Maud (Langmuir), 72
  William A., 91
Post, Julia, 305
  Sarah, 63
Pottenger, John, 279
  Mary (Beall), 279
  Sarah, 279
Potter, Anna Margaretta, 434
  Asa P., 193
  Caroline, 211
  Grace Josephine (Douglas), 193
  Harriet Maria, 434
  Henry C., 121
  Horatio, 187
  James Sheldon, 193
  John, 434
Poulter, Elizabeth, 315
  Pouncer, James, 273
Powell, James R., 120
Power, Emma (Jacobs), 450
  Marie Regina, 450
  Vincent W., 450
Powers, James Leake, 292, 296
  Lillie Elizabeth, 271

Powers—*Continued*
  Lucy (Calvert), 296
  Martha Ann (Nicklin), 292
  Poyntz, Susanna, 410
  Thomas, 410
Poythress, Martha (Ravenscroft), 153
  William, 153
Pratt, Benajah, 159
  Bethsheba, 159
  Dorothy, 489
  Eleanor (Montague), 493
  Eliza, 149
  Elizabeth, 498
  Elizabeth (Clark), 158
  Hannah, 489
  Hester (Clark), 159
  Isaac Reed, 248
  John, 490, 498
  Mary, 159
  Mary (Whitman), 488, 490
  Orin, 149
  Polly, 20
  Ruth E. (Capron), 149
  Sarah Frances, 248
  Sarah Williams (Ford), 248
  Thankful, 159
  William, 158
Prence, Thomas, 323
Prentice, Anne, 61
  Henry, 313
  Mary, 43
  Polly, 310
  Susanna (Brown), 313
Presby, Betsey, 380
  Betsy Walton (Flint), 380
  Dorothea, 380
  Elizabeth Ann (Husk) 381
  Frank Henry, 380, 381
  Hannah (Campbell), 380
  Harriet Myers (Cook), 380
  Ida M. (Taylor), 380
  Jesse Campbell, 380
  Joseph, 380
  Mildred, 380
  William Joseph Henry, 381
Prescott, Edith, 502
  Martha, 45
  William, 502
  William G., 502
  William Hickling, 502
Preston, Amanda, 487

Prestwood, George, 114
  Mary, 114
Price, ———, 366
  Barbara, 382
  Butler Delaplaine, 382, 384
  Chandler, 383, 384
  Clara Agnes (Gillmore), 382
  Eliza (Trippe), 445
  Elizabeth, 210, 383
  Elizabeth Arnold (Whaling), 382
  Elizabeth Senter, 382
  Elizabeth Senter (Huntt), 383, 384
  Ella Virginia, 384
  Ellen (Matlack), 383
  Ellen Matlack, 383
  Ethel Huntt, 382
  Evan, 257
  Fannie Maria, 384
  Gillmore Delaplaine, 382
  Hannah (Delpalaine), 383
  Henrietta, 200
  James, 445
  John, 383
  Jonathan, 383
  Mary, 383
  Mary (Chandler), 383
  Mary Gwynne, 382
  Rebecca (Hoover), 257
  Richard Butler, 383, 384
  Sarah, 383
  Sarah (Warfield), 366
  Susannah, 383
Priest, John, 261
  Mary, 261
Prime, Frederick, 304
  Laura, 305
  Mary Rutherfurd (Jay), 304
  Nathaniel, 305
Primmer, Mary E., 46
Prince, Frank, 210
  Jane, 392
  John, 210
  Mary, 210
  Rebecca, 380
  Thomas, 210
Pringle, Edward Jenkins, 259
  Mary Motte, 259
Prioleau, Elias, 140
  Hext, 140
  Providence Hext, 140
  Samuel, 140

INDEX

Proctor, Sarah, 189
Pryor, Lucy Atkinson, 155
Puddington, George, 363
Pulley, Mary, 12
Purdue, Betsey (Baker), 66
Prudence, 404
Purdy, ———, 66
Putnam, Aaron, 32
  Annie, 380
  B. A., 130
  Elizabeth (Avery), 32
  Emma, 32
  Hannah (———), 380
  Henry, 381
  Israel, 134
  John, 380, 381
  Kate Kirby, 130
  Mehitable, 380
  Nicholas, 381
  Priscilla (Gould), 381
  Rebecca (Prince), 380
  Richard, 381
  Robert, 381
  Roger, 381
  Rufus, 250
  Thomas, 381
  William, 381
Pyle, Cyrus, 112
  Isabel, 112
  Mary Bassett (Mumford), 112

Q

Quillian, Helen Bertha, 155

R

Rabineau, Josephine, 324
Radcliffe, Judith, 140
Raitt, Betsey (Ferguson), 87
  Clementin, 87
  John, 87
Ralls, Anne (Smither), 292
  Lydia Beck, 291, 293
  Nathaniel Beck, 292
Ramsden, Anne, 410
  John, 410
Ramsey, Nancy, 403
Rand, Abigail (Whitney), 496
  Alice (Sharp), 476
  Elizabeth Adeline (Kirtland), 298
  Hanson, 298
  John, 496

Rand—*Continued*
  Robert, 476
  Sarah, 398, 476, 484
  Sarah (Edenden), 476
  Sarah Elizabeth, 298
  Thomas, 398, 476
Randall, ———, 149
Randolph, John, 243
Rankin, Adams, 14
  Catherine, 501
  Elizabeth (Speed), 14
  Henry, 501
  Laura Maria (Wolcott), 501
  Robert G., 501
Rannells, Sara Jane, 465
Ransom, Elias, 467
Rapalje, Annatie Coerte (Van Voorhees), 458
  Jan, 458
Rappleye, Jacobus, 356
  Jane, 356
Rasby, Barbara (Saltonstall), 411
  Christopher, 411
Rash, Betsey, 98
Rathbone, Content (Brown), 190
  John, 190
  Martha, 190
  Phoebe (Clark), 159
  Sophia, 191
  Thomas, 159
Ratliff, Gulielma, 253
Ravenscroft, Martha, 153
Rawle, William, 441
Rawlins, Emily S., 369
  John A., 369
Rawson, Jerusha, 249
Raymond, Lydia, 174
  Richard, 214
Raynor, Abigail, 328
  John, 328
Razee, ———, 466
  Sarah (Whipple), 466
Read, Isaac, 455
  Martha, 466
  Mary, 41
  Thomas, 41, 51, 466
Reader, Thomas, 396
Reagan, Nancy, 504
Record, Hannah (Hobart), 264
  John, 264

Reed, Abigail, 397
  Abigail (Kendall), 397, 480
  Adeline, 26
  Amos, 329
  Ann (Hoo), 396
  Benjamin, 397, 480
  Eleazer, 185
  Elizabeth, 289, 297
  Elizabeth (Gennison), 396
  George, 328, 396, 480
  Giles, 297
  Isaac, 480
  Israel, 328
  Jane (Ellis), 251
  Katherine (Greville), 297
  Katherine A., 141
  Mabel Kendall, 328, 396, 480
  Mahala, 251
  Mary, 51
  Mary (Brockett), 396
  Mary (Cornwall), 396
  Mary (Stonehouse), 396
  Persis (Kendall), 328
  Rachel (Cumming), 185
  Rebecca, 477, 480
  Rebecca (Stone), 397, 480
  Ruth, 480, 489
  Sampson, 251
  Sarah, 490
  Susanna (Kendall), 329
  Thomas, 328, 396
  Timothy, 328
  William, 328, 396, 397, 480, 489
Rees, Elizabeth, 207
  Mary, 418
Reese, Sarah, 101
Reeve, Eliza A. E., 255
Reeves, Biddle, 306
  Elizabeth Thomas, 306
  Hannah, 164
  Ruthana (Thomas), 306
Reid, Ann Elizabeth, 504
  Clementina (Venable), 455
  Clementine S., 426
  Jane, 454
  William S., 455
Reikes, Robert, 36
Reinecker, Clara, 237
Remsen, Antie, 458
  Gertrude (Vanderbilt), 457
  Jacob, 457, 458, 459

INDEX

Remsen—*Continued*
Jannetje, 457
Maria (Van Voorhees), 459
Marretje Coerte, 458
Rench, Mary, 407
Renching, Ellen, 438
Richard, 438
Susan (Honeywood), 438
Rennolds, Elizabeth, 450
Henry Starkley, 450
Julia Louisa (Tubman), 450
William Daingerfield, 450
Renshaw, Sarah, 383
Revere, Paul, 266
Reynolds, Dorothy, 438
Joseph, 319
Mary, 319
Ruth, 495
Rhett, Alfred, 126
Rhinelander, John, 432
Julia (Stockton), 432
Rhoades, Anne G. (Wheelwright), 143
Elizabeth, 143
John Harsen, 143
Rhodes, Downes, 404
Frank, 71
Gertrude Lucile (La Rue), 71
Lincoln, 71
Mary (Baker), 71
Maud, 71
Monroe, 71
Nora, 71
Wheeler, 71
Rice, ———, 147
Ann (Churchill), 147
Caroline Elizabeth, 72
Edward, 215
Elizabeth Emmeline (Foster), 72
Emily, 150
John Abbott, 72
Mehitable, 477
Rich, Mary, 288
Richards, Deborah, 489
James, 412
Jerusha, 412
Mary, 489, 500
Richardson, ———, 363
Abigail (Farwell), 44
Celesta, 225
Deborah, 329

Richardson—*Continued*
Ebenezer, 330
Elizabeth (Bacon), 42
Elizabeth (Ewen), 367
Ezekiel, 329
Joanna, 42
John, 42
Joseph, 350
Levi, 44
Mary, 42, 51
Samuel, 42
Sarah, 42, 350
Sarah (Morris), 350
Susannah (Burgess), 363
Thomas, 42, 51
William, 367
Rickey, Amy (Olden), 6
Anne, 6
John, 6
Rider, Eliza, 26
Ridgeway, Abigail (Stockton), 430
Jacob, 430
Ridgley, Charles, 365
Henry, 280
Jane, 280
Jane (Westal), 280
Lydia (Warfield), 365
Sarah (Isaac), 280
Westal, 280
William, 280
Ridgway, Ann (Pharo), 350
Elizabeth (Chamberlain), 350
Elizabeth (Wright), 350
Jacob, 408
John, 350
Phoebe (Bellangee), 350
Phoebe Ann, 408
Richard, 350
Sarah, 350
Thomas, 350
Riffe, Elizabeth, 405
Riggs, Rachel, 364
Righton, Sarah (Biddle), 93
William, 93
Riker, Catherine Ann, 165
Rilie (?), Mary, 451
Ring, Susannah, 482
Ripley, Amelia Jane, 263, 266
Faith, 97
Jane (Molineux), 266
John, 263, 266

Ripley—*Continued*
Lydia (Hobart), 263
Nehemiah, 263
Risbrough, Mary Blake, 385
Ritchie, Albert, 117
Albert Cabell, 117
Elizabeth Caskie (Cabell), 117
Roach, Alice Margaret, 389
Alice Morgan (Blankson), 388
Allen, 387
Eliza Walter (Jones), 387
George Washington, 386
Martha (Scanlan), 386
Mary (Huddell), 386
Mary Edith, 389
Mary Fisher (Stellwagen), 385
Mary Huddell, 387
Mary Zemas (Thomas), 388
Isaac, 385, 386, 387, 389
Joseph Chandler, 387, 388
Joseph Huddell, 386, 387, 388, 389
Katherine Bankson, 389
Rebecca Huddell, 387
Thomas Bankson, 389
Thomas Randall, 387
Walter Thomas, 385, 388, 389
William, 386
Roane, Anne (Henry), 244
Spencer, 244
Robb, James Hampden, 339
Louisa, 339
Robbins, Alice (Brockway), 393
Ammi Ruhamah, 392, 393
Bertine, 394
Chandler, 392
Dorothea Le Baron, 391
Edward, 393
Eleanor Hartpence, 390
Elizabeth, 393
Elizabeth (Le Baron), 392
Elizabeth Bradford, 391
Elizabeth Kemp (Rutton), 394
Elizabeth M. (Oliver), 393
Fanny (Osborne), 393
Frances, 393

INDEX

Robbins—*Continued*
Frances Cleveland (Lamont, 391
Francis Le Baron, 390, 391, 393, 394
Hannah, 392
Hannah (Chandler), 392
Hannah (Foote), 392
Hannah Rebecca, 392
Hannah S. (Cooke), 393
Helen (Gill), 393
Helen Morton, 390
Henry Welles, 394
Howard Chandler, 390
Irene, 392
James Watson, 393
Jane (Mills), 392
Jane (Prince), 392
John, 391
Lucy Morton (Hartpence), 390
Mara, 393
Margaret Bradford, 390
Maria (Eggleston), 393
Mary (Brazier), 391
Mary Alice, 391
Mary Ann Haight (Wells), 393
Mary Louise (Bayles), 390
Mary Sherwood, 393
Mercy, 392
Nathaniel, 391, 392, 393
Philemon, 392, 393
Priscilla (Le Baron) Alden, 393
Rebecca, 391, 392
Rebecca (———), 391
Rebecca Hannah, 392
Richard, 391
Rose (Bignal), 393
Salome, 393
Salome (Robbins), 393
Samuel, 391, 393
Sarah, 190, 392, 393
Sarah Elizabeth, 394
Susan, 393
Thomas, 393, 394
Thomas Burr, 393
William, 393
Roberts, Elizabeth Fox, 408
Hugh, 408
Isabel, 292
John, 214

Roberts—*Continued*
Nancy L., 331
Samuel S., 107
Talitha (Bryan), 107
Robertson, Addie Crandall, 395
Amelia (Janes), 396
Daniel, 396
Elizabeth White (Crandall), 395, 399
Ewing Welch, 395, 396, 399
Jane Ruffin, 11
Jean, 243
Lou E., 395
Lydia (Strong), 396
Mary (Silver), 396
Mary D., 395
Nathan, 396
Robert, 395
Susannah, 396
Susannah (Robertson), 396
William, 243
Robins, Edward, 363
Elizabeth, 363
George, 440
Henrietta, Maria (Tilghman, 440
Obedience, 144
Robinson, Abigail (Bacon), 44
Carline, 376
Caroline (Potter), 211
Eliza (Pearce), 268
Frances (Robbins), 393
Jerusha (Minot), 359
John, 263
John McHenry, 8
John Mitchell, 211
Lemuel, 359
Lettie Reed, 8
Lucile Pearce, 268
Maria Louisa (Booker), 8
Mariana Stoughton (Emory, 211
Mariana Winder, 211
Peter, 211
Ralph, 211
Rosa Johnson, 276
Sarah (Mitchell), 211
Susan Jane (Avery), 33
Susannah Witham, 430
Thomas, 430
William, 33
William Wiltshire, 393

Robinson—*Continued*
Winthrop, 44
Worthington, 268
Roblot, Jeanne, 151
Rockey, Maria (Peddaick), 281
Rockwell, Daniel, 98
Esther (Bingham), 98
William, 214
Rockwood, Abigail, 20
Joanna (Ellis), 20
Nathaniel, 20
Rhoda, 21
Rodes, Anne E., 276
Roe, Delphine, 149
John, 149
Roelofs, ———, 456
Merghin Stevense (Van Voor Hees), 456
Roet, Katherine, 297
Rogers, Agnes, 364
Catherine Fletcher, 222
Ezekiel, 168
Florence (Wallingford), 222
Hanford Newell, 222
James Newell, 222
Jane Gardiner, 222
John, 142, 364, 367
Juliet (Gardiner), 222
Lauren Eastman, 227
Lydia (King), 491
Mary (Bryd), 226
Mary (Tall), 77
Mary Ann, 142
Mary Ann C. (Muhlenberg), 142
Nathaniel, 491
Nina Louise (Eastman), 226
Pelatiah, 77
Richard, 85
Sarah, 93
Sarah Maria, 77
Thomas Brown, 226
Wallace Brown, 226
Rood, Annie, 181
Rookard, ———, 293
Sarah (Calvert), 293
Roosa, Catharina (Moul), 371
Isaac, 371
Ropes, Dorothy (Bartlet), 83
John, 83

INDEX

Rose, Ann Maria, 220
  Cornelia Ward (Whipple) Davis, 469
  Elizabeth (Fulton), 220
  Francis M., 469
  John Whitney, 220
  Lucy Whitney, 220
  Martha Elizabeth, 220
  Royal Nelson, 220
  William Fulton, 220
Rosewell, Elizabeth, 412
  William, 412
Ross, Dorothy, 496
  Elizabeth, 94, 324
  James, 496
  John, 94, 324
  Josephine, 297
  Margaret (Young), 324
Rosser, Joseph Travis, 296
  Mary Landon Armistead, 296
  Mary Walker (Armistead), 296
Rosseter, Nathan, 90
  Rebekah, 90
  Sarah, 90
Rotch, Mary, 32
  William, 32
Rothrock, Abraham, 400, 401
  Ada, 404
  Adeline (———), 404
  Aileen, 400
  Alexander, 404
  Alice (Hudgins), 400
  Allen, 400
  Andrew, 405
  Ann Elita, 404
  Ann Maria, 402
  Anna (———), 404
  Anna Belle Crawford (Seymour), 403
  Anne Maria, 402
  Barbara (Weller), 401
  Benjamin, 402
  Boyd P., 403
  Catherine, 401, 402
  Catherine (Kuntz), 401
  Charity, 402, 404
  Charles, 405
  Clifford, 404
  David, 404
  Donald, 403
  Dorothy (Gump), 402

Rothrock—*Continued*
  Downes (Rhodes), 404
  Eleanore (Maquinet) Galatin, 401
  Elizabeth, 402, 404
  Elizabeth (Joslyn), 403
  Elizabeth (Riffe) Gilly, 405
  Ellen (———), 404
  Eva, 401
  Eva Elizabeth, 401
  Francis Blake, 400
  Frederick, 402
  George, 400, 401, 402, 403, 404
  George Test, 405
  Henry, 404, 405
  Henry R., 403
  Huling Herbert, 404
  Isabella, 404, 405
  Isabella (Test), 404
  Jacob, 401, 402, 404, 405
  James, 402
  James Huling, 404
  Jennie, 404
  Jessie, 404
  Johaanes, 401
  John, 400, 402, 404, 405
  Joseph, 402, 403
  Joseph Trimble, 401
  Ludwig, 400
  Margaret, 404
  Maria, 402
  Martha (Lobaugh), 400
  Mary, 404
  Mary (Young), 405
  Matilda (———), 404
  Mollie, 405
  Nancy (Ramsey), 403
  Nancy Alice, 400
  Olivia, 403
  Oscar, 403
  Peter, 402
  Phebe Brinton (Trimble), 401
  Philip, 400, 401, 402
  Philip Jacob, 403
  Prudence (Purdue) Thomas, 404
  Rebecca, 403
  Robert (Buckler), 404
  Russell, 405
  Salome Charity (Worley), 402

Rothrock—*Continued*
  Sarah (Yost), 403
  Susan, 404
  Susanna, 402, 403
  Thomas, 403, 404
  Valentine, 402
  Wilfred Leester, 403
  William, 403, 404, 405
  Wilson, 404, 405
Rouse, Hannah Anne (Park) Avery, Coyne, 38
  John Owen, 38
Rowan, Ann, 375
  John, 375
Rowland, ———, 198
  Elizabeth (Duke), 198
Royce, Hannah Churchill, 146
  Samuel, 146
Ruddy, Edward, 347
  Jane, 347
  Jonathan, 97
  Mary, 97
Rudicil, Lucy (Smither), 292
  John, 296
  Mary Catherine (Smith), 296
  Robert, 292
Rudston, Barbara, 410
  Walter, 410
Ruffin, Edward, 154
  Mary, 153
  Patsy, 154
  Robert, 153
Rundell, Jacob, 320
  Rachel (Lobdell), 320
Rush, Abraham, 207
  Ann, 407
  Ann (Evans), 207
  Anna Maria, 409
  Anne Emily, 408
  Aurelia, 407
  Aurelia (———), 406
  Benjamin, 207, 294, 407, 408, 431
  Catherine, 207
  Catherine E. (Murray), 408
  Catherine Eliza Murray, 408
  Edward, 206, 406
  Elizabeth, 205, 206, 207, 406, 407, 408
  Elizabeth (Dennis), 409
  Elizabeth (Hilton), 206
  Elizabeth (Hodges), 206

INDEX

Rush—*Continued*
Elizabeth (Rees), 207
Elizabeth Fox (Roberts), 408
Elizabeth Murray, 409
Elizabeth M. (Simpson), 408
Ella Day, 406
Ella Mary (Day), 406
Esther, 207
Esther (Carlisle), 206
Eugenia Frances (Hiester) Sheaff, 409
Frances (Decorne), 206
Francis, 206, 406
George, 207
Jacob, 205, 406, 407
James, 206, 406, 407, 408
James Irvine, 207
James Murray, 408, 409
Jane, 206, 406
John, 205, 206, 207, 406, 407, 408
John Hanger, 294
Joseph, 206, 207, 406, 407
Julia, 408, 409
Julia (Stockton), 407, 431
Julia Stockton, 409
Martha, 207
Martha (Wallace), 207
Mary, 206, 207, 408
Mary (———), 207
Mary (Rench), 407
Mary (Williams), 407
Mary Simpson, 204, 207
Mary Theresa de Leelen, 408
Nancy (Wilmer), 408
Phoebe Ann (Ridgway), 408
Rachel, 206, 407
Rachel (Peart), 206, 407
Rebecca, 207, 407
Rebecca (Jones), 207
Rebecca (Lincoln), 206
Richard, 406, 408, 409
Richard Henry, 409
Samuel, 408
Samuel W., 207
Sarah, 207
Sarah (Aurelia), 206
Sarah Anna (Blight), 409
Sarah Catherine, 409
Sarah Maynadier, 409
Stevenson, 407
Susan Bowdoin (Yerby), 409

Rush—*Continued*
Susanna, 206, 207, 406, 407, 408
Susanna (Hall), 407
Susanna (Lucas), 205, 406
Thomas, 205, 406, 407
William, 204, 205, 206, 207, 406, 407, 408
William Simpson, 408
Russell, Andrew, 334
Catherine Elkins (Musier), 271
Elizabeth (Henry) Campbell, 243
Ellen Forbes, 28
Henry Pierrepont, 271
Henry S., 28
Janet (Livingston), 334
Kate Taintor, 271
Mary, 298
Mary Ella, 323
Mary Forbes, 28
Sybil (Crosby), 170
William, 170, 243
William E., 81
Rust, Mary, 74, 83
Rutherfurd, Lucille, 97
Lucille Zoe (Tison), 97
Thomas Scott, 97
Rutledge, B. H., 119
Rutter, Joseph, 330
Mary, 330
Rutton, Elizabeth Kemp, 394
Ryder, Altje Stevense (Van Voor Hees), 457
Barrent Jurianz, 457
Jannetje, 459
Phebe, 459
Ryers, Hannah (Waln), 350
John, 350
Ryland, Kate Thompson (Hundley), 272
Leonard Gamble, 272

S

Sabells, Lucy, 330
Sabine, Emma, 300
Sacherell, Henry, 396
Sacket, Ann, 221
Sackett, Daniel, 220
John Fulton, 220
Levi Wallace, 221
Lucy, 221

Sackett—*Continued*
Nancy (Fulton), 220
Robert, 220
Roxana, 221
William Fulton, 221
Sage, Comfort, 169
Susanna, 19
St. John, Julia (Stockton), 435
Richard C., 435
St. Nicholas, Dorothy (Tilghman), 438
Thomas, 438
Sale, Annie, 285
Salisbury, Amanda, 149
Hiram, 467
Sarah Brayton (Whipple), 467
Saltonstall, Abigail, 412, 413
Abigail (Waldron), 413
Anna (White), 413
Anne, 411
Anne (Ramsden), 410
Anne Elizabeth, 414
Barbara, 411
Barbara (Rudston), 410
Caroline, 414
Caroline (Sanders), 413
Dorothy (Frizel), 412
Eleanor, 410
Eleanor (Brooks), 410
Elizabeth, 411, 412, 413, 415
Elizabeth (Ogden), 410
Elizabeth (Rosewell), 412
Elizabeth (Ward), 412
Elizabeth (West), 411
Elizabeth Baldwin (Dupec), 415
Endicott Peabody, 415
Frances Ann Fitch (Sherwood), 414
Frances Sherwood, 415
George, 411
Gilbert, 410
Grace, 411
Grace (Kaye), 411
Guerdon, 158
Gurdon, 412
Henry, 411
Isabel (———), 410
Jerusha (Richards), 412
John, 411, 412
Katharine, 415
Leverett, 410, 413, 414

INDEX

Saltonstall—*Continued*
  Lucy Sanders, 414
  Margaret, 411
  Margaret Ann (Savage), 414
  Martha (Wilfred), 411
  Mary, 410, 411, 413, 415
  Mary (Cooke), 413
  Mary (Jekyll), 413
  Mary (Whittingham) Clarke, 412
  Mary Cooke, 413
  Mary Elizabeth, 414
  Mary Elizabeth (Sanders), 414
  Matilda, 414
  Mehitabel (Wainwright), 412
  Middlecott Cooke, 413
  Muriel, 412
  Muriel (Gurdon), 411
  Muriel Gurdon, 410
  Nathaniel, 412, 413, 415
  Philip Leverett, 414, 415
  Richard, 195, 410, 411, 412, 413, 414
  Richard Gurdon, 414
  Richard Middlecott, 410, 414
  Robert, 411
  Rosamond, 411
  Rose, 451
  Rose Lee, 414
  Rose S. (Lee), 414
  Samuel, 410, 411
  Sarah, 413
  Susanna (Poyntz), 410
  Thomas, 411
  Ward, 413
  William, 413
Salvage, Catherine, 296
Sanders, Caroline, 413
  Catherine (Livingston), 338
  Jacob, 253
  John, 338
  Mary Elizabeth, 414
  Sarah (Hoover), 253
  Thomas, 413, 414
Sanderson, Abial, 416
  Abial (Bartlett), 416
  Abigail (Fiske), 417
  Benjamin, 416
  Clara Noyes (Sherwin), 416
  Edward, 416

Sanderson—*Continued*
  Esther, 416
  Hannah, 416
  Helen, 416
  John, 416, 417
  Jonathan, 416, 417
  Lucien, 416, 417
  Lydia (Morton), 417
  Marie, 416
  Mary (Curtiss), 417
  Mary (Drury), 417
  Mary (Eggleston), 416
  Mary (Osgood), 417
  Nathaniel, 417
  Robert, 416
  Samuel, 416
  Thomas, 416
Sands, Austin Ledyard, 211
  Mariana Emory (Fullam), 211
Sanford, Catherine Washington, 293
  Lucretia (Deming), 180
  Mary, 224
  Silas, 180
Sanger, Isaac, 36
  John, 35
  Mary (Park), 36
  Rebecca (Park), 35
Sargent, Annie P., 55
  Cushman, 498
  Ellerton Pratt (Whitney), 498
  Sarah Elizabeth, 55
  Sarah J. (Ames), 55
  Stephen P., 55
  Stephen Pillsbury, 55
Sarmiento, James, 95
  Jane Josephine, 95
Satterthwaite, Anne, 4
  Mary (Osborne), 5
  William, 5
Saulsbury, Eliza, 421
Saunders, Agnes, 397, 474
  Elizabeth, 499
  Janet, 397, 474
  Lillian, 256
  Thomas, 499
  William, 397, 474
Savage, Elizabeth, 486
  Margaret Ann, 414
  Samuel Stowe, 185
  Thomas, 144

Savile, Francis, 410
  George, 410
  Henry, 410
  Mary (Saltonstall), 410
Sawin, Eliza Adeline, 262
  Samuel, 262
Sawyer, Anna G., 26
  Josiah, 262
  Susanna, 262
Scandrett, Henry A., 469
  Jane Whiting (Whipple), 469
Scanlan, Martha, 386
  William, 386
Scarborough, Sarah, 245
Schaetzel, Katherine, 226
Schellinger, Catalyntje, 224
  Catherine, 63, 64
  Cornelia (Melyn), 65, 224
  Hannah, 65
  Jacob, 65
  Jacobus, 65, 224
  Mercy, 65
Schenck, Annatie (Pieters), 457
  Annatie Roelofse, 459
  Garret R., 458
  Jan Martense, 457
  Jannetje Stevense (Van Voor Hees), 457
  Mayke R., 457
  Neeltje Coert (Van Voorhees), 458
  Roelof Martense, 457
Schiefflein, Charles Miller, 142
  Mary Fredericka (Chisolm), 142
Schutt, Caspar C., 141
  Harriet Emily, 141
Schuyler, Adoniah, 336
  Alida, 334
  Gertrude (Van Rensselaer), 336
  Philip Pieterse, 334
  Sarah (Hodge), 224
Scott, ———, 21, 111, 153
  Abigail, 97
  Alexander, 244
  Anne (Bye), 111
  Caroline S., 232
  Charles, 455
  David, 320
  Elizabeth (Bennett) Crosby, 169
  Eunice, 21

INDEX

Scott—*Continued*
 Hannah, 312, 321
 James, 21
 John, 169, 334
 Marion (Livingston), 334
 Mary Embry, 455
 Merab Ann (Alexander), 21
 Octavia (Alexander), 21
 Philis, 343
 Rebecca, 465
 Rhoda, 21
 Rhoda (Rockwood), 21
 Sarah, 320
 Sarah Butler (Henry) Campbell, 244
 Willis R., 21
Scoville, Asenath, 180
Scull, John, 93
 Mary, 93
Seabrooke, Jemima (Gist), 239
 William, 239
Seabury, Martha Mary (Tubman), 451
 William T., 451
Seager, Joseph, 147
 Thankful (Hewit), 147
Searle, Abigail, 19
Seay, Elizabeth, 229
Seeley, Sally, 148
Selden, Eliza Armistead, 286
 Mary, 11
 Mary (Douglas), 190
 Mary Bowles (Armistead), 286
 Roger, 190
 Wilson Cary, 286
Sellick, John, 173
 Martha (Gould), 173
Seltzer, Sallie, 134
Senker, Henry V. L., 460
 Matilda Ackerman (Voorhees), 460
Senter, Eliza (Arnold), 383
 Isaac, 383
 Sarah Ann, 383
Sentney, Ada (Beard), 505
 Alonzo, 505
Servin, Anna Juliana, 370
Settle, ———, 293
 Jane, 293
 Jane (Calvert) Maddox, 293
 John Calvert, 293
 Sarah (Turner), 293

Seubering, Willempie Roeloffse, 456
Sewall, Elizabeth, 440
 Jane (Lowe), 288
 Mary, 441
 Nicholas, 363, 440, 441
 Susannah (Burgess), 363
Sewell, Jane, 289
Seymour, Alexina, 213
 Anna Belle Crawford, 403
 Charles, 492, 493
 Laura, 493
 Lucy, 493
 Lucy (Whitman), 492, 493
 Richard, 214
Seytie, ———, 459
Shafer, Mary, 369
Shand, Ann Jane, 231
 Peter Johnson, 231
Shapleigh, Abbie E., 86
 Abigail (Bartlet), 84
 Dorcas (Littlefield), 85
 Elizabeth (Bartlett), 86
 John, 84, 85
 Nicholas, 84
 Samuel, 86
 Sarah, 85
Sharp, Alice, 476
 Anice (Churchill), 148
 Chester, 148
 John, 479
 Martha, 479
 Martha (Vose), 479
 Robert, 479
Sharpe, John, 398
 Martha, 398
Shattuck, Mary, 313
Shatwell, Mary, 74
Shaw, John, 375
 Louis Agassiz, 414
 Madeline (Mitchell), 414
 Martha, 489
 Mary Elizabeth (Saltonstall), 414
 Naomi (Whitman), 489
 Sarah (Biddle) Penrose, 375
 Quincy Adams, 414
 William, 489
Shawhan, James, 149
 Martha Asenath (Churchill), 149

Sheaff, Eugenia Frances (Hiester), 409
 William, 409
Sheaffe, Margaret, 336
Shearer, James William, 105
Shedd, Elizabeth, 184
 Samuel, 184
Sheets, William, 253
Sheffield, Josephine Earl, 91
Shelden, Isaac, 215
Sheldon, Florence (Baker), 71
 Henry Earl, 71
Shelton, John, 244
 Sarah, 244
Shepard, Alexander, 249
 Ann (Arnold), 69
 Hannah, 94
 Jane Maria, 178
 John, 52
 Martha (Bacon), 52
 White, 69
Shepherd, Charles, 230
 Elizabeth (Gibbes), 230
 Emmett Albin, 113
Shepperson, Charles, 455
 Mildred C. (Venable), 455
Shercliffe, Anne (Spinke), 201
 John, 201
 Mary, 201
Sherman, Edward, 317
 Grace, 317
 Grace (Makin), 317
 Harriet, 21
Sherwin, Abigail (Bacon) Robinson, 44
 Clara Noyes, 416
 Elnathan, 44
 Mary A. (Howes), 416
 William F., 416
Sherwood, Anna, 393
 Elizabeth, 320
 Frances Ann Fitch, 414
 Hugh, 420, 444
 Margaret, 420
 Mary, 420, 444
 Susan, 444
Shewell, Julia C., 6
Shinn, John, 430
 Mary (Stockton), 430
 Sarah (Vinacomb), 347
 Thomas, 347, 430
 Unity, 347

INDEX

Shipman, Carline (Robinson), 376
　Mary Deming, 376
　Nathaniel, 376
Shippen, Anna, 339
　Anne Hume, 335
　Elizabeth Carter (Farley), 284
　Thomas Lee, 284
　William, 335
Shoemaker, George, 349
　Mary, 349
　Rebecca (Dilworth), 349
　Virginia, 144
Shoen, Allen McLee, 127
　Sarah Louise (Calhoun), 127
Sholdam, Alice, 472
　Thomas, 472
Shorey, Emily D., 86
Short, Peyton, 106
Shriver, Margaretta, 292
Shuart, Christian, 165
　Mary Ann, 165
Sibthorp, Ann (Waln) Dilworth, 348
　Christopher, 348
Silver, Mary, 396
Simcock, Benjamin, 348, 349
　Hannah (Waln) Hodges, 348
　Jacob, 349
　John, 348, 349
　Mary (Waln), 348
　Sarah (Waln), 349
Simkins, Maria, 127
Simmers Anabel, 70,
　Charles J., 70
　Edith Eliza, 70
　Fanny (Baker), 70
　J. Arthur, 70
Simmons, Caleb, 42
　Louisa, 68
　Peter, 164
　Sarah (Bacon), 42
　Sarah (?) (Corwin), 164
Simonds, Jane Hamilton (Calhoun), 125
　Joseph Webb, 125
Simonton, Sarah, 54
Simpson, ———, 366
　Elizabeth M., 408
　Evangeline (Marrs), 469
　Michael, 469

Simpson—*Continued*
　Sophia (Warfield), 366
　William, 408
Simvall, Bethia (Owen), 165
　Mary, 165
　William, 165
Singer, Anna Maria Musser, 135
　John, 133, 135
　Sarah, 133, 135
Sinnerd, Sarah L., 165
Skelton, Ruth, 330
Skinner, (Bailey), 422
　Adeline, 421
　Alexander Summerfield, 423
　Ann, 419, 423, 493
　Anne E., 423
　Annie, 423
　Beckie (Pattison), 423
　Benjamin, 424
　Birdie, 423
　Caroline P., 423
　Carrie (———), 421
　Cassandra (Woolford), 423
　Cassandra Jones, 423
　Cora, 422
　Edgar Martin, 422
　Eliza, 422
　Elizabeth, 419, 420, 421, 423, 445
　Elizabeth (———), 419
　Elizabeth (Colston), 419
　Elizabeth (Fookes) Stewart, 420
　Elizabeth (Jones), 420
　Eliza (Saulsbury), 421
　Ella, 423
　Emaline (Jones), 422
　Emily, 421
　Emily Margaret, 422
　Emma (Musselman), 423
　Emma Virginia, 422
　Esther, 419, 420
　Ethel Ann, 341
　Eugenia, 422
　Eugenia Woolford, 418
　Evelena Colston, 418
　Ferdinand Stansbury, 421
　Florence, 341
　Georgeanna (Mitchell), 418
　George W., 423
　Gertrude (Thompson), 423
　Hannah Bond (Jones), 421

Skinner—*Continued*
　Hannah Elizabeth, 421
　Harry G., 423
　Henry White, 424
　Hester (Le Compte) Fox, 419
　Howard, 423
　James, 423
　James Aquilla, 423
　James Fookes, 421
　Jane (Freeman), 423
　Jennie, 422
　Jeremiah Pattison, 423
　Jessie (Parker), 422
　Jessie Parker, 422
　John, 419, 420, 421
　John Jones, 422
　John O., 422
　Joseph, 421, 424
　Katharine, 421
　Lamden (———), 420
　Laurice Edward, 421
　Levin, 421
　Levin Philip, 448
　Levin Phillips, 418, 424
　Lucy (Hambleton), 420
　Margaret, 423, 424
　Margaret E., 423
　Marguerretta M. (Teal), 422
　Martha Ann (Wilson), 423
　Martin, 419
　Mary, 419, 420, 421, 423, 424
　Mary (———), 419
　Mary Elizabeth, 423
　Mary Eugenia (Willis), 418, 448
　Mary Florence (Stansbury), 421
　Mary Frances, 422
　Mary R., 423
　Mattie, 423
　Mattie (Mitchell), 422
　Maud Eugenia, 418, 448
　Maurice Edward, 421
　Mildred Lee, 418
　Mildred Lee (Wright), 418
　Milton Ellis, 422
　Mordecai, 420
　Nancy (Pattison), 421
　Nettie Esther (Howser), 421
　Philemon, 420, 424

INDEX

Skinner—*Continued*
Polly Hambleton, 420
Porter N., 341
Rachel, 420, 492
Richard Standley, 423
Robert Stansbury, 421
Ruth, 420
Ruth (Colton), 493
Sally Ann, 421
Samuel, 420, 421
Sarah, 419, 423
Sarah (————), 419
Sarah (Lee), 424
Sarah A. (Hurty), 423
Shirley Eugenia, 422
Susan, 424
Susan Ann (Phillips), 424
Susie (Phillips), 421
Thomas, 419, 420, 421, 422, 424
Thomas Richard, 424
Timothy, 493
Victoria (Jones), 421
Washington Hammond, 423
William, 419, 420, 421, 423, 424
William H., 423
William Henry, 424
William Howser, 421
William James, 421
William Woolford, 418
Zachariah, 421, 423, 424
Slaughter, Susan Clayton, 13
Sloane, Olive (Douglas), 190
Samuel, 190
Sloat, Alice M. (Hoover), 256
Elmer Elsworth Robert, 256
Nancy, 68
Slocum, Joanna, 354
Smith, ————, 14, 420
Alice, 466
Anna Maria (Tilghman) Goldsborough, 441
Anna Melvina, 294
Anne (Adams), 9
Anne (Prentice), 61
Anne Strother (Calvert), 295
Barbara, 198
Betsey, 464
Calla, 360
Charlotte (Douglas), 190
Charlotte (Izard), 283

Smith—*Continued*
Charlotte Georgina (Izard), 284
Christopher, 282
Clara (Weir), 294
Claudia, 284
Cornelia Wyntje, 61
Dorothy, 282
Elizabeth, 296, 453, 497
Elizabeth (Baker), 67
Elizabeth Speed, 16
Esther, 430
Ethan, 67
Frances M. (Bell), 294
Francis, 9
Issacher, 295
Jehiel, 32
John, 214, 465
John Perry, 294
John Ralls, 296
Joseph, 190, 360
Joseph Allen, 284
J. Speed, 276
Kesia (Wood), 32
Lewis Edward, 294
Lucy Anna (Allen), 296
Margaret Elizabeth (Massie), 294, 296
Margery, 5
Martha, 390
Mary, 486
Mary (Speed), 14
Mary Catherine, 296
Mary Elizabeth Frances, 294
Mary Skinner (Brown), 420
Mary Walker (Barret), 276
Matilda, 353
Oliver Hazard Perry, 294, 296
Peter S., 61
Peter Skenandoh, 61
Rebecca (Fairfield), 67
Robert, 441, 453
Robert A., 426
Robert Issacher, 294
Ruth, 32
Sabina Iowa (Miles), 255
Sally W. (Spencer), 426
Samuel, 464
Sarah (Adams), 10
Sarah (Whipple), 465
Sarah Letitia (Beatty), 353
Silas, 67

Smith—*Continued*
Tacy Jane, 107
Thomas Loughton, 284
Virginia Emma, 294
William, 4, 10, 14, 353
William Bernard, 294
William C., 255
William Loughton, 283
Smither, Evelina, 292
Gabriel, 292
Gabriella, 292
John, 274, 292
Lucy, 292
Priscilla, 295
Richard, 292
Smyth, Sarah, 441
Thomas, 441
Snediker, Jannetie, 457
Snow, Arthur Willard, 18
Katherine (White), 473
Marion Louise (Alexander), 18
Martin, 473
Soleiac, Marguerite, 305
Solomons, Alice Heyward (Izard), 285
John, 285
Sorrell, Anne, 209
Elizabeth, 209
Thomas, 209
Sotheron, Constance (Lambert), 168
Jane, 168
William, 168
Southall, Elizabeth, 10
Valentine Wood, 455
Sparhawk, Esther, 311
Nathaniel, 31
Patience (Newman), 31
Sybil, 31
Sparrow, Elizabeth, 363
Spaulding, Mary, 426
Olive, 189
Speakman, Anna (Jenkins), 112
Caroline, 112
Thomas, 112
Spear, Mary, 490
Spears, Bettie Thomas, 272
Fannie Poindexter, 272
Julian Austin, 272
Mary Willie, 272

INDEX

Spears—*Continued*
Rebecca Porterfield (Hundley), 272
Virginia Meredith (Turner), 272
William Edward, 272
Speed, ———, 425
——— (Smith), 14
Abby (Lemaster), 14
Ann (Bignall), 13
Ann Pope, 17
Ardell Hutchinson, 17
Eliza, 16
Elizabeth, 14
Elizabeth (Williamson), 17
Elizabeth Julia, 425
Elizabeth Julia (Spencer), 13
Emma (Keats), 17
Fannie (Henning), 16
Henry, 13, 14
Horace, 12
James, 11, 12, 13, 14, 16
Jane (Cochran), 16
Jessie St. John (Adams), 12
John, 11, 12, 13, 14, 16, 124
John Smith, 17
Joseph, 13
Joshua Fry, 11, 16
Lewis, 13
Lucy, 13
Lucy Fry, 16
Lucy Gilmer (Fry), 11, 14, 16
Margaret (Hawkins), 12
Margaret D. Phillips, 17
Martha, 13
Martha (Calhoun), 124
Martha Bell, 11, 17
Mary, 13, 14, 16, 124
Mary (Pulley), 12
Mary (Spencer), 13, 425
Mary Ellen Shellcross, 17
Mary McElroy (Allen), 13
Mary Minetry (Taylor), 12
Mathias, 13
Peachy Walker, 16
Philip, 17
Sarah, 13
Sarah (Baird), 13
Susan (Phillips), 17
Susan Clayton (Slaughter), 13

Speed—*Continued*
Susan Fry, 17
Thomas, 12, 13, 16
William, 12
William Pope, 16
Spencer, Ada Catherine, 426
Alice Eleanor (Manes), 426
Ann, 425
Ann (Douglas), 189
Catherine (Clements), 425
Clementine S. (Reid), 426
Colie Pierce, 426
Colin Stokes, 426
Eleanor Elizabeth, 427
Eliza Julia (Flournoy), 425
Eliza W. (Bouldin,) 426
Eliza W. (Fennell), 426
Elizabeth (Clark), 159, 160
Elizabeth Julia, 13, 425, 426
Elizabeth Williams, 426
Elvira H., 426
Ezra, 160
Flournoy Poindexter, 426, 427
Frances (Pearce), 426
Frances A., 426
Gideon, 425
Harriet G., 426
Henry, 426
Henry Martin, 426
Jane, 426
Jane P., 426
Jared, 161, 188
Jessie, 426
John, 425
John James Robertson, 426
Joseph, 159
Judith, 425
Lelia Matilda, 426
Leslie Louise, 427
Lois (Hill), 425
Louisa Stokes (Neal), 426
Louisa Virginia, 426
Lucy (Watkins), 425
Lydia, 185
Manly Lyle, 425
Martha F., 426
Martha Owen, 425
Mary, 13, 425
Mary (Spaulding), 426
Mary Frances, 426
Matilda Cole, 426
Matthew Lyle, 425, 426, 427

Spencer—*Continued*
Mehitable, 161
Rebecca (Parker) Clark, 158
Sallie W. (Bouldin), 426
Sally (Watkins), 425
Sally W., 426
Samuel F., 425
Samuel Graham, 426
Sarah (Douglas), 188
Sarah Watkins, 426
Sion, 425
Susan Rives, 426
Susanna, 41
Thomas, 158, 159, 425
Thomas Cole, 426
Thomas James, 426
Spiller, Anne Sophia, 296
Anne Strother (Calvert) Smith, 295
Henry, 295
Martha Elvira, 296
Nehemiah, 296
Spinke, Anne, 201
Spotswood, Alexander, 244
Anne Butler (Brayne), 244
Dorothea, 244
Unity (West) Dandridge, 244
William, 244
Sprackling, Adam, 438
Margery, 438
Sprague, Catherine, 307
Jerusha, 98
Spring, Anne, 36
Sprinkle, Cokie V., 427
Eleanor Elizabeth, 427
Eleanor Elizabeth (Spencer), 427
Stafford, Anne, 297
Staigg, Anne (Atkinson), 28
Elizabeth, 27
Richard Morell, 28
Stamper, Rebecca (Rush), 407
Thomas, 407
Stanley, Abigail, 492
Constance Robertson, 395
Eliza (Bragg), 395
Elizabeth, 296
George Albert, 395
Joseph, 395
Lou E. (Robertson), 395
Stannard, Ada (Clark), 160
Ephraim, 159

INDEX

Stannard—*Continued*
  Job, 160
  Sarah (Clark), 159
Stansbury, Elleanor (Foreman), 421
  James, 421
  Mary Florence, 421
  Tobias, 239
Staple, Harriet L., 191
Staplefort, Dorothy, 449
  Raymond, 449
Staples, Abigail, 85
  Blanche, E., 47
  Emma, 47
  Stephen, 47
Stark, John, 189
Starkweather, Robert, 214
Starr, Abigail, 195
  Peter, 392
  Sarah (Robbins), 392
Steadman, Jean (Calhoun), 127
  John, 127
Stearns, Alfred, 68
  Arvilla (King), 68
  Daniel, 68
  George, 68
  George W., 68
  Isaac, 397, 480
  John Baker, 68
  Louisa (Simmons), 68
  Mary, 480
  Nancy (Sloat), 68
  Sarah, 397, 480
  Sophia (Baker), 68
Stebbins, Rowland, 215
Steele, Ann (Welles), 180
  David, 294
  Hannah, 180
  Honour (Deming), 180
  James, 180
  M. Elizabeth, 143
  Prudence, 180
  Samuel, 180
Stein, John, 134
  Sabina (Capp), 134
Stellwagen, Annie Eliza (Carpenter), 385
  Henry S., 385
  Mary Ann (Cook), 385
  Mary Fisher, 385
  Thomas Cook, 385
Stephenson, Elizabeth, 504

Sterling, J. Edward N., 200
  Lynwood J., 200
  Margaret Martine (Duke), 200
Sterrett, James, 238
  Mary, 238
Stevens, Bartlett, 77
  Emily Burton, 326
  John, 214, 335
  John Sanborn, 77
  Marjory, 326
  Mary, 335
  Sarah Maria (Bartlett), 77
Stevenson, Carolyn (James) Young, 502
  Elizabeth (Rush), 206, 407
  Elizabeth Tallman, 457
  Hannah, 502
  Rachel (Rush), 206, 407
  Robert Hooper, 502
  Timothy, 206, 407
Stewart, Alexander T., 361
  Ann (Skinner), 423
  Colin, 423
  Content, 190
  Dixon, 183
  Elizabeth, 139
  Elizabeth (Fookes), 420
  George (?), 189
  Hannah Caroline, 362
  Jane, 371
  John Keith, 183
  John Travillian, 420
  Lucil Mast (Dixon), 183
  Ralph William, 183
  Samuel, 190
  Sarah (Douglas), 189
  Susanne, 220
Stickney, Davis, 24
  Jonathan, 44
  Lydia, 25
  Lydia (Atkinson), 25
  Mary Roads, 44
  Richard, 25
  Sara (Atkinson), 24
  Wealthy Chase, 44
Stiles, ———, 478
  Nancy (White), 478
Stillwell, Lillian E., 135
Stimpson, Andrew, 476
Stimson, Alice Mary, 79
  Alice Wheaton (Bartlett), 79
  Barbara Bartlett, 79

Stimson—*Continued*
  Dorothy, 79
  Henry Albert, 79
  Henry Bartlett, 79
  Julia Catherine, 79
  Lucile Hinkle, 79
  Philip Moen, 79
Stitt, Ida Estelle, 133, 136
  Sarah Wilkinson (Wall), 136
  Seth Bunker, 136
Stockett, Catherine, 363
Stockton, ——— (Milnor), 431
  Abigail, 430, 431, 432
  Abigail (———), 429
  Abigail (Phillips), 430
  Ann (Doughty), 430
  Ann (Petty), 430
  Anna Margaretta (Potter), 434
  Annis, 432, 434
  Annis (Boudinot), 431
  Bayard, 430
  Caroline, 432, 434
  Caroline Bayard (Dodd), 434
  Catherine (Cumming), 431
  Catherine Elizabeth, 434
  Clemence Eliza (Finch), 435
  Elizabeth, 430
  Elizabeth (Doughty), 430
  Ellen Rosemary, 435
  Esther (Smith), 430
  George Finch, 435
  Hannah, 430
  Harriet Maria, 434
  Harriet Maria (Potter), 434
  Helen Beryl (Gove), 428
  Helen Clemence Carolyn, 428
  Henry Haines, 435
  Horatio, 432
  Jack Potter, 428, 435
  Job, 430
  John, 429, 430, 431
  John Potter, 434, 435
  Joseph, 430
  Julia, 407, 431, 432, 434, 435
  Louise (Haines), 435
  Lucius Horatio, 431
  Mary, 430, 432, 434
  Mary (Field), 432

INDEX

Stockton—*Continued*
  Mary (Hibbets), 431
  Mary (Leeds), 429
  Mary F., 432
  Philip, 431
  Rachel (Stout), 430
  Randall, 429
  Rebecca, 431
  Rebecca (Phillips), 430
  Richard, 407, 428, 429, 430, 431, 432, 434, 435
  Richard Finch, 428
  Robert, 430
  Robert Field, 428, 432, 434, 435
  Saidee, 435
  Samuel, 430
  Samuel William, 431
  Samuel Witham, 432
  Sara (Marks), 435
  Sarah, 430
  Susan, 432
  Susan B. (Dodd), 434
  Susanna, 431
  Susannah Witham (Robinson), 430
  Thomas, 430
  Thomas Coates, 429
  Violet, 435
  William Bradford, 432
Stoddard, Charles, 91
  Esther (Warham), 492
  Mary, 91
  Mary (Noble) Porter, 91
  Sarah, 492
  Solomon, 492
Stokes, Anna H., 94
  Elizabeth, 350
  John, 350
  Susan S., 5
Stone, Dorcas (Jones), 480
  Elizabeth, 289
  Gregory, 397
  Rebecca, 397, 480
  Samuel, 397, 480
  Sarah (Stearns), 397
  Verlinda Sprigg (Cotton), 289
  William, 289
Stonehouse, Mary, 396
Stopham, Assoline, 82
Stoolhoff, Magdalen Hulst, 226
Stoothoff, Achia, 456

Story, Elizabeth, 367
  Harriet, 157
Stoughton, Elizabeth, 501
  Hannah, 358
  Israel, 358
  John, 501
Stout, Joseph, 430
  Rachel, 430
  Ruth, 430
Stowell, Caleb, 266
  Emeline (Hobard or Hubbard), 266
  John, 264
  Mary (Beal), 264
Stowitz, Rhoda Ann, 213
Strange, ———, 543
  Mary (Venable) Moreman, 453
Stratton, Daniel, 224
  David, 224
  Jemima (Howell), 224
  John, 224
  Mary (Gardiner), 224
Stribling, Francis Taliaferro, 297
  Olive Caldwell (Jackson), 297
Stringer, Lydia (Warfield), 365
  Samuel, 365
Strode, Martha, 105
Strong, Elizabeth (Whitman), 492
  Eunice (Whitman), 492
  Hephzibah (Wolcott), 500
  John, 214, 492, 500
  Lydia, 396
  Thomas, 492
Strother, Ann, 295
  Anne (Strother), 295
  Delia, 296
  Enoch, 296
  Francis, 290, 295
  John, 295
  Mary, 290
  Mary (Key), 296
  Mary Wade, 295
  Mary Willis (Wade), 295
  Susannah (Dabney), 290, 295
Strycker, Altje, 458
  Ida (Huybrechts), 458
  Jacobus Gerritsen, 458
  Jane, 68

Stuart, James, 249
  Martha, 165
  Mehitable, 249
Sturdevant, Mary, 31
Stuyvesant, ——— (Kip), 136
  Peter, 136
Styles, Amy, 148
Suert, Olfrets, 165
Summers, Elizabeth (Alexander), 19
  John, 19
Sumner, Elizabeth (Minot), 359
  William, 359
Sunderland, Benjamin Cosmo, 281
  Mary Gertrude (Isaac), 281
Sutherland, Alexander, 138
  Ann, 191
  Muriel (Chisholme), 138
  Solomon, 191
  Tamma (Thompson), 191
Sutliff, Clark, 317
  Elizabeth (Eaton), 317
Sutton, Amos, 266
  Elizabeth Williams (Hobard or Hubbard) Colman, 266
Suydam, Geertie or Charity, 459
  George, 459
  Jane (Van Voorhies), 459
  Willemtje, 458
Swain, Martha, 347
Swan, Betsey L., 20
  Ella A., 362
  Jabez, 162
  Mehitable, 162
Swasey, Charlotte, 26
Sweet, ———, 221
Swift, Anna Greenleaf (Winsor), 28
  Heman, 148
  John Baker, 28
  Martha, 28
Swinton, Mary, 143
  William, 143
Swynford, Katherine (Roet), 297
Sylvester, Hannah, 249
  Hannah (Bartlett), 249
  Joseph, 249
Syme, John, 243
  Sarah (Winston), 243

INDEX

Symonds, Mark, 215
Sympson, Alexander, 457
  Jannetje Stevense (Van Voor Hees), Schenck, 457

T

Taggart, Jennie, 218
Tailer, Edward N., 339
  Mary, 339
Tainter, Elizabeth (Warren), 463
  Jonathan, 463
Talbot, Anne, 289
  Daniel, 359
  Dorothy (Calvert), 288
  Elizabeth, 289
  Elizabeth (Ewen), 367
  Frances, 288, 289
  Frances (Talbot), 288
  Frances (Wogan), 288
  Grace (Calvert), 288
  James, 288
  John, 288
  Mary, 289
  Mary (Tobin), 288
  Richard, 288, 367
  Robert, 288
  Sophia (Minot), 359
  Susan, 289
  Valentine, 288
Talcott, Joseph, 179
  Rachel, 499
  Sarah (Deming), 179
Tall, Mary, 77
Talley, Eugenia, 234
Talmage, Mary Rebecca Halsey (Avery), 33
  T. De Witt, 33
Taney, Michael, 198
Tankersley, Florence C., (Calhoun), 128
  John T., 128
Tapping, Mary (Woodmansey), 30
Tarball, Abigail, 495
Tarkington, Pauline, 505
Tasker, ———, 289
  Anne (Calvert) Brooke, Brent, Marsham, 289
Tatlock, John, 494
  Lucy Beman (Whitman), 494

Tatum, Joseph, 207
  Mary (Rush), 207
Tayler, Abigail, 438
  Francis, 438
Taylor, Abigail, 43
  Alexander F., 245
  Alva May, 112
  Anna (Alexander), 20
  Benjamin Field, 112
  Bessie, 362, 367
  Bushrod, 292
  Deborah, 89, 111
  Deborah (Bye), 111
  Delia M., 160
  Elizabeth (Dickinson), 112
  Elvira (Jett), 292
  Elvira Bruce (Henry) Higginbotham, 245
  Ida M., 380
  John, 67
  L. T., 128
  Mary, 89, 261
  Mary Minetry, 12
  Rebecca, 43
  Reuben, 89
  Samuel, 20
  Sarah (White), 485
  Sarah Caroline, 128
  Stephen, 485
  Sydney W., 367
  Thomas, 89
  William, 111
  Zachary, 290
Teal, Margueretta M., 422
Temple, Alice, 328
  Christopher, 328
  Eleanor, 225
  Julia, 478
Ten Broeck, Christina, 337
  Dirck, 337
Tennent, Catherine (Calhoun), 129
  William, 129
Terhune, Albert, 459
  Albert Albertse, 457
  Altje (Van Voorhees), 459
  Annatie Roelofse (Schenck), 459
  Hendrickje Stevense (Van Voor Hees) Kierstead, 457
  Jan Albertse, 459
Terry, Juan C., 443
  Lucy Adeline, 443

Test, Charity (Rothrock), 402
  George, 402, 404
  Isabella, 404
  Margaret (Wogan), 402, 404
  Maria, 402
Tewksbury, ———, 75
Thaxter, Elizabeth (Jacob), 298
  John, 298
Thayer, Caroline S., 231
Thomas, ———, 421
  ——— (Conger), 362
  Ann (Gibbes), 230
  Anna Augusta (Claiborne), 154
  Benjamin Gibbes, 233
  Caroline Elizabeth, 233
  Charles Follen, 112
  Deborah (Jacob), 299
  Dwight, 233
  Edward, 230
  Eleanor Walter, 233
  Emma I. (Wolfe), 233
  Fannie, 201
  Frances (Bacon), 44
  Gabriel, 154
  Harold, 233
  Harriet Couturier, 233
  Hasell, 233
  John, 366, 490
  John Gallagher, 388
  John M., 362
  John P., 232
  John Peyre Thomas, 233
  Joseph, 44
  Josephine (Beylle), 388
  Juliet Elliott, 233
  Louisa Dandridge, 154
  Lydia (Whitman), 490
  Margaret (White), 473
  Mary, 362, 366
  Mary (Hutchins), 367
  Mary Caroline (Gibbes), 232
  Mary Gibbes, 233
  Mary S. (Waties), 233
  Mary Zema, 388
  Nathaniel, 299
  Philip, 367
  Philip Francis, 446
  Prudence (Purdue), 404
  Robert Gibbes, 233
  Ruth Anna (Bye), 112
  Ruthana, 306

INDEX

Thomas—*Continued*
  Sally Ann (Skinner), 421
  Samuel, 367, 473
  Sarah (Harrison), 367
  Sarah (Henry), 243
  Sophie Kerr, 446
  Thomas, 243
  Walter Couturier, 233
Thompson, ———, 241
  Anne Claiborne (McIlwaine, 156
  Asahel, 493
  Cyrus, 251
  Emily (Baker), 69
  George D., 392
  Gertrude, 423
  Harriet, 387
  Irene (Robbins), 392
  James, 69
  Julia Elizabeth Adams, 156
  Mary Jane, 27
  Ruth (Whitman), 493
  Susan Jeannette, 79
  Tamma, 191
  William, 215
  William McIlwaine, 156
  William Taliaferro, 156
Thomson, Margaret Jane, 449
Thorne, George, 293
  Jane (Settle), 293
  Mary, 293
  Mary (Calvert), 293
  Nicholas, 293
Thornton, Francis, 11
  Lucy W., 11
  Mildred, 15
  Sarah (Innes), 11
Thoroughgood, Adam, 144
Thorpe, Margarey, 49
  William, 49
Thurston, David, 52
Tidd, John, 327
  Mary, 327
Tileston, Grace, 91
Tilghman, Abigail (Tayler), 438
  Agnes, 442
  Angela, 442
  Anna (Francis), 440
  Anna (Lloyd), 440
  Anna Maria, 440, 441, 442
  Anna Maria (Lloyd), 439

Tilghman—*Continued*
  Anna Maria (McMurtrie), 442
  Anna Maria (Tilghman), 441
  Anna Maria (Turbutt), 441
  Benjamin, 441, 442
  Benjamin Chew, 442
  Charles, 438
  Deborah, 439
  Dionysia (———), 437
  Dorothy, 438
  Dorothy (Reynolds), 438
  Edith, 442
  Edward, 438, 440, 441, 442
  Elizabeth, 441
  Elizabeth (Chew), 441
  Elizabeth (Packnam), 438
  Elizabeth (Tilghman), 441
  Ellen (Renching), 438
  Emily, 442
  Emily (Cadwalader), 441
  Francis, 438
  Gabriela, 437
  Gabriela (De Potestad), 437
  Henrietta Maria, 440
  Henrietta Maria (Tilghman), 440
  Henry, 438
  Isabel (Avery), 437
  James, 440
  Joan, 438
  Joan (———), 437
  Joan (Amherst), 437
  Joan (Amias), 438
  John, 437
  Juliana (Carroll), 441
  Julyan (Pordage), 437
  Katherine (Ingersoll), 442
  Lambard, 438
  Lloyd, 440
  Mabel (Murphy), 439
  Margaret, 440
  Margaret (Brewer), 438
  Margaret (Lloyd), 439, 440
  Margaret (Tilghman), 440
  Margery (Sprackling), 438
  Mary, 439, 440, 441
  Mary (Bere), 438
  Mary (Foxley), 439
  Mary (Tilghman), 440, 441
  Mary Anna, 441
  Matthew, 440, 441

Tilghman—*Continued*
  Matthew Ward, 440
  Oswald, 438
  Philemon, 439
  Ralph, 437
  Rebecca, 439
  Rebecca (Waln), 441
  Richard, 437, 439, 440, 441
  Richard Albert, 442
  Samuel, 439
  Sarah (Smyth), 441
  Susan, 442
  Susan Price (Toland), 442
  Susanna, 441
  Susanna (Frisby), 439
  Susanna (Whetenhall), 438
  Tench, 441
  Thomas, 437
  Whetenhall, 438
  William, 437, 438, 439, 440
  William McMurtrie, 442
Tillman, Edward, 125
  Kitty (Calhoun), 125
Tillotson, Margaret (Livingston), 335
  Thomas, 335
Tillott, Helena, 49
Tilly, Mary (Gibbes), 230
  William, 230
Tilton, Unity, 351
Tinkham, Madeleine, 353
Tisdale, James, 31
  Mary (Avery), 31
Tison, Lucille Zoe, 97
Titcomb, Elizabeth, 74, 83
  Joan (Bartlet), 82
  Joanna (Bartlett), 73
  Tirza, 74, 83
  William, 73, 82
Tobin, Mary, 288
Todd, ———, 426
  Elizabeth Julia (Spencer), 426
Toland, Susan Price, 442
Tolliver, Jennie, 503
Tompkins, Daniel D., 67
Toney, Caroline, 286
Tong, Mary, 336
Tonnyhill, Rebecca, 125
Toppan, Elizabeth (Atkinson), 25
  Michael, 25

INDEX

Topping, Ann, 63
Thomas, 63, 64
Torrey, John, 489
Mary (Whitman), 489
Tourtellot, Israel, 300
Mercy (Jacob), 300
Tower, ———, 466
Deborah (Whipple), 466
Hannah, 466
John, 466
Margaret (Ibrook), 466
Towle, Charles Sibell, 267
Elizabeth de Peyster, 267
Florence Hastings (Hubbard), 267
Francis Bartram, 267
Francis Ellingwood, 267
George Sibell, 267
John Alden, 267
Priscilla Alden, 267
Town, Electa (Churchill), 148
Clark, 148
Townes, Henry, 129
Lucretia Ann (Calhoun), 129
Townsend, Charles, 251
John, 354
Mathilda, 396
Sarah, 396
Thomas, 354
Towson, Ann Tolly, 445
William, 445
Tracy, Annie (Rood), 181
Deborah (Bingham), 97
Ezekiel, 181
Hezekiah, 181
Jesse, 190
Martha (Douglas), 190
Sarah (Deming), 181
Stephen, 97
Thankful, 181
Travaissa, ———, 190
Travers, Elizabeth, 449
Sarah, 10
Treat, Elizabeth, 499
Honor, 178
James, 179
Rebecca, 179
Rebecca (Latimer), 179
Richard, 178
Robert, 158
Sarah, 491
Trenholm, Edward L., 143
Eliza Bonsall (Holmes), 143

Trenholm—*Continued*
George A., 143
Glover Holmes, 143
Julia (Chisolm), 143
Tressenrider, Eliza, 504
Trewnwall, Alice, 228
Jane H. (Brinton), 401
Joseph, 401
Phebe Brinton, 401
Triplet, Mary, 149
Triplett, George, 293
Sarah Calvert (Lindsay), 293
Trippe, Amelia, 445
Andrew Cross, 444
Ann Tolly (Towson), 445
Caroline Augusta (McConky), 444
Caroline Ennalls, 447
Catherine D. (Bowie), 446
Charles White, 443, 447
Edward, 444, 445, 446
Edward Richard, 445
Edward Thomas, 446
Eliza, 445
Elizabeth, 443, 444
Elizabeth (Barney), 445
Elizabeth (Gibson), 445
Elizabeth (Noel), 445
Elizabeth (Pennell), 444
Elizabeth (Skinner), 445
Elizabeth (Trippe), 443
Elizabeth H. (Darrow), 446
Frances, 238, 445
Frances (Holliday), 445
Francis (Brooke), 443
Frederick Louis, 447
Frederick Wright, 447
Harriet (Edmondson), 446
Henrietta, 444, 445
Henry, 443, 444
James, 444, 446
Jean, 445
John, 444, 445, 446
Joseph Ennalls, 446, 447
Joseph Everett, 444, 445, 447
Juan Terry, 443
Julian, 447
Katherine Louise, 443
Levin, 445
Lucy Adeline (Terry), 443
Margaret, 445

Trippe—*Continued*
Margaret Helen, 446
Mary, 446
Mary (Ennalls), 446
Mary (Noel), 445
Mary (Pennell), 444
Mary Caroline, 446
Mary Dawes (Grafton) McConky, 444
Mary Harriett, 446
Mary Louise (White), 447
Mary Pennell, 444
Mary Suzannah, 446
May, 445
Nicholas, 443
Nicholas Hammond, 446
Rachel Elizabeth, 445
Richard, 445, 446
Richard Henry, 446
Richard John, 446
Robert H., 446
Sarah (Noel), Byus, 444
Sarah E., 445
Sarah E. (Trippe), 445
Sarah Elizabeth, 446
Sarah Patterson (Cross), 444
Sophie Kerr (Thomas), 446
Susan (Sherwood) Hambleton, 444
Susannah (Herron), 444
William, 444, 445, 446
William Henderson, 447
William James, 446
Trowbridge, Cyrus, 467
Nancy (Whipple), 467
True, Charlotte, 76
Reuben, 75
Rhoda (Bartlett), 75
Truesdell, Marilla Etta, 225
Trumbull, John, 492
Sarah (Whitman), 492
Tryon, Ruth, 147
Tubman, Benjamin Gaither Keene, 449
Benjamin Lynn Lachlin, 449
Carrie (Coskery), 450
Clarence Eugene, 450
Dorothy (Staplefort), 449
Dorothy Keene, 418, 448
Eleanor (———), 448
Elizabeth (Travers), 449

INDEX

Tubman—*Continued*
Elizabeth Willis, 418, 448
Ellen Louise, 451
E. Nellie (Covey), 451
Eugene Francis, 450
Eugene Power, 450
Frances Ann, 450
Frances Halley, 450
Francis Joseph, 450
Gladys (Halley), 450
Granville Lloyd, 451
Henry Francis, 450
Henry Harrison, 450
John, 449
Julia Keene, 451
Julia Louisa, 450
Julian Le Roy, 451
Margaret Jane (Thomson), 449
Marie Ann, 450
Marie Regina (Power), 450
Martha Mary, 451
Mary, 449
Mary (Rilie (?)), 451
Mary Gaither (Keene), 449
Mary Henrietta, 451
Mary Imogene (Berry), 450
Mary Keene, 418, 448
Mary Naomi (Willis), 451
Maud Eugenia (Skinner), 418, 448
Nancy (———), 449
Nannie (Hammond), 449
Nellie Lucille, 451
Richard, 448
Richard Hammond, 450
Robert Constantine, 451
Robert Eugene, 418, 448, 451
Robert Francis, 449, 451
Robert Keene, 450
Roberta (Keen), 449
Rosalie Eugenia Berry, 450
Samuel Alexander, 449, 450
Sarah (Keene), 448
Susan (Keene), 449
Vincent Alexander, 450
William Billingsley Keene, 449
Tucker, Anne Sophia (Jackson), 297
Deborah, 254

Tucker—*Continued*
Judith, 249
Robert J., 297
Tuckerman, John Francis, 414
Lucy Sanders (Saltonstall), 414
Tufts, Deborah (Frothingham), 331
Eliza B. (Kendall), 331
Emma, 331
Helen E., 331
Nathan, 331
William, 331
William Clark, 331
Tunnicliff, Alonzo, 67
Fanny (Baker), 67
Louisa, 67
Tupper, Thankful, 482
Turbutt, Anna Maria, 441
William, 441
Turgis, Susan (Cabell), 114
Thomas, 114
Turner, Agnes (Mumford), 197
Barker, 201
Catherine (Herter), 197
Eleanor (Whitman), 490
Elizabeth, 489
Fannie (Thomas), 201
Jane, 159, 348
Joseph Joshua, 197
Joshua Joseph, 197
Katherine Marie, 197
Lilian Paret, 201
Margaret, 324
Matthew, 197
Nazareth (Hobart), 263
Robert, 263
Sarah, 293
Virginia Meredith, 272
William, 197, 490
Turney, Jane, 228
Thomas, 228
Tuthill, ———, 63
Abigail (Baker), 63
Tweed, A. C., 57
Mary Virginia, 144
Robert, 144
Virginia (Shoemaker), 144
Twohig, Elizabeth (Calvert), 295
John, 295
Twyman, Mary (Walker), 275

U

Uden, Anne, 228
Uhlhorn, Frederick, 161
Harriet Elizabeth, 161
Maria (Goodrich), 161
Underhill, Lydia, 142
Unthank, Christopher, 354
Mary, 354
Susanna, 354
Updegraff, Laura Rebecca, 59
Upton, Ann, 495
Urann, Henry Wilson, 21
Jane, 21
Thomas, 21
Utz, Mary, 504

V

Vail, Irena (Churchill), 149
Lucius, 149
Valette, Mary (Jay), 302
Peter, 302
Van Brugh, Catherine, 336
Peter, 336
Van Brunt, Altje Coerte (Van Voorhees) Willemse, 458
Catherine, 459
Joost Rutgertse, 458
Van Cortlandt, Frances (Jay), 302
Frederick, 302
Mary, 302
Van Couwenhoven, Aeltie Lambertse (Cool), 458
Gerrit Wolfertse, 458
Marretje Gerritse, 458
Vanderbilt, Gertrude, 457
Ida, 458
Van Der Schure, Helena, 457
Van Duyckhuysen, Achia (Stoothoff), 456
Anna, 456
Jan Teunissen, 456
Van Duzee, Alonzo John, 182
Hannah Keith (Judson) Deming, 182
Van Dyck, Achaias, 458
Barbara, 458
Catherine, 456
Jannetje (Lamberts), 458
Van Eeghen, Geertruide Margarethe Jacoba, 109

INDEX

Van Horne, Ann Mary, 339
  Cornelius Gerrit, 336
  Cornelius J., 302
  Elizabeth, 338
  Johanna (Livingston), 336
  Judith (Jay), 302
  Van Keuren, ———, 68
  Sarah (Baker), 68
Van Loon, Jannecken Gertiste, 456
Van Noortstrand, Hans, 456
  Jannecken Gertiste, 456
Van Nostrand, Antie (Van Voorhees), 459
  Catherine Hansen, 456
  Rem Garretse, 459
Van Nuyse, Auke Janse, 457
  Femmetje Aukes, 457
  Magdalena (Pieterse), 457
Van Pelt, Elizabeth (Gray), 68
  Samuel, 68
Van Poelien, Jane, 469
Van Rensselaer, Alida (Schuyler), 334
  Catherine (Livingston), 337
  Edith (Biddle), 95
  Gertrude, 336
  Kiliaen, 336
  Nicholas, 334
  Peter, 66
  Philip Schuyler, 95
  Stephen, 337
Van Voorhees, Abraham, 459
  Agatha (Janse), 458
  Albert Coerte, 458
  Altje, 459
  Altje Coerte, 458
  Annatie Coerte, 458
  Antie, 459
  Antie (Remsen), 458
  Barbara (Van Dyck), 458
  Coert, 458
  Coert Stevense, 458
  Cornelius Coerte, 458
  Gerrit Coerte, 458
  Grietje (Wyckoff), 458
  Ida (Vanderbilt), 458
  Jan Lucasse, 457
  Johannes Coerte, 458
  John, 459
  Lucresy, 459
  Maria, 459
  Marretje Coerte, 458

Van Voorhees—*Continued*
  Marretje Gerritse (Van Couwenhoven), 458
  Mayke R. (Schenck), 457
  Mensie (Janse), 458
  Neeltje Coerte, 458
  Sara, 459
  Sara Willemse (Cornell), 458
  Sarah (Van Vleit), 458
  Steven Coerte, 458
  Willemtje (Pieters), 458
  Willemtje (Suydam), 458
Van Voor Hees, Abraham Stevense, 458
  Albert Stevense, 457
  Altje (Strycker), 458
  Altje Stevense, 457
  Anna (Van Duyckhuysen), 456
  Barrentje (Willemse), 457
  Catherine (Van Dyck), 456
  Catherine (Voorhees), 457
  Catherine Hansen (Van Nostrand), 456
  Coert, 456
  Cornelia Reiniers (Wizzel-Penning), 457
  Elizabeth Tallman (Stevenson), 457
  Femmetje Rukes (Van Nuyse), 457
  Helena (Van Der Schure), 457
  Hendrickje Stevense, 457
  Hendrickjen Stevense, 456
  Jan Lucasse, 456
  Jan Stevense, 457
  Jannetje (Remsen), 457
  Jannetje Minnes (Faddans), 456
  Jannetje Stevense, 457
  John P., 457
  Lucas Stevense, 456
  Mary (———), 457
  Mayke R. (Schenck), 457
  Merghin Stevense, 456
  Peter, 457
  Petrus, 457
  Steven Coerte, 456
  Tilletje Reiniers (Wizzel-Penning), 457
  Willempie Roeloffse (Seubering), 456

Van Voorhies, Adrianna (Voorhees), 459
  Catherine (Van Brunt), 459
  Eva, 457, 459
  Geertie or Charity (Suydam), 459
  Jacobus, 459
  Jane, 459
  Jannetje (Ryder), 459
  John, 459
  John S., 459
  Lucas, 459
  Phebe (Johnson), 459
  Phebe (Ryder), 459
  Seytie, 459
  Stephen, 459
  Stephen J., 459
  Stephen S., 459
  Van Vleit, Sarah, 458
Van Wyck, Hannah (Ker), 316
  Theodorus, 316
Varnum, George, 326
  James M., 326
  John, 413
  Joseph B., 326
  Mary Cooke (Saltonstall), 413
Vaughn, Abraham, 239
  Edith (Gist), 239
  Lois, 219
  Lydia, 253
Veitch, Ann, 334
Vemcomb, Sarah (Stockton) Jones, 430
  William, 430
Venable, ———, 320
  Abraham, 452, 453
  Abraham W., 454
  Abraham Woodson, 454
  Agnes, 453, 455
  Agnes (Moorman), 453
  Agnes Catherine, 455
  Andrew Reid, 454
  Ann, 453
  Ann (Clark), 453
  Anna, 454
  Anne, 453, 455
  Cantey McDowell, 452
  Charles, 453, 455
  Charles Scott, 452, 455
  Clementina, 455
  Cordelia (Kingsbury), 454
  Elizabeth, 453

INDEX

Venable—*Continued*
Elizabeth (Lewis) Nix, 452
Elizabeth (Michaux), 452
Elizabeth (Smith), 453
Elizabeth (Woodson), 453
Elizabeth G., 455
Elizabeth Thornton (Carrington), 455
Elizabeth W., 454
Emily, 454
Emily (Carrington), 454
Frances, 453
Frances J., 455
Frances Preston, 452, 455
Frances W. (Nautz), 453
George Carrington, 454
Henningham, 455
Hugh Lewis, 453
Isabella, 454
Isabella Alston (Brown), 454
Isabella Brown, 454
James, 453
Jane (Reid), 454
John, 453
John Manning, 452
Joseph, 452
Judith (Morton), 453
Louis Manning, 452
Louisa J., 454
Margaret, 116, 454
Margaret (Moseley), 454
Margaret Cantey (McDowell), 455
Margaret Read, 455
Martha, 453
Martha (Davis), 452
Martha (Venable), 453
Martha Daniel, 454
Mary, 453
Mary (Martin), 453
Mary (Morton), 453
Mary C., 454, 455
Mary Carrington, 454
Mary Embry (Scott), 455
Mary Grace, 454
Mary M. (Southall) Brown, 455
Mary P., 455
Mary P. (Venable), 455
Mary S. (Carrington), 453
Mildred C., 455
Nathaniel, 453
Nathaniel A., 455

Venable—*Continued*
Nathaniel E., 454, 455
Nathaniel W., 455
Paul Carrington, 454, 455
Richard, 453
Sally Charlton (Manning), 452
Sally Tucker, 454
Sally Tucker (Venable), 454
Samuel Frederick, 454
Samuel Woodson, 453, 454, 455
Sarah Scott, 455
Tennessee (Marr), 455
Thomas, 453
Thomas Frederick, 455
William, 453
William G., 454
William L., 453
Vetch, ———, 334
Margaret (Livingston), 334
Victor, Margaret A., 107
Viles, Frances M., 464
Vinacomb, Sarah, 347
Vining, Sarah, 489
Vinton, David H., 305
Harriette Arnold, 305
Vipont, Grace, 110
John, 110
Volz, Elizabeth, 281
Von Jagermann, Frances (Whitman), 494
Hans C. G., 494
Voorhees, Adrianna, 459
Annie Elizabeth (Cole), 460
Archibald Craig, 460
Catherine, 457
Charles Ashley, 435
Edward Craig, 460
Elizabeth, 460
Ethel Margaret (Feindall), 456
Eva (Van Voorhies), 457, 459
George Van Wickle, 456, 460
Gitty Jane, 457, 460
Gitty Jane (Voorhees), 460
Hannah C. (Corwin), 460
Johannah, 460
John, 460
John G., 457
John P., 460

Voorhees—*Continued*
Lucas, 459
Matilda Ackerman, 460
Minna (Cortelyou), 460
Peter L., 457, 459
Phebe, 460
Phebe Ann, 460
Stephen, 460
Stephen S., 460
Syche Ann, 460
Violet (Stockton), 435
Voie, Elizabeth A. (Hoover), 256
Jesse Walter, 256
Vose, Martha, 479
Robert, 479
Sarah, 479
Vrenne, Mary, 159

W

Waddell, Catherine (Calhoun) 129
Moses, 124, 129
Waddill, Mary Susan, 113
Wade, Jonathan, 168
Mary Willis, 295
Matilda (Smith), 353
Prudence, 168
Susanna, 168
Wadsworth, Mary Heath (Atkinson), 28
Peleg, 250
Richard Goodwin, 28
Wager, Elizabeth, 467
Henry, 467
Wainwright, Francis, 214
Mehitabel, 412
Simon, 412
Wait, Alida, 369
Anne E. (Knapp), 369
Annie, 370
Augustus, 370
Charles D., 369
Effie, 369
Emily S. (Rawlins), 369
George W., 369
Lucille Rawlins, 370
Martha, 369
Mary (Welch), 369
Mary E., 369
Samuel, 369
Thomas, 369
Wesley, 369

INDEX

Waldron, Abigail, 413
Wales, Polly, 98
Walker, Charles, 279
  Clarissa, 76
  Elizabeth, 16
  Elizabeth (Moore), 15
  Francis, 16
  John, 15
  Lucy, 15
  Martha, 16
  Mary, 15, 275
  Mildred, 16
  Mildred (Thornton), 15
  Peachy, 9, 14, 15, 16
  Rebecca (Isacke), 279
  Reuben, 16
  Sarah, 16
  Susan, 15
  Thomas, 9, 15, 16
  Timothy, 76
Wall, Sarah Wilkinson, 136
Wallace, Martha, 207
  Rachel, 444
Waller, ———, 234
  Elizabeth, 234
Wallingford, Florence, 222
Waln, Ada (Allmendinger), 351
  Ann, 348, 350
  Ann (Hall), 349
  Anna, 351
  Anne, 349
  Anne (Heath), 349
  Caroline (Mount), 351
  Elizabeth, 349, 350, 351
  Elizabeth (Armitt), 350
  Elizabeth (Stokes), 350
  Ellen, 349
  Hannah, 348, 350
  Jacob Shoemaker, 350
  Jane, 348, 349
  Jane (Mifflin), 349
  Jane (Rudd), 347
  Jane (Turner), 348
  John, 349
  John Ridgway, 351
  Joseph, 349, 350
  Margaret, 348
  Maria (Kirby), 351
  Mary, 348, 349, 350
  Mary (Shoemaker), 349
  Mary Ann (Allen), 351
  Nicholas, 348, 349, 350, 351
  Rebecca, 350, 441

Waln—*Continued*
  Rebecca (Coffin), 349
  Richard, 347, 348, 349, 350, 351
  Robert, 349
  Sarah, 349, 351
  Sarah (Morris), 350
  Sarah (Richardson), 350
  Sarah (Ridgway), 350
  Susanna, 349
  Susannah (Paul), 349
  Unity (Tilton), 351
  William, 349
Walsh, Edward, 426
  Susan Rives (Spencer), 426
Walton, Edward, 199
  Elizabeth (Deming), 180
  John, 199
  Mary (Duke), 199
  Randolph, 199
  Roland, 199
  Silas, 180
Ward, Agnes (Biddle), 95
  Charlotte Ferris, 191
  Cornelia De Koven, 192
  Dudley Livingstone, 192
  Edward Smith, 192
  Elizabeth, 412
  Emma Wilder, 191
  Frank A., 191
  Frank Hawley, 191
  George Merritt, 192
  James W., 95
  John, 412
  Joyce, 157
  Mary, 157
  Mary (Tilghman), 439
  Mary Antoinette, 192
  Mary Hawley (Douglas), 191
  Matthew, 439
  Matthew Tilghman, 439
  Sarah, 469
  Sutherland Douglas, 192
  William, 214
  William Douglas, 191
Wardell, Elialim, 93
  Lydia, 93
  Thomas, 93
Ware, ———, 181, 363
  Margaret (Burgess), 363
  Martha B., 281
  Mary Roach, 281

Warfield, Alexander, 364, 365, 366
  Ann, 366
  Anne, 364, 366
  Assantha (Waters), 366
  Azel, 366
  Basil, 366
  Benjamin, 365
  Charles, 364, 365, 366, 367
  David, 365, 367
  Davidge, 366
  Dennis, 365, 367
  Dinah, 366
  Dinah (Davidge), 365
  Edward, 364
  Elijah, 365, 367
  Elinor, 365
  Elinor (Browne), 365
  Elizabeth, 364, 366
  Elizabeth (Warfield), 366
  John, 365
  Joshua, 366
  Launcelot, 364, 365, 367
  Lydia, 365
  Marion (Caldwell), 365
  Mary, 364, 366
  Mary (Gaither), 364
  Philemon, 366
  Rachel, 365
  Rachel (Riggs), 364
  Rezin, 364, 366
  Richard, 364, 365
  Ruth, 365
  Ruth (Crutchley), 365
  Sarah, 364, 366
  Sarah (Gaither), 364
  Sarah (Gambrill), 365
  Seth, 364
  Sophia, 366
Warham, Esther, 492
  Mary (Gibbes), 230
  William C., 230
Warner, Andrew, 215
  Eliphalet, 165
  Eliza, 62
  Elizabeth, 161
  Elizabeth (Corwin), 165
  Elizabeth Harrison, 214
  Henry, 62
  Isabella (Rothrock), 405
  John, 161, 214
  Mary, 191

INDEX

Warner—*Continued*
  Nathan, 405
  Priscilla, 183
Warren, Abigail, 463, 464
  Abigail (Livermore), 463
  Abijah, 463
  Allen, 426
  Amos, 463
  Ann, 32, 463
  Anne, 464
  Betsey (Smith), 464
  Beulah, 463
  Charlotte Elizabeth (Bacon), 462
  Cyrus, 464
  Daniel, 462, 463
  Ebenezer, 463
  Elisha, 463
  Eliza, 464
  Elizabeth, 462, 463
  Ellen Elizabeth, 464
  Frances M. (Viles), 464
  George W., 464
  Grace, 463
  Hannah, 463
  Isaac, 463, 464
  Jane (Spencer), 426
  John, 313, 462, 463
  John Benjamin, 464
  Joshua, 463
  Josiah, 463
  Lydia, 463
  Margaret, 462
  Margaret (———), 462
  Martha, 175
  Mary, 462, 463, 464
  Mary (Barron), 462
  Mary (Brown), 463
  Mary (Browne), 313
  Micah, 463
  Michal (Jennison) Bloise 462
  Nathan, 462, 464
  Nehemiah, 463, 464
  Prudence, 463
  Richard, 31, 32, 249, 326, 462
  Sally (Wyman), 464
  Samuel, 464
  Sarah, 351, 463, 464
  Sarah (Abbott), 463
  Sarah Boynton, 464
  Sarah Boynton (Warren), 464
  Susanna, 463

Warriner, Ruth, 54
  William, 54
Warwick, Anna Calvert (Jackson), 297
  James B., 297
Washburn, Edward A., 187
Washington, George, 15, 123, 135, 144, 239
  Mildred, 123
Waters, Assantha, 366
  Carlos, 451
  Edward, 144
  Fanny C., 39
  Leon Wilson, 451
  Marguerite, 451
  Mary Henrietta (Tubman), 451
  Matilda (Broughton), 451
  Nathan, 364
  Robert Custis, 451
  Robert E., 451
  Robert Francis Tubman, 451
  Susannah (Gaither), 364
Wathen, Mary Priscilla (Duke), 200
  Robert H., 200
Waties, Mary S., 233
Watkins, Agnes (Venable), 455
  Ann (Venable), 453
  Anna (Alexander), 20
  Elizabeth Edmunds, 246
  Elizabeth W. (Venable), 454
  Henry E., 455
  Henry W., 269
  James, 295
  Justus, 269
  Lucy, 425
  Mary (Calvert), 295
  Mary Willie (Spears), 272
  Sally, 425
  Theodore, 20
  Thomas, 425, 453
  Walter Abbott, 272
  William Morton, 454
Watrous, Abram, 158
  Rebecca (Clark), 158
Watson, Abigail (Saltonstall), 413
  Annie Leslie, 154
  Catherine, 149
  George, 413
  Helen M., 45
  Margaret, 105

Way, John, 195
  Lucy, 195
Waymire, Elizabeth, 253
  Elizabeth (Hoover), 253
  Frederick, 253
Weaver, Anna, 361
  Elizabeth Ker (Johnson), 309
  Henry, 404
  Mary, 404
  Mary (Rothrock), 404
  Walter Reed, 309
Webb, Abigail, 321, 322
  Abner, 321
  Benjamin, 321
  Benjamin Deford, 141
  Bethia, 322
  Bethia (Adams), 321
  Catherine Ellen, 104
  Christopher, 312, 320, 321
  Eliphalet, 322
  George, 197
  Hannah, 321
  Hannah (Scott), 312, 321
  Humility (———), 320
  Jemima, 322
  Jennie, 197
  John, 321
  Joseph, 321
  Judith, 321
  Judith (Howard), 310, 321
  Katherine Prioleau (Chisholm), 141
  Mary, 174, 312, 321
  Mary (Adams), 321
  May (Trippe), 445
  Mildred Rees (Woolford) 418
  Napthali, 321
  Nathan, 321
  Nathaniel, 312, 321
  Peter, 321, 445
  P. Watson, 418
  Rebecca, 312, 321
  Samuel, 312, 321
  Sarah, 310, 321, 322
  Stephen, 322
  Thomas, 321
  Virginia, 418
  Zebulon, 310, 312, 321
Webbe, Anne, 474
Webber, Philomelia, 86

INDEX

Webster, Abigail, 148
  Abigail (Alexander), 19
  Alice Bridge, 467
  Daniel, 467
  Hannah, 75
  John, 74, 206, 407, 488
  Mary, 74
  Mary (Shatwell), 74
  Susanna (Rush), 206
  Thomas, 19
Weed, Phebe, 224
Weightman, Ann Walker, 347
  William, 347
Weir, Clara, 294
Welch, Mary, 369
Welcher, Alice Lee, 34
  Amy Ogden, 34
  Emma Parke Avery, 34
  Fannie Falconer (Avery), 34, 38
  Lester Groome, 34
  Manfred Philester, 34, 38
Weldon, Mary E., 154
Welker, Daniel, 504
  Nancy (Reagan), 504
  Salome, 504
Weller, Anna Catryna (Moul), 371
  Anna Juliana, 371
  Barbara, 401
  Catherine, 371
  Henrich, 371
  Lea, 371
  Phillipus, 371
  Wilhelimne, 371
Welles, ———, 393
  Ann, 180
  Elisha, 180
  Lydia (Deming), 180
  Thomas, 19
Wellington, Benjamin, 313
  Lydia (Browne), 313
Wells, ———, 164, 485
  Abigail (Whitman), 492
  Deborah, 164
  Ebenezer, 492
  Edward, 162
  Frederic DeWitt, 305
  Georgina (Betts), 91
  Georgina Lawrence, 91
  Grace (Tileston), 91
  Hannah, 492
  Henry, 393

Wells—*Continued*
  John, 91
  Mary, 350
  Mary (White), 485
  Mary Ann Haight, 393
  Rachel (Skinner), 492
  Rossiter Betts, 91
  Thomas Tileston, 91
Wentworth, John 75, 85
  Sarah (Bartlet), 85
West, ———, 32
  Alice Lee, 414
  Anne, 153
  Bartholomew, 354
  Benjamin, 15
  Benjamin H., 360
  Bertha A., 256
  Catherine (Almy), 354
  Elizabeth, 411
  Elizabeth Augusta (Minot) 360
  George Saltonstall, 414
  George Webb, 414
  John, 153
  Mary (Avery), 32
  Rose Lee (Saltonstall), 414
  Thomas, 411
  Unity, 244
Westal, Alice, 280
  George, 280
  Jane, 280
Westcott, Elizabeth (Dunton), 205, 207
  John H., 205, 207
  Lorenzo, 205, 207
  Mary (Dunton), 205, 207
Westerlo, Catherine (Livingston) Van Rensselaer, 337
  Dominie Eilardus, 337
Weston, Heloise, 233
Wetherby, Eliza (Corwin), 165
  Henry Corwin, 165
Whaling, Elizabeth Arnold, 382
Wharton, Joanna, 92
Wheeler, Deborah (Whitney), 496
  Eunice Amelia, 160
  Fanny, 70
  George, 294
  Grattan Henry, 70
  Hannah (Drury), 160
  Jacob, 160
  Jonathan, 189

Wheeler—*Continued*
  Joseph, 496
  Lydia (Calvert), 294
  Rebecca, 189, 358
  Sarah, 159, 189
  Timothy, 358
Wheelock, Ruth, 54
Wheelwright, Anne G., 143
  John, 23
Whelen, Laura, 96
Whetenhall, Alice (Birkley), 438
  Dorothy (Fane) 438
  George, 438
  Susanna, 438
  Thomas, 438
Whilock, Eleazer, 173
Whipple, Abigail, 466
  Abraham, 467
  Aida Mae (Bulger), 465
  Alice (Angell), 465
  Alice (Smith), 466
  Alice Bridge (Webster), 467
  Amy, 466, 467
  Ann Frances, 467
  Anna, 466
  Benjamin, 466, 467
  Benjamin Brayton, 467
  Charles Henry, 465, 469
  Cornelia (Wright, 469
  Cornelia Ward, 469
  Cynthia, 467
  David, 466, 467
  David Wager, 468
  Deborah, 466
  Deborah (Bucklin), 466
  Eleazer, 465
  Elizabeth (Wager), 467
  Esther, 467
  Evangeline (Marrs) Simpson, 469
  Evelyn Elizabeth (McLean), 465
  Frances Ransom, 469
  Francis Ransom, 468
  George, 467
  George Brayton, 468
  Hannah, 466
  Hannah (Brown), 466
  Hannah (Tower), 466
  Helen (Dawson), 271
  Helen Dorothy, 271

INDEX

Whipple—*Continued*
Henry Benjamin, 465, 467, 468
Israel, 466
Jane Whiting, 469
Jeremiah, 466
John, 465, 468
John Hall, 467, 469
Jonathan, 466, 467
Joseph, 466, 467
Katherine Nelson (Meade), 465
Lydia, 467
Margaret (Angell), 466
Martha, 467
Martha (Read), 466
Mary, 466
Mary (———), 466
Mary (Arnold), 467
Mary (Harris), 465
Mary (Jennison), 467
Mary (Olney), 465
Mary (Wilmarth), 466
Mary Goodridge (Gould), 465
Mary J. (Mills), 468
Nancy, 467
Nathan Frank, 271
Nathaniel McLean, 465
Otis, 467
Rebecca (Scott), 465
Ruth (Matthewson), 466
Sally (Baker), 467
Samuel, 465
Sarah, 465, 466
Sarah (———), 465
Sarah (Corey), 467
Sarah (Hearnden), 466
Sarah Brayton, 467
Sarah Elizabeth, 469
Simon, 467
Susan Letitia, 468
Susanna, 467
Susanna (Hall), 467
Susanna (Whipple), 467
Walter Frank, 271
William, 466
Whit, Johannis, 472
White, ———, 363
Adam, 397, 472
Abigail, 476, 477
Abigail (Croft), 486
Abigail (Cutting), 398

White—*Continued*
Abigail (Muzzey), 397, 398, 477, 479, 480, 484
Agnes, 474, 475
Agnes (———), 472
Agnes (Barker), 473
Agnes (Wright), 397, 474
Alexander, 473
Alice (Sholdam), 472
Alice (Wood), 473
Allan Temple, 479
Amanda (Preston), 487
Amasa, 477
Andree, 474
Ann (Burgess), 363
Anna, 413
Anne, 474
Anne (Webbe), 474
Annie (Evans), 470, 481
Bartholomew, 472
Benjamin, 477, 489
Betty (Crosby), 170
Carolyn Elizabeth (Hall), 485
Charles Davis, 479
Cyrus, 487
Daniel, 485, 486
David, 170
Davy, 473
Deacon Joseph, 484
Dorothy, 475
Ebenezer, 478
Eldad, 486
Elizabeth, 31, 230, 476, 477, 485, 486
Elizabeth (———), 486
Elizabeth (Savage), 486
Ellen, 474
Ellen (Wright), 474
Esther, 485
Experience (King), 491
Fanny, 98
Francis Wayland, 478
Gabriel, 474
Hannah, 476, 478, 485
Hannah (Day), 486
Hannah (Estabrook), 478, 479, 480, 484
Hannah Mandana, 478
Isaac, 231, 361
Jacob, 485, 486
Janet (Saunders), 397, 474
Joel, 398, 477

White—*Continued*
Johanna, 474
Johanna (Lydden), 397, 473
Johannis, 397, 472, 474
John, 397, 398, 472, 473, 474, 476, 477, 479, 484, 485, 486
John Bradshaw, 477
Jonab, 477
Joseph, 398, 478, 479, 480, 481, 483, 486
Joseph Estabrook, 478
Joseph Nelson, 397, 399, 470, 479, 480, 481, 482, 483, 484
Josiah, 486
Julia, 231
Julia Davis (Long), 478, 479, 480, 481, 482, 484
Julia Matilda, 479
Julia Temple (Long), 483
Katharine, 397
Katharine (White), 397
Ketherine, 473
Madeleine Evans, 470
Margaret, 473, 474
Margaret (Early), 398, 475
Martha (Coit) Mould, 486
Mary, 475, 476, 477, 485, 486
Mary (———), 485
Mary (Browne), 475
Mary (Frothingham), 398, 475, 476, 484
Mary (Smith), 486
Mary Louise, 447
Matilda (Davis), 478, 479, 480, 481, 482, 483, 484
Mehitable, 485
Mehitable (Rice), 477
Mollie, 477
Nancy, 477, 478
Nancy (Morrison), 361
Nathaniel, 485, 486
Nellie Mandana, 479
Nelson Davis, 470, 478, 479, 480, 481, 482, 483, 484
Nicholas, 472, 491
Percival Wayland, 479
Persis Arminda, 478
Petrus, 472
Polly, 478
Rachel Burnet, 470

INDEX 595

White—*Continued*
Ralph, 474
Rand, 477
Rebeccca (White), 487
Ricardus, 472
Robert, 472, 473, 476, 477, 487
Roberto, 472
Robertus, 397, 471, 473
Samuel, 476
Sarah, 476, 477, 485, 486
Sarah (Crow), 485
Sarah (Rand), 398, 476, 484
Serena, 395, 398
Sibillab, 477
Silence (Baldwin), 477
Susan, 185
Susanna (Whitman), 489
Sybilla, 477
Sybilla (Buckminster), 398, 477, 479, 484
Thaddeus, 477
Thomas, 397, 398, 474, 475, 476, 477, 478, 479, 480, 484
Walter, 397, 398, 474, 475
Willelmus, 397, 471, 472
William, 397, 472, 473, 474, 476, 487
William Gardner, 485, 487
Windsor Newton, 478
Winifred Evans, 470
Zadoc, 470
Zadoc Long, 478
Whitehead, ———, 93
Asa, 501
Caroline H., 190
Mary, 153
Mary Ann Goodrich (Wolcott), 501
Penelope (Biddle), 93
Philip, 153
Whitlock, Sarah (Davenport) Maltby, 173
Whitman, Abiah 490
Abigail, 492
Abigail (Abbott), 493
Abigail (Burnham), 489
Abigail (Butler), 493
Abigail (Byram), 489
Abigail (Hollis), 489
Abigail (Pantry), 492
Abigail (Stanley), 492

Whitman—*Continued*
Abijah, 488
Anna, 493
Anna Maria (Bulkeley), 493
Anne (Skinner), 493
Charles Addison, 494
Charles Seymour, 488, 492, 494
Damaris (Carmen), 491
Deborah (Richards), 489
Dorcas (Green) Chitty, 492
Dorothy (Pratt), 489
Ebenezer, 489
Eleanor, 490, 493
Eleanor (Montague) Pratt, 493
Elizabeth, 490, 492
Elizabeth (Turner), 489
Elnathan, 491, 492
Eunice, 492, 493
Experience, 489
Frances, 494
Hannah, 489, 490
Hannah (Pratt), 489
Hannah (Wells), 492
James, 493
Joanna, 491
John, 488, 489, 490, 491, 492, 493
John Munroe, 494
John Pantry, 493
John Seymour, 494
Judah, 488
Judith, 491
Laura (Seymour), 493
Lillie (Arne), 494
Lucy, 492, 493
Lucy (Seymour), 493
Lucy Beman, 494
Lucy Skinner, 493
Lydia, 490
Maria Louise, 494
Mary, 488, 489, 490, 492
Mary (Cary), 489
Mary (Conant), 489
Mary (Ford), 490
Mary (Graves), 492
Mary (Richards), 489
Mary Eva, 494
Mercy, 299
Naomi, 489
Nicholas, 489
Olive, 488

Whitman—*Continued*
Olive (Hitchcock), 488
Rebecca (Manley), 490
Ruth, 489, 493
Ruth (———), 489
Ruth (Pittee), 490
Ruth (Reed), 489
Samuel, 489, 491, 492, 493
Sarah, 488, 489, 491, 492, 493
Sarah (Alcock), 299, 491
Sarah (Reed), 490
Sarah (Stoddard), 492
Sarah (Treat), 491
Sarah (Vining), 489
Seymour, 493
Solomon, 492
Susanna, 489
Susanna (Cole), 492
Thomas, 489
Timothy, 493
Zachariah, 299
Zachary, 490
Zechariah, 488, 490, 491
Whitney, Abigail, 496, 497
Abigail (Bridge), 496
Abigail (Cutler), 497
Abigail (Tarball), 495
Anna, 497
Barrett, 496
Bathsheba (Heston), 497
Benjamin, 496, 497
Betsy (Derby), 497
Bezaleel, 496
Caleb, 496
Caroline Elizabeth, 498
Constance, 498
Cyrus, 497
Daniel, 331
David, 497
Deborah, 496
Dinah, 497
Dolly, 331
Dorothy (Ross), 496
Dwight, 495
Eben, 497
Eleazer, 496
Eli, 495
Elinor (———), 495
Elizabeth, 496, 498
Elizabeth (Adams), 496
Elizabeth (Lawrence), 496
Elizabeth (Pratt), 498

INDEX

Whitney—*Continued*
  Elizabeth (Smith), 497
  Ellerton Pratt, 498
  Elnathan, 496
  Emily Burton (Stevens), 326
  Fanny (Lawrence), 498
  George, 497
  George Hayward, 495
  Georgina (Hayward), 495
  Henry, 498
  Henry Austin, 498
  Henry Lawrence, 495, 498
  Isaiah, 496
  James, 497
  Jane (———), 496
  Job, 497
  John, 326, 331, 495, 496, 497
  Jonathan, 495
  Joseph, 497, 498
  Joseph Cutler, 495, 498
  Joshua, 495
  Judah (Clement), 495
  Kate Varnum, 326
  Lucy (Perkins), 498
  Lydia, 497
  Lydia (———), 495
  Lydia (Jones), 495
  Martha, 496
  Martha (Coldham), 495
  Mary, 52, 495, 496
  Mary (———), 495
  Mary (Brewer), 497
  Mary (Holman), 496
  Mary (Kendall), 496
  Mary (Poor), 496
  Mercy (———), 497
  Nathan, 496
  Nathaniel, 495
  Persis, 497
  Polly, 497
  Richard, 495
  Robert Upton, 495
  Rufus Hayden, 326
  Ruth (Perkins), 497
  Ruth (Reynolds), 495
  Samuel, 497
  Samuel Austin, 497
  Sarah, 496, 497
  Sarah (Barrett), 496
  Sarah (Woodward), 496
  Sarah Josephine, 498
  Silas, 331
  Solomon, 497

Whitney—*Continued*
  Susanna, 496
  Tabitha, 212
  Thomas, 495, 496
  Timothy, 497
  William, 497
  William Collins, 495
Whitredd, William, 214
Whitte (White), Willelmi, 471
Whittemore, Abigail (Park) 36
  Benjamin, 329
  Francis, 35
  Hannah, 185
  Isabel (Park), 35
  John, 329
  Nathaniel, 36
  Ruth (Basset), 329
  Sarah (Kendall), 329
  Thomas, 329
Whittingham, Mary, 412
  William, 412
Whittle, Eleanor, 364
Whyt, Petrus, 472
Whyte de Alnewyk, Robert, 397
  Robertus, 473
  Willelmi, 473
  William, 473
Wickendon, William, 167
Wickham, ———, 147
  Elizabeth, 165
  Sarah (Churchill), 147
Wigg, Ann, 229
Wilber, Charles W., 345
  Sarah Alexander (Lyman), 345
Wilbur, Cornelius, 185
  Lucinda (Cummings), 185
Wilcox, Anna Maria, 116
  Caroline, 465
Wild, Hannah (Minot), 359
  Joseph, 359
  Rachel, 359
Wilder, Lucy, 261
Wildman, Abiah, 147
Wilemsen Duercant, Derike, 223
  Hachim (Bastians), 223
  Mary, 223
Wiley, Anna Campbell (Kelton), 325
  Harvey W., 325
Wilfred, Martha, 411

Wilkins, John D., 154
  Maria (Claiborne), 154
Wilkinson, Lawrence, 133
Willard, Daniel, 180
  Dorothy, 180
  Dorothy (Deming), 180
  Margery, 482
  Richard, 482
  Simon, 482
Willemse, Altje Coerte (Van Voorhees), 458
  Barrantje, 457
  Johannes, 458
  Merghin Stevense (Van Voor Hees) Roelofs, 456
  Remmelt, 456
Willett, Marinus, 66
Williams, Abigail (Davenport), 173
  Aileen (Rothrock), 400
  Catherine, 431
  Charles, 294
  Ebenezer, 491
  Edith (Cromwell) Gist, 236
  Eliza (Fairfield), 67
  Elizabeth, 159, 190, 400
  Elizabeth (Abbott), 4
  Elizabeth (Calvert), 294
  Ellen Green, 11
  George, 4
  George W., 131
  Hannah (Douglas), 189
  Henry J., 408
  Hezekiah, 4
  John, 400
  Joseph, 236
  Judith (King), 491
  Julia (Rush), 408
  Julia Davie (Izard), 285
  Keziah, 225
  Louis, 400
  Lucius, 67
  Mariann (Wolcott), 500
  Mary, 407
  Mary (Abbott) Ellis, 4
  Mary Wentworth, 77
  Maud Rothrock, 400
  Roger, 167
  Sarah (Abbott), 4
  Sarah Porter, 131
  Stephen, 173
  Thomas, 189, 500
  William T., 285

INDEX

Williamson, Anne, 375
 Charles, 67
 Elizabeth, 17
 Joseph Biddle, 375
 Lucresy (Van Voorhees), 459
 Nicholas, 459
Willis, Henry, 123, 144
 Lewis, 144
 Mary Eugenia, 418, 448
 Mary Naomi, 451
 Mildred (Washington), 123, 144
 William W., 451
Willoughby, Elizabeth, 297
Willoughby de Broke, Edward, 297
 Margaret (De Neville), 297
Wills, Anna (Waln), 351
 Benajah P., 351
 Edith Russell, 323
 George Edward, 323
 Mabel, 351
 Mary Ella (Russell), 323
 Richard Waln, 351
Wilmarth, Mary, 466
Wilmer, Nancy, 408
 Rebecca (Tilghman), 439
 Simon, 439
Wilson, ———, 255
 Ann (Chisholme), 140
 Ann Isabell (Gibbes) How, 231
 Anne Jane (Shand), 231
 Caleb, 360
 Catherine (Baird), 59
 Clara, 60
 David Shield, 59
 Eliza (Gibbes), 231
 Elizabeth (Venable), 453
 Emily Thurston, 232
 Frank E., 255
 George, 59
 Goodrich, 453
 Hannah, 175
 Harriet Chisolm (Cain), 231
 Henry Ravenel, 231
 Hugh H., 60
 James H., 426
 James M., 231
 James Mazyck, 231, 232
 Jane, 59
 John, 231
 Julia (White), 231

Wilson—*Continued*
 Martha (Minot), 360
 Martha Ann, 423
 Mary (Browne), 199
 Mary (Jay), 255
 Mary How, 231
 Mary Philip, 230
 Mary Susan (Gibbes), 231
 Matilda Cole (Spencer), 426
 Nancy, 21
 Nanna Shand, 232
 Peter Johnson Shand, 231
 Rebecca E. (Miles), 255
 Rebecca Wright, 232
 Robert, 140, 231
 Samuel, 232
 Sarah (Baird), 59
 Sue Guignard, 231
 Susan Ravenel, 232
 Susan Wilson (Gibbes), 231, 232
Wilton, Alice, 63
Winder, Mariana Stoughton, 211
Winfrey, Frances A. (Spencer), 426
 Jesse, 426
Winship, Edward, 328
 Elizabeth (Kendall), 328
 Ephraim, 328
Winslow, Elizabeth Capen (Hubbard), 267
 Eunice (Fulton), 220
 George Carlos, 267
 Joseph, 44, 220
 Millicent, 253
Winsor, Anna Greenleaf, 28
 Anna Greenleaf (Atkinson), 28
 Edward Atkinson, 28
 Ernest, 28
 Helen, 28
 Percival, 28
Winston, Dorothea Spotswood (Dandridge) Henry, 244
 Dorothea Spotswood (Henry), 244
 Edmund, 244
 Geddes, 10
 George Dabney, 244
 Isaac, 243
 Margaret, 10

Winston—*Continued*
 Mary (Dabney), 243
 Sarah, 243
Winthrop, Fitz John, 334
 Honora Elizabeth Temple, 357
 John, 158, 195
 Mary, 334
 Thomas Lindall, 357
Wirt, Mary Frances, 400
 William, 15
Wiseman, Henry, 387
 Mary, 387
 Thomas, 387
Wisner, Anthony D., 226
 Elizabeth Gardiner, 226
 Frank Gardiner, 226
 Frank George, 226
 George Brockway, 226
 George E. D., 226
 Katherine (Schaetzel), 226
 Louise Gardiner, 226
 Mary Elizabeth (Hemple), 226
Wister, Mary (Waln), 350
 Richard, 350
 Sarah (Wyatt), 350
 Thomas, 350
Wiswall, Mary (Minot), 359
 Oliver, 359
Witham, Ann, 430
 Robert, 430
Witherington, Thos., 49
Witherow, Cecil Calvert, 292
 Lavinia (Jett), 292
 Thomas Scott, 292
Withington, Mary, 314
Witt, Benjamin, 54
 Olivia (Campbell), 54
Wittum, John, 84
 Peter, 84
Wizzel-Penning, Cornelia Reiniers, 457
 Jannetie (Snediker), 457
 Reinier, 457
 Tilletje Reiniers, 457
Wolcott, Abby Woolsey (Howland), 501
 Abiah, (Hawley), 500
 Alexander, 500
 Anna, 499
 Catherine (Rankin), 501
 Charles Moseley, 501

INDEX

Wolcott—*Continued*
Chauncey Goodrich, 501
Christopher, 499
Cornelia (Frothingham), 501, 502
Edith (Prescott), 502
Elizabeth, 499, 500, 501
Elizabeth (Huntington), 501
Elizabeth (Saunders), 499
Elizabeth (Stoughton), 501
Elizabeth (Treat), 499
Epaphras, 500
Erastus, 500
Eunice (Colton) Ely, 500
Frederick, 501
Frederick Henry, 501
George, 499
Hannah, 499
Hannah (Stevenson), 502
Hannah (Wolcott), 499
Hannah Huntington, 501
Harriet (Frothingham), 501
Henry, 499
Henry Griswold, 501
Hephzibah, 500
Huntington Frothingham, 502
Jane (Allyn), 499
Jerusha, 500
Jerusha (Wolcott), 500
Joanna, 499
Joanna (Cook), 499
John, 499, 500
Joshua Huntington, 501
Josiah, 500
Laura, 501
Laura (Collins), 500
Laura Maria, 501
Lydia (Atwater), 500
Marah (Newberry), 500
Mariann, 500
Martha, 499
Martha (Pitkin), 499
Mary, 499, 500
Mary (Allyn), 500
Mary (Richards), 500
Mary Ann, 501
Mary Ann Goodrich, 501
Mary E. (Goodrich), 501
Mary Frances, 501
Oliver, 500, 501, 502
Rachel (Talcott), 499
Robert Stevenson, 502

Wolcott—*Continued*
Roger, 499, 500, 502
Sally Worthington (Goodrich) Cooke, 501
Samuel, 500
Samuel Hungtington, 502
Sarah, 500
Sarah (Chester), 499
Sarah (Drake), 500
Sarah (Newberry), 499
Sarah Elizabeth Chase (Merchant), 501
Simon, 499
Ursula, 500
William, 500
William Prescott, 502
Wolfe, Amanda Louise (Burton), 503
Andrew, 504
Ann Elizabeth (Reid), 504
Ann Marie, 505
Belle (Dobbins), 505
Bertha Frances, 503
Blanche Martin, 503
Clara Louise, 503
Clay, 505
David, 504
Eliza (Tressenrider), 504
Elizabeth, 504
Elizabeth (Burford), 504
Elizabeth (Stephenson), 504
Elmer Burton, 503
Emma I., 233
Flavius Joseph, 503, 505
Frank Beard, 505
George, 504
George Washington, 504
George Wendell, 503, 504
Henry, 504
Iras Louise, 503
Jacob, 504
Jessie (Bass), 503
John, 504
John Henry, 504
Joseph, 504
Lee B., 505
Leonidas Oliver Perry, 505
Lucinda Ann, 505
Lucy Frances (Beard), 505
Mahitabel (Mitchell), 504
Marcus Aurelius, 505
Margaret, 504
Margaret (Edleman), 504

Wolfe—*Continued*
Mary (Miller), 504
Mary (Utz), 504
Mary Ann (Aurand), 504
Mary Margaret (Conrad), 504
Michael, 504
Nancy (Haggerday), 504
Nancy Margaret, 505
Peter, 504
Philip, 504
Roscoe Burton, 503
Roy, 505
Salome (Welker), 504
Samuel, 504
Sarah, 504
Sophia (Zillhart), 504
Susan, 504
Wogan, Frances, 288
Margaret, 402, 404
Wolley, Elizabeth, 172
Wolseley, Anne, 289
Womack, Mary C. (Venable), 455
William L., 455
Wood, Abigail (Bacon), 42
Alice, 473
Charles Blake, 18
David, 295
Elizabeth (Barret), 276
Elizabeth (Twyman), 275
Elizabeth Blake, 18
Ellena (Israel), 275
George Twymon, 276
Henry Crittenden, 276
Henry Crutcher, 276
James, 291
Jane Calvert (Kaylor), 295
John, 275
Josiah, 42
Kesia, 32
Lizzie Boyle, 276
Lucy (Henry), 243
Marietta Gridley (Bowman), 18
Mary, 52
Mary (Davenport), 173
Mary Walker, 272, 275
Nathaniel, 173
Polly, 218
Sarah Anne (Calvert), 291
Thomas John, 276

INDEX

599

Wood—*Continued*
  Valentine, 243
  William J., 275
Woodbridge, Hannah Rebecca
  (Robbins) Keep, 392
  Jahleel, 392
Woodbury, William, 215
Woodford, Thomas, 214
Woodhouse, Henry, 480
  Millicent, 480
Woodman, Abigail (Atkinson), 24
  Jonathan, 24
  Margaret, 74
Woodmansey, Mary, 30
  Robert, 30
Woodruff, Matthew, 214
Woods, John, 215
  Marguerite, 286
  Willie Anne, 291
Woodson, Elizabeth, 453
  Richard, 453
  Virginia, 245
Woodward, ———, 366
  Dinah (Warfield), 366
  George, 496
  Hannah W., 11
  James T., 280
  Jane (Ridgley), 280
  John, 391, 505
  Lucinda Ann (Wolfe), 505
  Lydia, 173
  Mary, 229
  Rebecca (Robbins), 391
  Rignal D., 280
  Sarah, 496
  William, 280
Woodworth, Charlotte (Norton), 150
  Joel Cyrenus, 150
  Sarah Erminie, 150
Woolens, Jesse, 111
  Mary Anne, 111
Wooley, Hannah, 160
  Hester Ann, 70
Woolford, Amelia (Trippe), 445
  Benjamin Whitely, 422
  Cassandra, 423
  Emma Virginia (Skinner), 422
  Evelena Colston (Skinner), 418

Woolford—*Continued*
  George Whitefield, 418
  Ida Stengle (Hooper), 422
  James, 445
  John, 418
  Mabel, 418
  Mary (Rees), 418
  Mildred Rees, 418
  Miles Hogan, 418
Woolley, Amasa, 20
  Mary (Alexander), 20
Worden, Mehitable (Hinckley), 31
  Sarah, 181
Work, Isabella, 361
Worley, Daniel, 402
  Maria, 402
  Salome Charity, 402
Worster, Lydia F., 86
Worth, Judith, 25
Worthington, Edward, 178
  Jane Maria (Shepard), 178
  Mary Colebrook, 178
Wright, Agnes, 397, 474
  Anne, 168
  Azubah, 20
  Benjamin, 19, 469
  Boykin, 117
  Boykin Cable, 117
  Constance Cabell, 117
  Cornelia, 469
  Elijah, 253
  Elizabeth, 5, 350, 474
  Ellen, 474
  Hannah, 147
  Hannah (Bacon), 52
  Joseph, 179
  Joseph O., 418
  Margaret (Lee), 418
  Margaret Constance, 117
  Marguerite Cabell, 117
  Martin, 474
  Mercy (Deming), 179
  Mildred Lee, 418
  Nathaniel, 52
  Prudence (Deming), 180
  Samuel, 214
  Sarah, 184
  Sarah (Ward), 469
  Susanna (Hoover), 253
  Thomas, 179, 180, 214
  Walter, 474

Writzell, Hester Maria (Harvey), 257
  Walter E., 257
Wroth, Elizabeth, 288
  Mary (Rich), 288
  Thomas, 288
Wurts, Laura (Jay), 305
  Pemberton, 305
Wyatt, Sarah, 350
  Susan, 116
Wyckoff, Catherine (Nevius), 458
  Garret Pieterse, 458
  Grietje, 458
Wyer, Ann, 217
  Elizabeth (Minot), 359
  Thomas, 359
Wylie, Elizabeth, 41, 50
Wyllys, George, 488
Wyman, Amos, 330
  Benjamin, 43, 464
  Elizabeth (Hancock), 43
  Francis, 42
  Judith, 43
  Judith (Pierce), 43
  Sally, 464
Wymond, Adah, 117
Wynne, Martha (Buttall), 368
  Thomas, 368
Wythe, George, 243

Y

Yarborough, ———, 129
Yarbrough, ———, 426
  Jane (Spencer) Warren, 426
Yates, ———, 365
  Ann, 238
  Rachel (Warfield), 365
Yeagley, John H., 403
  Rebecca Elizabeth (Buckingham), 403
Yeardley, George, 144
Yeatman, ———, 114
  Elizabeth (Cabell), 114
Yerby, George, 409
  Susan Bowdoin, 409
Yost, Sarah, 403
Yorke, Daniel, 51
  Sarah (Bacon), 51
Youille, Jane, 245
Young, Anna Belle (Morrison), 362

Young—*Continued*
  Anne, 273
  Carolyn (James), 502
  David, 362
  Margaret, 324
  Martha, 223
  Mary, 405
  Mary E. (Hundley), 273
  Jacob, 405
  John J., 310

Young—*Continued*
  Robert E., 273
  Sarah (Johnson), 310
  Thomas, 223
Yount, ———, 253
  Catherine, 253
  Catherine (Hoover), 254
  Henry, 254
  Michal, 254
  Rebecca, 254

Z

Zesline, Jos., 204
Zichy, Ladislaus, 70
  Mary (Knapp), 70
Zillhart, Sophia, 504
Zimmerman, Elizabeth, 134
Zorrahn, Constance (Whitney), 498
  Franz Edward, 498